AF208179

HERMITAGE
ERMITAGE
EREMITAGE

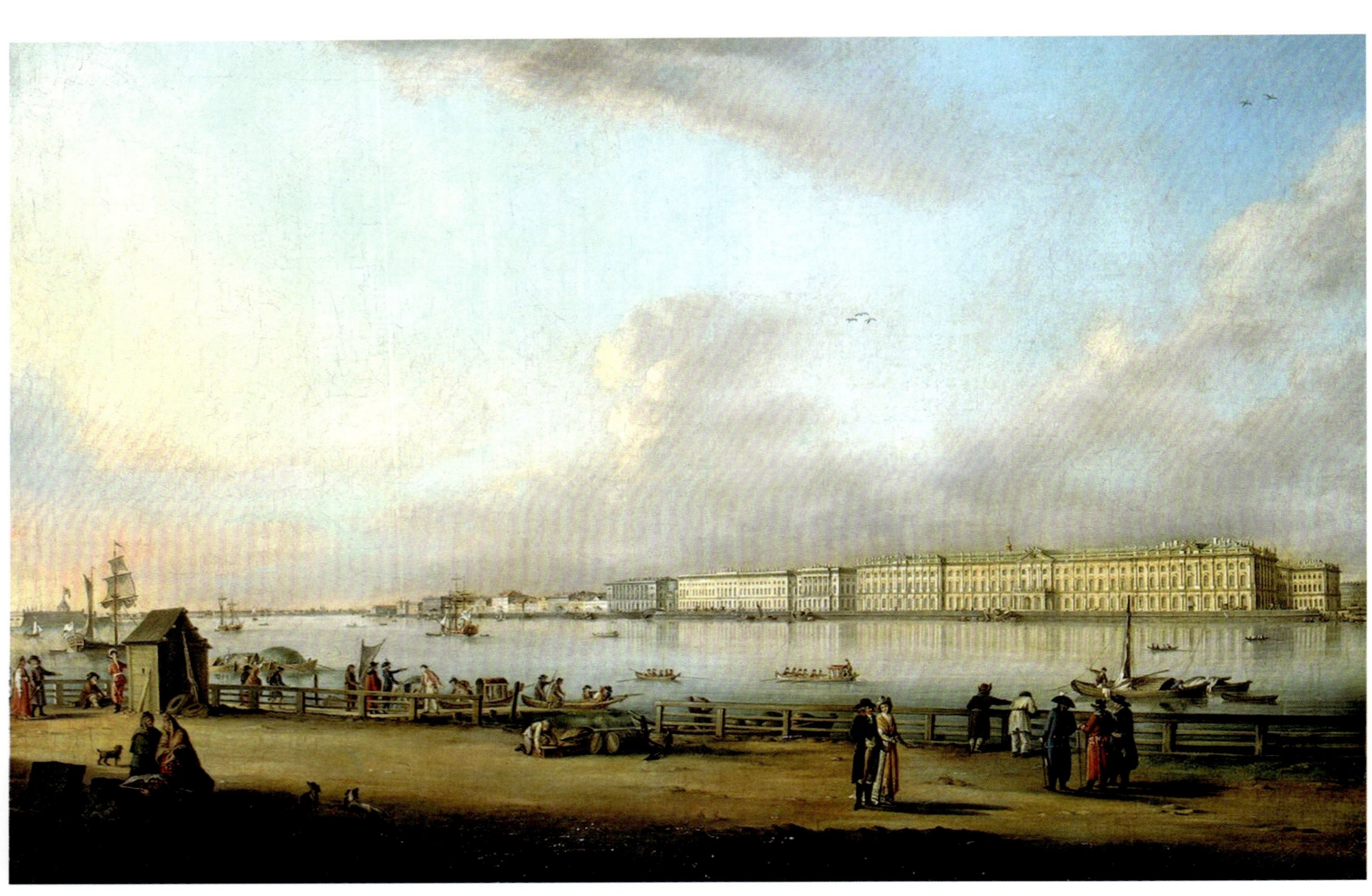

HAJO DÜCHTING

HERMITAGE
ERMITAGE
EREMITAGE

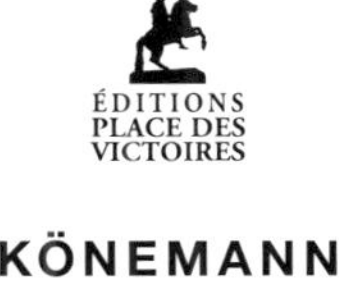

ÉDITIONS
PLACE DES
VICTOIRES

KÖNEMANN

p. 2

Johann Georg Mayr (1760–1816)

The Winter Palace seen from Vasilyevsky Island
Vue du palais d'Hiver depuis l'île Vassilievski
Der Winterpalast von der Wassiljewski-Insel aus
El Palacio de Invierno visto desde la Isla Vassilyevski
O Palácio de Inverno Visto da Ilha de Vassiliev
Het Winterpaleis vanaf het Vassiljevski-eiland
1796, Oil on canvas/Huile sur toile, 77 × 117 cm

KÖNEMANN
© 2017 koenemann.com GmbH
www.koenemann.com

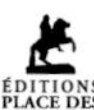

© Éditions Place des Victoires
6, rue du Mail – 75002 Paris
www.victoires.com
ISBN : 978-2-8099-1692-8
Dépôt légal : 2ᵉ trimestre 2019

Concept, Project Management: koenemann.com GmbH
Text: Hajo Düchting
Editing: Uta Hasekamp

Translation into French: Denis-Armand Canal
Translations into English, Spanish, Portuguese, Dutch:

TEXTCASE
info@textcase.nl
textcase.de   textcase.eu

Layout: Christoph Eiden
Picture credits: Bridgeman Images

ISBN: 978-3-7419-2417-0

Printed in China by Shenzen Hua Xin Colour-printing & Platemaking Co., Ltd

Contents Sommaire Inhalt Índice Índice Inhoud

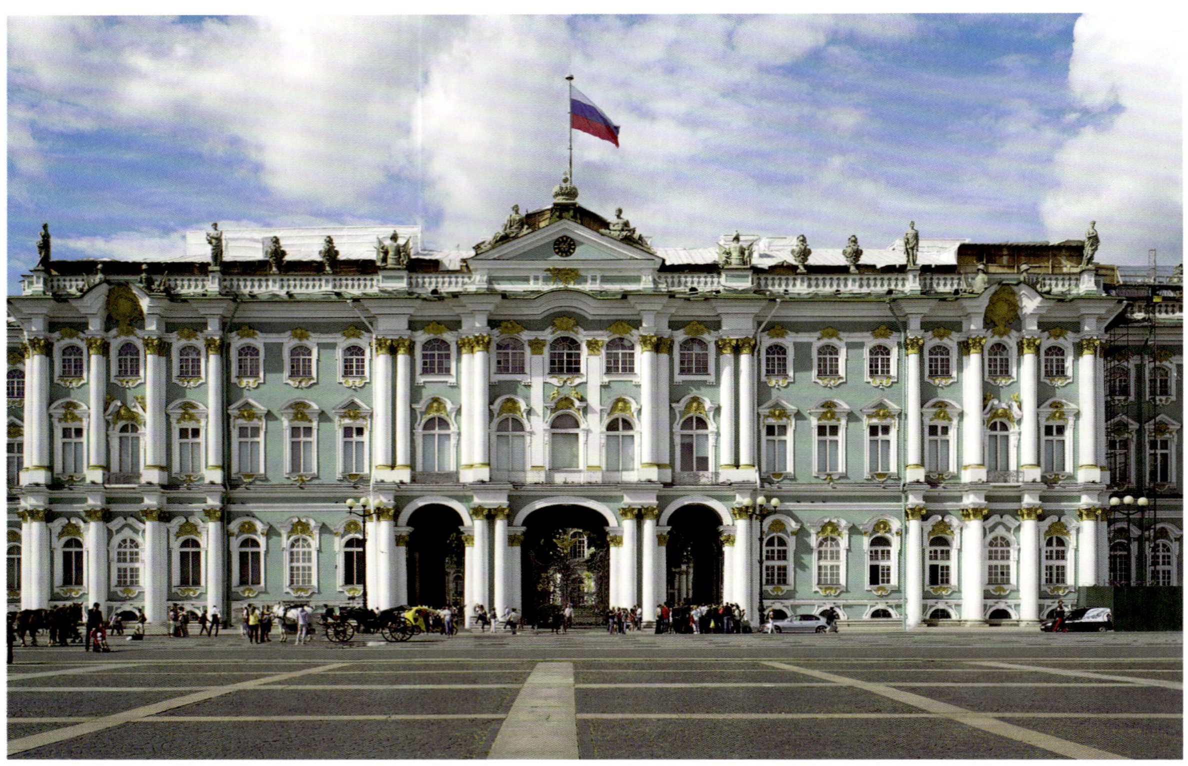

The Hermitage in St. Petersburg

St. Petersburg's Hermitage Museum (French *ermitage:* Place of solitude, hermitage) is one of the largest and most important art museums in the world and boasts a rich history. The buildings in which the museum is located include the Small Hermitage, the Old Hermitage, the New Hermitage, the famous Winter Palace, and the Hermitage Theatre. The museum, founded by Russian Czar Catherine II in 1764 to hold her private collection, has been open to the public since 1852 and now displays more than 60,000 pieces at any time in about 350 rooms. In addition to the archaeological and decorative arts collections, it is museum's extraordinary collection of European paintings from the early Renaissance to the modern era that attracts millions of visitors each year. A large part of the Russian art has since been given to the Russian Museum, but the Hermitage still holds high quality collections of Russian icons, costumes, and jewelry from the Fabergé workshop. Only a small fraction of the three million or so works can be displayed at any time; the rest are kept in storage. The museum has about 2,500 employees.

L'Ermitage de Saint-Pétersbourg

À Saint-Pétersbourg, l'Ermitage – qui en français désigne un lieu écarté ou une retraite d'ermite – est l'un des plus grands et des plus importants musées du monde, riche aussi d'une histoire mouvementée. L'ensemble homonyme de bâtiments – dans lequel se déploie le musée – comporte, à côté du Petit, du Vieil et du Nouvel Ermitage, le célèbre palais d'Hiver et le théâtre de l'Ermitage. Fondé en 1764 comme collection privée de l'impératrice Catherine II, le musée est accessible au public depuis 1852 et présente aujourd'hui plus de 60 000 pièces, dans quelque 350 salles d'exposition. À côté des collections d'archéologie et d'artisanat d'art, c'est surtout l'extraordinaire collection de peintures européennes – de la Haute Renaissance à la période moderne – qui attire chaque année des millions de visiteurs. Une grande partie de l'art russe jadis rassemblé a été transféré au Musée russe, mais l'Ermitage conserve toujours de remarquables collections dans ce domaine, comme des icônes et des costumes russes, ainsi que des chefs-d'œuvre de l'atelier Fabergé. Une fraction seulement des collections peut être exposée : presque trois millions d'œuvres sont conservées dans les réserves. Lesdites collections sont confiées aux soins de 2 500 collaborateurs.

Die Eremitage in St. Petersburg

Die Eremitage in St. Petersburg (frz. *ermitage:* Ort der Einsamkeit, Einsiedelei) ist eines der wichtigsten und größten Kunstmuseen der Welt mit einer bewegten Geschichte. Das gleichnamige Gebäudeensemble, in dem sich das Museum befindet, umfasst neben der Kleinen, der Alten und der Neuen Eremitage den berühmten Winterpalast (oder Winterpalais) und das Eremitage-Theater. Das Museum, das im Jahre 1764 als private Sammlung von der russischen Kaiserin Katharina II. begründet wurde, ist seit 1852 für die Öffentlichkeit zugänglich und präsentiert heute in etwa 350 Räumen mehr als 60.000 Exponate. Neben den archäologischen und kunsthandwerklichen Sammlungen zieht besonders die außerordentliche Sammlung europäischer Gemälde von der Frührenaissance bis zur Moderne jedes Jahr Millionen Besucher an. Ein Großteil der einst gesammelten russischen Kunst wurde dem Russischen Museum überlassen, doch befinden sich in der Eremitage nach wie vor qualitätsvolle Kollektionen wie beispielsweise russische Ikonen und Kostüme sowie Prunkstücke aus der Fabergé-Werkstatt. Ausgestellt werden kann nur ein Bruchteil der Sammlung, fast drei Millionen weitere Kunstwerke werden in den Depots aufbewahrt. Die Sammlungen werden von 2500 Mitarbeitern betreut.

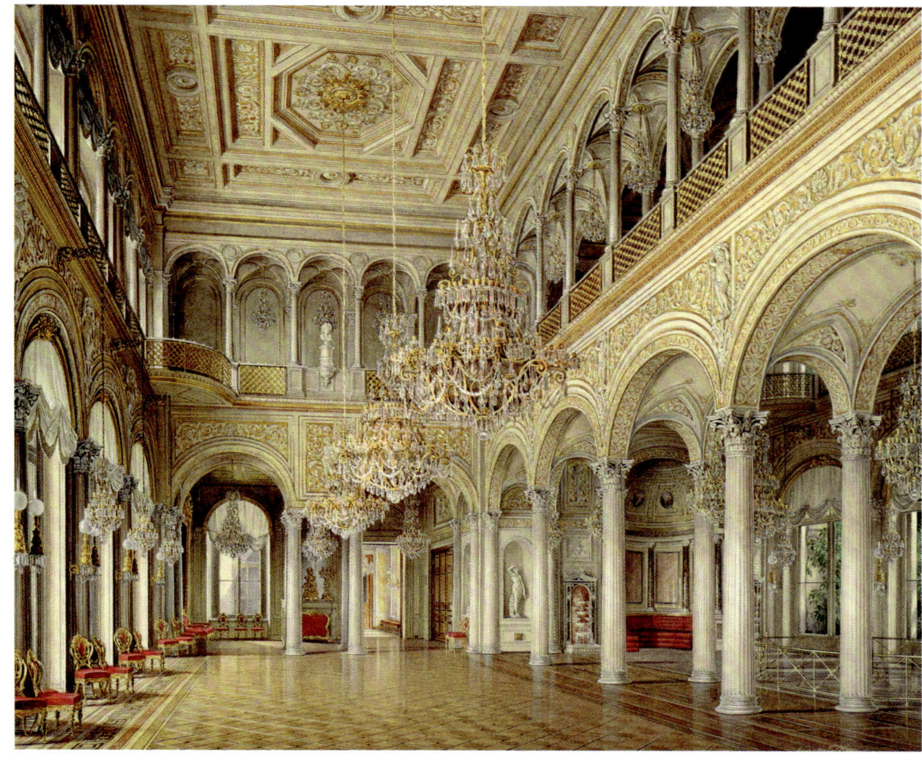

El Hermitage en San Petersburgo

El Hermitage en San Petersburgo (del francés *ermitage:* ermita, refugio del ermitaño) es uno de los museos de arte más grandes e importantes del mundo, con una historia ciertamente agitada. El conjunto de edificios del mismo nombre en el que se encuentra el museo incluye junto al Pequeño Hermitago, el Viejo, el Nuevo, el famoso Palacio de invierno y el teatro del Hermitage. El museo, fundado en 1764 como colección privada por la emperatriz rusa Catalina II, está abierto al público desde 1852 y presenta hoy en sus casi 350 salas más de 60.000 piezas. Junto a las colecciones arqueológicas y artesanales es especialmente su extraordinaria colección de pintura europea, que abarca desde el Renacimiento temprano hasta la era moderna, la que atrae cada año a millones de visitantes. Una gran parte del arte ruso de su colección fue donado al Museo Ruso, pero aún se conservan en el Hermitage algunas colecciones de valor por ejemplo de iconos y vestidos rusos así como joyas del taller de Fabergé. Actualmente solo puede exponerse una parte de la colección, y tres millones de obras de arte se guardan por el momento en los almacenes del museo. Unos 2500 trabajadores se ocupan de las colecciones.

O Hermitage em São Petersburgo

O Hermitage em São Petersburgo (fr. *ermitage:* local da solidão, eremitério) é um dos maiores e mais importantes museus de arte do mundo com uma história atribulada. Além do Pequeno, do Antigo e do Novo Hermitage, o conjunto de edifícios homónimo, no qual se encontra o museu, abrange igualmente o célebre Palácio de Inverno e o Teatro do Hermitage. O museu fundado em 1764 enquanto coleção particular da imperatriz Catarina II da Rússia está aberto ao público desde 1852 e apresenta atualmente mais de 60.000 peças de exposição em cerca de 350 salas. Além das coleções arqueológicas e artesanais, a extraordinária coleção de pintura europeia, que vai desde o Primeiro Renascimento até ao Modernismo, atrai especialmente todos os anos milhões de visitantes. Uma grande parte da arte russa outrora colecionada foi cedida ao Museu Russo, contando porém o Hermitage de qualquer modo com coleções de elevada qualidade, como, por exemplo, ícones e vestuário russo, bem como luxuosas peças da oficina Fabergé. Apenas é possível expor uma fração da coleção, encontrando-se quase três milhões de outras obras de arte conservadas nos depósitos. As coleções são preservadas por 2500 colaboradores.

De Hermitage in Sint Petersburg

De Hermitage in Sint Petersburg (van het Franse *ermitage,* 'eenzame plek, kluizenaarswoning') is een van de belangrijkste en grootste kunstmusea ter wereld. Het heeft een bewogen geschiedenis. Tot het gelijknamige gebouwencomplex waarin het musea zich bevindt, behoren naast de Kleine, de Oude en de Nieuwe Hermitage ook het beroemde Winterpaleis en het Hermitage Theater. Het museum, dat in 1764 is ontstaan uit de privéverzameling van de Russische tsarina Catharina de Grote, is sinds 1852 voor het brede publiek toegankelijk en toont nu in ongeveer 350 pronkzalen meer dan 60.000 kunstvoorwerpen. Naast de archeologische en kunstnijverheidscollecties trekt vooral de buitengewone collectie van Europese schilderijen uit de vroege renaissance tot de moderne tijd elk jaar weer miljoenen bezoekers. In het museum is het grootste deel van de eertijds bijeengebrachte Russische kunst ondergebracht, maar de Hermitage-collectie omvat net als vroeger ook topcollecties van bijvoorbeeld Russische iconen en kostuums, maar ook pronkstukken uit de Fabergé-fabrieken. Slechts een klein deel van de collectie kan worden tentoongesteld; bijna drie miljoen kunstwerken worden in de depots bewaard. Bij het beheer en behoud van de collectie zijn 2500 medewerkers betrokken.

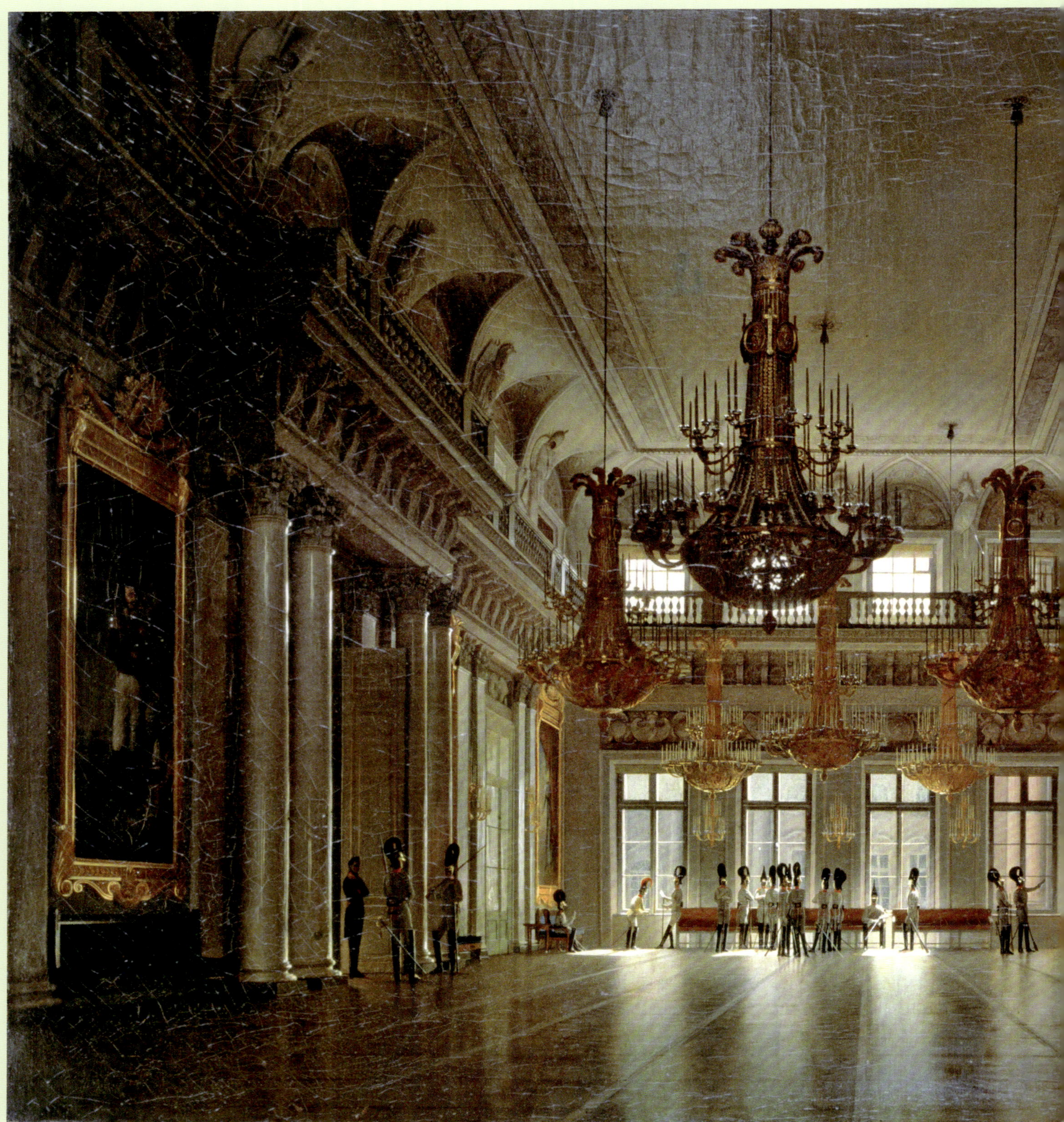

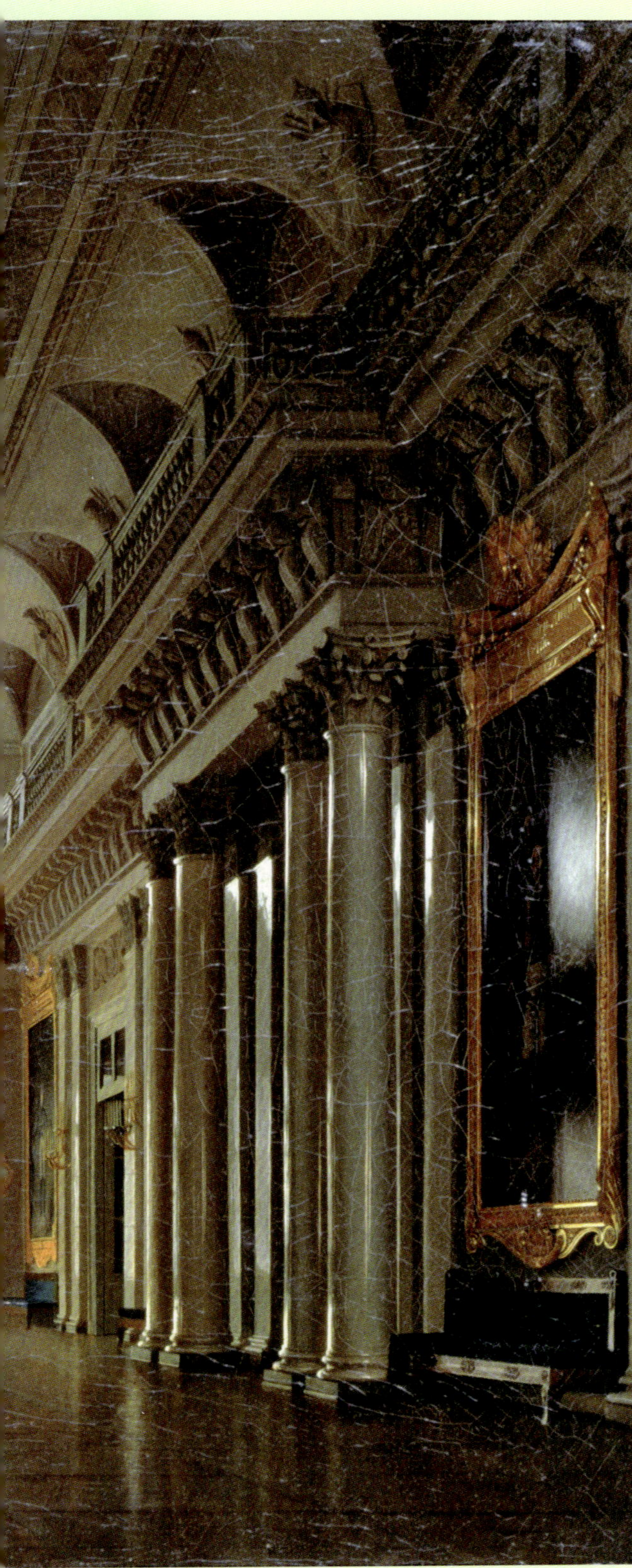

Sergei Konstantinowitsch Sarjanko (1818–70)

The Field Marshal Hall

La Salle des maréchaux au palais d'Hiver

Der Feldmarschall-Saal

La sala del mariscal de campo

O Salão do Marechal-de-Campo

De Veldmaarschalkzaal

c. 1836, Oil on canvas/Huile sur toile, 81 × 109 cm

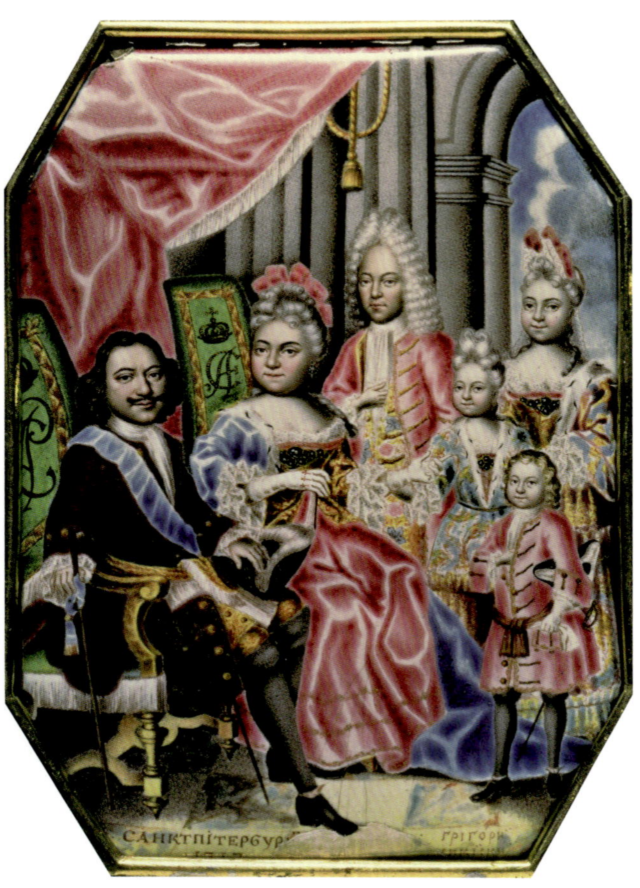

Grigori Semjonowitsch Musikijski (c. 1670 – c. 1739)

The Family of Peter I the Great

La famille de Pierre Ier le Grand

Die Familie von Peter I. dem Großen

La familia de Pedro I el Grande

A Família de Pedro I. o Grande

De familie van Peter I de Grote

c. 1716/17, Enamel/Miniature, émail sur plaque de cuivre

The History of the Hermitage

Today's Hermitage owes its magnificent building on the banks of the River Neva to Russian Czar Catherine the Great (Catherine II) (1729–1796, reign 1762–1796). She had the **Small Hermitage** built between 1764 and 1769 to plans by Jean-Baptiste Vallin de la Mothé. Architect Georg Friedrich Velthen supervised the construction. The Small Hermitage is adjacent to the Winter Palace. It has southern and northern pavilions (the latter on the banks of the river), connected with galleries added later. In the 19th century, the Small Hermitage underwent significant modification. Next door, Velthen built the **Old Hermitage** between 1771 and 1787, with a gallery wing along the Winter Canal added in 1782–83. Giacomo Quarenghi erected the **Hermitage Theatre** between 1783 and 1787. The **New Hermitage** is much newer, having been built between 1842 and 1851 to plans by Leo von Klenze.

The architecture and the precious collection of paintings at the Hermitage are both due to Catherine the Great's vision. The base collection was established in 1764 with 225 paintings that she purchased from

L'histoire de l'Ermitage

L'Ermitage actuel doit ses prestigieux bâtiments, au bord de la Néva, à l'impératrice russe Catherine II ou Catherine la Grande (1729–1796), tsarine à partir de 1762. En 1764–1769, elle fit d'abord construire le **Petit Ermitage** sur les plans de l'architecte français Jean-Baptiste Vallin de la Mothe et sous la supervision de l'architecte allemand Georg Friedrich Veldten. Cet ensemble de bâtiments – jouxtant le palais d'Hiver remanié à partir de 1754 – se compose d'un pavillon sud et d'un pavillon nord sur la Néva, reliés ensuite par des galeries. Tous les corps de bâtiment du Petit Ermitage ont été fortement remaniés au XIXe siècle. En 1771–1787, Veldten construisit l'**Ancien Ermitage** qui reçut en 1782–1783 une aile en galerie le long du canal d'Hiver. En 1783–1787, l'architecte italien Giacomo Quarenghi construisit non loin de là le **théâtre de l'Ermitage.** Enfin, longtemps après la mort de Catherine II, le **Nouvel Ermitage** fut construit sur des plans de l'architecte allemand Leo von Klenze.

Outre l'architecture, la précieuse collection de tableaux remonte aussi à la Grande Catherine. Le noyau

Zur Geschichte

Die heutige Eremitage verdankt ihre prächtigen Gebäude an der Newa der russischen Kaiserin Katharina II. oder Katharina der Großen (1729–1796, seit 1762 Kaiserin). 1764–1769 wurde auf ihren Wunsch nach Plänen von Jean-Baptiste Vallin de la Mothe die **Kleine Eremitage** erbaut, ausführender Architekt war Georg Friedrich Velthen. Dieser Gebäudekomplex, der an den ab 1754 neu errichteten Winterpalast grenzt, besteht aus einem Süd- und einem zur Newa gelegenen Nordpavillon sowie etwas später gebauten Verbindungsgalerien. Im 19. Jahrhundert wurden alle Bestandteile der Kleinen Eremitage stark verändert. Daneben erbaute Velthen 1771–1787 die **Alte Eremitage,** die 1782/83 einen Galerieflügel am Winterkanal erhielt. Giacomo Quarenghi errichtete 1783–1787 das **Eremitage-Theater.** Die **Neue Eremitage** entstand lange nach Katharinas Tod 1842–1851 nach Plänen von Leo von Klenze.

Nicht nur die Architektur, auch die kostbare Gemäldesammlung geht auf Katharina die Große zurück. Den Grundstock bildeten 1764 die 225 Gemälde,

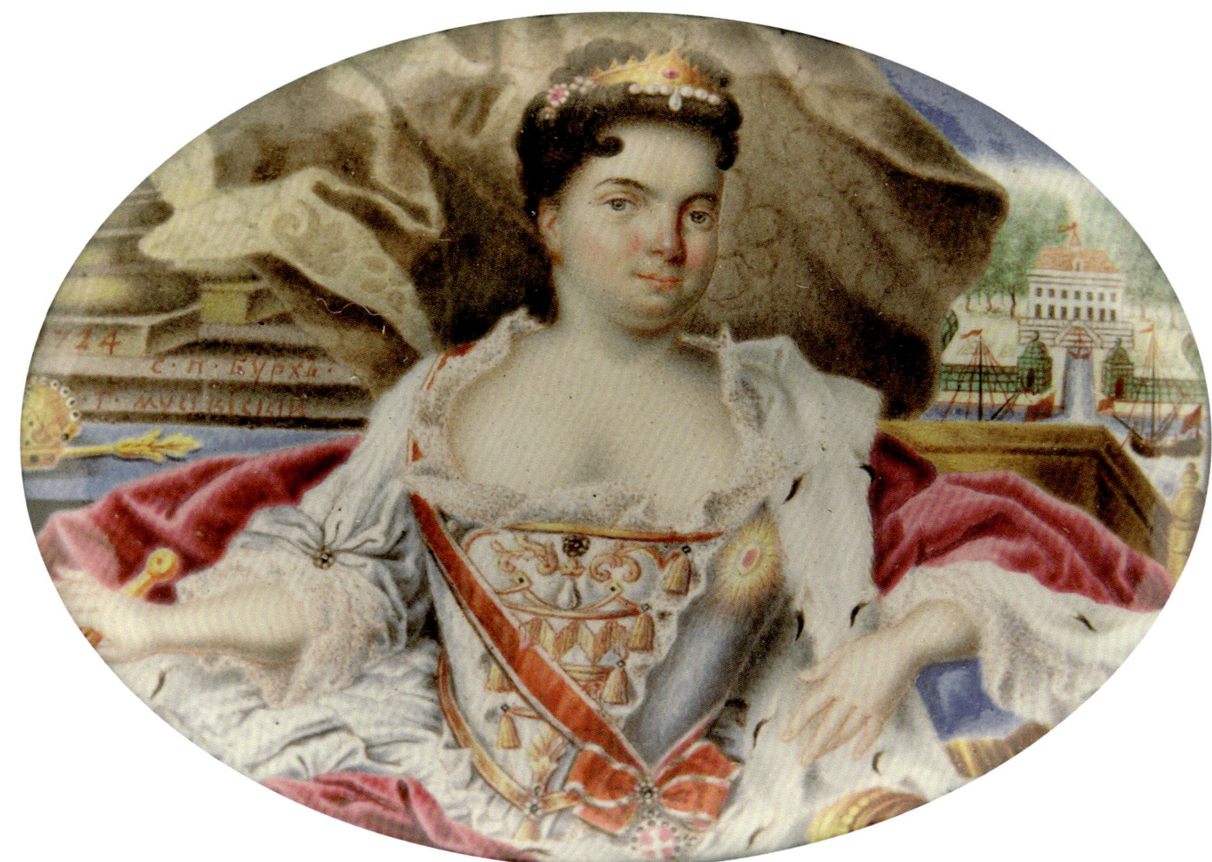

Historia

El actual Hermitage debe sus fabulosos edificios en el Nevá a la emperatriz rusa Catalina II, Catalina la Grande (1729–1796, emperatriz desde 1762). En 1764–1769, por orden suya y diseñado por Jean-Baptiste Vallin de la Mothe, el arquitecto Georg Friedrich Velthen construyó el **Pequeño Hermitage.** Este complejo de edificios colindaba con el recién construido (1754) Palacio de Invierno, contando con un pabellón sur y uno norte que daba al Nevá, y posteriormente se realizaron galerías de unión entre ellos. En el siglo XIX se cambiaron radicalmente todas las partes del Pequeño Hermitage. Junto a este Velthen construyó en 1771–1787 el **Antiguo Hermitage,** que fue ampliado en 1782/83 con una galería colindante al canal de Invierno. Giacomo Quarenghi construyó en 1783–1787 el **Teatro del Hermitage. El Nuevo Hermitage** se construyó ya tras la muerte de Catalina, en 1842–1851, sobre planos de Leo von Klenze.

A Catalina la Grande se deben no solo los edificios, sino también la valiosa colección de pintura. El núcleo de la misma ascendía en 1764 a 225 pinturas que

Sobre a história

O Hermitage deve os seus imponentes edifícios à margem do rio Neva à imperatriz Catarina II da Rússia ou Catarina a Grande (1729–1796, imperatriz desde 1762). Entre 1764 e 1769 foi construído a seu pedido o **Pequeno Hermitage** segundo o projeto de Jean-Baptiste Vallin de la Mothe, tendo sido Georg Friedrich Velthen o arquiteto executante. Este complexo de edifícios, contíguo ao Palácio de Inverno erigido de novo a partir de 1754, é constituído por um pavilhão situado a sul e um pavilhão a norte do rio Neva, bem como pelas galerias de ligação construídas um pouco mais tarde. No século XIX todas as partes constituintes do Pequeno Hermitage foram fortemente alteradas. Ao lado, Velthen construiu entre 1771 e 1787 o **Antigo Hermitage,** que em 1782/83 obteve uma ala com galeria junto ao canal de inverno. Giacomo Quarenghi edificou o **Teatro Hermitage** entre 1783 e 1787. O **Novo Hermitage** surgiu muito depois da morte de Catarina em 1842–1851 segundo o projeto de Leo von Klenze.

Não é apenas a arquitetura, mas também a valiosa coleção de pinturas que provém de Catarina a Grande.

Over de geschiedenis

De huidige Hermitage dankt de prachtige gebouwen aan de Neva aan de Russische tsarina Catharina II of Catharina de Grote (1729–1796, vanaf 1762 tsarina). Van 1764 tot 1769 werd op haar verzoek naar een ontwerp van Jean-Baptiste Vallin de la Mothe de **Kleine Hermitage** gebouwd. Uitvoerend architect was Georg Friedrich Veldten, ook bekend als Yuri Felten. Dit gebouwencomplex, dat grenst aan het vanaf 1754 nieuw gebouwde Winterpaleis bestaat uit een Zuid- en een aan de Neva gelegen Noord-Paviljoen plus iets later toegevoegde verbindingsgalerijen. In de 19de eeuw werden alle onderdelen van de Kleine Hermitage ingrijpend veranderd. Daarnaast bouwde Felten van 1771 tot 1787 de **Oude Hermitage,** die in 1782–1783 een galerijvleugel aan het Winterkanaal kreeg. Giacomo Quarenghi bouwde van 1783 tot 1787 het **Hermitage Theater.** De **Nieuwe Hermitage** dateert van lang na Catharina's dood en werd van 1842 tot 1851 naar ontwerpen van Leo von Klenze gebouwd.

Niet alleen de architectuur, ook de kostbare schilderijenverzameling is ontstaan op initiatief van

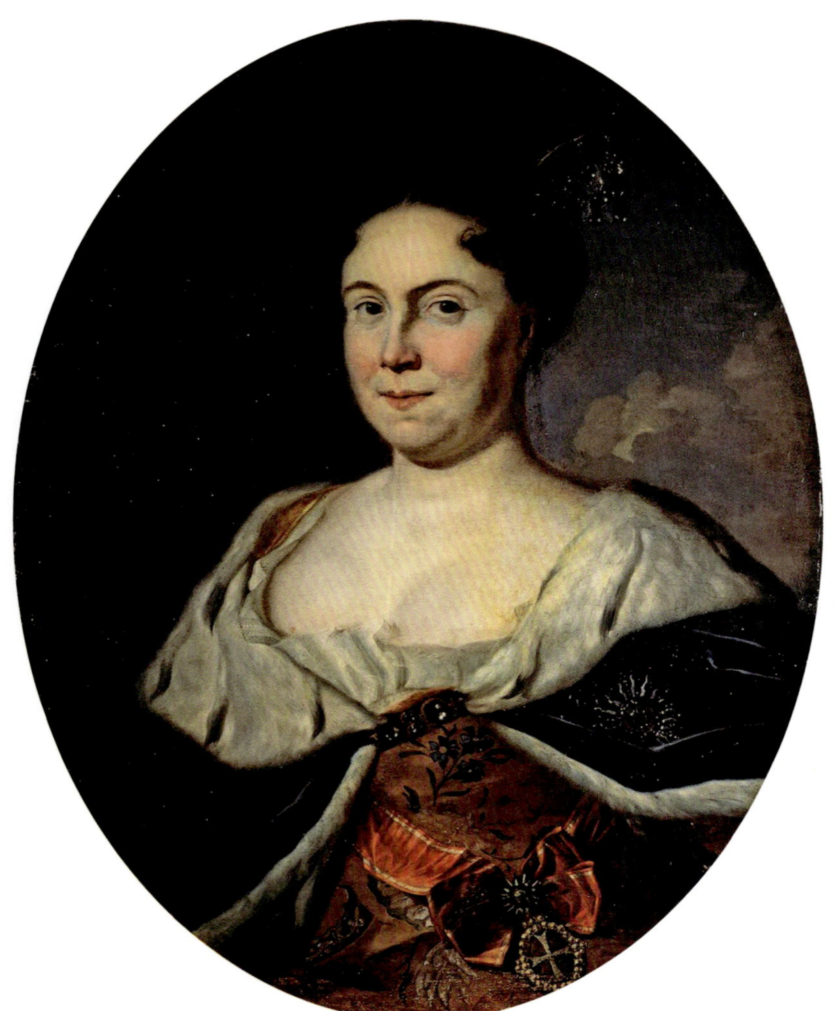

Berlin art dealer Johann Ernst Gotzkowsky. Catherine then bought nearly 1,000 paintings a year later from the estate of Saxon Prime Minister Count Heinrich von Brühl.

Various other rounds of purchases grew the collection to 3,996 paintings from various European schools: In 1779, she purchased the collection of British Prime Minister Robert Walpole and then acquired 119 largely Dutch and Flemish works from the collection of Count Baudouin, including nine paintings by Rembrandt as well as works by Van Dyck, van Ostade, Ruisdael, and Teniers the Younger.

Catherine's successors were likewise committed to building the Hermitage collection. Throughout the nineteenth century, they systematically purchased works of art. In the first half of the century, various local and Middle Eastern archaeological pieces were added. In

initial est constitué par les 225 tableaux achetés en 1764 au marchand d'art berlinois Johann Ernst Gotzkowsky. Un an plus tard, Catherine II put acquérir, pour 80 000 thalers, presque mille tableaux de la succession du comte Heinrich von Brühl, Premier ministre de Saxe.

L'acquisition de divers lots de tableaux permit à la collection d'atteindre 3 996 peintures de différentes écoles européennes, du vivant même de Catherine II. En 1779, elle réussit à acheter la collection rassemblée par le Premier ministre britannique Robert Walpole ; en 1781, elle acquit 119 toiles hollandaises et flamandes de la collection du comte Baudouin, dont neuf toiles de Rembrandt et des œuvres de van Dyck, van Ostade, Ruysdael et Teniers le Jeune.

Les successeurs de Catherine II sur le trône de Russie s'engagèrent aussi avec constance pour les collections d'art de l'Ermitage. Pendant tout le XIXe siècle, ils

die sie von dem Berliner Kunsthändler Johann Ernst Gotzkowsky erwarb, sowie fast 1000 Bilder, die Katharina ein Jahr später, 1765, für 80.000 Taler aus dem Nachlass des sächsischen Premierministers Graf Heinrich von Brühl erhalten konnte.

Durch den Kauf verschiedener Konvolute wuchs die Sammlung zu Lebzeiten Katharinas der Großen auf 3996 Gemälde verschiedener europäischer Schulen an. 1779 gelang der Ankauf der Kollektion, die der britische Premierminister Robert Walpole zusammengetragen hatte, 1781 wurden 119 Gemälde vor allem niederländischer und flämischer Schulen aus der Sammlung des Grafen Baudouin erworben, darunter neun Gemälde von Rembrandt sowie Bilder von van Dyck, van Ostade, Ruisdael und Teniers d. J.

Auch die Nachfolger Katharinas auf dem russischen Kaiserthron engagierten sich sehr für die

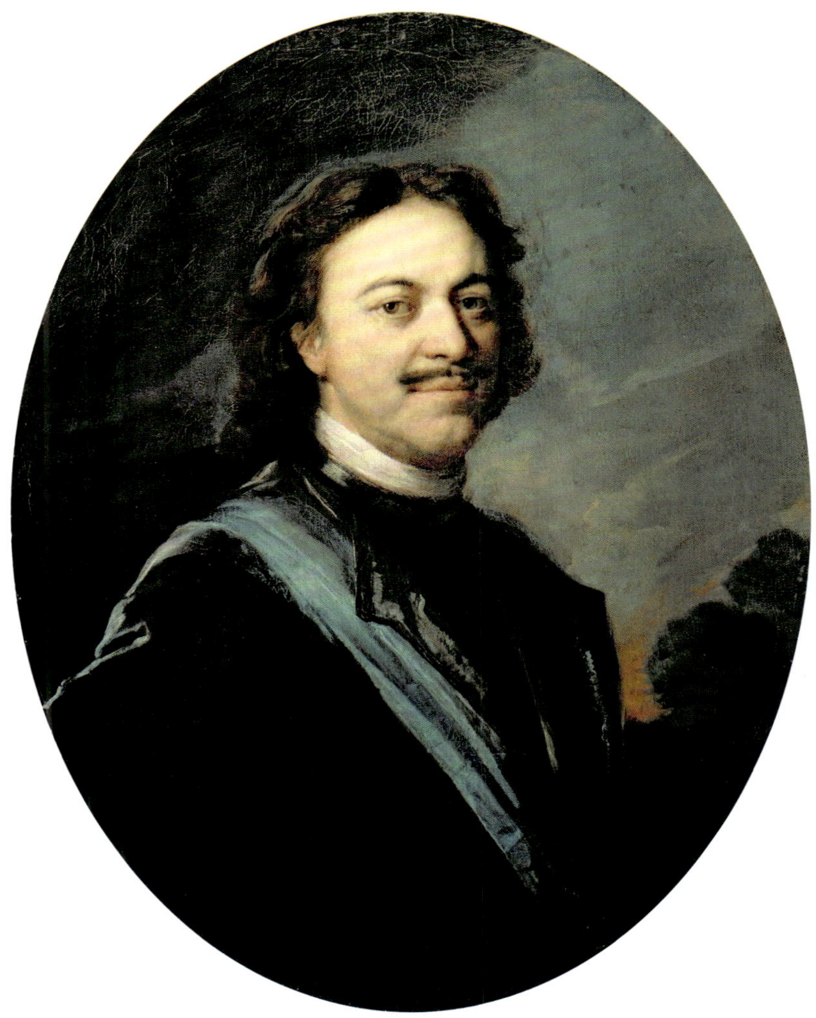

compró del marchante de arte berlinés Johann Ernst Gotzkovsky, así como otros 1000 cuadros que Catalina compró por 80.000 táleros un año más tarde, en 1765, a los sucesores del primer ministro sajón el Conde Heinrich von Brühl.

Con la compra de varias colecciones la colección creció durante la vida de Catalina la Grande hasta abarcar 3996 pinturas de diversas escuelas europeas. En 1779 se consiguió comprar la colección del primer ministro británico Robert Walpole, en 1781 se compraron 119 cuadros en su mayoría de las escuelas flamenca y holandesa al conde Baudouin, entre los cuales había 9 de Rembrandt así como otros de van Dyck, van Ostade, Ruisdael y Teniers el Joven .

También las sucesoras de Catalina en el trono imperial ruso se dedicaron con esmero a la colección de arte del Hermitage. Compraron de forma

O rés-do-chão era constituído em 1764 pelas 225 pinturas que a mesma adquiriu ao comerciante de arte berlinense, Johann Ernst Gotzkowsky, bem como quase 1000 pinturas que Catarina conseguiu obter um ano mais tarde, em 1765, por 80.000 táleres do legado do Primeiro-ministro da Saxónia, o Conde Heinrich von Brühl.

Através da compra de vários convolutos, a coleção subiu ao longo da vida de Catarina a Grande para 3996 pinturas de diferentes escolas europeias. Em 1779 realizou-se a compra da coleção, que o Primeiro-ministro britânico Robert Walpole havia reunido, em 1781 foram adquiridas 119 pinturas, sobretudo de escolas holandesas e flamengas da coleção do Conde Baudouin, entre elas, nove pinturas de Rembrandt, bem como obras de van Dyck, van Ostade, Ruisdael e Teniers d.J.

De igual modo, os sucessores de Catarina ao trono russo empenharam-se muito em manter a coleção de

Catharina de Grote. De basis van de collectie wordt gevormd door de 225 schilderijen die zij van de Berlijnse kunsthandelaar Johann Ernst Gotzkowsky kreeg, net als bijna 1000 beelden die Catharina een jaar later, in 1765, voor 80.000 daalders uit de nalatenschap van de Saksische premier Graaf Heinrich von Brühl kon kopen.

Door de koop van diverse convoluten breidde de kunstverzameling zich nog tijdens het leven van Catharina de Grote verder uit tot 3996 schilderijen uit verschillende Europese schilderscholen. In 1779 werd de aankoop van de collectie van de Britse premier Robert Walpole succesvol afgerond, in 1781 werden 119 schilderijen van met name schilders uit de Hollandse School en de Vlaamse School uit de collectie van Graaf Baudouin verworven, waaronder negen werken van Rembrandt en prenten van Van Dyck, Van Ostade, Ruisdael en Teniers de Jonge.

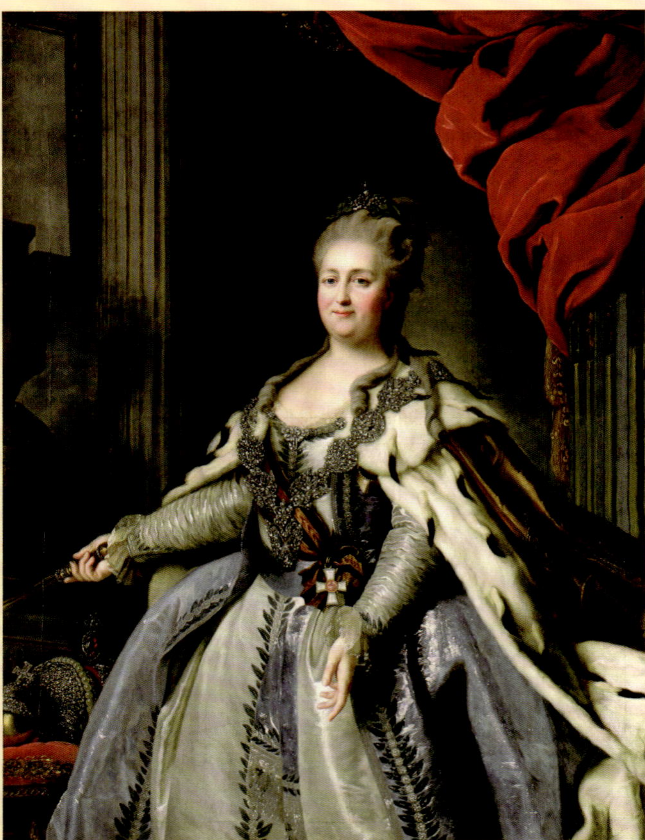

Catherine the Great and her Hermitage Complex

The first structure to be completed in the complex, the South Pavilion of the Small Hermitage, lived up to its name and served as a place for Catherine the Great to retreat from life in the court. This is where she hung the first pieces she had acquired to serve as the backdrop to the intimate, informal gatherings known as "little hermitages" that she would host there. Catherine's chambers soon became too small for her steadily growing art collection, leading not only to the construction of the connecting galleries to the Northern Pavilion, but also the adjacent building, originally called the Great Hermitage (and later rechristened the Old Hermitage when the New Hermitage was built). This building was not only a place for Catherine to display her collection, but also became the venue for Catherine's "great hermitages", full-on receptions where the Czar would welcome up to 200 guests at a time. These "hermitages" also came to include stage performances which initially took place in a small theatre in the Great Hermitage. Later, they were moved to the purpose-built Hermitage Theatre.

Catherine et ses « ermitages »

Le premier bâtiment de l'ensemble architectural – le pavillon sud du Petit Ermitage – servait de lieu de retraite à la Grande Catherine. Elle y installa les premières œuvres d'art acquises par elle et y organisait aussi des soirées à la fois intimes et informelles qu'elle appelait ses « petits ermitages », nom dont on désigna bientôt le bâtiment. Mais les pièces en furent bientôt trop petites pour sa collection d'art, en augmentation constante. Pour cette raison on construisit non seulement les galeries de liaison avec le pavillon nord, mais aussi le bâtiment adjacent, baptisé d'abord « Grand Ermitage », et plus tard « Vieil Ermitage » après la construction du Nouvel Ermitage. Ce bâtiment servait non seulement à la présentation des collections, mais aussi pour les prestigieuses réceptions des « grands ermitages » auxquelles la tsarine conviait parfois jusqu'à deux cents invités. Ces soirées incluaient souvent des représentations théâtrales qui se déroulèrent d'abord dans un petit théâtre aménagé dans le Grand Ermitage, puis plus tard au théâtre de l'Ermitage spécialement construit à cette fin.

Katharina und ihre „Ermitagen"

Der erste Eremitage-Bau, der Südpavillon der Kleinen Eremitage, diente Katharina der Großen als Rückzugsort. Hier brachte sie die ersten von ihr erworbenen Kunstwerke unter und veranstaltete intime, zwanglose Gesellschaften, die „Kleinen Ermitagen", nach denen dann auch das Gebäude selbst bezeichnet wurde. Doch waren die Räume für Katharinas stetig wachsende Kunstsammlung bald zu klein, weshalb für diese nicht nur die Verbindungsgalerien zum Nordpavillon errichtet wurden, sondern auch der angrenzende Bau, der zunächst als Große Eremitage und später (nach dem Bau der Neuen Eremitage) als Alte Eremitage bezeichnet wurde. Dieses Gebäude diente nicht nur der Präsentation von Kunst, sondern war auch Schauplatz der prunkvollen „Großen Ermitagen", Empfänge, an denen bis zu 200 Gäste der Kaiserin aufwarteten. Zu Katharinas „Ermitagen" gehörten auch Theateraufführungen. Diese fanden zunächst in einem kleinen Theater in der Großen (Alten) Ermitage statt, später im eigens erbauten Eremitage-Theater.

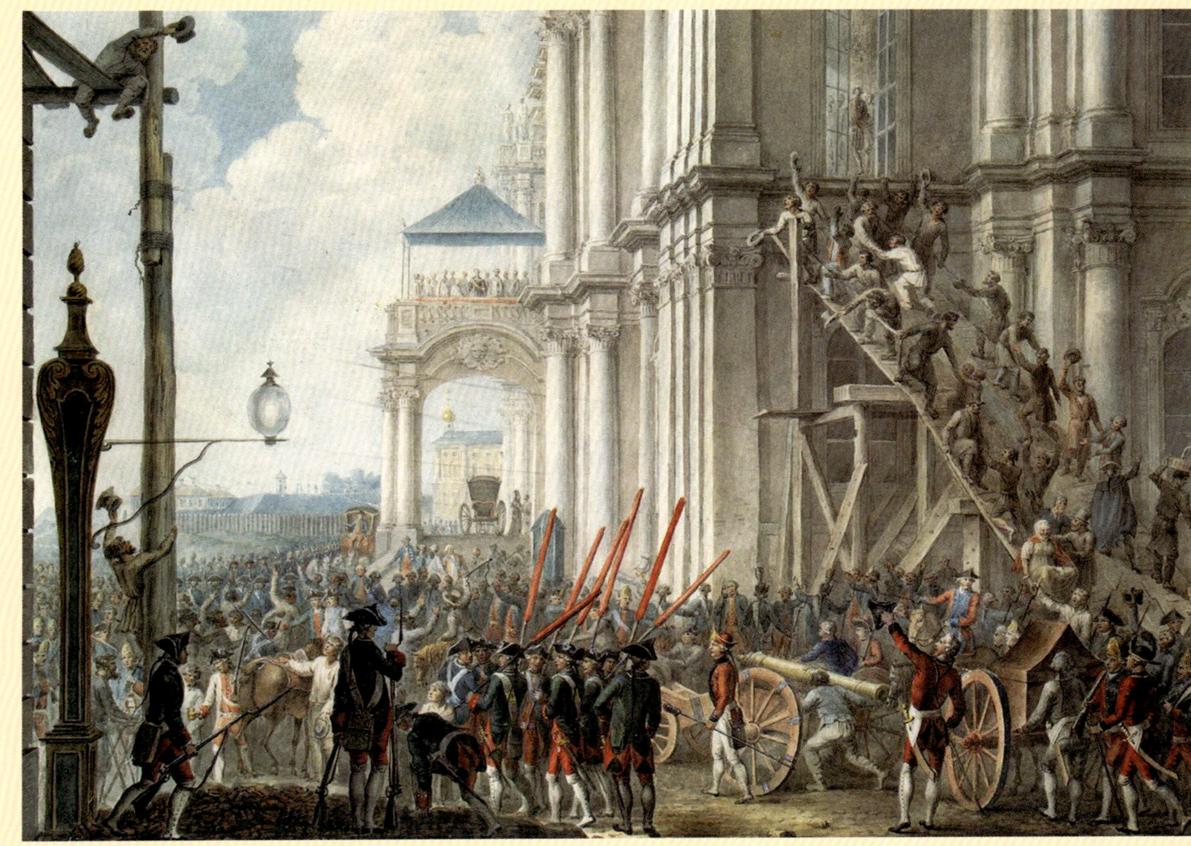

Catalina y sus "Hermitages"

El primer edificio del Hermitage, el pabellón sur del Pequeño Hermitage, sirvió como lugar de retiro para Catalina. Aquí trajo las primeras obras de arte que adquirió, organizando veladas íntimas e informales, sus "Pequeños Hermitages", que acabarían por dar nombre al edificio. Pero estas estancias rápidamente se volvieron demasiado pequeñas para la colección de Catalina, constantemente en crecimiento, por lo que se construyeron no ya solo las galerías de conexión al pabellón norte, sino también un edificio anexo que sería conocido como el Gran Hermitage y posteriormente, tras la construcción del Nuevo Hermitage, el Viejo Hermitage. Este edificio servía no solo para exponer arte, sino que era además escenario de los fastuosos "Grandes Hermitages", recepciones con hasta 200 invitados de la emperatriz. Parte de los "Hermitages" de Catalina eran representaciones teatrales. Al principio estas se presentaban en un pequeño teatro del Gran (Viejo) Hermitage, y después en el propio Teatro del Hermitage, construido a tal efecto.

Catarina e os seus "Hermitages"

A primeira construção do Hermitage, o pavilhão sul do Pequeno Hermitage, servia a Catarina a Grande de espaço de retiro. Aqui, a imperatriz acolheu as primeiras obras de arte que adquiriu e organizou reuniões íntimas e informais, os "pequenos hermitages", segundo os quais também o próprio edifício obteve o seu nome. Porém, os espaços tornaram-se, desde logo, pequenos para a coleção de arte de Catarina em permanente crescimento, pelo que não só foram construídas as galerias de ligação ao pavilhão norte, como também se realizou a edificação limítrofe, que inicialmente era designada de Grande Hermitage e mais tarde (depois da construção do Novo Hermitage) de Antigo Hermitage. Este edifício não só servia para a apresentação da arte, sendo também o local dos magníficos "Grandes Hermitages", ou seja, receções nas quais a imperatriz era esperada por até 200 convidados. Dos "Hermitages" de Catarina faziam também parte apresentações de teatro. Estas realizavam-se inicialmente no teatro pequeno no Grande (Velho) Hermitage e, mais tarde, no Teatro Hermitage especificamente edificado para esse fim.

Catharina en haar 'hermitages'

Het eerste Hermitage-gebouw, het Zuid-Paviljoen van de Kleine Hermitage, was letterlijk bedoeld als een kluizenaarswoning waar de tsarina zich kon terugtrekken. Hier bracht ze de eerste aangekochte kunstwerken onder en organiseerde ze intieme, vrijblijvende soirées, de 'kleine hermitages', waarmee ook het gebouw zelf werd aangeduid. Maar de vertrekken waren al snel te klein voor Catharina's almaar groter wordende kunstverzameling. Daarom werden er niet alleen verbindingsgalerijen naar het Noord-Paviljoen gebouwd, maar verrees ook de wat al snel de Grote Hermitage en later (na de bouw van de Nieuwe Hermitage) de Oude Hermitage werd genoemd. In dit gebouw werd niet alleen kunst tentoongesteld; het was ook het toneel van grote galabijeenkomsten, de 'grote hermitages', ontvangsten waarbij de tsarina tot 200 gasten verwelkomde. Bij Catharina's 'hermitages' hoorden ook theatervoorstellingen. Die vonden eerst plaats in een klein theater in de Grote (of Oude) Hermitage, later in het in haar opdracht gebouwde Hermitage Theater.

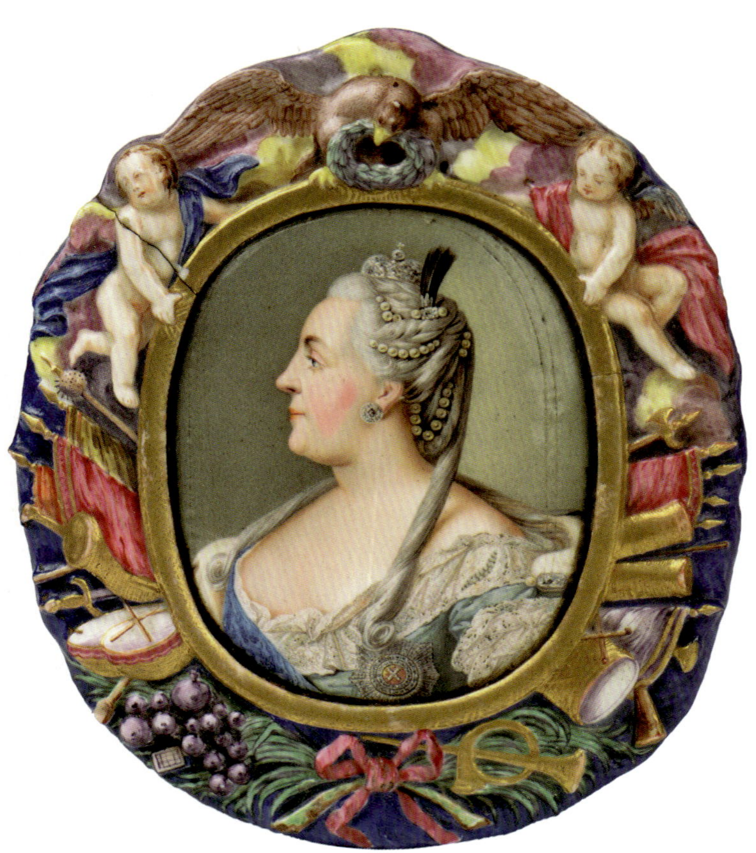

1825, additional space was dedicated to a collection of eighteenth-century Russian art, with the works displayed by school.

The collections remained exclusively open to courtiers until Czar Nicholas I officially separated the imperial residence and the Hermitage collection on February 17, 1852, making the latter available to the public for the first time in the newly erected New Hermitage.

The world wars and the political and social upheavals of the 20th century had a direct impact on the Hermitage. The intensive collection activities of the 19th and early 20th centuries reached a high point in 1914 with the acquisition of the *Madonna with the Flower (Madonna Benois)* by Leonardo da Vinci. The First World War abruptly interrupted this work. Many of the works were taken to Moscow and only retrieved after the war with great difficulty, although the galleries continued to operate. After the possessions of the Russian aristocracy were expropriated in the aftermath of the 1917 October Revolution, many high-quality private collections as well as art from churches were transferred to the Hermitage. Its holdings quadrupled

achetèrent méthodiquement des œuvres d'art ; des objets archéologiques et des pièces orientales s'y ajoutèrent dans la première moitié du siècle. Les tsars accentuèrent aussi les efforts de présentation méthodique, en classant et en accrochant les tableaux par écoles.

Jusqu'au milieu du siècle, les collections n'étaient ouvertes qu'aux membres de la Cour. Le 17 février 1852, le tsar Nicolas Ier sépara la résidence impériale de la collection de l'Ermitage, cette dernière – transformée ainsi en musée – devenant pour la première fois accessible au public dans le Nouvel Ermitage récemment construit.

Les guerres mondiales et les bouleversements politiques et sociaux du XXe siècle eurent un impact direct sur l'Ermitage. L'intense activité de collection du XIXe siècle et du début du XXe – atteignant son apogée en 1914 avec l'acquisition de la *Madone Benois* de Léonard de Vinci – fut brutalement interrompue par la Première Guerre mondiale. Une grande partie des collections fut déménagée à Moscou (d'où elles ne revinrent que très difficilement, après la guerre), mais la galerie de tableaux resta sur place. Les biens de la

Kunstsammlung der Eremitage. Sie kauften während des gesamten 19. Jahrhunderts systematisch Kunstwerke an – so kamen in der ersten Jahrhunderthälfte archäologische und orientalische Exponate hinzu; 1825 wurden Räume der russischen Kunst des 18. Jahrhunderts gewidmet – und verfolgten auch in der Präsentation eine Systematik: Die Gemälde wurden nun nach Schulen gehängt.

Bis zu dieser Zeit standen die Sammlungen nur Mitgliedern des Hofes offen. Am 17. Februar 1852 trennte Nikolaus I. die kaiserliche Residenz und die Eremitage-Sammlung, wodurch Letztere als Museum in der gerade erbauten Neuen Eremitage erstmals der Öffentlichkeit zugänglich wurde.

Die Weltkriege sowie die politischen und gesellschaftlichen Umwälzungen des 20. Jahrhunderts wirkten sich direkt auf die Eremitage aus. Die intensive Sammeltätigkeit des 19. und beginnenden 20. Jahrhunderts – ein Höhepunkt war 1914 der Erwerb der *Madonna mit der Blume (Madonna Benois)* von Leonardo da Vinci – wurde durch den Ersten Weltkrieg jäh unterbrochen. Ein Großteil der Schätze wurde nach Moskau gebracht (von wo sie nach Kriegsende

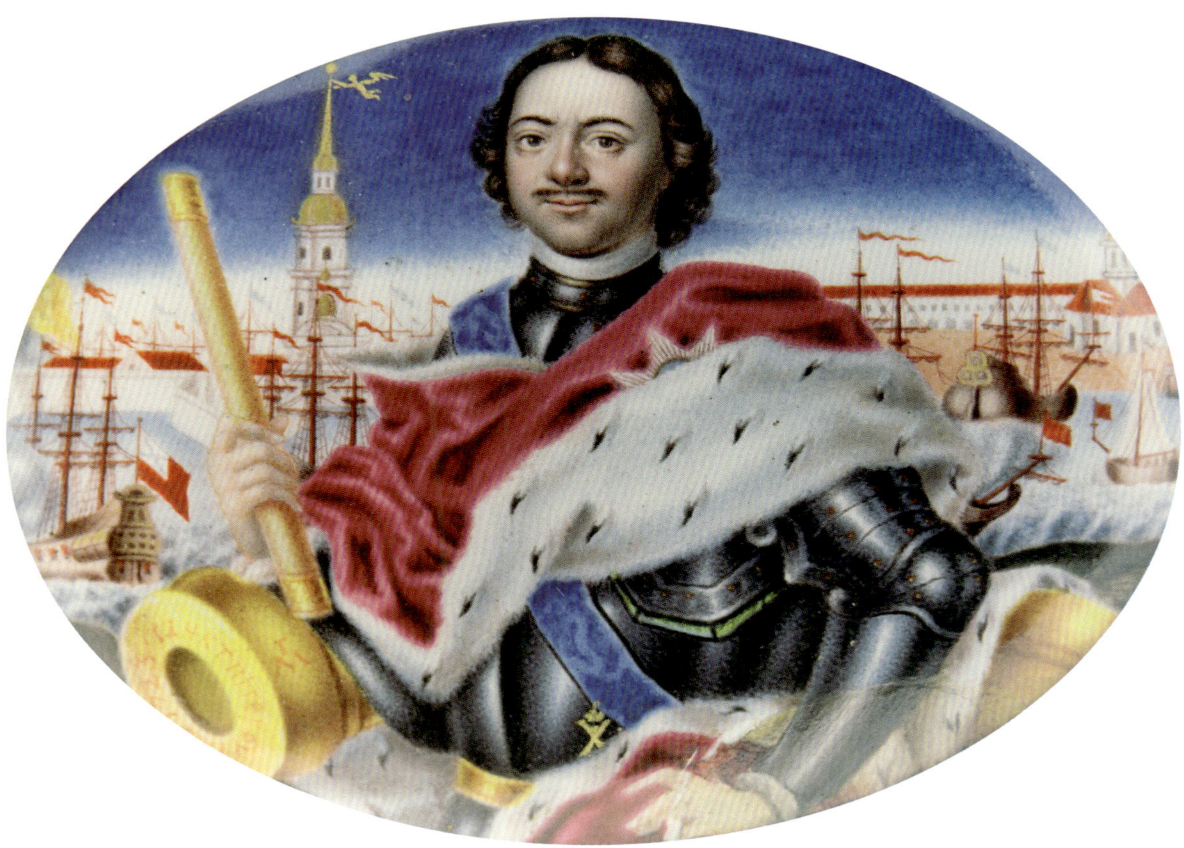

sistemática durante el XIX obras de arte -así llegaron
durante la primera mitad del siglo piezas orientales
y arqueológicas; en 1825 se dedicaron algunas salas al
arte ruso del XVIII – y se sistematizó la presentación:
empezaron a colocarse las pinturas por escuelas.

Hasta este momento la colección estaba únicamente
abierta a miembros de la corte. El 17 de febrero de 1852
Nicolás I separó la residencia imperial de la colección
del Hermitage, por lo que esta última se hizo accesible
al público como museo en el recién construido Nuevo
Hermitage.

Las guerras mundiales y los cambios políticos y
sociales del XX tuvieron una influencia directa en el
Hermitage. La intensa actividad de coleccionismo
del XIX y XX -con un punto álgido en la adquisición
en 1914 de la *Virgen de la flor (Madonna Benois)* de
Leonardo da Vinci- se vio interrumpida abruptamente
por la Primera Guerra Mundial. Una gran parte de
los tesoros se llevó a Moscú (de donde, tras el fin de la
guerra, costó mucho recuperarlos); la galería de pintura
sin embargo se mantuvo intacta en su lugar. Dado
que después de la Revolución de Octubre de 1917 se
expropió a la nobleza, se transfirieron al Hermitage en

arte do Hermitage. Ao longo de todo o século XIX
foram adquirindo sistematicamente obras de arte.
Assim, na primeira metade do século, juntaram-se
objetos de exposição arqueológicos e orientais. Em
1825, havia salas dedicadas à arte russa do século
XVIII, que também na sua apresentação seguiam uma
sistematização: as pinturas eram agora suspensas por
escolas.

Até esta época, apenas os membros da corte tinham
acesso às coleções. A 17 de fevereiro de 1852 Nicolau I.
separou a residência imperial da coleção Hermitage,
pelo que esta última passou a estar acessível ao público
pela primeira vez no Novo Hermitage precisamente
erigido.

As Guerras Mundiais, bem como as revoluções
políticas e sociais do século XX tiveram uma
repercussão direta sobre o Hermitage. A intensa
atividade de colecionismo do século XIX e do início
do século XX, tendo sido o seu ponto alto a compra da
obra *Madona com Flor (Virgem Benois)* de Leonardo da
Vinci em 1914, foi repentinamente interrompida devido
à Primeira Guerra Mundial. Uma grande parte dos
tesouros foi levada para Moscovo (de onde após o fim

Ook Catharina's opvolgers op de Russische
keizerstroon verbonden hun naam aan de kunstcollectie
van de Hermitage. Ze kochten gedurende de hele
19de eeuw systematisch kunstwerken aan. Zo werd de
kunstverzameling in de eerste helft van de 19de eeuw
met archeologische en oriëntaalse kunst uitgebreid; in
1825 werden zalen ingericht met 18de-eeuwse Russische
kunst. Daarnaast werd met het oog op de presentatie
van de collectie een systematiek ingevoerd: de werken
werden voortaan naar schilderschool gegroepeerd.

Tot die tijd hadden alleen leden van het Hof toegang
tot de collecties. Op 17 februari 1852 scheidde Nicolaas
I de tsarenresidentie en de Hermitage-verzameling,
waarna de kunstcollectie in de kort daarna als museum
gebouwde Nieuwe Hermitage voor het brede publiek
toegankelijk werd.

De wereldoorlogen en de politieke en
maatschappelijke omwentelingen van de 20ste
eeuw waren direct van invloed op de Hermitage.
De intensieve verzamelactiviteit in de 19de en de
vroege 20ste eeuw – een hoogtepunt was in 1914 de
aankoop van de *Madonna met een bloem (Madonna
Benois)* van Leonardo da Vinci – werd door de Eerste

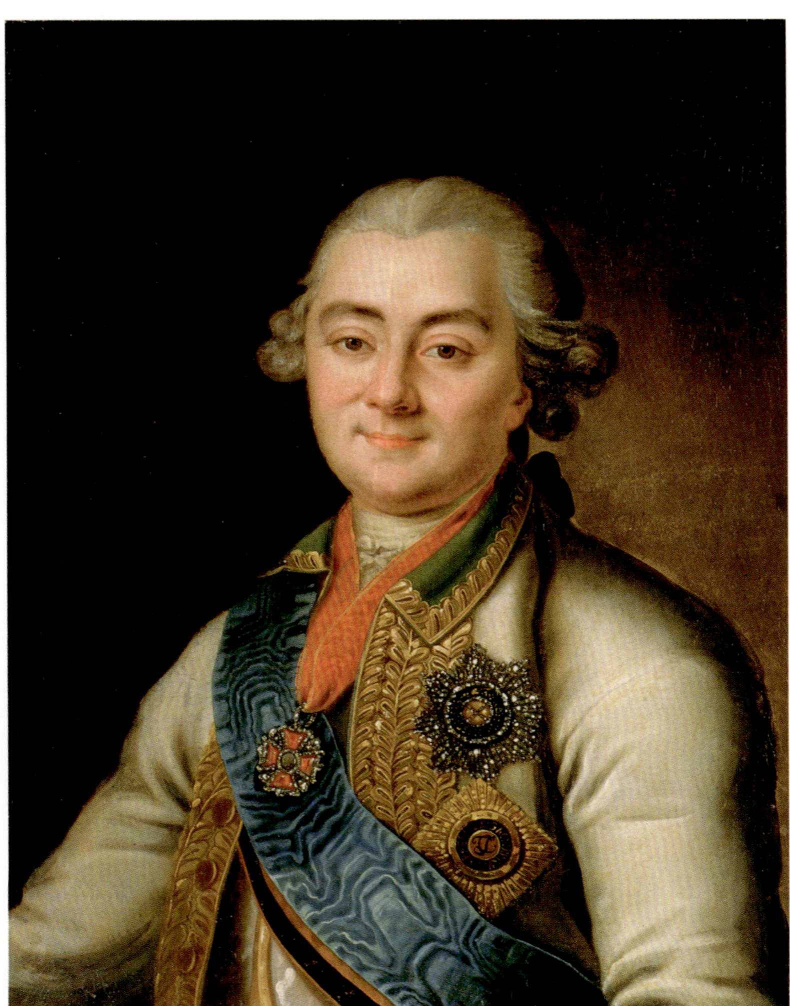

and represented an even greater range than ever before. In the early 1920s, the entire building was opened to the public and the Winter Palace was used for film screenings and lectures. The first major exhibition to open in the Hermitage concerned the art of ancient Egypt in 1920, but this was also the time when the long-term decimation of the collections started in earnest. In 1927, the government ordered 770 paintings be taken from storage and put on display permanently in Moscow's Pushkin Museum. Other works were sent to provincial capitals that wanted to claim some of the glory of the former Czarist capital. In the 1920s and 1930s, no fewer than 2,880 paintings were sold to foreign buyers to raise hard currency.

In Summer 1941 as the invading German forces approached the city, most of the collection of more than one million works of art was taken to Yekaterinburg

noblesse russe et du clergé ayant été confisqués après la révolution d'Octobre, les collections de l'Ermitage s'enrichirent de très nombreux objets et œuvres de valeur, en élargissant du même coup leur ampleur et leur portée. Au début des années 1920, l'ensemble des bâtiments était accessible au public et le palais d'Hiver servait à des projections de films et à des conférences. Dès 1920, une exposition sur l'Égypte ancienne avait ouvert la série de ces présentations publiques. Mais c'est aussi à cette époque que commence le démantèlement des collections : en 1927, 770 tableaux – tirés des dépôts, mais aussi des cimaises – doivent être remis à ce qui deviendra le musée Pouchkine de Moscou, et d'autres œuvres sont dévolues à des musées de province, dans des villes désireuses de récupérer une partie au moins du prestige de l'ancienne capitale, après la Première Guerre mondiale. Par ailleurs, dans les décennies 1920

nur mit Mühe zurückerhalten werden konnten); die Bildergalerie blieb allerdings an Ort und Stelle. Da nach der Oktoberrevolution 1917 der russische Adel enteignet wurde, wurden in der Folgezeit qualitätsvolle adlige Privatsammlungen wie auch Kunst aus Kirchen in die Eremitage überführt, sodass sich die Bestände schließlich vervierfachten und ihr Spektrum größer war denn je. Anfang der 1920er-Jahre war das gesamte Gebäudeensemble der Öffentlichkeit zugänglich, auch der Winterpalast wurde für Filmvorführungen und Vortragsveranstaltungen genutzt. Den Auftakt für die in der Eremitage gezeigten Ausstellungen hatte bereits 1920 eine Schau über das alte Ägypten gemacht. Doch begann in dieser Zeit auch die nachhaltige Dezimierung der Sammlungen: 1927 mussten 770 Gemälde aus dem Depot und der ständigen Ausstellung dem Puschkin-Museum in Moskau und weitere Werke Provinzmuseen

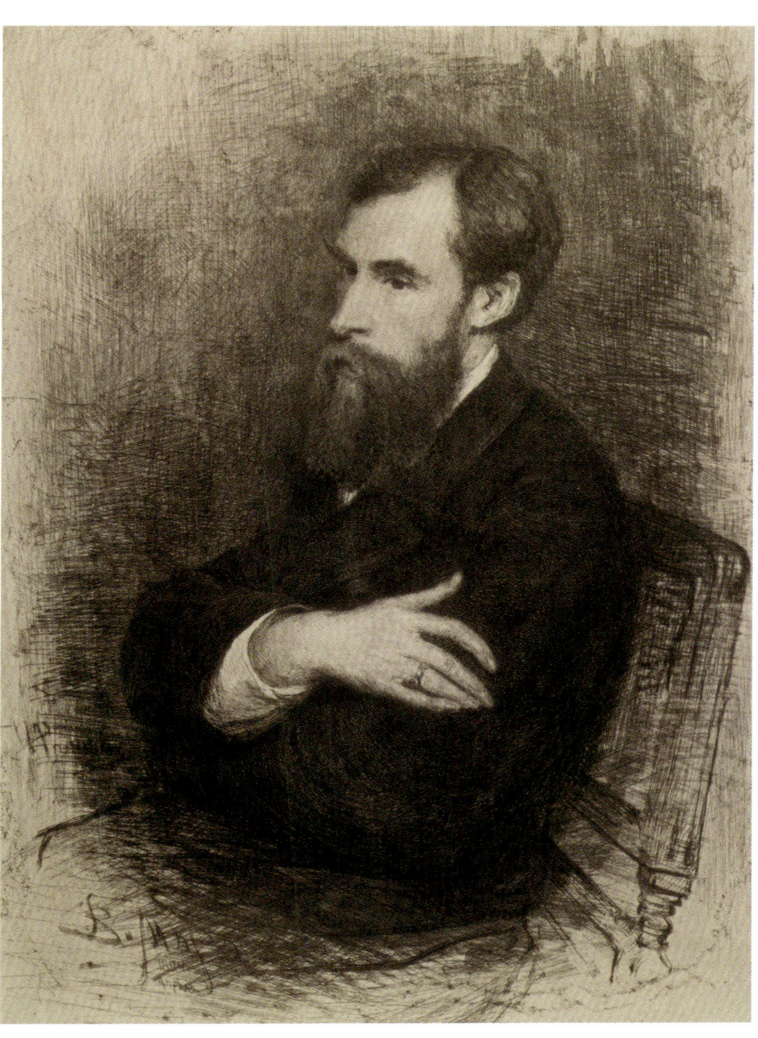

los tiempos posteriores a la misma valiosas colecciones privadas y arte sacro, de manera que el número de sus piezas se cuadriplicó y su espectro fue más amplio de lo que había sido hasta entonces. A principios de los años veinte se permitió el acceso del público al complejo de edificios, y también se usó el Palacio de Invierno para mostrar películas y para eventos y conferencias. Como comienzo a la muestra de exposiciones en el Hermitage se mostró en 1920 una exposición sobre el antiguo Egipto. Y sin embargo al mismo tiempo comenzó una reducción sostenida de las colecciones: en 1927 se llevaron 770 pinturas del almacén y la colección permanente al Museo Puschkin de Moscú y otros museos de provincia recibieron asimismo otras obras; se llevaron a ciudades que, tras la Primera Guerra Mundial, querían tener algo del resplandor de la antigua capital San Petersburgo. En los años 20 y 30 se enviaron

da guerra foram recuperadas obras apenas com muito esforço). Porém, a galeria de pinturas não saiu do sítio. Uma vez que a aristocracia russa foi expropriada após a Revolução de Outubro de 1917, coleções particulares aristocratas de elevada qualidade, bem como objetos de arte das igrejas foram transferidos nos anos seguintes para o Hermitage, de modo a que o inventário quadruplicou finalmente, passando o seu âmbito a ser maior do que nunca. No início dos anos de 1920, todo o conjunto de edifícios estava aberto ao público e até o Palácio de Inverno era utilizado para apresentações de filmes e colóquios. O início das exposições exibidas no Hermitage ocorreu, desde logo, em 1920 através de uma exibição sobre o antigo Egito. No entanto, nesta altura começou também a dizimação prolongada das coleções: em 1927, 770 pinturas do depósito e da exposição permanente tiveram de ser cedidas ao Museu Pushkin

Wereldoorlog abrupt onderbroken. Het merendeel van de kunstschatten werd naar Moskou gebracht (vanwaar ze na de oorlog maar met moeite weer naar Sint-Petersburg teruggehaald konden worden); de prentengalerij daarentegen bleef waar hij was. Omdat de Russische adel na de Oktoberrevolutie in 1917 onteigend werd, vonden in de daaropvolgende periode kwalitatief hoogstaande adellijke privécollecties en kerkschatten een heenkomen in de Hermitage, waardoor de omvang van de kunstverzameling uiteindelijk verviervoudigde en een groter spectrum dan ooit daarvoor besloeg. Begin jaren 1920 was het gehele gebouwencomplex voor het brede publiek toegankelijk en werd ook het Winterpaleis voor filmvertoningen en lezingen gebruikt. De opmaat tot de in de Hermitage georganiseerde tentoonstellingen werd al in 1920 gegeven in de vorm van een expositie over het oude Egypte. Toch markeerde

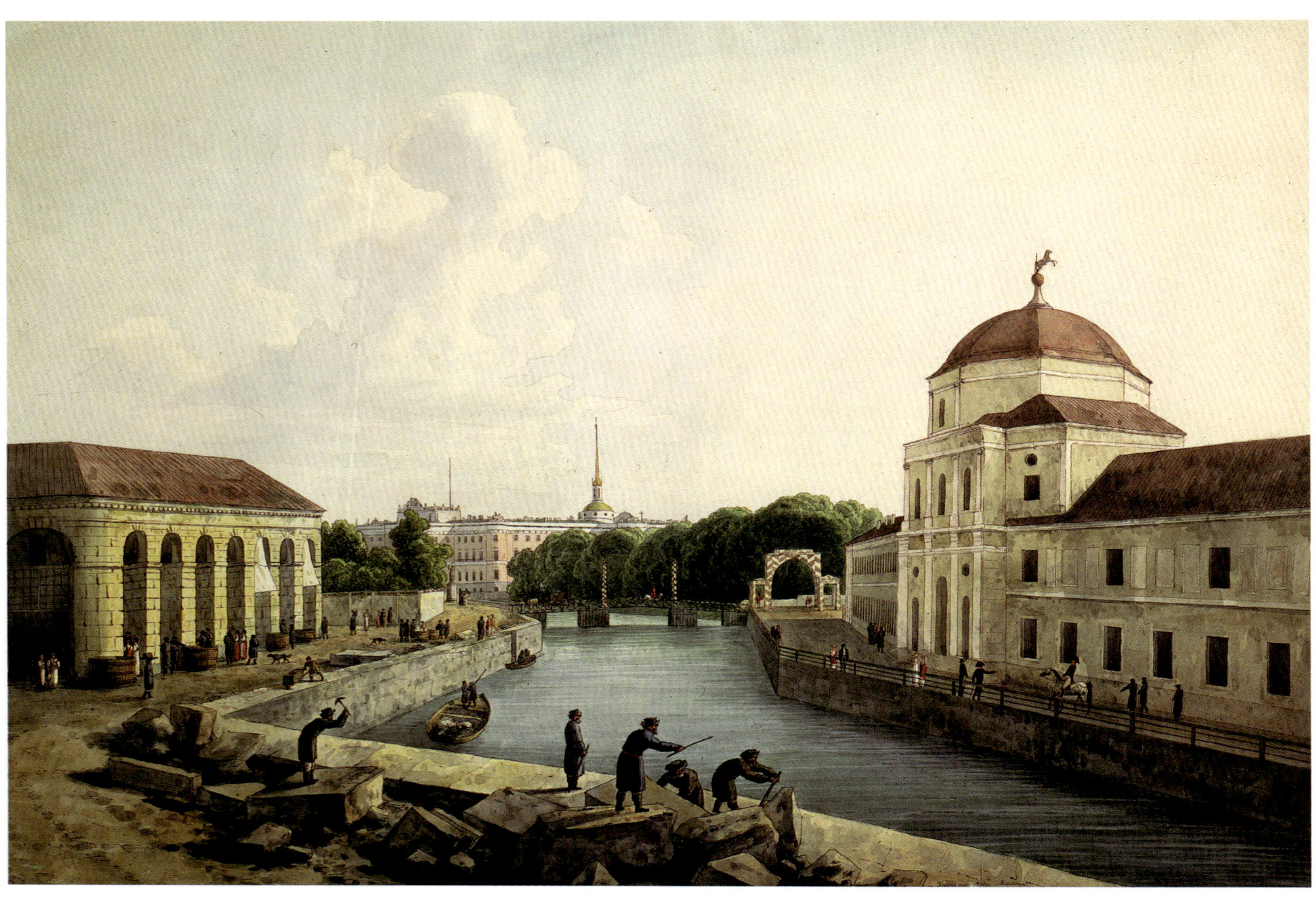

in the Urals, while what was left was stored in the museum's cellars. It was not long before the German army began its merciless siege of Leningrad which lasted until January 1944. The buildings of the Hermitage were badly damaged by artillery fire and bombs, but, after makeshift repairs, the first exhibition after the city's liberation opened in November 1944, featuring the works that had been kept in the museum's cellars. A year later, the rest of the collection was returned and the museum was officially reopened.

Another important event in the history of the Hermitage Museum came in 1948 when 316 pieces of Modernist art were transferred to Leningrad from Moscow's Museum of Modern Western European Art. These were primarily works that had once belonged to Shchukin and Morozov, the two great collectors in pre-Revolution Moscow, including important early Modernist pieces by the likes of Monet, Renoir, Cézanne, Gauguin, Matisse, Picasso, and Malevich.

et 1930, ce ne sont pas moins de 2 880 tableaux de l'Ermitage qui partent à l'étranger en échange de devises.

Pendant la Seconde Guerre mondiale, dès l'été 1941, plus d'un million d'œuvres d'art – soit la plus grande partie des collections – sont mises en lieu sûr à Sverdlovsk (aujourd'hui Iékaterinbourg), dans l'Oural ; le reste est entreposé dans les caves. Peu de temps après commence l'impitoyable siège de Léningrad par l'armée allemande, qui va durer jusqu'en janvier 1944. Les bâtiments de l'Ermitage sont alors lourdement endommagés par des tirs d'artillerie et des bombardements aériens, mais dès novembre 1944, dans des bâtiments sommairement remis en état, une première exposition est organisée avec les œuvres restées sur place. Un an plus tard, l'ensemble du musée est solennellement rouvert, avec toutes les œuvres qui y sont revenues.

Une nouvelle étape importante dans l'histoire de l'Ermitage intervient en 1948, avec le transfert

überlassen werden; sie kamen in Städte, die nach dem Ersten Weltkrieg an der Pracht der ehemaligen Hauptstadt St. Petersburg teilhaben wollten. In den 1920er- und 1930er-Jahren gelangten nicht weniger als 2880 Gemälde der Eremitage gegen Devisen ins Ausland.

Während des Zweiten Weltkriegs wurde im Sommer 1941 mehr als eine Million Kunstwerke, der größte Teil der Sammlung, nach Swerdlowsk (heute Jekaterinburg) im Ural gebracht, ein kleinerer Teil verblieb in den Kellern. Nur wenig später begann die erbarmungslose Belagerung Leningrads durch die deutsche Wehrmacht, die bis zum Januar 1944 andauern sollte.

Die Gebäude der Eremitage wurden in dieser Zeit durch Artilleriebeschuss und Fliegerbomben stark beschädigt, doch fand in den nur notdürftig instand gesetzten Gebäuden bereits im November 1944 eine erste Ausstellung mit den hier verbliebenen Werken statt; ein Jahr später wurde das gesamte Museum

Andrei Jefimowitsch Martynow (1768–1826)

View of the Moika and the Imperial Stables

La Moïka le long des écuries impériales

Blick auf die Moika und die kaiserlichen Stallungen

Vista del Moika y de los establos imperiales

Vista sobre o Rio Moika e os Estábulos Imperiais

Uitzicht op de Mojka en de keizerlijke stallen

1809, Watercolor on paper, Chinese ink/Aquarelle sur papier, encre de Chine, 60 × 86 cm

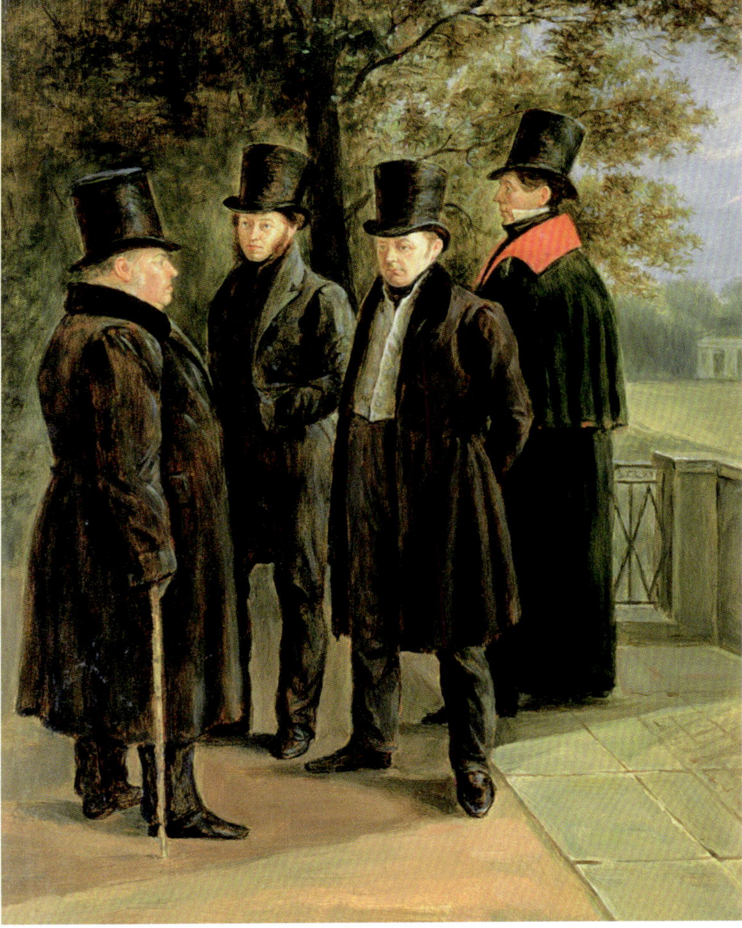

Grigori Tschernezow (1802–65)

The Writers Alexander Pushkin, Ivan Krylov, Vasily Zhukovsky and Nikolay Gnedich

Les Poètes Alexandre Pouchkine, Ivan Krylov, Vassili Joukovski et Nikolai Gnedich

Die Dichter Alexander Puschkin, Iwan Krylow, Wassili Schukowski und Nikolai Gneditsch

Los poetas Alexander Puschkin, Ivan Krylow, Vasily Schukovski y Nikolai Gnedich

Os Poetas Alexander Pushkin, Ivan Krylov, Vasily Zhukovsky e Nikolai Gneditsch

De dichter Aleksander Poesjkin, Ivan Krylov, Wassili Sjukovski en Nikolai Gneditsj

n.d., Oil on canvas/Huile sur toile, 27,2 × 28,2 cm

al extranjero no menos de 2880 cuadros a cambio de divisa.

Durante la Segunda Guerra Mundial, en el verano de 1941, se llevaron más de un millón de obras (la mayor parte de la colección) a Sverdlovsk, hoy en día Ekaterimburgo, en los Urales, dejando una parte más pequeña en los sótanos del museo. Un poco más tarde comenzó el despiadado asedio de Leningrado a manos de la Wehrmacht alemana, que duraría hasta enero de 1944. Los edificios del Hermitage recibieron daños importantes por el fuego de artillería y bombas de la aviación, y sin embargo en los edificios mantenidos de manera provisional se montó en noviembre de 1944 una primera exposición con las piezas que habían quedado; un año más tarde el museo reabriría por todo lo alto, ya con las obras retornadas.

Otro acontecimiento importante en la historia del Hermitage fue el transporte, en 1948, de 316 cuadros de arte moderno del museo de arte moderno europeo

em Moscovo e outras obras a museus da província. As obras foram para cidades que após a Primeira Guerra Mundial queriam fazer parte da magnificência da antiga capital de São Petersburgo. Nos anos de 1920 e 1930, não menos de 2880 pinturas do Hermitage foram parar ao estrangeiro em troca de divisas.

Durante a Segunda Guerra Mundial, mais de um milhão de obras de arte, ou seja, a parte maior da coleção, foi transferida no verão de 1941 para Sverdlovsk (atualmente Ecaterimburgo) nos Montes Urais, tendo uma parte mais pequena permanecido nas caves. Apenas um pouco mais tarde começou a impiedosa ocupação de Leningrado através das forças armadas alemãs, que havia de perdurar até janeiro de 1944. Os edifícios do Hermitage ficaram fortemente danificados nesta altura através dos disparos de artilharia e das bombas aéreas, tendo porém sido realizada uma primeira exposição em novembro de 1944 nos edifícios precariamente recuperados com as obras

deze periode ook het begin van de aanhoudende krimp van de collectie: in 1927 verhuisden 770 schilderijen uit het depot en de permanente tentoonstellingen naar het Poesjkinmuseum in Moskou en andere musea in de provincie; ze kwamen in steden terecht die na de Eerste Wereldoorlog wilden delen in de pracht en praal van de voormalige hoofdstad Sint-Petersburg. In de jaren 1920 en 1930 werden niet minder dan 2880 schilderijen uit de Hermitage in het buitenland tegen deviezen geruild.

In de Tweede Wereldoorlog werd in de zomer van 1941 ruim een miljoen kunstwerken, het grootste deel van de collectie, overgebracht naar Sverdlovsk (nu Jekaterinburg) in de Oeral, een kleiner deel werd in kelders opgeslagen. Kort daarna begon de meedogenloze belegering van Leningrad door de Duitse Wehrmacht, die tot in januari 1944 zou duren. Het Hermitage-complex werd in deze periode door artilleriebeschietingen en vliegtuigbommen zwaar beschadigd, maar toch vond in de zo goed en zo kwaad

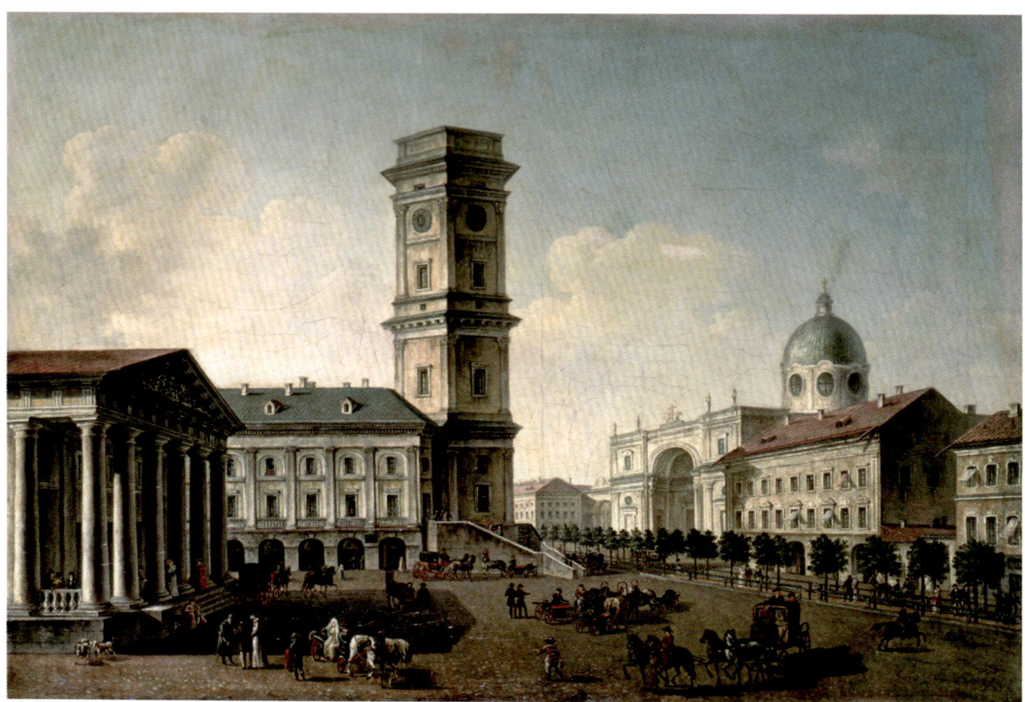

The Hermitage also became the destination for works originally stolen by the German army during the war and later discovered by the Red Army. Art looted from Germany, including parts of the Wettin Dynasty Treasury which had been buried at Moritzburg Palace near Dresden, was also brought to Leningrad by the Red Army.

Since 1996, the Hermitage has been officially under the auspices of the Russian president, but receives relatively little state support. Despite unrelenting visitor traffic, the museum suffers under constant financial difficulties. Support has, however, come from abroad. For example, the Hermitage works with the Solomon R. Guggenheim Foundation (and operated the Guggenheim Hermitage Museum in Las Vegas between 2001 and 2008). Hermitage Amsterdam opened in 2004 to put on special exhibitions of works from the Hermitage collections.

à Leningrad de 316 tableaux modernes depuis la collection du musée de Moscou dédié aux arts de l'Occident. Il s'agit pour l'essentiel de peintures appartenant aux collections de deux grands mécènes de l'époque impériale, Sergueï Chtchoukine et Ivan Morozov, qui comprenaient des œuvres capitales, de Monet à Malevitch en passant par Renoir, Cézanne, Gauguin, Matisse et Picasso. À cela viennent s'ajouter des œuvres d'art pillées par la Wehrmacht pendant la guerre et récupérées par l'Armée Rouge, ainsi que du butin artistique de guerre.

Depuis 1996, l'Ermitage est officiellement placé sous le patronage du président de la Fédération de Russie, mais il est relativement peu subventionné par l'État et souffre d'un perpétuel manque d'argent, malgré les flots incessants de visiteurs qui s'y pressent. Le soutien vient entre autres de l'étranger : c'est ainsi que l'Ermitage travaille en collaboration avec la Fondation Solomon R. Guggenheim (qui a financé de 2001 à 2008 le Guggenheim Hermitage Museum de Las Vegas) ; 2004 a vu l'ouverture de l'Hermitage Amsterdam, succursale néerlandaise de l'Ermitage qui présente par roulement des œuvres venues de Saint-Pétersbourg, dans le cadre d'expositions spéciales.

mit den zurückgekehrten Kunstwerken feierlich wiedereröffnet.

Eines weiteres wichtiges Ereignis in der Geschichte der Eremitage war 1948 die Überführung von 316 Gemälden moderner Kunst aus dem Museum neuer westeuropäischer Kunst in Moskau nach Leningrad. Es handelte sich in erster Linie um Werke aus den Sammlungen der beiden großen Moskauer Sammler Schtschukin und Morosow, bedeutende Gemälde aus den Anfangsjahren der Moderne von Monet, Renoir, Cézanne, Gauguin, Matisse bis Picasso und Malewitsch. Zudem gelangten Kunstwerke in die Eremitage, welche die deutsche Wehrmacht im Zweiten Weltkrieg geraubt und die Rote Armee wieder aufgespürte hatte, sowie Beutekunst aus Deutschland.

Seit 1996 befindet sich die Eremitage offiziell unter der Schirmherrschaft des russischen Präsidenten, wird vom Staat aber relativ wenig gefördert und leidet trotz nicht nachlassender Besucherströme unter ständiger Geldnot. Unterstützung kommt unter anderem aus dem Ausland: So arbeitet die Eremitage mit der Solomon R. Guggenheim Foundation zusammen (die 2001–2008 das Guggenheim Hermitage Museum in Las Vegas finanzierte); 2004 eröffnete das Hermitage Amsterdam, das im Rahmen von Sonderausstellungen Werke aus der Eremitage zeigt.

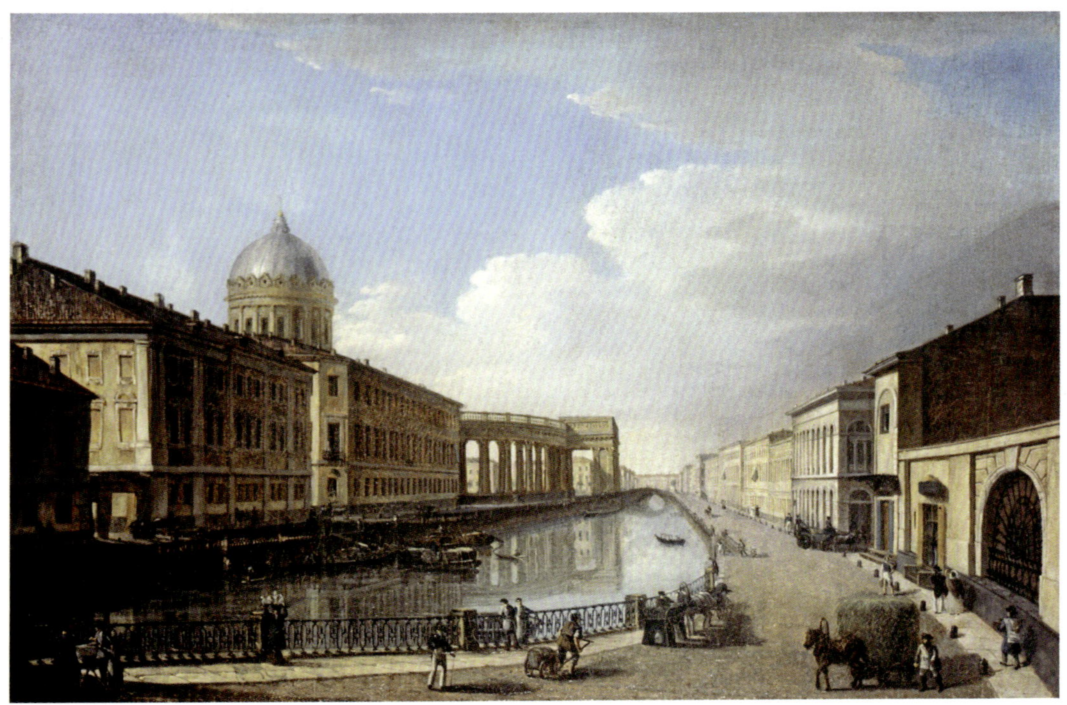

occidental en Moscú a Leningrado. Se trataba sobre todo de obras de las colecciones de los grandes coleccionistas moscovitas Schtschukin y Morosov, pinturas significativas de los inicios de la modernidad como Monet, Renoir, Cézanne, Gauguin, Matisse, hasta Picasso o Malévich. Algunas de estas obras acabaron en el Hermitage, habiendo sido robadas por la Wehrmacht alemana y restituidas por el ejército rojo, así como arte saqueado de Alemania.

Desde 1996 el Hermitage se encuentra bajo el auspicio del presidente ruso, si bien recibe poca ayuda estatal lo que le lleva a un estado de constante necesidad a pesar del flujo de visitantes que no decrece. Los apoyos llegan sobre todo del extranjero: así, el Hermitage colabora con la Fundación Solomon R. Guggenheim (que financió en 2001–2008 el Guggenheim Hermitage Museum en Las Vegas); en 2004 abrió sus puertas el Hermitage Amsterdam, que muestra en exposiciones extraordinarias obras del Hermitage.

aqui remanescentes. Um ano depois todo o museu foi festivamente reaberto com as obras de arte recuperadas.

Um outro acontecimento importante na história do Hermitage foi a transferência em 1948 de 316 pinturas de arte moderna do Museu da Nova Arte da Europa Ocidental em Moscovo para Leningrado. Trataram-se principalmente de obras das coleções dos dois grandes colecionadores moscovitas, Shchukin e Morozov, designadamente, pinturas relevantes do início do Modernismo desde Monet, Renoir, Cézanne, Gauguin, Matisse até Picasso e Malevich. Além disso, ao Hermitage chegaram obras de arte que haviam sido roubadas pelas forças armadas alemãs durante a Segunda Guerra Mundial e que o Exército Vermelho conseguiu encontrar novamente, assim como obras de arte pilhadas da Alemanha.

Desde 1996 que o Hermitage se encontra oficialmente sob o protetorado do Presidente russo. No entanto, o museu é relativamente pouco promovido pelo estado e sofre permanentemente de falta de meios financeiros, embora o grande número de visitantes não pare de crescer. O apoio vem, entre outros, do estrangeiro, trabalhando assim o Hermitage juntamente com a Fundação Solomon R. Guggenheim (que entre 2001 e 2008 financiou o Museu Guggenheim Hermitage em Las Vegas). Em 2004 abriu o Hermitage Amesterdão, que no âmbito de exposições especiais exibe obras do Hermitage.

als het ging herstelde gebouwen al in november 1944 een eerste tentoonstelling plaats van de achtergebleven schilderijen. Een jaar later, na terugkeer van de kunstwerken, werd het hele museum feestelijk heropend.

Een ander belangrijk moment in de geschiedenis van de Hermitage was de komst in 1948 van 316 moderne schilderijen uit het Staatsmuseum voor Nieuwe West-Europese Kunst in Moskou naar Leningrad. Het ging in eerste instantie om werken uit de kunstverzamelingen van de twee grote Moskouse kunstverzamelaars Sjtsjoekin en Morosov, en betrof belangrijke schilderijen uit de beginjaren van de moderne tijd van Monet, Renoir, Cézanne, Gauguin, Matisse tot Picasso en Malevitsj. Daarnaast kwamen kunstwerken in de Hermitage terecht die in de Tweede Wereldoorlog door de Duitse Wehrmacht geroofd en door het Rode Leger opgespoord waren, evenals in Duitsland buitgemaakte kunst.

Sinds 1996 staat de Hermitage officieel onder beschermheerschap van de Russische president. Toch doet de Russische staat relatief weinig voor het museum, dat ondanks de niet-aflatende bezoekersstromen onder aanhoudend geldgebrek gebukt gaat. Ondersteuning komt onder andere uit het buitenland. Zo werkt de Hermitage samen met de Solomon R. Guggenheim Foundation (die in 2001–2008 het Guggenheim Hermitage Museum in Las Vegas financierde) en werd in 2004 de Hermitage Amsterdam geopend dat bijzondere exposities van kunstwerken uit de Hermitage organiseert.

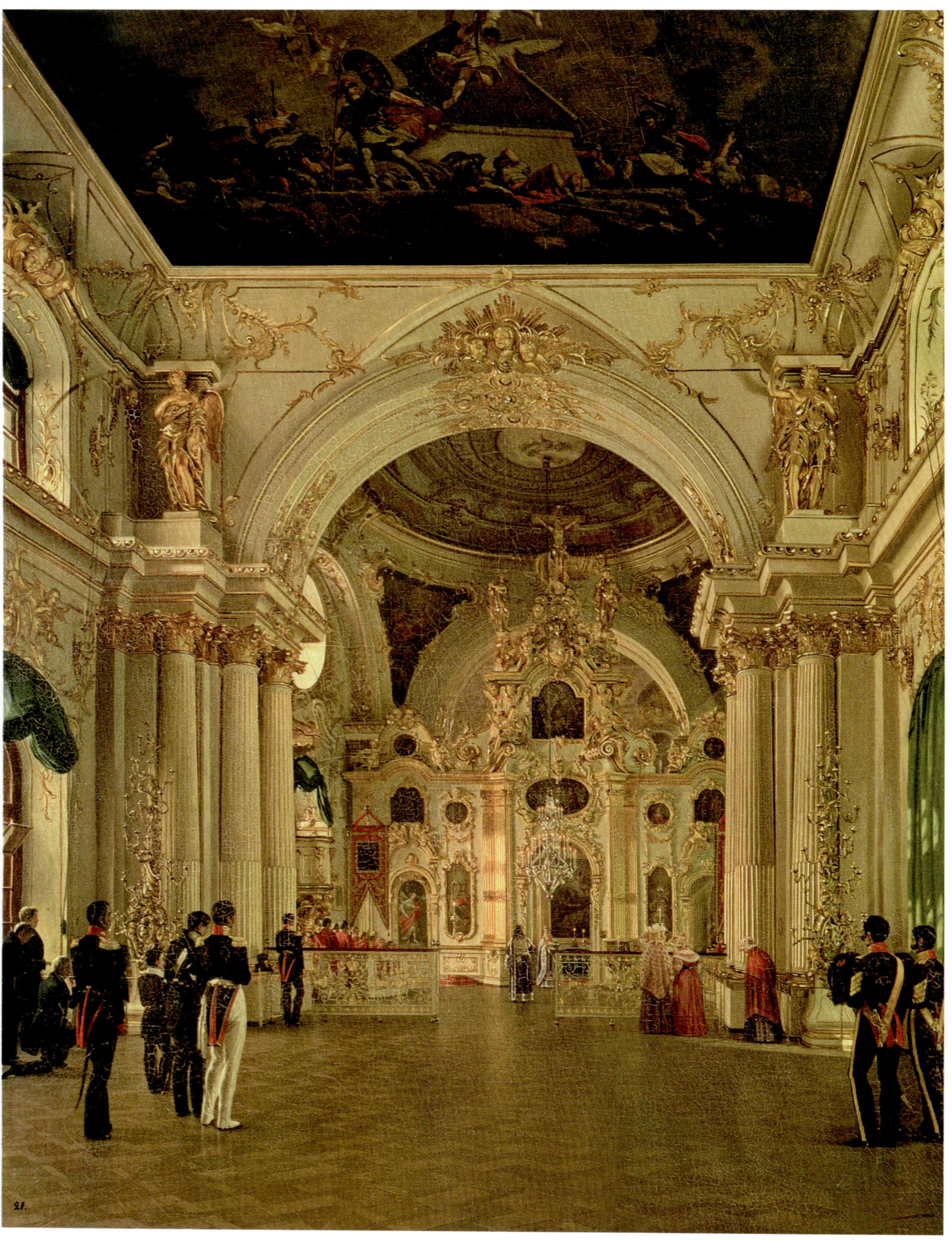

Alexei Wassiljewitsch
Tyranow (1808–59)

The Great Church of
the Winter Palace

La Grande Église
du palais d'Hiver

Die Große Kirche
im Winterpalast

La gran iglesia del
Palacio de Invierno

A Grande Igreja no
Palácio de Inverno

De Grote Kerk in
het Winterpaleis

1829, Oil on canvas/Huile
sur toile, 146 × 108 cm

24

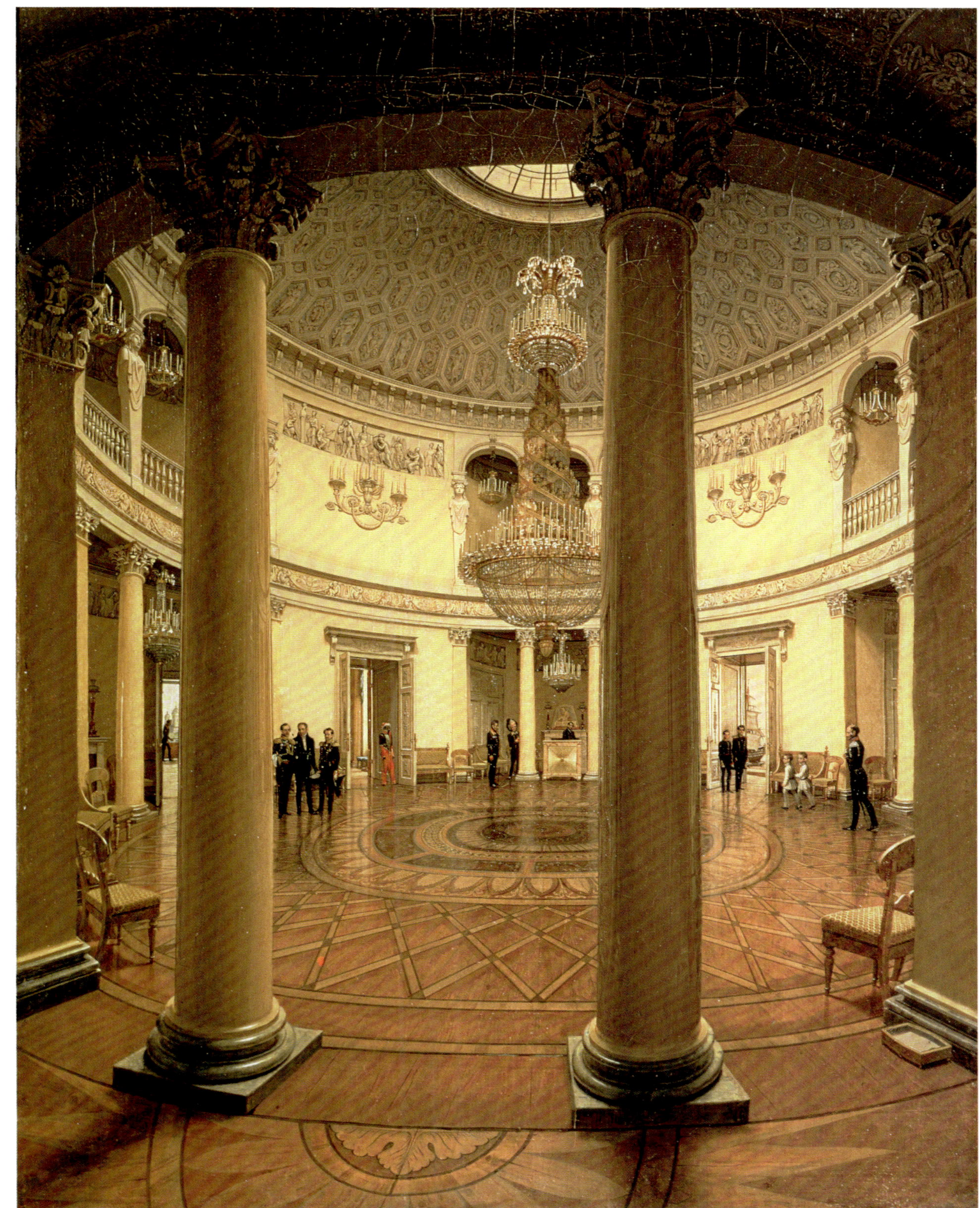

Jefim Tucharinow

The Rotunda in
the Winter Palace

La Rotonde du
palais d'Hiver

Die Rotunde im
Winterpalais

La rotonda
del Palacio de
Invierno

A Rotunda no
Palácio de Inverno

De Rotunda in
het Winterpaleis

1834, Oil on
canvas/Huile sur
toile, 104 × 82 cm

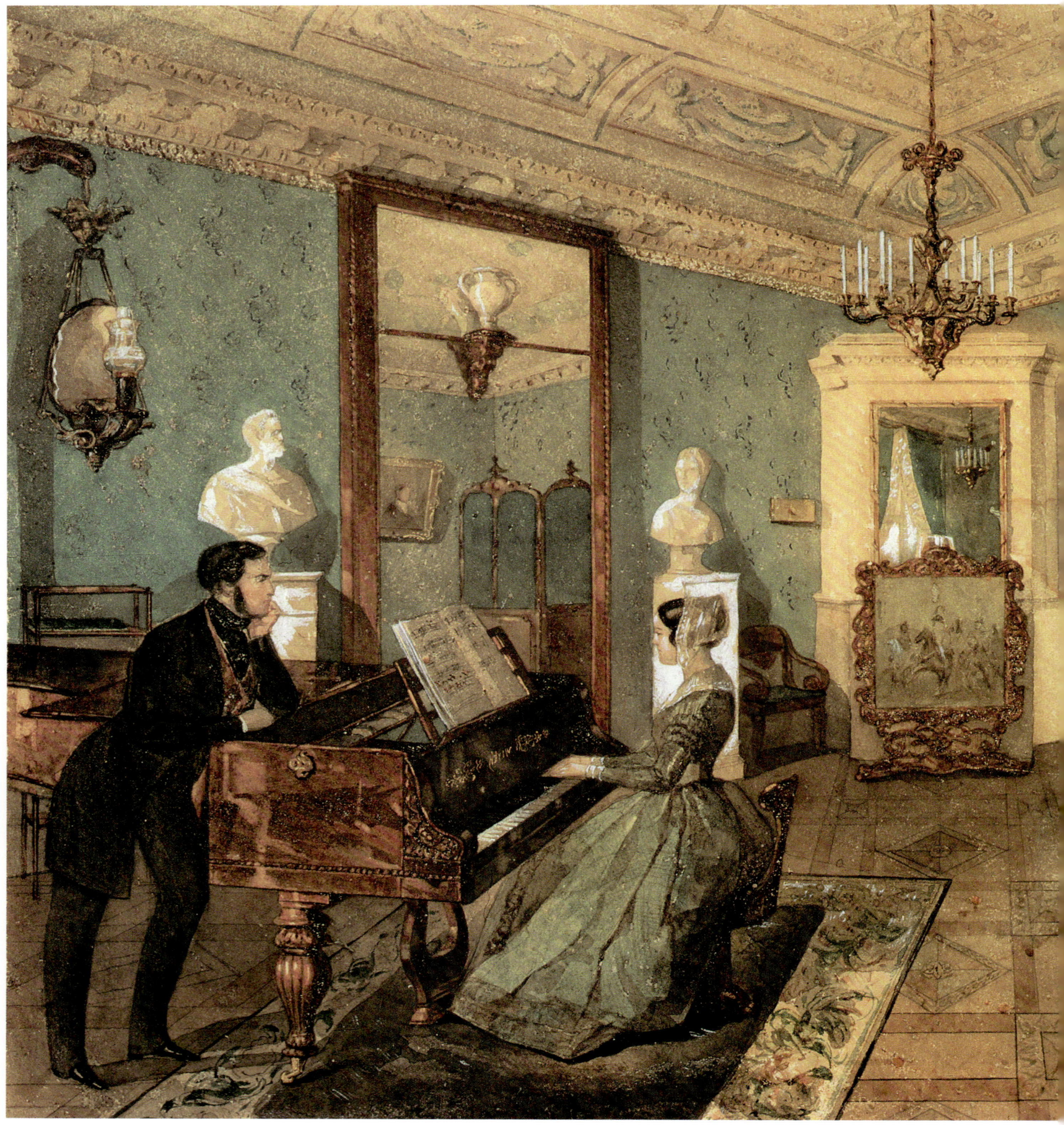

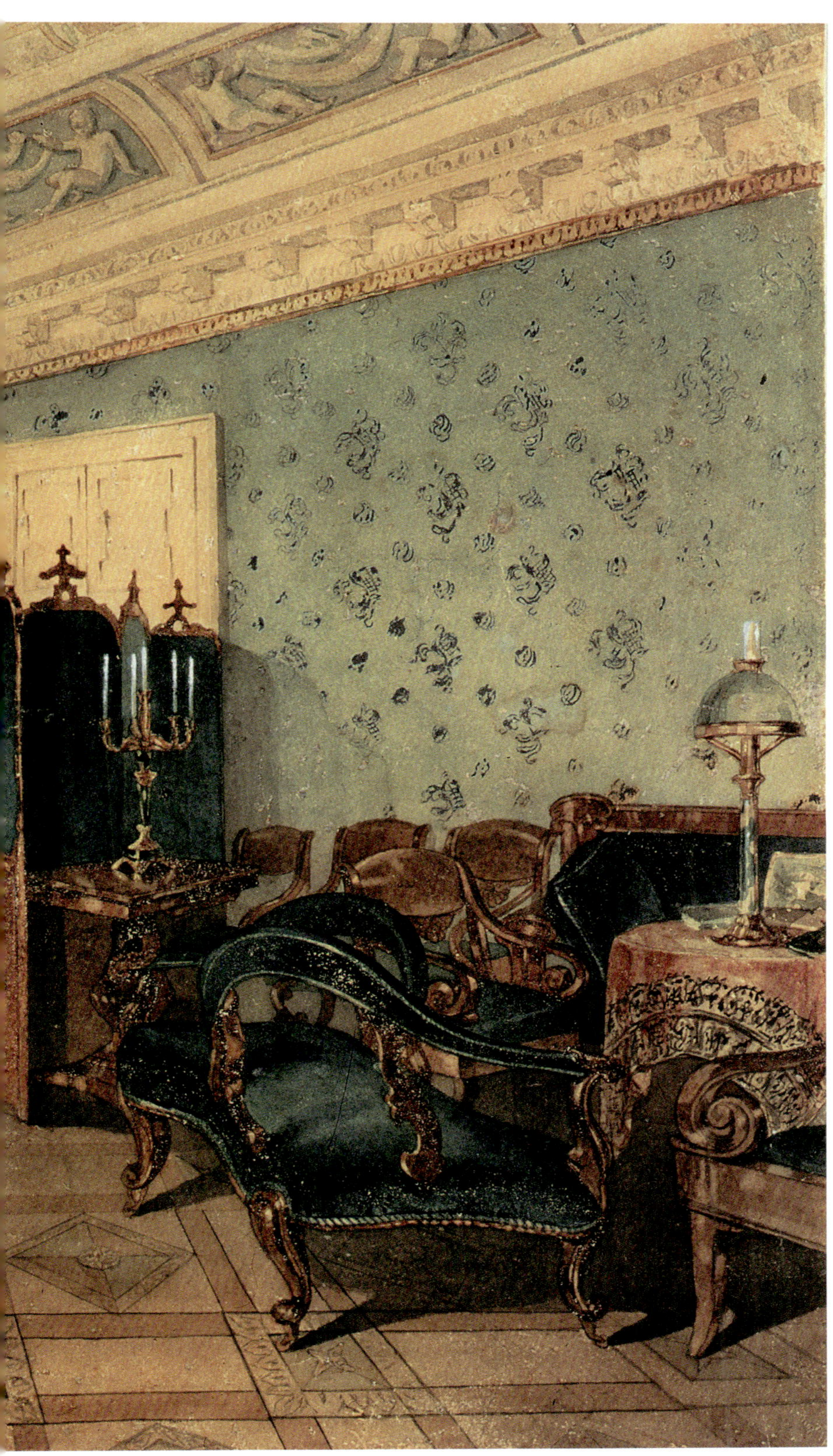

Pjotr Fjodorowitsch Sokolow (c. 1787–1848)

Salon in the House of Baron Stieglitz in St. Petersburg

Le Salon de la maison du baron Alexandre Stieglitz à Saint-Pétersbourg

Salon im Haus des Baron Stieglitz in St. Petersburg

Salón en la casa del Barón Stieglitz en San Petersburgo

Salão na Casa do Barão de Stieglitz em São Petersburgo

Salon in het huis van baron Stieglitz in Sint-Petersburg

1841, Watercolour on paper/Aquarelle sur papier, 24 × 35,5 cm

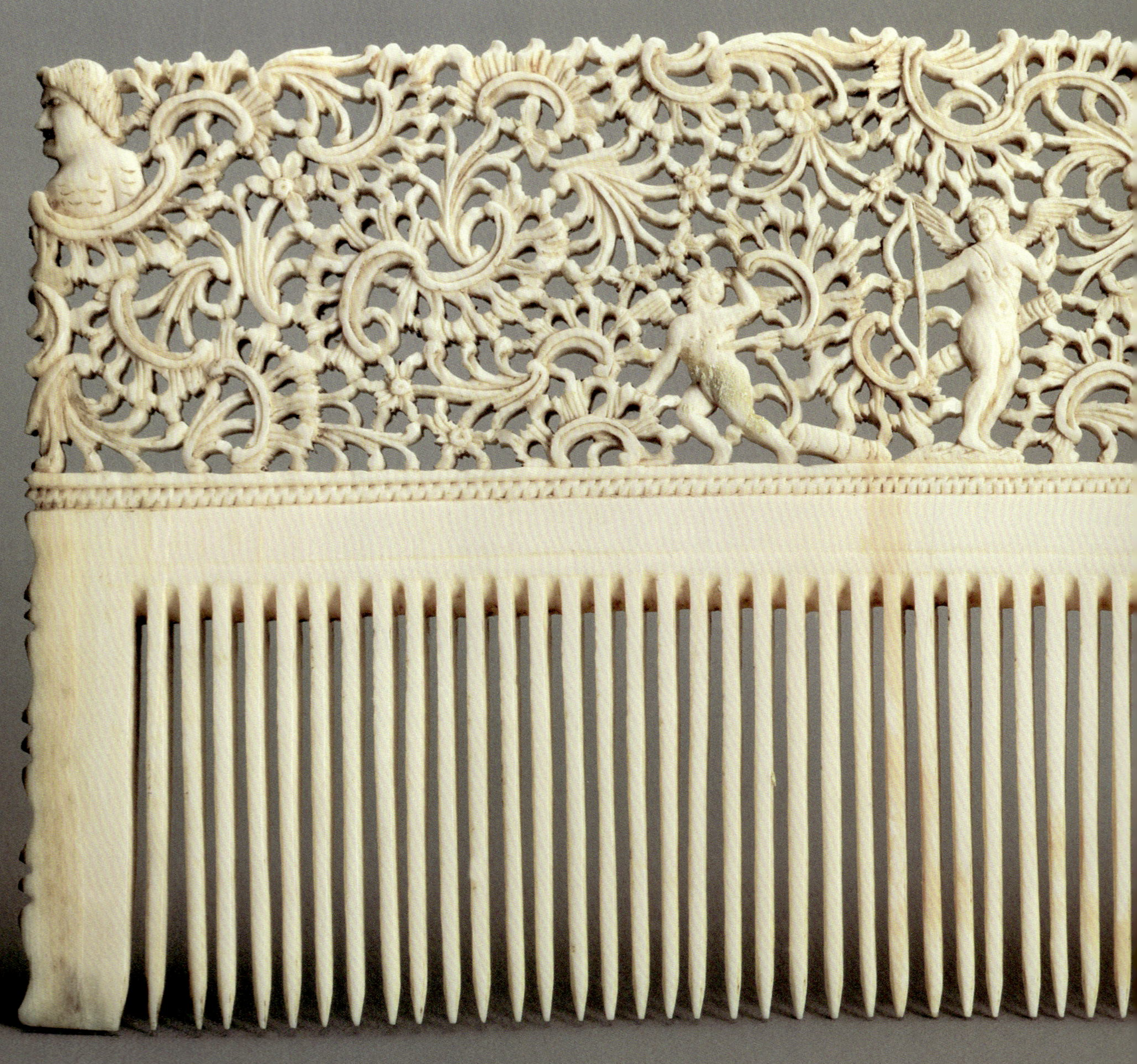

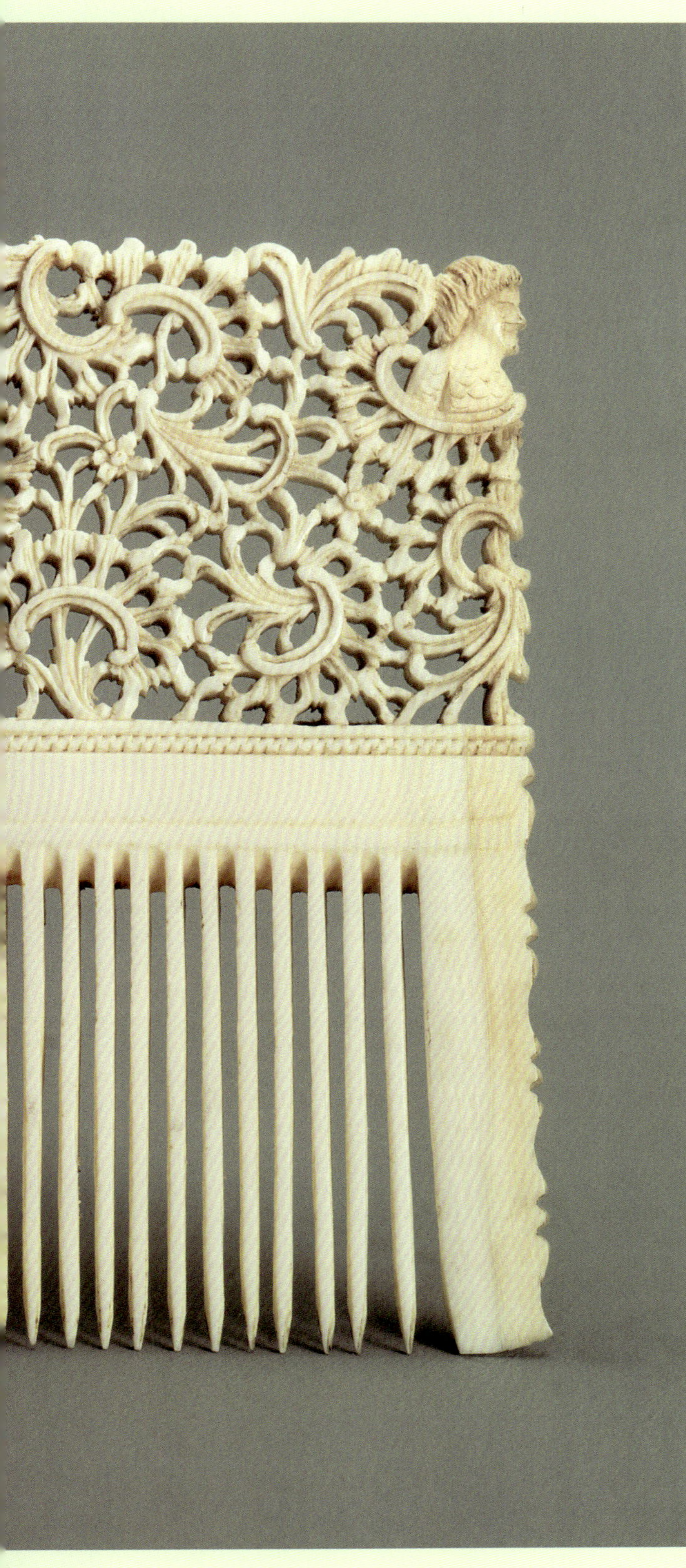

Russia/Russie
Ornamental comb
Peigne
Kamm mit ornamentierter Griffplatte
Peine con mango ornamentado
Pente com Punho Ornamental
Kam met versierde handgreep
1750–70, Walrus ivory/Os sculpté, 14 × 9 cm

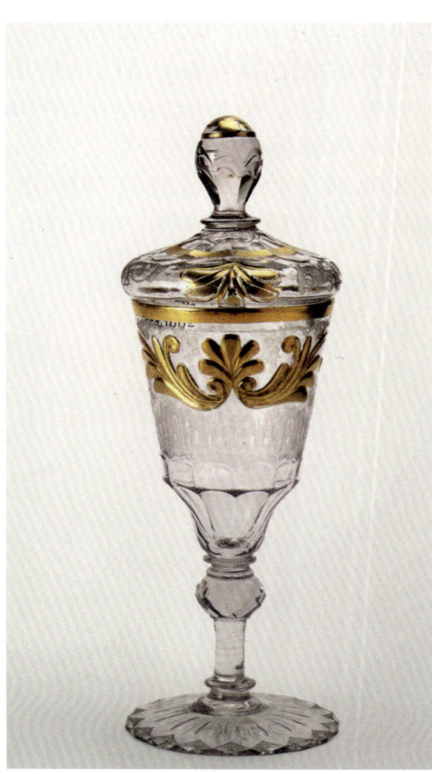

Archaeology and Applied Arts

It is impossible at this point to go into detail about all of the collections at the Hermitage, given that they include 65,000 pieces on display at any time in about 350 rooms. The departments are diverse, ranging from antiquity through the cultures of the Middle East, the Caucasus, and Central Asia, to the art of Western Europe, Russia, and East Asia.

Applied arts are especially well-represented, including furniture, carpets, tapestries, ceramics, and no fewer than 14,000 pieces of porcelain from most major manufacturers, glass from Venice, Germany, and Spain, and medieval church wares. Invaluable is the collection of gold treasures of the Scythians with numerous precious pieces of jewelry. The treasury showcases gold and jewelry pieces that go back more than 4,000 years. The collection of Russian costumes from the 18th to the 20th centuries includes some 300 garments once worn by Czar Peter the Great.

The Hermitage also holds some 12,000 pieces of sculpture.

The museum holds such a vast collection that all of it could not possibly be sampled in this volume. For this reason, the focus here is on European painting.

Archéologie et artisanat d'art

Il est impossible ici d'aborder toutes les richesses de l'Ermitage, avec ses 350 salles d'exposition et ses quelque 65 000 pièces exposées. Les départements sont multiples et couvrent de l'Antiquité à l'art de l'Extrême-Orient en passant par les cultures du Moyen-Orient, du Caucase et de l'Asie centrale, ainsi que l'art d'Europe occidentale et de Russie.

Les arts appliqués sont généreusement représentés : on peut y voir des meubles, des tapis et des tapisseries, de la céramique et pas moins de 14 000 porcelaines des plus grandes manufactures, de la verrerie de Venise, d'Allemagne et d'Espagne, des objets liturgiques du Moyen Âge. La collection des trésors des Scythes est d'une valeur incommensurable, avec ses nombreuses parures en or massif. La salle du Trésor présente des chefs-d'œuvre d'orfèvrerie et de joaillerie, dont certaines pièces remontent au IIIe millénaire avant Jésus-Christ. La collection de costumes russes (du XVIIIe au XXe siècle) compte entre autres trois cents habits de Pierre le Grand.

L'Ermitage possède en outre quelque 12 000 sculptures qui en font une des plus riches collections du monde dans ce domaine.

Il est impossible d'illustrer la totalité des objets exposés dans ce volume. La peinture européenne y occupe donc une place prépondérante.

Archäologie und Kunsthandwerk

Es ist an dieser Stelle unmöglich, auf alle Sammlungen der Eremitage mit ihren 350 Schauräumen mit rund 65.000 Exponaten einzugehen. Die Abteilungen sind vielfältig und reichen von der Antike über orientalische, kaukasische und zentralasiatische Kulturen bis zur Kunst Westeuropas, Russlands und des Fernen Ostens.

Umfangreich vertreten ist die angewandte Kunst: Zu sehen sind unter anderem Möbel, Teppiche und Tapisserien, Keramik und nicht weniger als 14.000 Porzellane aus den meisten bedeutenden Manufakturen, Glas aus Venedig, Deutschland und Spanien sowie Kirchengerät des Mittelalters. Von unschätzbarem Wert ist die Sammlung von Goldschätzen der Skythen mit zahlreichen Schmuckpreziosen. In der Schatzkammer werden Goldschmiede- und Juwelierarbeiten seit dem 3. Jahrtausend v. Chr. präsentiert. Die Sammlung russischer Kostüme des 18. bis 20. Jahrhunderts nennt unter anderem 300 Gewänder von Peter dem Großen ihr Eigen.

Darüber hinaus besitzt die Eremitage mit etwa 12.000 Arbeiten auch eine umfangreiche Skulpturensammlung.

Die gesamte Bandbreite der Exponate kann in diesem Band nicht beleuchtet werden. Daher bildet die europäische Malerei hier den Schwerpunkt.

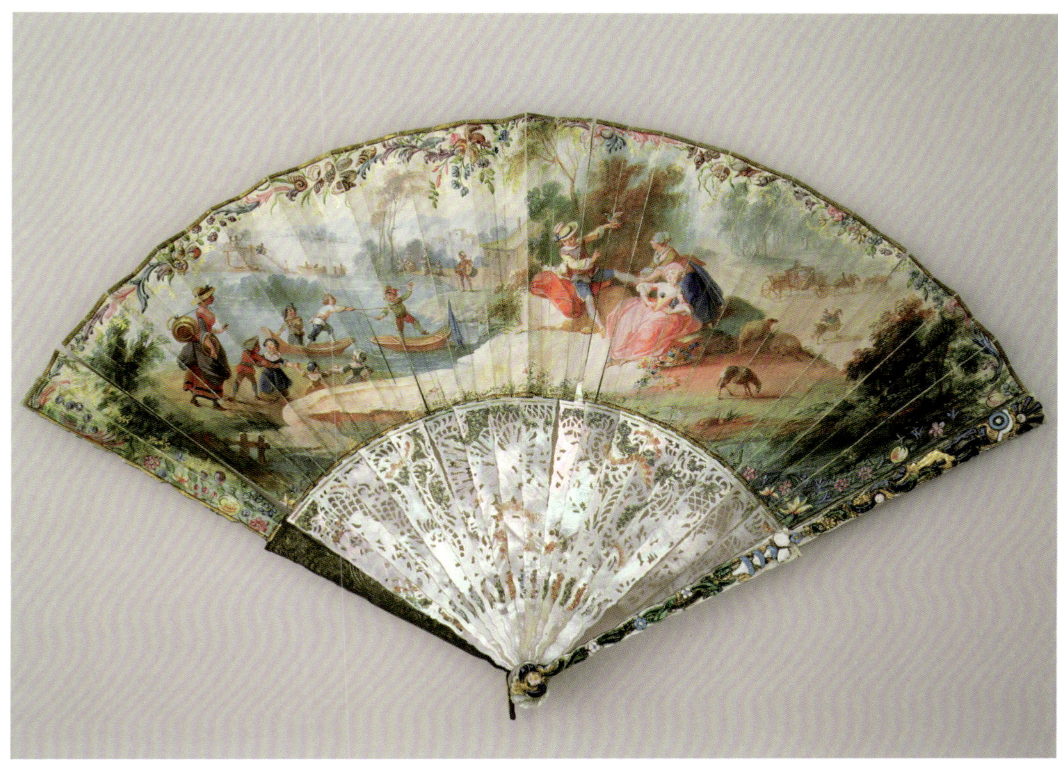

Delespine (fl. 1730–45)

Fan with a courtly scene

Éventail orné d'une scène galante

Fächer mit höfischer Szene

Abanicos con escenas de cortesanos

Leques com Cena da Corte

Waaier met hoftaferelen

1744, Gouache on parchment/
Gouache sur parchemin

Arqueología y artesanía

Es imposible entrar aquí al detalle en las colecciones
del Hermitage, con sus 350 salas y 65.000 piezas.
Los departamentos son múltiples y abarcan desde la
Antigüedad, pasando por culturas orientales, caucásicas
y centroasiáticas hasta el arte de Europa Occidental,
Rusia y el Lejano Oriente.

Las artes aplicadas están especialmente bien
representadas: pueden verse aquí, entre otros, muebles,
alfombras y tapicerías, cerámica y no menos de
14.000 piezas de porcelana de las manufacturas más
importantes, cristal veneciano, de Alemania y España,
así como objetos litúrgicos de la Edad Media. La
colección de tesoros de los escitas, con su multitud de
joyas, es de un valor incalculable. En la sala del tesoro se
muestran trabajos de orfebrería y joyas que datan desde
el tercer milenio a.C. La colección de vestimentas rusas
de los siglos XVIII a XX expone entre otros alrededor
de 300 piezas del propio Pedro el Grande.

Además de todo esto el Hermitage posee con sus
12.000 piezas una exhaustivas colecciones de escultura.

Toda la diversidad de obra expuesta no puede ser
examinada en este volumen. Así que aquí concederemos
prioridad a la pintura europea.

Arqueologia e obras artesanais

Aqui será impossível abordae de uma forma
aprofundada todas as coleções do Hermitage com as
suas 350 salas de exposição e cerca de 65.000 objetos de
arte. As secções são diversas e vão desde a Antiguidade,
passando pelas culturas do Oriente, do Cáucaso e da
Ásia Central até à arte da Europa Ocidental, da Rússia e
do Extremo Oriente.

A arte utilitária está abundantemente representada:
podem ser vistos, entre outros, móveis, tapetes
e tapeçarias, cerâmica e não menos do que
14.000 porcelanas oriundas das mais importantes
manufaturas, vidro de Veneza, Alemanha e Espanha,
bem como objetos de igrejas da Idade Média. De um
valor incalculável é a coleção de tesouros de ouro dos
Citas com inúmeras preciosidades de joalharia. No
tesouro são apresentados trabalhos de ourives e de
joalheiros desde o século III a. C. A coleção de trajes
russos do século XVIII ao século XX contém, entre
outros, 300 roupagens de Pedro o Grande.

Para além disso, o Hermitage possui também
uma abrangente coleção de esculturas com cerca de
12.000 trabalhos.

É impossível iluminar todo o espectro das obras
expostas neste volume. Portanto, a pintura europeia
formará aqui o ponto central.

Archeologie en kunstnijverheid

Het is onmogelijk om alle collecties van de Hermitage
met zijn 350 pronkzalen met 65.000 kunstwerken te
belichten. Het aantal afdelingen is groot en omvat
zowel de antieke, oriëntaalse, Kaukasische en Centraal-
Aziatische culturen als de kunst van West-Europa,
Rusland en het Verre Oosten.

Bijzonder goed vertegenwoordigd is de toegepaste
kunst: te zien zijn onder andere meubels, tapijten
en wandtapijten, keramiek en niet minder dan
14.000 porseleinen objecten uit alle beroemde
porseleinfabrieken, glas uit Venetië, Duitsland en
Spanje, maar ook kerkelijke kunstvoorwerpen. Van
onschatbare waarde zijn de goudschatten van de
Scythen waartoe een groot aantal kostbare sieraden
behoort. In de schatkamer worden goudsmeedkunst
en juwelen vanaf 3000 v.C. tentoongesteld. De collectie
Russische kostuums van de 18de tot de 20ste eeuw telt
onder andere 300 gewaden van Peter de Grote zelf.

Daarenboven bezit de Hermitage met ongeveer
12.000 werken een omvangrijke beeldencollectie.

De totale omvang van de tentoongestelde werken kan
niet in één boek worden belicht. Daarom ligt de nadruk
hier op de Europese schilderkunst

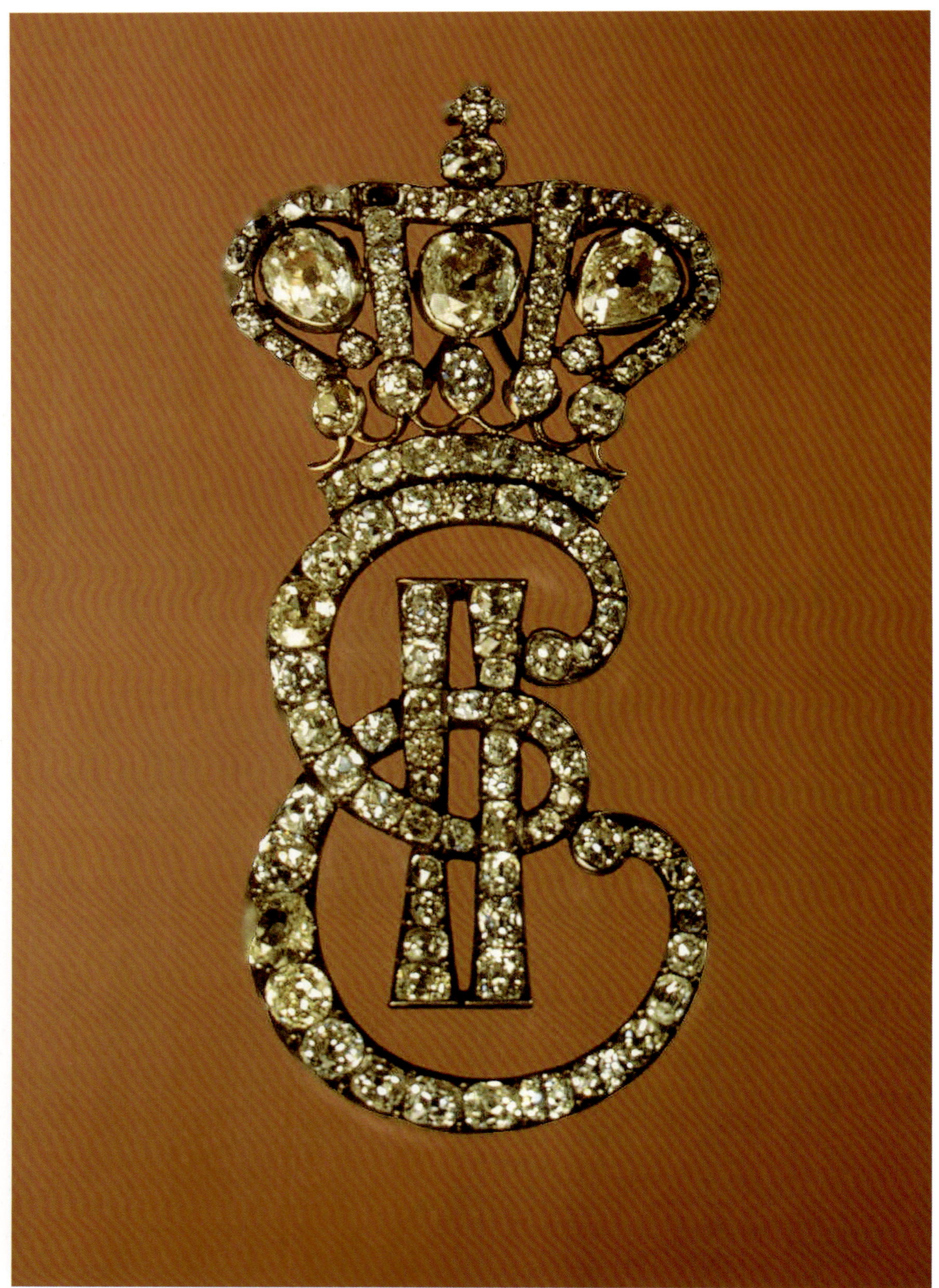

Russia/Russie
Brooch for a lady-in-waiting
Broche d'une dame d'honneur
Ehrenbrosche einer Dame
Broche para una dama de honor
Broche de uma Dama de Honor
Broche voor een dame d'honneur
c. 1770–80, Diamonds/Diamants

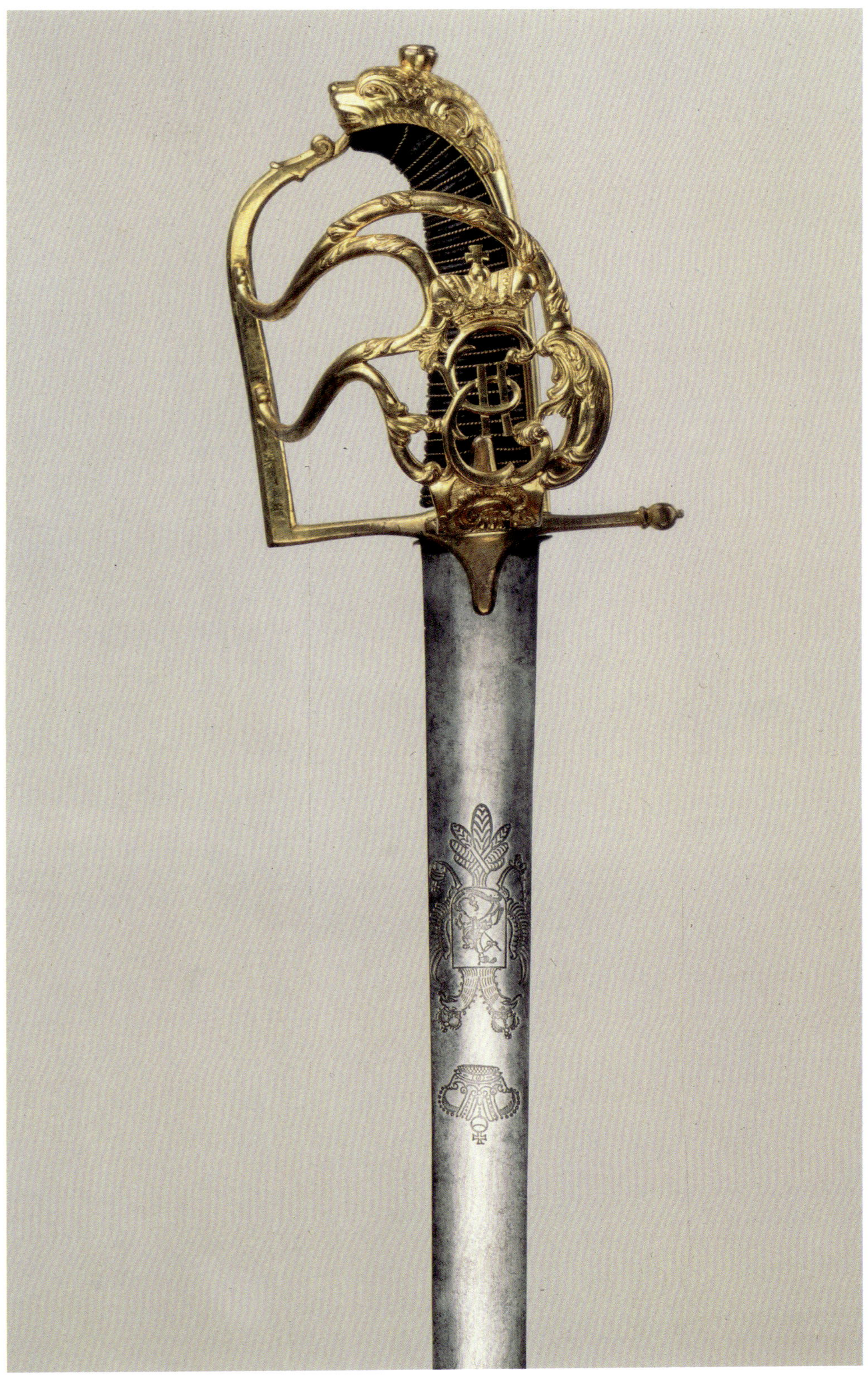

Russia/Russie

Officer's sword with double-headed eagle and
St. George under the imperial crown

Sabre d'officier, orné d'un aigle à deux têtes et
saint Georges sous la couronne impériale

Offiziersschwert mit Doppeladler und dem
heiligen Georg unter der Kaiserkrone

Espada de oficial con águila bicéfala y
san Jorge bajo la corona imperial

Espada de Oficial com Águia Dupla e
São Jorge sob a Coroa Imperial

Officierszwaard met dubbelkoppige aardelaar
en Sint-Joris op de keizerstroon

18th Century/XVIIIᵉ siècle, Steel, bronze, copper
and gold/Acier, bronze, cuivre et plaqué or

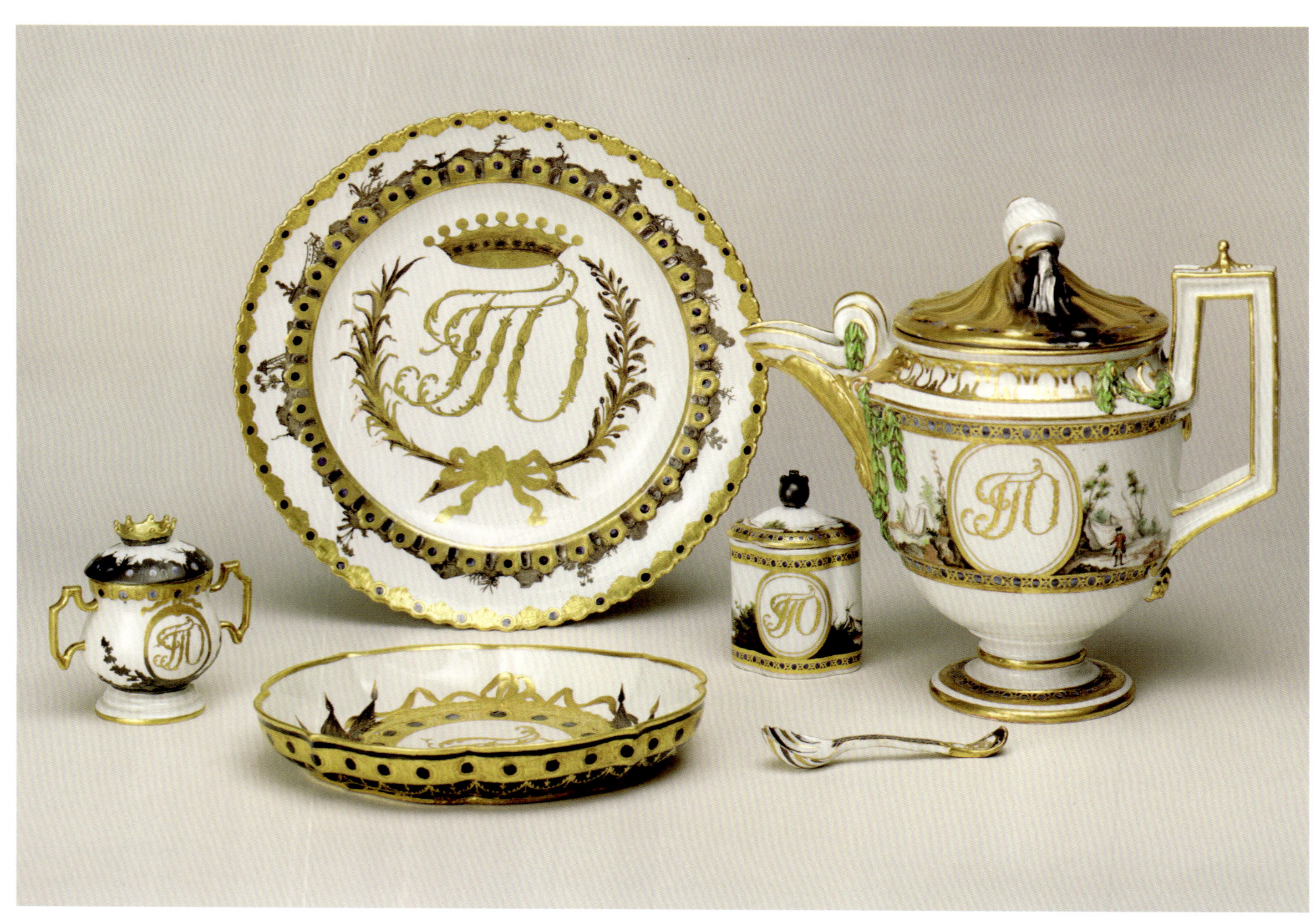

Andrei & Polozow Gerassimow

Orlov Tea Service

Service à thé Orlov

Orlow-Teegeschirr

Juego de té Orlov

Serviço de Chá de Orlov

Orlov-theeservies

c. 1765, Porcelain/Porcelaine

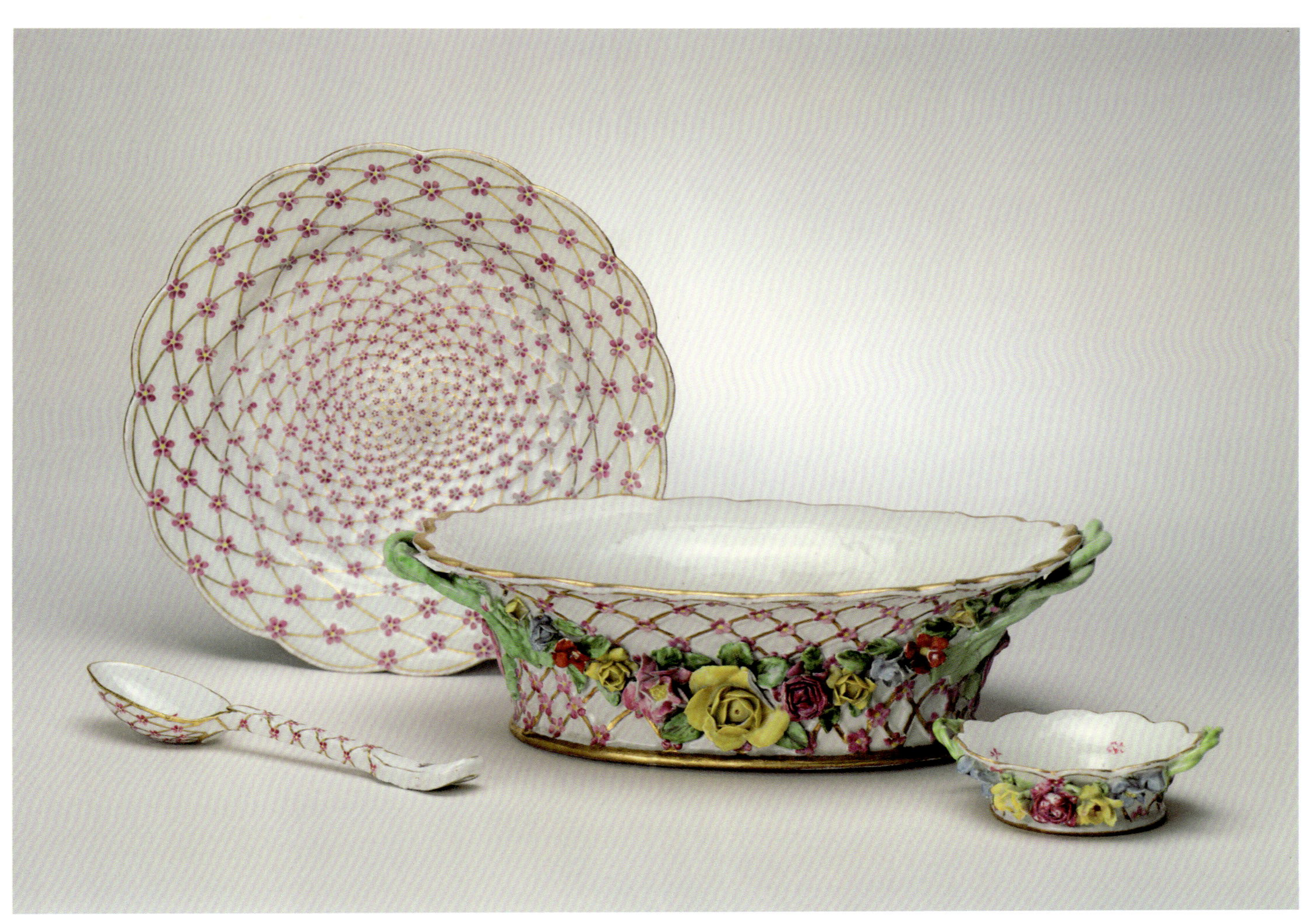

Parts of the Czarina Elizaveta Petrovna Service

Élément du service de l'impératrice Elizabeth Petrovna

Teile aus dem Service der Kaiserin Jelisaweta Petrowna

Piezas del servicio de la emperatriz Yelisaveta Petrovna

Peças de um Serviço da Imperatriz Isabel da Rússia (Elisabete Petrovna)

Deel uit het servies van tsarina Elisabeth (Jelisaveta) Petrovna

1756, Porcelain/Porcelaine

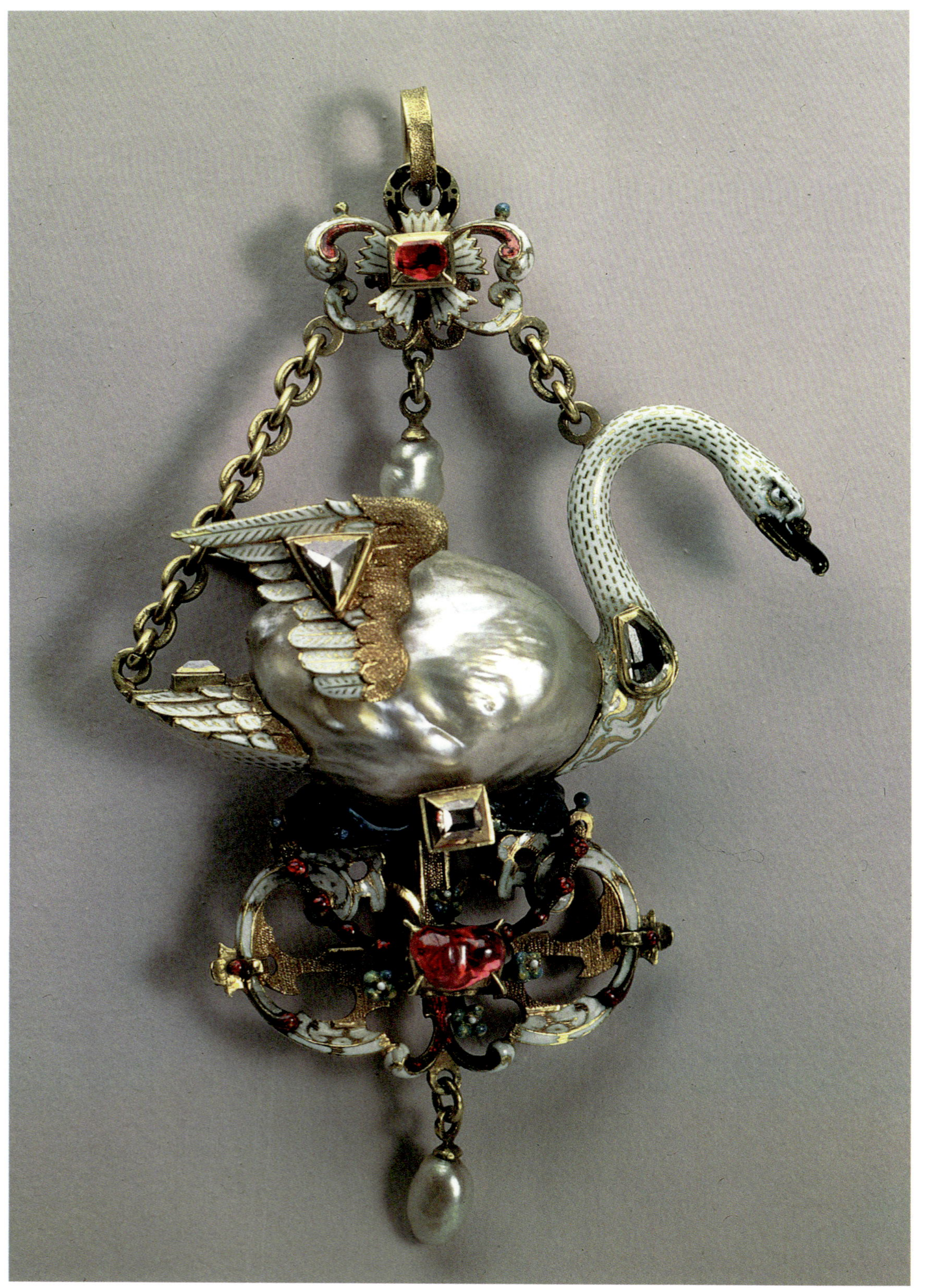

Netherlands/Pays-Bas
Swan Pendant
Pendentif cygne
Anhänger mit Schwan
Colgante con cisne
Pendente com Cisne
Hanger met zwaan
c. 1590, Gold, enamel, diamonds, emeralds, ruby and perls/Or, émail, diamants incrustés, émeraudes, rubis et perles, 9,2 × 5,9 cm

Fabergé jewelry/Atelier Fabergé
Cornflowers and Ears of Wheat
Bleuets et tiges d'avoine
Kornblumen und Ähren
Flores y mazorcas de maíz
Fidalguinhos e Espigas
Korenbloemen en aren
1880, Gold, rock-crystal and polished diamonds/Or, cristal de roche et diamants coupés

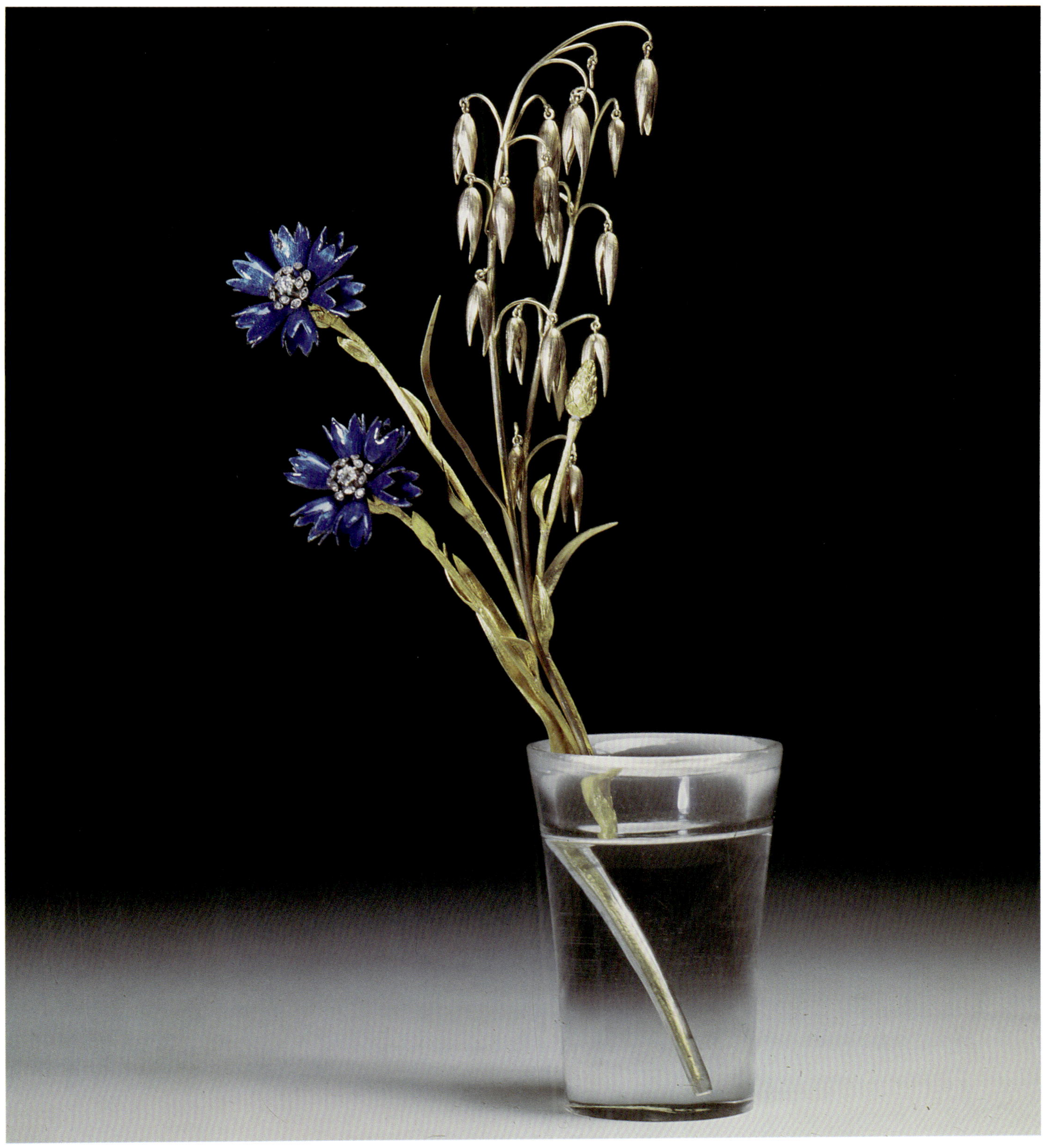

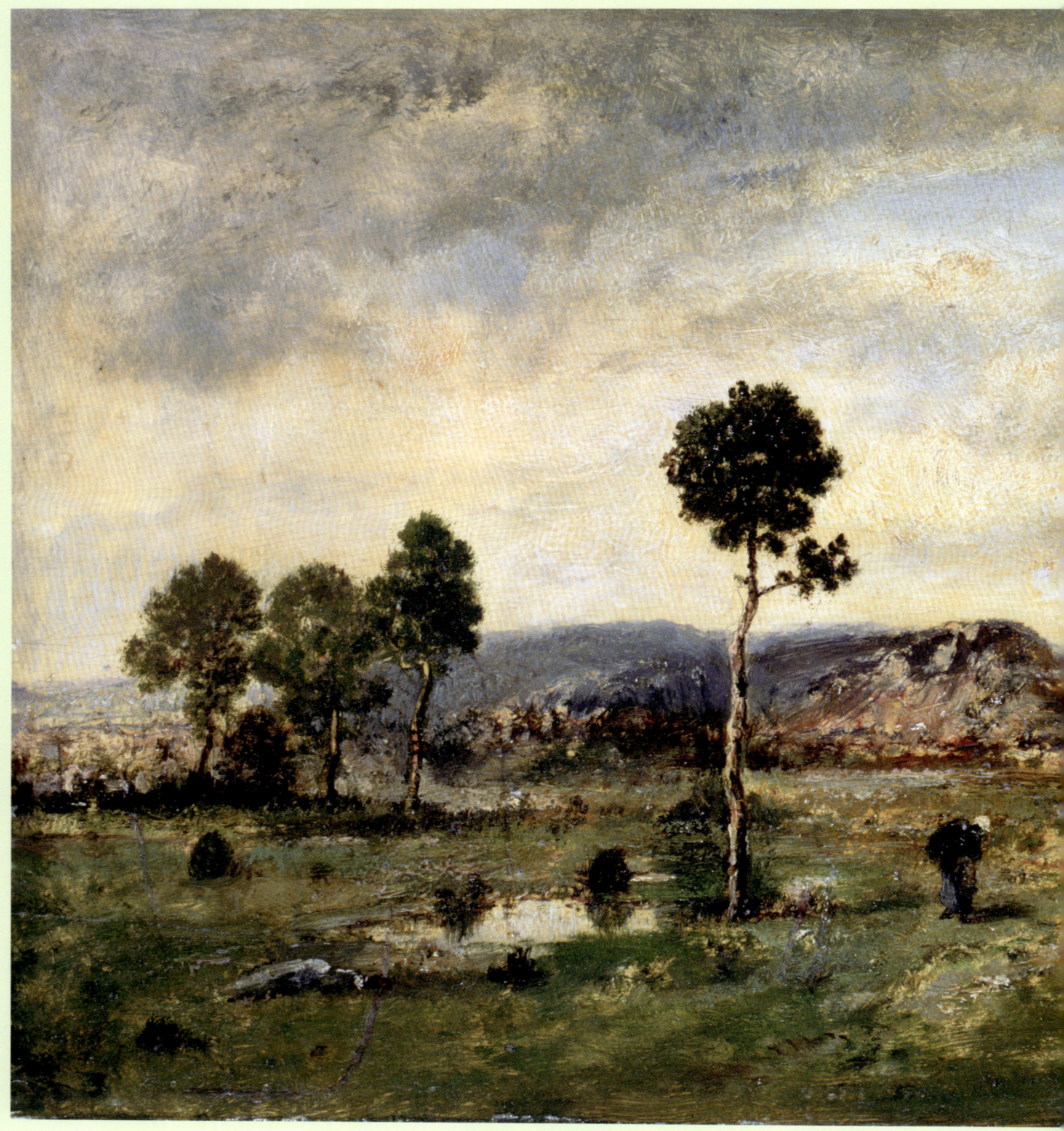

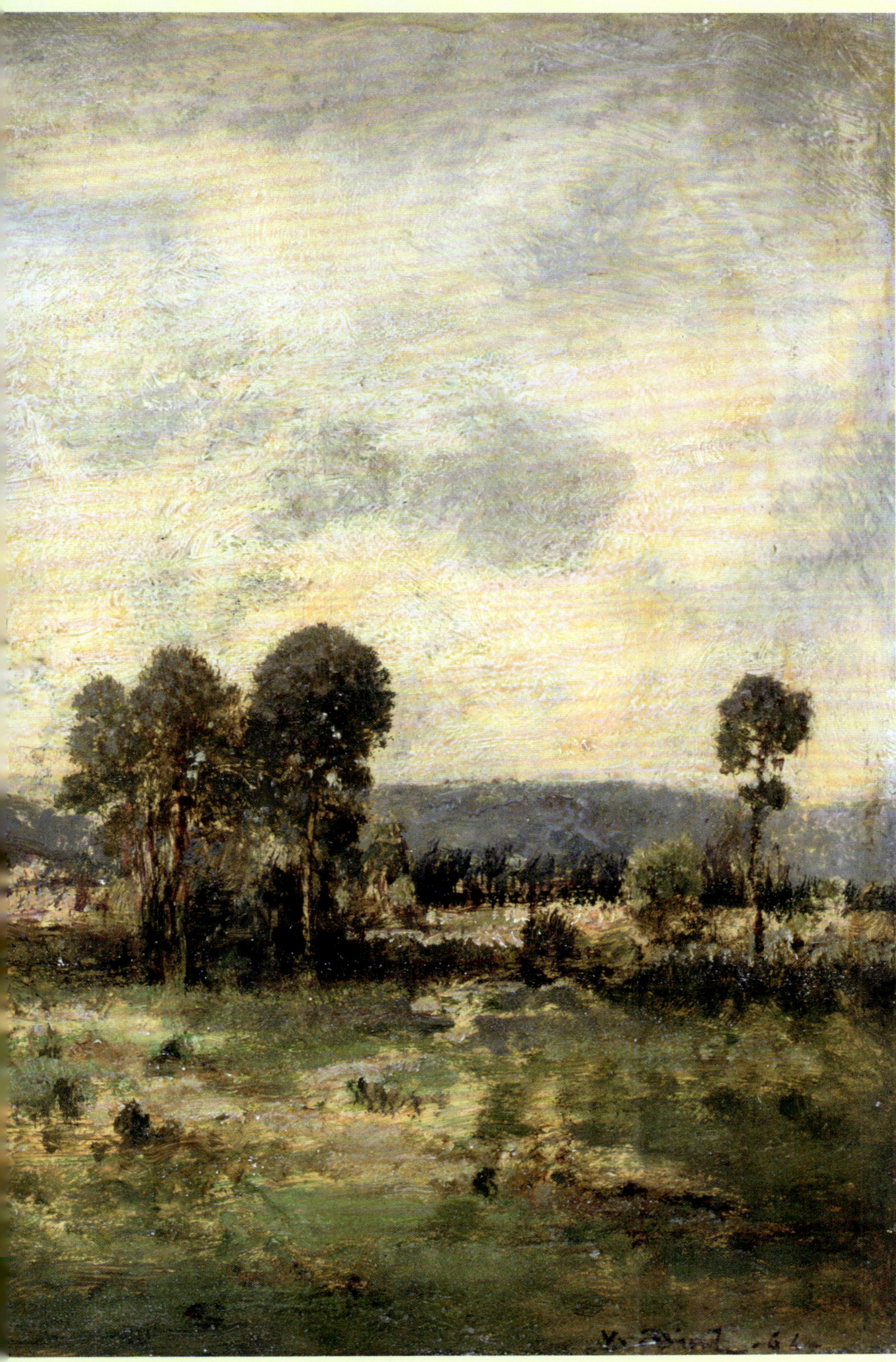

Narcisso Virgilio Díaz de la Peña (1807–76)
Landscape with Pines
Paysage avec un pin
Landschaft mit Kiefer
Paisaje con pinos
Paisagem com Pinheiros
Landschap met pijnbomen
1864, Oil on canvas/Huile sur toile, 21,5 × 33,5 cm

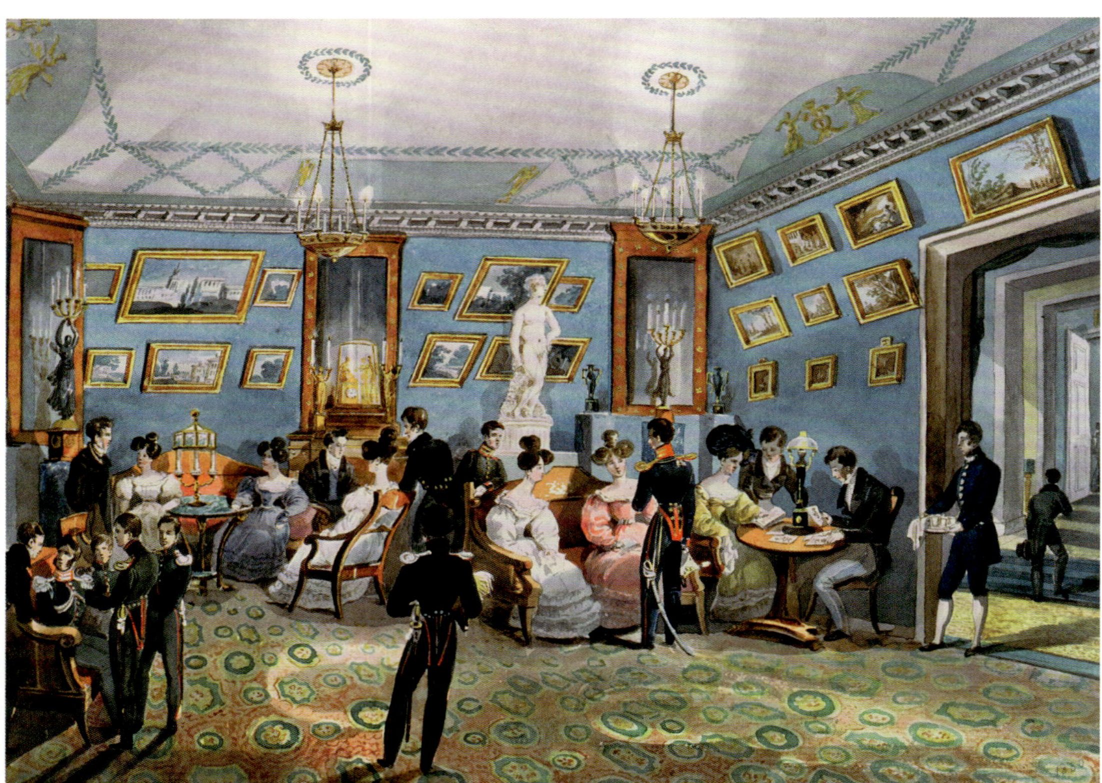

European Painting

Of central importance, and always at the center of the czars' collecting activities, are the galleries with examples from every European school of painting. Skillful diplomacy and advice from art connoisseurs like Denis Diderot and Melchior Grimm led Catherine the Great to assemble one of the most important collections of European art, which has been continually expanded in the more than two centuries hence.

In addition to the purchases of entire collections as discussed above, the Russian czars also maintained contacts with the artists themselves who gladly sent masterpieces to the court in hope for future commissions. For example, Chardin painted the still life *The Attributes of the Arts* for Catherine. It was brought to Russia by sculptor Etienne-Maurice Falconet, who was also worked for the czar.

The manner in which the works are displayed also dates from this period: the Petersburg hanging style crams works of artworks into tight spaces, often covering walls in their entirety. This style, also known as "salon hanging," was not invented in St. Petersburg, however, but instead has been popular since the Renaissance. But the Hermitage is one of the few museums which preserves this practice.

La peinture européenne

La galerie de tableaux – toujours au centre du collectionnisme des tsars – est d'une importance primordiale, avec des œuvres capitales de toutes les écoles européennes. L'habileté diplomatique et les conseils d'excellents connaisseurs comme les encyclopédistes Denis Diderot et Melchior Grimm ont permis à Catherine II d'agrandir constamment ses collections avec grand nombre de chefs-d'œuvre de la peinture européenne.

À côté des achats de collections complètes, la Cour impériale russe entretenait des contacts avec les artistes eux-mêmes à qui elle commandait souvent des œuvres destinées à la galerie de peinture. Chardin peignit par exemple pour elle une nature morte – *Les Attributs des arts et les récompenses qui leur sont attribuées* – que le sculpteur Falconet (au service de la tsarine) lui apporta en Russie.

Cette époque est caractérisée, dans la présentation des salles, par une juxtaposition serrées des œuvres sur les murs qu'elles finissent souvent par couvrir complètement – technique d'exposition dite depuis « accrochage pétersbourgeois ». Cette forme de présentation pléthorique et ostentatoire remonte en fait à la Renaissance, mais l'Ermitage est l'un des rares

Europäische Malerei

Von zentraler Bedeutung, und immer schon Mittelpunkt der Sammlertätigkeit der russischen Kaiser, ist die Gemäldegalerie mit wichtigen Werken aus allen europäischen Schulen. Durch geschickte Diplomatie und Beratung durch Kunstkenner wie Denis Diderot und Melchior Grimm konnte Katharina die Große bedeutende Sammlungen mit europäischen Kunstwerken erwerben, die ständig erweitert wurden.

Neben den bereits erwähnten Ankäufen kompletter Sammlungen unterhielt der russische Hof auch Kontakte zu den Künstlern selbst, die, mit Aufträgen bedacht, ihre Werke der Gemäldegalerie überließen. Chardin malte zum Beispiel im Auftrag Katharinas das *Stillleben mit Attributen der Künste,* das der ebenfalls für die Kaiserin tätige Bildhauer Etienne-Maurice Falconet nach Russland überbrachte.

Aus dieser Zeit stammt die in vielen Sälen zu sehende Präsentation der Werke: Die sogenannte Petersburger Hängung drängt die Kunstwerke auf engem Raum zusammen, sodass sie häufig ganze Wände bedecken. Diese auch als Salonhängung bezeichnete Form der Darbietung von Kunstwerken geht nicht auf St. Petersburg zurück, sondern war seit der Renaissance häufig, da man sie als besonders repräsentativ empfand.

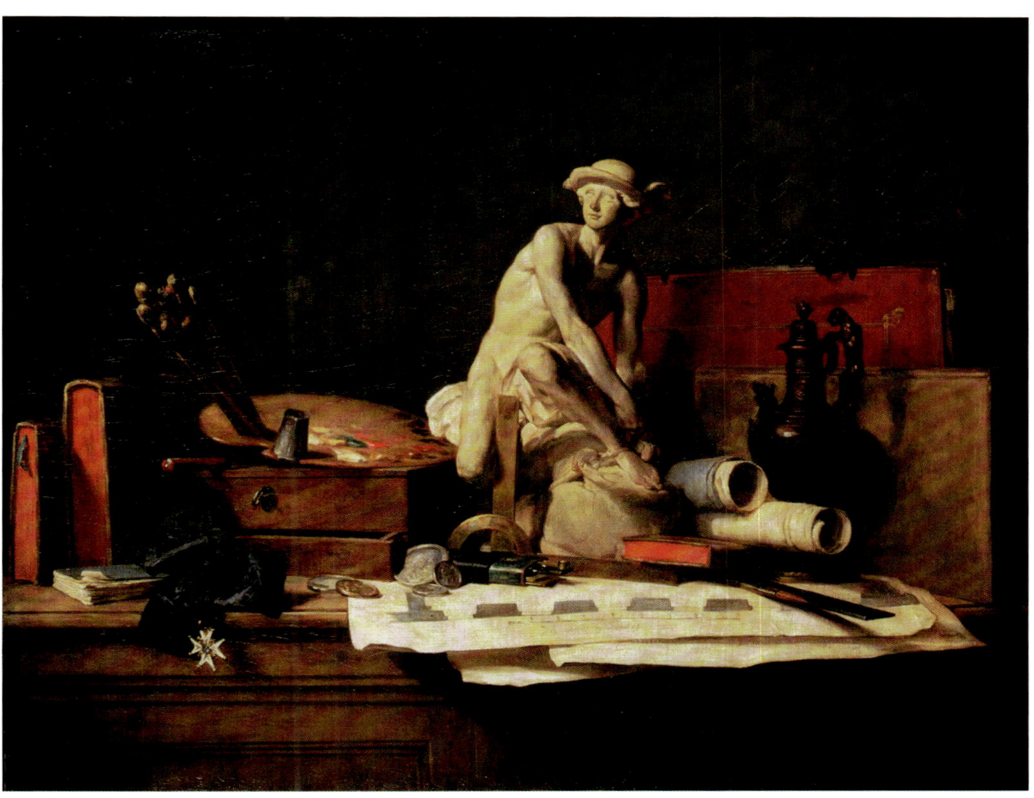

Pintura europea

La galería de pintura con sus importantes obras de todas las escuelas europeas fue siempre de una importancia fundamental, eje central de la actividad coleccionista del emperador. Gracias a una habilidosa diplomacia y a la asesoría de especialistas en arte como Denis Diderot o Melchior Grimm, Catalina la Grande puedo hacerse con colecciones importantes de obras de arte europeas, que fueron expandidas constantemente.

Además de las mencionadas adquisiciones de colecciones completas, la corte rusa mantenía contacto con los propios artistas quienes, con vistas a encargos, cedían sus obras a la galería de pintura. Chardin por ejemplo pintó por encargo de Catalina el bodegón *Los atributos de las artes* que el escultor Etienne-Maurice Falconet, receptor igualmente de encargos de la emperatriz, llevó a Rusia.

De esta época proviene la presentación de las obras tal y como se ve en muchas salas: el estilo conocido como Petersburgo concentra los cuadros en un espacio reducido, de forma que a menudo ocupan paredes enteras. Este forma de presentar cuadros, denominada también de salón, no surge en San Peterburgo, sino que era común desde el Renacimiento, cuando se la consideraba especialmente impresionante. El Hermitage

Pintura europeia

De uma importância central e desde sempre o centro da atividade do colecionismo dos imperadores russos é a galeria de pinturas com obras importantes de todas as escolas de arte europeias. Através de uma hábil diplomacia e do aconselhamento de conhecedores de arte, como Denis Diderot e Melchior Grimm, Catarina a Grande conseguiu adquirir coleções importantes com obras de arte europeias, que eram constantemente ampliadas.

Além das aquisições já mencionadas de coleções completas, a corte russa mantinha também contacto com os próprios artistas, aos quais eram atribuídas encomendas e que assim deixavam as suas obras à galeria de pintura. Chardin pintou, por exemplo, mediante a ordem de Catarina a obra *Natureza-Morta com Atributos das Artes,* que o escultor Etienne-Maurice Falconet, que também trabalhava para a Imperatriz, trouxe para a Rússia.

Desta época tem origem a forma de apresentação das obras que pode ser vista em muitas salas. A designada de exposição de quadros ao estilo de São Petersburgo adensa as obras de arte num pequeno espaço, de modo a que frequentemente estas cubram paredes inteiras. Esta forma de apresentação de obras

Europese schilderkunst

Van cruciaal belang en van begin af aan de grootste focus van de verzamelactiviteiten van de Russische keizerin, is de schilderijengalerij met belangrijke werken uit alle Europese schilderscholen. Door behendig diplomatiek optreden en adviesoverleg met kunstkenners als Denis Diderot en Melchior Grimm kon Catharina de Grote belangrijke collecties Europese kunstwerken verwerven die vervolgens voortdurend werden uitgebreid.

Naast de al genoemde aankopen van complete collecties onderhield het Russische hof ook contacten met kunstenaars zelf, die – met opdrachten op zak – hun werken aan de schilderijengalerij ter beschikking stelden. Chardin schilderde bijvoorbeeld in opdracht van Catharina het stilleven *De attributen van de kunst,* dat de eveneens voor de tsarina werkzame beeldhouwer Etienne-Maurice Falconet naar Rusland bracht.

Uit deze tijd stamt de in veel zalen gebruikte manier waarop de werken worden getoond: in de zogeheten Petersburg-opstelling worden de kunstwerken zo dicht op elkaar gehangen dat ze vaak hele wanden bedekken. Deze ook wel 'salonopstelling' genoemde manier van schilderijen presenteren komt van oorsprong niet uit Sint-Petersburg, en was sinds de renaissance populair

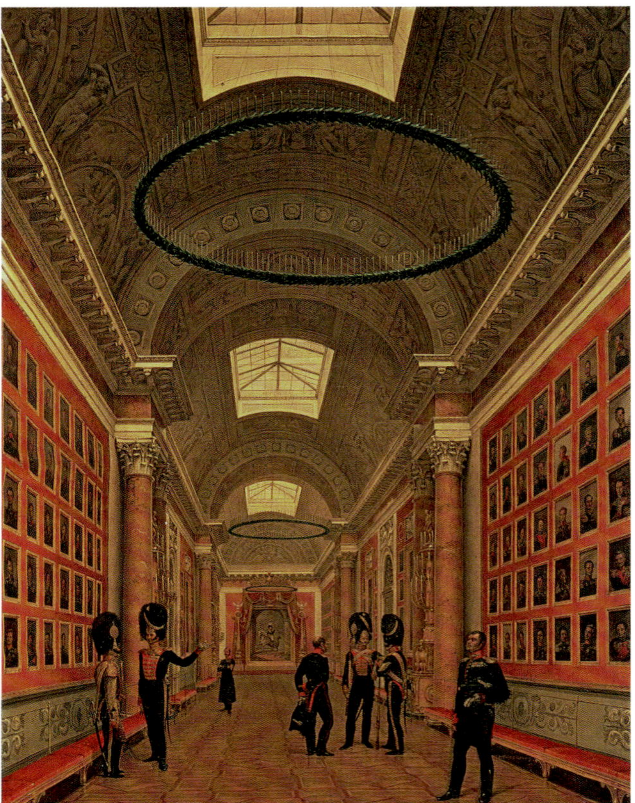

In addition to paintings, the Hermitage has a large collection of drawings and 50,000 prints from different eras made using a variety of techniques. Only a small fraction of the works held by the Hermitage is on display at any time; the rest are held in storage.

This precious collection of paintings has established the Hermitage's reputation as one of the most important museums in the world, but the architectural ensemble on the banks of the Neva is also a masterpiece of world architecture. This magical triad of important paintings, treasures from around the world, and architecture attracts an ever-growing stream of visitors each year to St. Petersburg, a city full of wonders shaped by its rich history.

musées mondiaux dans lesquels cet accrochage a été maintenu.

L'Ermitage possède également une très vaste collection de dessins et plus de 50 000 estampes et gravures de différentes techniques et époques. Une partie seulement est exposée en permanence et/ou par roulement, de même que pour les 7 000 tableaux de la galerie de peinture. En dehors des œuvres les plus importantes ainsi présentées, le reste des trésors est soigneusement gardé dans les magasins des réserves.

À elle seule, l'inestimable collection de peinture a établi la renommée de l'Ermitage comme l'un des trois plus importants musées du monde. Reste que le complexe architectural au bord de la Néva appartient aussi aux réalisations majeures de l'architecture mondiale. Cette fabuleuse triade – tableaux essentiels, objets précieux du monde entier et architecture – attire chaque année des visiteurs de plus en plus nombreux à Saint-Pétersbourg, ville magique au passé prestigieux.

Doch ist die Eremitage eines der wenigen Museen, in der sich diese Hängung erhalten hat.

Neben der Malerei besitzt die Eremitage eine große Sammlung von Zeichnungen und über 50.000 Druckgrafiken verschiedener Techniken und Epochen. Ständig zu sehen ist nur ein Bruchteil – wie auch von den 7000 Bildern der Gemäldegalerie nur die bedeutendsten ausgestellt sind und der Rest in den Depoträumen aufbewahrt wird.

Allein diese unschätzbar kostbare Gemäldesammlung hat den Ruf der Eremitage als eines der bedeutendsten Museen in der ganzen Welt gefestigt. Aber auch das architektonische Ensemble an der Newa gehört zu den Meisterleistungen der Weltarchitektur. Dieser märchenhafte Dreiklang – bedeutende Gemälde, Preziosen aus aller Welt und die Architektur – lockt jedes Jahr mehr Besucher nach St. Petersburg, der Wunderstadt mit ihrer reichen Vergangenheit.

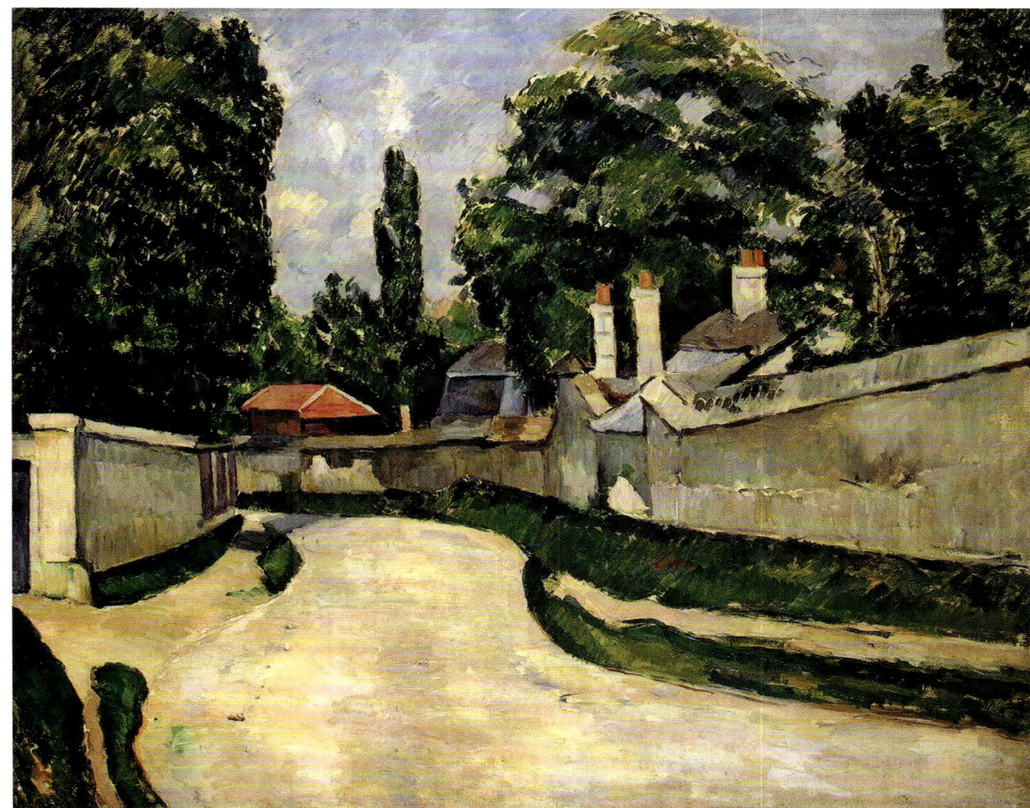

sin embargo es uno de los pocos museos que ha mantenido este estilo.

Además de su colección de pintura el Hermitage posee una amplia colección de dibujos y más de 50.000 trabajos de imprenta de diversas técnicas y épocas. Normalmente solo puede verse una pequeña parte de las mismas: como en el caso de las 7000 pinturas de la colección solo las más importantes se exponen, guardándose el resto en los espacios de almacenamiento.

Solo esta colección de pintura de valor incalculable ha otorgado al Hermitage un lugar como uno de los museos más importantes de todo el mundo, pero el propio conjunto arquitectónico en el Nevá también es una obra maestra de la arquitectura mundial. Este triángulo de ensueño -pinturas importantes, joyas de todo el mundo y arquitectura- atrae cada año a más visitantes a San Petersburgo, la ciudad de las maravillas con su glorioso pasado.

de arte também denominada de suspensão ao estilo de salão não remonta a São Petersburgo, tendo sido já comum no Renascimento, uma vez que era considerada especialmente representativa. Com efeito, o Hermitage é um dos poucos museus que conservou esta forma de pendurar quadros na parede.

Além da pintura, o Hermitage possui uma grande coleção de desenhos e mais de 50.000 trabalhos gráficos de impressão de diferentes técnicas e épocas. Apenas uma fração é que pode ser permanente vista, tal como acontece também com as 7000 obras da galeria de pinturas das quais apenas estão expostas as mais importantes, estando as restantes conservadas nos espaços de depósito.

Somente esta coleção de pinturas incalculavelmente valiosa consolidou a fama do Hermitage no sentido de este ser um dos museus mais importantes de todo o mundo. No entanto, também o conjunto arquitetónico à margem do rio Neva faz parte das contribuições mestres da arquitetura mundial. Esta tríade fabulosa, designadamente, as pinturas importantes, as preciosidades de todo o mundo e a arquitetura, atrai todos os anos cada vez mais visitantes a São Petersburgo, a cidade miraculosa com o seu copioso passado.

omdat hij als representatief werd ervaren. De Hermitage is daarentegen wel een van de weinige musea waarin deze opstelling nog altijd wordt toegepast.

Naast de schilderijenverzamelingen bezit de Hermitage ook een grote collectie tekeningen en meer dan 50.000 prenten uit verschillende perioden uit de geschiedenis. In de vaste tentoonstelling is daarvan maar een fractie opgenomen – net zoals ook van de 7000 schilderijen uit de schilderijengalerij alleen de belangrijkste worden getoond en de rest in depots is opgeslagen.

Met deze onschatbaar kostbare kunstverzamelingen vestigde de Hermitage zijn reputatie als een van de belangrijkste musea ter wereld. Maar ook het Hermitage-complex aan de Neva zelf behoort tot de meesterwerken van de wereldarchitectuur. Deze sprookjesachtige drieklank – belangrijke schilderijen, kostbaarheden van overal ter wereld, de architectuur – trekt elk jaar weer meer bezoekers naar Sint-Petersburg, de stad der wonderen met zijn rijke verleden.

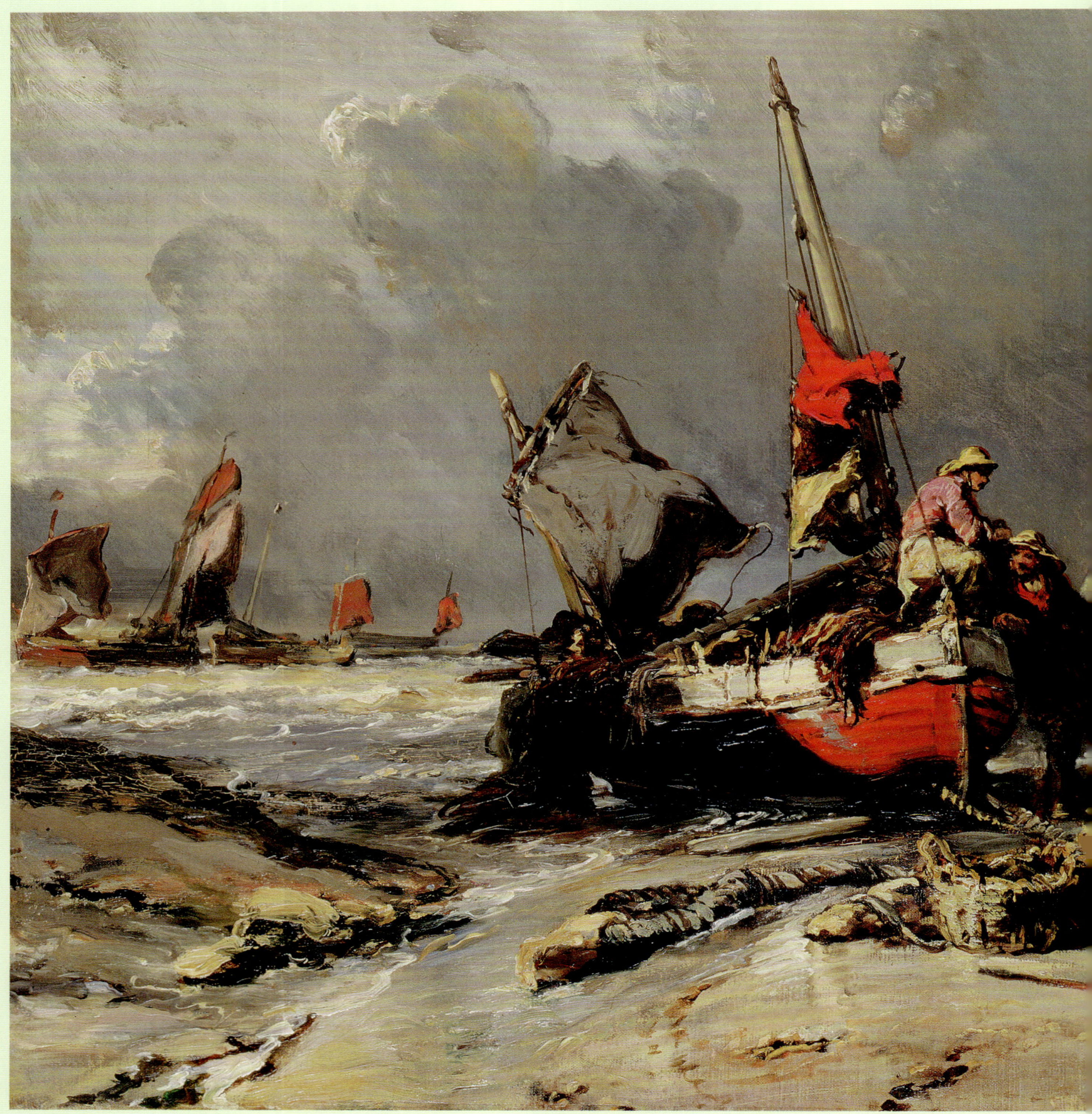

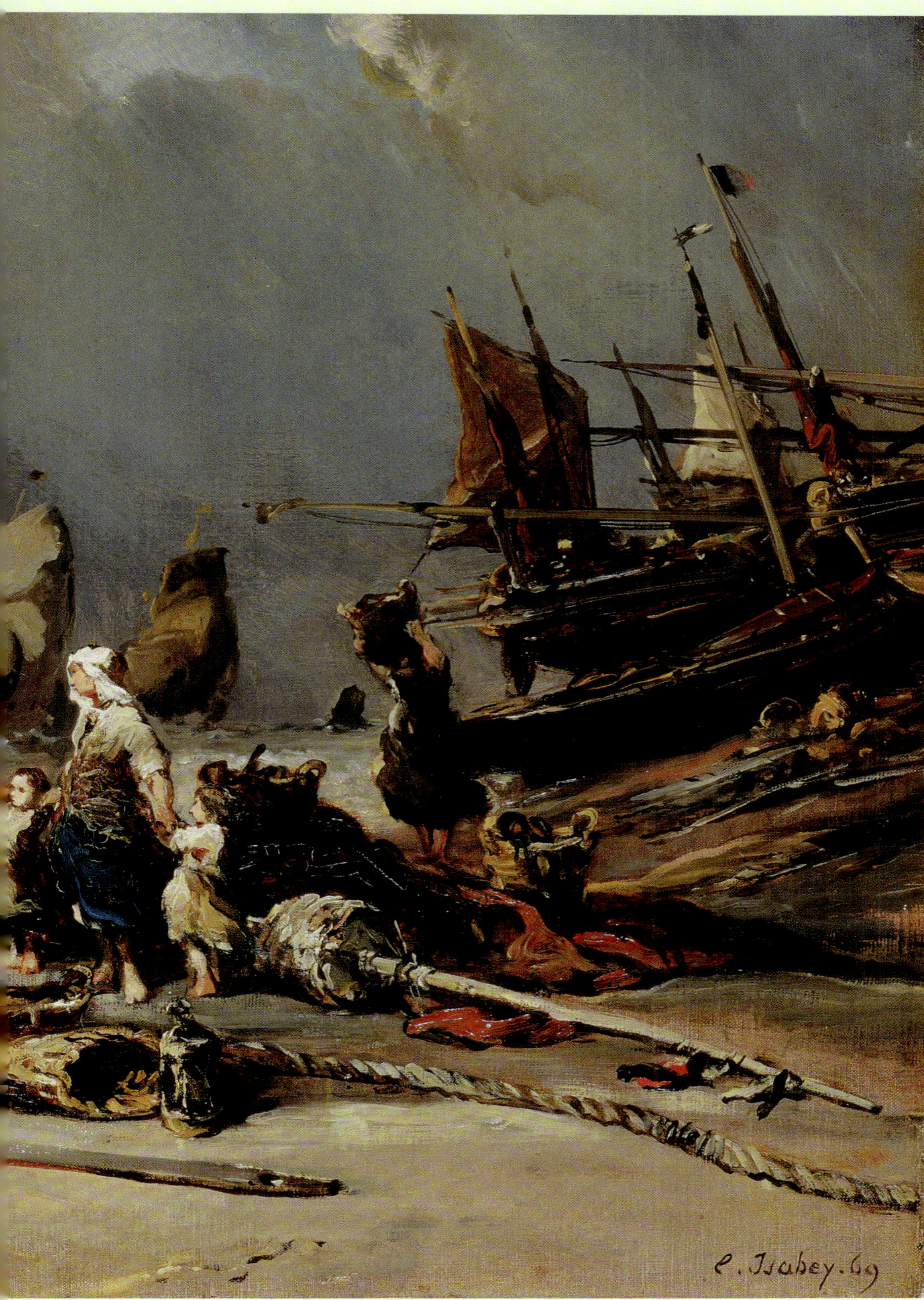

FRENCH PAINTING
LA PEINTURE FRANÇAISE
FRANZÖSISCHE MALEREI
PINTURA FRANCESA
PINTURA FRANCESA
FRANSE SCHILDERKUNST

Eugène Isabey (1803–86)
After the Storm
Après la tempête
Nach dem Sturm
Tras la tormenta
Depois da Tempestade
Na de storm
1869, Oil on canvas/Huile sur toile, 36,5 × 60 cm

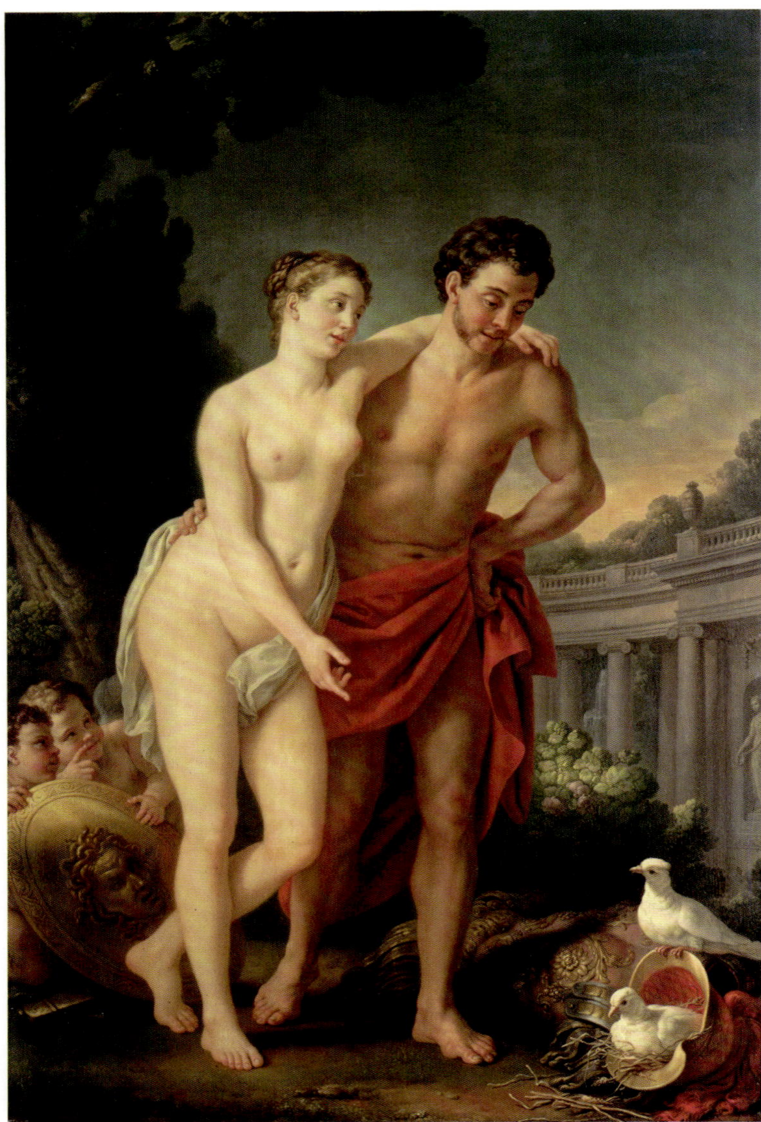

French Painting

The Hermitage's collection of classic French painting is outstanding, including works by Nicolas Poussin, Claude Lorrain, the Le Nain brothers, Antoine Watteau, François Boucher, Jean-Honoré Fragonard, Hubert Robert, Jean-Baptiste Greuze, and Jean Siméon Chardin. The museum's collection of early Modernist works has also become well known, with exemplars from Impressionism (Monet, Renoir, Sisley, Cézanne, Gauguin) to Fauvism and Cubism. In 2014, the collection was relocated to the General Staff Building across Palace Square from the Hermitage.

La peinture française

La sélection de peinture classique française est très remarquable, avec des toiles de Nicolas Poussin, de Claude Lorrain, des frères Le Nain, d'Antoine Watteau, de François Boucher, de Jean-Honoré Fragonard, d'Hubert Robert, de Jean-Baptiste Greuze et de Jean Siméon Chardin. L'ensemble de tableaux des débuts de la peinture moderne est tout aussi remarquable, de l'impressionnisme (Monet, Renoir, Sisley, Pissarro, Cézanne, Gauguin) au cubisme en passant par le fauvisme. Depuis 2014, cette section est installée dans le bâtiment d'État-Major, en face de l'Ermitage, sur la place du Palais.

Französische Malerei

Hervorragend ist die Auswahl an klassischer französischer Malerei. Darunter befinden sich Werke von Nicolas Poussin, Claude Lorrain, Gemälde der Gebrüder Le Nain, von Jean-Antoine Watteau, François Boucher, Jean-Honoré Fragonard, Hubert Robert, Jean-Baptiste Greuze und Jean Siméon Chardin. Besonders bekannt wurde die Sammlung früher moderner Malerei – vom Impressionismus (Monet, Renoir, Sisley, Cézanne, Gauguin) bis zum Fauvismus und Kubismus. Sie befindet sich seit 2014 im der Eremitage am Palastplatz gegenüberliegenden Generalstabsgebäude.

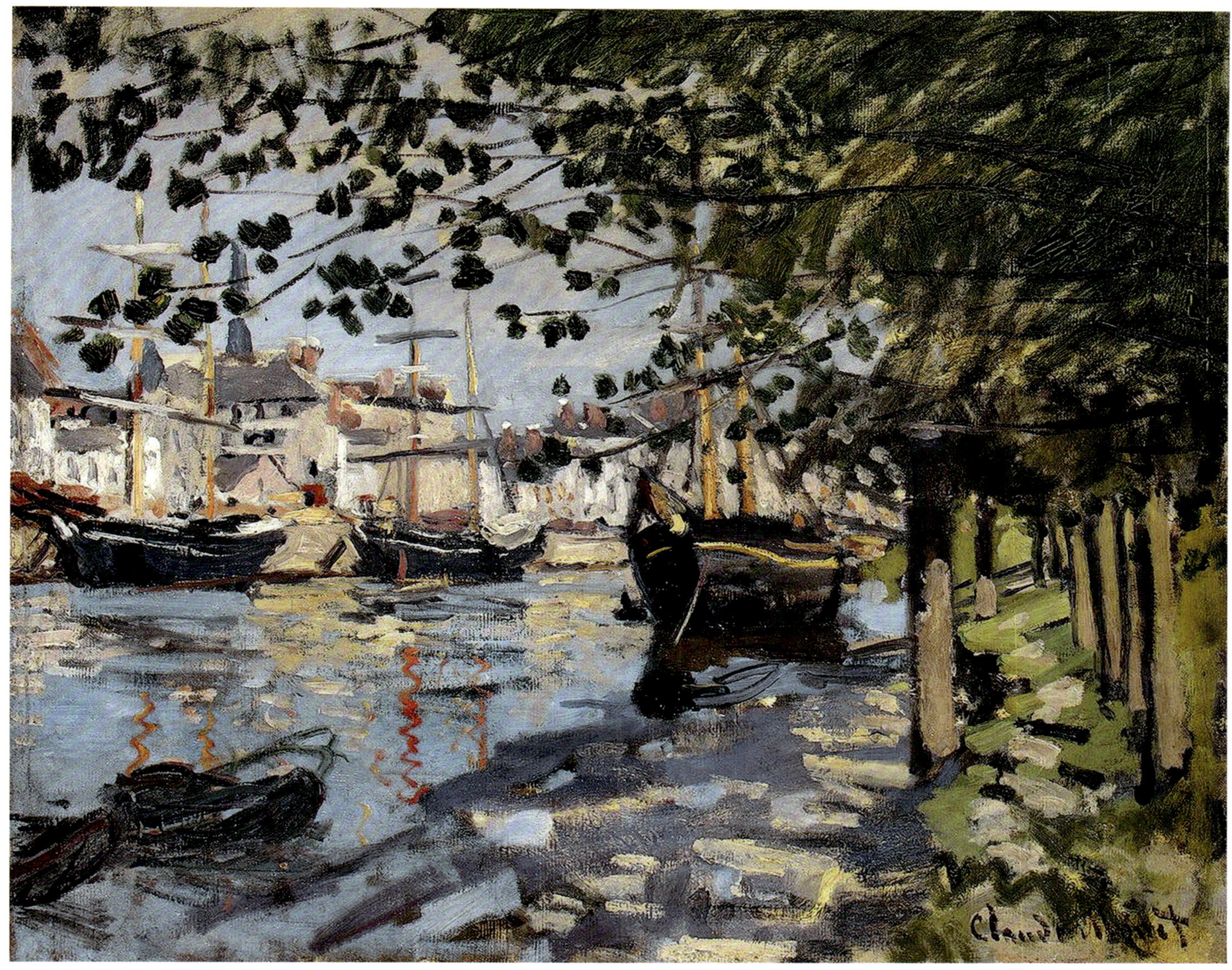

Pintura francesa

La selección de pintura clásica francesa es especialmente extraordinaria. Hay obras de Nicolas Poussin, Claude Lorrain, cuadros de los hermanos Le Nain, de Antoine Watteau, François Boucher, Jean-Honoré Fragonard, Hubert Robert, Jean-Baptiste Greuze y Jean Siméon Chardin. La colección de pintura de inicios de la modernidad se hizo especialmente famosa, desde el impresionismo (Monet, Renoir, Sisley, Cézanne, Gauguin) hasta el fauvismo y cubismo. Esta se encuentra desde 2014 en el edificio del Estado Mayor, frente al Hermitage en la plaza del palacio.

Pintura francesa

A seleção de pintura francesa clássica é excelente. Entre as pinturas, encontram-se obras de Nicolas Poussin, Claude Lorrain, pinturas dos irmãos Le Nain, de Jean-Antoine Watteau, François Boucher, Jean-Honoré Fragonard, Hubert Robert, Jean-Baptiste Greuze e Jean Siméon Chardin. A coleção da pintura moderna inicial, desde o Impressionismo (Monet, Renoir, Sisley, Cézanne, Gauguin) até ao Fauvismo e o Cubismo, tornou-se especialmente famosa. A coleção encontra-se desde 2014 no Hermitage no edifício do Palácio do Estado Maior situado em frente à Praça do Palácio.

Franse schilderkunst

Ronduit indrukwekkend is de collectie klassieke Franse schilderkunst. Daartoe behoren werken van Nicolas Poussin, Claude Lorrain, schilderijen van de gebroeders Le Nain, van Antoine Watteau, François Boucher, Jean-Honoré Fragonard, Hubert Robert, Jean-Baptiste Greuze en Jean-Baptiste Siméon Chardin. Vooral bekend werd de verzameling vroege moderne schilderkunst – van impressionisme (Monet, Renoir, Sisley, Cézanne, Gauguin) tot fauvisme en kubisme. Deze collectie is sinds 2014 ondergebracht in het Generale Stafgebouw tegenover de Hermitage aan het Paleisplein.

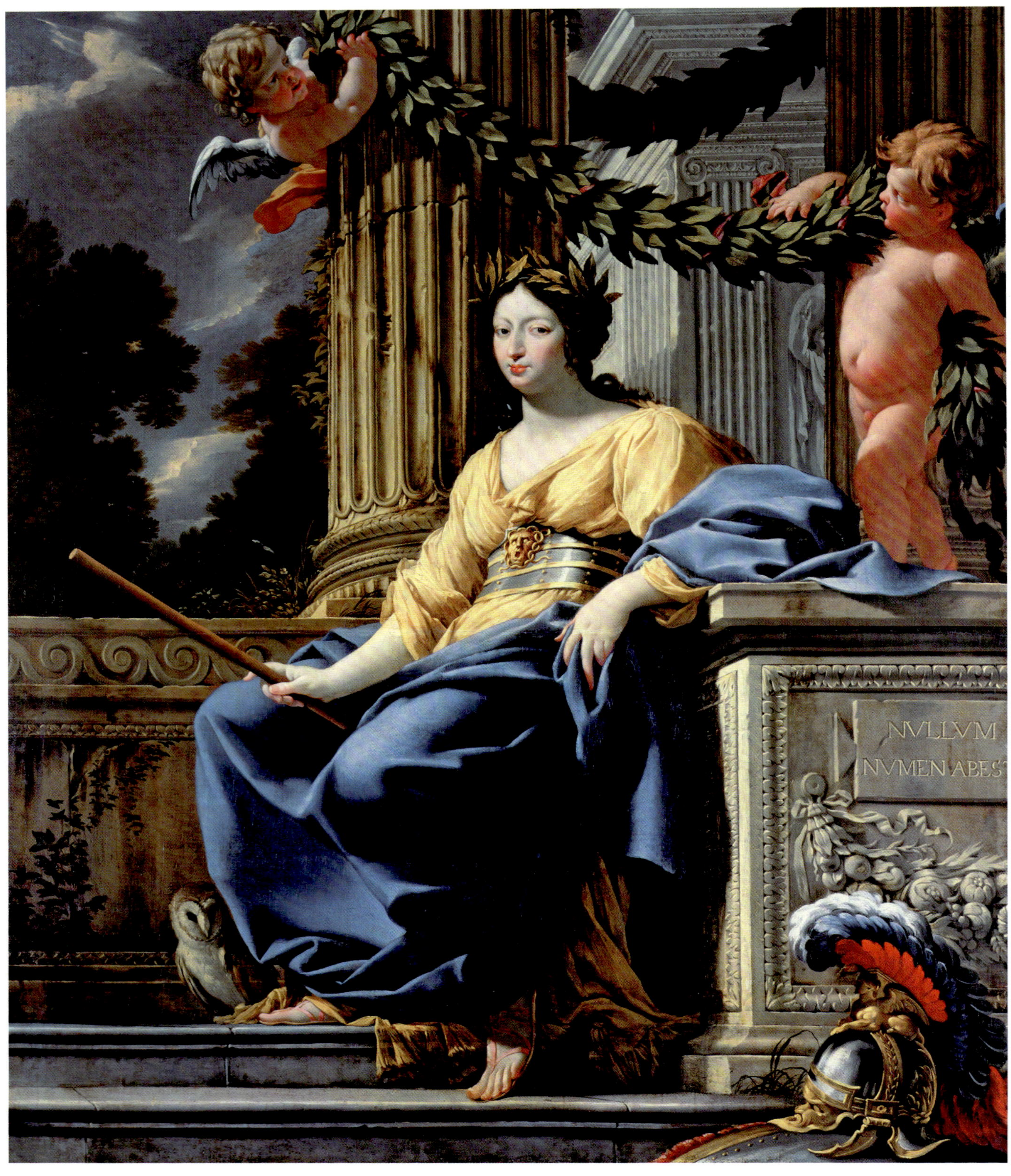

NVLLVM
NVMEN ABES

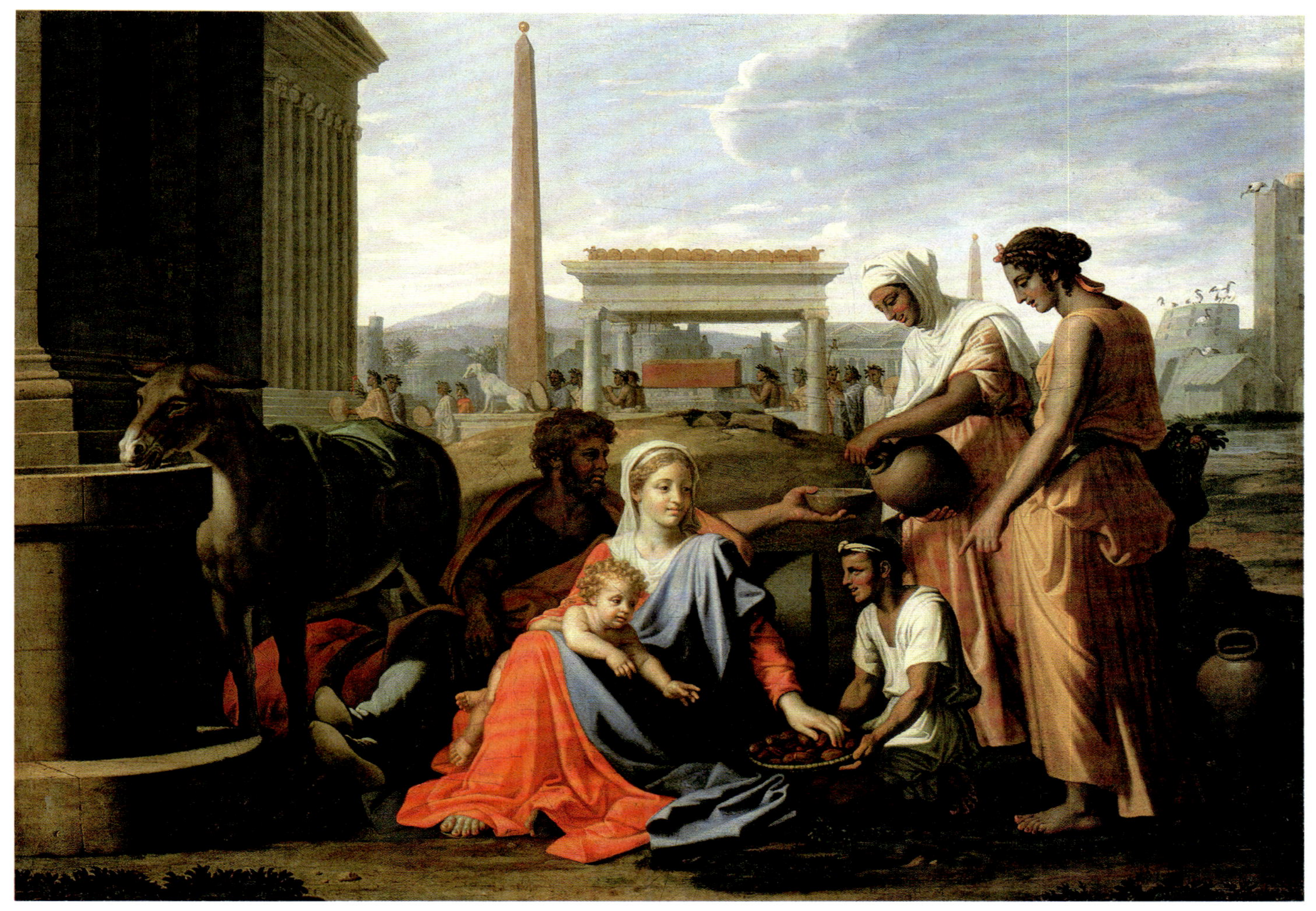

Nicolas Poussin (1594–1665)

Rest on the Flight into Egypt

Le Repos pendant la fuite en Égypte

Ruhe auf der Flucht nach Ägypten

Un descanso durante la huida a Egipto

Descanso na Fuga para o Egito

Rust tijdens de vlucht naar Egypte

1655–57, Oil on canvas/Huile sur toile, 105 × 145 cm

Simon Vouet (1590–1649)

Allegorical Portrait of Anne of Austria

Portrait allégorique d'Anne d'Autriche

Allegorisches Porträt der Anna von Österreich

Retrato alegórico de Ana de Austria

Retrato Alegórico de Ana da Áustria

Allegorisch portret van Anna van Oostenrijk

c. 1643, Oil on canvas/Huile sur toile, 202 × 172 cm

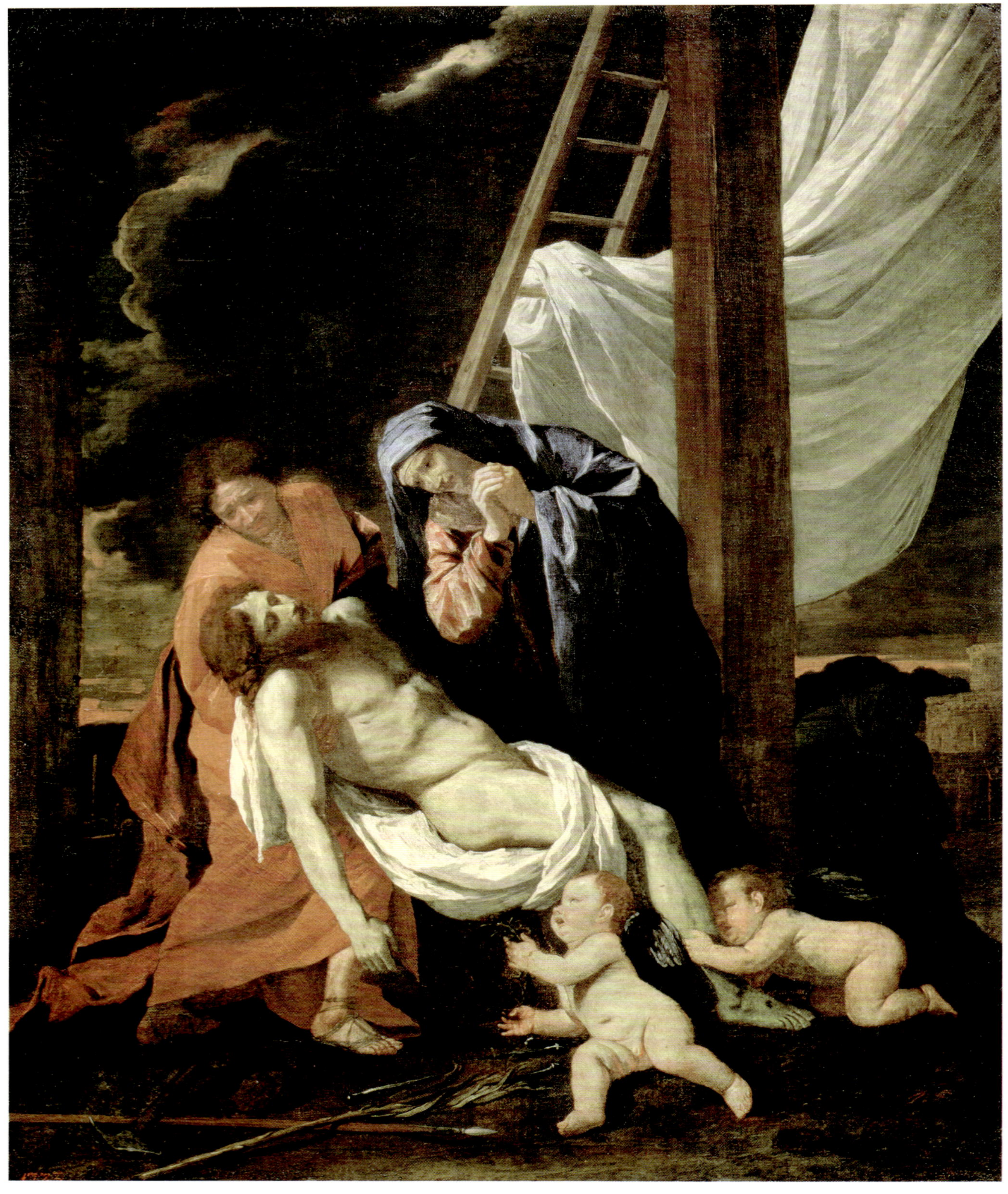

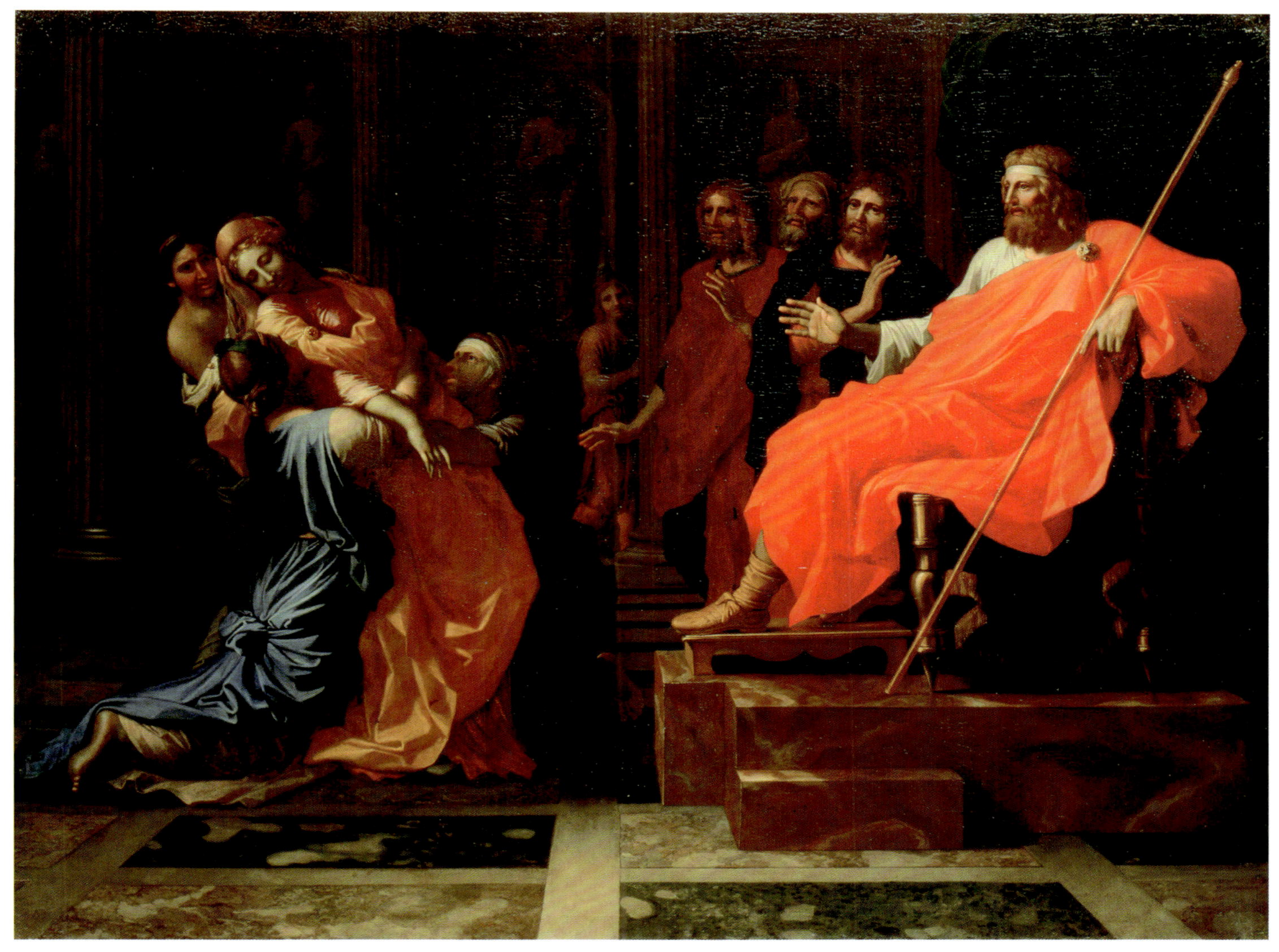

Nicolas Poussin (1594–1665)

The Deposition from the Cross

Descente de Croix

Die Kreuzabnahme

La deposición

A Deposição da Cruz

De Kruisafneming

c. 1630, Oil on canvas/Huile sur toile, 119,5 × 99 cm

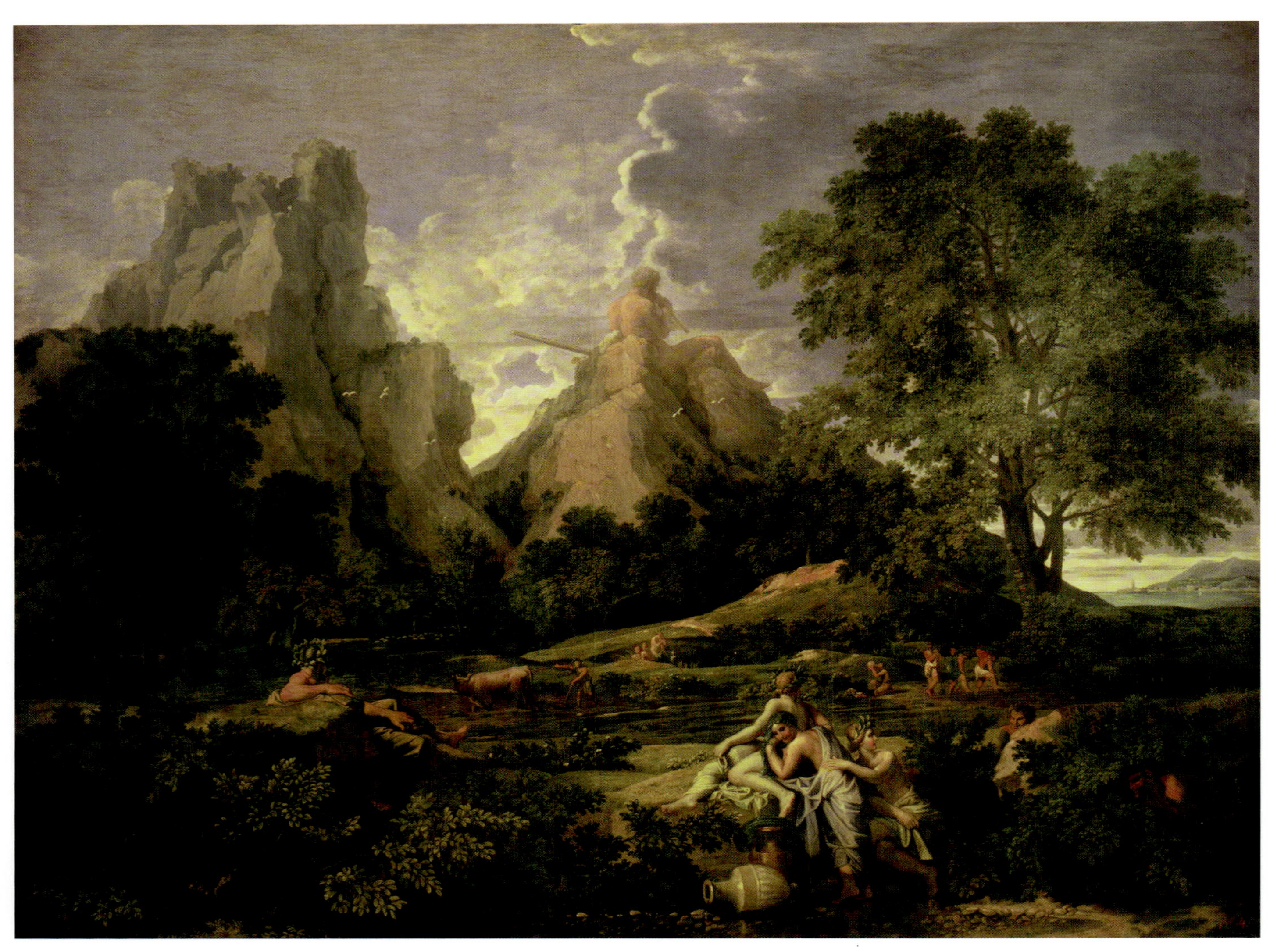

Nicolas Poussin (1594–1665)

Landscape with Polyphemus

Paysage avec Polyphème

Landschaft mit Polyphem

Paisaje con Polifemo

Paisagem com Polifemo

Landschap met Polyphemos

1649, Oil on canvas/Huile sur toile, 155 × 199 cm

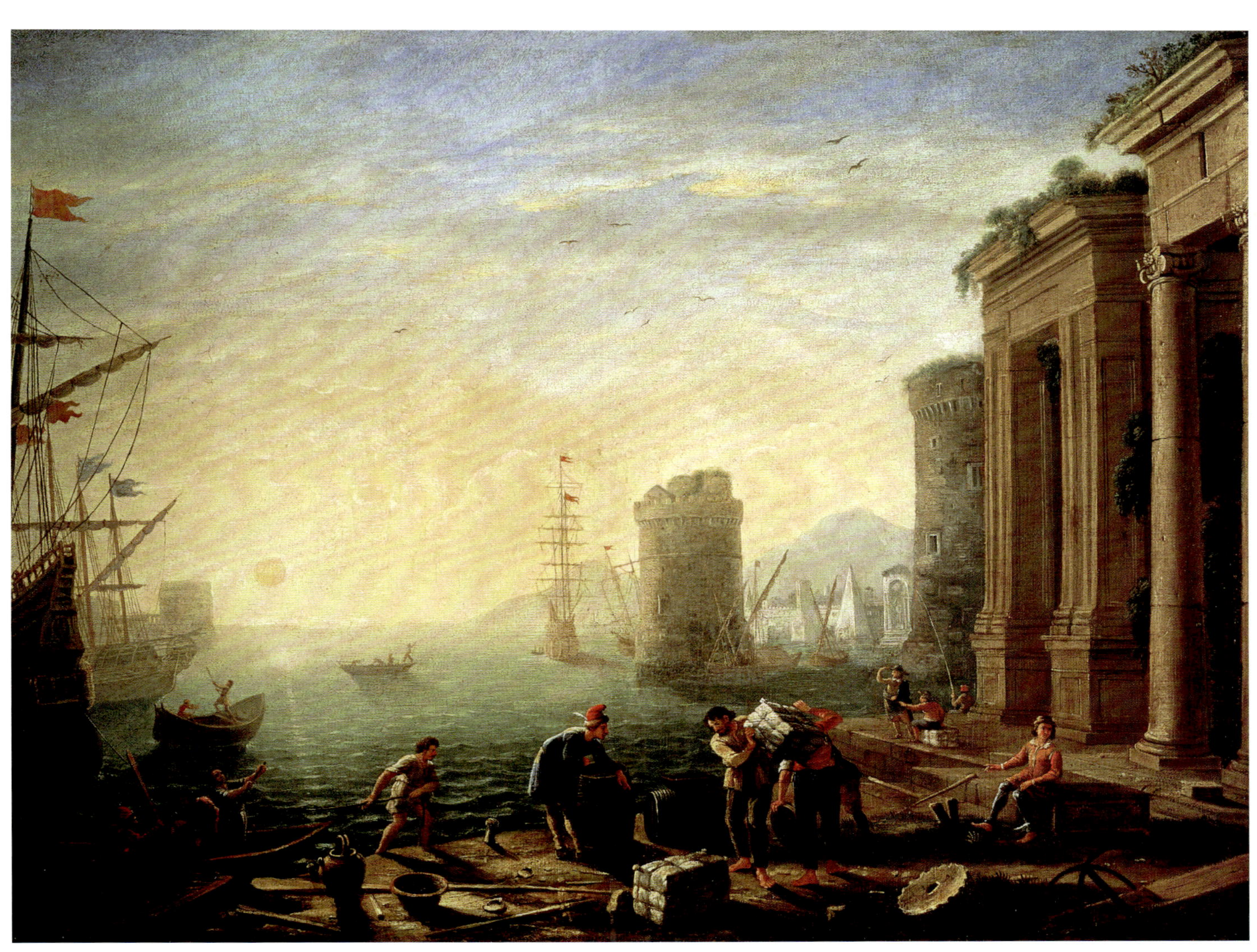

Claude Lorrain (Claude Gellée) (1600–82)

Morning at the Port

Le Matin dans un port

Morgen am Hafen

Mañana en el puerto

Manhã no Porto

Ochtend in de haven

c. 1630–40, Oil on canvas/Huile sur toile, 73 × 98 cm

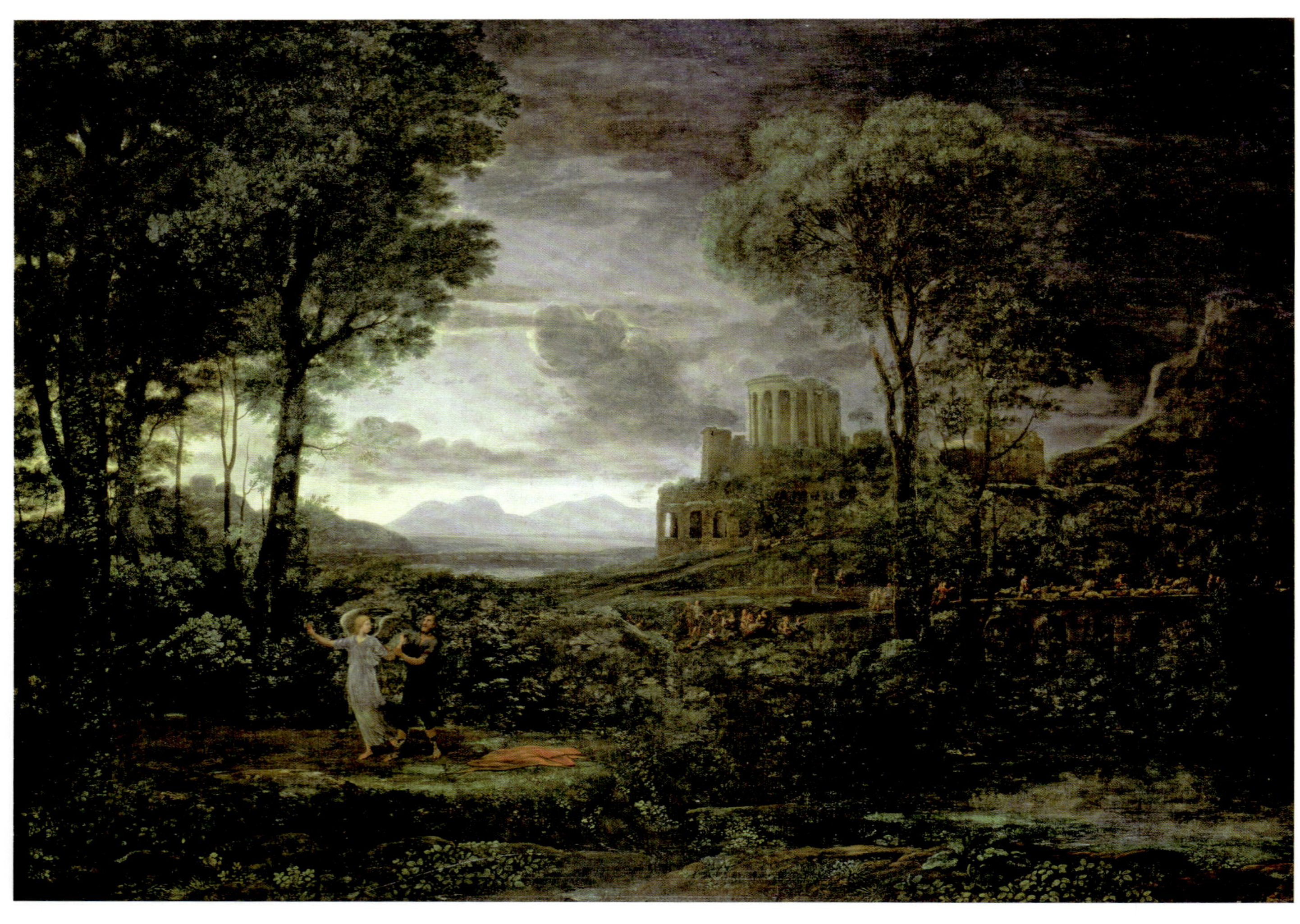

Claude Lorrain (Claude Gellée) (1600–82)

Landscape with Jacob Wrestling the Angel (Night)

Paysage avec Jacob luttant avec l'ange (Nuit)

Landschaft mit Jakobs Kampf mit dem Engel (Die Nacht)

Paisaje con la lucha de Jacob con el ángel (La noche)

Paisagem com a Luta de Jacó com o Anjo (A Noite)

Landschap met Jacobs gevecht met de engel (De Nacht)

1672, Oil on canvas/Huile sur toile, 113 × 157 cm

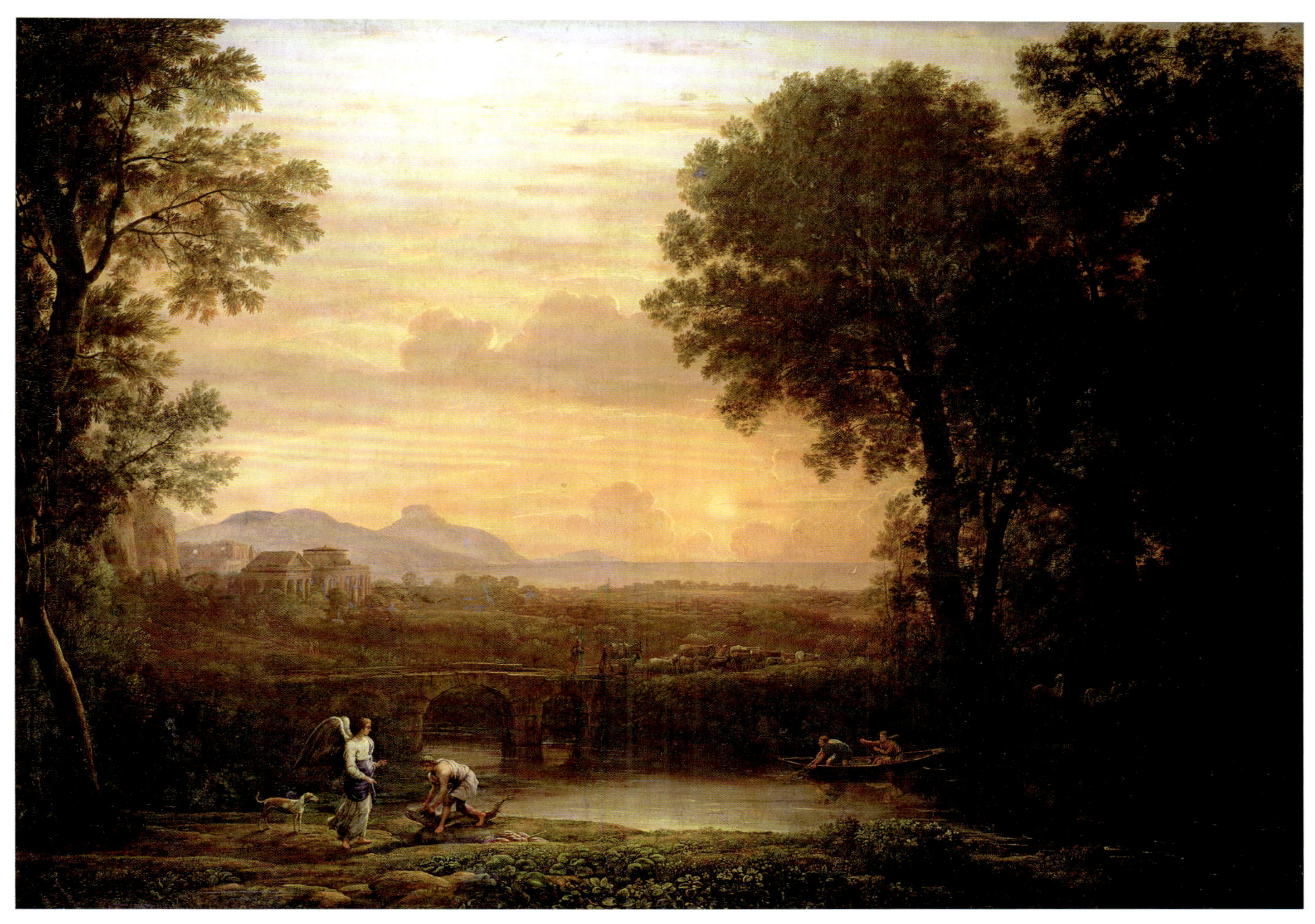

Claude Lorrain (Claude Gellée) (1600–82)

Landscape with Tobias and Angle

Paysage avec Jacob luttant avec l'ange (Soir)

Landschaft mit Tobias und dem Engel

Paisaje con Tobías y el angel

Paisagem com Tobias e o Anjo

Landschap met Tobias en de engel

1663, Oil on canvas/Huile sur toile, 116 × 153,5 cm

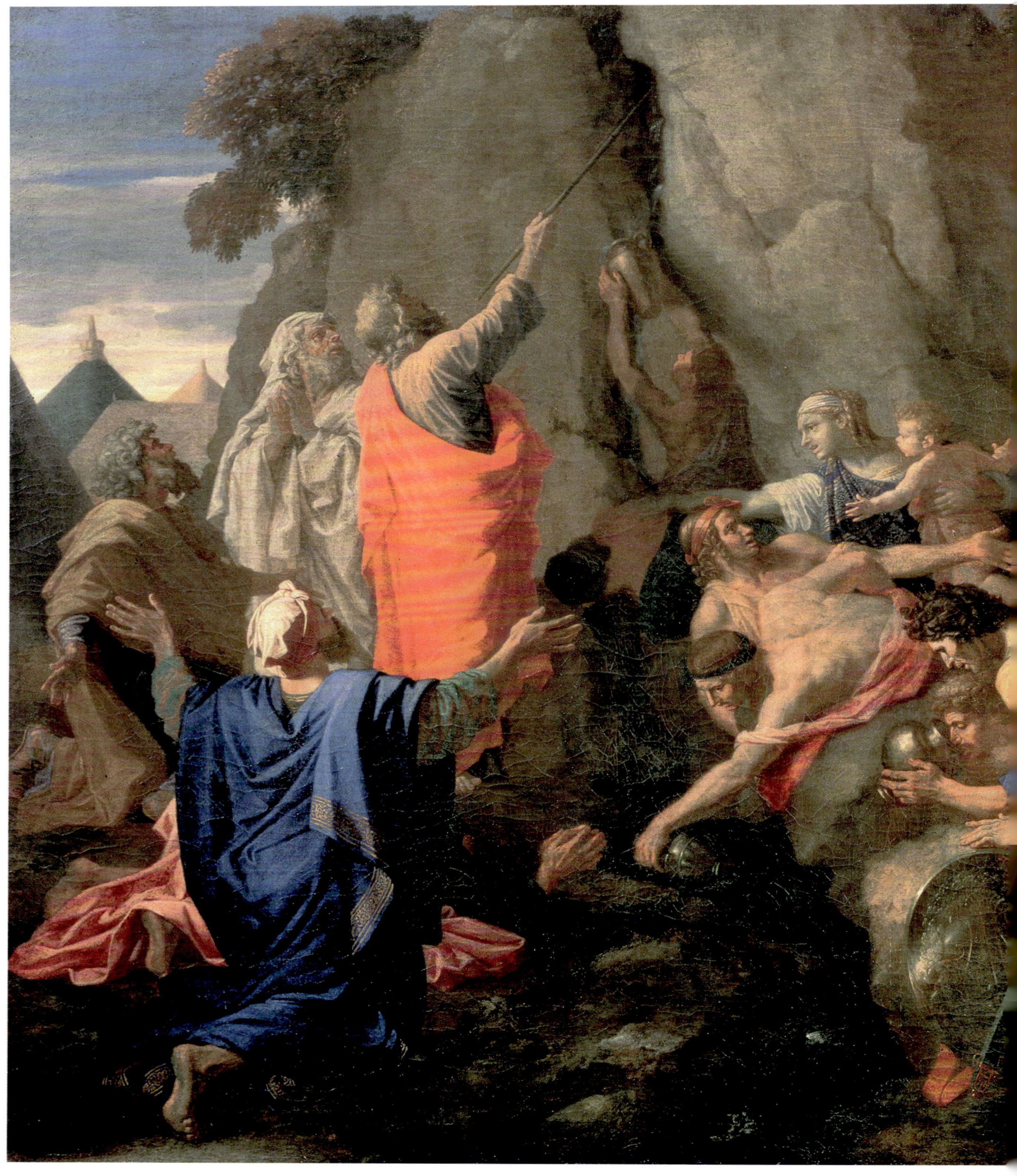

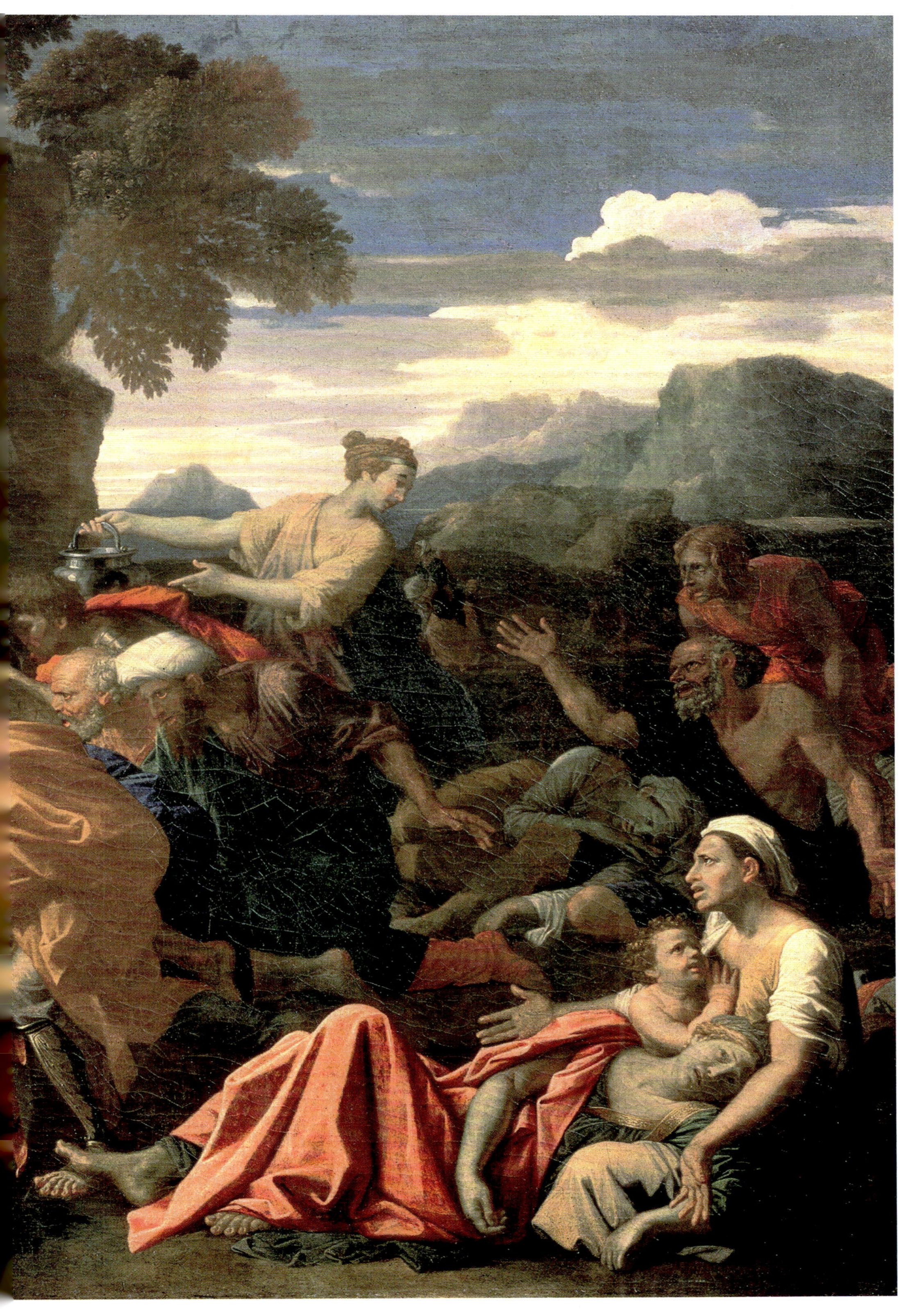

Nicolas Poussin (1594–1665)
Moses Striking Water from the Rock
Moïse frappant le rocher
Moses schlägt Wasser aus dem Felsen
Moisés extrae agua de la roca
Moisés Faz Brotar Água da Rocha
Mozes slaat water uit de rots
1649, Oil on canvas/Huile sur toile, 122,5 × 191 cm

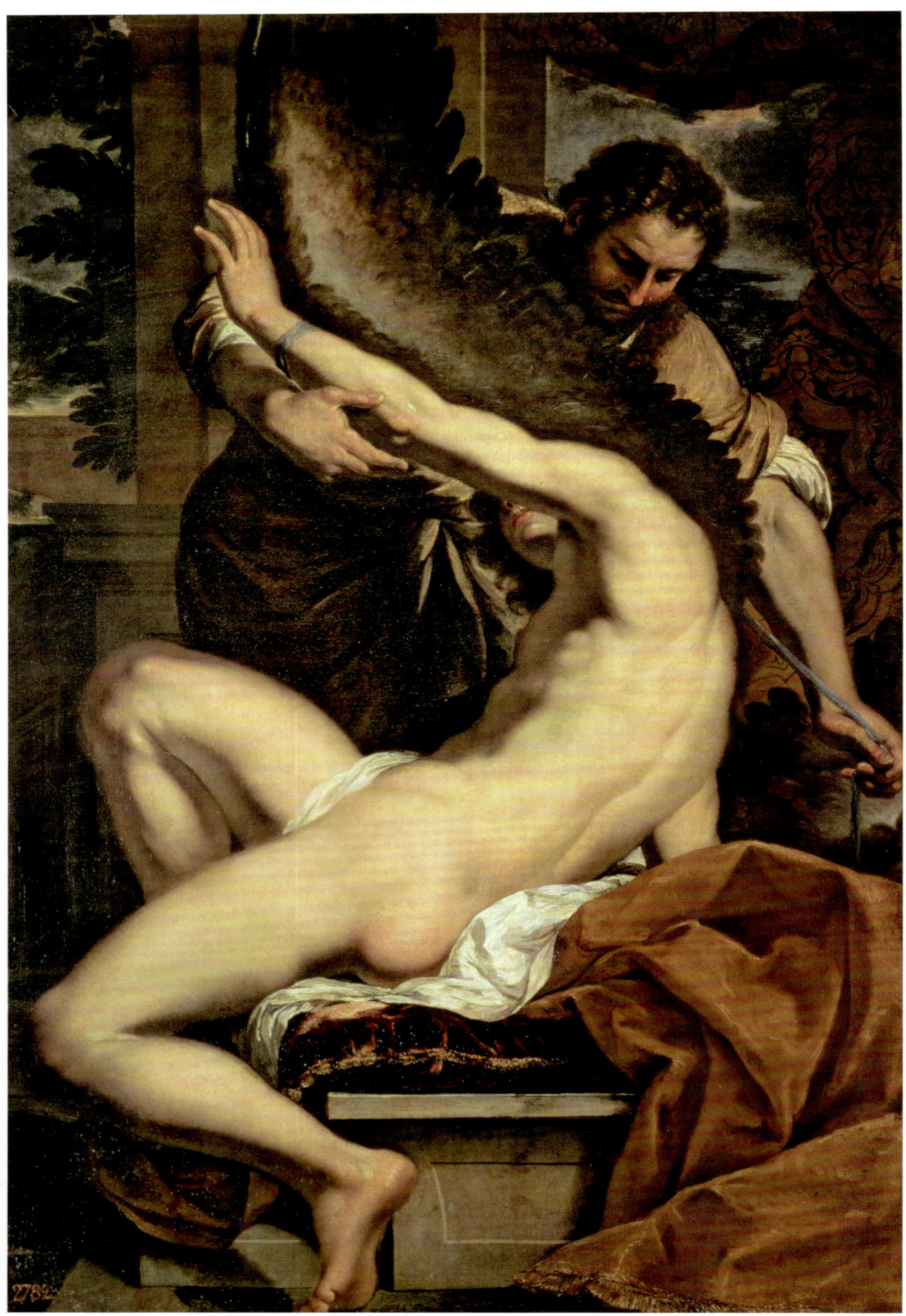

Charles Le Brun (1619−90)

Daedalus and Icarus

Dédale et Icare

Dädalus und Ikarus

Dédalo e Ícaro

Dédalo e Ícaro

Daedalos en Icaros

c.1645/46, Oil on canvas/Huile sur toile, 190 × 124 cm

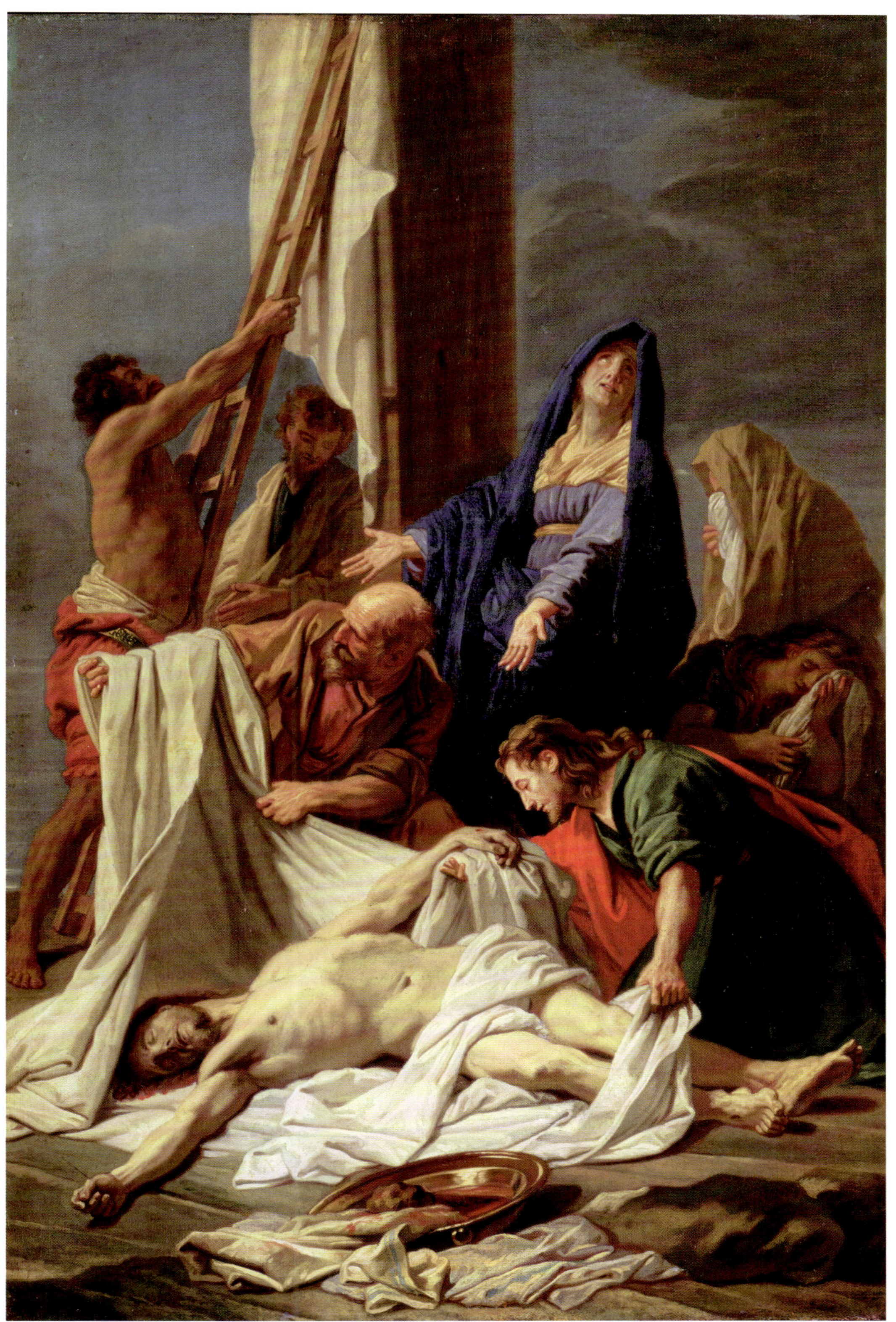

Jean-Baptiste Jouvenet (1644–1717)
The Deposition from the Cross
La Descente de croix
Die Kreuzabnahme
La deposición
A Deposição da Cruz
De Kruisafneming

1704–09, Oil on canvas/
Huile sur toile, 98 × 62 cm

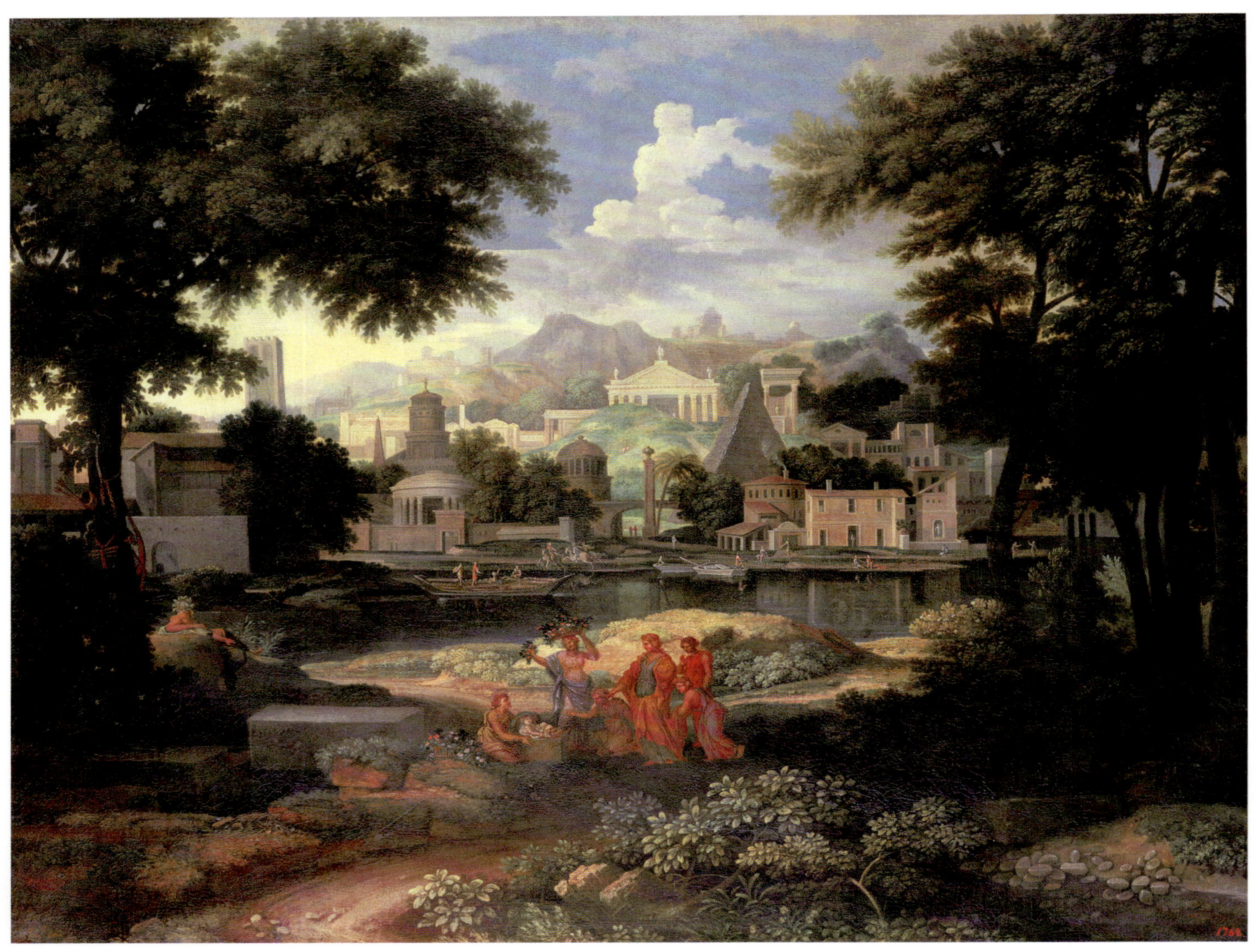

Étienne Allegrain (1644–1736)

Landscape with the Finding of Moses

Paysage avec Moïse sauvé des eaux

Landschaft mit der Auffindung des Mosesknaben

Paisaje con el descubrimiento del niño Moisés

Paisagem com Moisés Salvo das Águas

Landschap met de kleine Mozes die uit de Nijl wordt gered

Last quarter of the 17th–first third of the 18th century/Fin du XVIIᵉ–début de XVIIIᵉ siècle, Oil on canvas/Huile sur toile, 88 × 114,8 cm

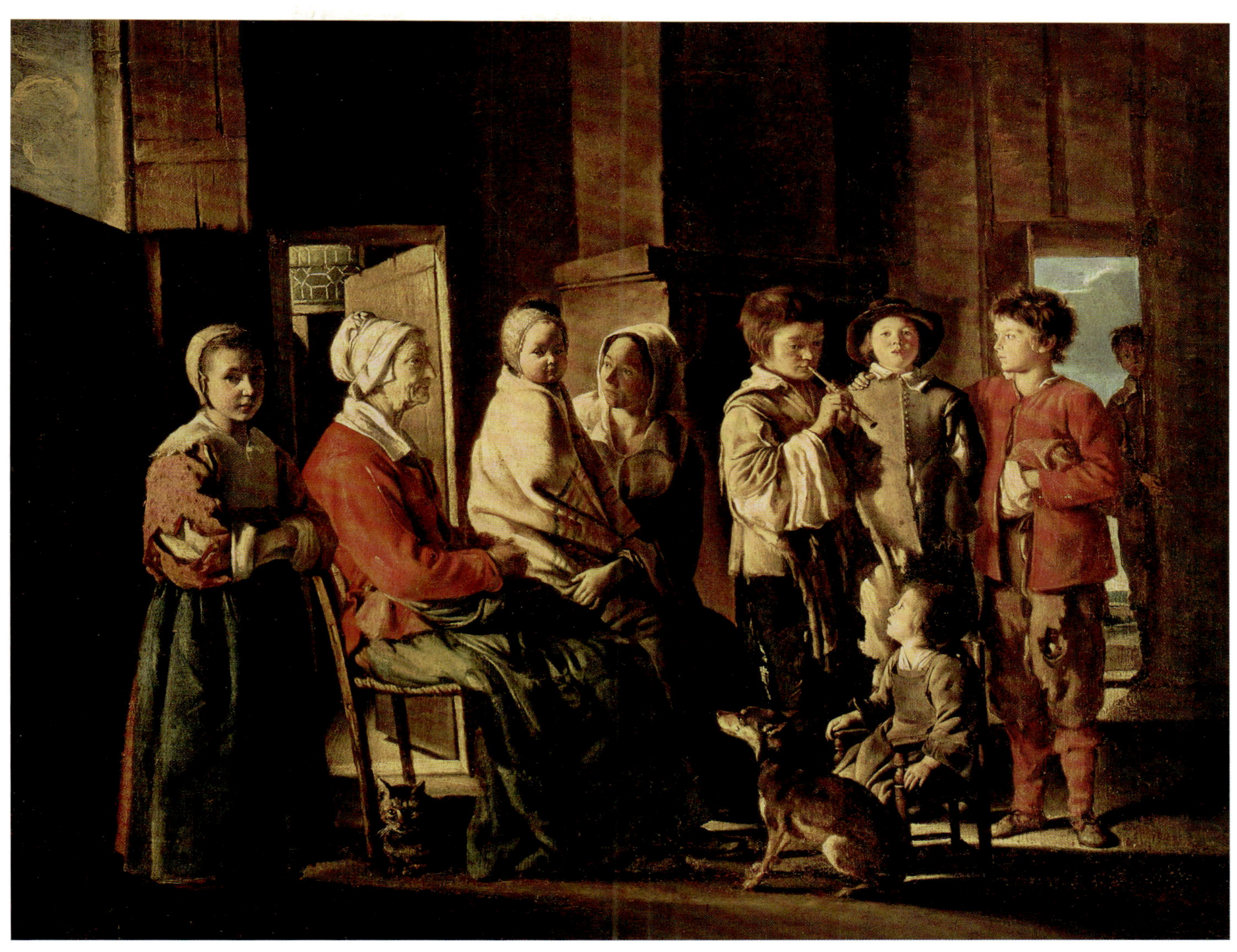

Louis Le Nain (1593–1648)

Visiting Grandmother

La Visite à la grand-mère

Der Besuch bei der Großmutter

La visita a la abuela

A Visita da Avó

Het bezoek aan de grootmoeder

c. 1645–48, Oil on canvas/Huile sur toile, 58 × 73 cm

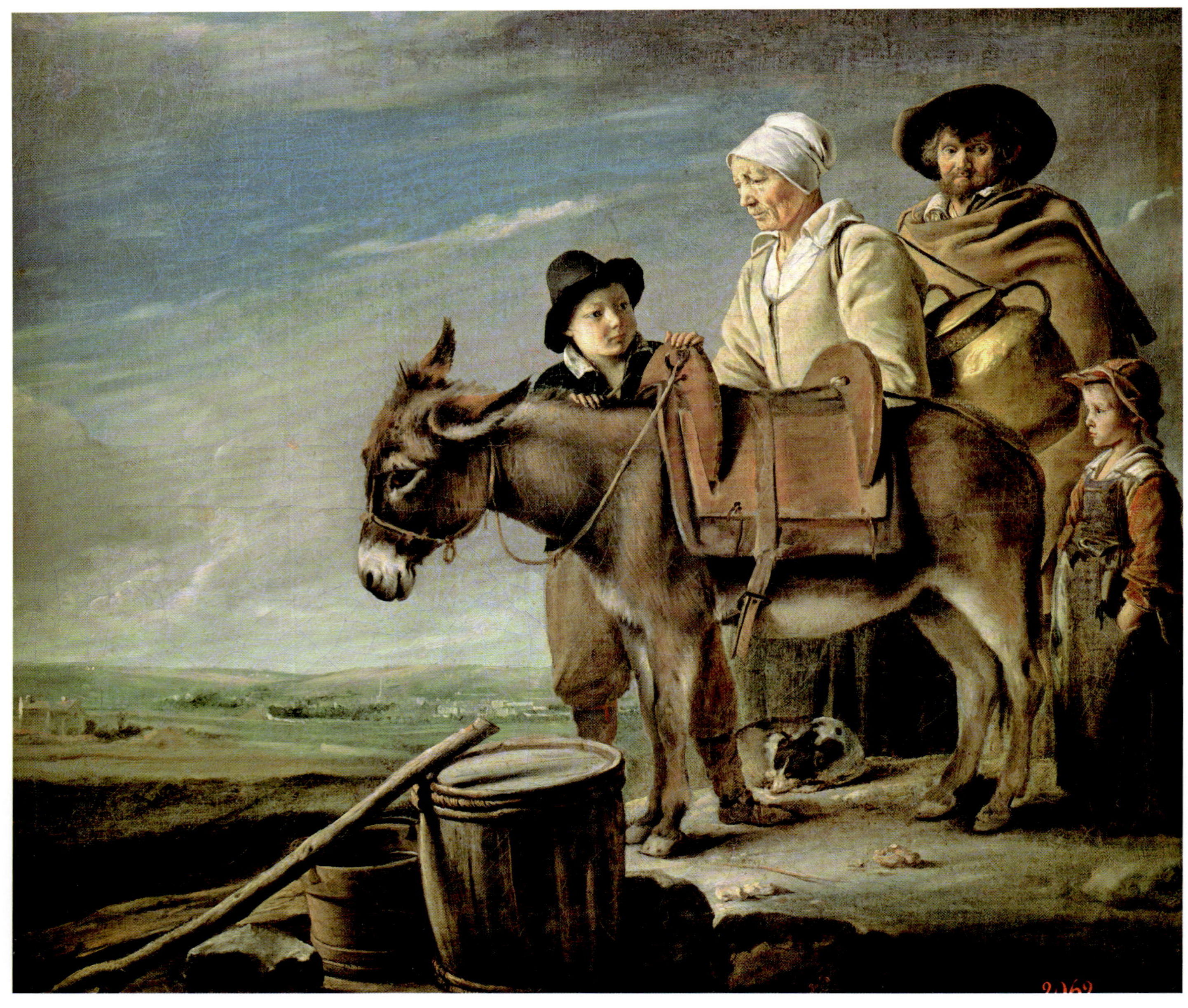

Louis Le Nain (1593–1648)

The Donkey

La Famille de la laitière

Der Esel

El asno

O Burro

De ezel

c. 1641, Oil on canvas/Huile sur toile, 51 × 59 cm

Hyacinthe Rigaud (1659–1743)

Portrait of a Scholar

Portrait d'homme dit « d'un savant »

Bildnis eines Gelehrten

Retrato de un estudioso

Retrato de um Sábio

Portert van een geleerde

17th Century/XVIIᵉ siècle, Oil on canvas/Huile sur toile, 80 × 65 cm

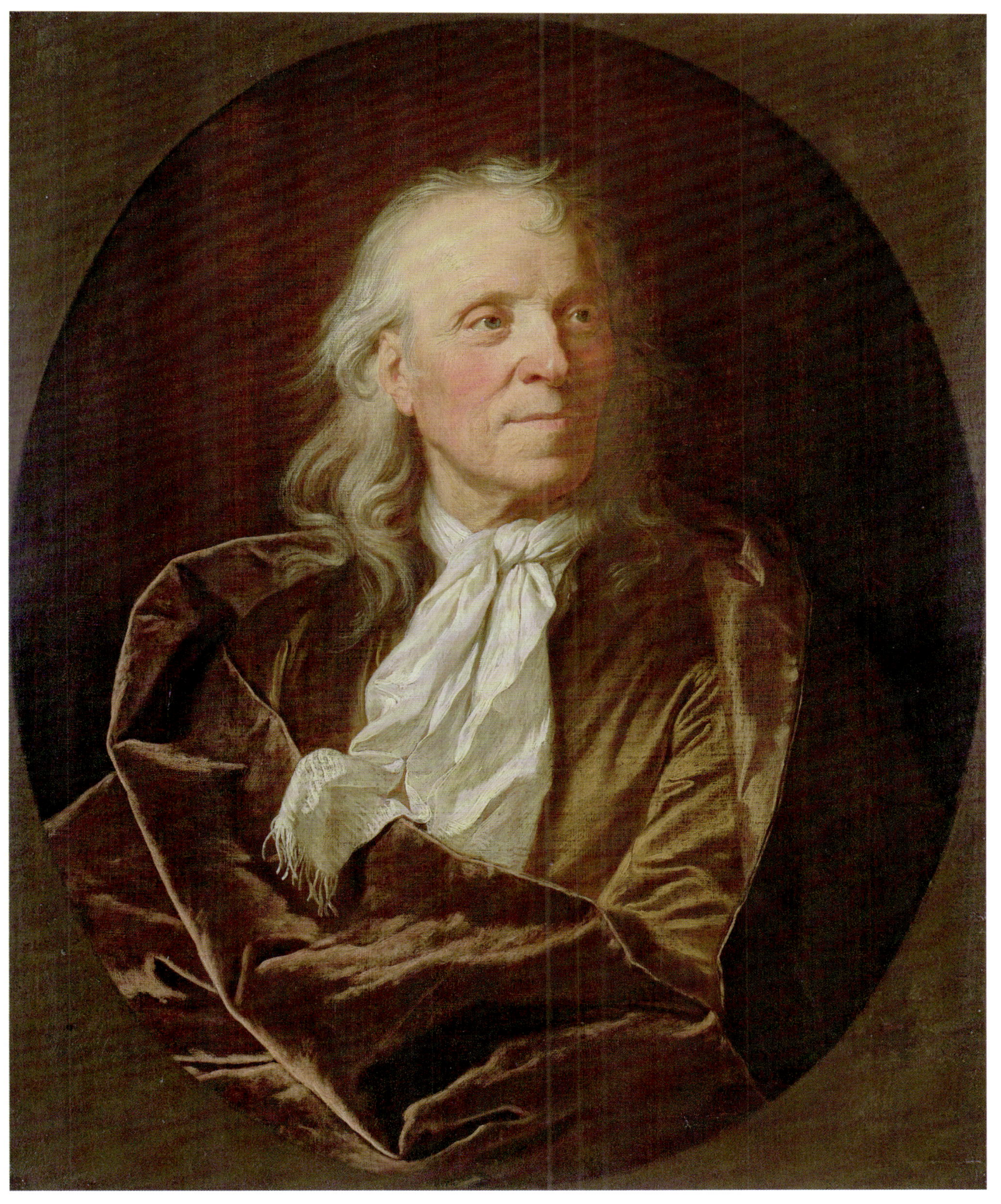

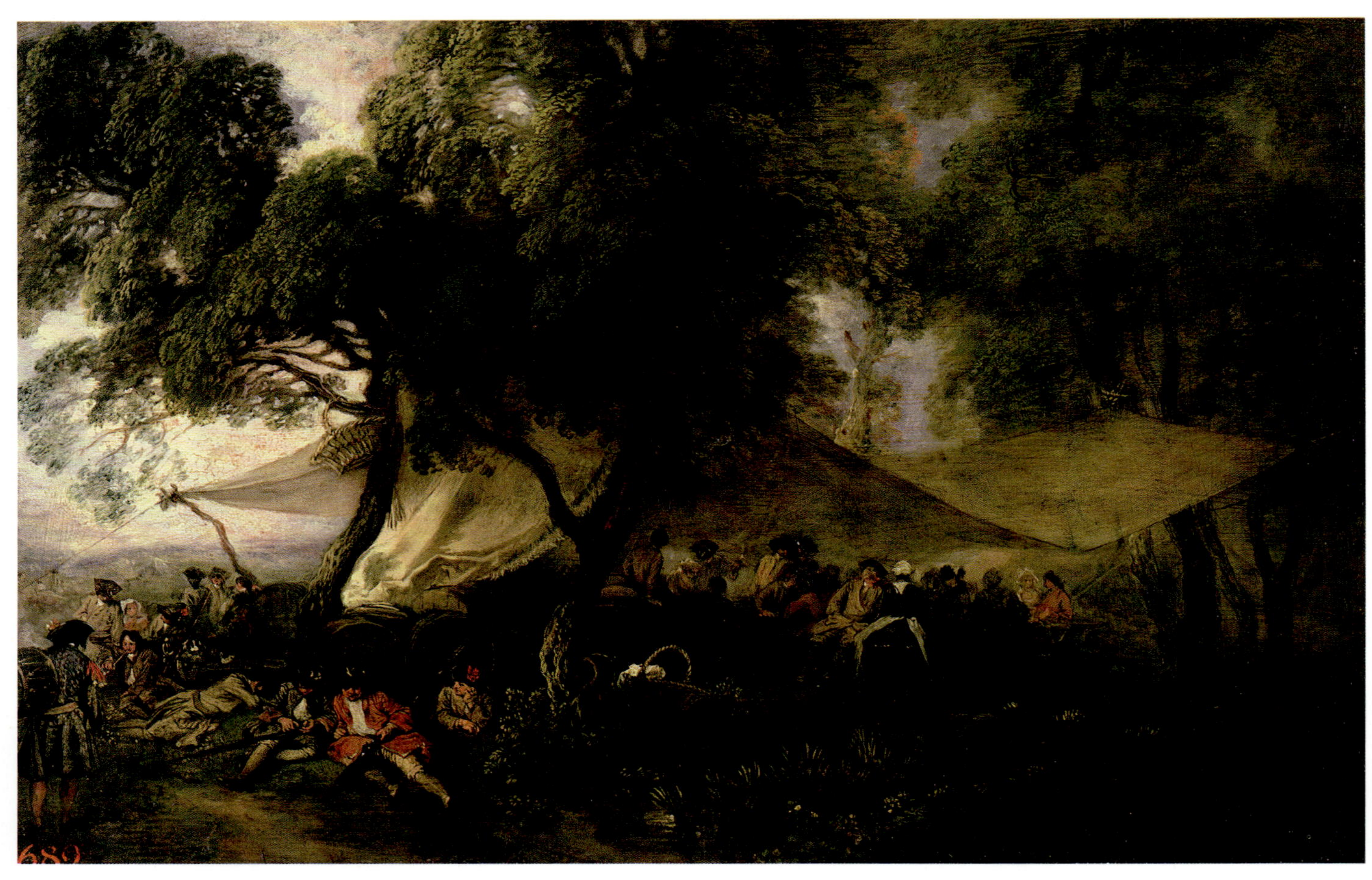

Jean-Antoine Watteau (1684–1721)

Respite from War

Les Délassements de la guerre

Ruhepause vom Krieg

Pausa antes de la guerra

Descanso da Guerra

Rustpauze in de oorlog

1715, Oil on copper/Huile sur cuivre, 21,5 × 33,5 cm

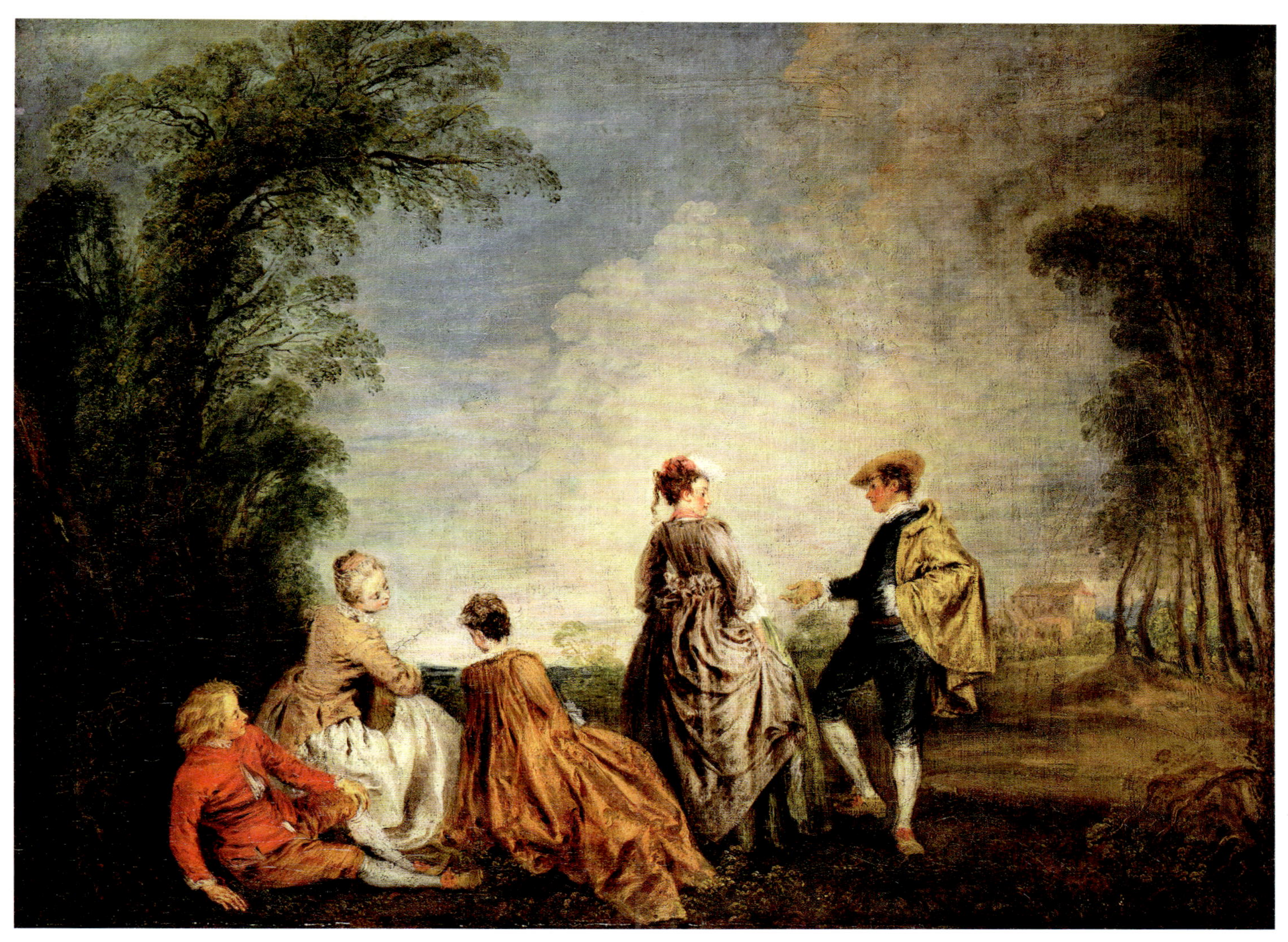

Jean-Antoine Watteau (1684–1721)

An Embarassing Proposal

La Proposition embarrassante

Der verwirrende Antrag

Una propuesta confusa

A Proposta Embaraçosa

Een pijnlijk aanzoek

1715/16, Oil on canvas/Huile sur toile, 65 × 84,5 cm

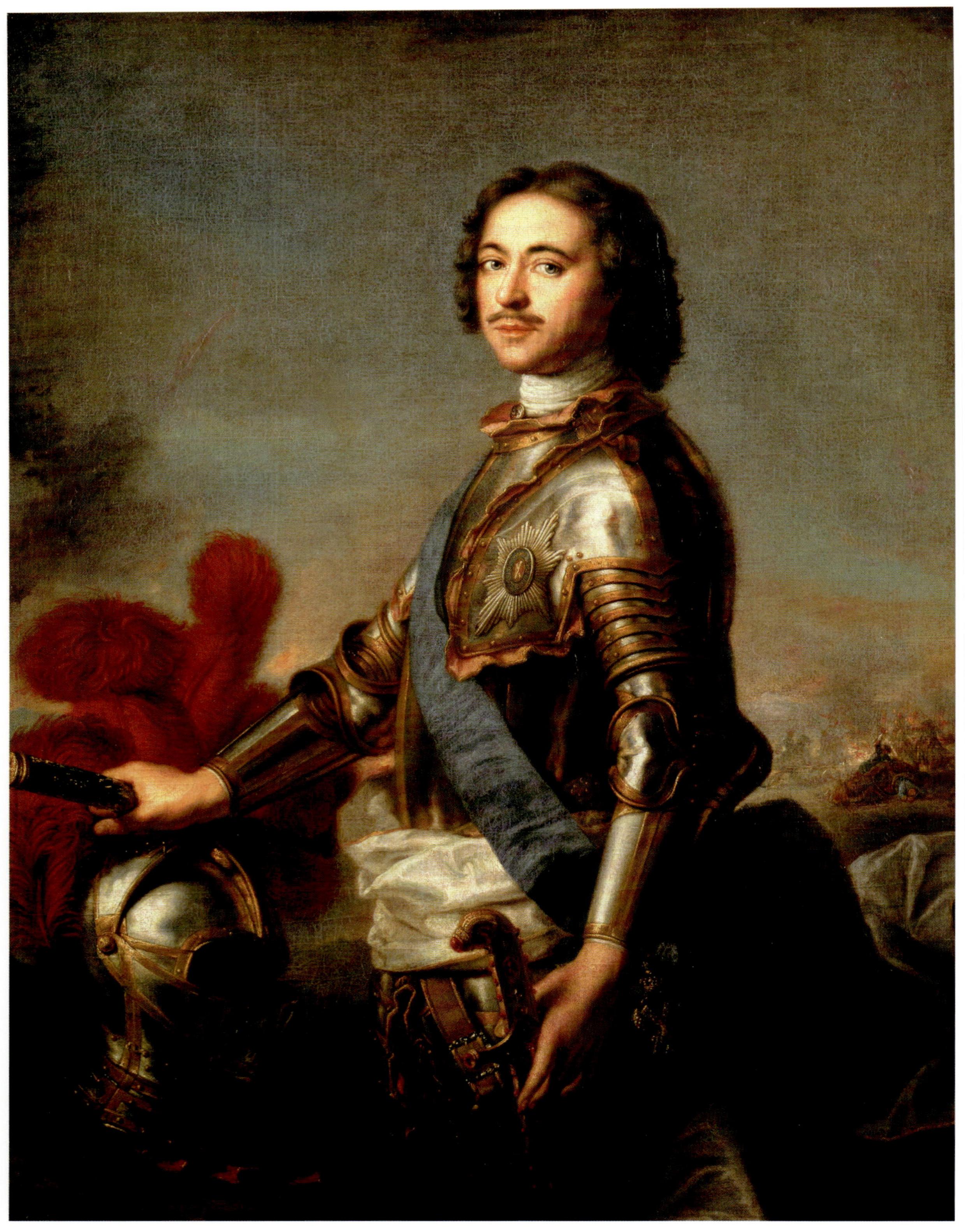

Jean-Marc Nattier
(1685–1766)

Peter I *or* Peter
the Great

Pierre le Grand

Peter I. *oder* Peter
der Große

Pedro I *o* Pedro
el Grande

Pedro I *ou* Pedro
o Grande

Peter I *of* Peter
de Grote

1717, Oil on canvas/
Huile sur toile,
142,5 × 110 cm

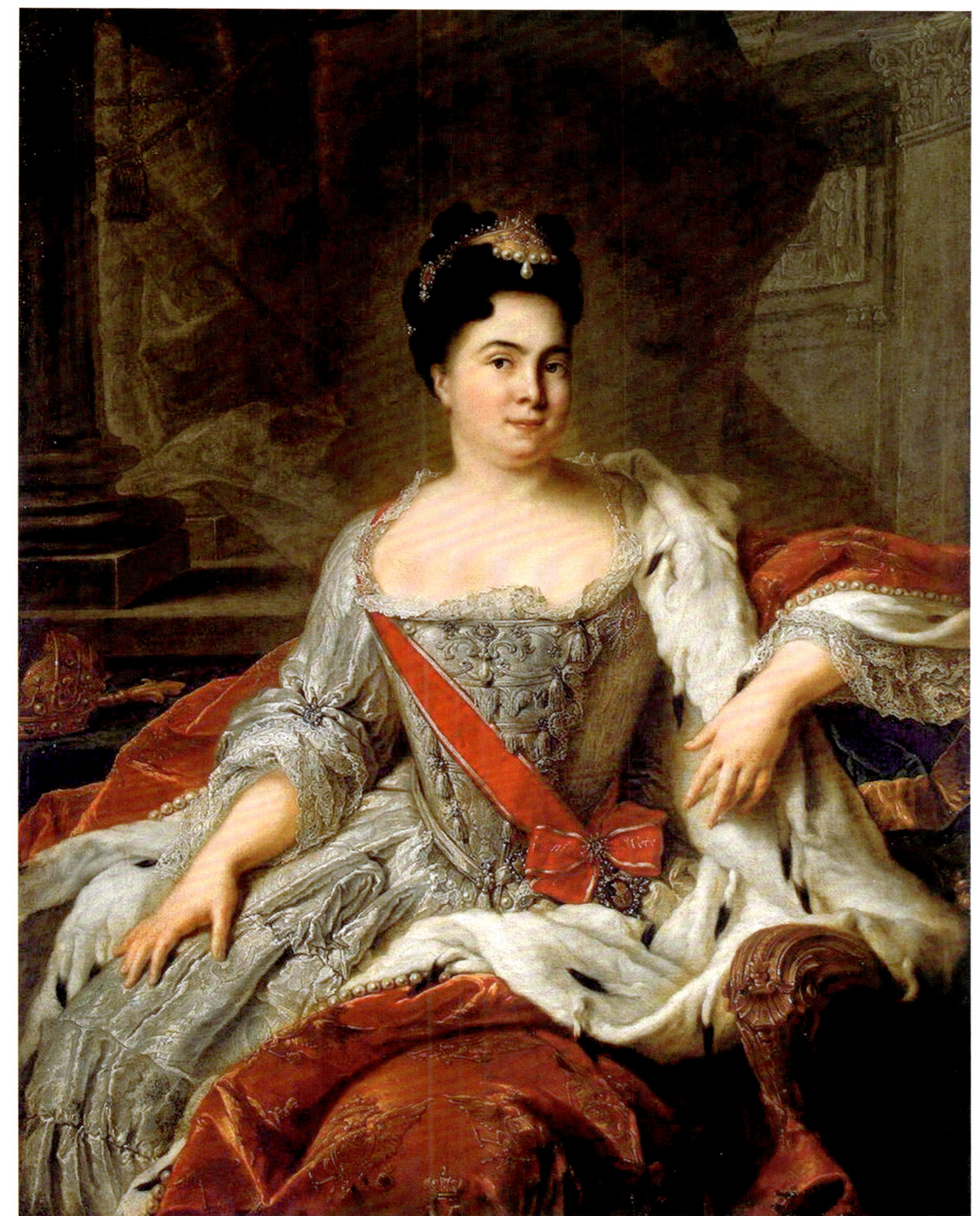

Jean-Marc Nattier
(1685–1766)

Catherine I

Catherine Ire
de Russie

Katharina I.

Catalina I

Catarina I

Catharina I

1717, Oil on canvas/
Huile sur toile,
142,5 × 110 cm

This piece is one of Chardin's first genre paintings which he would show in the Paris Salon (the official art exhibition of the *Académie des Beaux-Arts* held in the Louvre).

Chardin focuses here on portraying everyday life. The woman at the wash tub looks tired and exhausted by the long hours standing with her arms immersed in soapy water up to her elbows. The boy, meanwhile, is chasing bubbles. His humble origin is revealed in the ragged robe. A door opens to show a second woman hanging laundry in an adjoining room. The subtle browns show Chardin's mastery of color.

Esta imagen es una de las primeras pinturas costumbristas de Chardin, que mostró en el Salon (la exposición oficial de la *Acádemie des Beaux-Arts* en el Louvre parisino).

Chardin se dedica en esta imagen al mundo cotidiano. La mujer en el lavadero parece agotada tras horas de exposición al aire cargado de agua enjabonada. El niño se entretiene, despreocupado, con las pompas de jabón. Su procedencia humilde queda explicitada por sus ropas andrajosas. Una puerta abierta nos muestra una segunda mujer, que cuelga la colada en otra habitación. El sutil uso de tonos marrones nos descubren a Chardin como un maestro del color.

Ce tableau appartient aux premières scènes de genre du peintre, qu'il présenta au Salon – exposition annuelle officielle de l'Académie des Beaux-Arts.

Chardin s'attache ici à montrer le quotidien. La jeune femme penchée sur le baquet, dans la vapeur de la lessive, paraît assez lasse. Assis devant elle, un garçonnet insouciant joue à faire des bulles de savon. Les haillons dont il est vêtu traduisent la pauvreté de sa condition. Par la porte ouverte, on aperçoit une seconde femme en train de suspendre du linge, dans la pièce adjacente. Les camaïeux subtils de tons bruns attestent un maître du coloris.

Esta pintura pertence às primeiras obras de género de Chardin, que o mesmo exibiu no Salão (a exposição de arte oficial realizada no Louvre parisiense pela Academia de Belas Artes).

Nesta obra, Chardin dedica-se também ao mundo do quotidiano. A mulher numa pia parece cansada e fatigada por estar horas a fio em pé na bruma da barrela de sabão. Contrariamente, o pequeno ocupa-se despreocupadamente com bolas de sabão. A sua origem pobre caracteriza-se através das roupas esfarrapadas. Uma porta abre-se para uma segunda mulher, que pendura a roupa numa sala adjacente. Os subtis tons de castanho demonstram que Chardin era também um mestre da cor.

Dieses Bild gehört zu den ersten Genrebildern Chardins, die er im Salon (der im Pariser Louvre stattfindenden offiziellen Kunstausstellung der *Acádemie des Beaux-Arts*) zeigte.

Chardin widmet sich auch in diesem Bild der Welt des Alltags. Die Frau am Waschtrog wirkt durch das stundenlange Stehen im Dunst der Seifenlauge müde und erschöpft. Der Junge beschäftigt sich dagegen unbekümmert mit Seifenblasen. Seine ärmliche Herkunft ist durch das zerlumpte Gewand gekennzeichnet. Eine Tür öffnet sich auf eine zweite Frau, die Wäsche in einem Nebenraum aufhängt. Die subtilen Brauntöne weisen Chardin auch als einen Meister der Farbe aus.

De wasvrouw behoort tot de eerste genrestukken van Chardin, die hij toonde in de Salon (de officiële kunsttentoonstelling van de *Académie des Beaux-Arts* in het Parijse Louvre).

Chardin put ook voor dit schilderij uit de wereld van alledag. De vrouw aan de wastobbe raakt moe en uitgeput door het urenlange werk in de zeepwaterdampen. Het jongetje zit daarentegen onbezorgd bellen te blazen. Aan zijn armzalige lompen is zijn afkomst af te lezen. Door de geopende deur is een tweede vrouw te zien die in een nevenruimte was ophangt. De subtiele bruintinten illustreren Chardins meesterlijk kleurgebruik.

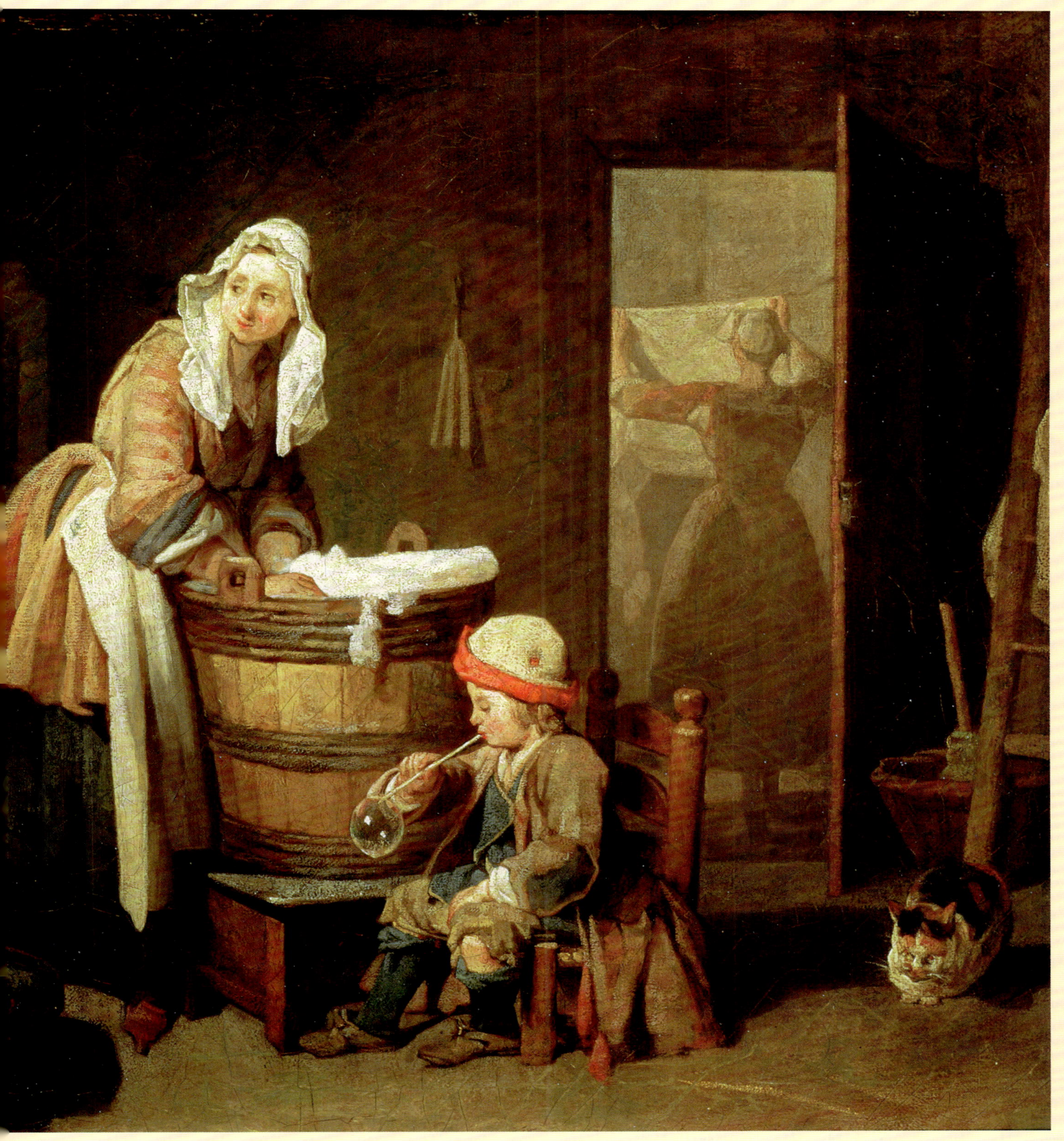

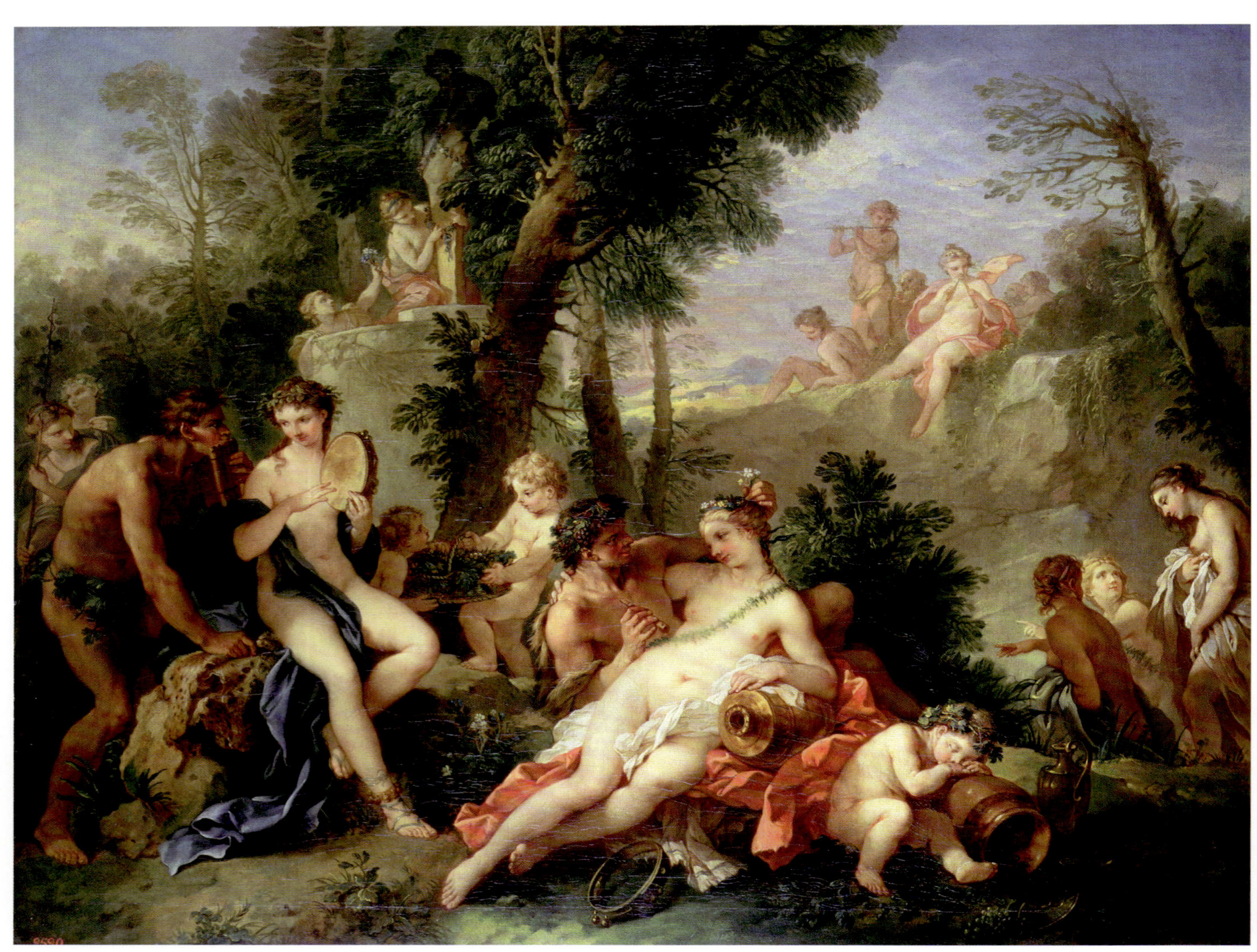

Charles-Joseph Natoir (1700–77)

Bacchus and Ariadne

Bacchus et Ariane

Bacchus und Ariadne

Bacco y Ariadna

Baco e Ariadne

Bacchus en Ariadne

c. 1742, Oil on canvas/Huile sur toile, 91 × 120 cm

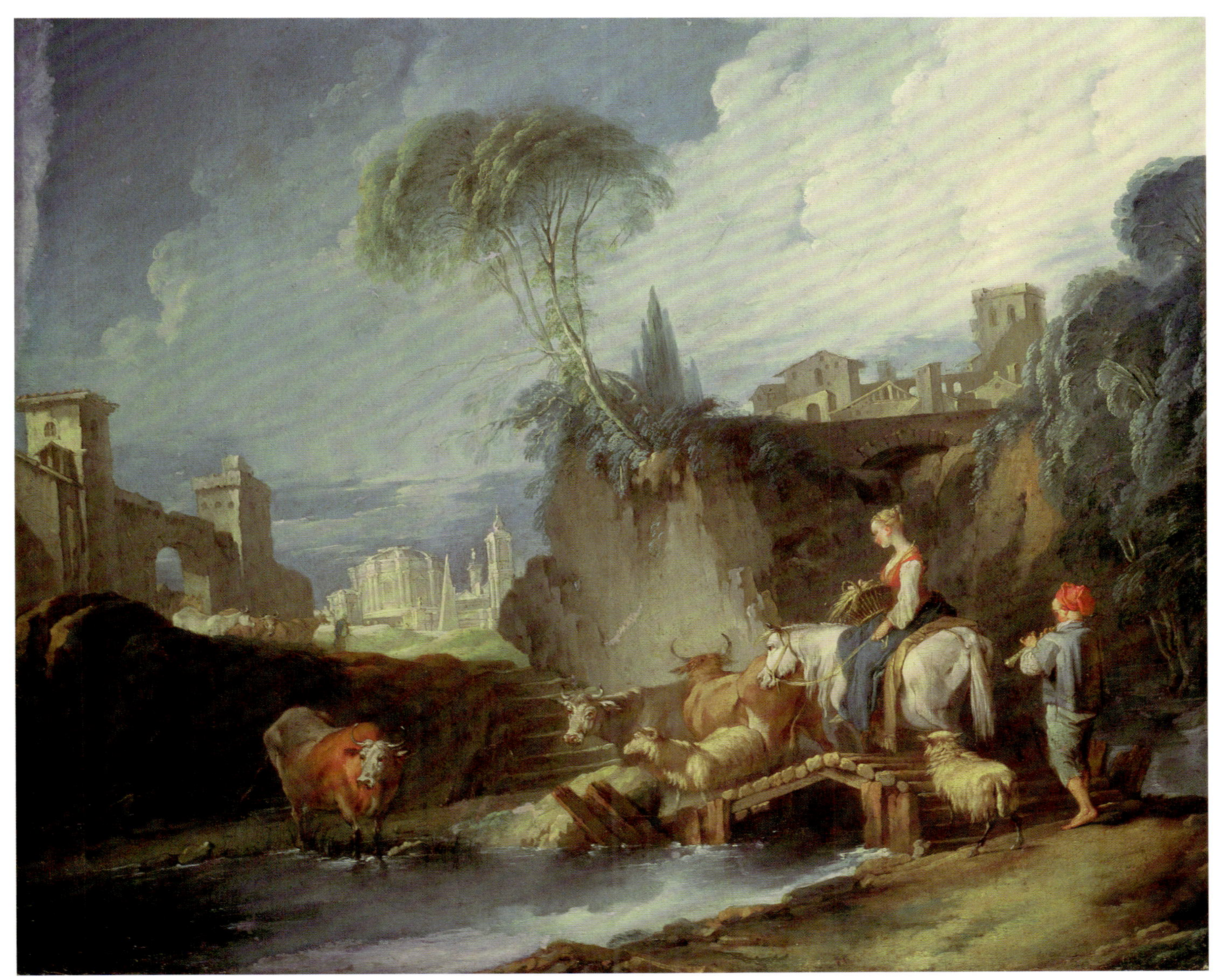

François Boucher (1703–70)

Crossing the Bridge

Le Pont

Die Überquerung der Brücke

Cruzando el puente

A Travessia da Ponte

De oversteek over de brug

1730, Oil on canvas/Huile sur toile, 59 × 72 cm

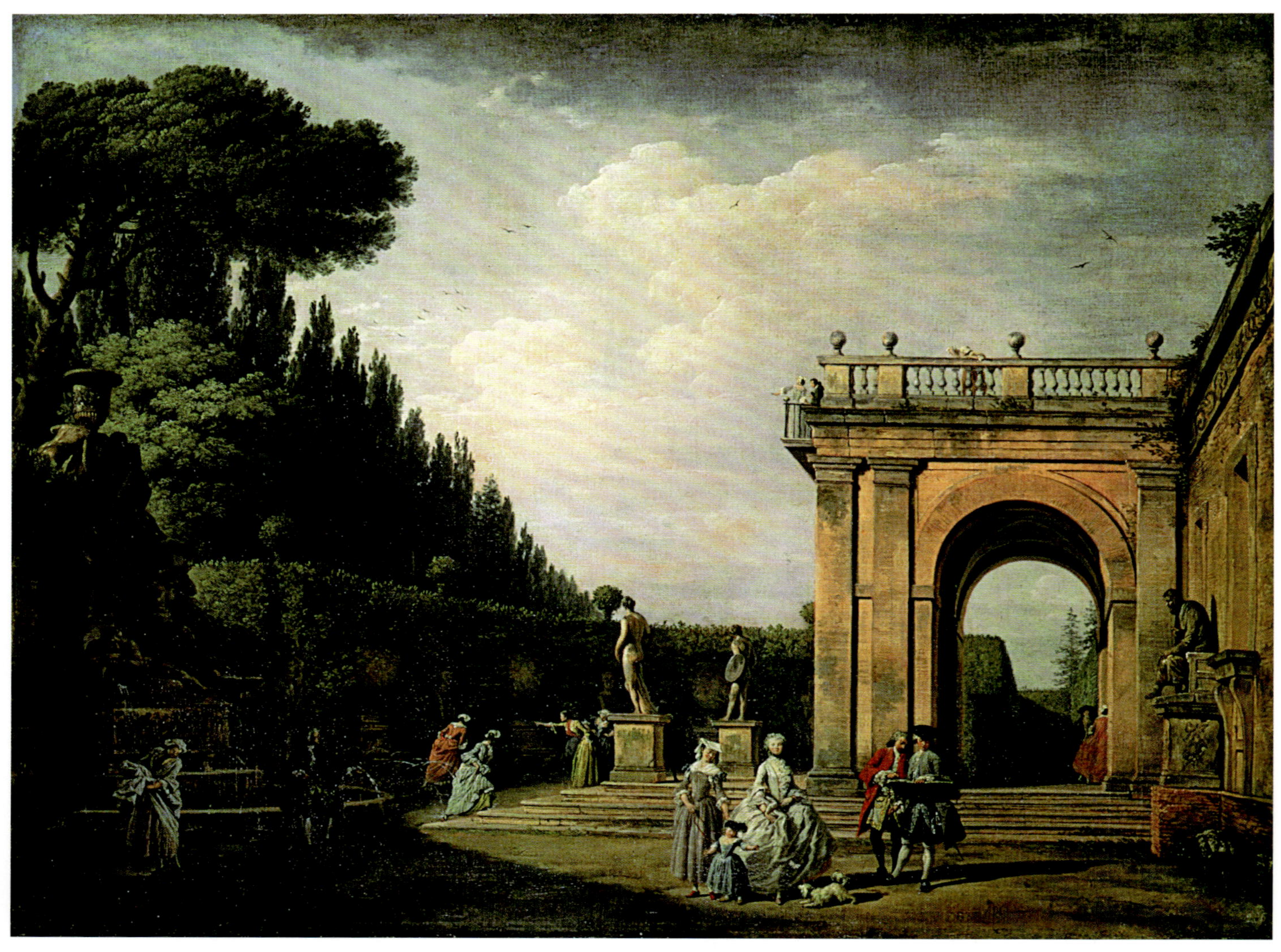

Claude Joseph Vernet (1714–89)

The Gardens of the Villa Ludovisi in Rome

Jardins de la villa Ludovisi

Die Gärten der Villa Ludovisi in Rom

Los jardines de la Villa Ludovisi en Roma

Os Jardins da Vila Ludovisi em Roma

De tuinen van Villa Ludovisi in Rome

1749, Oil on canvas/Huile sur toile, 74,5 × 99,5 cm

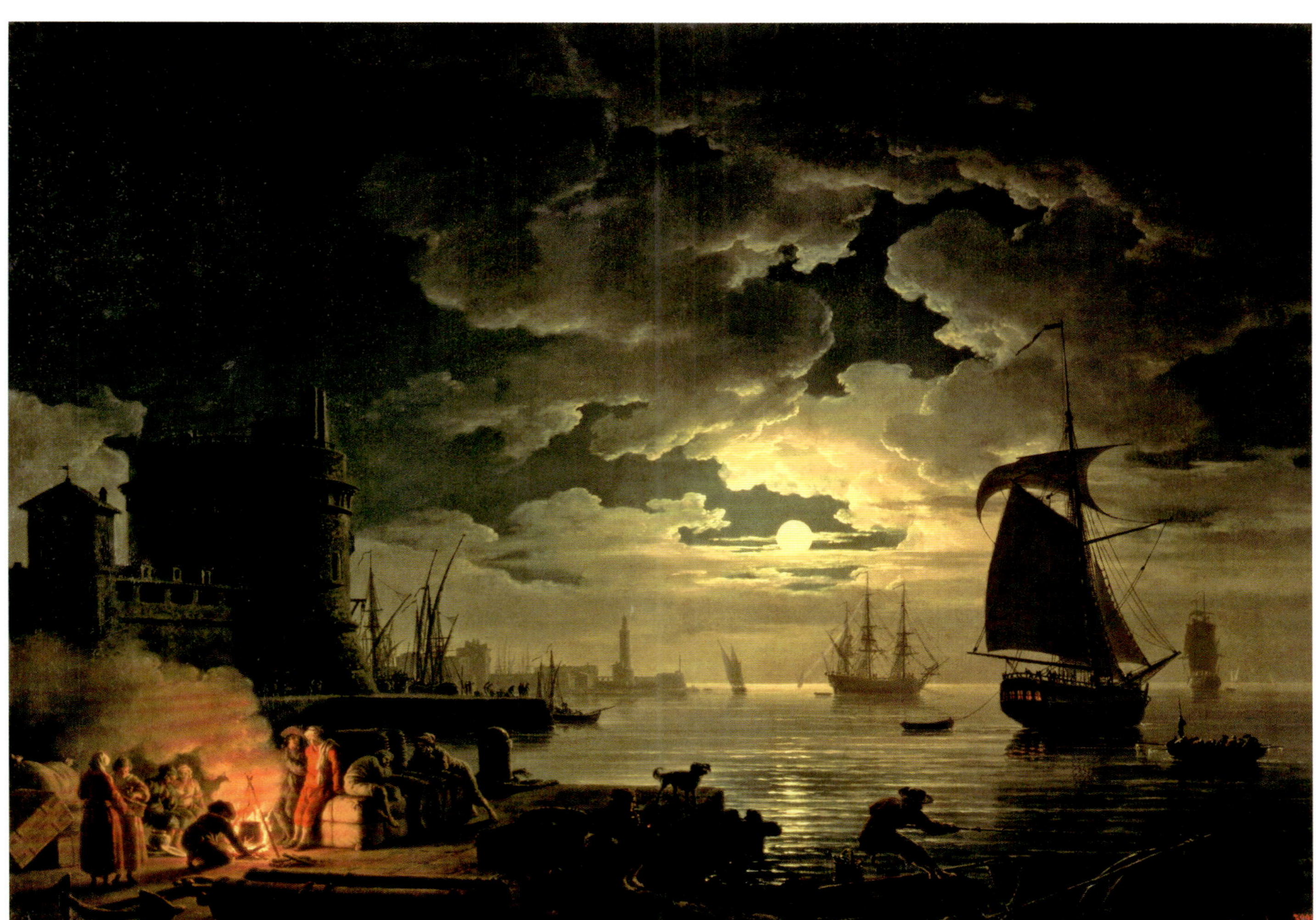

Claude Joseph Vernet (1714–89)

The Port of Palermo

L'Entrée du port de Palerme au clair de lune

Der Hafen von Palermo

El puerto de Palermo

O Porto de Palermo

De haven van Palermo

1769, Oil on canvas/Huile sur toile, 99,5 × 138 cm

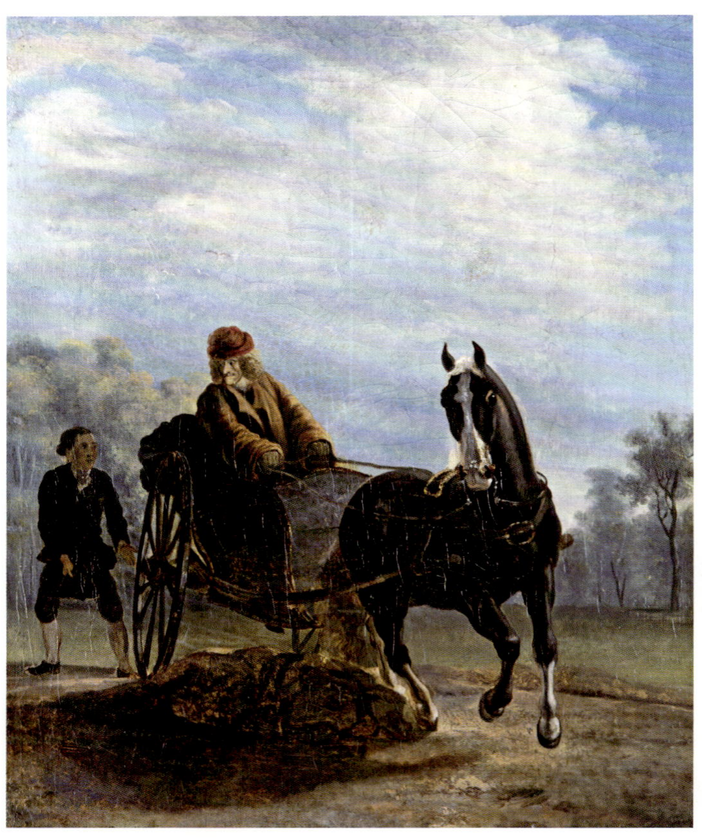

Jean Huber, **dit** *Huber-Voltaire (1721–86)*

Voltaire in a Buggy near Ferney

Voltaire en cabriolet

Voltaire in einem Einspänner bei Ferney

Voltaire en una carretilla en Ferney

Voltaire num Coche em Ferney

Voltaire in een cabriolet bij Ferney

1750–75, Oil on canvas/Huile sur toile, 62 × 51,5 cm

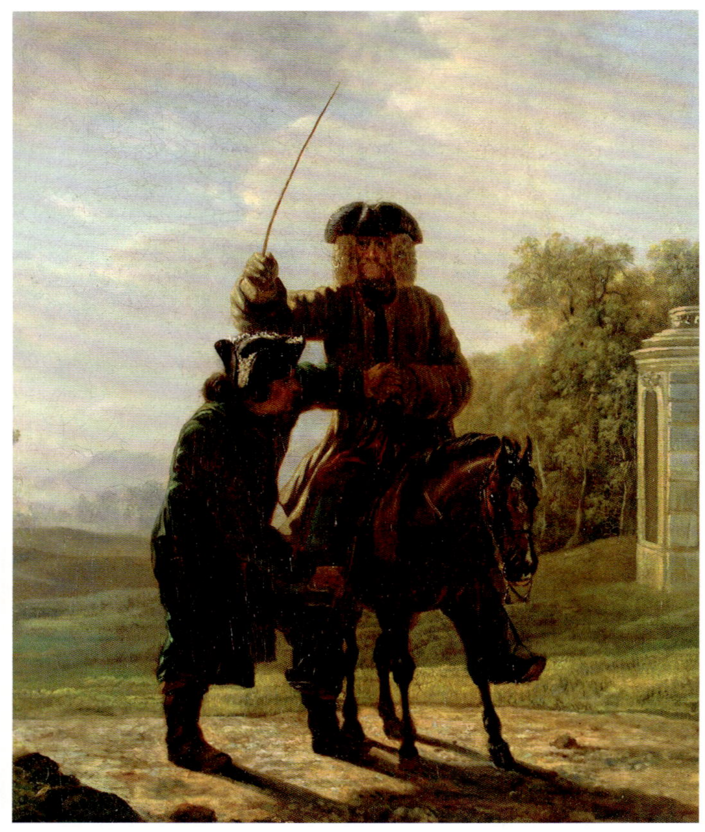

Jean Huber, **dit** *Huber-Voltaire (1721–86)*

Voltaire on Horseback

Voltaire à cheval

Voltaire zu Pferde

Voltaire a caballo

Voltaire a Cavalo

Voltaire te paard

c. 1750–75, Oil on canvas/Huile sur toile, 62 × 51 cm

Jean Huber, **dit** *Huber-Voltaire (1721–86)*

Voltaire Playing Chess

Voltaire jouant aux échecs avec le père Adam

Voltaire beim Schachspiel

Voltaire jugando al ajedrez

Voltaire Jogando Xadrez

Voltaire bij het schaakspel

1768, Oil on canvas/Huile sur toile, 53 × 44 cm

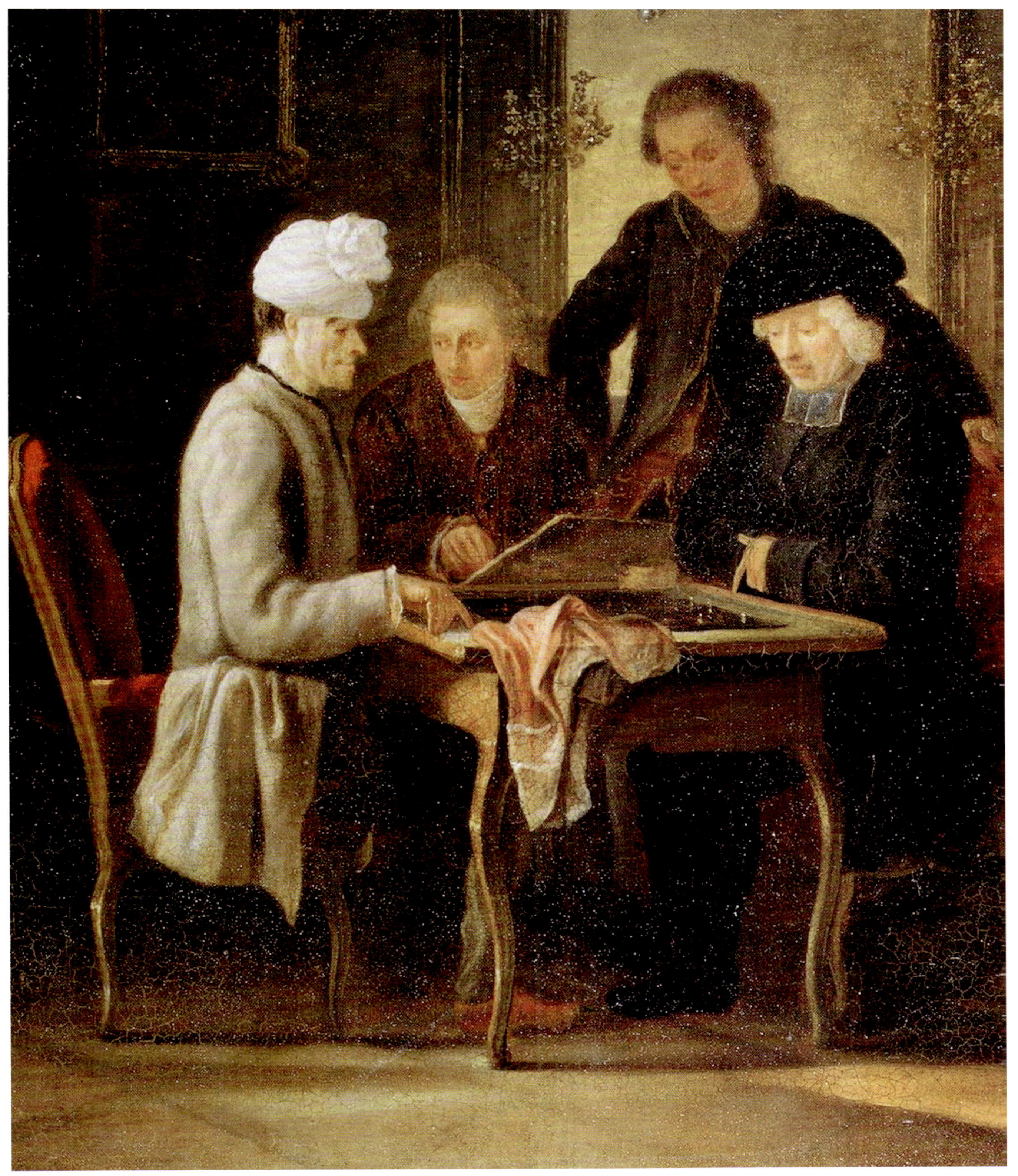

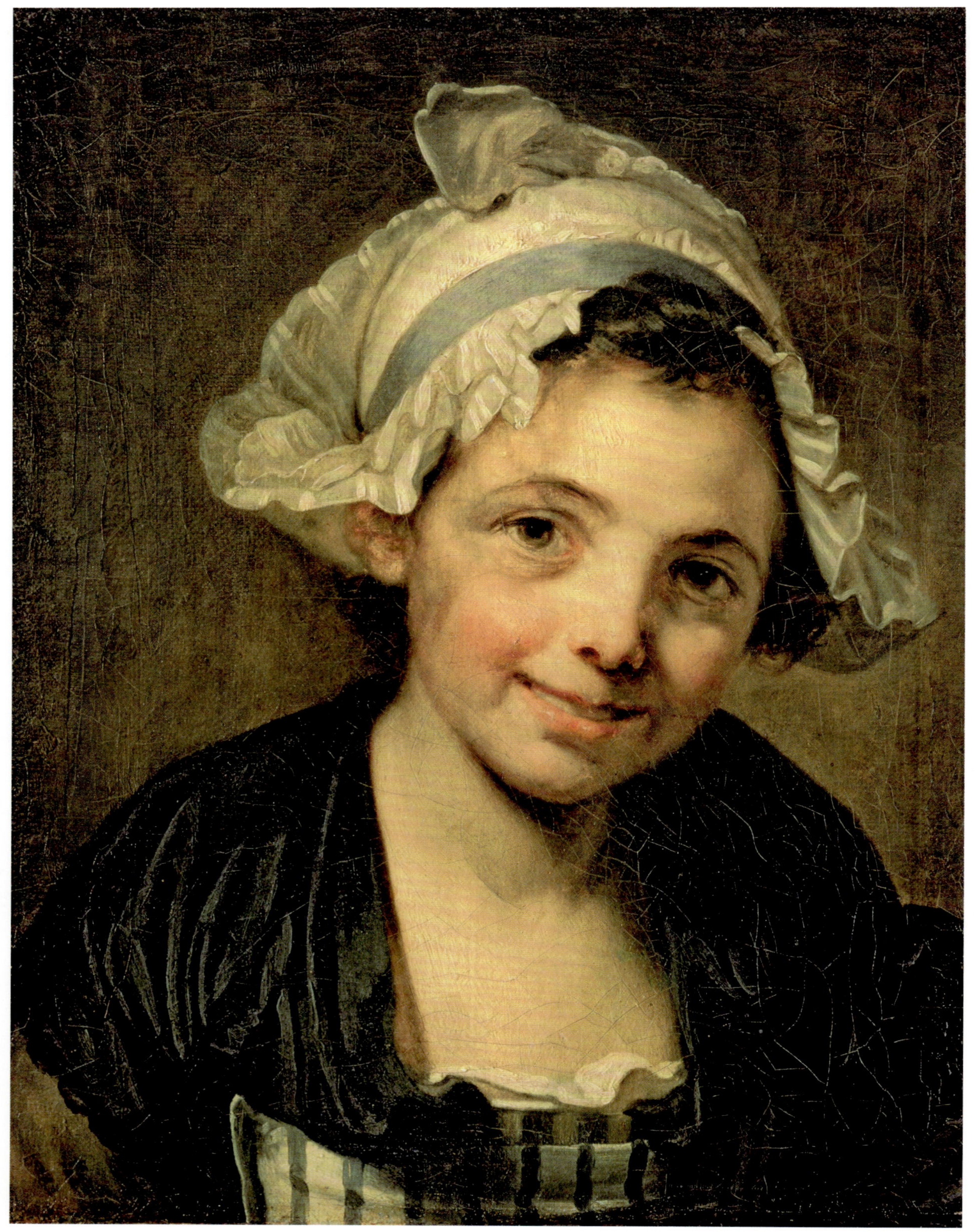

*Jean-Baptiste
Greuze (1725–1805)*

Girl in a Bonnet

Tête de jeune fille
avec une coiffe

Mädchen mit Haube

Niña con cofia

Menina com Touca

Meisje met kapje

1760–68, Oil on
canvas/Huile sur
toile, 41 × 33 cm

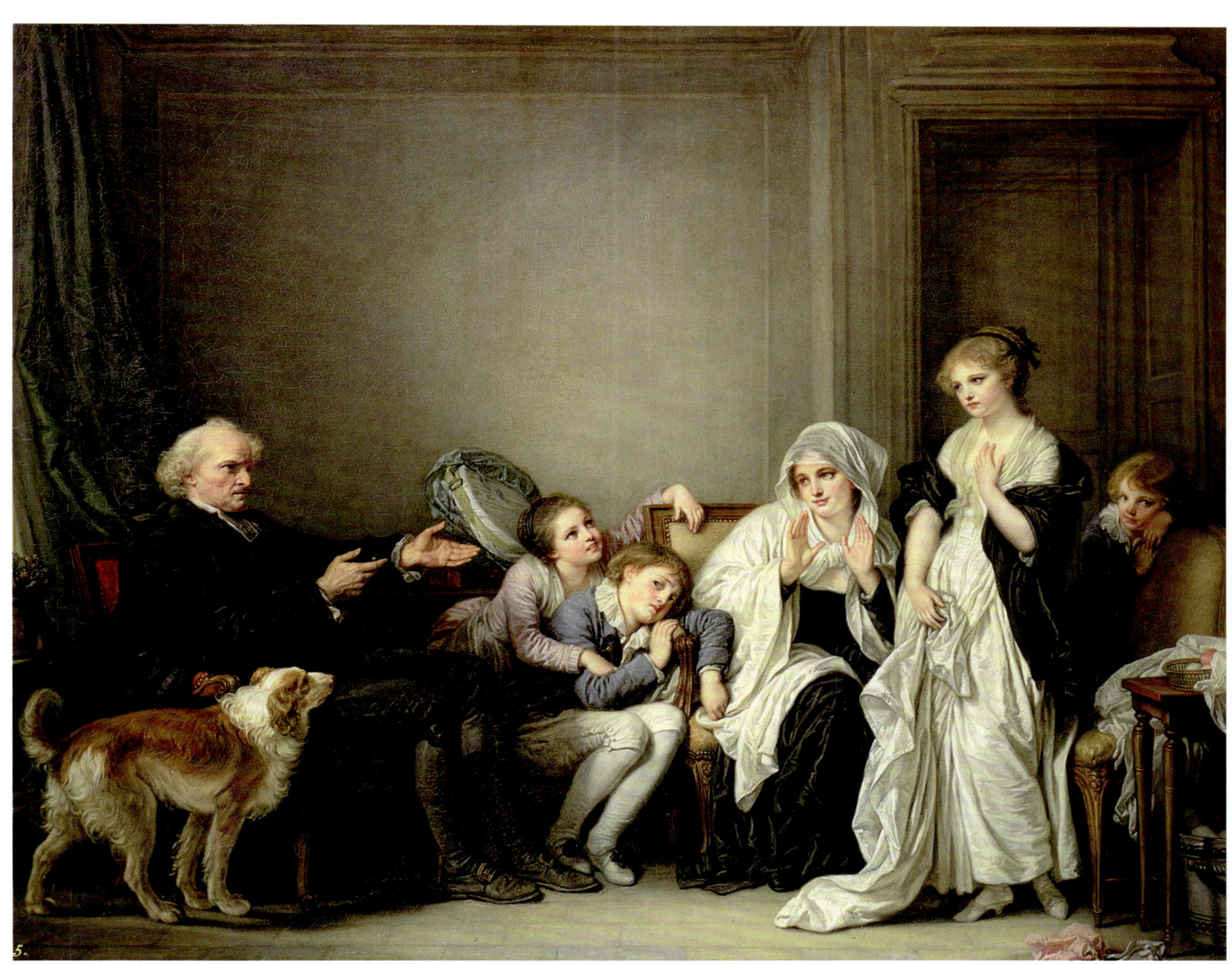

Jean-Baptiste Greuze (1725–1805)

The Widow and Her Priest

La Veuve et son curé

Die Witwe und ihr Priester

La viuda y su confesor

A Viúva e o seu Padre

Op bezoek bij de priester

1786, Oil on canvas/Huile sur toile, 128 × 160,5 cm

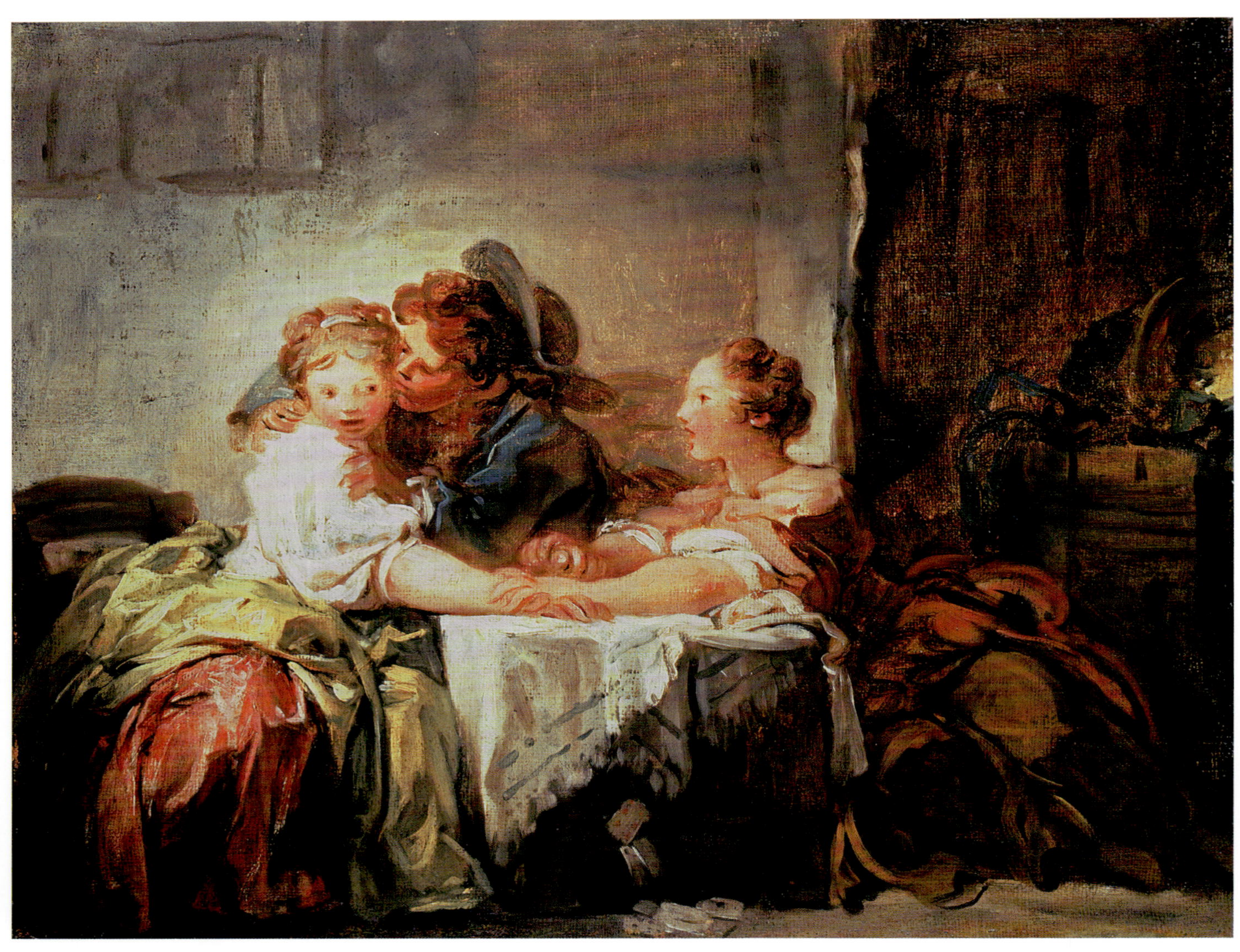

Jean-Honoré Fragonard (1732–1806)

The Prize of a Kiss

Le Baiser gagné

Der Preis des Kusses

El precio del beso

O Preço do Beijo

De prijs van een kus

1760, Oil on canvas/Huile sur toile, 47 × 60 cm

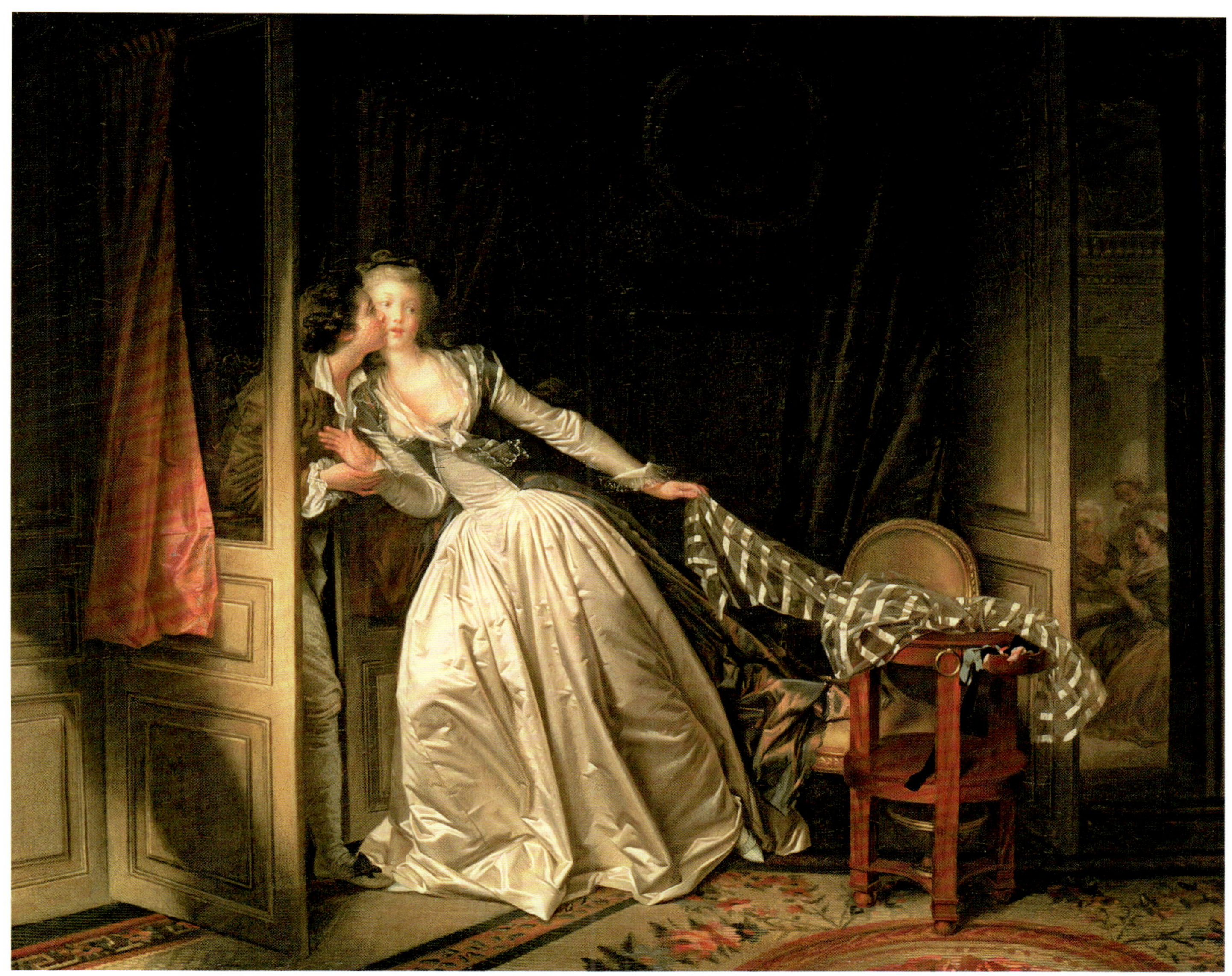

Jean-Honoré Fragonard (1732–1806)

The Stolen Kiss

Le Baiser à la dérobée

Der verspielte Einsatz (Der geraubte Kuss)

El beso robado

O Beijo Roubado

De gestolen kus

c. 1788, Oil on canvas/Huile sur toile, 45 × 55 cm

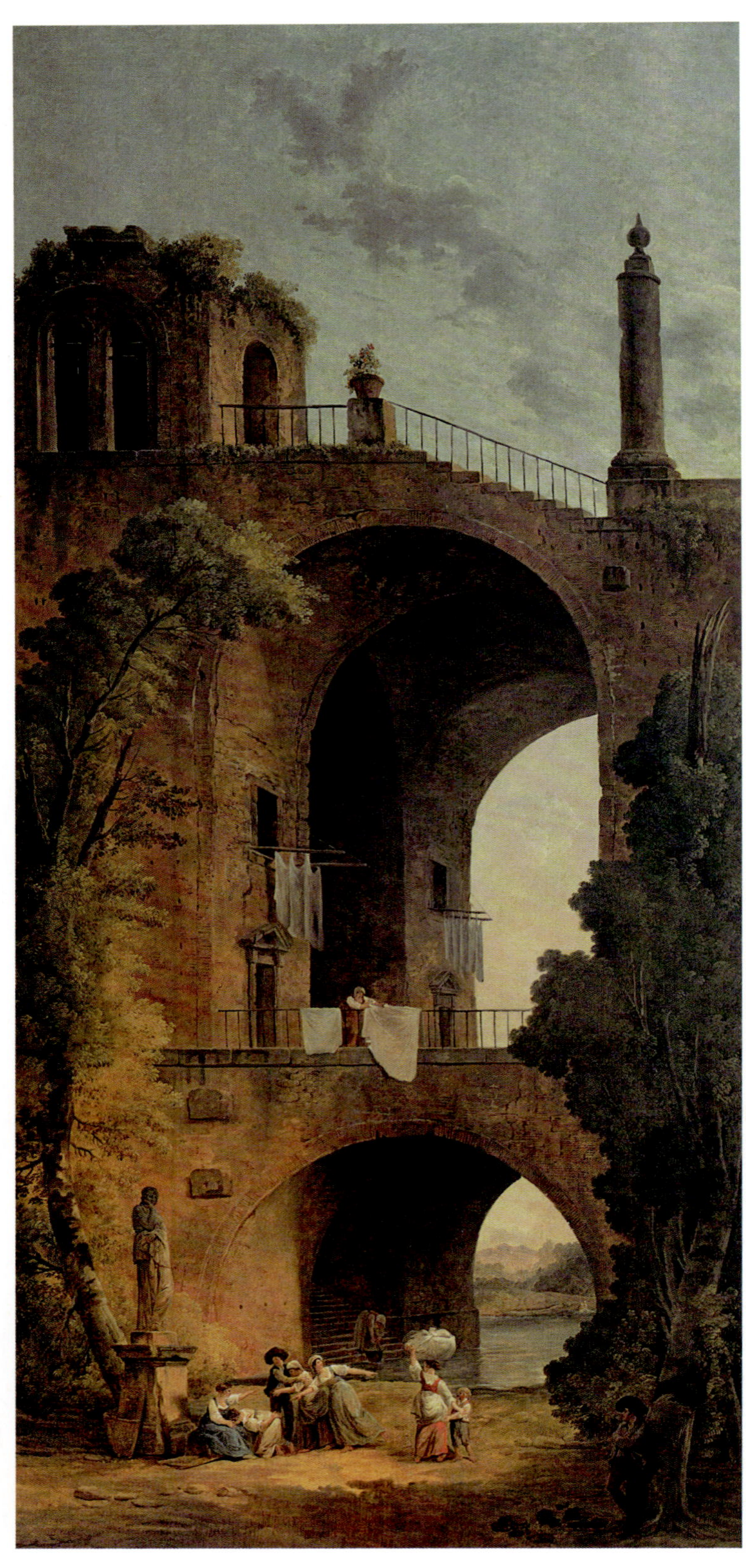

Hubert Robert (1733–1808)

Landscape with Ruins

Paysage avec des ruines

Landschaft mit Ruinen

Paisaje con ruina

Paisagem com Ruinas

Landschap met ruïnes

1802, Oil on canvas/Huile sur toile, 311 × 147 cm

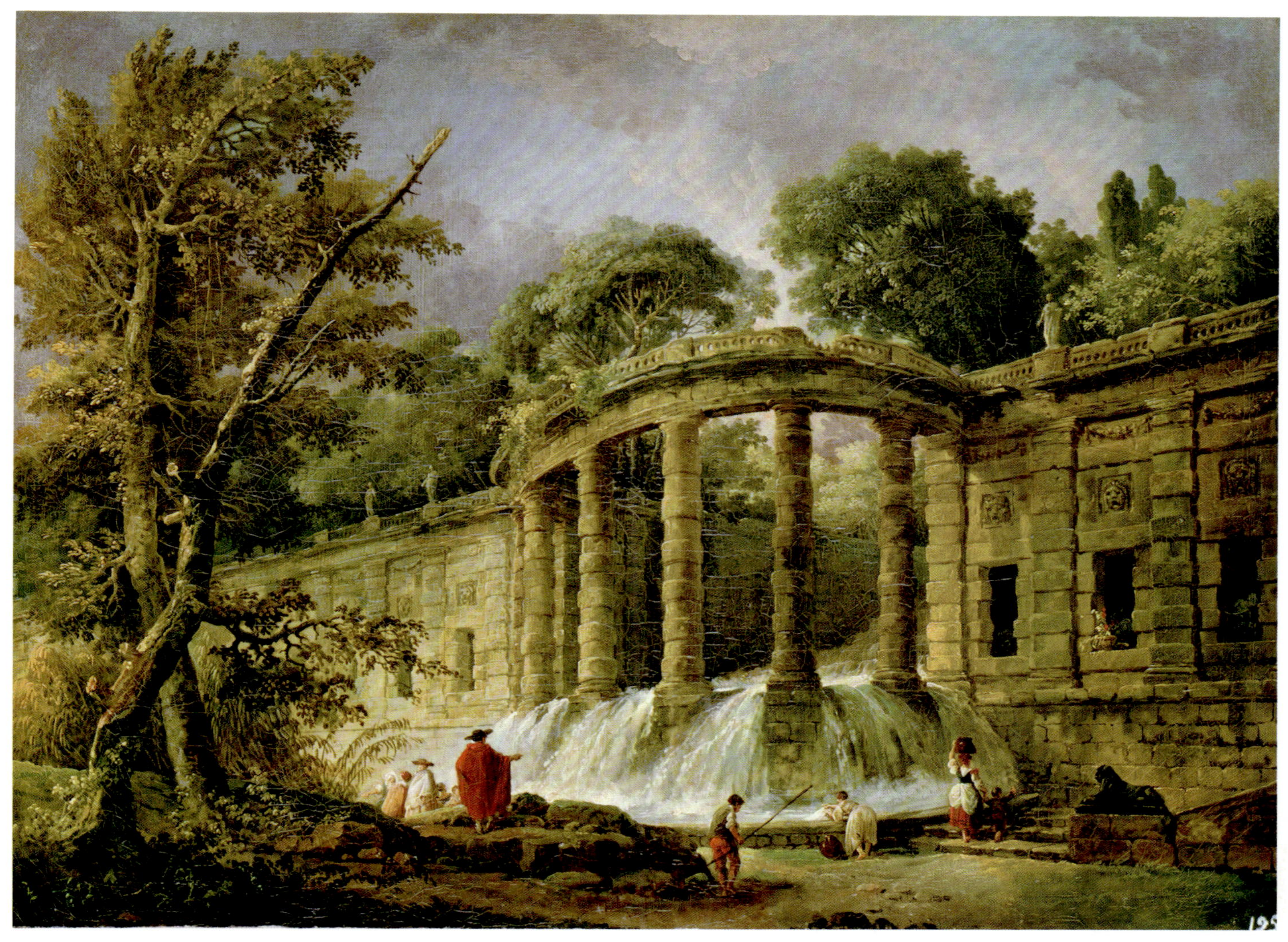

Hubert Robert (1733–1808)

Pavilion with Cascade

Pavillon avec cascade

Pavillon mit Kaskade

Pabellón con cascada

Pavilhão com Cascata

Paviljoen met waterval

c. 1767, Oil on canvas/Huile sur toile, 53 × 61 cm

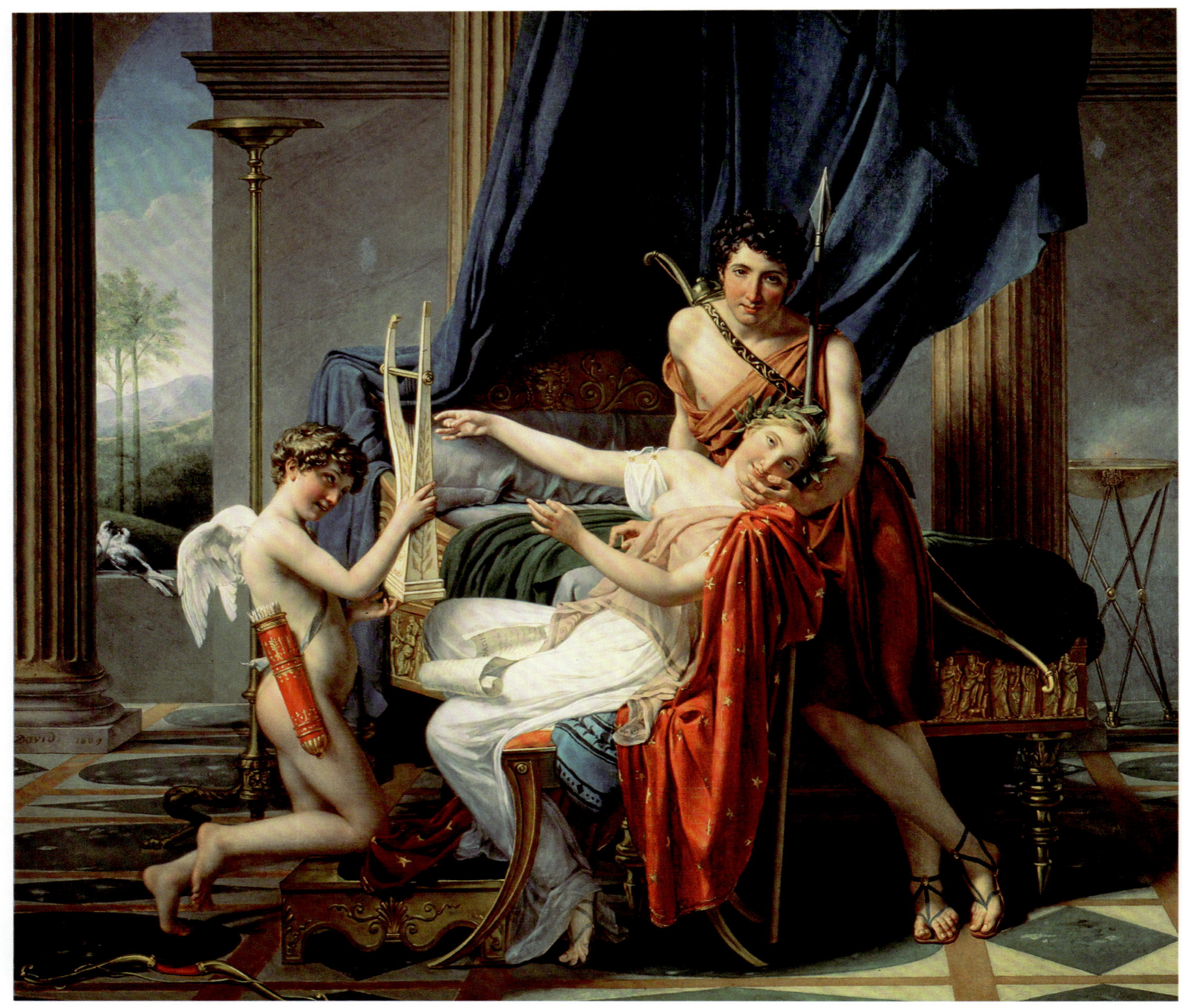

Jacques-Louis David (1748–1825)

Sappho and Phaon

Sapho et Phaon

Sappho und Phaon

Safo y Faón

Safo e Faón

Sappho en Phaon

1809, Oil on canvas/Huile sur toile, 225,3 × 262 cm

Élisabeth Louise Vigée-Lebrun (1755–1842)

Prince Alexander Borisovich Kurakin

Portrait du prince Alexandre Kourakin

Fürst Alexander Borrissowitsch Kurakin

Príncipe Alexander Borrissovich Kurakin

Príncipe Alexandre Borisovich Kurakin

Vorst Alexander Borissovitsj Koerakin

1797, Oil on canvas/Huile sur toile, 96 × 76 cm

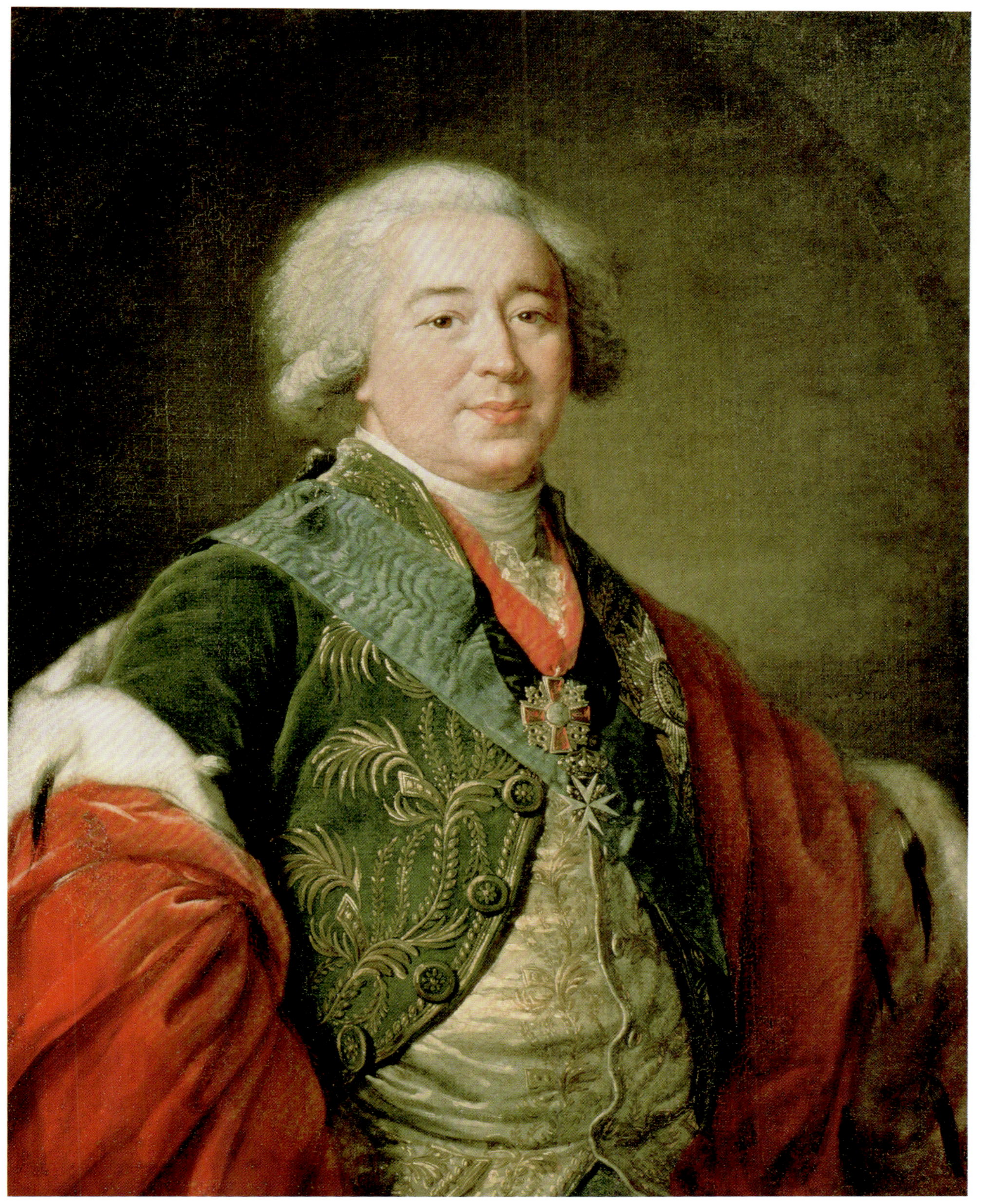

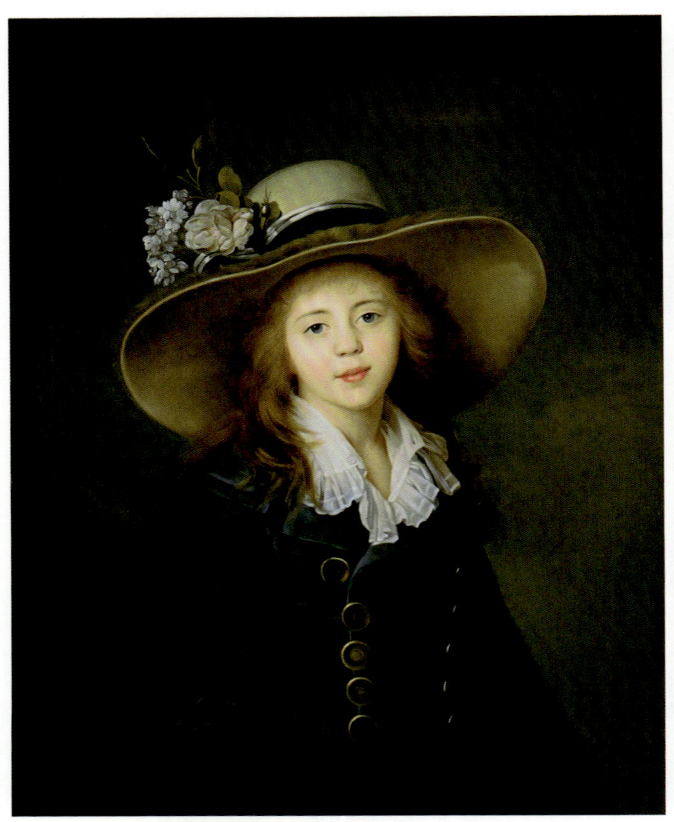

Jean-Louis Voille (1744–c. 1804)

Ekaterina Stroganova as a Child

Portrait de jeune fille au chapeau

Ekaterina Stroganowa als Kind

Ecaterina Stroganova de niña

Ekaterina Stroganova em Criança

Portret van Ekaterina Stroganov als kind

1781/82, Oil on canvas/Huile sur toile, 85 × 68 cm

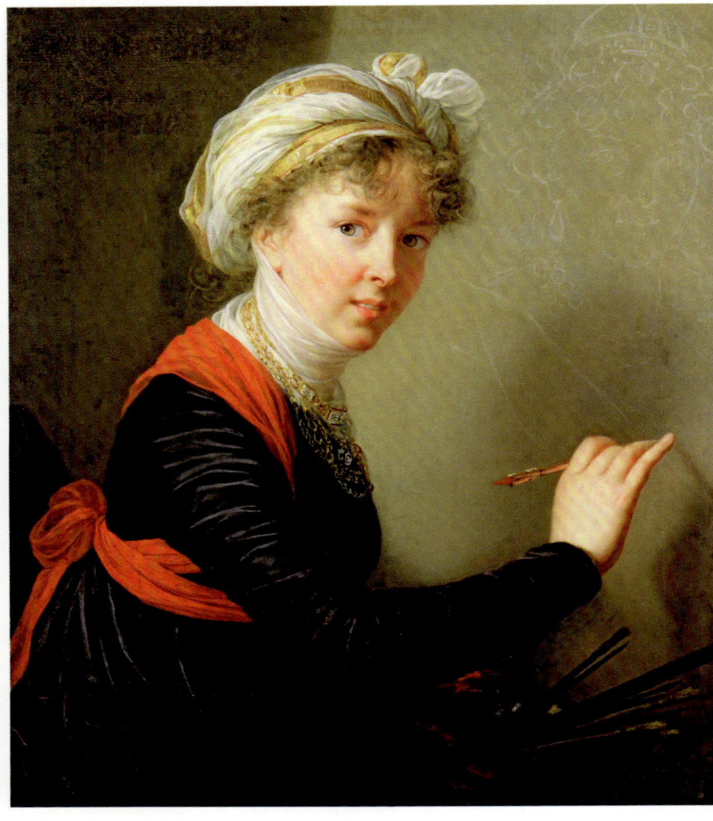

Élisabeth Louise Vigée-Lebrun (1755–1842)

Self-Portrait

Autoportrait

Selbstbildnis

Autorretrato

Autorretrato

Zelfportret

1800, Oil on canvas/Huile sur toile, 78,5 × 68 cm

Élisabeth Louise Vigée-Lebrun (1755–1842)

The Grand Duchesses Alexandra Pavlovna and Helena Pavlovna of Russia

Les Grandes-duchesses Alexandra Pavlovna et Helena Pavlovna de Russie

Die Großherzoginnen Alexandra Pawlowna und Helena Pawlowna von Russland

Las grandes duquesas de Rusia Alexandra Pavlovna y Helena Pavlovna

As Grandes Duquesas Alexandra Pavlovna e Helena Pavlovna da Rússia

De groothertoginnen Alexandra Pavlovna en Helena Pavlovna van Rusland

1796, Oil on canvas/Huile sur toile, 99 × 99 cm

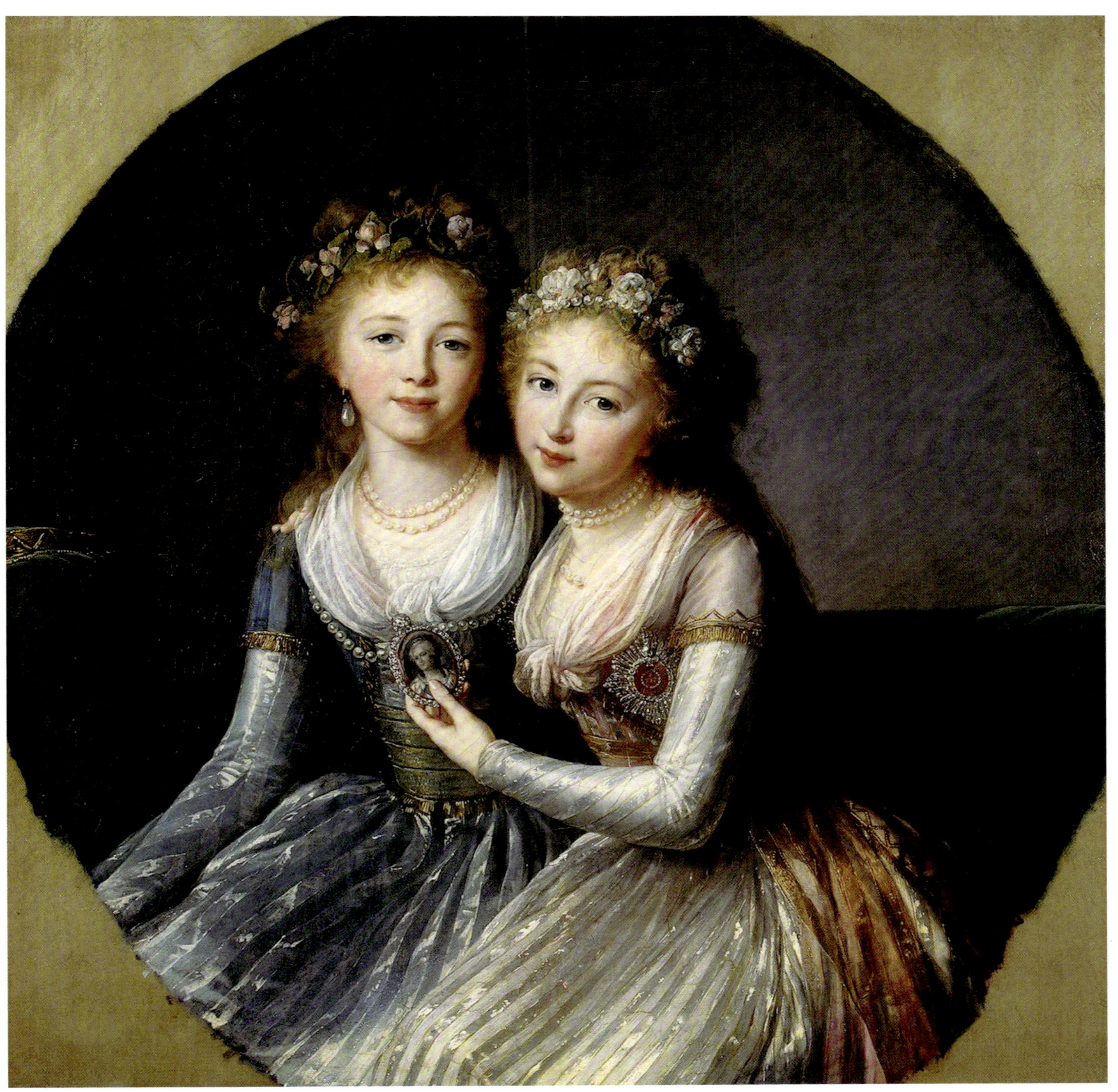

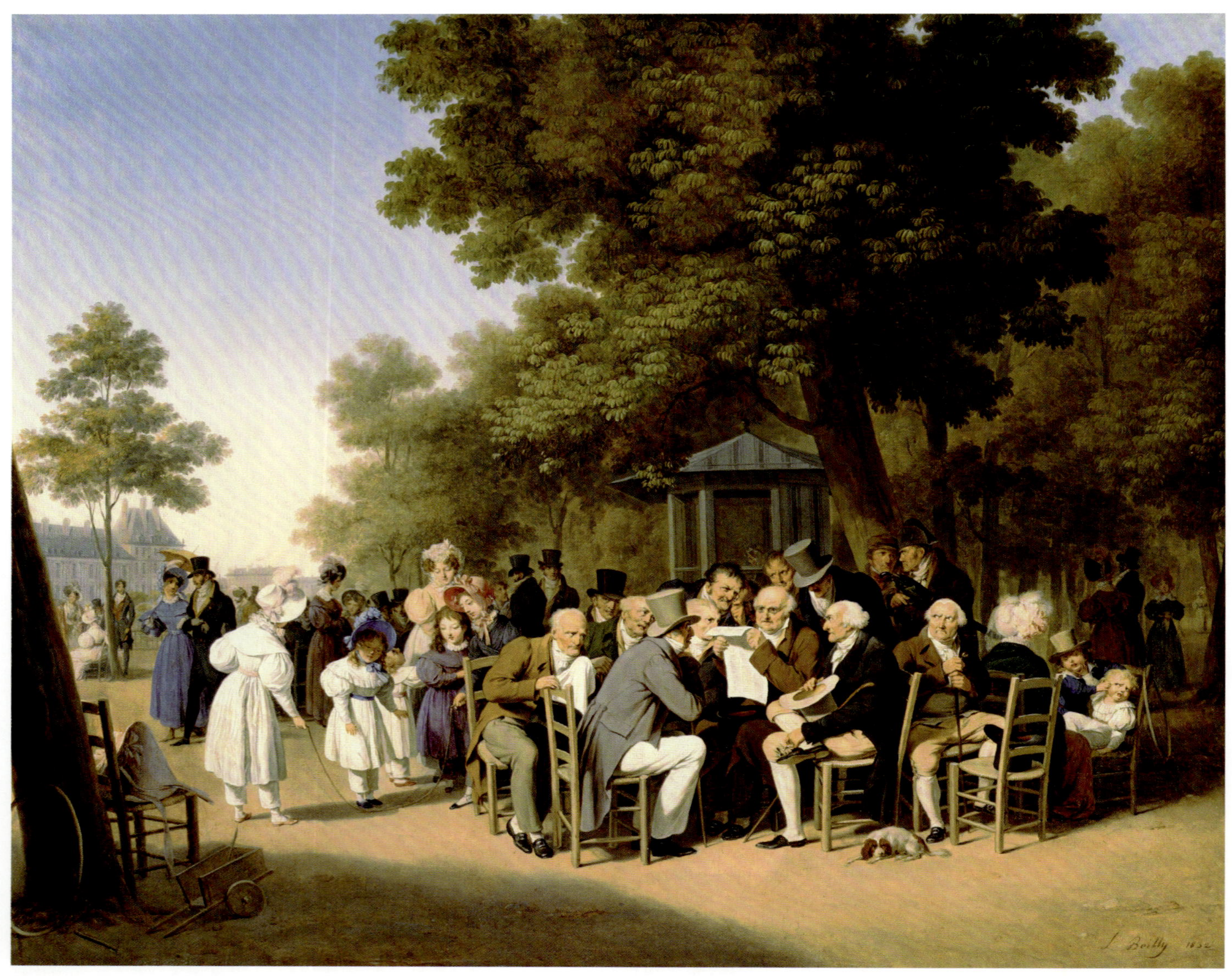

Louis Léopold Boilly (1761–1845)

Amateur Politicians in the Tuileries

Politiciens dans le jardin des Tuileries

Die Freizeit-Politiker in den Tuilerien

Políticos en las Tullerías

Políticos no Jardim das Tulherias

Politici in de Tuileriën

1832, Oil on canvas/Huile sur toile, 50 × 60,5 cm

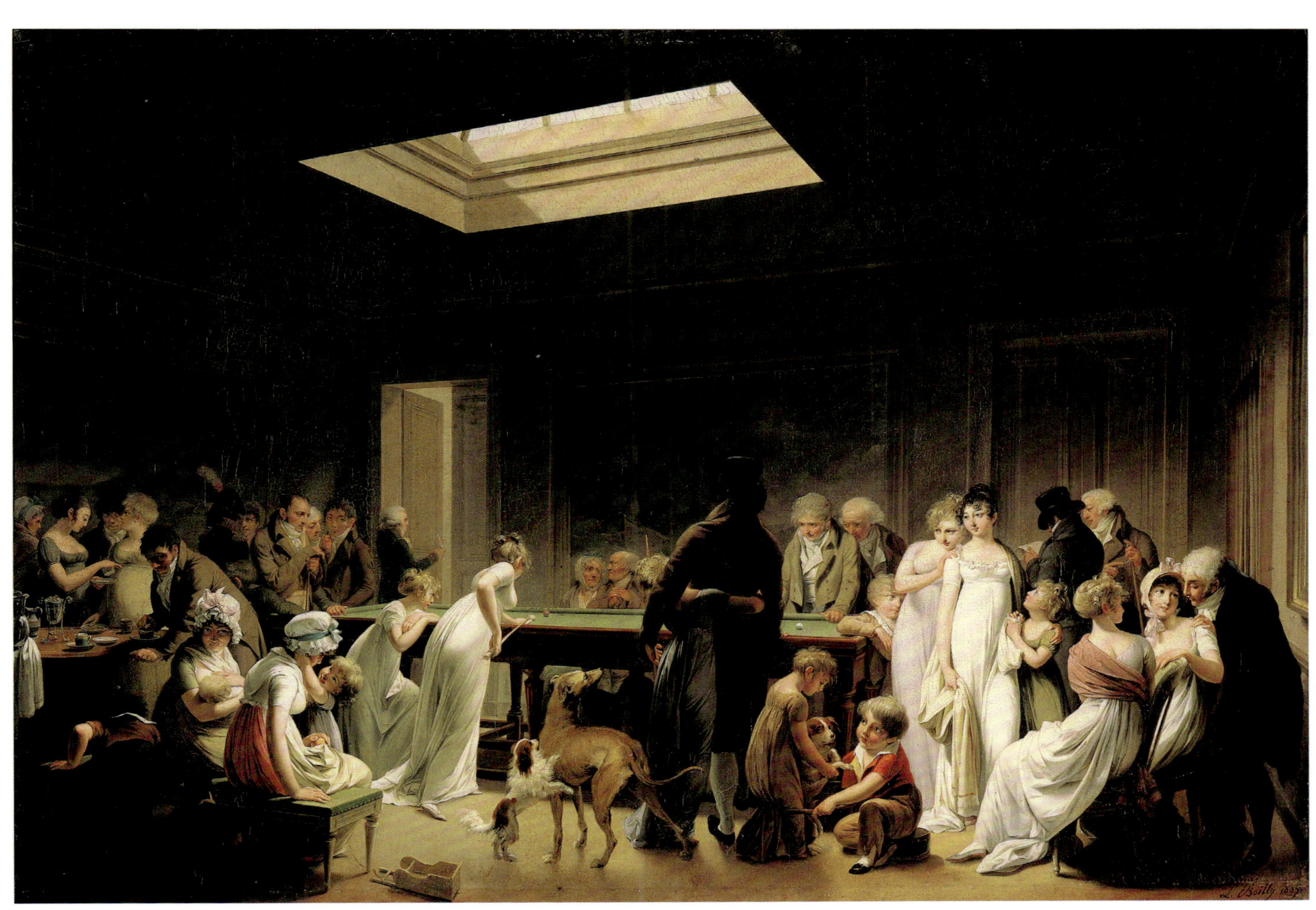

Louis Léopold Boilly (1761–1845)

The Billiards Game

Le Billard

Das Billiardspiel

El juego de billar

O Jogo de Bilhar

Het biljardspel

1807, Oil on canvas/Huile sur toile, 56 × 81 cm

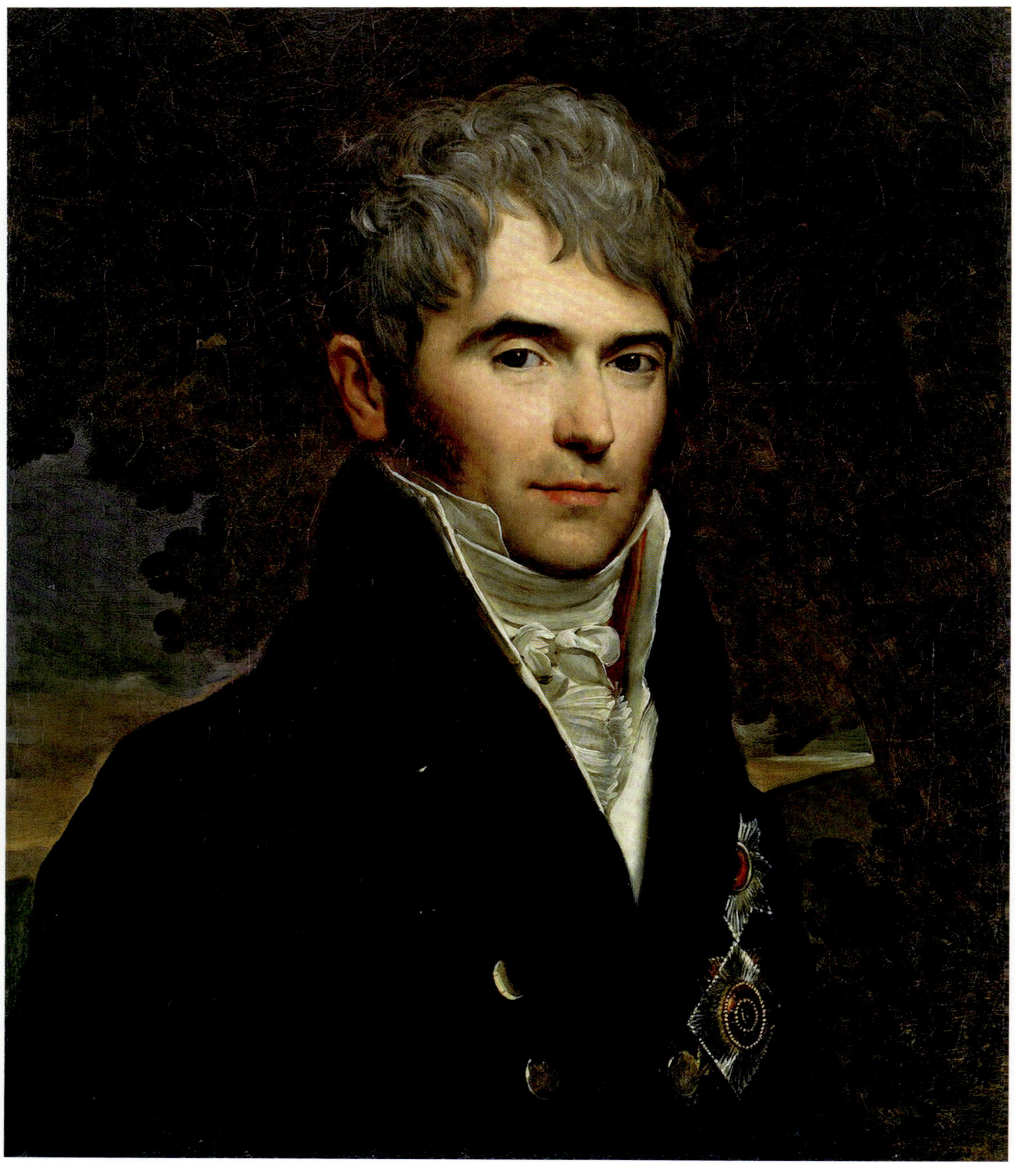

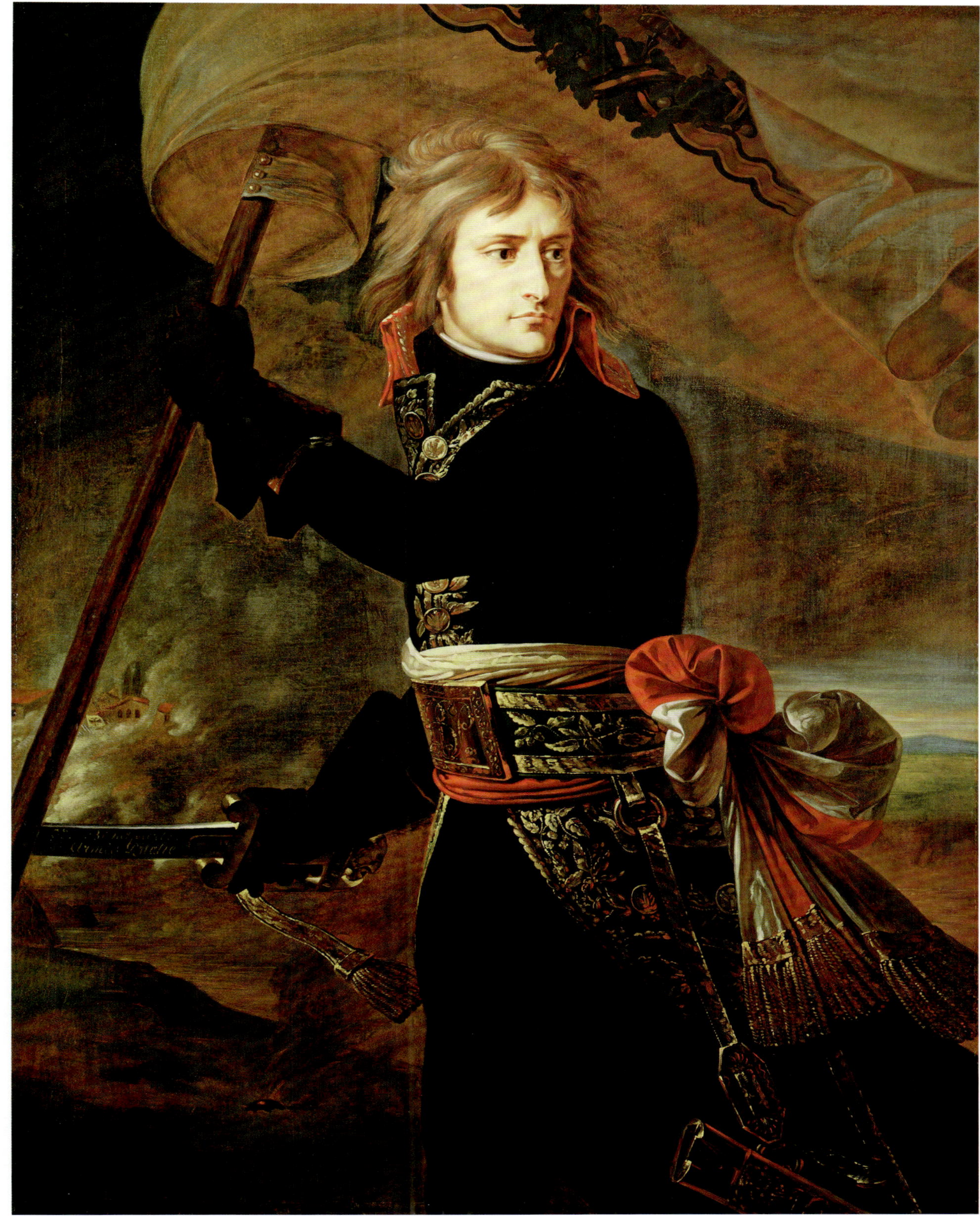

*François Pascal
Simon Gérard,
dit Baron Gérard*
(1770–1837)

Count Viktor
Pavlovich
Kochubey

Portrait du comte
Viktor Kochubey

Graf Wiktor
Pawlowitsch
Kotschubei

El Conde Viktor
Pavlovich
Kochubei

Conde Victor
Pavlovitch
Kotchoubeï

Graaf Viktor
Pavlovitsj
Kotsjubej

1809, Oil on
canvas/Huile sur
toile, 66 × 55,5 cm

*Antoine-Jean
Gros (1771–1835)*

Napoleon on the
Bridge of Arcole

Bonaparte au
pont d'Arcole

Napoleon auf
der Brücke
von Arcole

Napoleón en el
puente de Arcole

Napoleão na
Ponte de Arcole

Napoleon op de
brug van Arcole

c. 1796/97, Oil on
canvas/Huile sur
toile, 134 × 104 cm

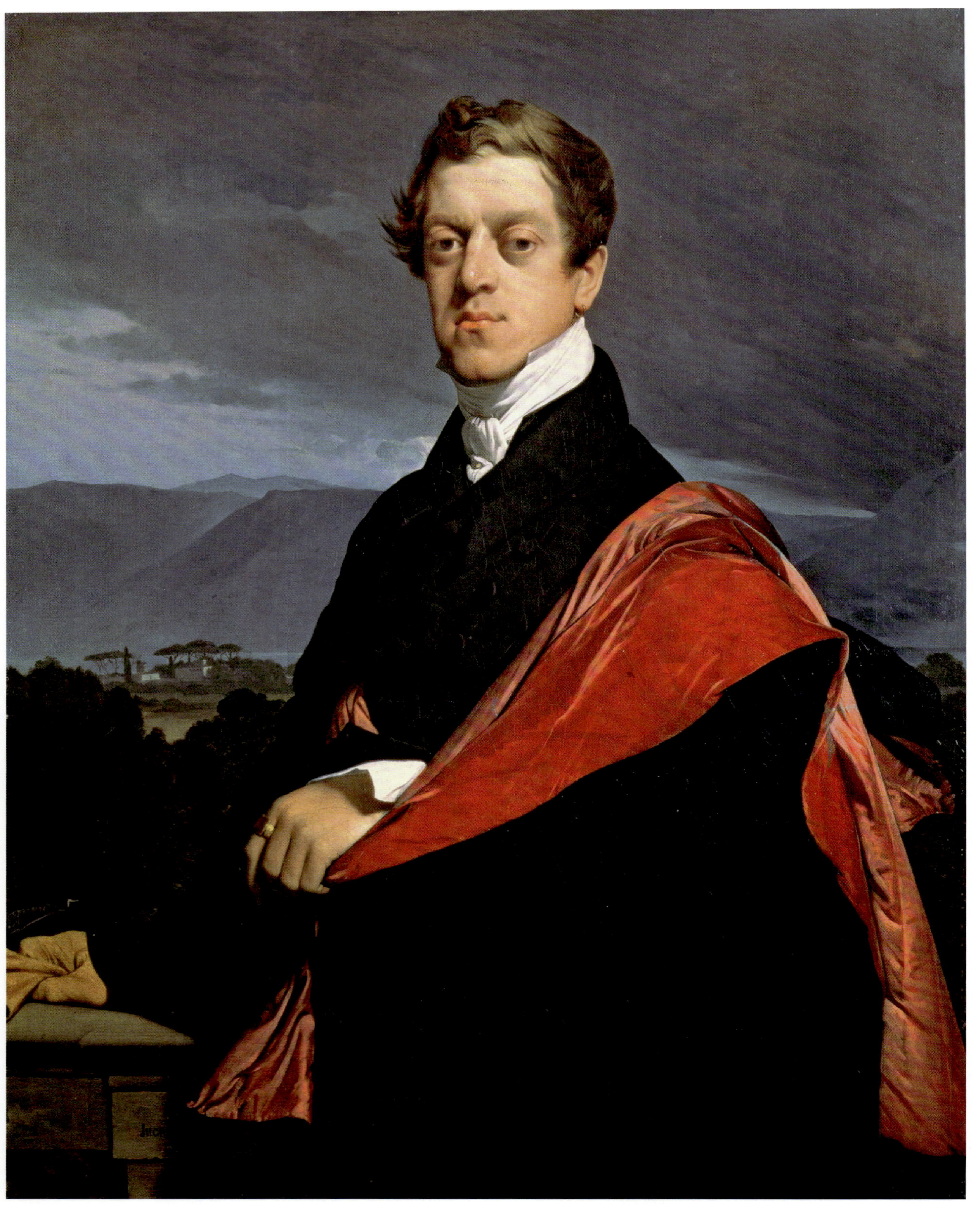

Jean Auguste Dominique Ingres
(1780–1867)

Count Nikolai Dmitrievich Guriev

Le Comte Nikolaï Gouriev

Graf Nikolai Dmitrijewitsch Guriew

El Conde Nikolai Dmitriyevich Guriev

Conde Nikolai Dmitrievich Guriev

Graaf Nikolai Dmitrijevitsj Goerjev

1821, Oil on canvas/ Huile sur toile, 107 × 86 cm

Émile Jean Horace Vernet
(1789–1863)

Self-Portrait

Autoportrait

Selbstbildnis

Autorretrato

Autorretrato

Zelfportret

1835, Oil on canvas/ Huile sur toile, 47 × 39 cm

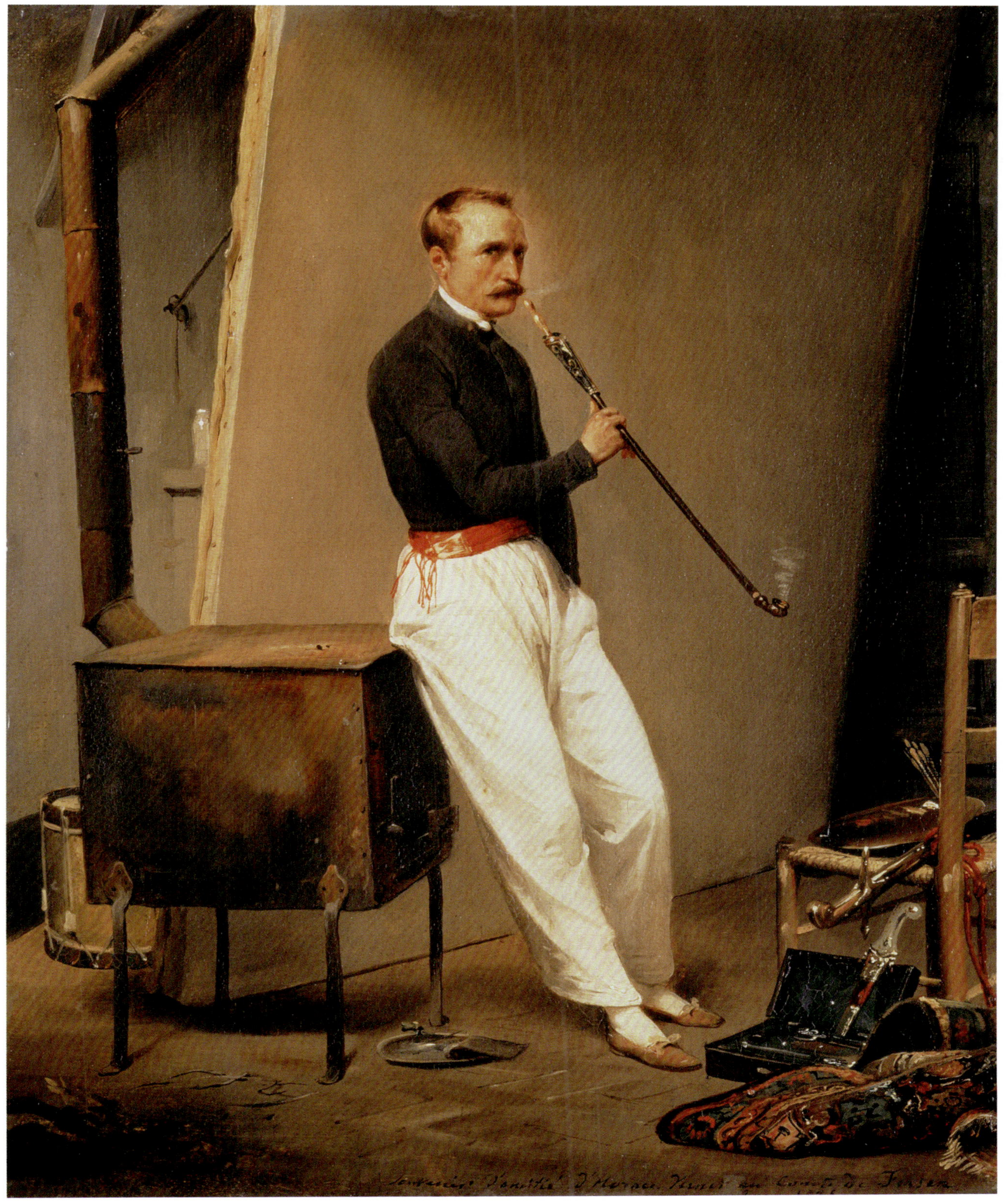

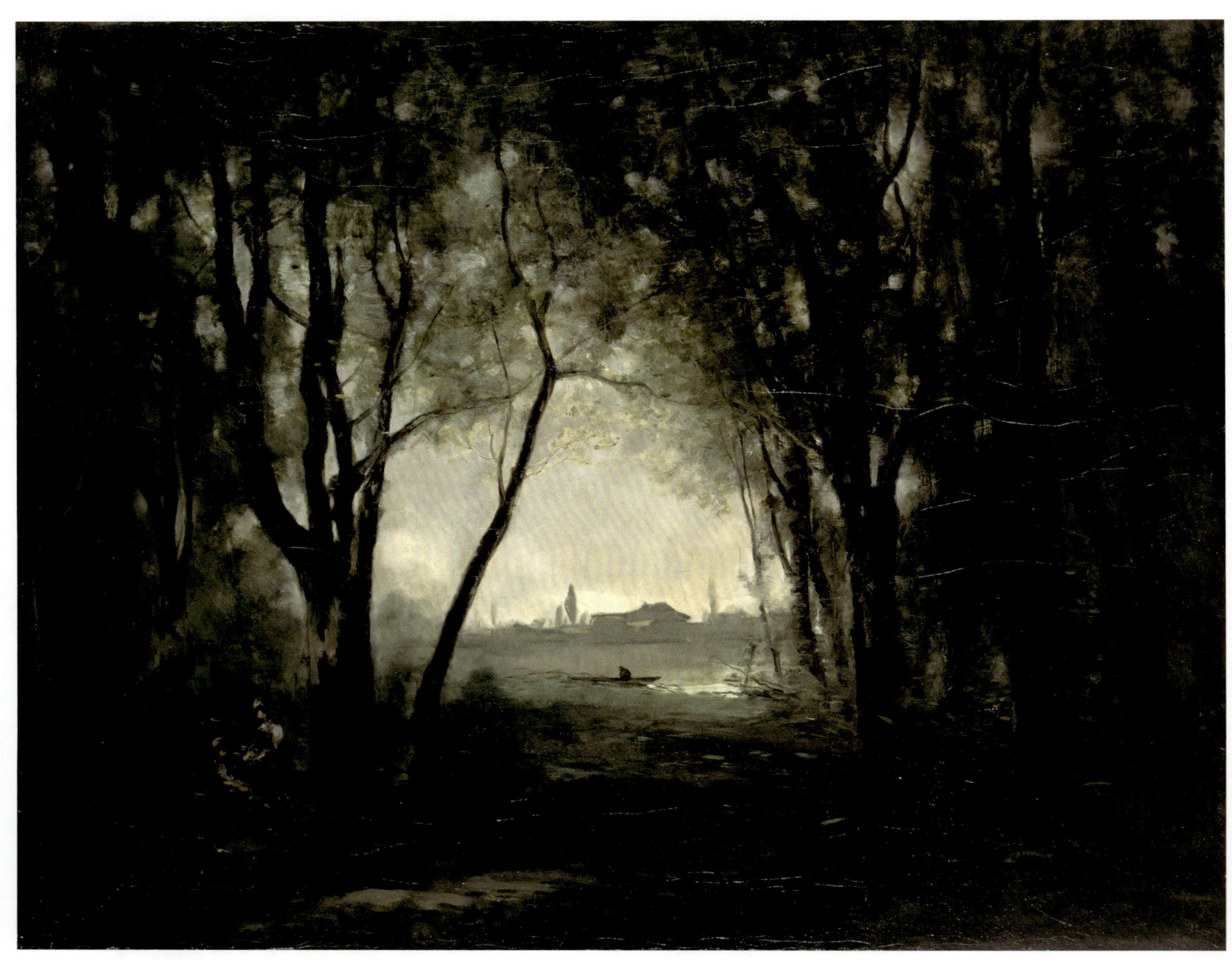

Jean-Baptiste Camille Corot (1796–1875)
Landscape with Lake
Paysage au lac
Landschaft mit See
Paisaje marítimo
Paisagem com Mar
Landschap met meer
c. 1860–70, Oil on canvas/Huile sur toile, 63 × 65,5 cm

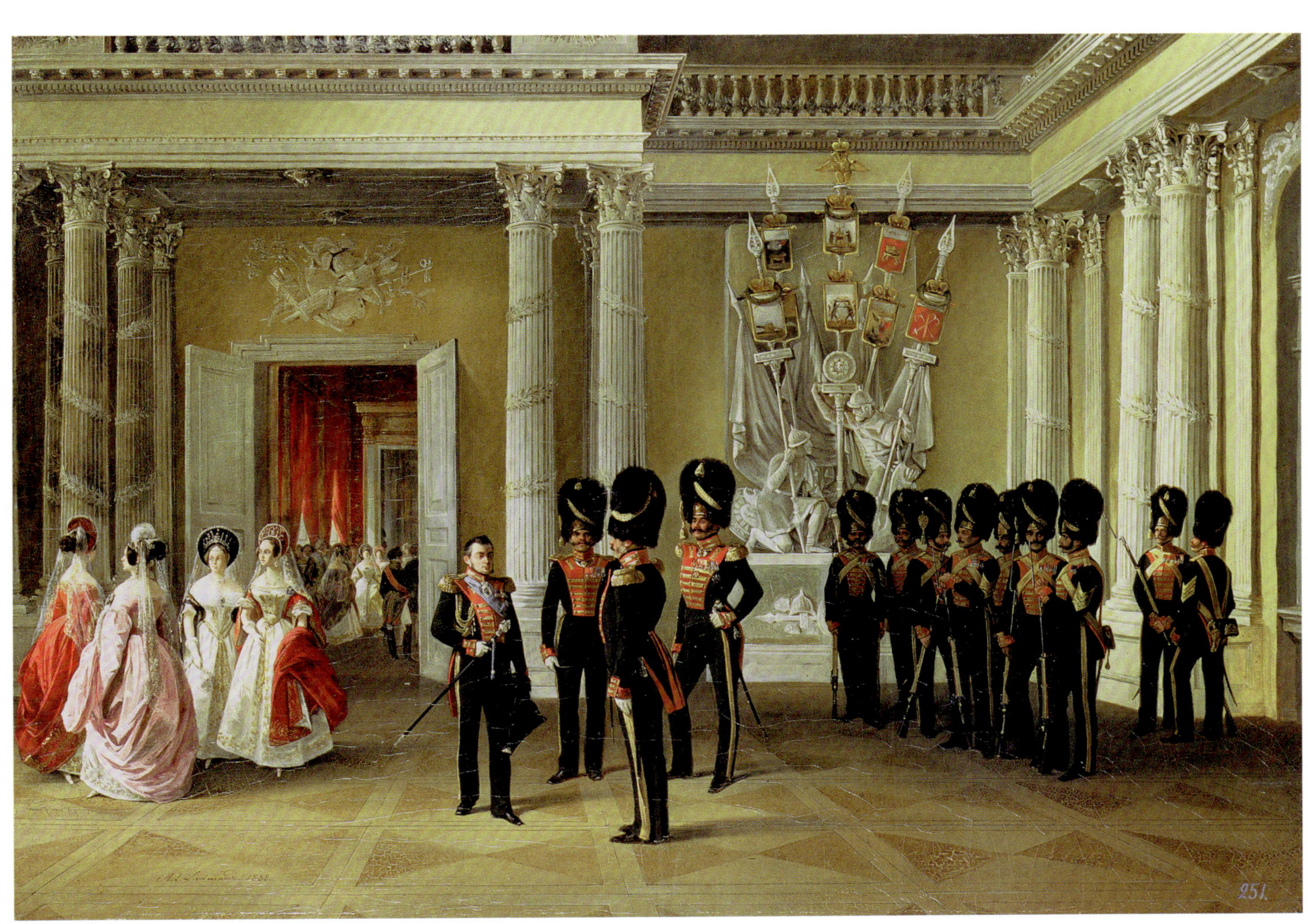

Adolphe Ladurner (1798–1856)

The Heraldic Hall in the Winter Palace

La Salle Blanche du palais d'Hiver

Der Wappensaal im Winterpalast

La sala de armas en el Palacio de Invierno

O Salão de Armas no Palácio de Inverno

De wapenzaal in het Winterpaleis

1838, Oil on canvas/Huile sur toile, 69 × 96 cm

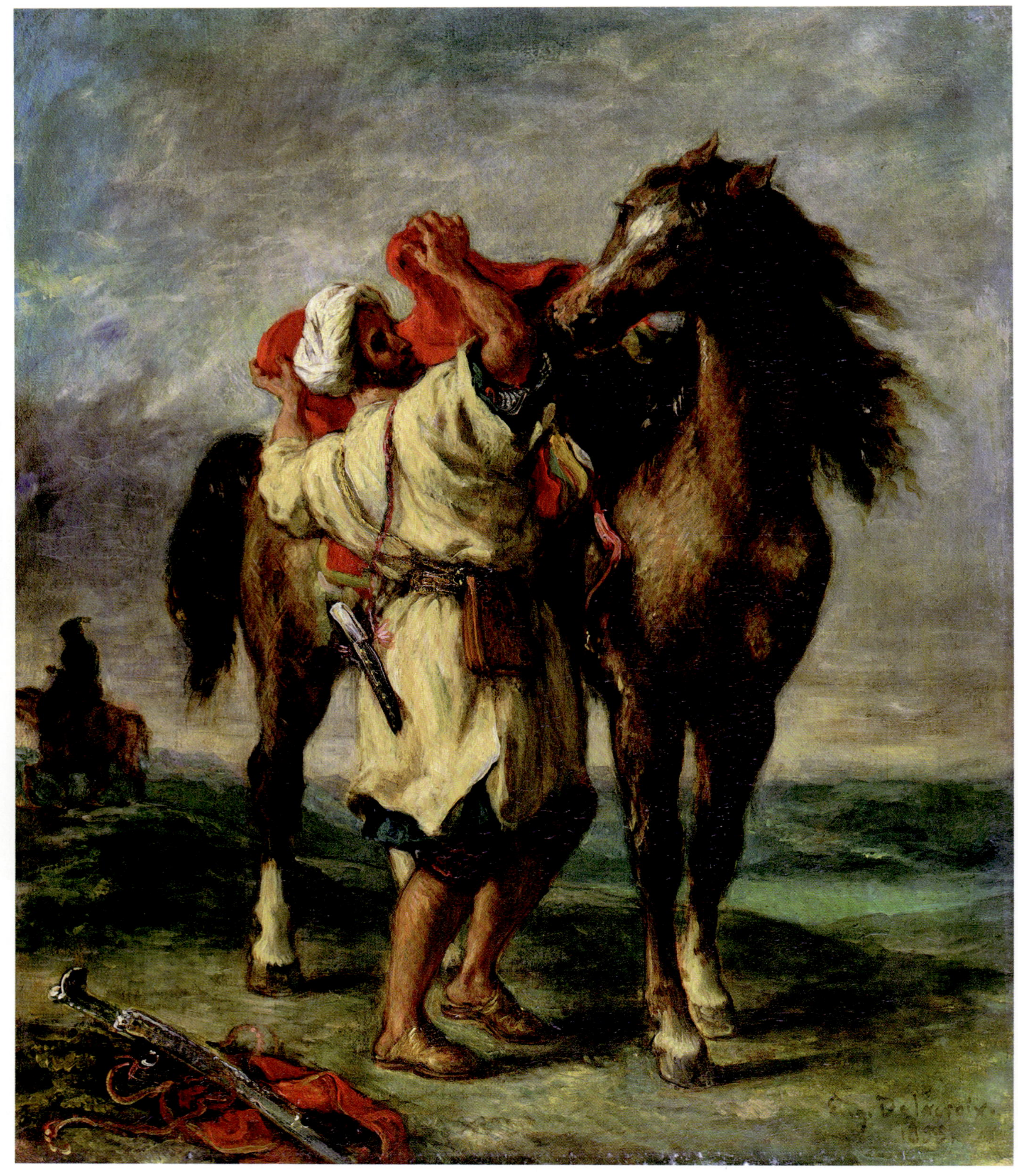

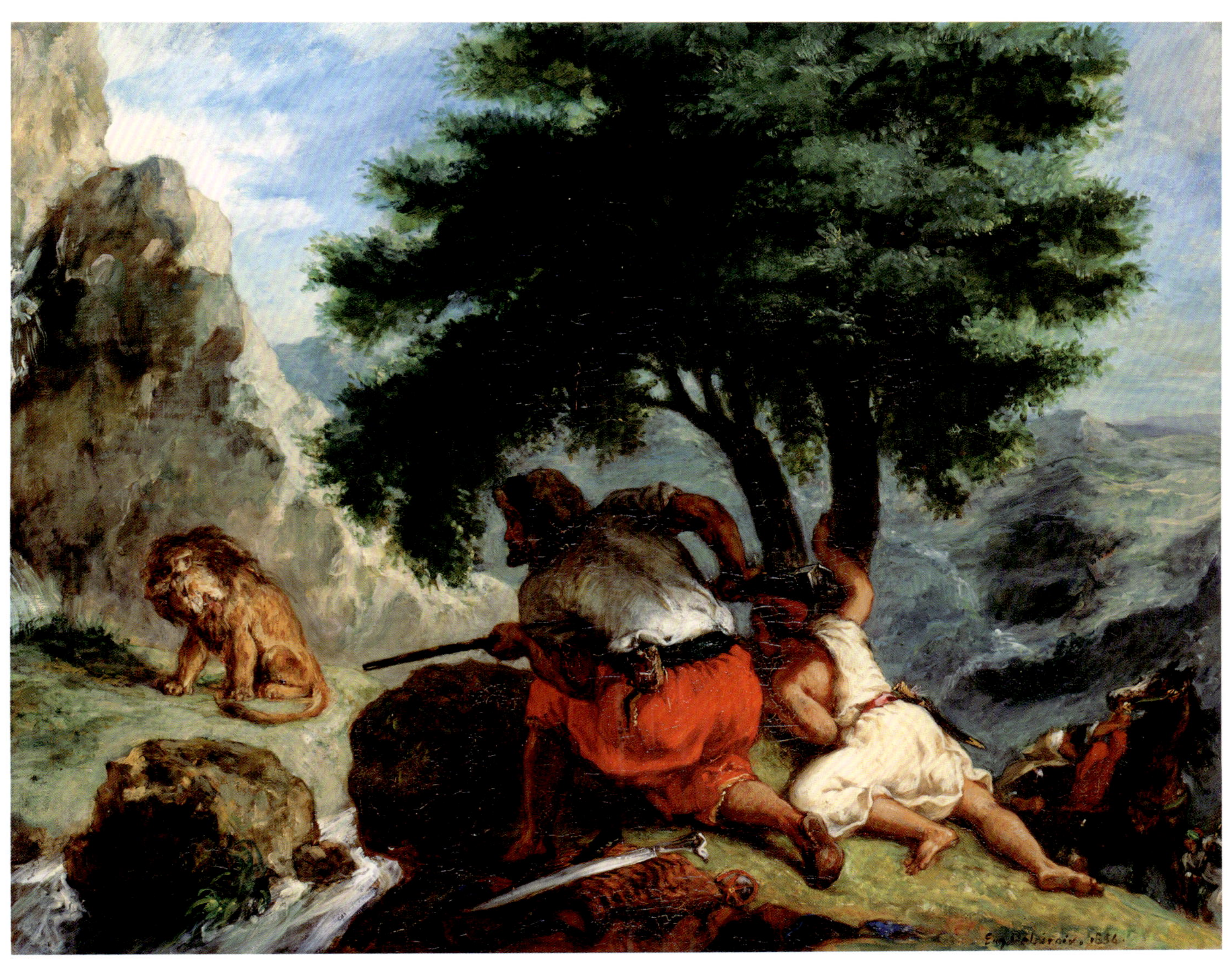

Eugène Delacroix (1798–1863)
Moroccan Saddling His Horse
Marocain sellant son cheval
Marokkaner beim Satteln seines Pferdes
Marroquí ensillando su caballo
Marroquino a Pôr a Sela ao seu Cavalo
Een Marokkaan bij het zadelen van de paarden
1855, Oil on canvas/Huile sur toile, 56 × 47 cm

Eugène Delacroix (1798–1863)
Lion Hunt in Morocco
Chasse au lion au Maroc
Löwenjagd in Marokko
Caza de leones en Marruecos
Caça ao Leão em Marrocos
Leeuwenjacht in Marokko
1854, Oil on canvas/Huile sur toile, 74 × 92 cm

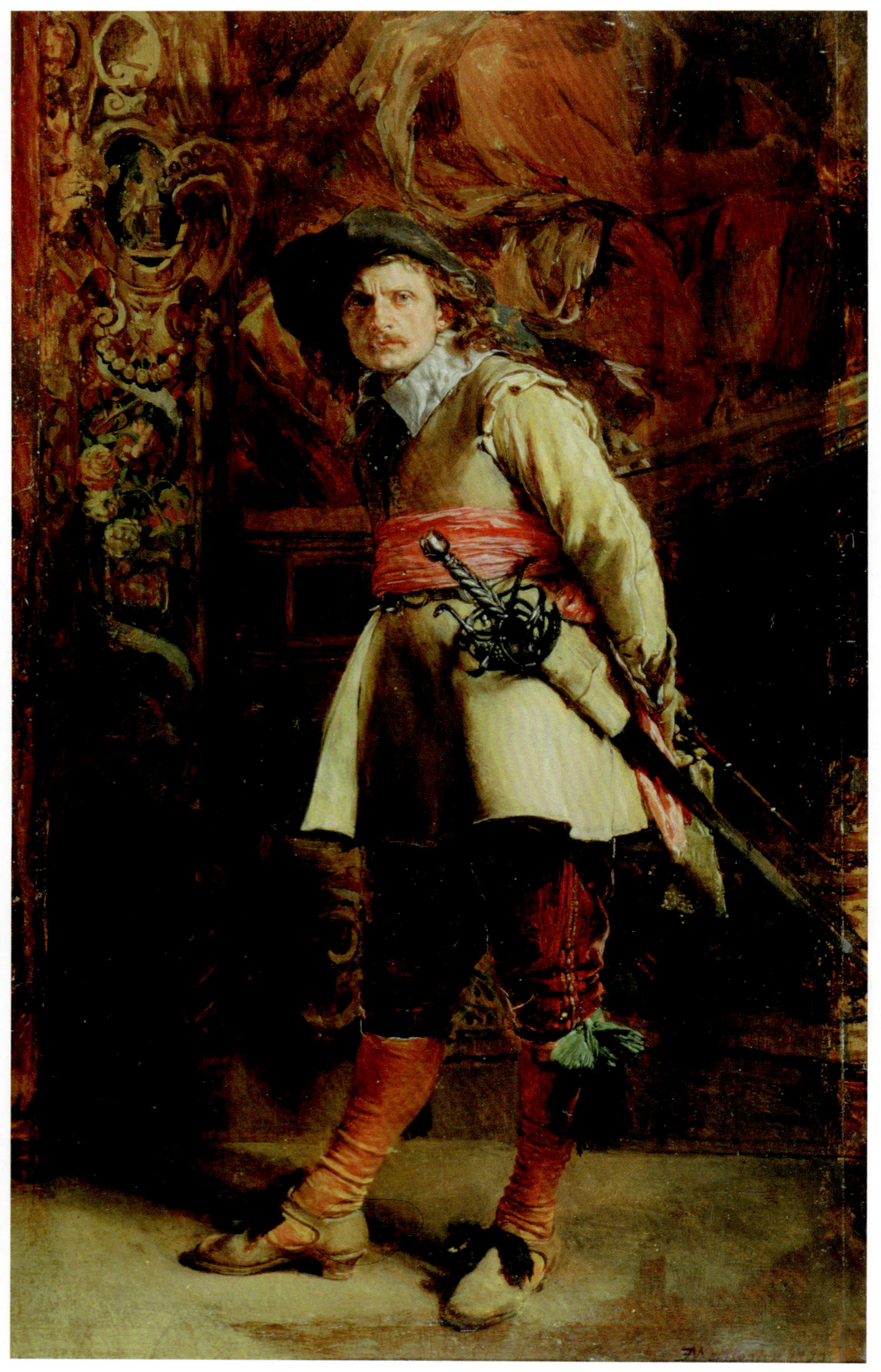

Ernest Meissonier (1815–91)

Musketeer

Mousquetaire

Musketier

Mosquetero

Mosqueteiro

Musketier

1870, Oil on canvas/Huile sur toile, 24,5 × 15 cm

Philippe Rousseau (1816–87)

The Rat Who Retired from the World

Le Rat qui s'est retiré du monde

Die Ratte, die sich vor der Welt zurückzog

La rata ermitaña

O Rato Eremita

De kluizenaar-rat

c. 1860–69, Oil on canvas/Huile sur toile, 25,5 × 21,5 cm

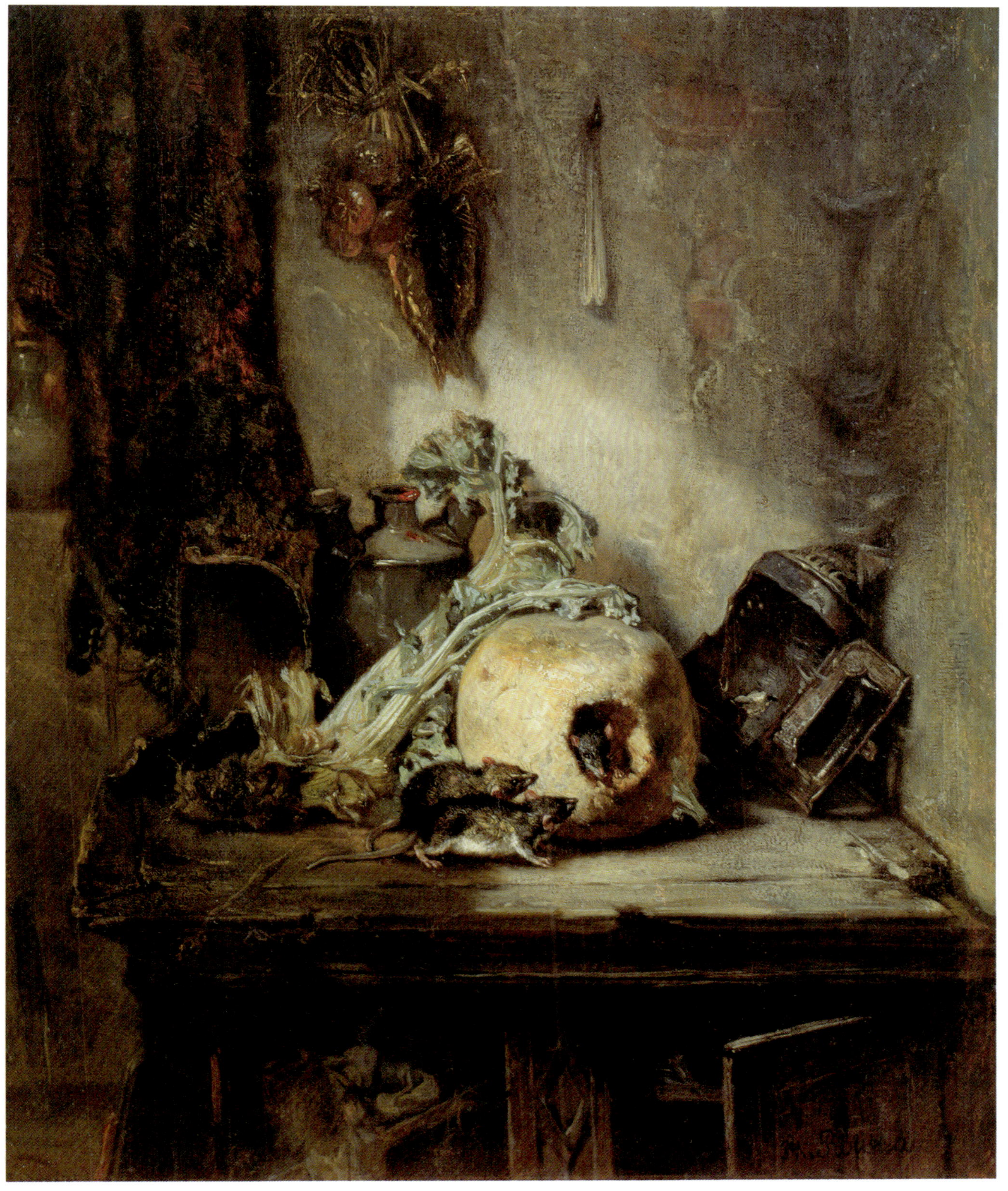

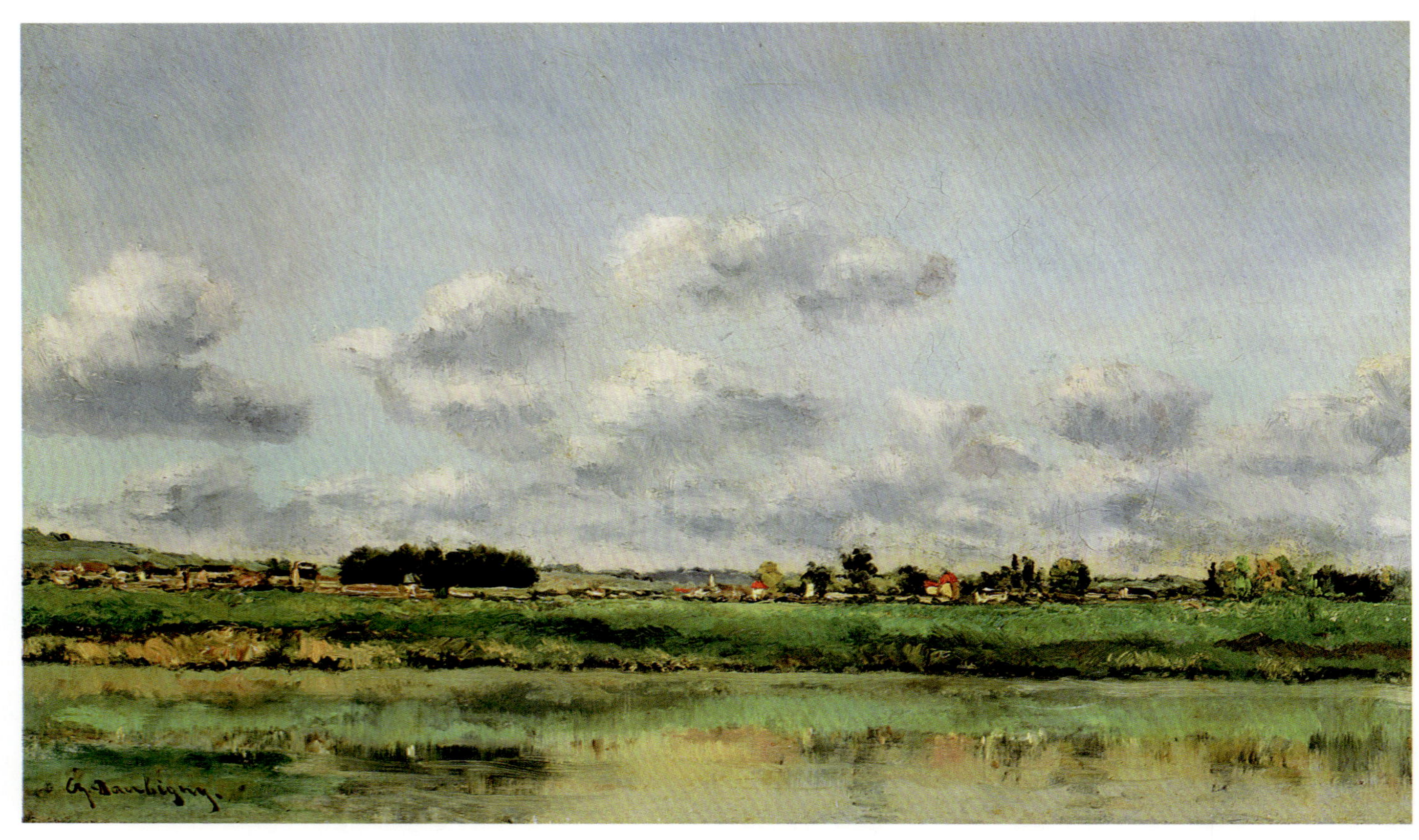

Charles-François Daubigny (1817–78)

The Banks of the Loing

Au bord du Loing

Das Ufer des Loing

A orillas del Loing

A Margem do Loing

De oever van de Loing

c. 1850, Oil on canvas/Huile sur toile, 25,5 × 41 cm

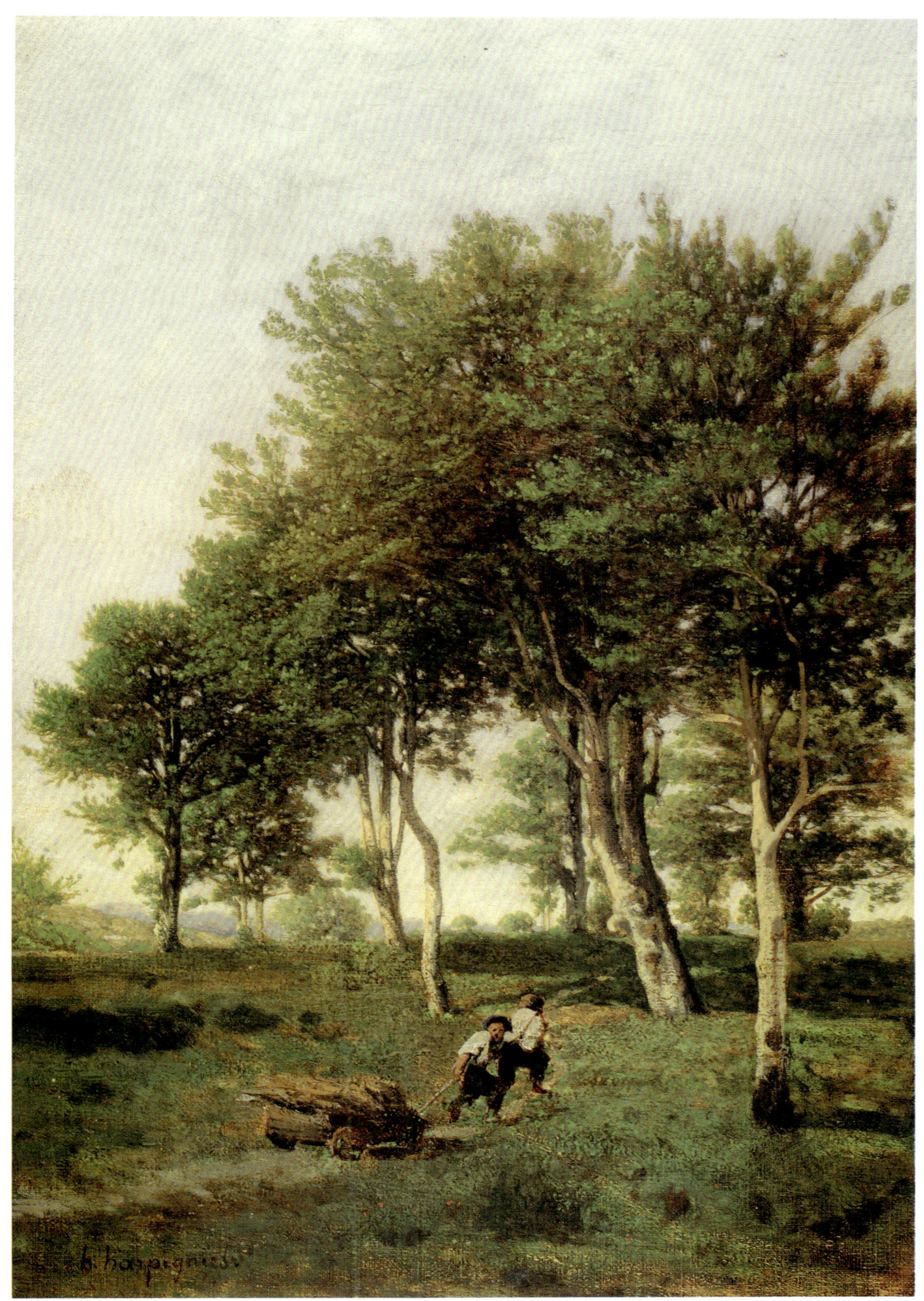

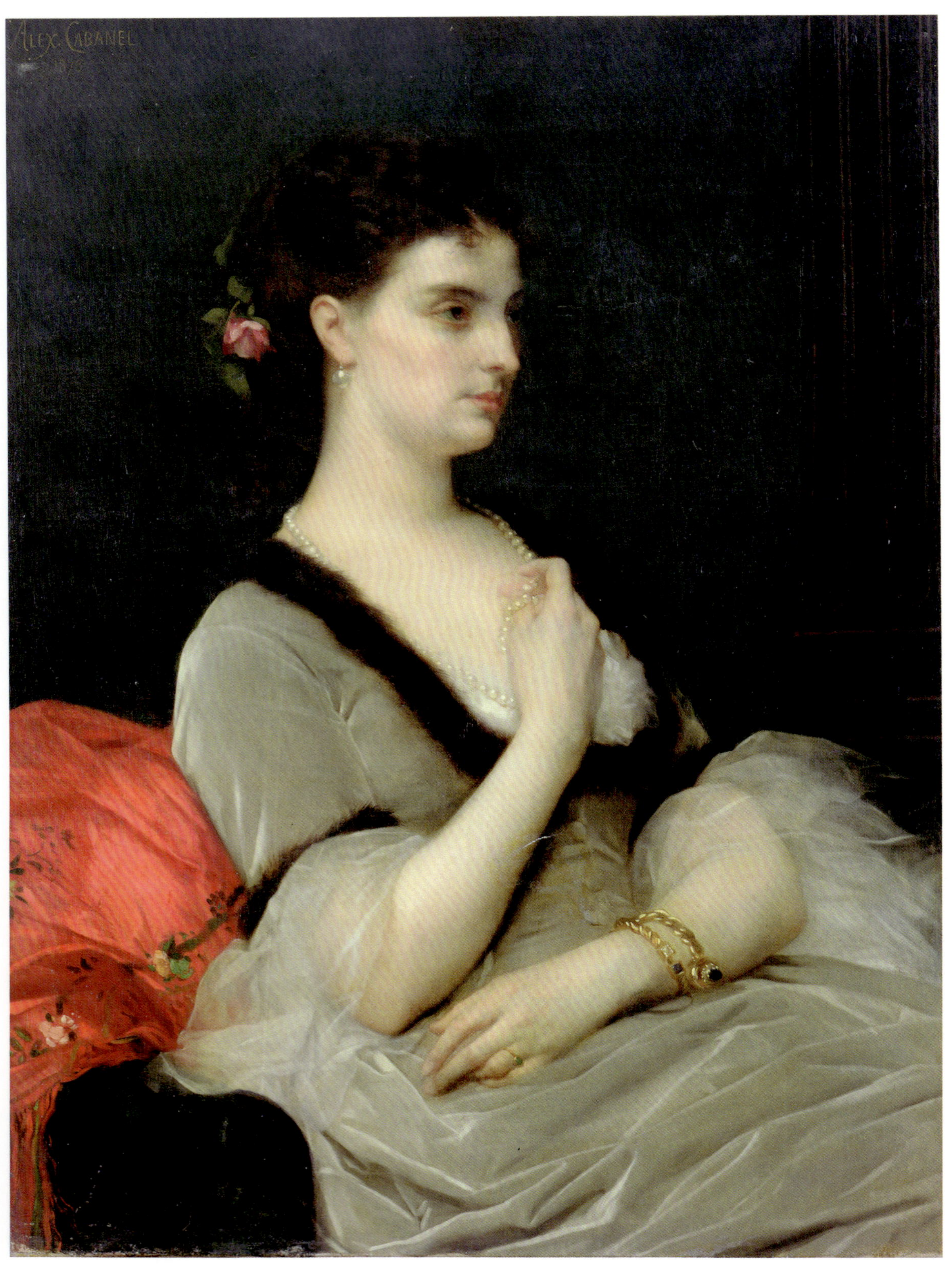

Alexandre Cabanel
(1823–89)

Princess Elizabeth
Vorontsova-Dashkova

Portrait de la comtesse
Elizabeth Vorontsova-
Dashkova

Fürstin Jelisaweta
Woronzowa-Daschkowa

La Princesa Yelisaveta
Voronzova-Daschkova

Princesa Catarina
Vorontsova-Dashkova

Vorstin Elisabeth
(Jelisaveta) Voronzova-
Dasjkova

1873, Oil on canvas/Huile
sur toile, 99 × 73 cm

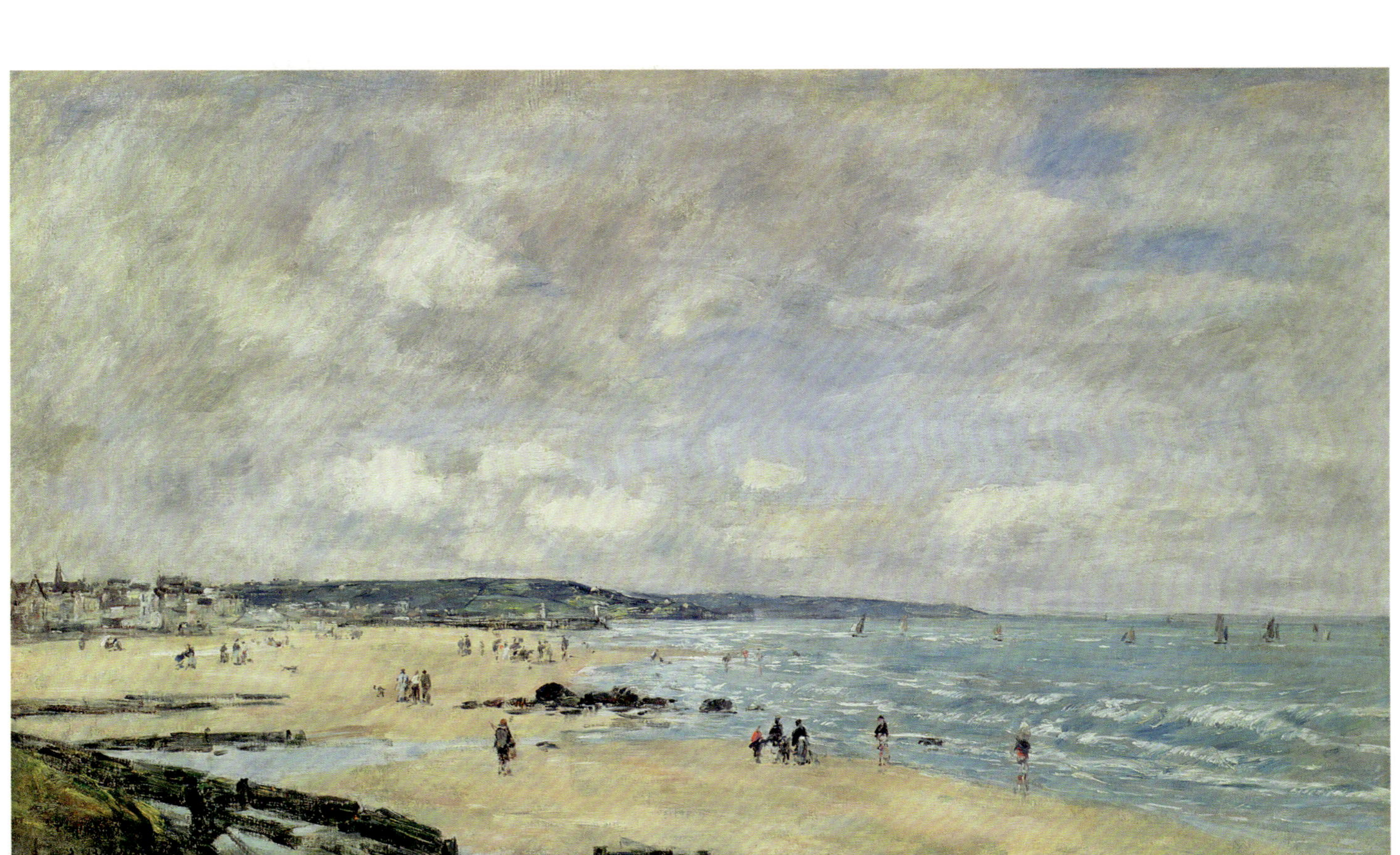

Eugène Louis Boudin (1824–98)

Beach at Trouville

La Plage à Trouville

Strand von Trouville

En la playa de Trouville

Praia de Trouville

Strand bij Trouville

1893, Oil on canvas/Huile sur toile, 56 × 91 cm

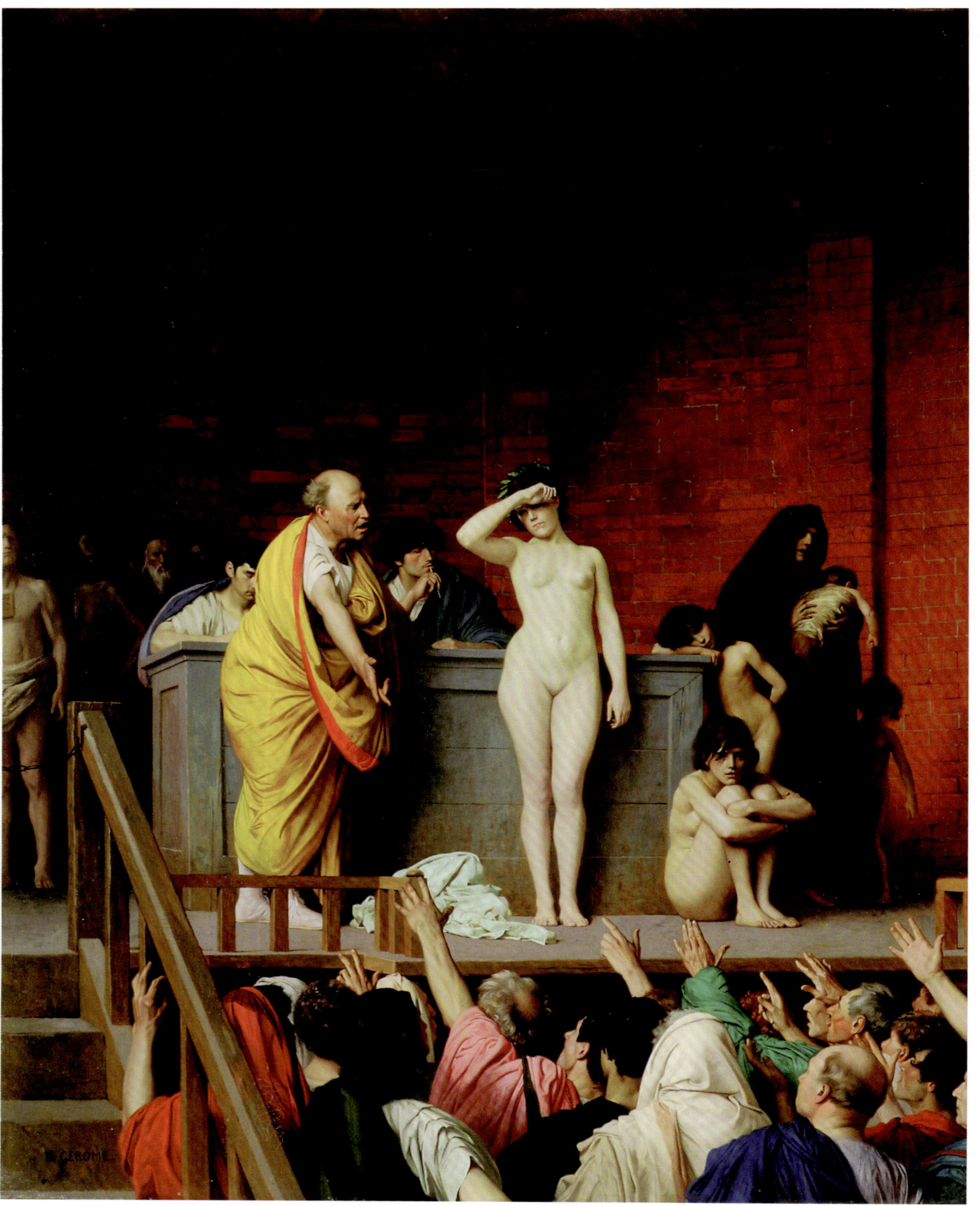

Jean-Léon Gérôme (1824–1904)

Slave Market in Rome

Vente d'esclaves à Rome

Sklavenmarkt in Rom

Mercado de esclavos en Roma

Mercado de Escravos em Roma

Slavenmarkt in Rome

1884, Oil on canvas/ Huile sur toile, 92 × 74 cm

Jean-Léon Gérôme (1824–1904)

Pool in a Harem

Une piscine dans le harem

Wasserbecken in einem Harem

Lavabo en un harén

Piscina num Harém

Bad in een harem

c. 1876, Oil on canvas/ Huile sur toile, 73,5 × 62 cm

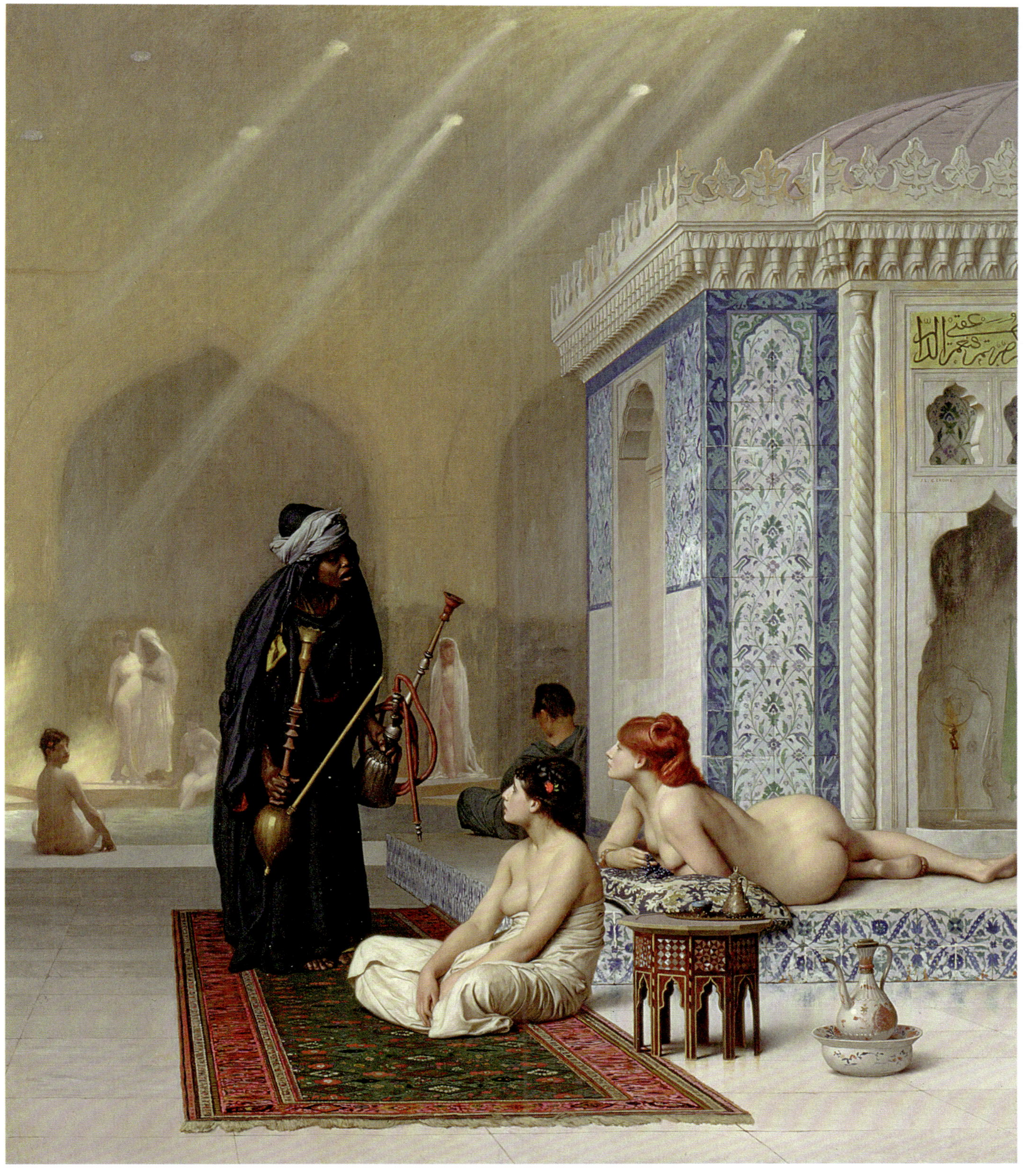

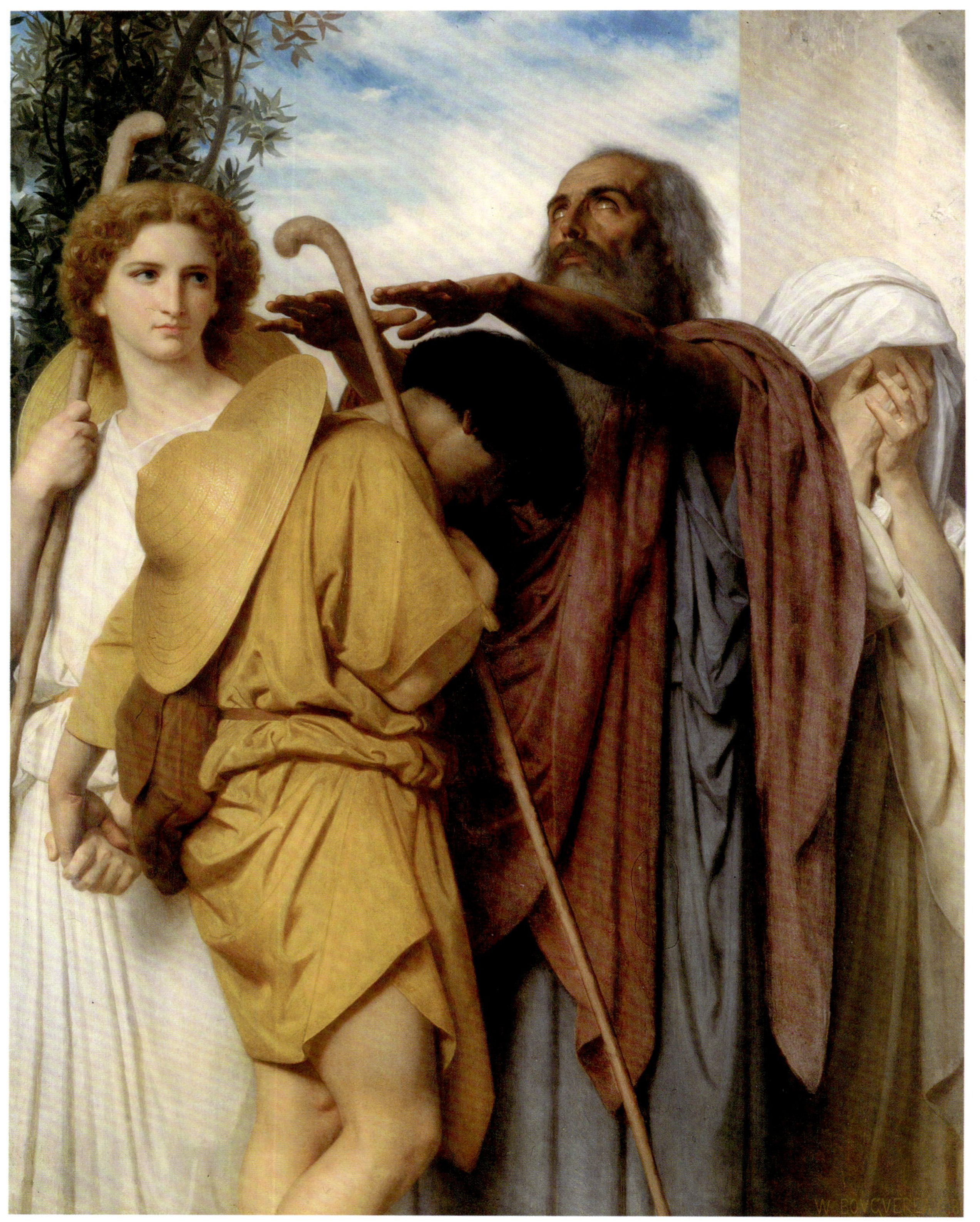

William
Bouguereau
(1825–1905)

Tobias Receiving
His Father's
Blessing

*Les Adieux de
Tobias à son père*

**Tobias erhält
den Segen
seines Vaters**

Tobías recibe
la bendición
de su padre

Tobias Recebe a
Bênção do Pai

Tobias krijgt
de zegen van
zijn vader

1860, Oil on canvas/
Huile sur toile,
153 × 119 cm

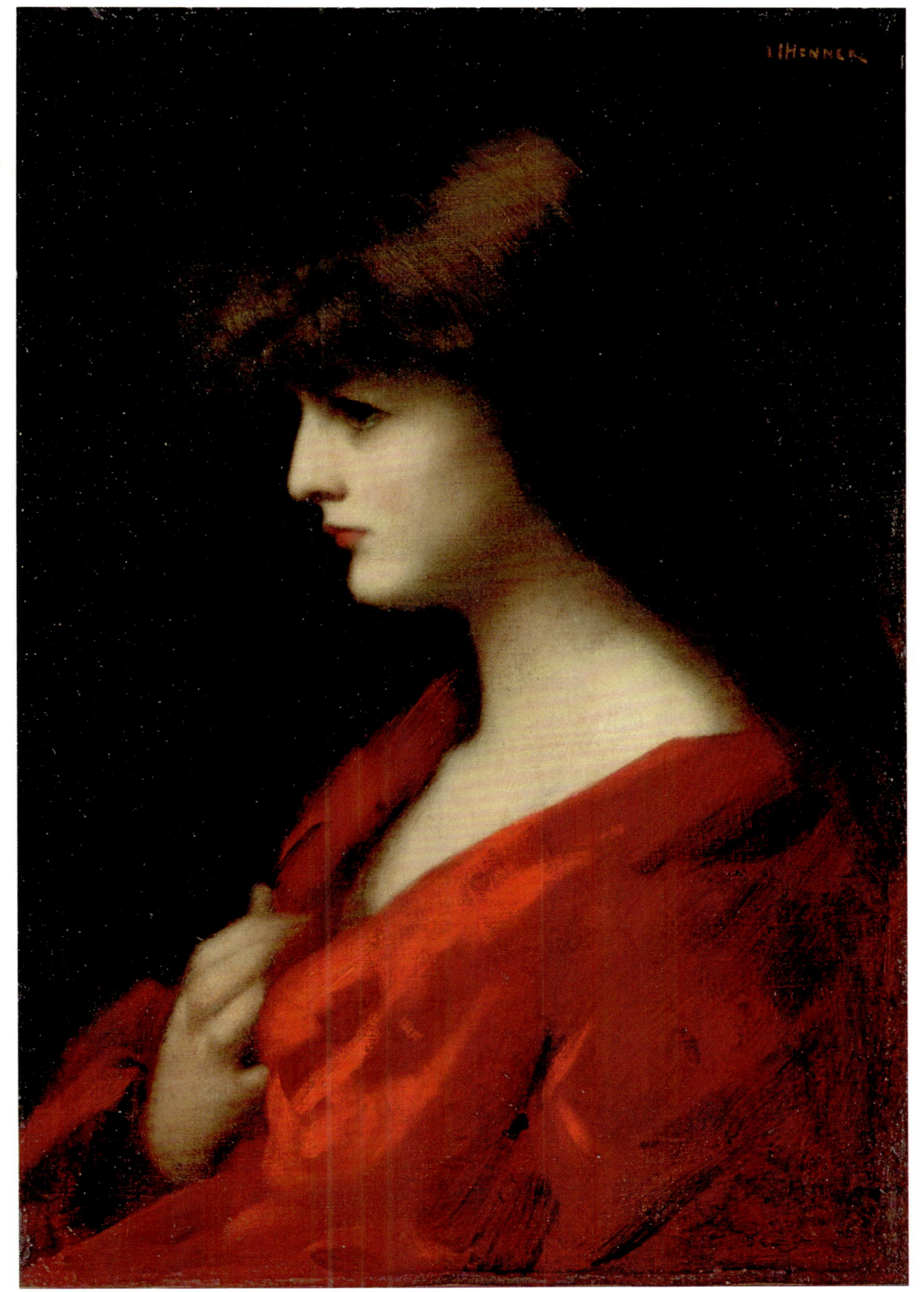

Jean-Jacques Henner (1829–1905)
Study of a Woman in Red
Étude d'une femme en rouge
Studie einer Frau in Rot
Estudio de mujer en rojo
Estudo de uma Mulher de Vermelho
Studie van een vrouw in rood
c. 1890, Oil on canvas/Huile
sur toile, 55 × 38 cm

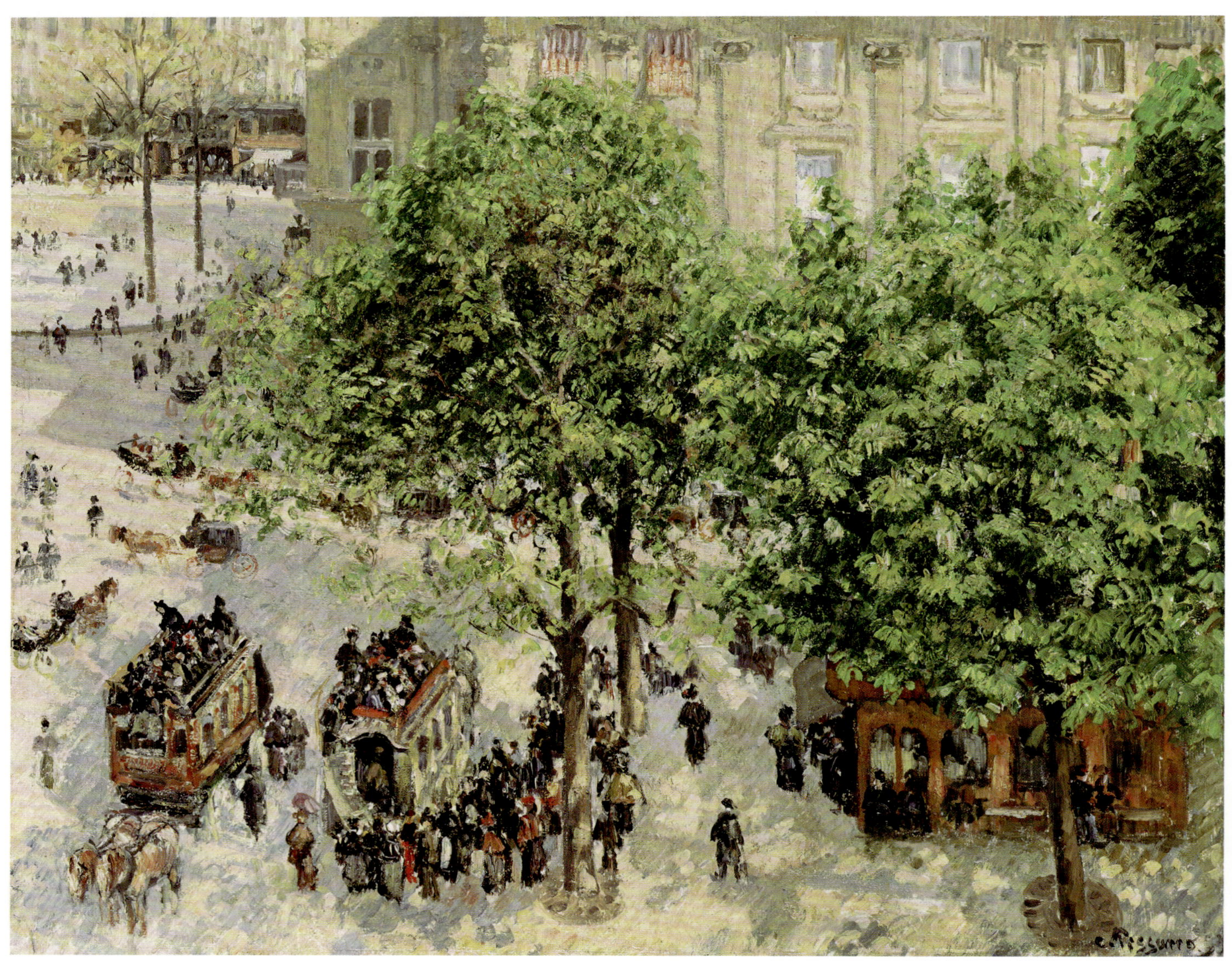

Camille Pissarro (1830–1903)
Place du Théâtre-Français in the Spring
Place du Théâtre Français en été
Place du Théâtre-Français im Frühling
La Place du Théâtre-Français en primavera
Place du Théâtre-Français na Primavera
Place du Théâtre-Français in het voorjaar
1898, Oil on canvas/Huile sur toile, 65,5 × 81,5 cm

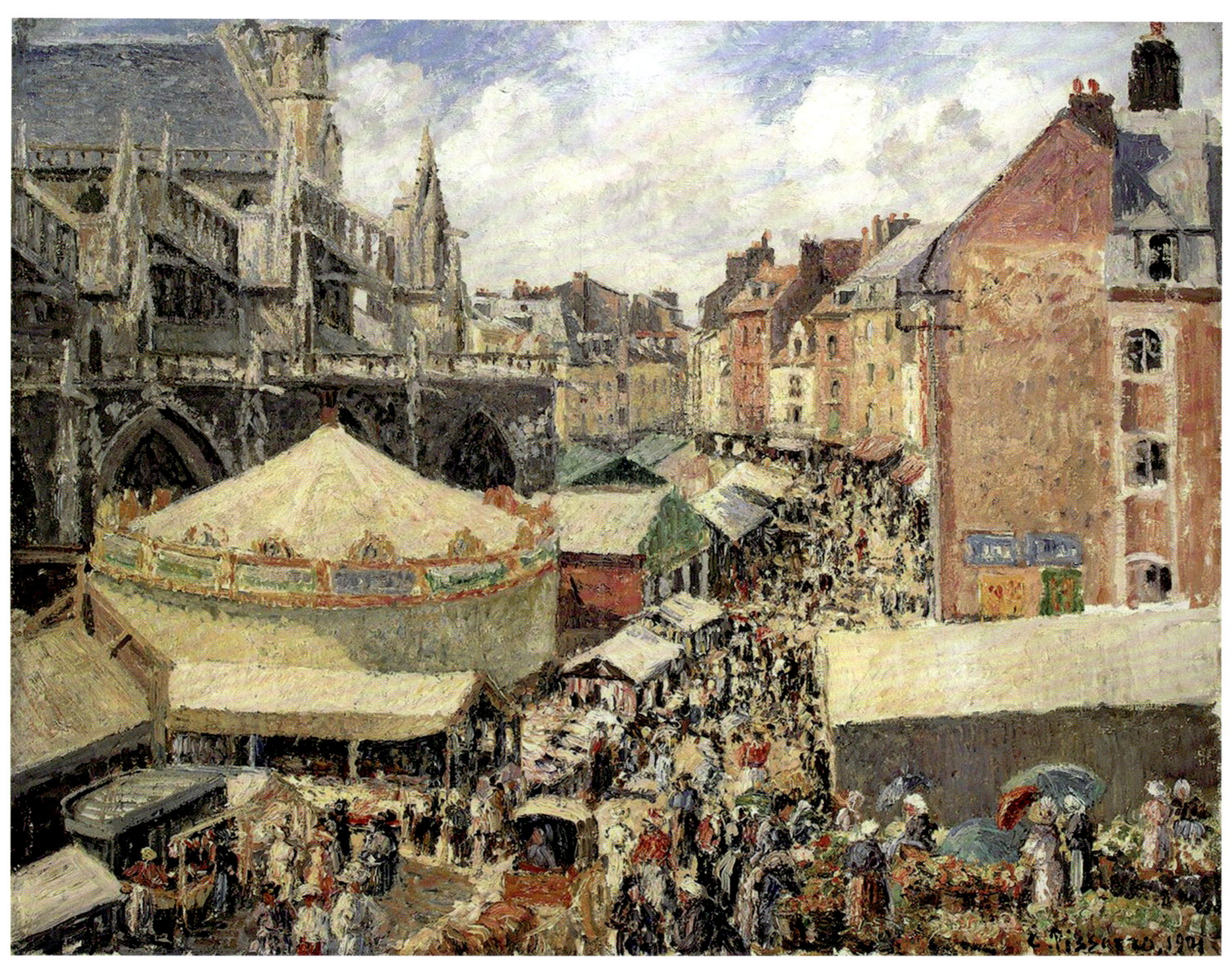

Camille Pissarro (1830–1903)

Fair in Dieppe, Sun, Morning

La Foire de Dieppe, soleil du matin

Jahrmarkt in Dieppe, Sonne, Morgen

Feria en Dieppe al sol, por la mañana

Mercado Anual em Dieppe, Sol, Manhã

De kermis in Dieppe, op een zonnige morgen

1901, Oil on canvas/Huile sur toile, 65,3 × 81,5 cm

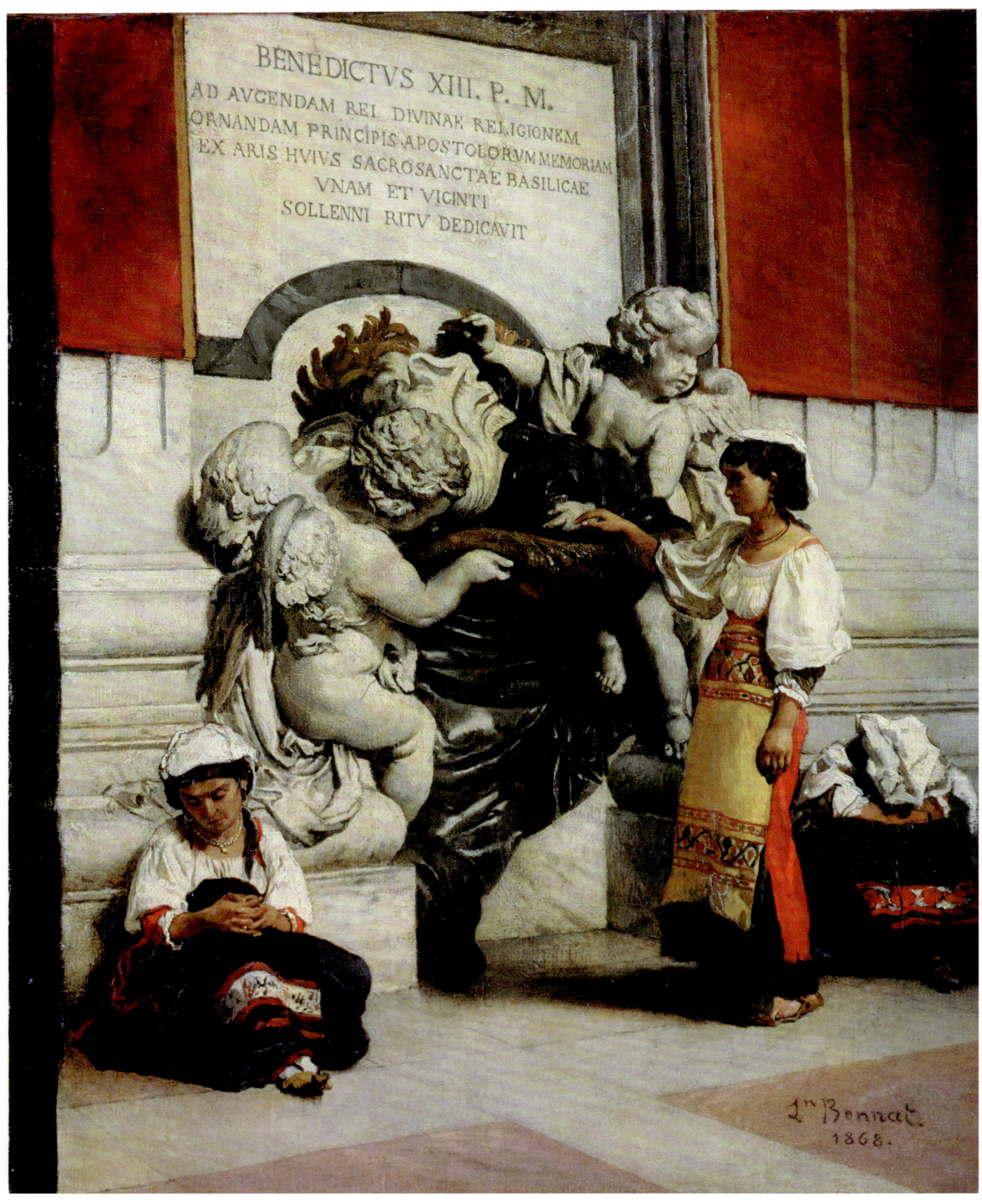
BENEDICTVS XIII. P. M.
AD AVGENDAM REI DIVINAE RELIGIONEM
ORNANDAM PRINCIPIS APOSTOLORVM MEMORIAM
EX ARIS HVIVS SACROSANCTAE BASILICAE
VNAM ET VICINTI
SOLLENNI RITV DEDICAVIT

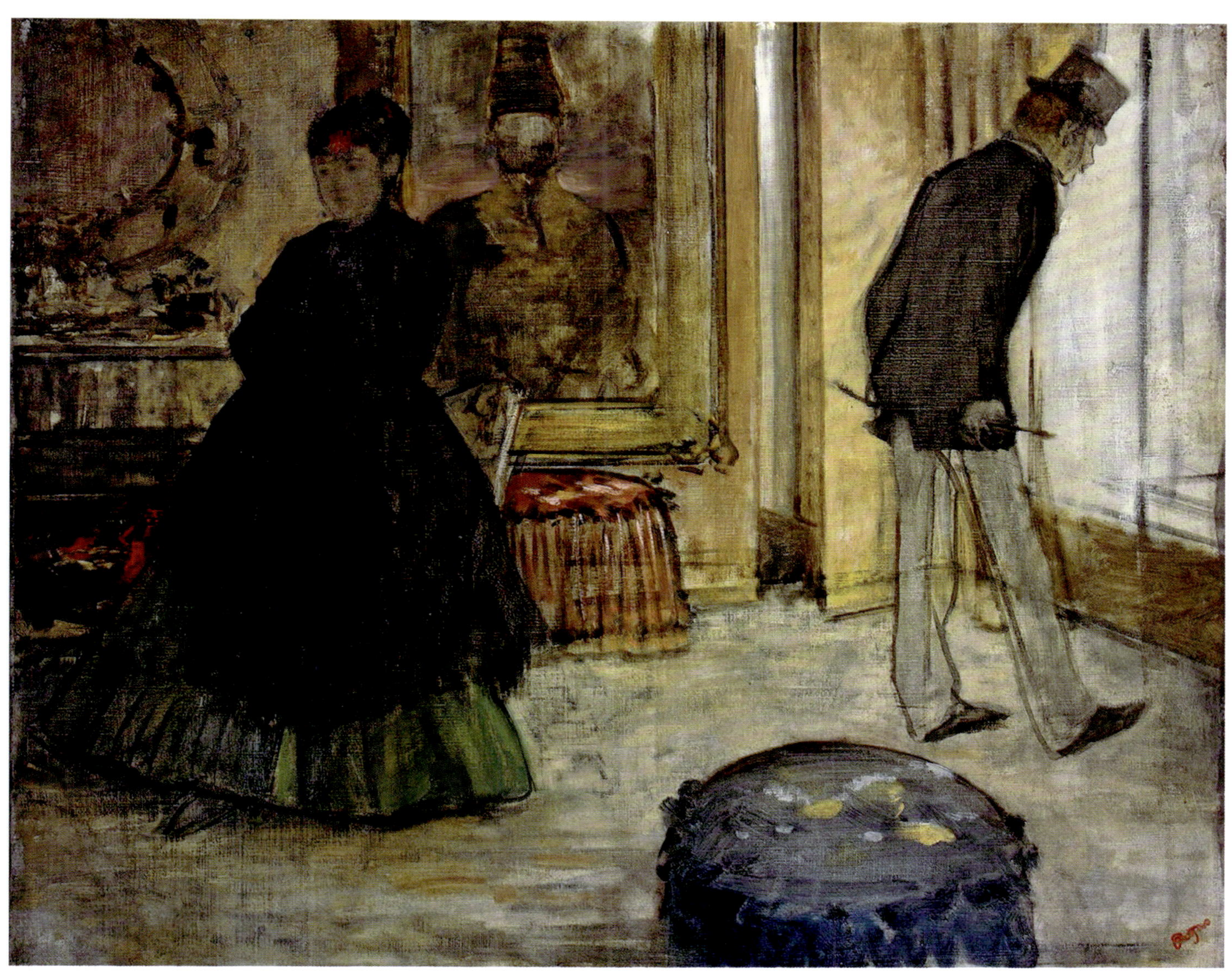

Léon Bonnat (1833–1922)

Fountain at St. Peter's in Rome

Fontaine à la basilique Saint-Pierre de Rome

Brunnen am Petersdom in Rom

Fuentes en la basílica de San Pedro, Roma

Fonte na Catedral de São Pedro em Roma

Fontein bij de Sint-Pieter in Rome

1868, Oil on canvas/Huile sur toile, 46 × 38 cm

Edgar Degas (1834–1917)

Interior with Two Figures

Intérieur avec deux personnages

Interieur mit zwei Figuren

Interior con dos personajes

Interior com Duas Figuras

Interieur met twee figuren

c. 1869, Oil on canvas/Huile sur toile, 59,5 × 73,2 cm

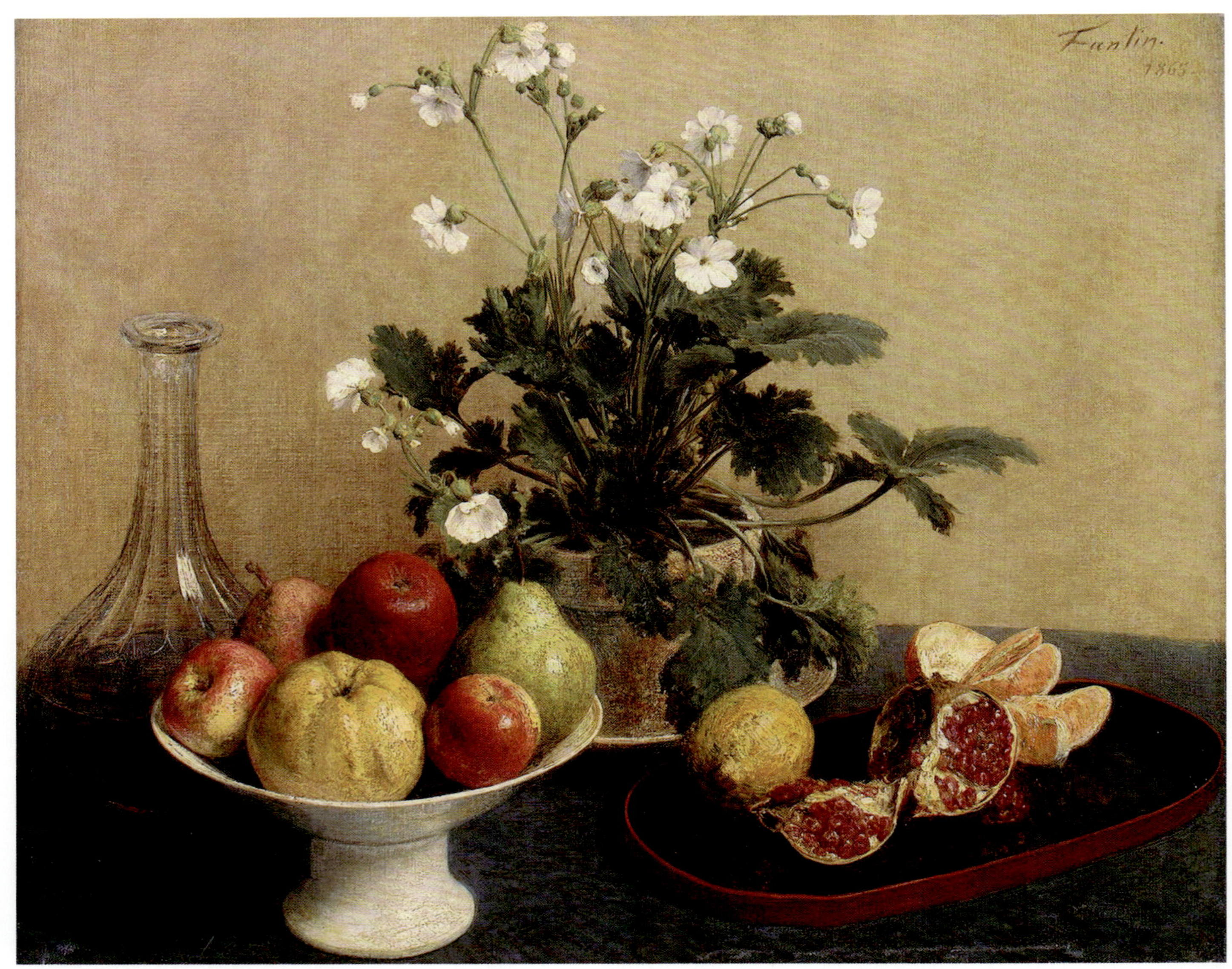

Henri Fantin-Latour (1836–1904)

Flowers, Fruit Basket, and Carafe

Nature morte avec fleurs, coupe de fruit et carafe

Blumen, Obstschale und Karaffe

Flores, frutero y jarra

Flores, Taça de Fruta e Garrafa

Bloemen, fruitschaal en karaf

1865, Oil on canvas/Huile sur toile, 55 × 68,5 cm

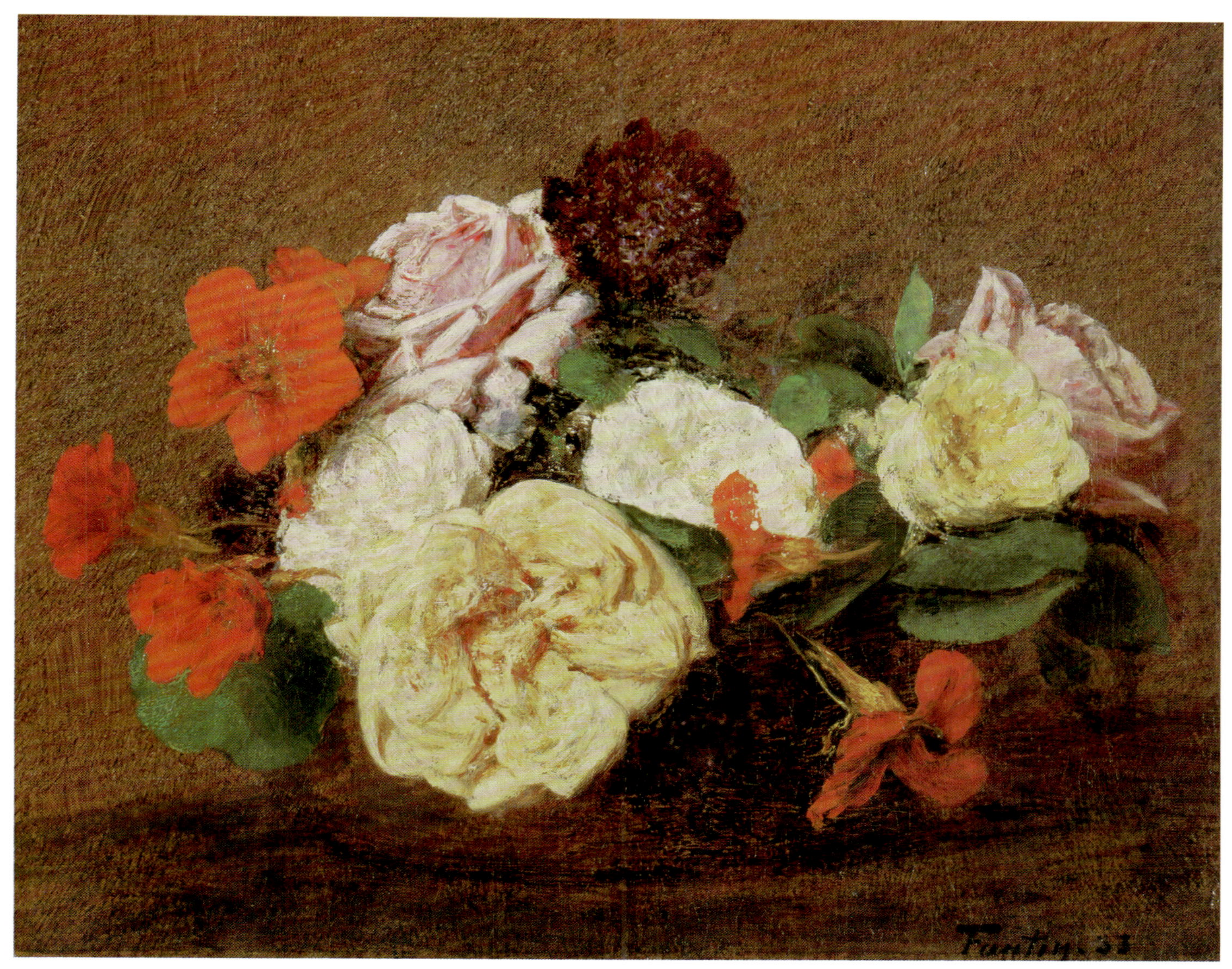

Henri Fantin-Latour (1836–1904)

Roses and Nasturtiums in a Vase

Bouquet de roses et capucines dans un vase

Rosen und Kapuzinerkresse in einer Vase

Rosas y capuchinas en un jarrón

Rosas e Nastúrcios num Jarro

Rozen en bloemen van waterkers in een vaas

1883, Oil on canvas/Huile sur toile, 28 × 36 cm

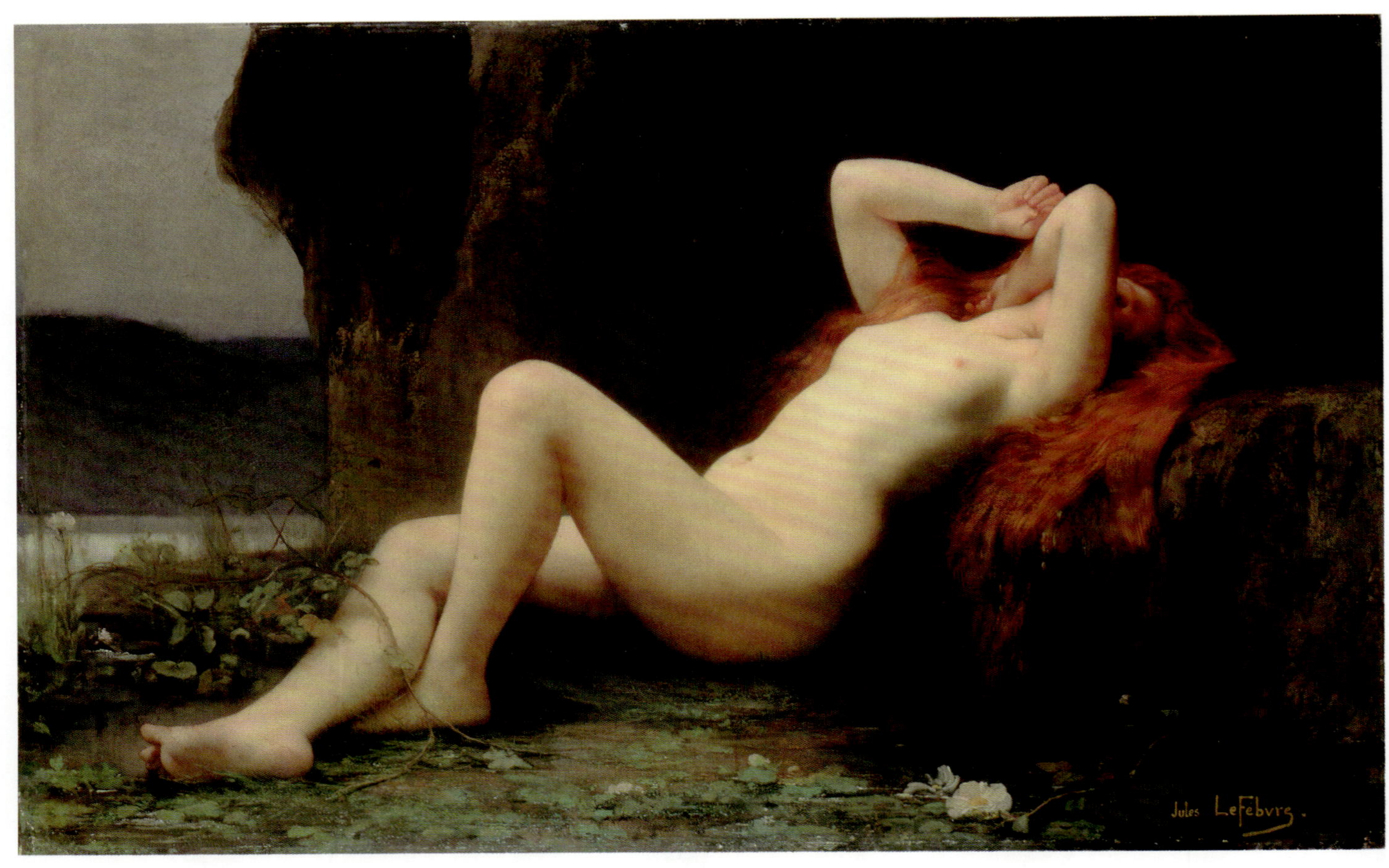

Jules Joseph Lefèbvre (1836–1912)

Mary Magdalene in the Grotto

Marie Madeleine dans la grotte

Maria Magdalena in der Grotte

María Magdalena en la cueva

Maria Madalena na Gruta

Maria Magdalena in de grot

1876, Oil on canvas/Huile sur toile, 71,5 × 113,5 cm

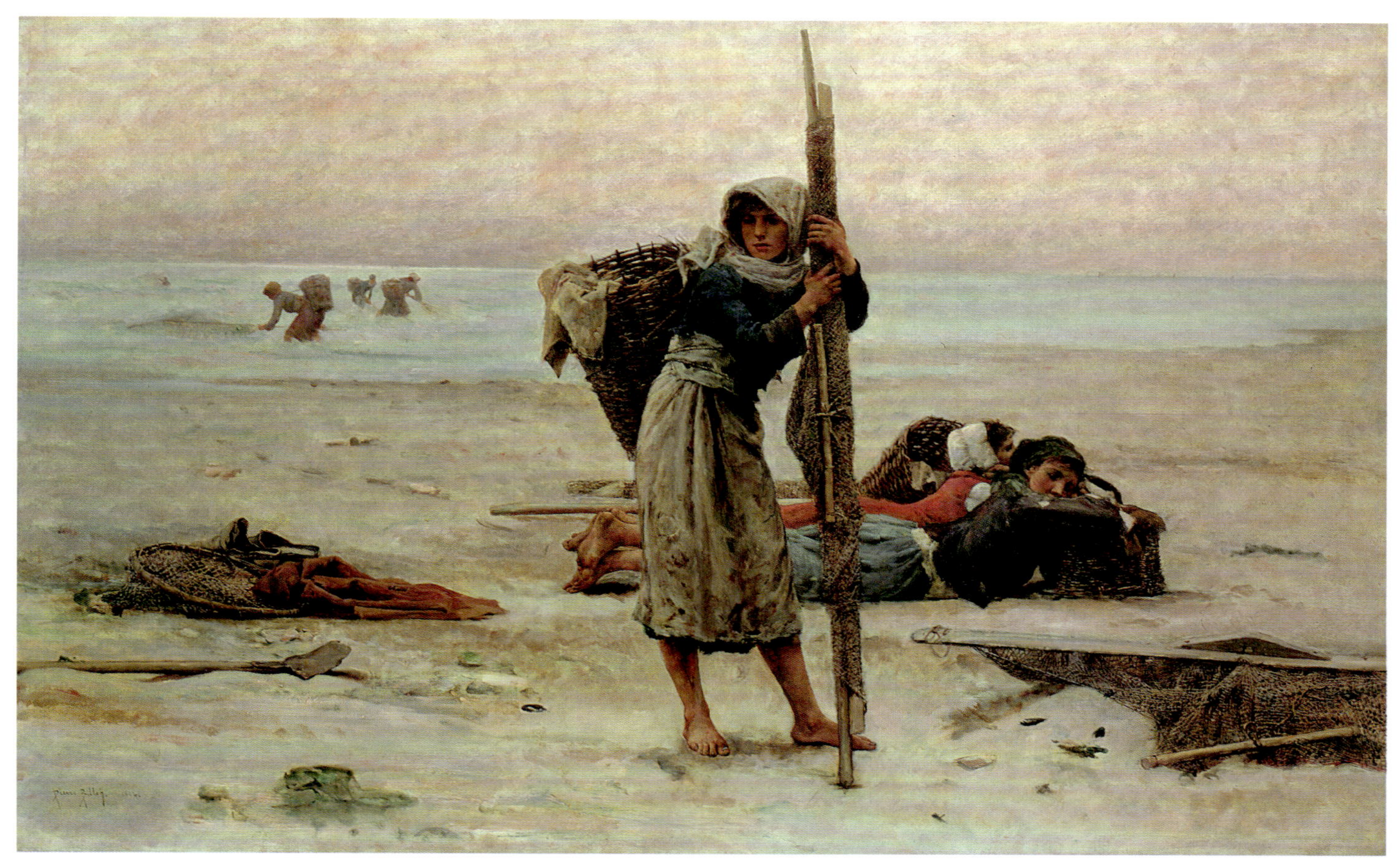

Pierre Billet (1837–1922)

Oyster Fishing

Ramasseuse d'huîtres

Austernfischen

Pescadores de ostras

Apanha de Ostras

Oestervisserij

1884, Oil on canvas/Huile sur toile, 115 × 180 cm

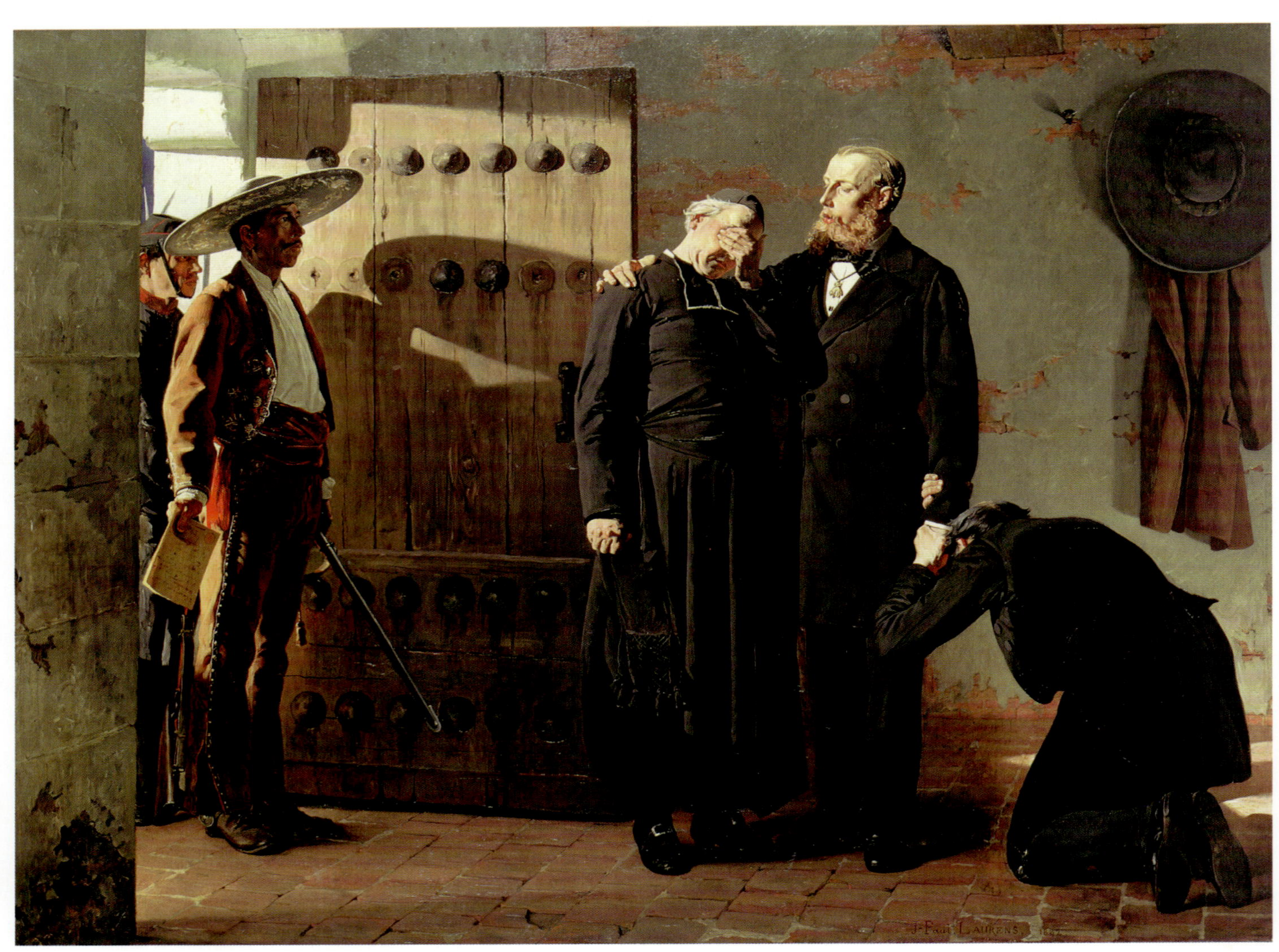

Jean-Paul Laurens (1838–1921)

The Final Moments of Emperor Maximilian of Mexico

L'Empereur Maximilien du Mexique avant son exécution

Die letzten Momente des Kaisers Maximilian von Mexiko

Los últimos momentos del emperador Maximiliano de México

Os Últimos Momentos do Imperador Maximiliano do México

De laatste momenten van keizer Maximiliaan van Mexico

1882, Oil on canvas/Huile sur toile, 222 × 303 cm

Paul Cézanne (1839–1906)

Self-Portrait

Autoportrait

Selbstbildnis

Autorretrato

Autorretrato

Zelfportret

1880/81, Oil on canvas/Huile sur toile, 55.5 × 45.5 cm

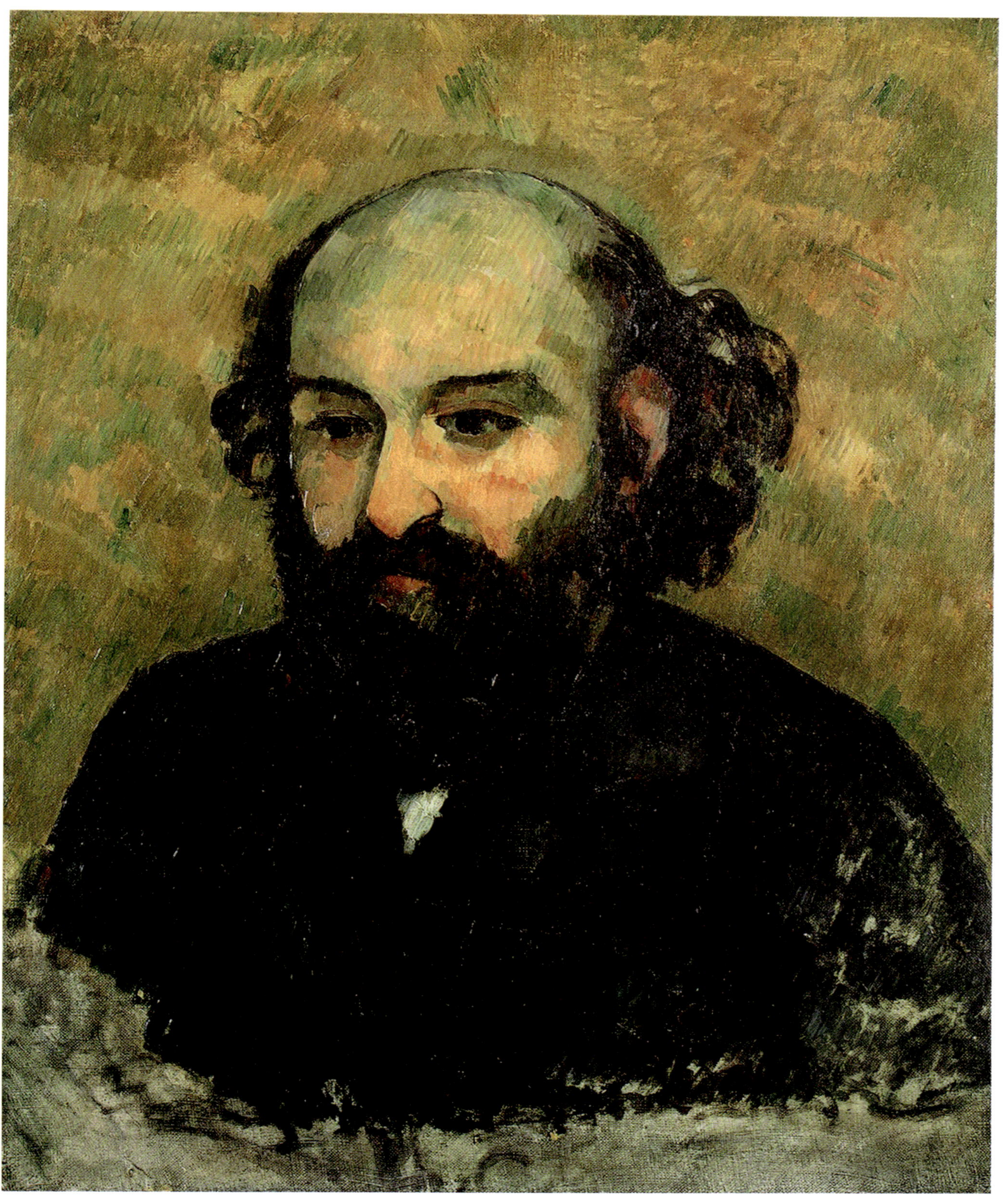

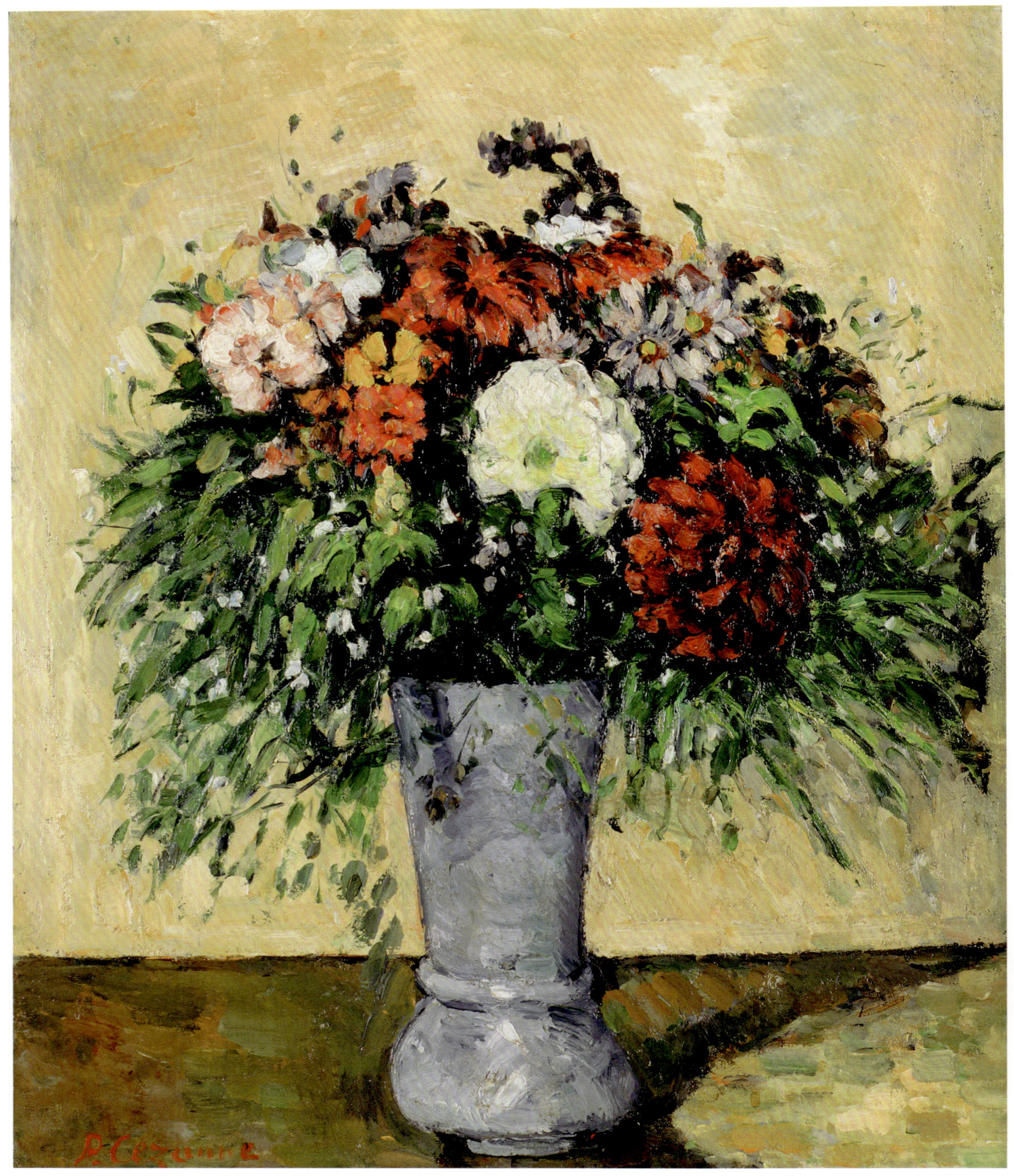

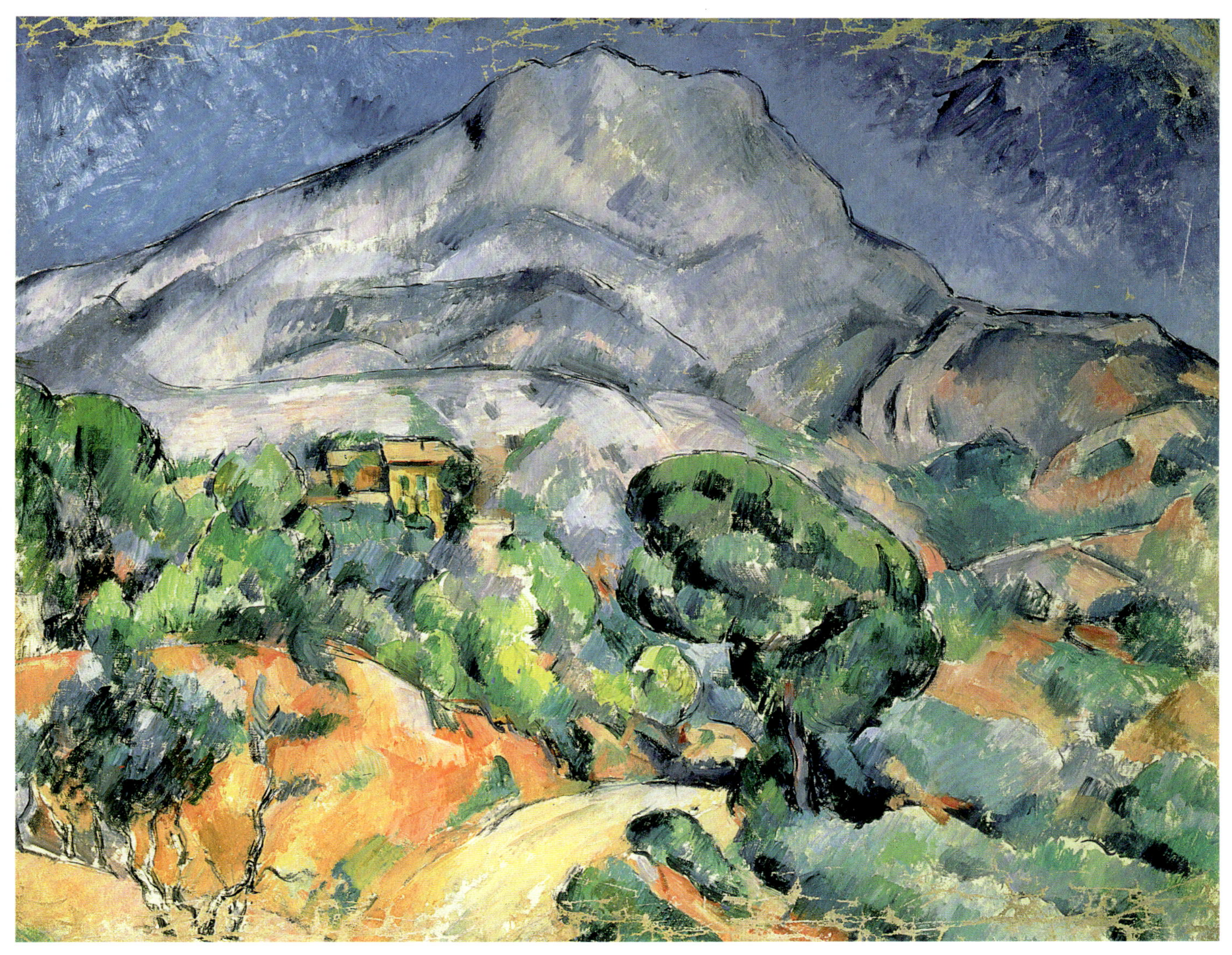

Paul Cézanne (1839–1906)

Bouquet in a Blue Vase

Fleurs dans un vase bleu

Blumenstrauß in blauer Vase

Ramo de flores en jarrón azul

Ramo de Flores num Jarro Azul

Boeket in blauwe vaas

c. 1873–75, Oil on canvas/Huile sur toile, 55,2 × 46 cm

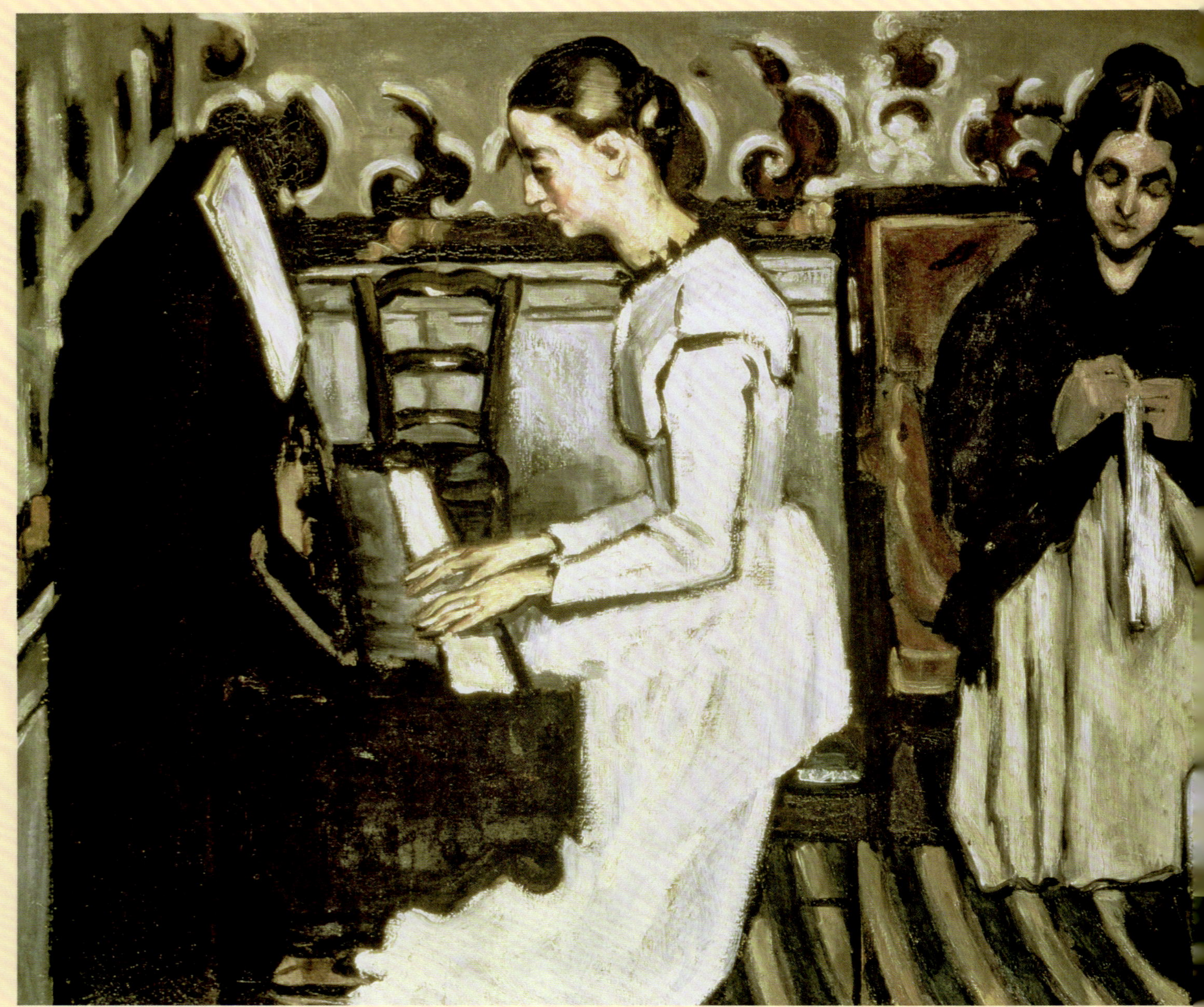

Paul Cézanne (1839–1906)

Girls at the Piano (Tannhäuser Overture)

Jeune fille au piano *ou* L'ouverture du Tannhäuser

Mädchen am Klavier (Tannhäuser-Overtüre)

Jovencita al piano (Obertura de Tannhäuser)

Jovem ao Piano (Abertura de Tannhäuser)

Meisje aan de piano (Ouverture uit Tannhäuser)

c. 1868, Oil on canvas/Huile sur toile, 57,8 × 92,5 cm

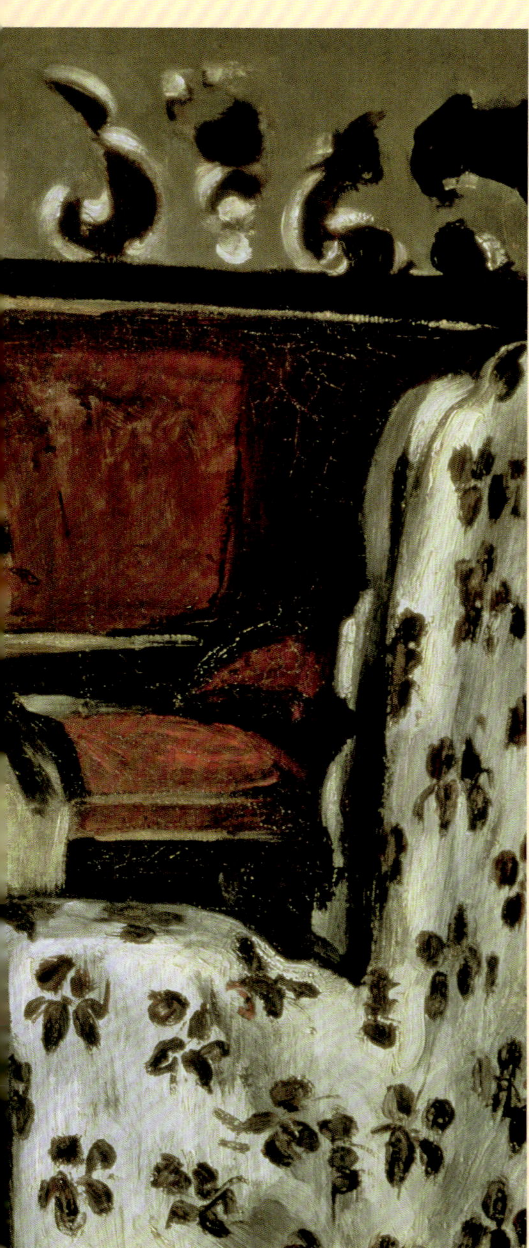

This portrait shows the domestic idyll back home in Aix which Cézanne had fled from to Paris, but still often found himself missing. A young woman sits at the piano (it is questionable whether it is Cézanne's older sister), with Cézanne's mother sewing behind her. A large wing-back chair, which another piece tells us was his father's, sits in the right-hand corner, cut off by the frame. This is a reference to the empty space in Cézanne's life, which is still occupied by his father and which he is not yet capable of filling.

Ce tableau donne à voir cette idylle d'intimité familiale que Cézanne avait fuie à Aix, mais qui lui manquait souvent à Paris. Une jeune fille – peut-être la sœur aînée du peintre ? – est assise au piano ; derrière elle, à droite, Madame Cézanne mère est occupée à coudre. Un grand fauteuil confortable – identifié comme celui du père d'après d'autres toiles de l'artiste – est coupé par l'encadrement du tableau, suggestion possible d'un « vide » que le peintre n'est pas encore en mesure de remplir.

Das Bild zeigt jene häusliche Idylle, der Cézanne aus Aix entflohen war, in Paris aber oft vermisste. Am Klavier sitzt eine junge Frau (wobei es fraglich ist, ob es sich um Cézannes ältere Schwester handelt), hinter ihr Cézannes nähende Mutter. Ein großer Ohrensessel – der anhand anderer Bilder des Künstlers als der seines Vaters zu identifizieren ist – wird rechts vom Bildrand überschnitten, ein Hinweis auf die Leerstelle in Cézannes Leben, die noch vom Vater besetzt wird und die einzunehmen er noch nicht imstande ist.

La imagen muestra el idilio hogareño del que había escapado Cézanne, pero que echaba de menos a menudo desde París. Una joven se sienta al piano (es cuestionable si se trata de la hermana mayor de Cézanne), y tras ella la madre de Cézanne cose. Un gran sillón orejero -el cual podemos identificar como perteneciente a su padre gracias a otros cuadros- desaparece por el lado derecho, indicio de un espacio en la vida de Cézanne que todavía llena su padre y que él no está todavía en condiciones de ocupar.

A pintura mostra aquele idílio doméstico do qual Cézanne fugiu em Aix, mas do qual o artista também sentia frequentemente saudades em Paris. Uma jovem mulher está sentada ao piano (sendo questionável se não se trata da irmã mais velha de Cézanne), atrás dela a mãe de Cézanne faz trabalhos de costura. Uma grande poltrona, que com base noutras obras do artista poderá ser identificada como sendo a de seu pai, encontra-se cortada à direita pela margem do quadro, tratando-se de uma indicação do espaço vazio na vida de Cézanne, que ainda é ocupado pelo pai e que o artista ainda não se sente preparado a preencher.

Dit schilderij toont een huiselijk tafereel dat Cézanne uit Aix was ontvlucht, maar dat hij in Parijs vaak miste. Aan de piano zit een jonge vrouw (misschien Cézannes oudere zuster) en achter haar zit Cézannes moeder te naaien. De grote fauteuil met de hoofdsteunen – die aan de hand van andere schilderijen van de schilder als zijn vaders stoel is herkend – wordt door de rechterkant van het schilderij afgesneden, een verwijzing naar de lege plaats die Cézannes vader nog in zijn leven inneemt en die hijzelf niet kan innemen omdat hij daartoe nog niet in staat is.

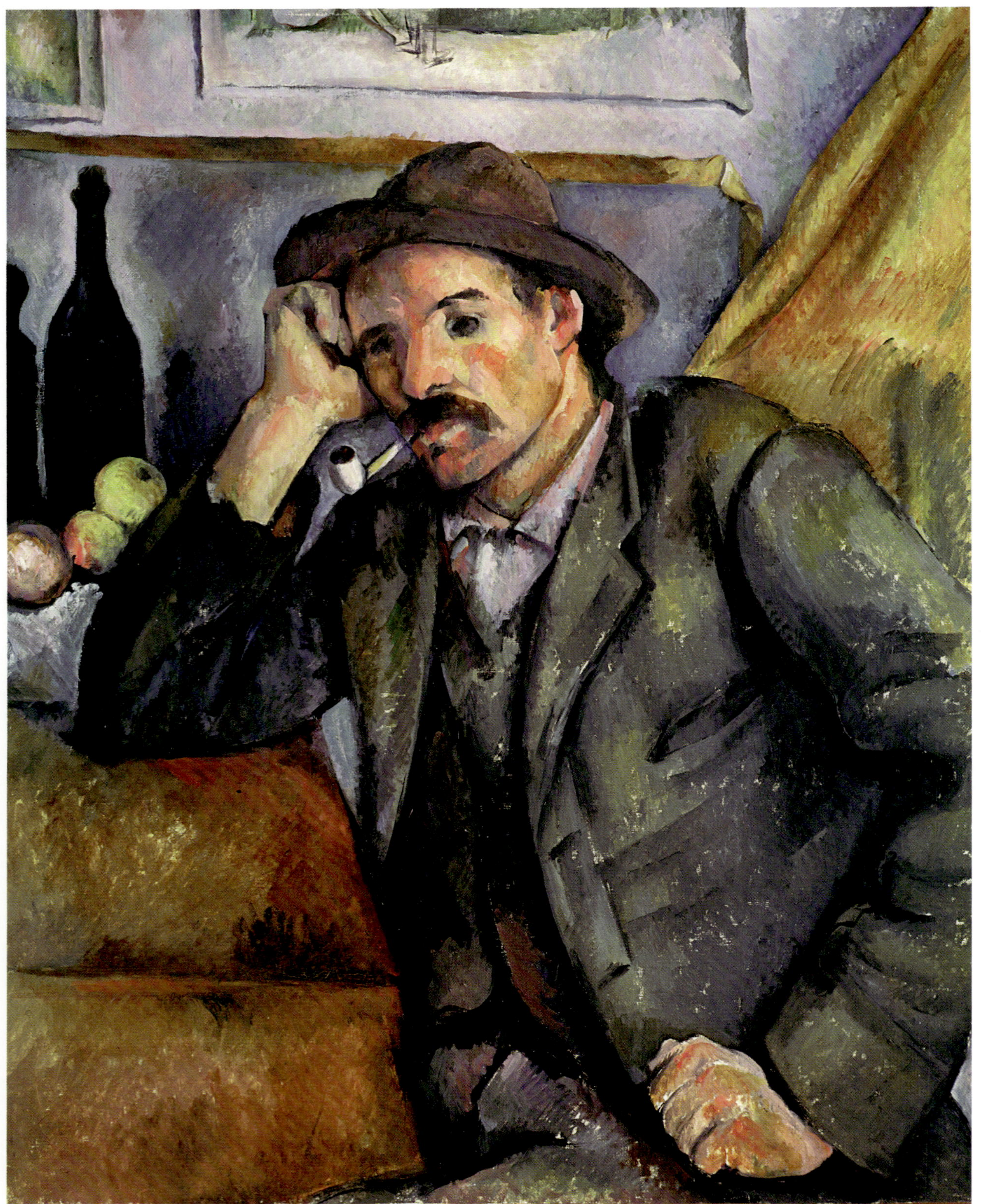

*Paul Cézanne
(1839–1906)*

The Smoker

Le Fumeur

Der Raucher

El fumador

O Fumador

De roker

c. 1890–92,
Oil on canvas/
Huile sur toile,
92,5 × 73,5 cm

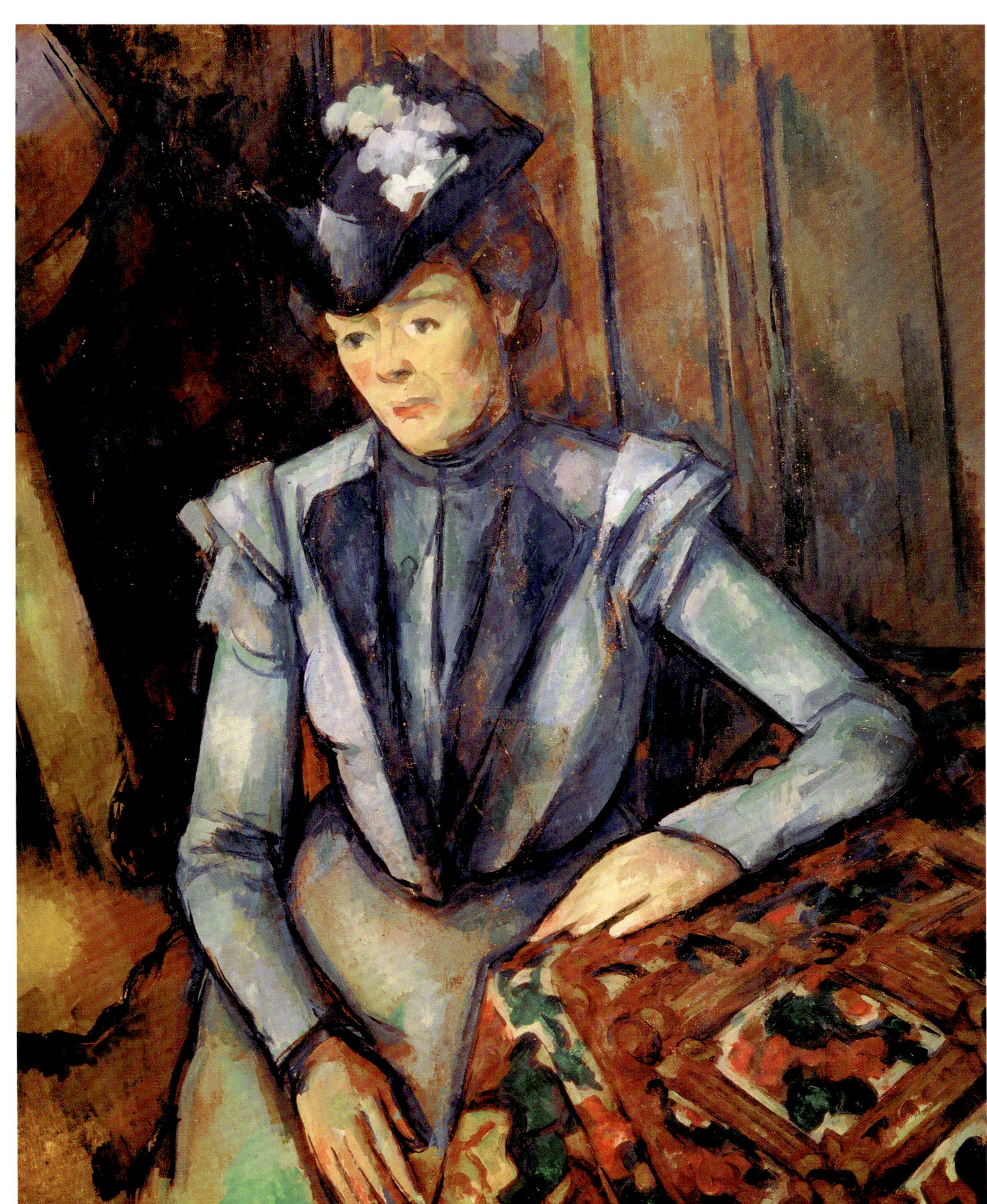

Paul Cézanne
(1839–1906)

The Woman in
Blue (Madame
Cézanne)

Femme en
bleu (madame
Cézanne)

Die Frau in
Blau (Mme
Cézanne)

La mujer de
azul (Mme
Cézanne)

A Mulher de
Azul (Mme
Cézanne)

De vrouw in
blauw (Mme
Cézanne)

1900–02, Oil
on canvas/
Huile sur toile,
90 × 73,5 cm

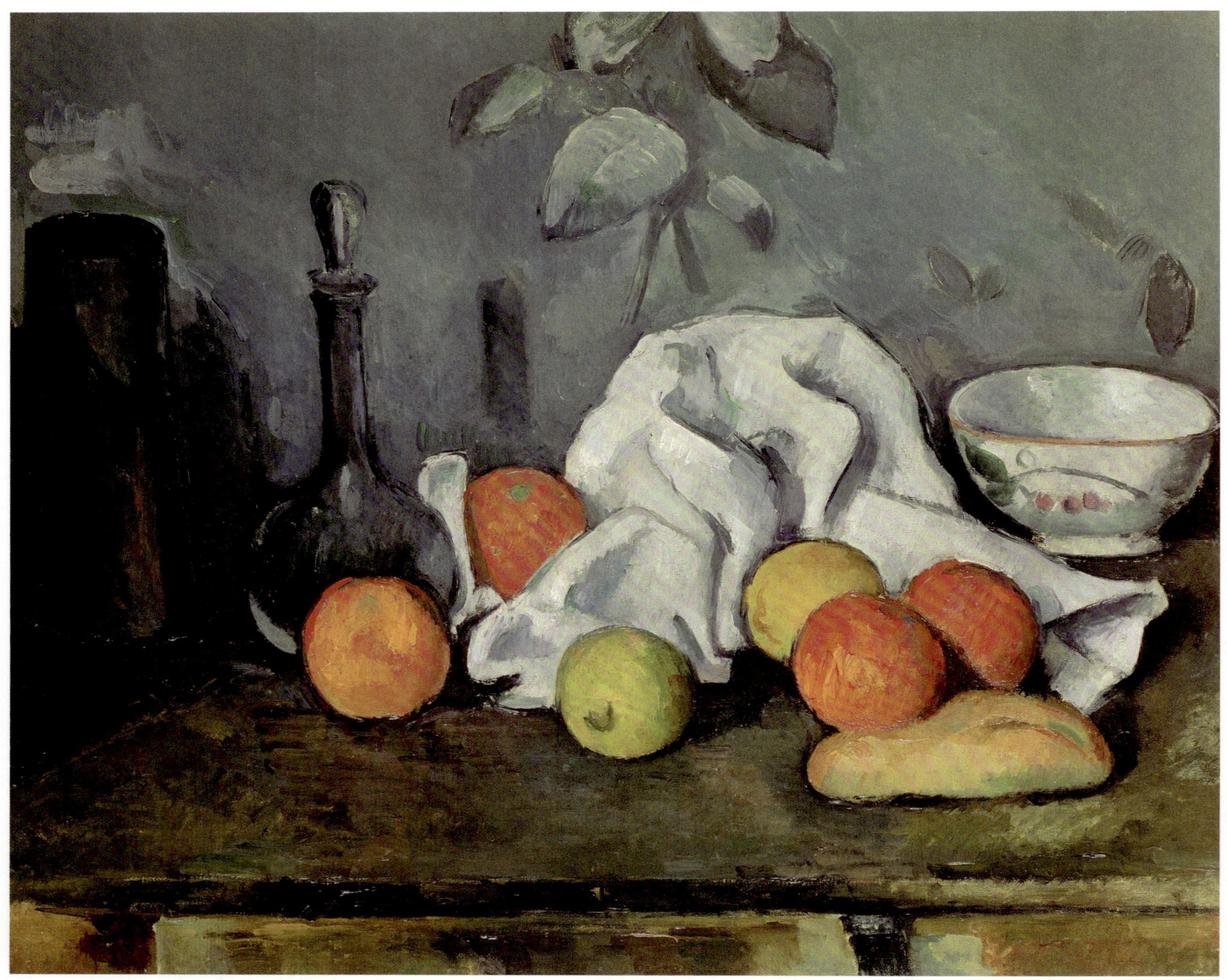

Paul Cézanne (1839–1906)

Still Life with Fruit

Nature morte aux fruits

Stillleben mit Früchten

Bodegón con frutos

Natureza-Morta com Frutos

Stilleven met vruchten

1879/80, Oil on canvas/Huile sur toile, 45 × 55,3 cm

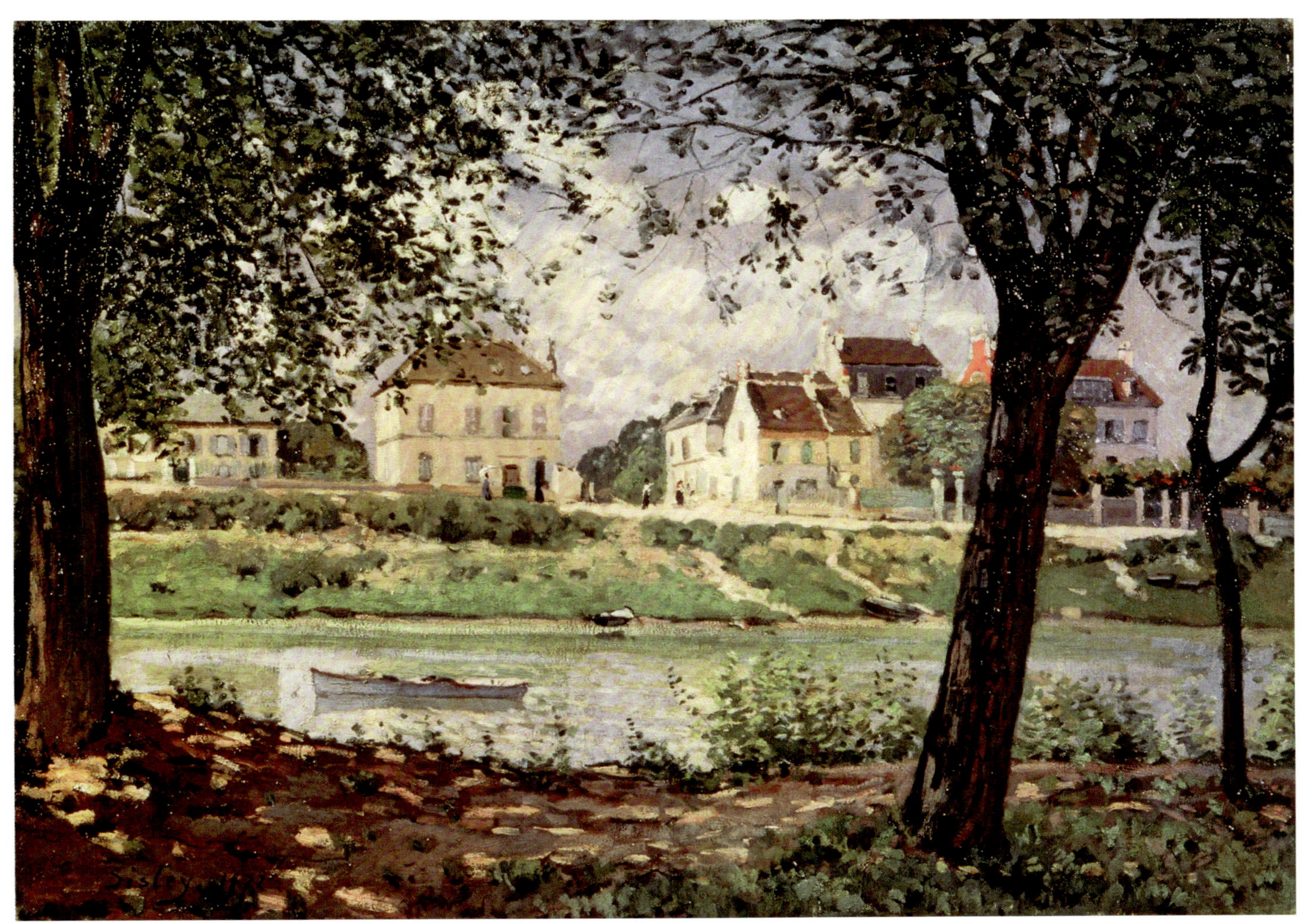

Alfred Sisley (1839−99)

Villeneuve-la-Garenne (Village on the Seine)

Villeneuve-la-Garenne (Village au bord de la Seine)

Villeneuve-la-Garenne (Dorf an der Seine)

Villeneuve-la-Garenne (Pueblo a orilla del Sena)

Villeneuve-la-Garenne (Aldeia junto ao Seine)

Villeneuve-la-Garenne (Dorp aan de Seine)

1872, Oil on canvas/Huile sur toile, 59 × 80,5 cm

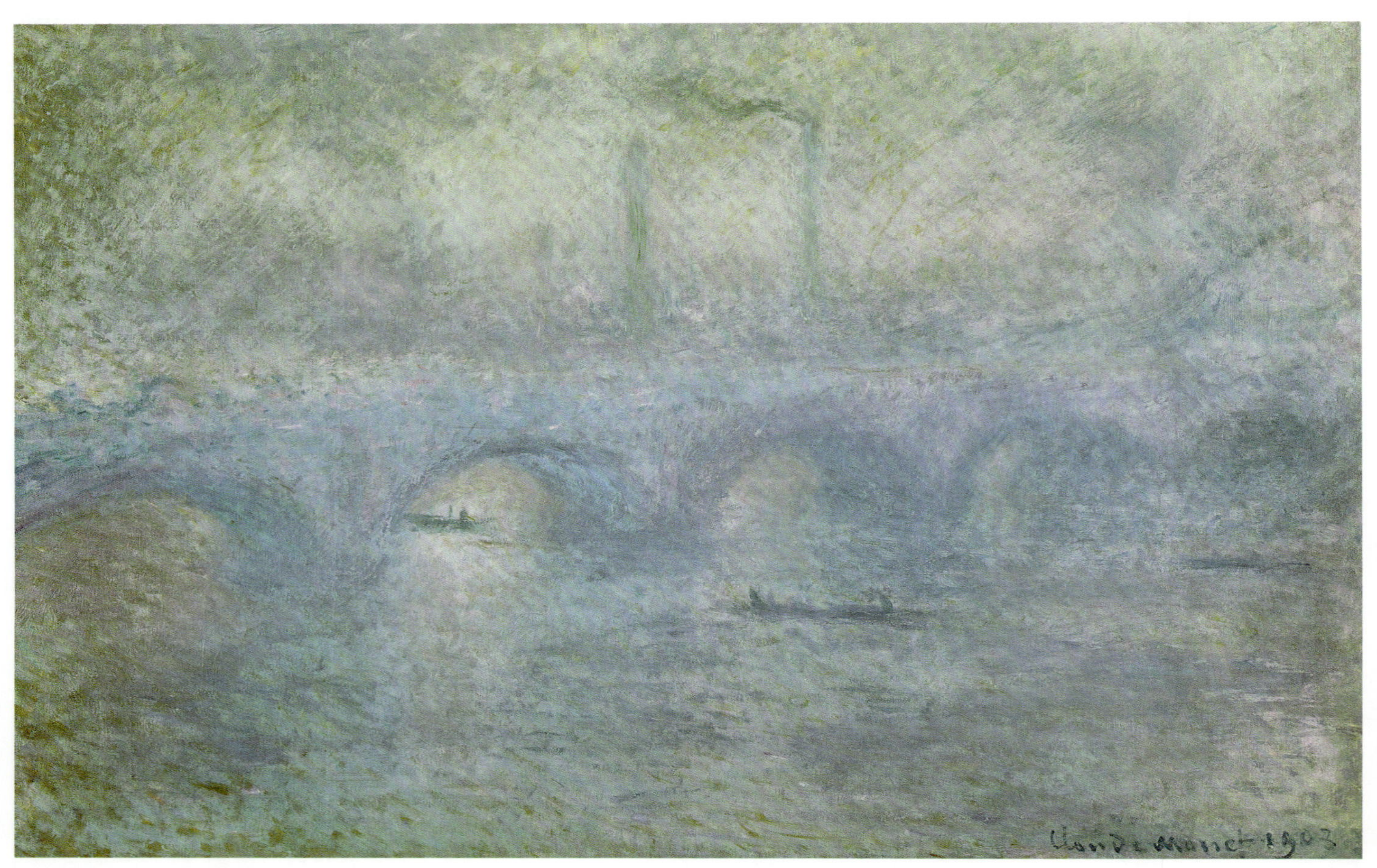

Claude Monet (1840–1926)

Waterloo Bridge in the Fog

Le Pont de Waterloo

Waterloo Bridge im Nebel

El puente de Waterloo en la niebla

Ponte de Waterloo no Nevoeiro

Waterloo Bridge in de mist

1903, Oil on canvas/Huile sur toile, 65,3 × 101 cm

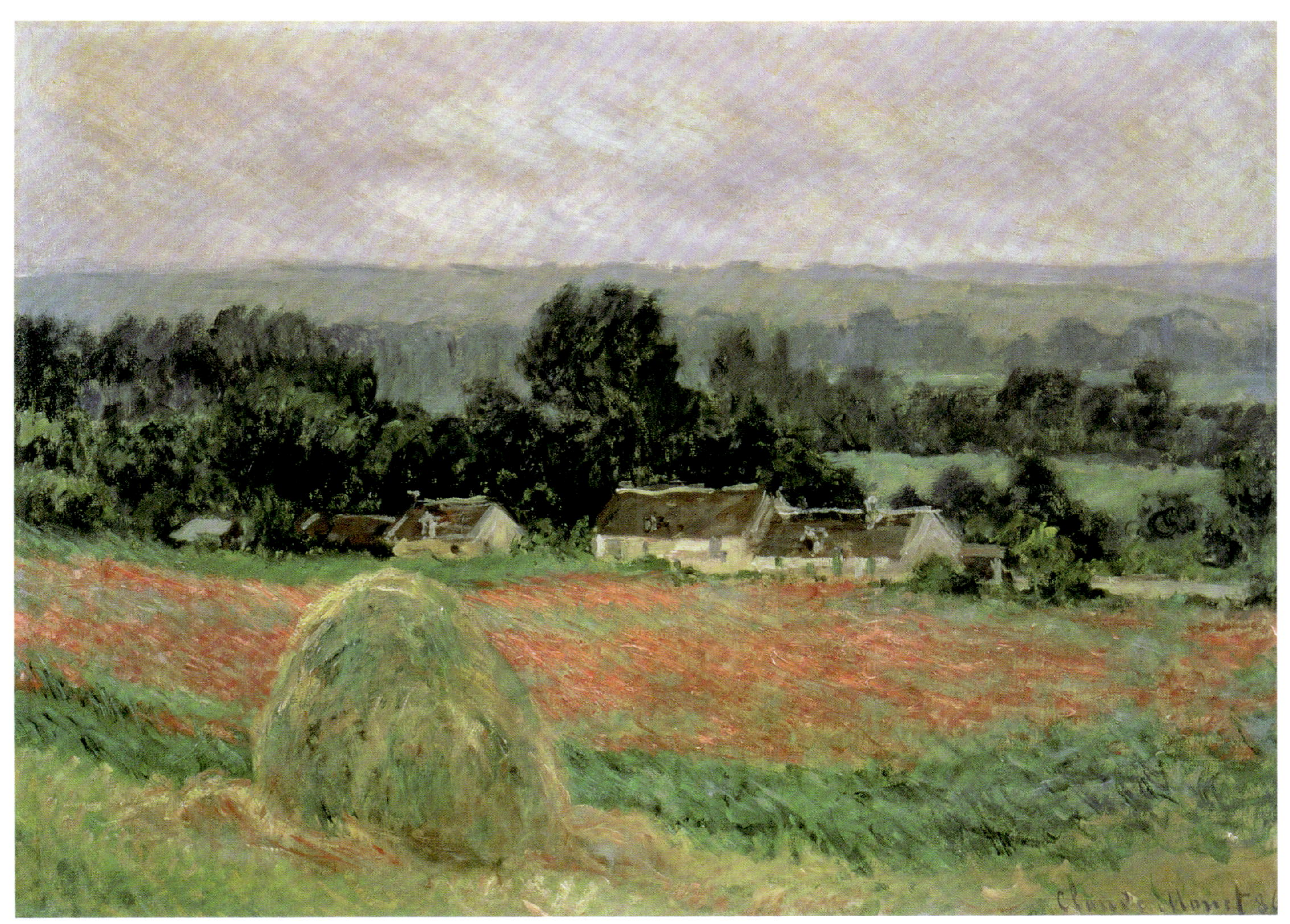

Claude Monet (1840–1926)

Haystack in Giverny

Meule à Giverny

Heuhaufen in Giverny

Montón de heno en Giverny

Fardo de Palha em Giverny

Hooiberg in Giverny

1886, Oil on canvas/Huile sur toile, 60,5 × 81,5 cm

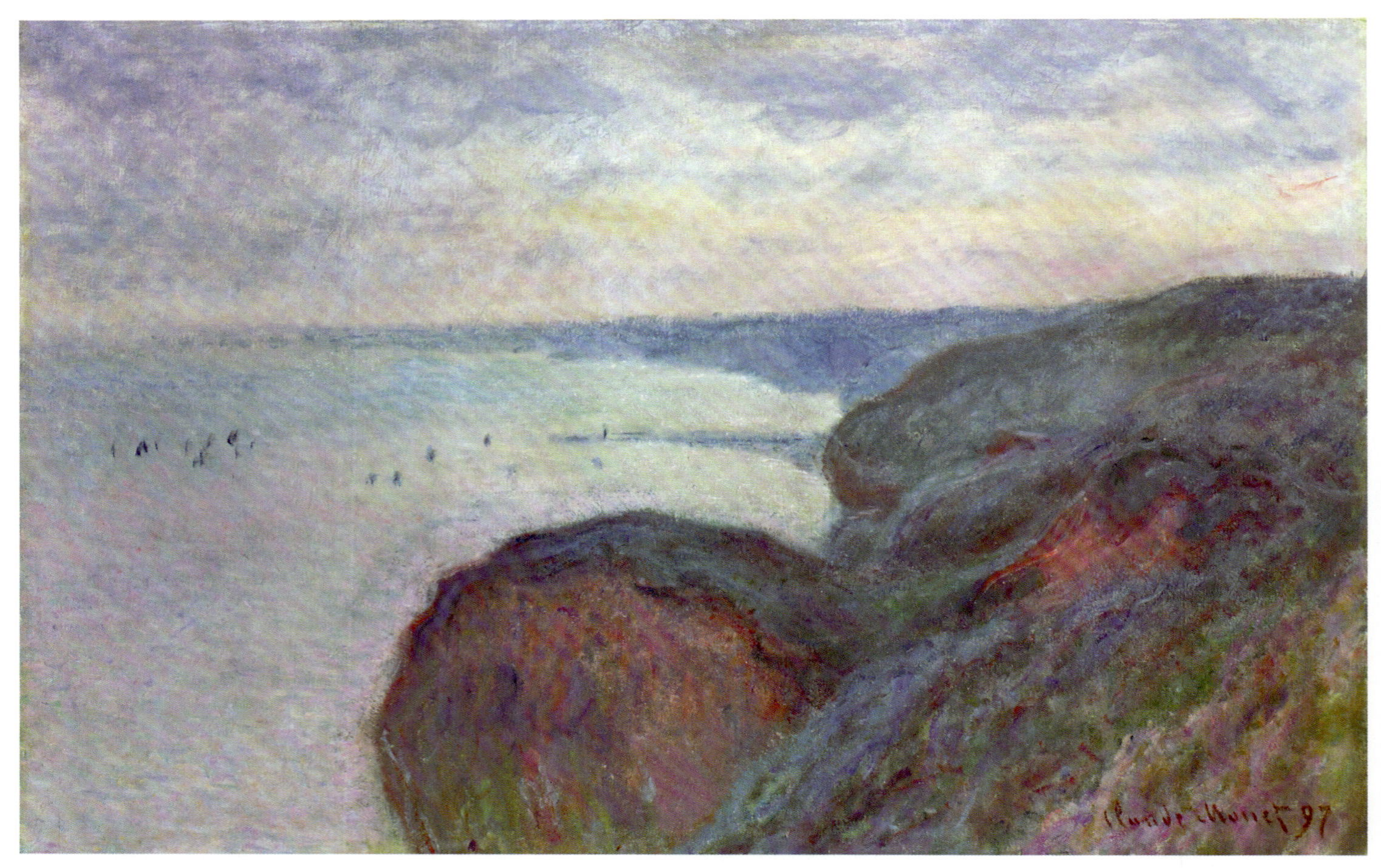

Claude Monet (1840–1926)

Cliffs at Dieppe

Les Falaises près de Dieppe

Klippen bei Dieppe

Los acantilados en Dieppe

Escarpas em Dieppe

Kliffen bij Dieppe

1897, Oil on canvas/Huile sur toile, 65,5 × 100,5 cm

Claude Monet (1840–1926)

Meadows in Giverny

Prairie à Giverny

Wiesen in Giverny

Jardín de Giverny

Prados em Giverny

Weiden in Giverny

1888, Oil on canvas/Huile sur toile, 92,5 × 81,5 cm

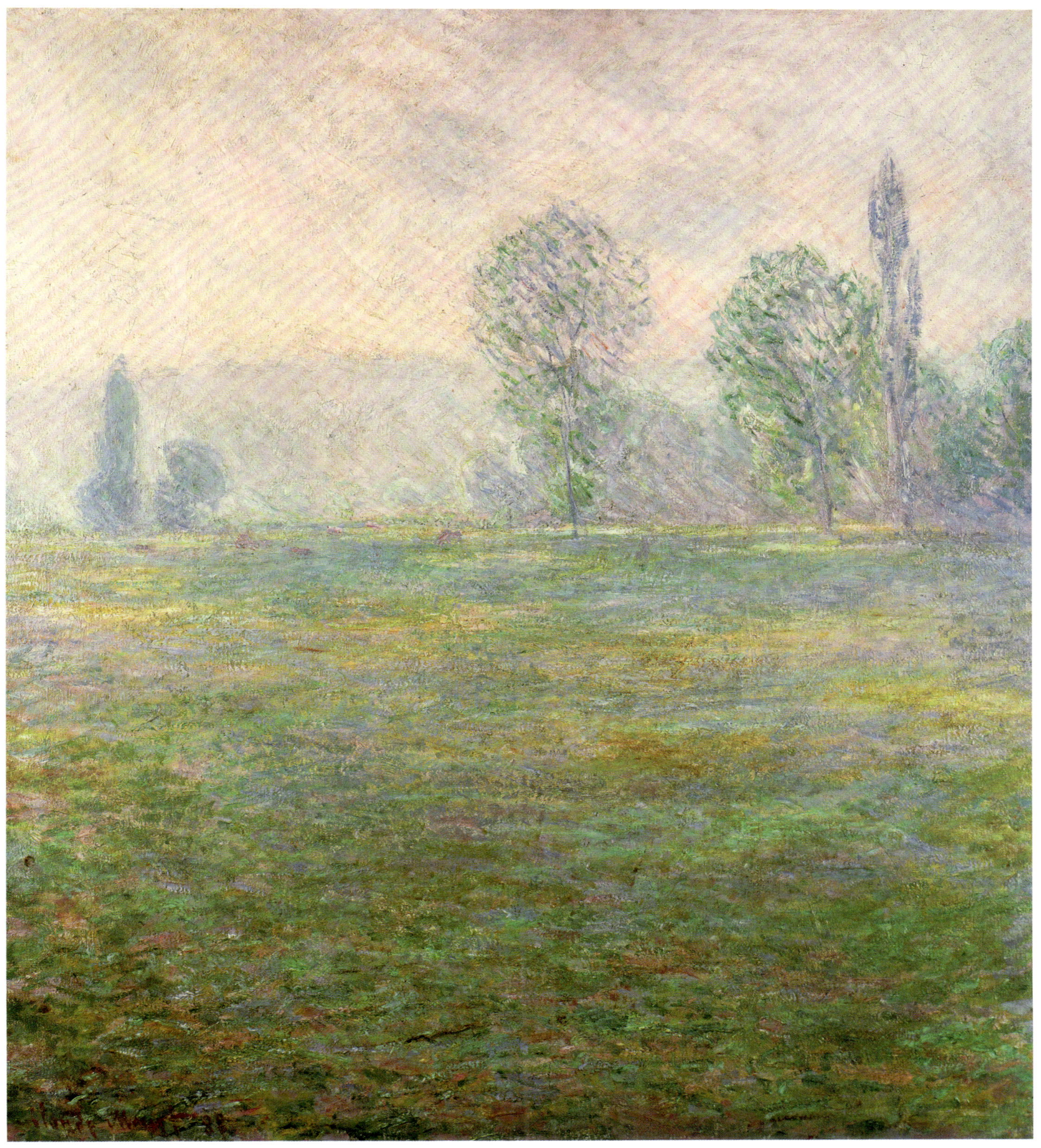

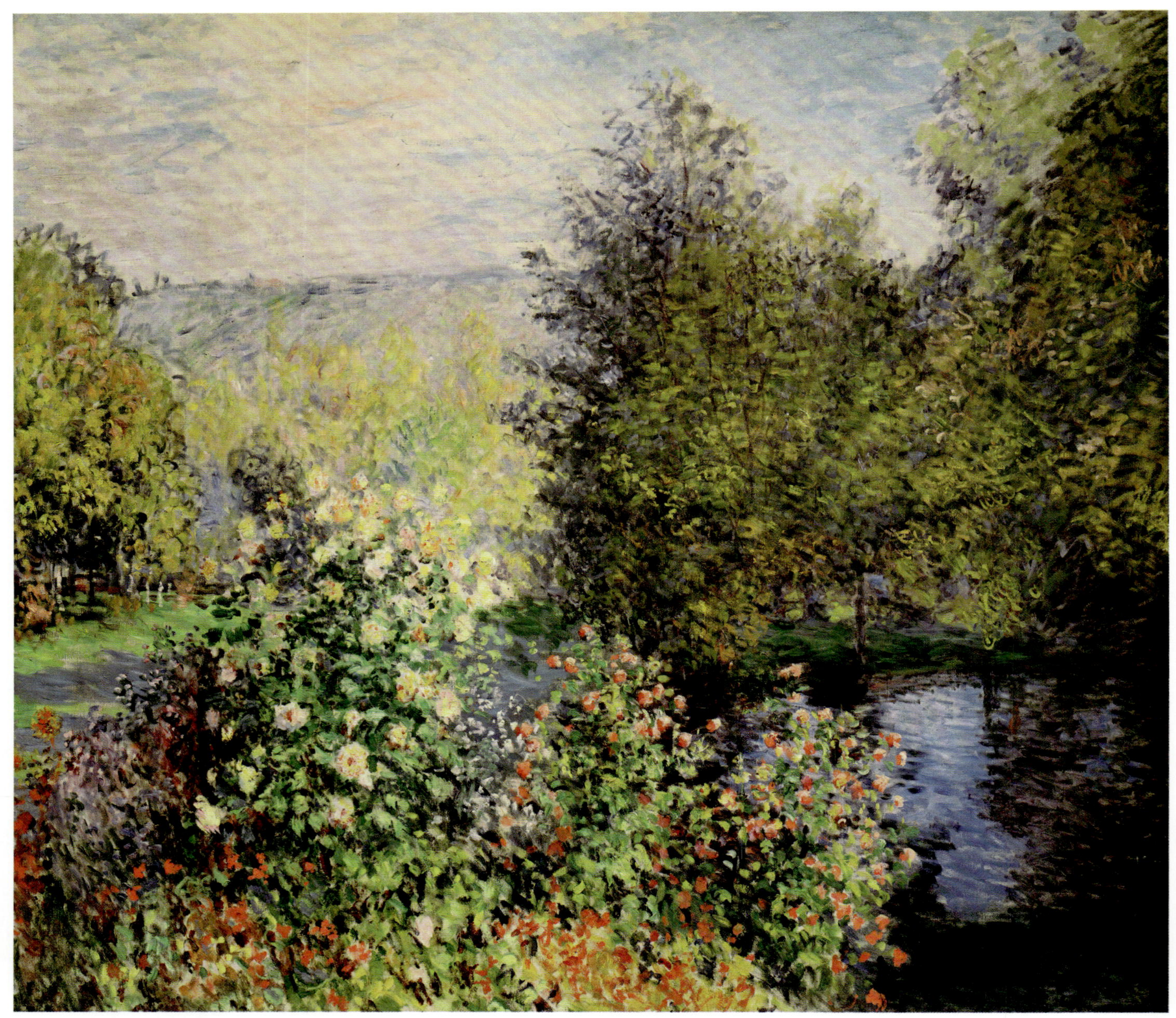

Claude Monet (1840–1926)

Corner of the Garden in Montgeron

Coin de jardin à Montgeron

Stiller Winkel im Garten von Montgeron

Rincón tranquilo en el jardín de Montgeron

Canto Tranquilo no Jardim de Montgeron

Een stil hoekje in de tuin van Montgeron

1876/77, Oil on canvas/Huile sur toile, 175 × 194 cm

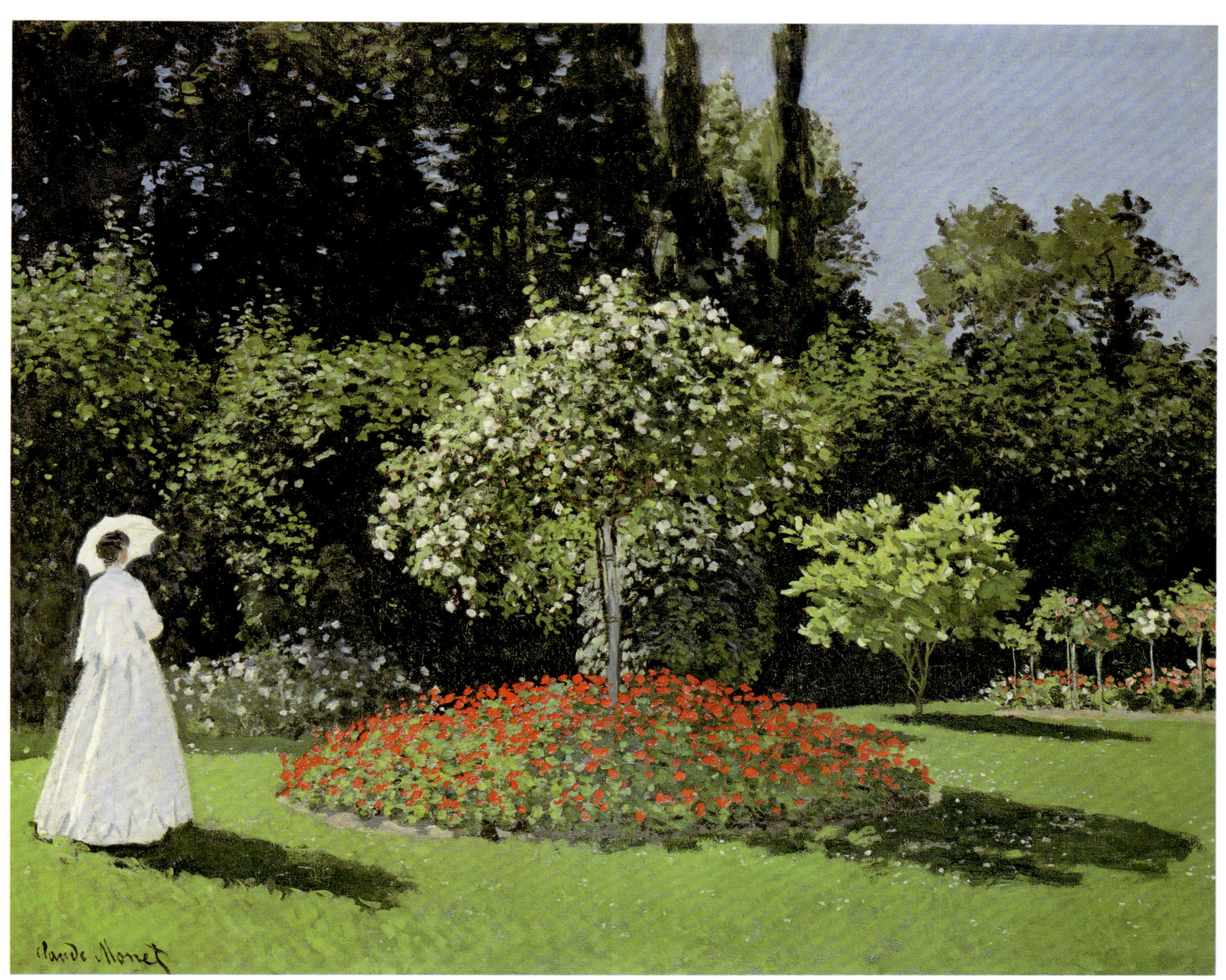

Claude Monet (1840–1926)

Jeanne-Marguerite Lecadre in the Garden

La Dame en blanc au jardin (Jeanne-Marguerite Lecadre)

Jeanne-Marguerite Lecadre im Garten

Jeanne Marie Lecadre en el jardín

Jeanne-Marguerite Lecadre no Jardim

Jeanne-Marguerite Lecadre in de tuin

1867, Oil on canvas/Huile sur toile, 82 × 101 cm

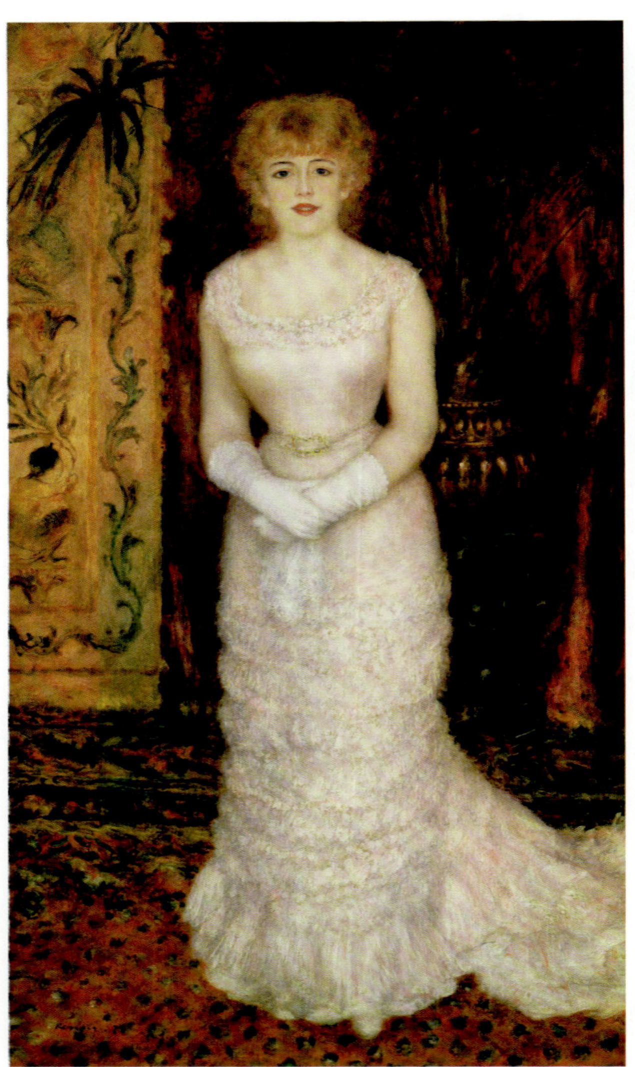

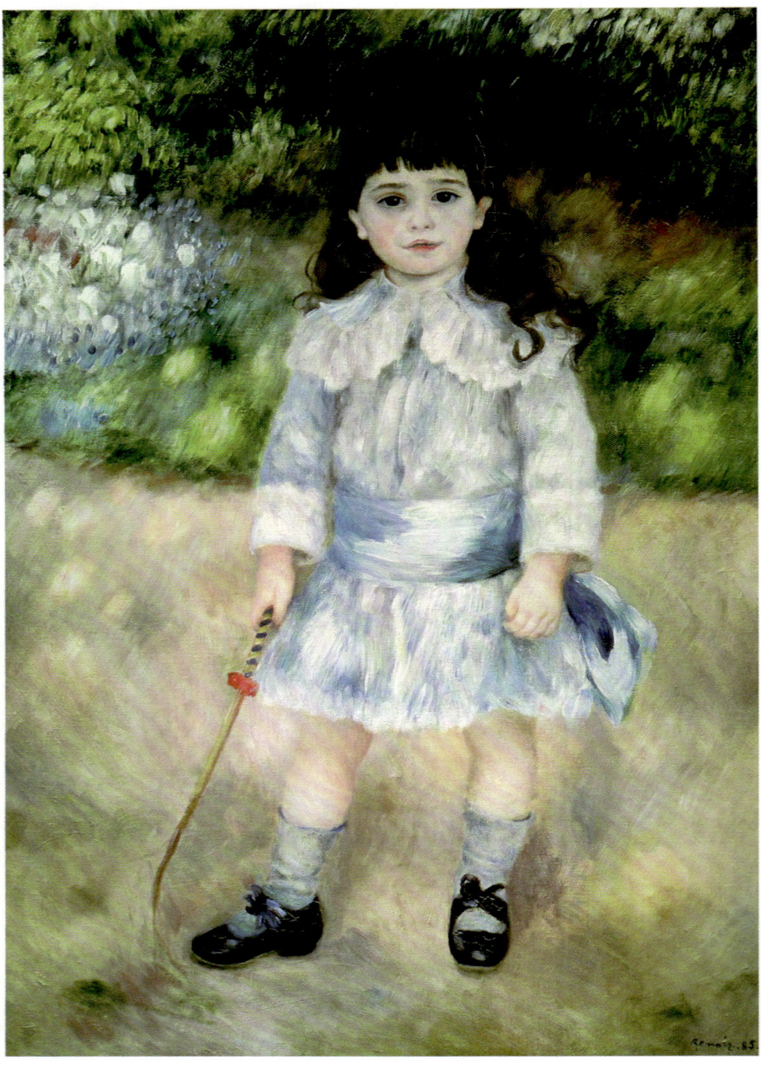

Auguste Renoir (1841–1919)

Jeanne Samary

1878, Oil on canvas/Huile sur toile, 174 × 105 cm

Auguste Renoir (1841–1919)

Child with Whip

L'Enfant au fouet

Kind mit Peitsche

Niña con látigo

Menino com Chicote

Kind met zweep

1885, Oil on canvas/Huile sur toile, 105 × 75 cm

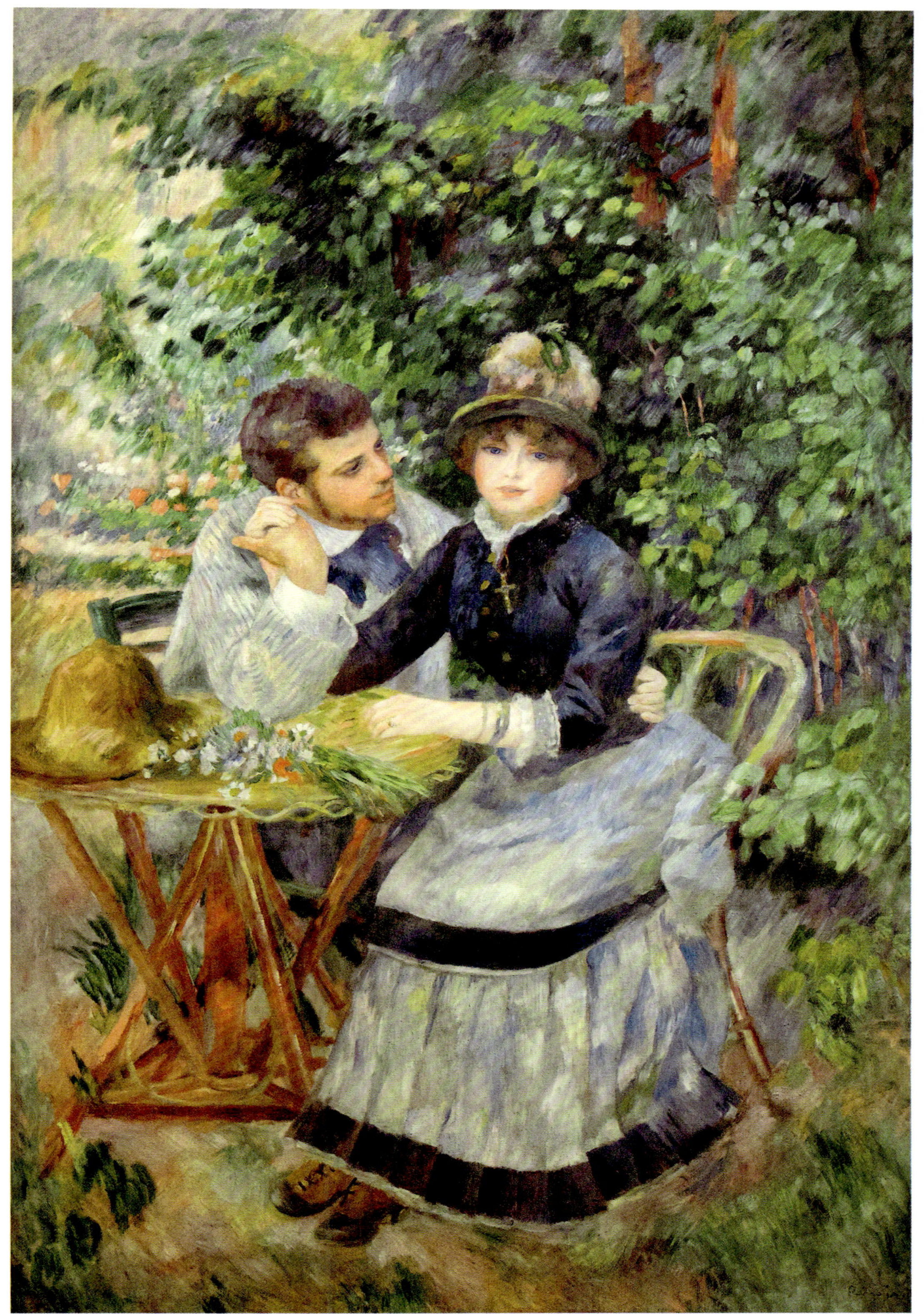

Auguste Renoir (1841–1919)

In the Garden

Dans le jardin

Im Garten

En el jardín

No Jardim

In de tuin

1885, Oil on canvas/Huile sur
toile, 170,5 × 112,5 cm

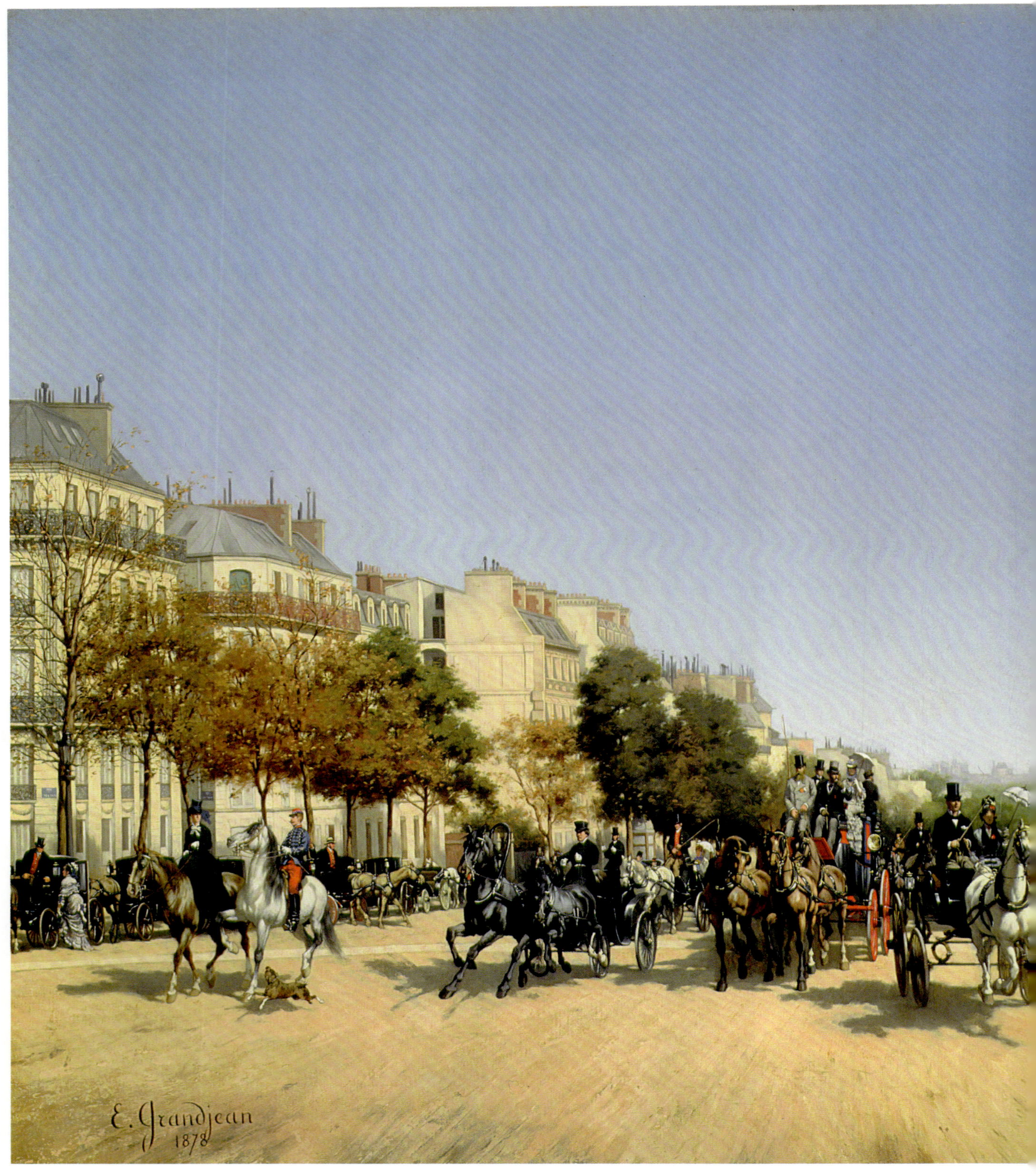
E. Grandjean
1878

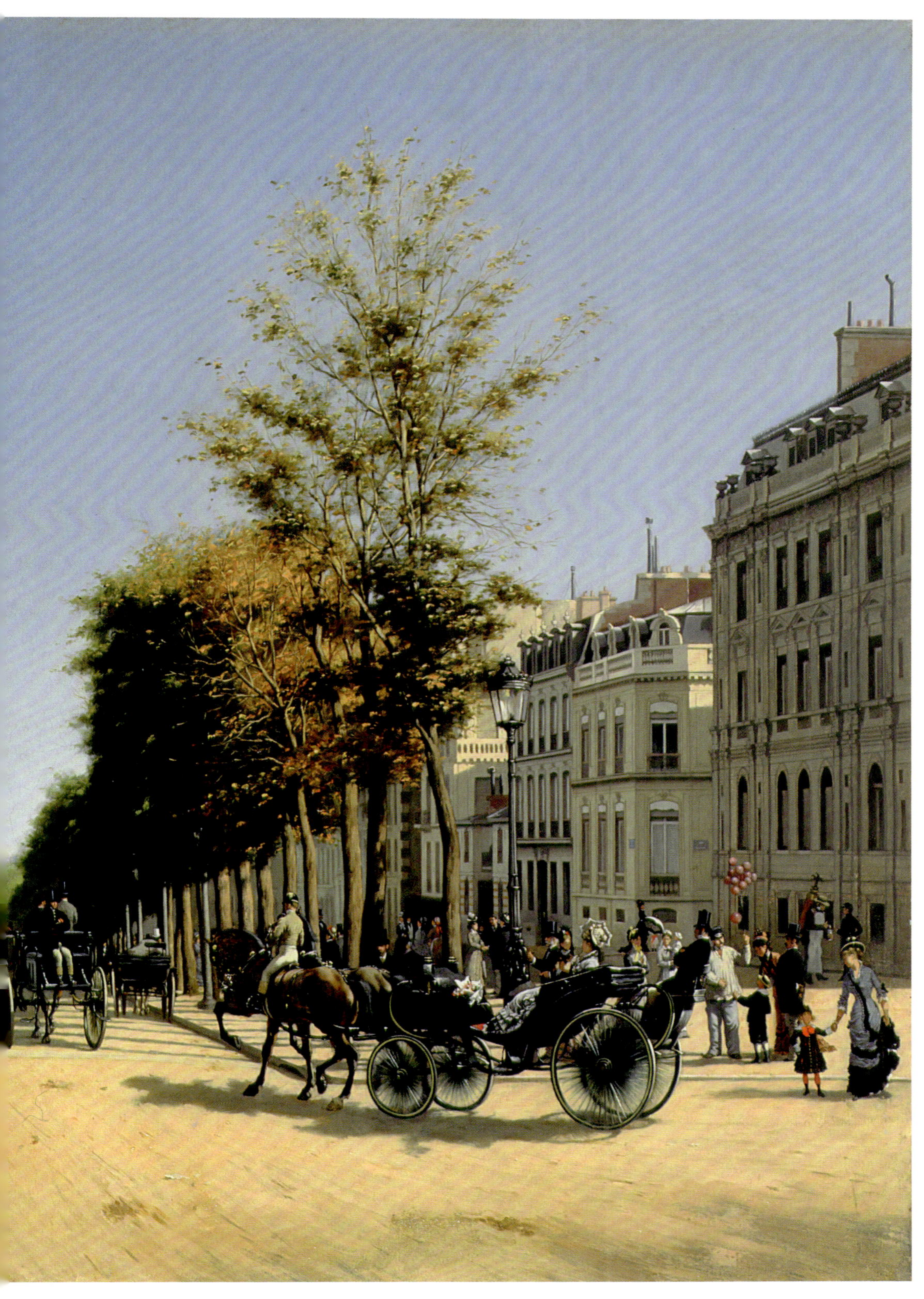

Edmond Georges Grandjean
(1844–1908)

The Champs-Elysées from
the Place de l'Etoile

Vue des Champs-Élysées
depuis la place de l'Étoile

Die Champs-Elysées von
der Place de l'Etoile aus

Los Campos Elíseos vistos
desde la Place de l'Etoile

Os Campos Elísios a partir
da Place de l'Etoile

De Champs-Elysées vanaf
de Place de l'Étoile

1878, Oil on canvas/Huile sur
toile, 85,5 × 136,5 cm

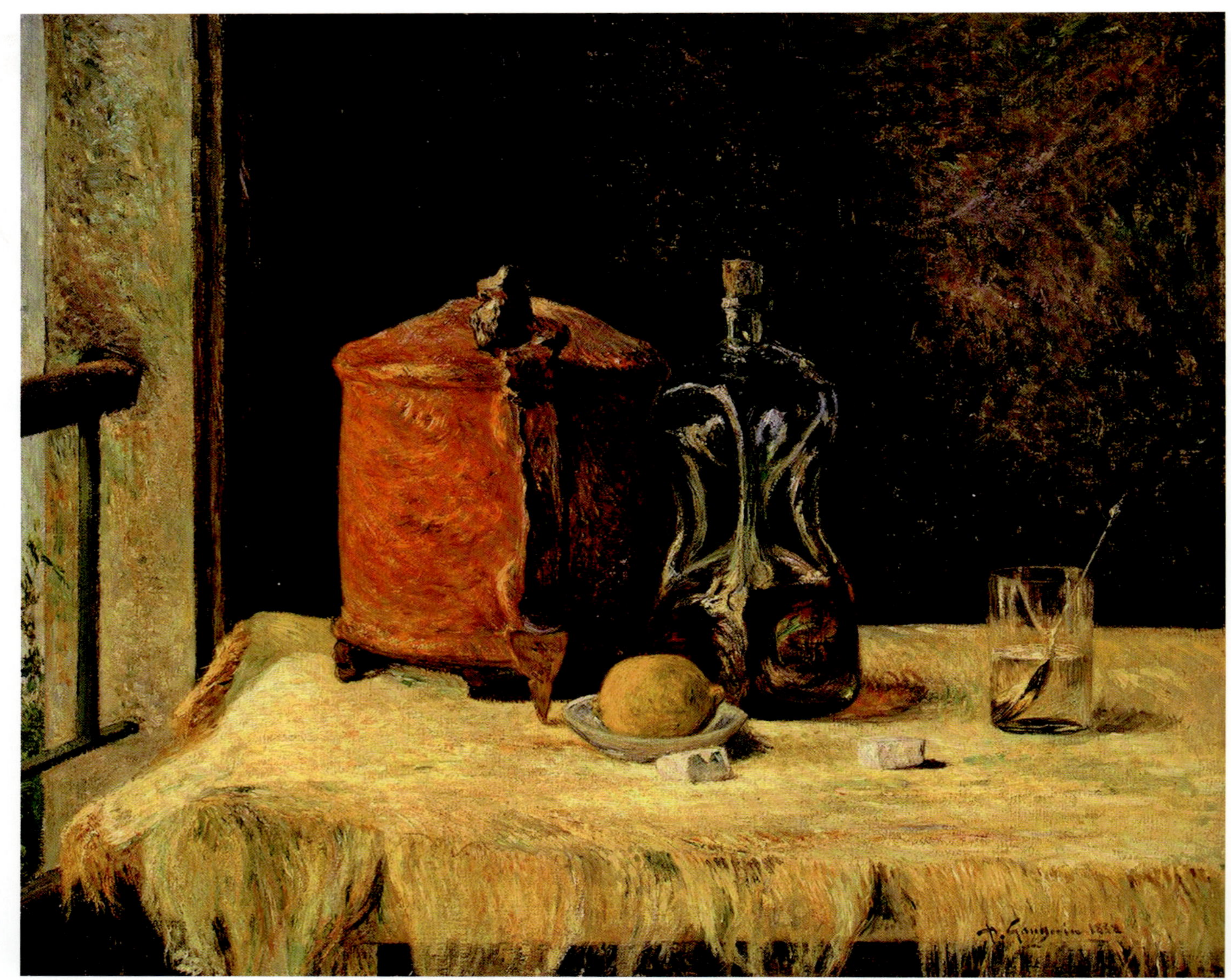

Paul Gauguin (1848–1903)

At the Window

À la fenêtre, nature morte

Am Fenster

En la ventana

À Janela

Aan het raam

1882, Oil on canvas/Huile sur toile, 54 × 65,3 cm

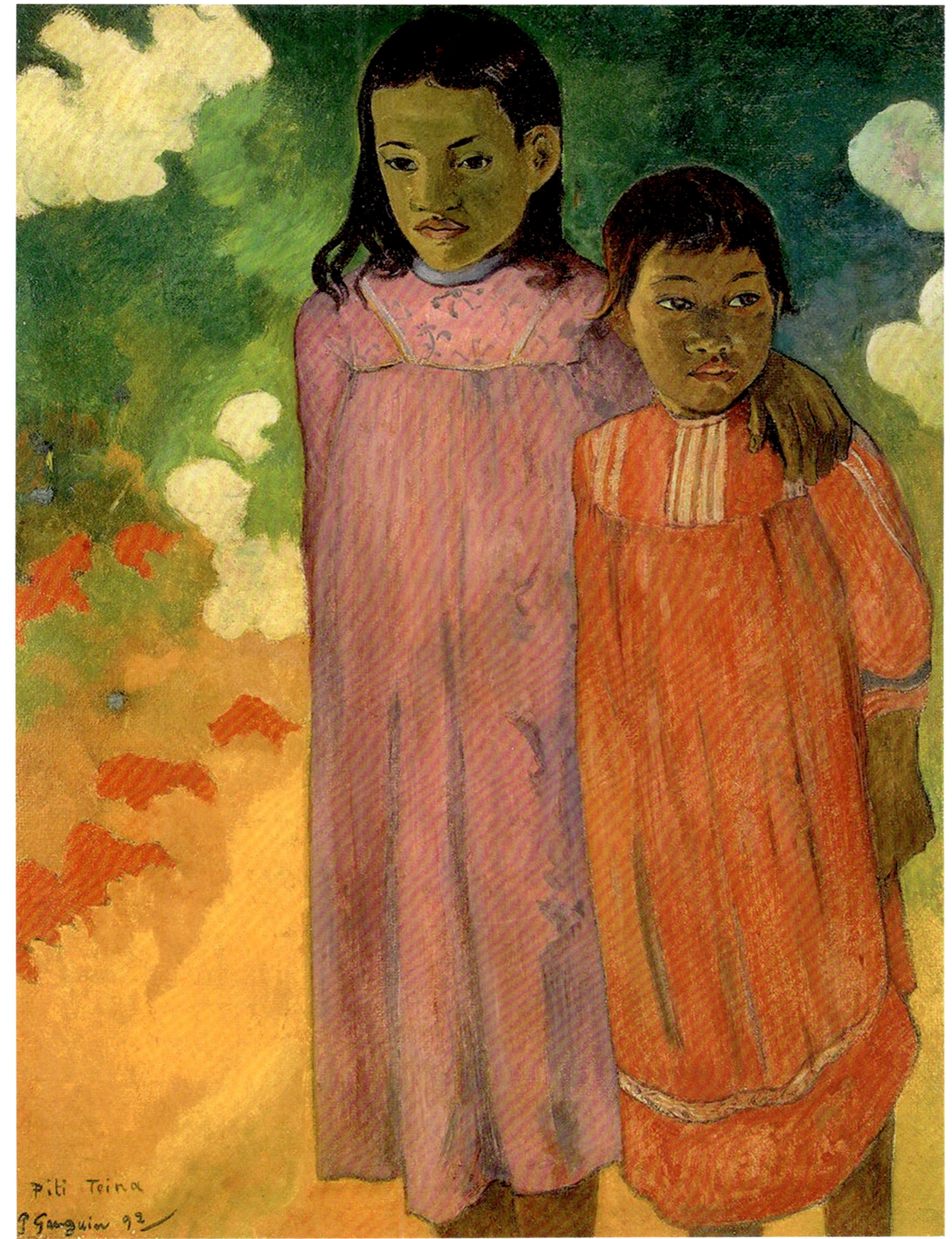

Paul Gauguin (1848–1903)
Piti Teina (Two Sisters)
Piti Teina (Les Deux Sœurs)
Piti Teina (Zwei Schwestern)
Piti Teina (Dos hermanas)
Piti Teina (Duas Irmãs)
Piti Teina (Twee zussen)
1892, Oil on canvas/Huile
sur toile, 90,5 × 67,5 cm

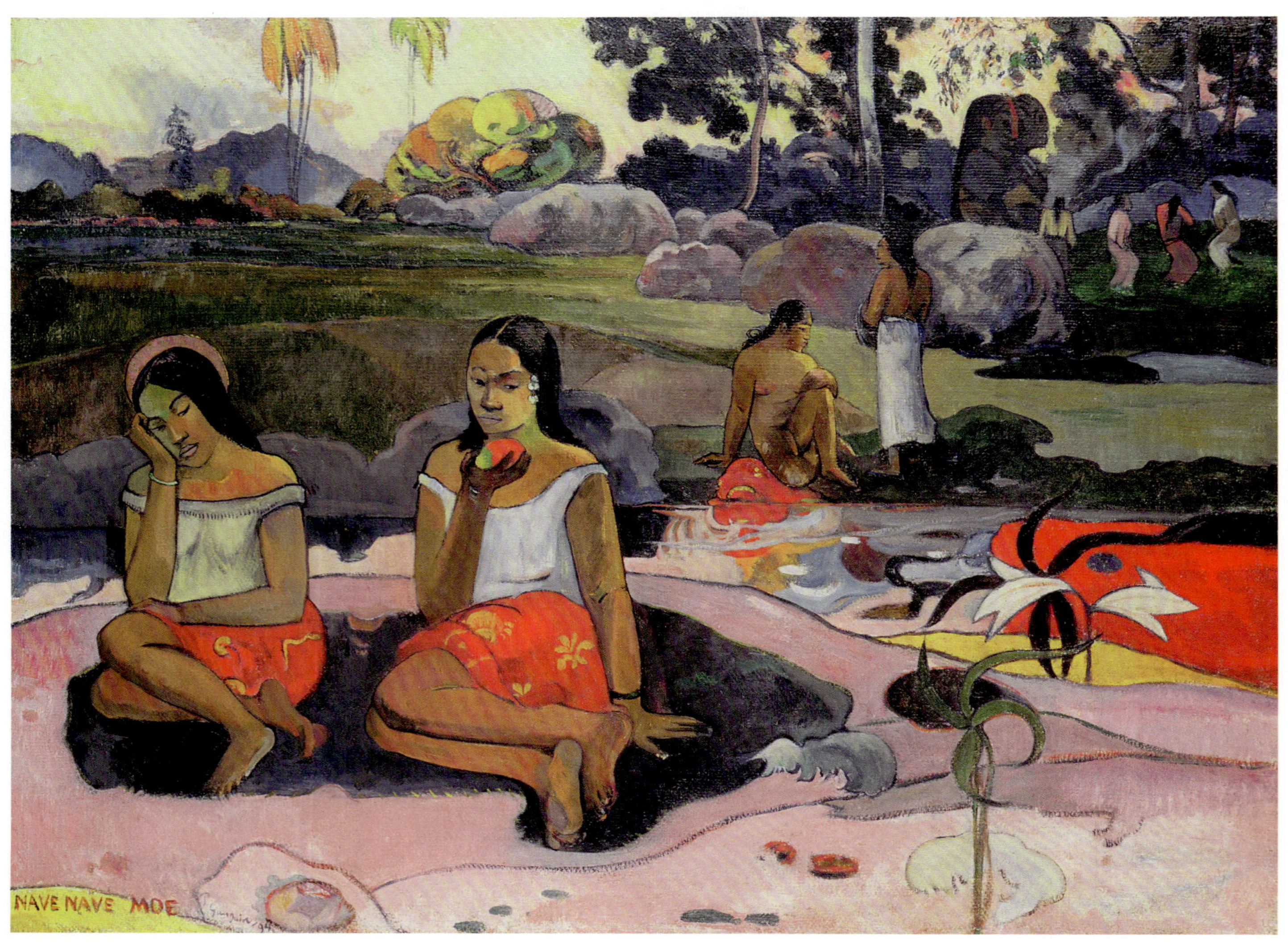

Paul Gauguin (1848–1903)

Nave Nave Moe (Sacred Spring)

Nave Nave Moe (Joie de se reposer)

Nave Nave Moe (Heiliger Frühling)

Nave Nave Moe (Primavera Santa)

Nave Nave Moe (Santa Primavera)

Nave Nave Moe (Heilige lente)

1894, Oil on canvas/Huile sur toile, 74 × 100 cm

Paul Gauguin (1848–1903)

Tahitian Woman with Fruit

Femme au fruit

Tahitische Frau mit Frucht

Mujer tahitiana con fruto

Mulher do Tahiti com Fruto

Tahitiaanse vrouw met mango

1893, Oil on canvas/Huile sur toile, 92,5 × 73,5 cm

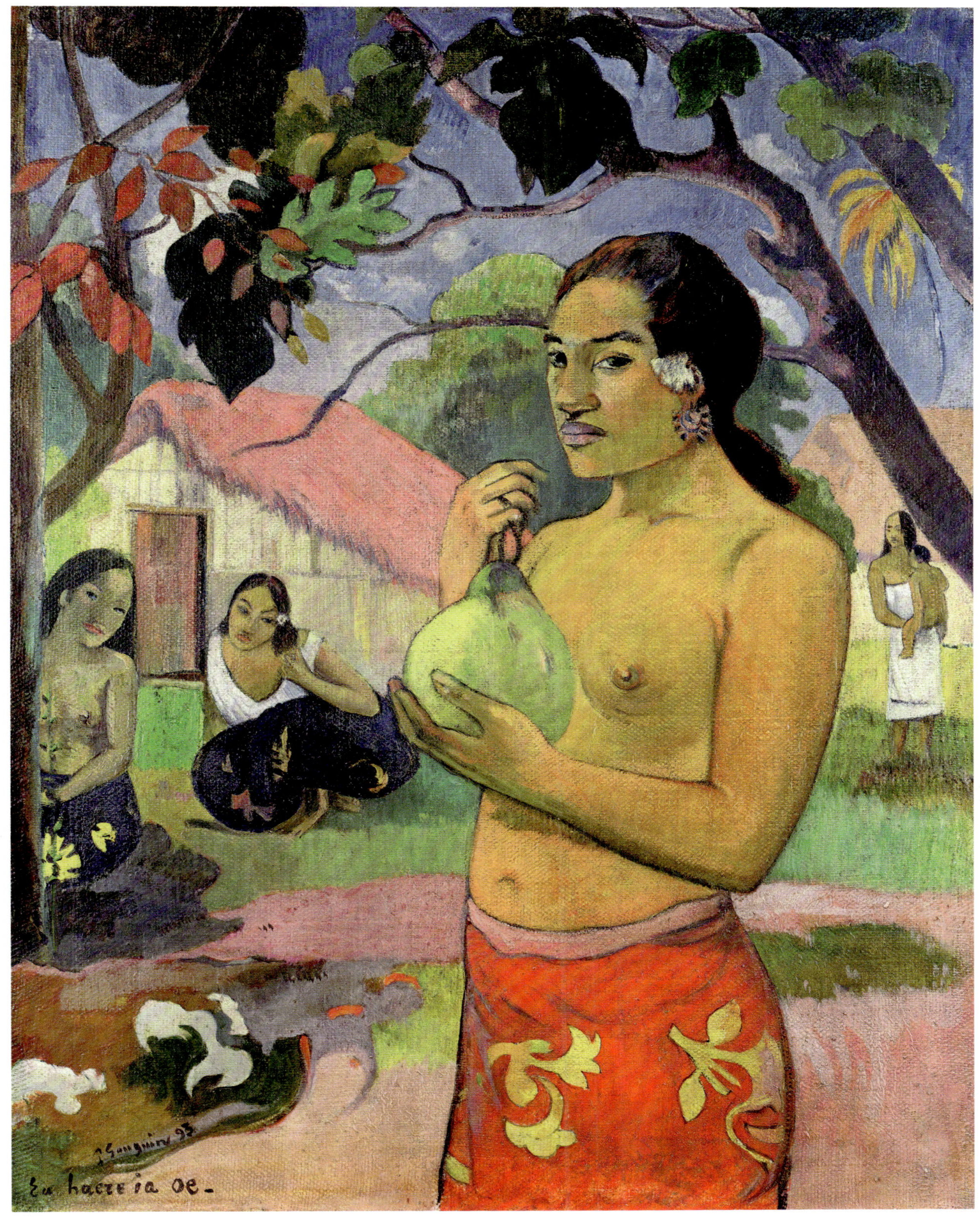

P Gauguin 93
Eu haere ia oe.

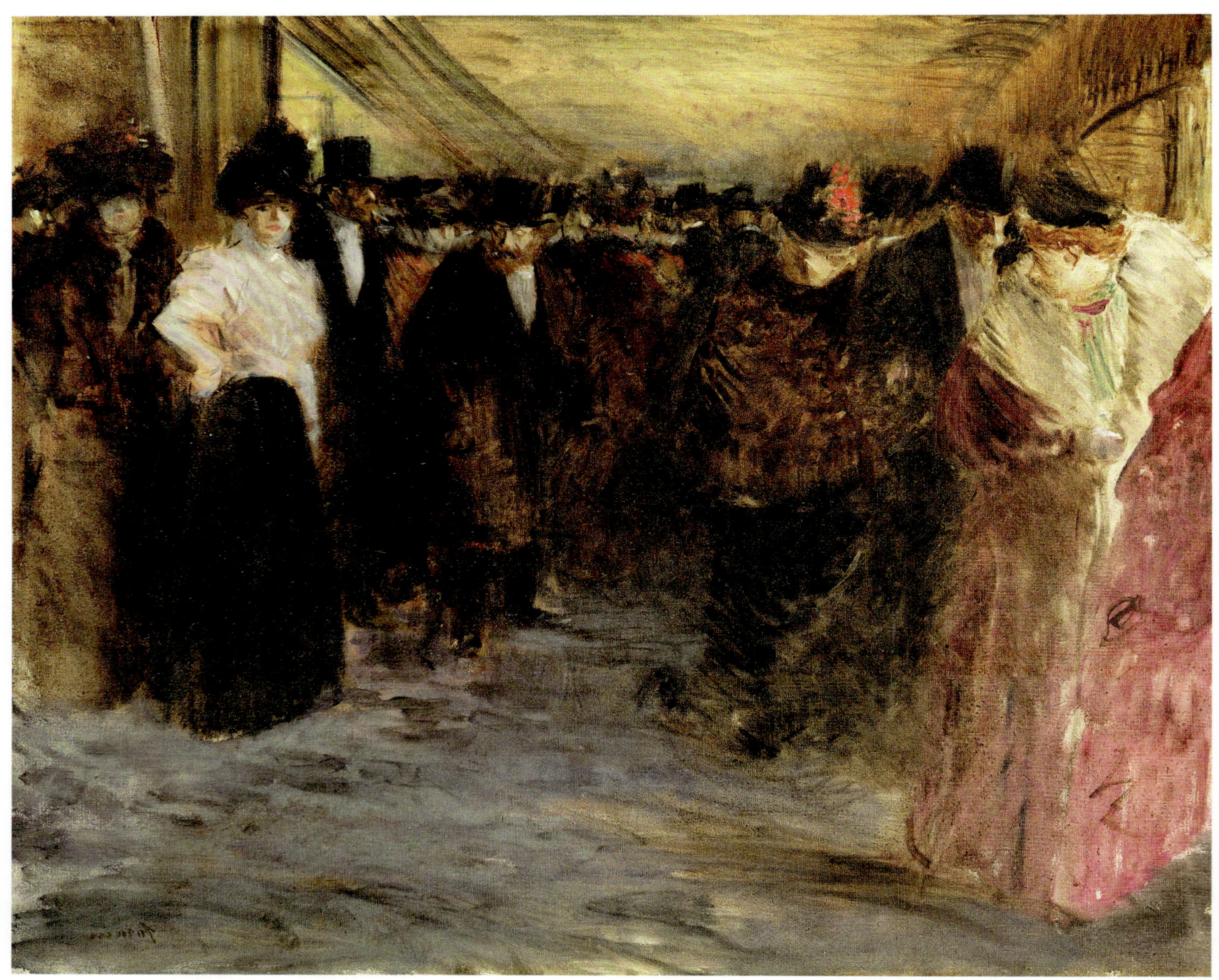

Jean-Louis Forain (1852–1931)
At the Music Hall
Music-Hall
Im Varieté
En el Varieté
No Teatro de Variedades
In het variététheater
c. 1895/96, Oil on canvas/Huile sur toile, 50,5 × 61 cm

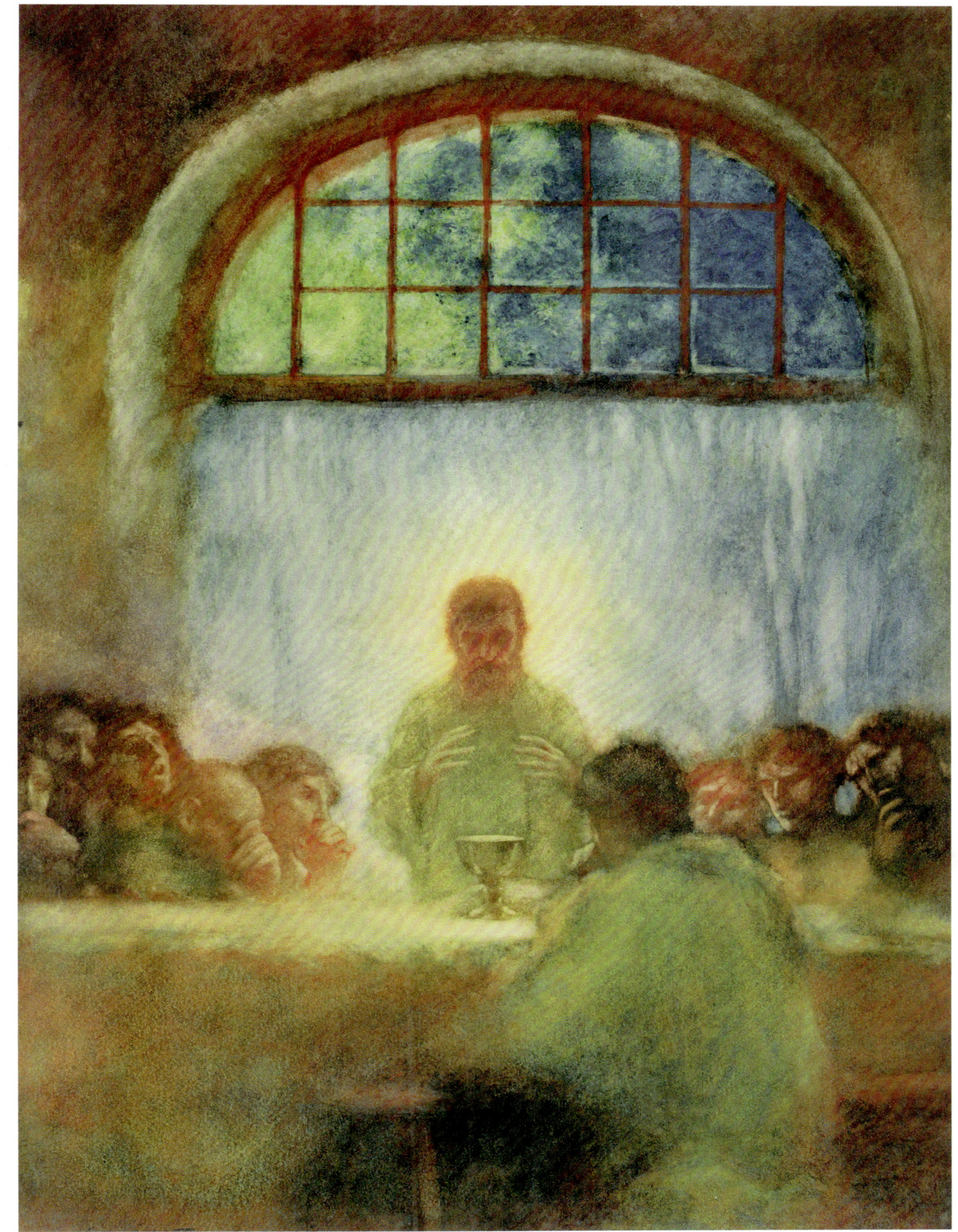

Gaston de La Touche
(1854–1913)
The Last Supper
Le Dernier Souper
Das letzte Abendmahl
La última cena
A Última Ceia
Het laatste avondmaal
1897, Oil on canvas/Huile
sur toile, 78,3 × 56 cm

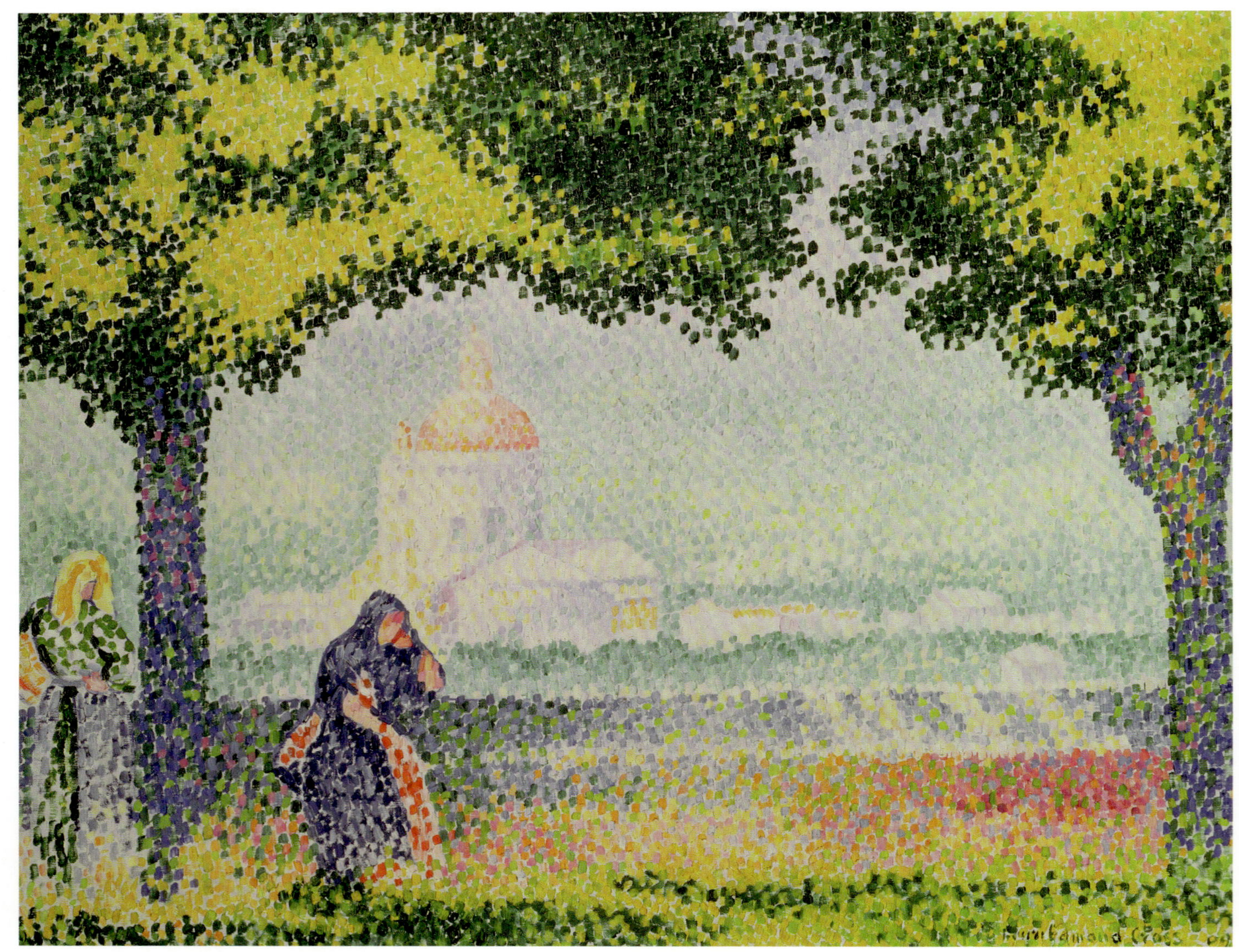

Henri-Edmond Cross (1856–1910)

View of the Church of Santa Maria degli Angeli in Assisi

Vue de l'église Santa Maria degli Angeli près d'Assise

Ansicht der Kirche Santa Maria degli Angeli bei Assisi

Vista de la iglesia de Santa Maria degli Angeli en Asís

Vista da Igreja Santa Maria degli Angeli em Assis

Uitzicht op de Santa Maria degli Angeli bij Assisi

1909, Oil on canvas/Huile sur toile, 73,5 × 92 cm

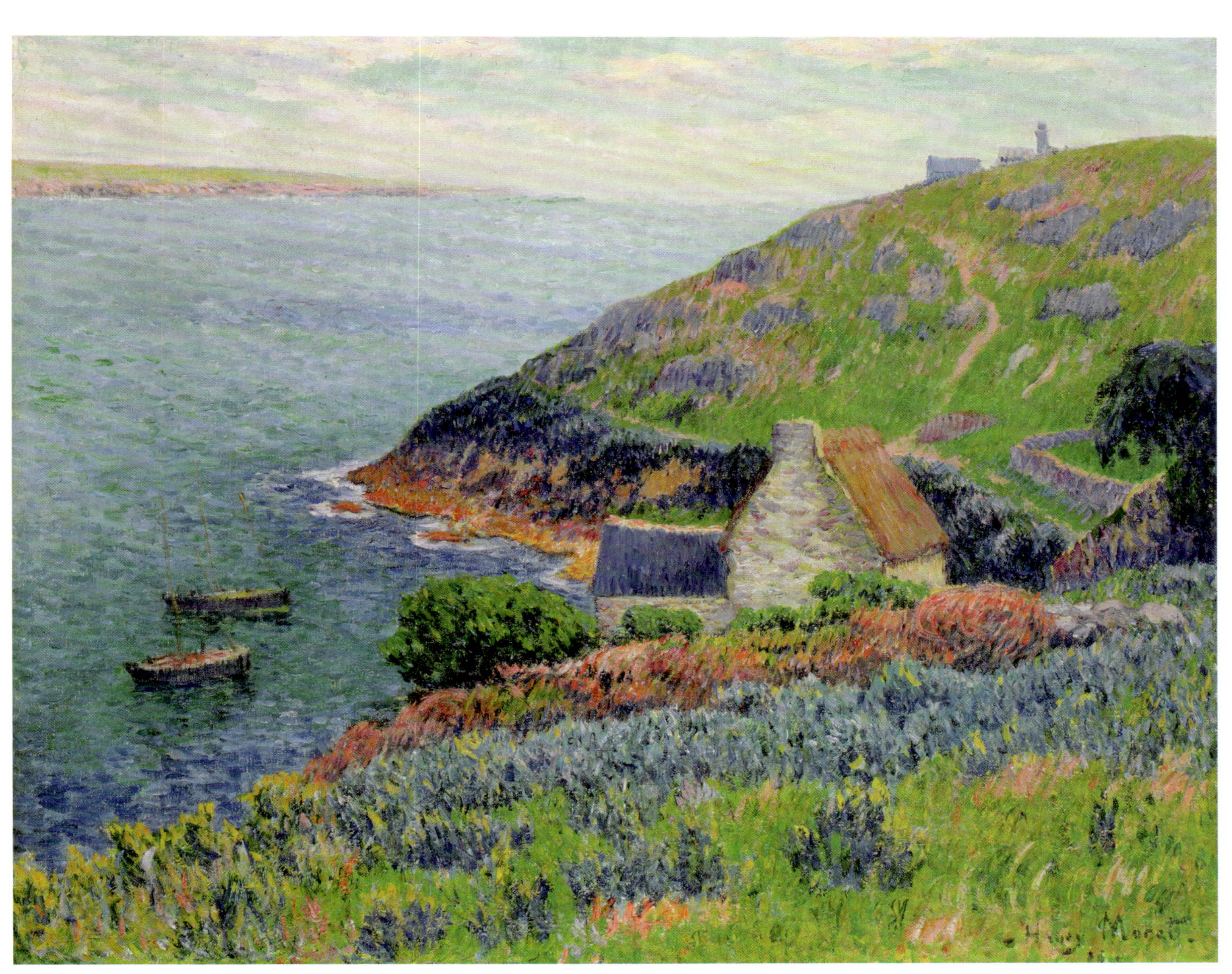

Henry Moret (1856–1913)

Port Manec'h

1896, Oil on canvas/Huile sur toile, 60,5 × 73,5 cm

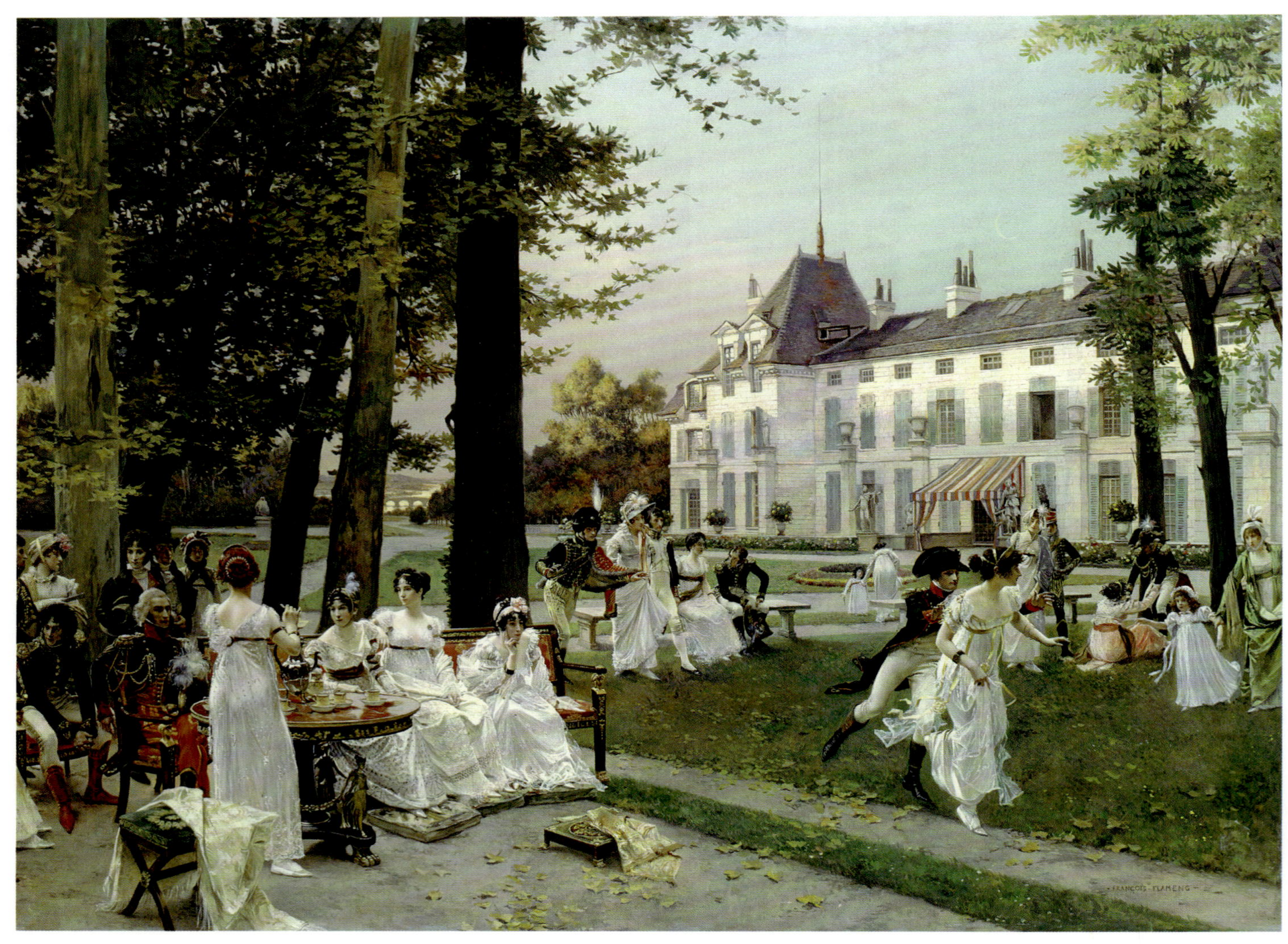

François Flameng (1856–1923)

Reception at Malmaison

Réception à Malmaison en 1802

Empfang in Malmaison

Recepción en Malmaison

Receção em Malmaison

Ontvangst in Malmaison

c. 1894, Oil on canvas/Huile sur toile, 106 × 139 cm

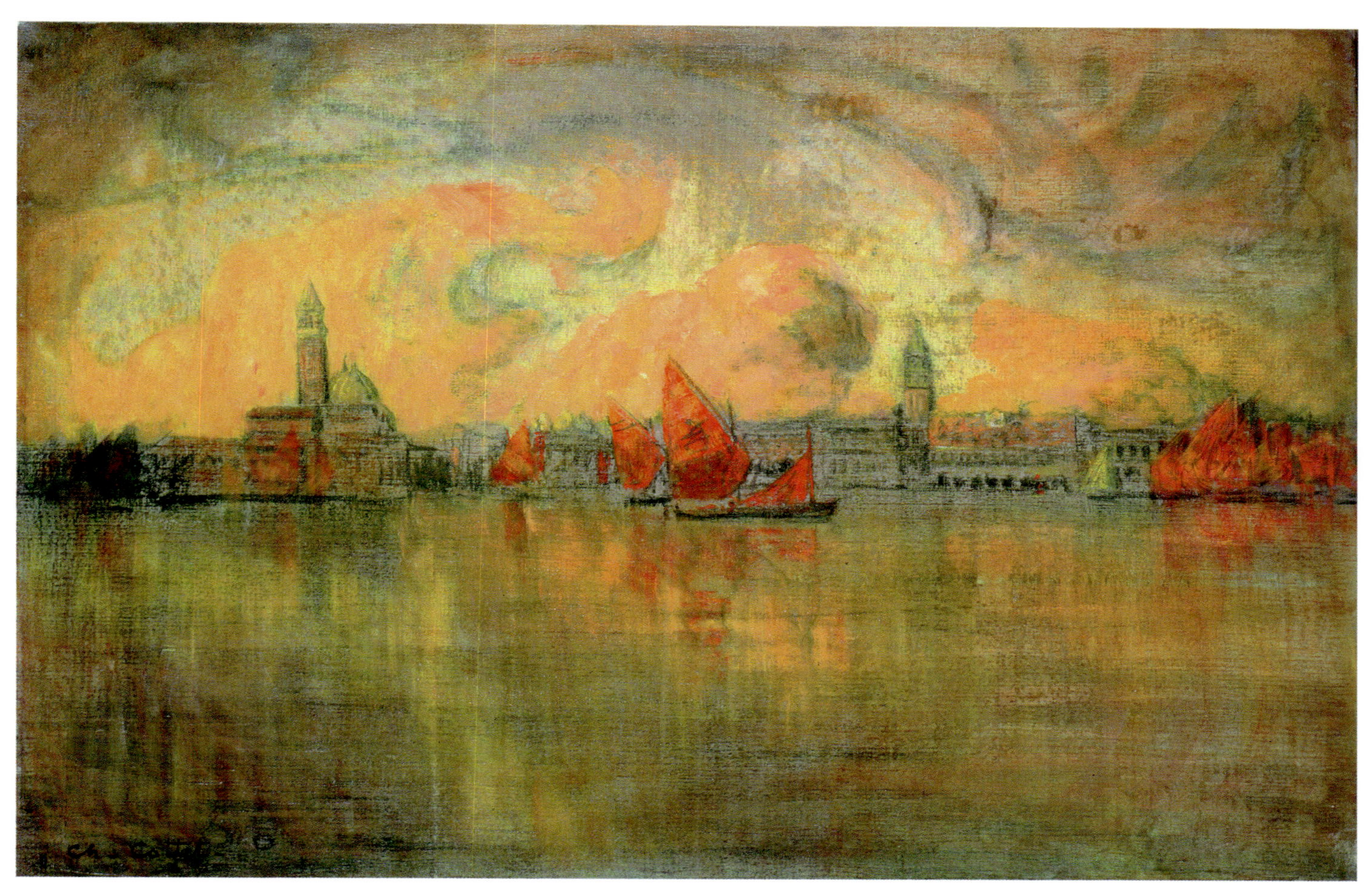

Georges Seurat (1859–91)

View of Fort Samson

Vue de Fort Samson

Ansicht von Fort Samson

Vista de Fort Samson

Vista de Fort Samson

Uitzicht op Fort Samson

1885, Oil on canvas/Huile sur toile, 65 × 81,5 cm

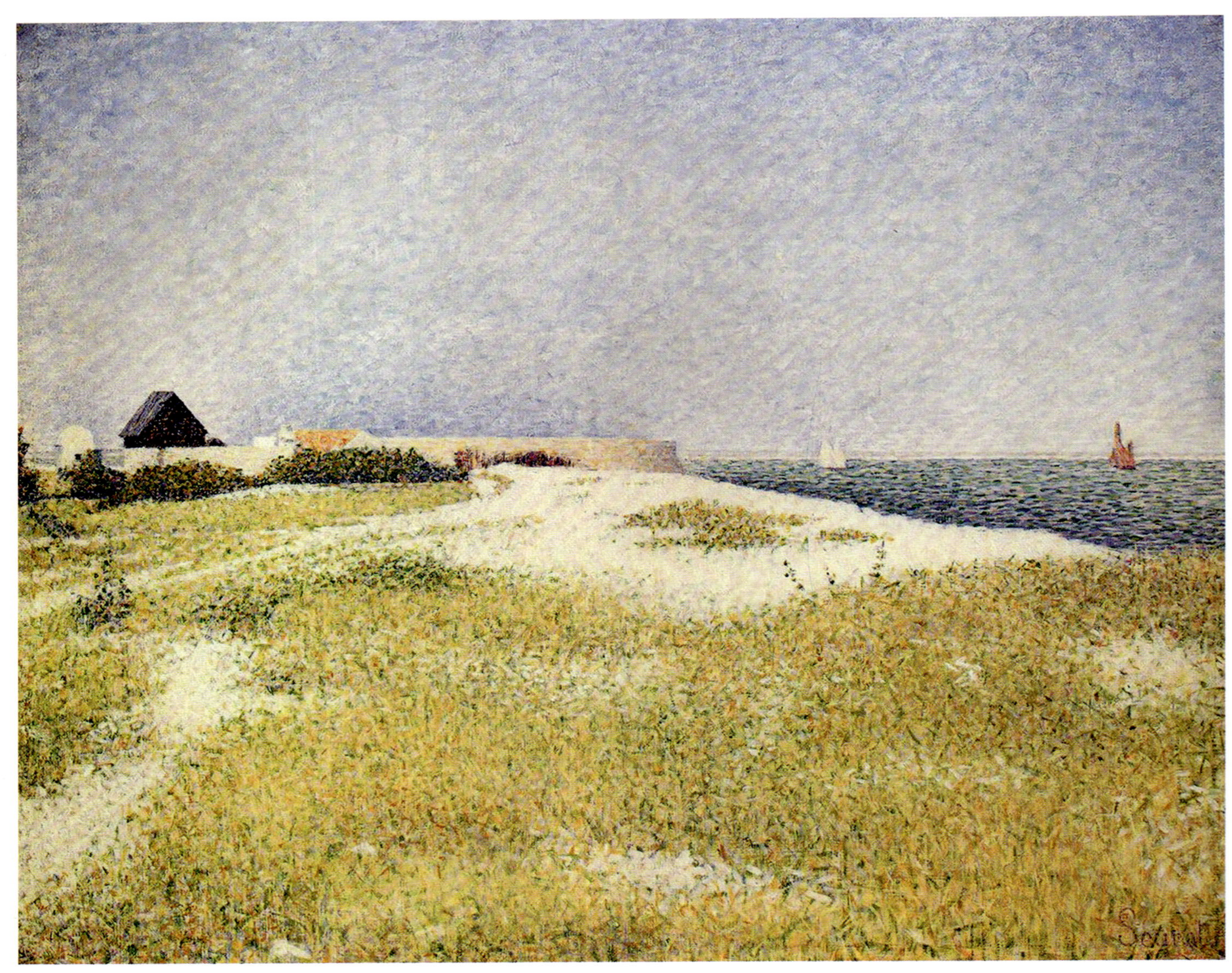

Charles Cottet (1863–1925)

Venice Seen from the Sea

Venise vue de la mer

Venedig vom Meer aus gesehen

Venecia vista desde el mar

Veneza Vista do Mar

Uitzicht op Venetië vanaf zee

1896, Oil on canvas/Huile sur toile, 55 × 82 cm

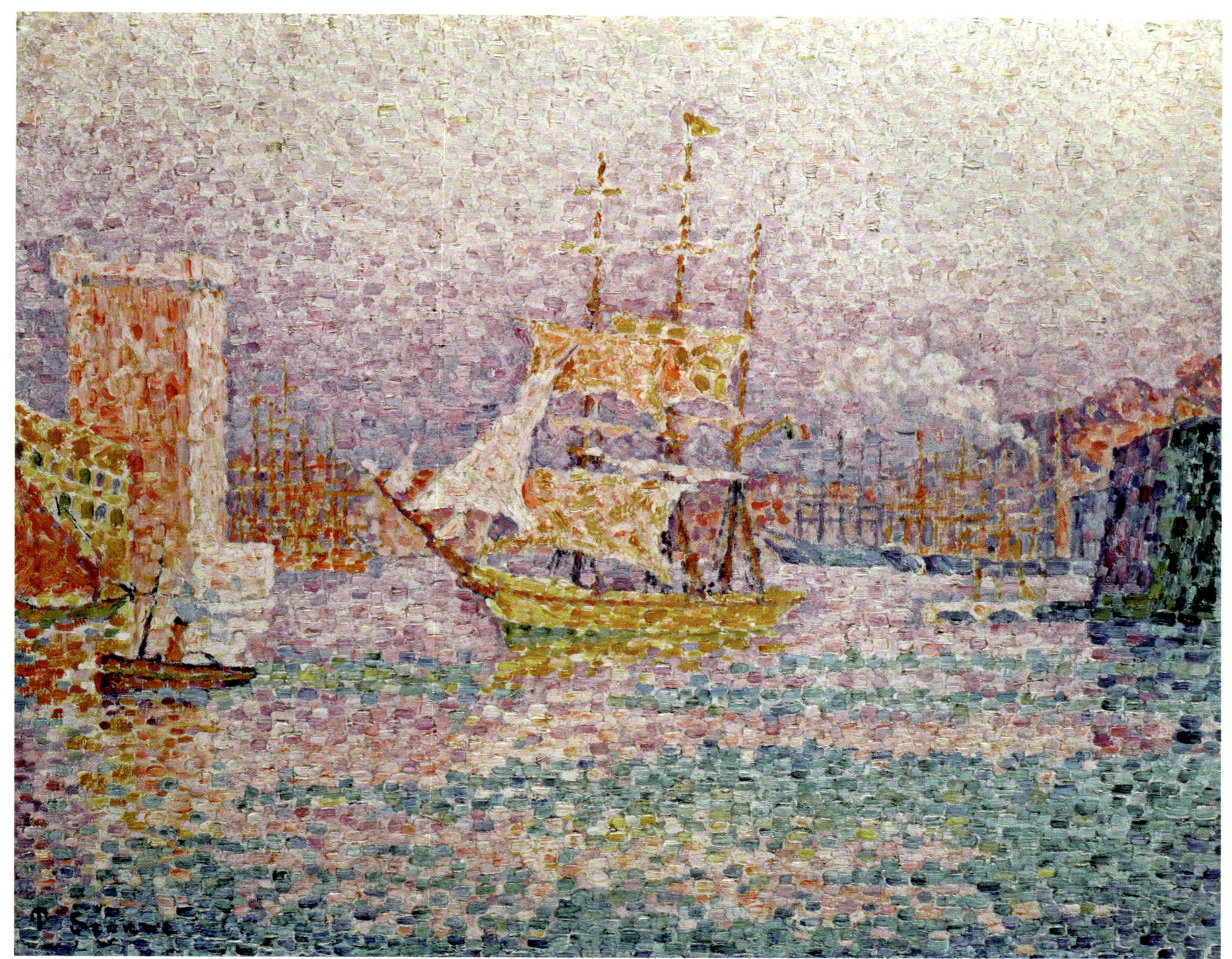

Paul Signac (1863–1935)

The Port of Marseille

Le Port de Marseille

Der Hafen von Marseille

El puerto de Marsella

O Porto de Marselha

De haven van Marseille

1907, Oil on canvas/Huile sur toile, 46 × 55 cm

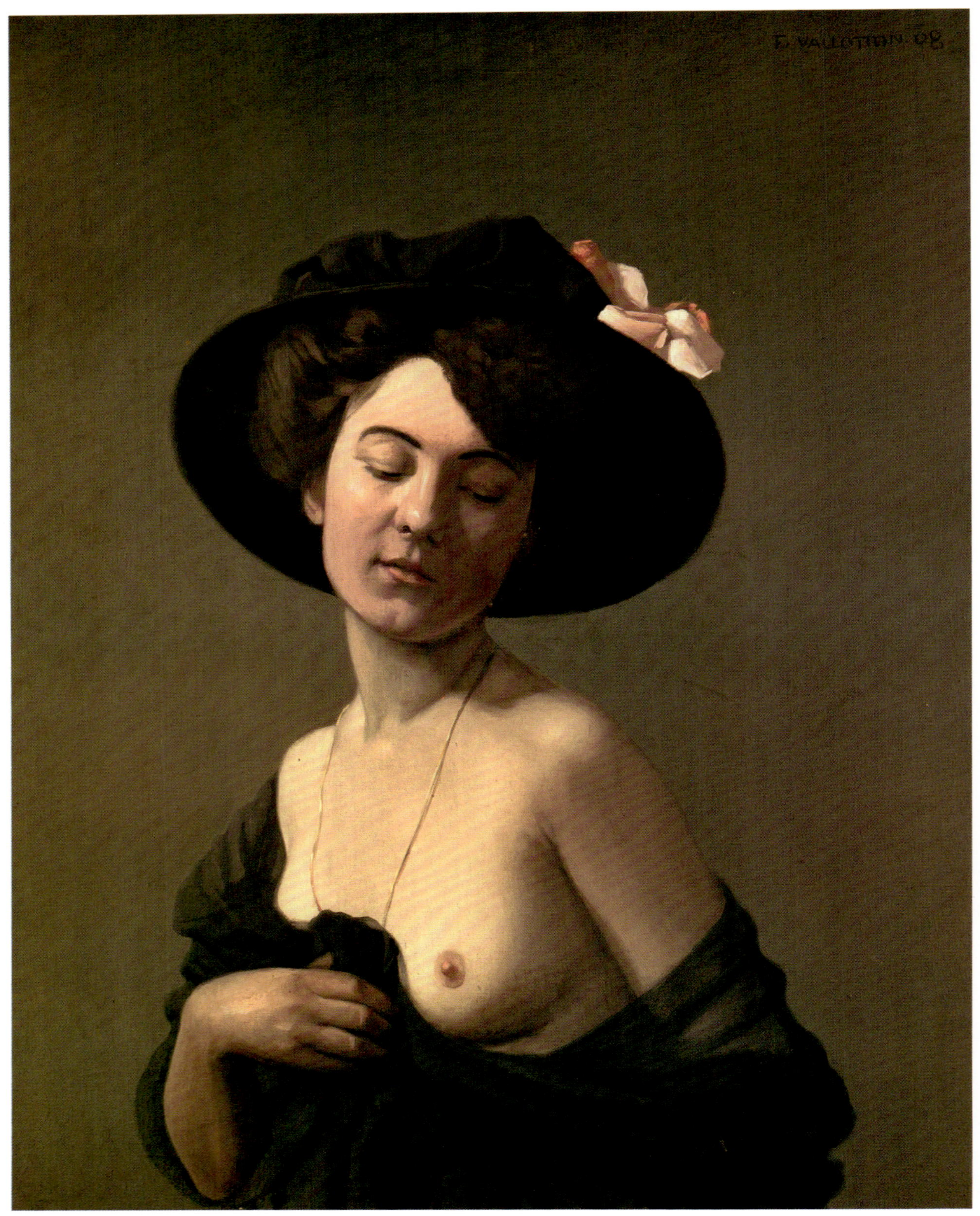

F. VALLOTTON. 08

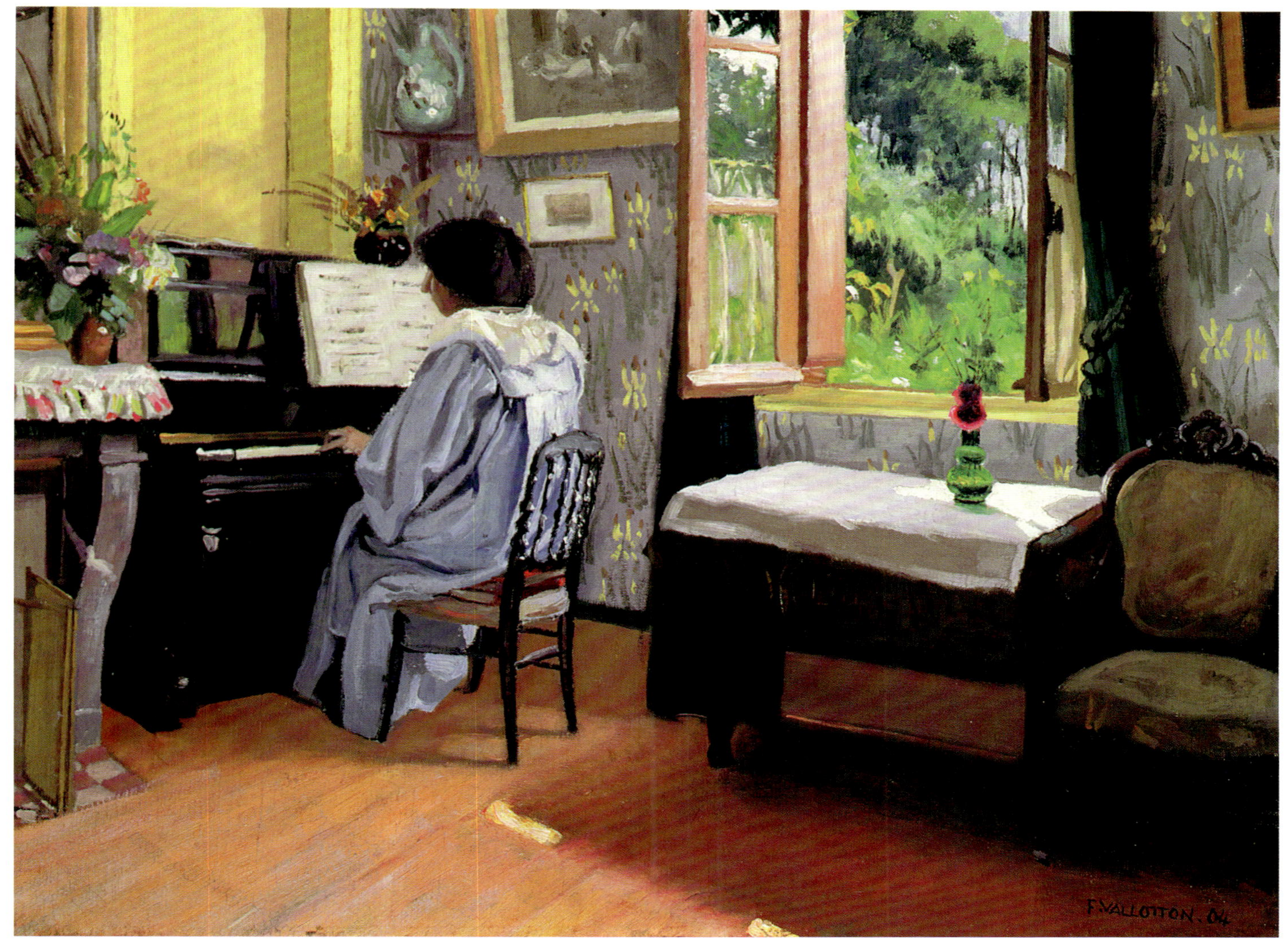

Félix Vallotton (1865–1925)
Woman at the Piano
Femme au piano (madame Vallotton)
Frau am Klavier
Mujer al piano
Mulher ao Piano
Vrouw aan de piano
1904, Oil on canvas/Huile sur toile, 43,5 × 57 cm

Félix Vallotton (1865–1925)
Woman with Hat
Femme au chapeau noir
Frau mit Hut
Mujer con sombrero
Mulher com Chapéu
Vrouw met hoed
1908, Oil on canvas/Huile sur toile, 81,3 × 65 cm

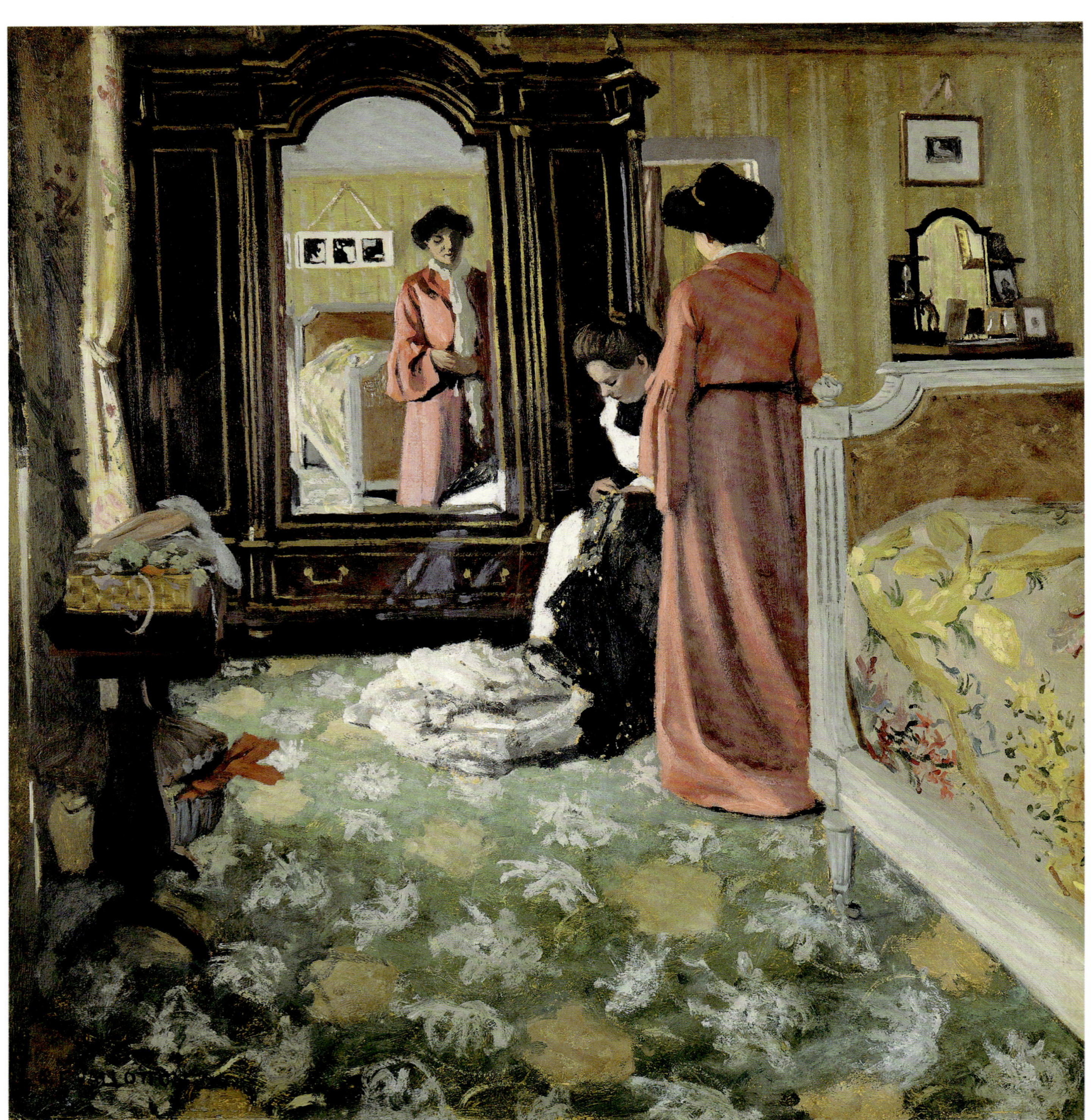

Félix Vallotton (1865–1925)

Interior

Intérieur

Interieur

Interior

Interior

Interieur

1903/04, Oil on canvas/
Huile sur carton, 61 × 56 cm

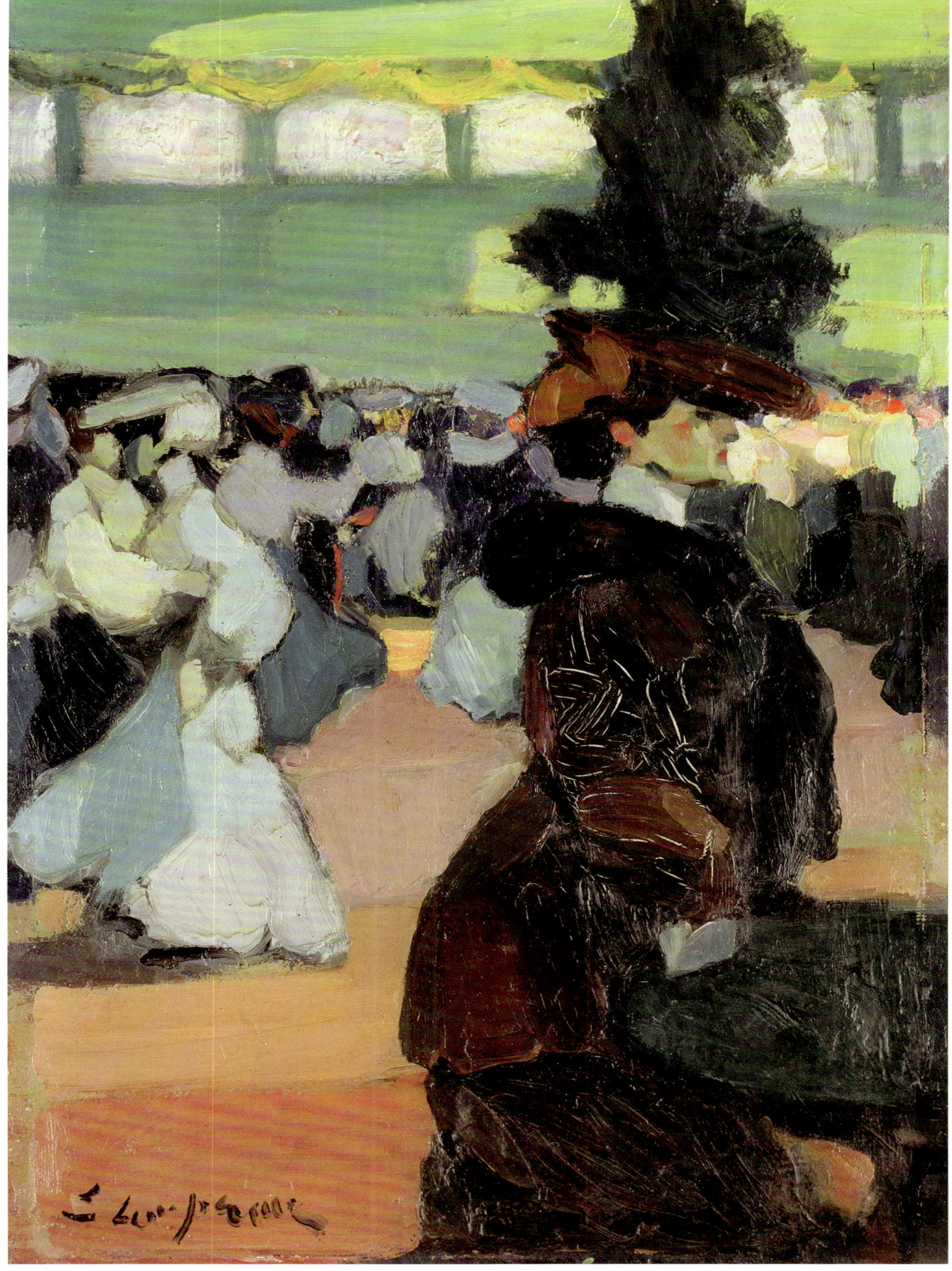

*Edmond Lempereur
(1876–1909)*

Bar Tabarin

1905, Oil on canvas/Huile
sur toile, 46,5 × 33,5 cm

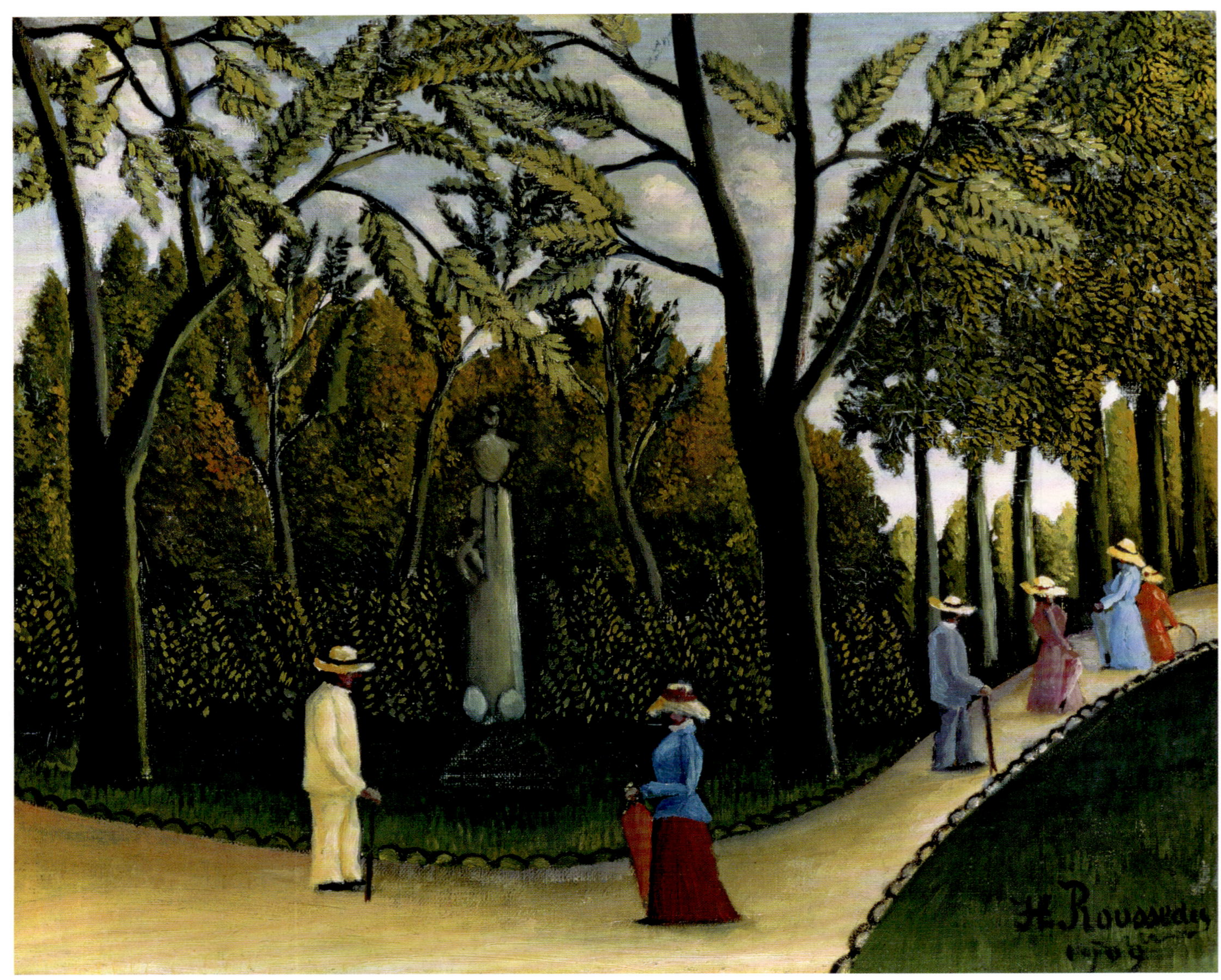

Henri Rousseau (Le Douanier) (1844–1910)

The Chopin Monument in the Jardin du Luxembourg

Jardin du Luxembourg. Monument de Chopin

Das Chopin-Denkmal im Jardin du Luxembourg

El monumento a Chopin en el Jardin du Luxembourg

O Monumento a Chopin no Jardim du Luxembourg

Het Chopin-monument in de Jardin du Luxembourg

1909, Oil on canvas/Huile sur toile, 38 × 47 cm

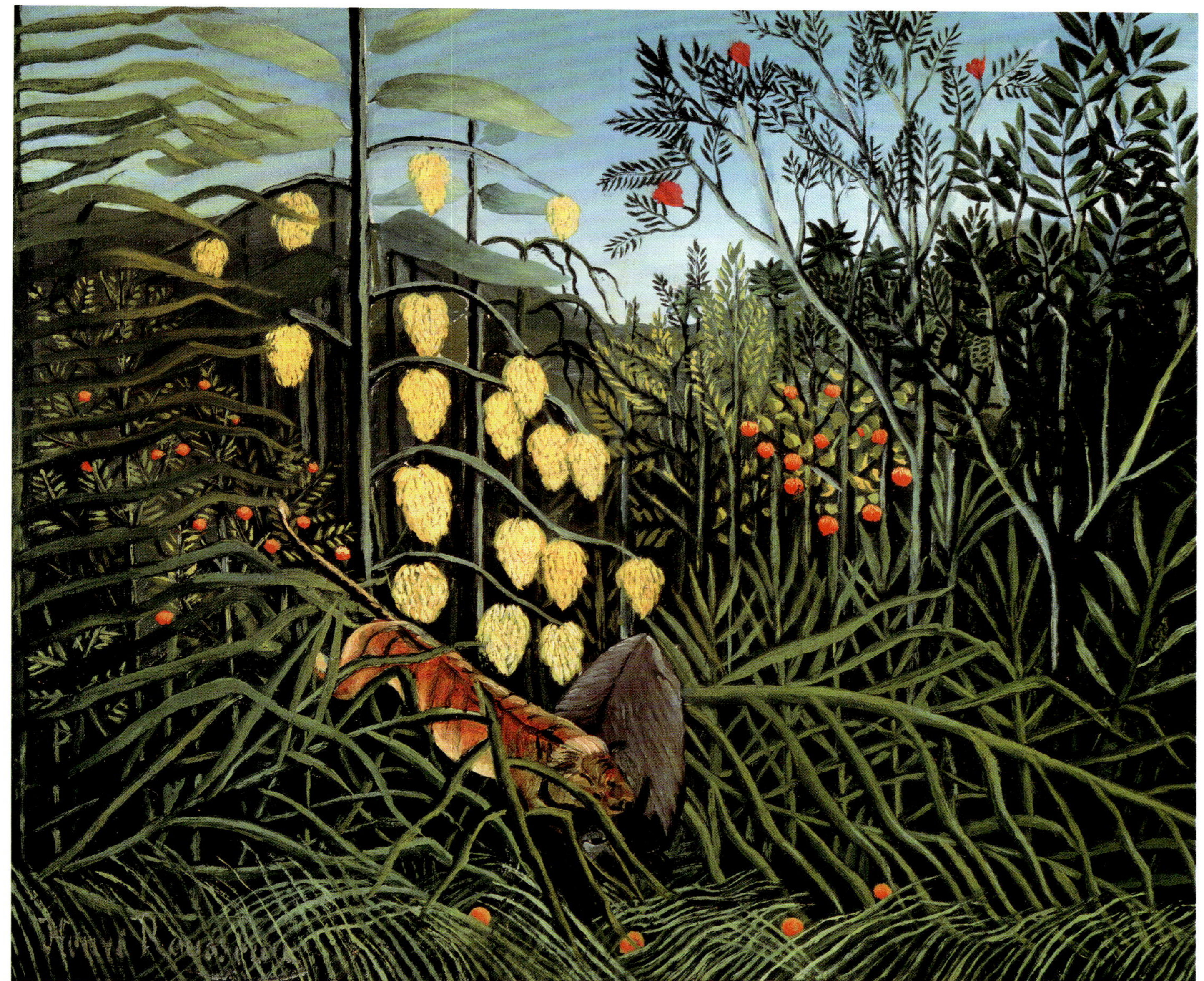

Henri Rousseau (Le Douanier) (1844–1910)

In the Jungle: Tiger and Buffalo in a Life-and-Death Struggle

Dans la forêt tropicale. Combat du tigre et du taureau

Im Urwald: Kampf zwischen Tiger und Büffel

En la jungla: Lucha entre tigres y búfalos

Na Selva: Luta entre Tigre e Búfalo

In het oerwoud: strijd tussen tijger en buffel

c. 1908/09, Oil on canvas/Huile sur toile, 46 × 55 cm

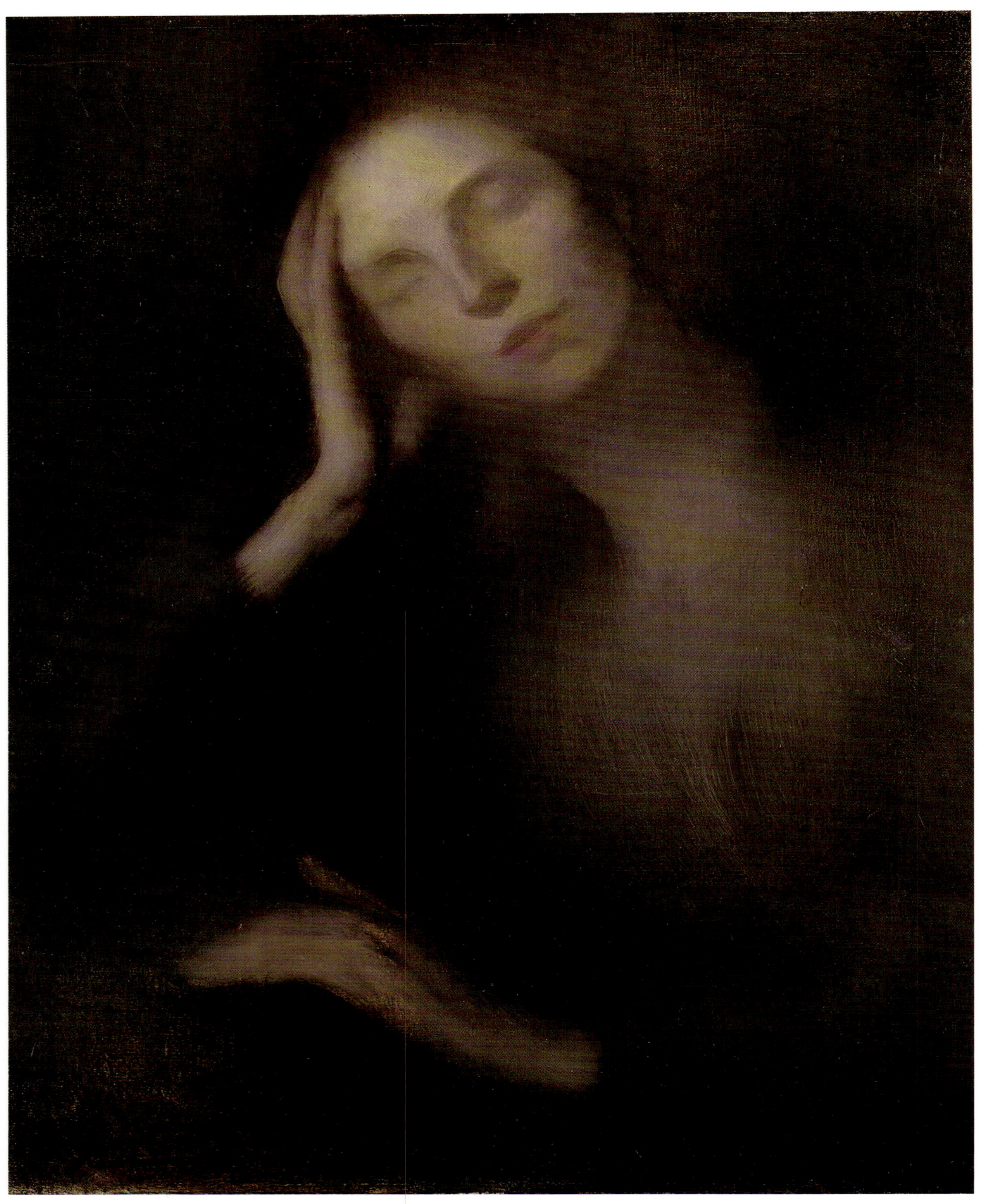

Eugène Carrière (1849–1906)

Woman at a Table

Femme accoudée sur une table

Frau, sich auf einen Tisch stützend

Mujer apoyada sobre una mesa

Mulher Apoiando-se numa Mesa

Vrouw leunend op tafel

c. 1893, Oil on canvas/ Huile sur toile, 65 × 54 cm

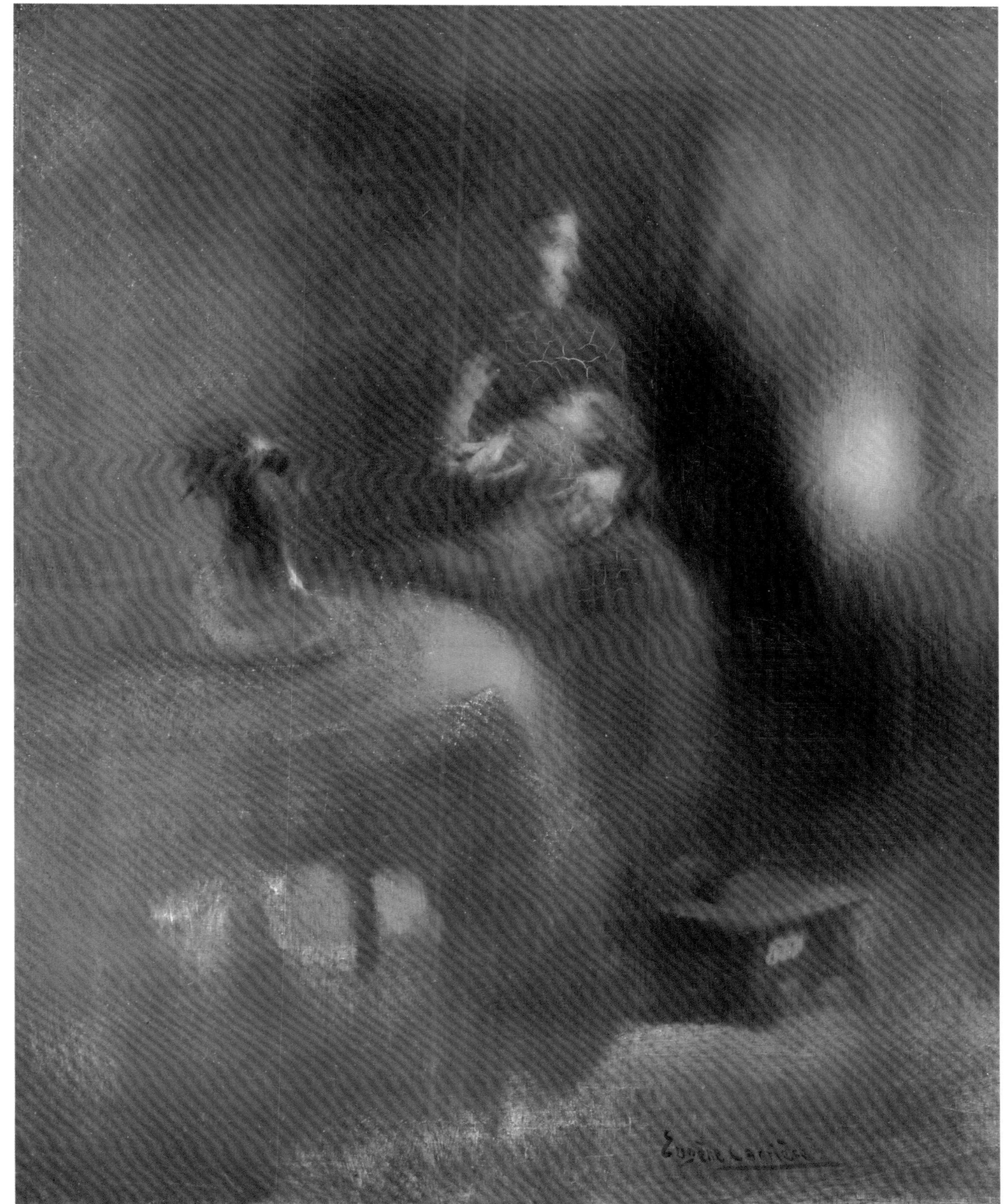

*Eugène
Carrière
(1849–1906)*

Woman
with Child

Femme avec
un enfant sur
ses genoux

Frau mit
Kleinkind

Mujer con
niño

Mulher com
Criança

Vrouw
met kind

c. 1890, Oil
on canvas/
Huile sur toile,
61,3 × 50 cm

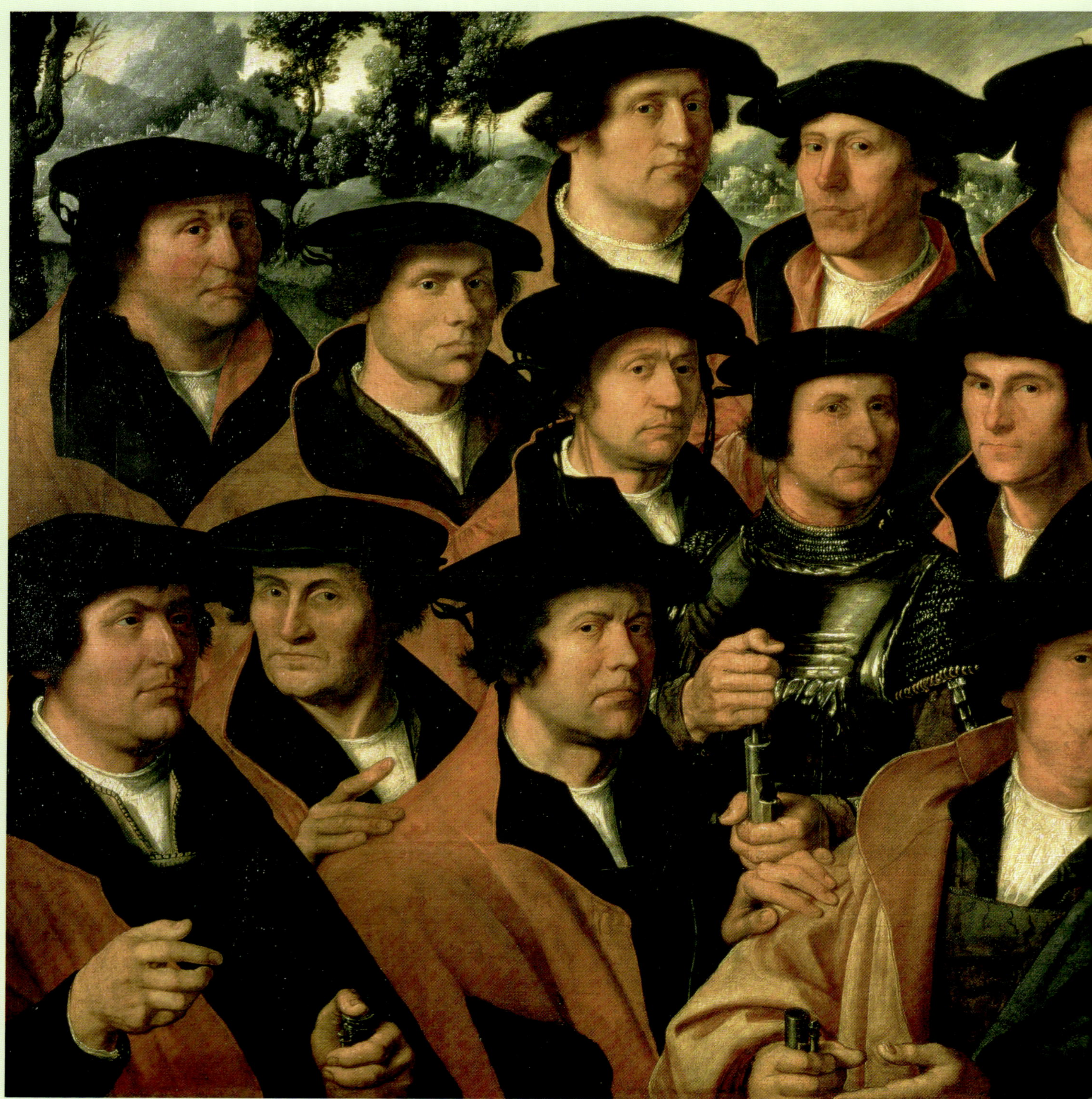

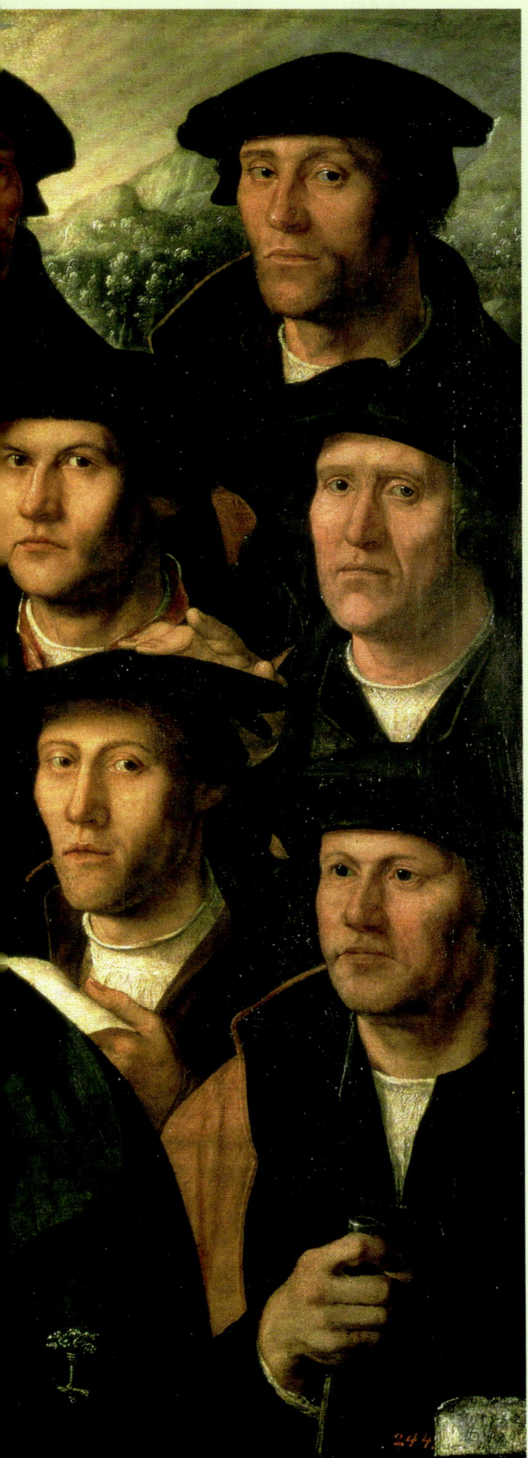

EARLY NETHERLANDISH PAINTING OF THE 15TH AND 16TH CENTURIES
LES PRIMITIFS FLAMANDS DES XVE ET XVIE SIÈCLES
ALTNIEDERLÄNDISCHE MALEREI DES 15. UND 16. JAHRHUNDERTS
PINTURA FLAMENCA PRIMITIVA DE LOS SIGLOS XV Y XVI
PINTURA HOLANDESA ANTIGA DO SÉCULO XV E XVI
VROEGNEDERLANDSE SCHILDERKUNST VAN DE 15E EN 16E EEUW

Dirk Jacobsz (1497–1567)

The Shooting Guild of Amsterdam

La Corporation des arquebusiers d'Amsterdam

Die Schützengilde von Amsterdam

La Corporación de Arcabuceros de Ámsterdam

Retrato de Grupo da Companhia de Tiro de Amsterdão

De schutterij van Amsterdam

1532, Oil on canvas, transferred from panel/Huile sur toile transposée d'un bois, 115 × 160 cm

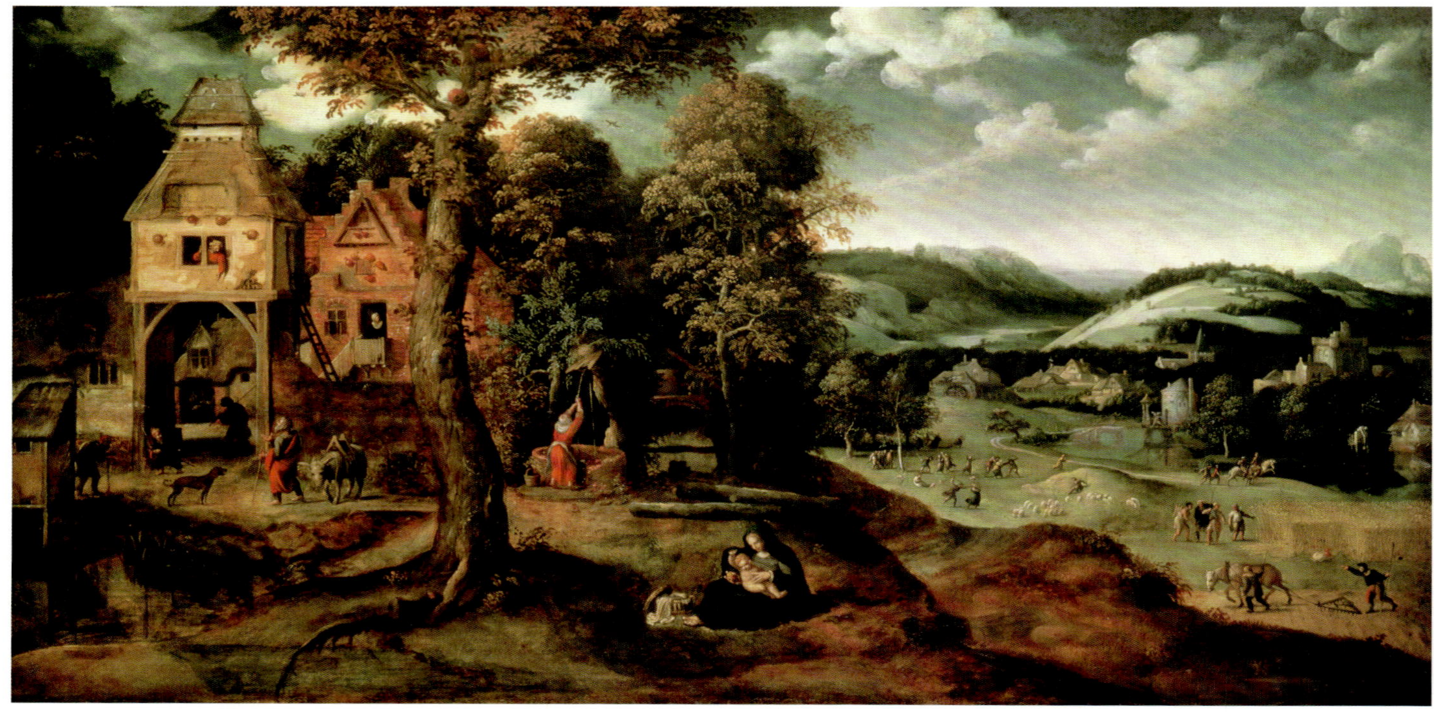

Joachim Patinir (attr.) (1483–1524)
Rest on the Flight into Egypt
Paysage avec la fuite en Égypte
Ruhe auf der Flucht nach Ägypten
Un descanso durante la huida a Egipto
Descanso na Fuga para o Egito
Rust tijdens de vlucht naar Egypte
c. 1524, Oil on canvas/Huile sur toile, 51 × 96 cm

Gerard David (c. 1460–1523)
The Lamentation
La Vierge embrassant le Christ mort
Beweinung Christi
La lamentación
Lamentação de Cristo
Bewening van Christus
n. d., Oil on canvas/Huile sur toile, 11,4 × 16,2 cm

Early Netherlandish Painting of the 15th and 16th Centuries

The collection of early Netherlandish paintings comprises around 100 works. *Saint Luke Drawing the Madonna* by Rogier van der Weyden is, together with Rober Campin's *diptych,* one of the pearls of this collection, complemented by works by Lucas van Leyden, Dirk Jacobs, and other masters. This impressive collection also includes several thousand drawings and prints.

Les primitifs flamands des XVe et XVIe siècles

La collection des primitifs flamands comporte une centaine de tableaux. À côté du *Diptyque* de Robert Campin, le *Saint Luc dessinant la Vierge* de Rogier van der Weyden compte parmi les perles de cette collection, complétée par des œuvres de Lucas van Leyden, Dirk Jacobs et autres maîtres – à quoi s'ajoutent plusieurs milliers de dessins et d'estampes.

Altniederländische Malerei des 15. und 16. Jahrhunderts

Die Sammlung altniederländischer Malerei umfasst rund 100 Werke. *Der heilige Lukas zeichnet die Madonna* von Rogier van der Weyden zählt neben dem *Diptychon* Robert Campins zu den Perlen dieser Sammlung, die durch Werke von Lucas van Leyden, Dirk Jacobs und weiteren Meistern ergänzt wird. Einige Tausend Zeichnungen und Drucke runden die eindrucksvolle Sammlung ab.

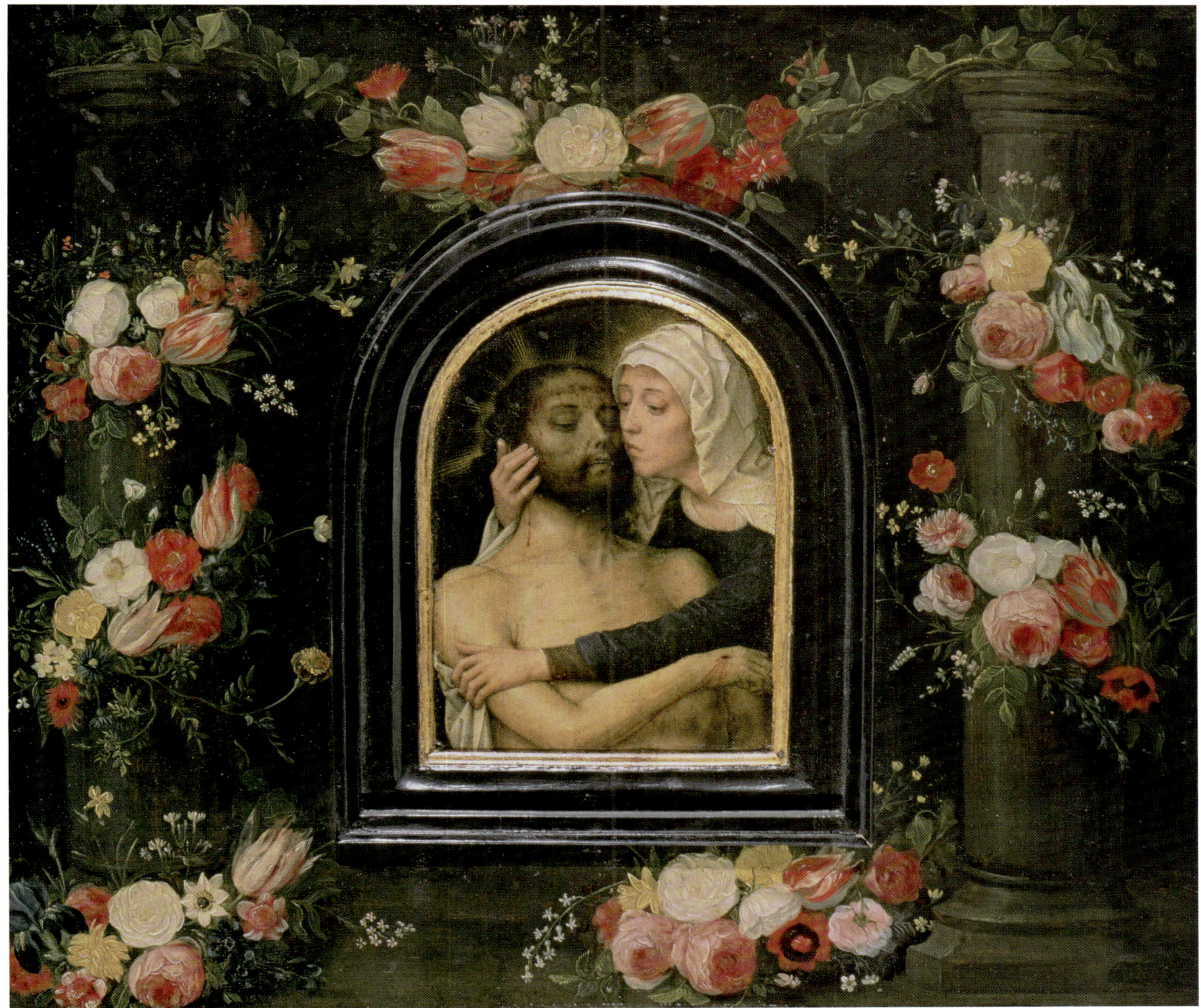

Pintura flamenca primitiva
de los siglos XV y XVI

La colección de pintura flamenca primitiva incluye unas 100 obras. *San Lucas pintando a la Virgen* de Rogier van der Weyden, junto con el *díptico* de Robert Campins, es una de las perlas de esta colección que se complementa con obras de Lucas van Leyden, Dirk Jacobs y otros maestros. Completan la impresionante colección varios miles de dibujos y grabados.

Pintura holandesa antiga
do século XV e XVI

A coleção de pintura holandesa antiga abrange cerca de 100 obras. Além do *díptico* de Robert Campin, a pintura *São Lucas Desenhando a Virgem* de Rogier van der Weyden está entre as pérolas desta coleção, que é completada através de obras de Lucas van Leyden, Dirk Jacobs e de outros mestres. Alguns milhares de desenhos e impressões complementam a impressionante coleção.

Vroegnederlandse schilderkunst
van de 15e en 16e eeuw

De collectie vroegnederlandse schilderkunst omvat rond honderd werken. *Sint-Lucas tekent het portret van de Madonna* van Rogier van der Weyden behoort naast het *tweeluik* van Robert Campin tot de topstukken van de collectie, die ook werken van Lucas van Leyden, Dirk Jacobs en andere meesters omvat. De imposante collectie wordt aangevuld met circa duizend tekeningen en prenten.

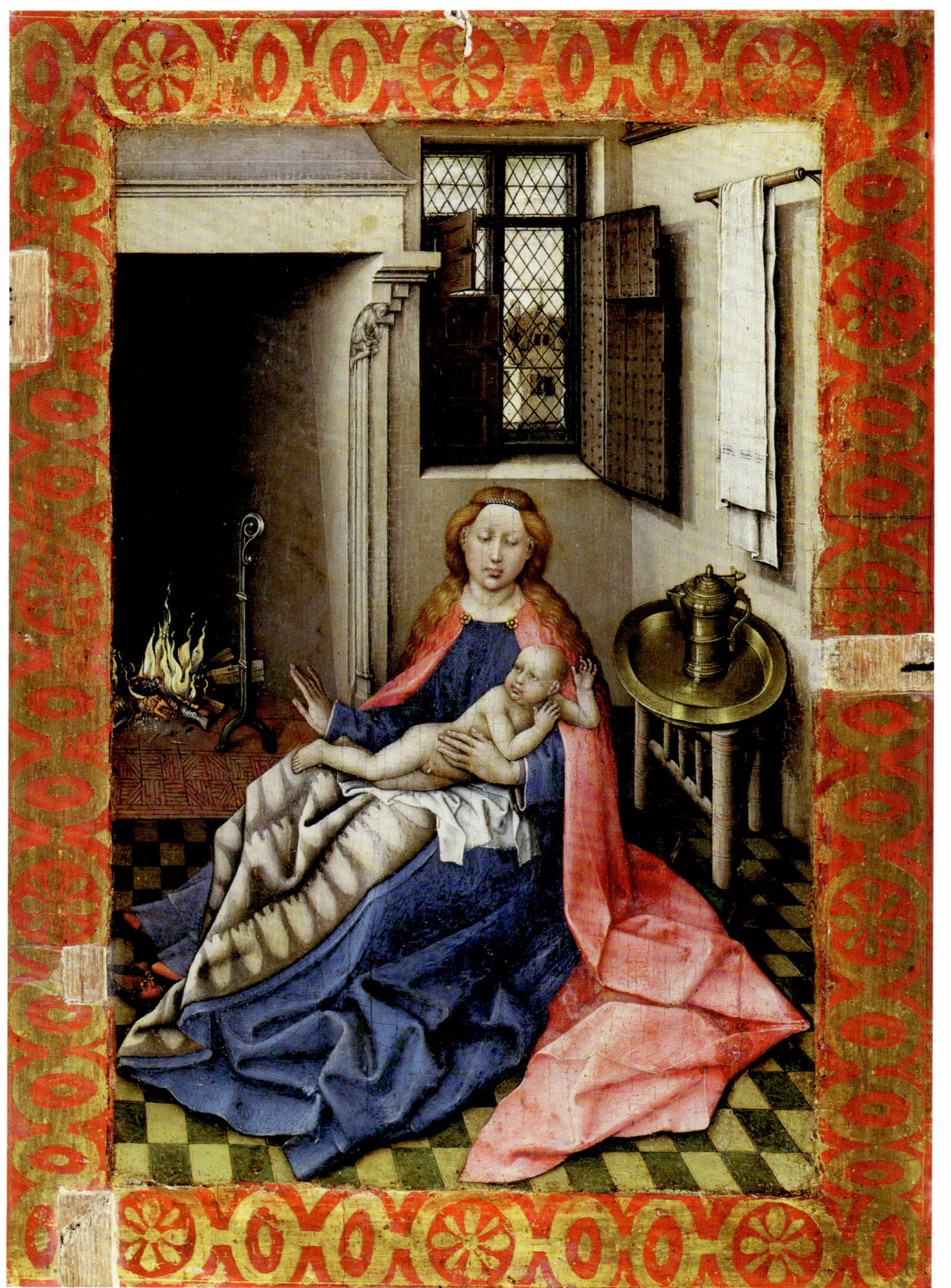

Robert Campin (Master of Flémalle/la Maître de Flémalle) (c. 1378–1444)

Madonna and Child in Front of a Fireplace

La Vierge à l'Enfant, dit aussi La Vierge à la cheminée

Muttergottes und Kind vor einer Feuerstelle

Virgen y niño delante de una chimenea

Virgem e Menino diante da Lareira

Madonna en kind voor een haard

1430, Tempera on wood/Tempera sur bois, 34,3 × 24,5 cm

Anonymous/Anonyme

Hell

L'Enfer

Die Hölle

El infierno

O Inferno

De hel

First decade of the 16th century/ Premier tiers du XVIe siècle, Oil on wood/Huile sur bois, 39,7 × 38,5 cm

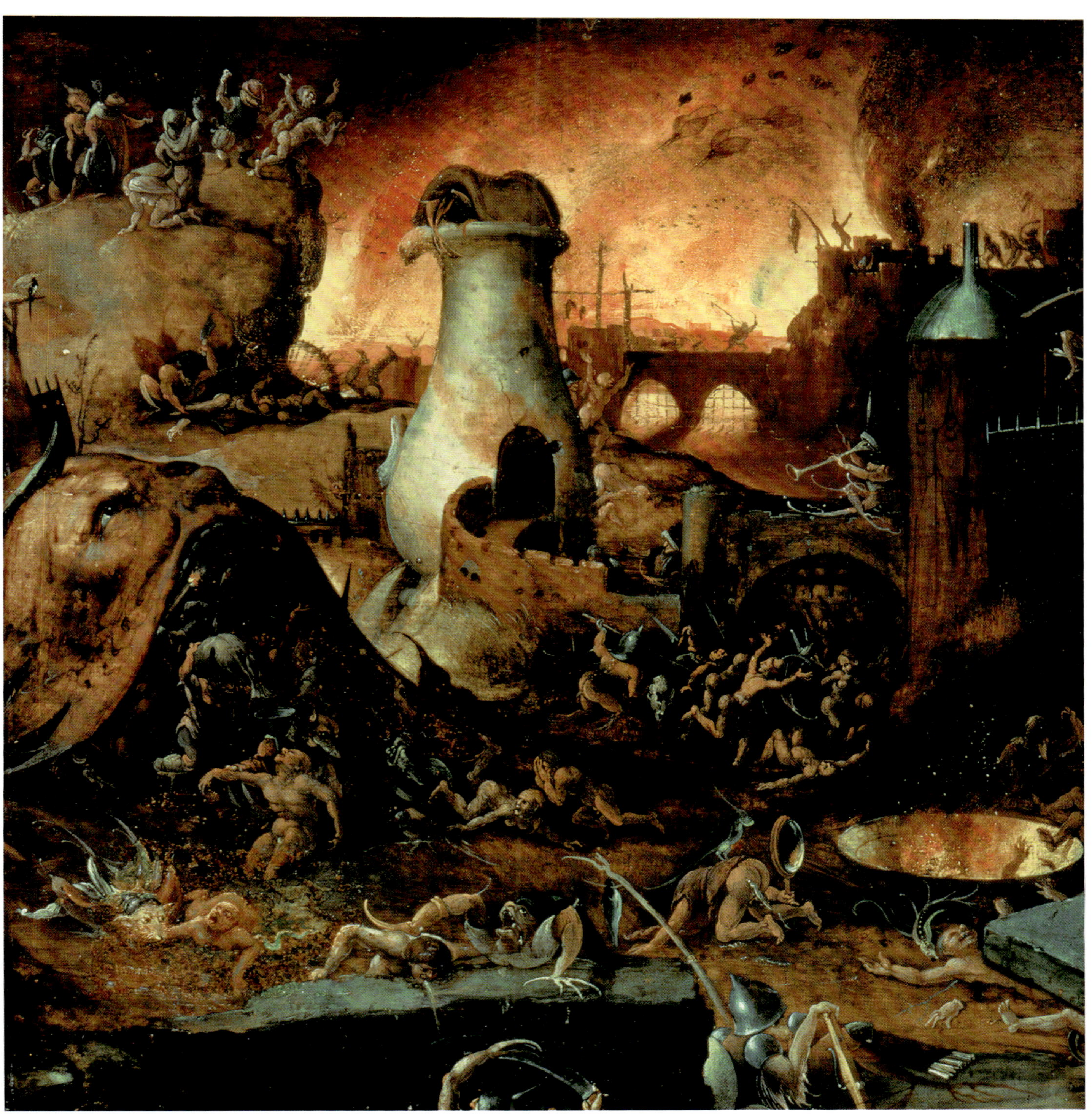

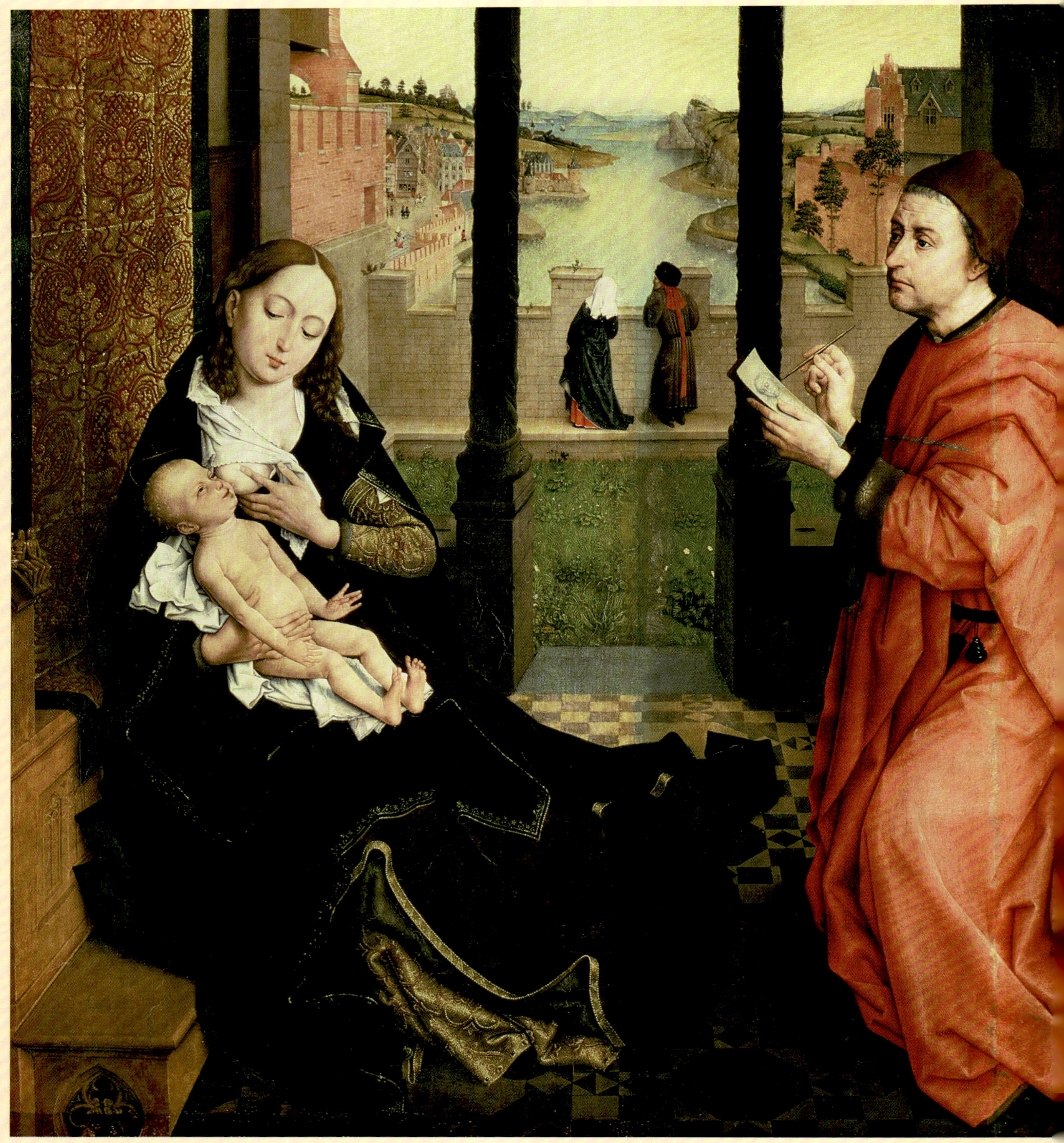

One highlight of the collection is this Flemish masterpiece. Using the new technique of oil painting, van der Weyden managed to show the finest nuances of each color and thus create a credible plasticity through his use of chiaroscuro modeling. The interior space with the Madonna and St. Luke opens out onto a vast panorama of a city, a river, and blurred, bluish mountains off in the distance.

Ce tableau de maître flamand est une des pièces phares de la collection. Grâce à la nouvelle technique de la peinture à l'huile, van der Weyden réussit à traduire les nuances les plus délicates des valeurs tonales et le subtil modelé du clair-obscur lui permet d'obtenir une parfaite crédibilité de la plastique. L'espace intérieur où se trouvent la Vierge à l'Enfant et saint Luc s'ouvre par une triple baie sur un vaste panorama avec une ville traversée par un fleuve et un horizon de montagnes se dissolvant dans des lointains bleutés.

Ein Höhepunkt der Sammlung ist dieses Bild des flämischen Meisters. Mit Hilfe der neuen Technik der Ölmalerei gelang es van der Weyden, sämtliche Farbwerte in feinste Nuancen übergehen zu lassen und zudem durch die Hell-Dunkel-Modellierung glaubwürdige Plastizität zu erzielen. Der Innenraum mit der Madonna und dem heiligen Lukas öffnet sich auf ein weites Panorama mit einer Stadt, einem Flusslauf und in der Ferne bläulich verschwimmenden Bergen.

Esta imagen del maestro flamenco es uno de los puntos álgidos de la colección. Ayudándose con la nueva técnica de la pintura al óleo van der Weyden consigue obtener matices finísimos que hacen que las transiciones entre colores, y con ellas el modelado de claroscuros, ganen una plasticidad altamente realista. El interior con la Virgen y San Lucas se abre a una panorámica que muestra una ciudad, el curso de un río y montañas en la lejanía desvaneciéndose en tonos azulados.

Esta obra do mestre flamengo consiste num apogeu da coleção. Com o auxílio da nova técnica da pintura a óleo, van der Weyden conseguiu transferir toda a cromaticidade para as mais delicadas nuances e ainda alcançar uma plasticidade plausível através da modelação do claro-escuro. O espaço interior com a Virgem e São Lucas abre-se num vasto panorama com uma cidade, o correr de um rio e montes esbatidos a azul ao longe.

Een van de topstukken uit de collectie is dit schilderij van de Vlaamse meester. Met behulp van een nieuwe techniek in de olieverfschilderkunst lukte het Van der Weyden om alle kleuren in de subtielste nuances aan te brengen en door licht-donker-contrasten de beeldende kracht bovendien geloofwaardig te laten zijn. Vanuit de ruimte met de Madonna en de heilige Lucas ontvouwt zich een weids panorama met een stad, een rivier en in de verte blauwig vervagende bergen.

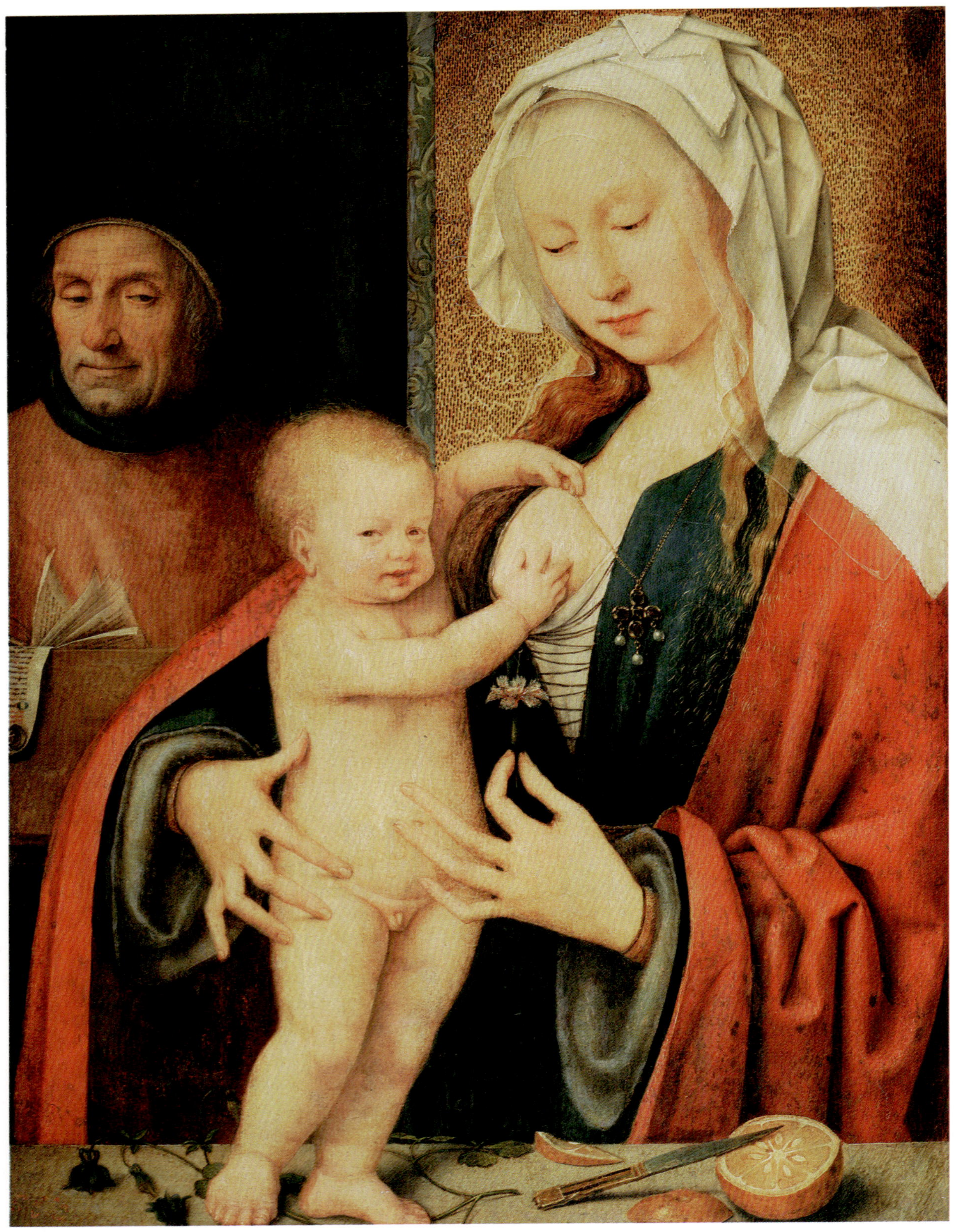

Joos van Cleve
(c. 1485–c. 1541)
The Holy Family
La Sainte Famille
Die Heilige Familie
La Sagrada Familia
A Sagrada Família
De Heilige Familie

n. d., Oil on canvas/Huile
sur toile, 42,5 × 31,5 cm

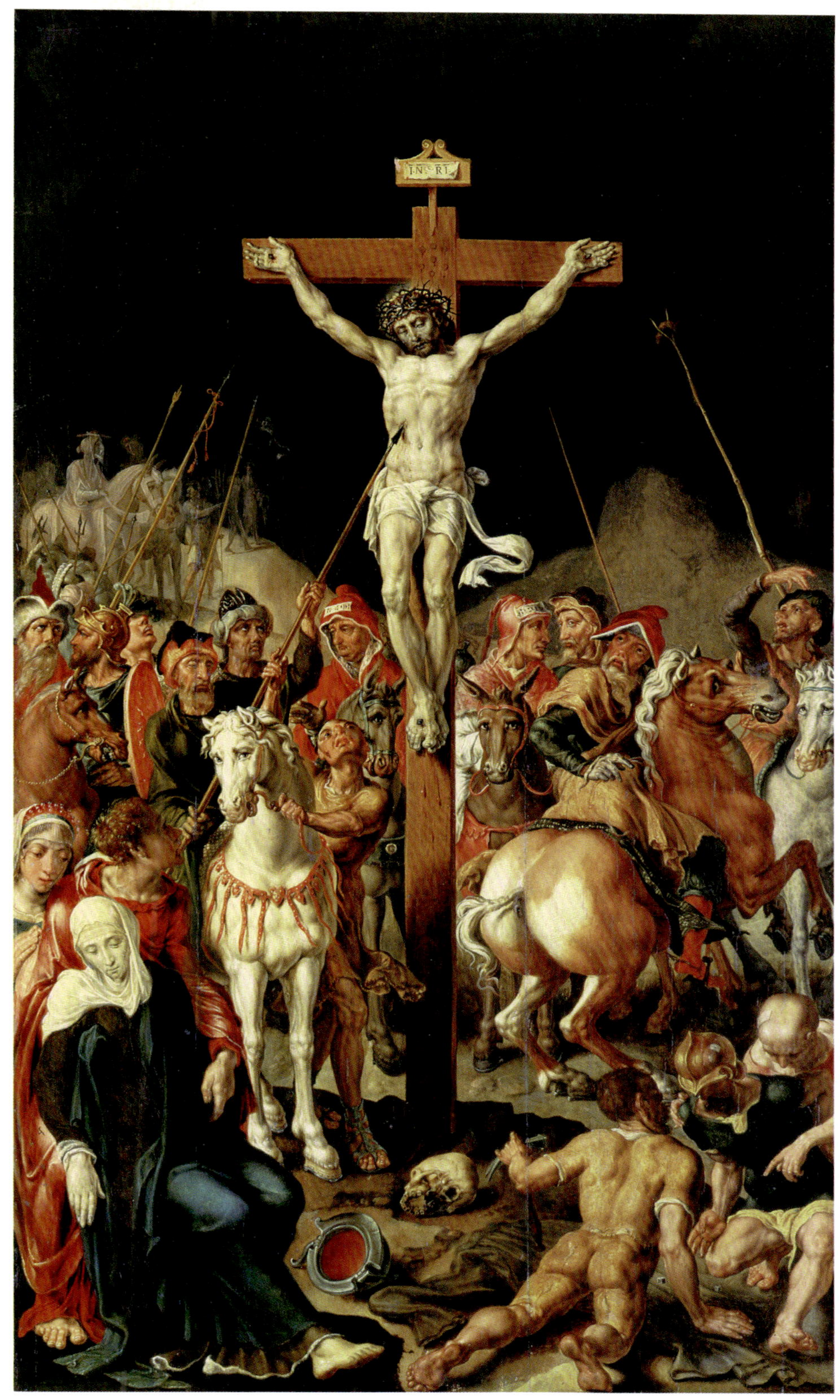

Maerten van Heemskerck (1498–1574)

Calvary

Calvaire

Kalvarienberg

El Calvario (Gólgota)

O Monte do Calvário

Calvarieberg

c. 1545–50, Oil on canvas/Huile sur toile, 100,7 × 86,3 cm

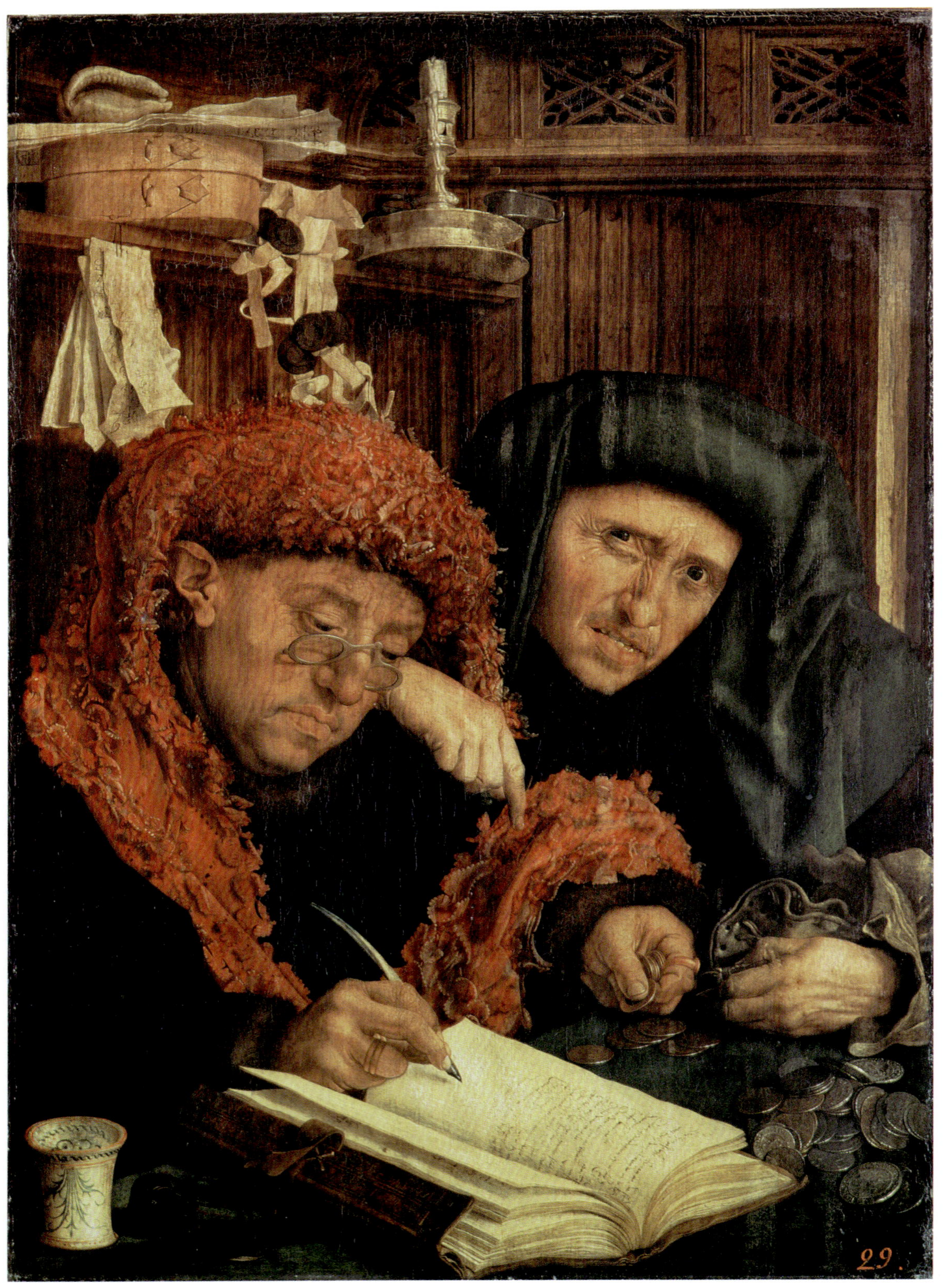

Marinus van Reymerswaele
(c. 1490–1567)

The Tax Collectors

Les Collecteurs d'impôts

Die Steuereintreiber

Los recaudadores de impuestos

Os Coletores de Impostos

De belastinginners

n.d., Oil on wood/Huile sur bois, 84,3 × 59,6 cm

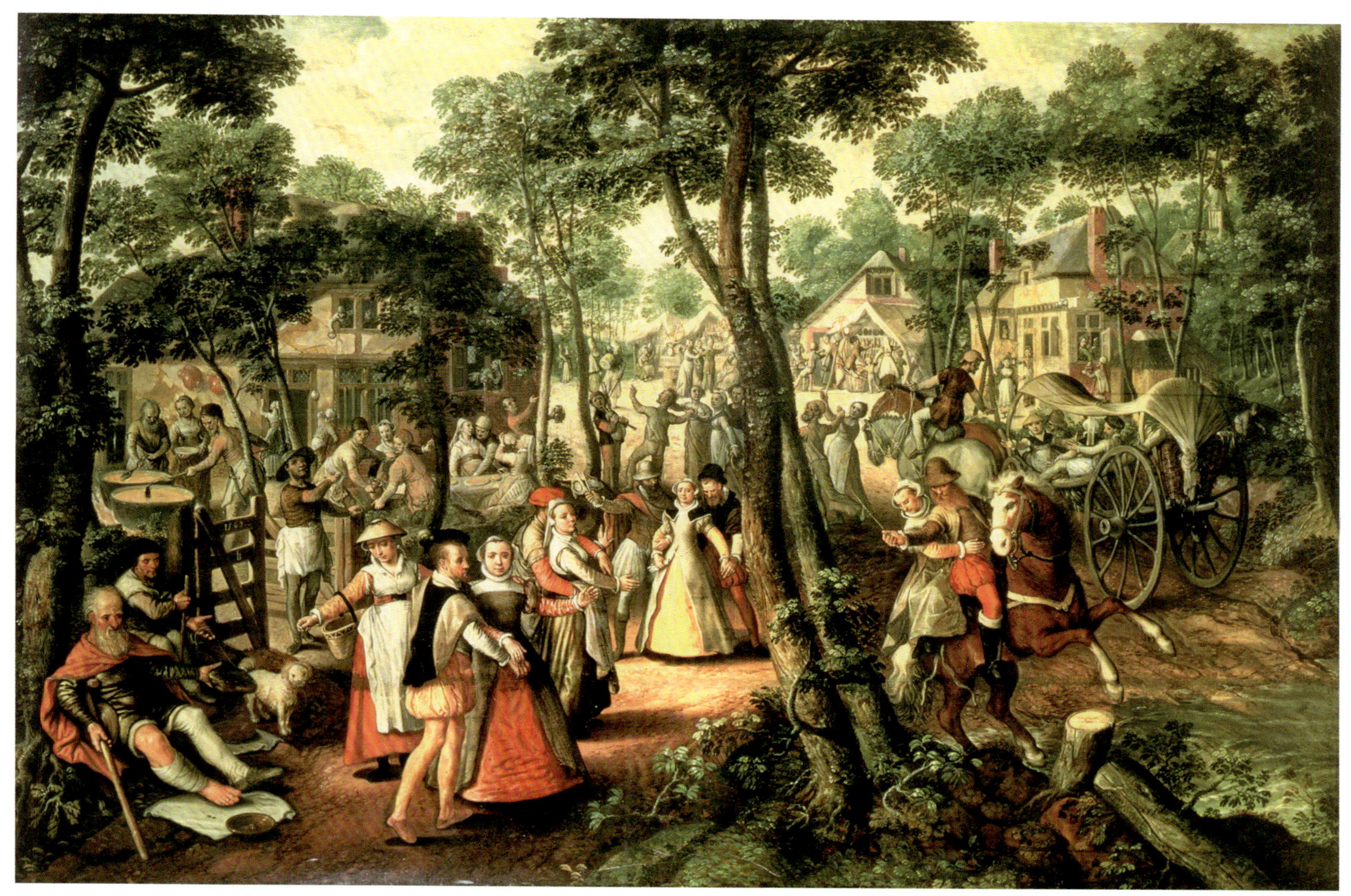

Joachim Beuckelaer or/ou Bueckelaer (c. 1530–73)

Country Festival

Kermesse

Ländliches Fest

Fiesta campestre

Festa no Campo

Landelijk feest

1563, Oil on canvas/Huile sur toile, 112 × 163,5 cm

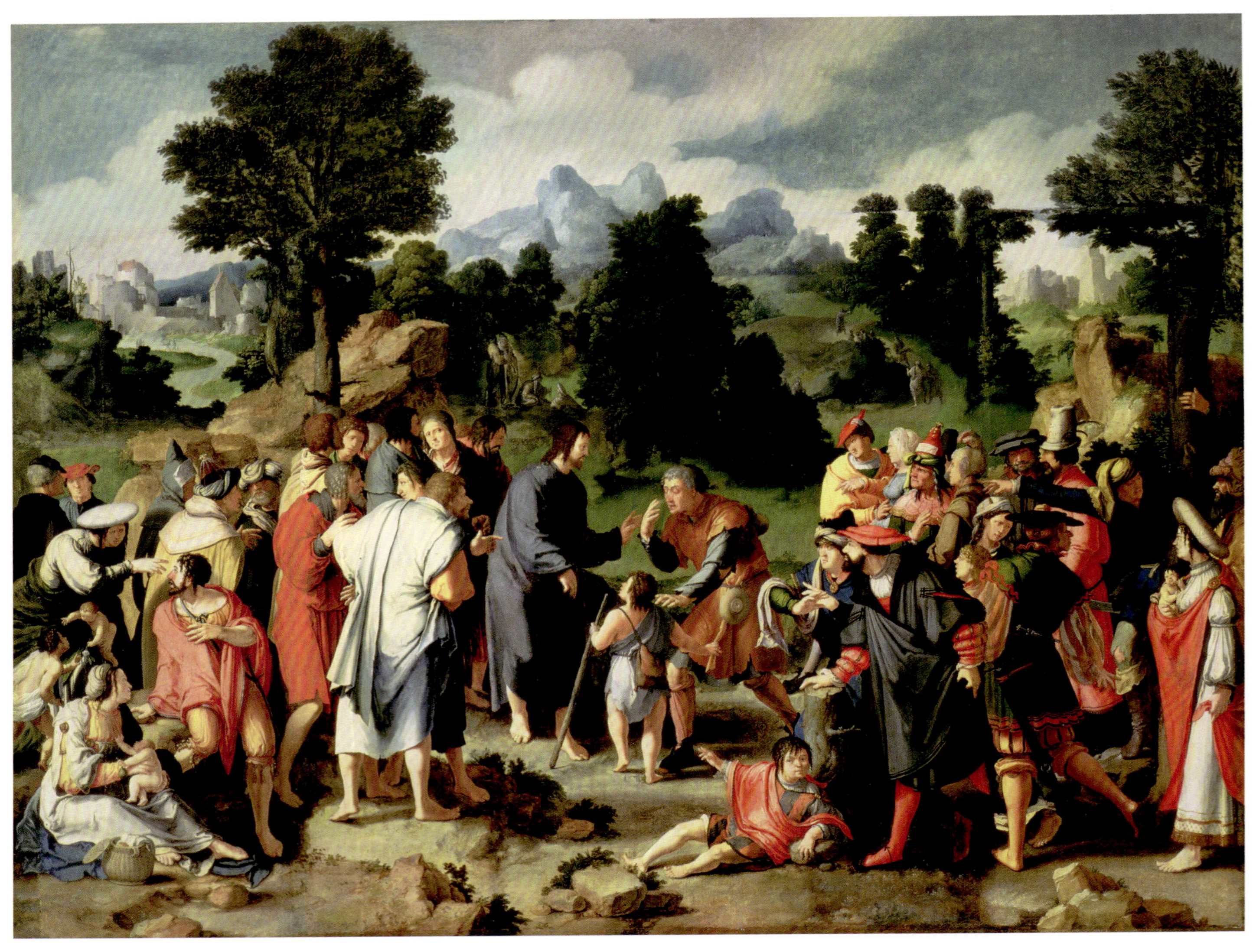

Lucas van Leyden (c. 1494–1533)

The Healing of the Blind Man of Jericho

La Guérison de l'aveugle de Jéricho (triptyque, panneau central)

Die Heilung des Blinden von Jericho

La curación del ciego de Jericó

A Cura do Cego de Jericó

De genezing van de blinde van Jericho

1531, Oil on canvas/Huile sur toile, 115,7 × 150 cm

Lucas van Leyden (c. 1494–1533)

The Healing of the Blind Man of Jericho (left and right side panel)

La Guérison de l'aveugle de Jéricho (triptyque, panneau de gauche et droite)

Die Heilung des Blinden von Jericho (linker und rechter Seitenflügel)

La curación del ciego de Jericó (tabla izquierda y derecha)

A Cura do Cego de Jericó (painel esquerdo e direito)

De genezing van de blinde van Jericho (linker- en rechterzijpaneel)

1531, Oil on canvas/Huile sur toile, 89 × 33,5 cm

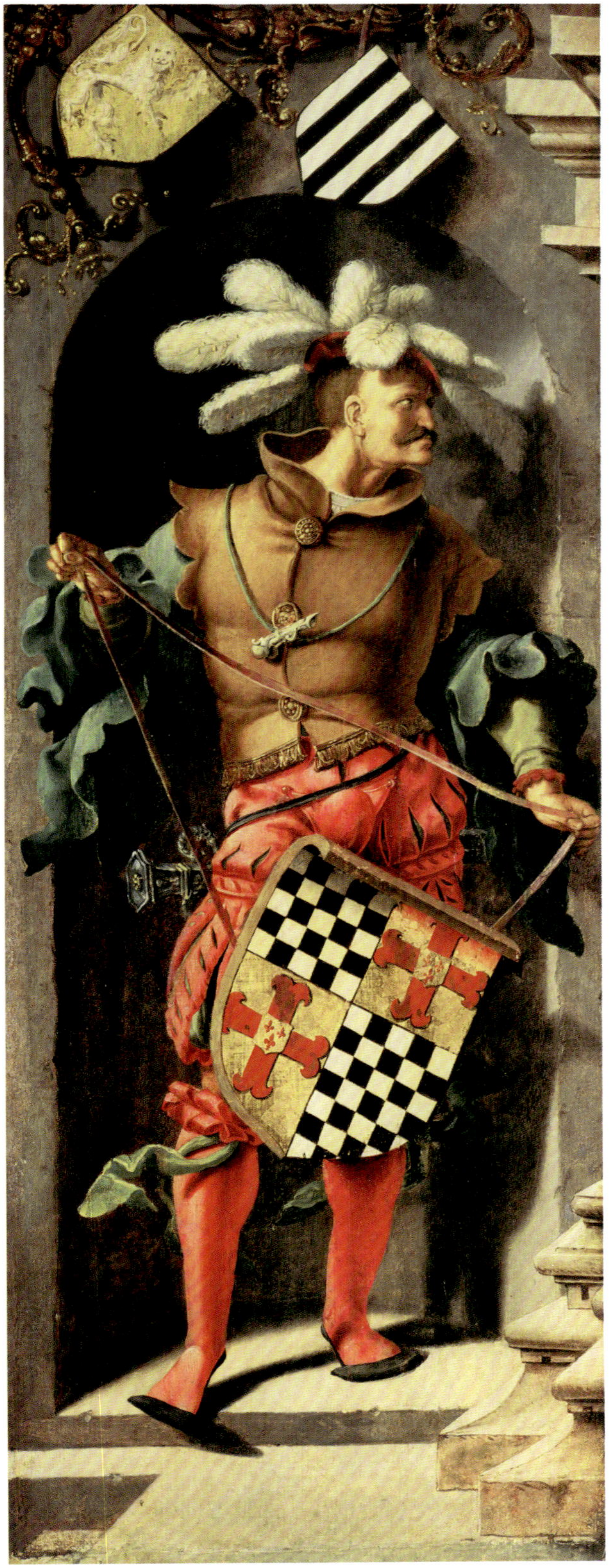

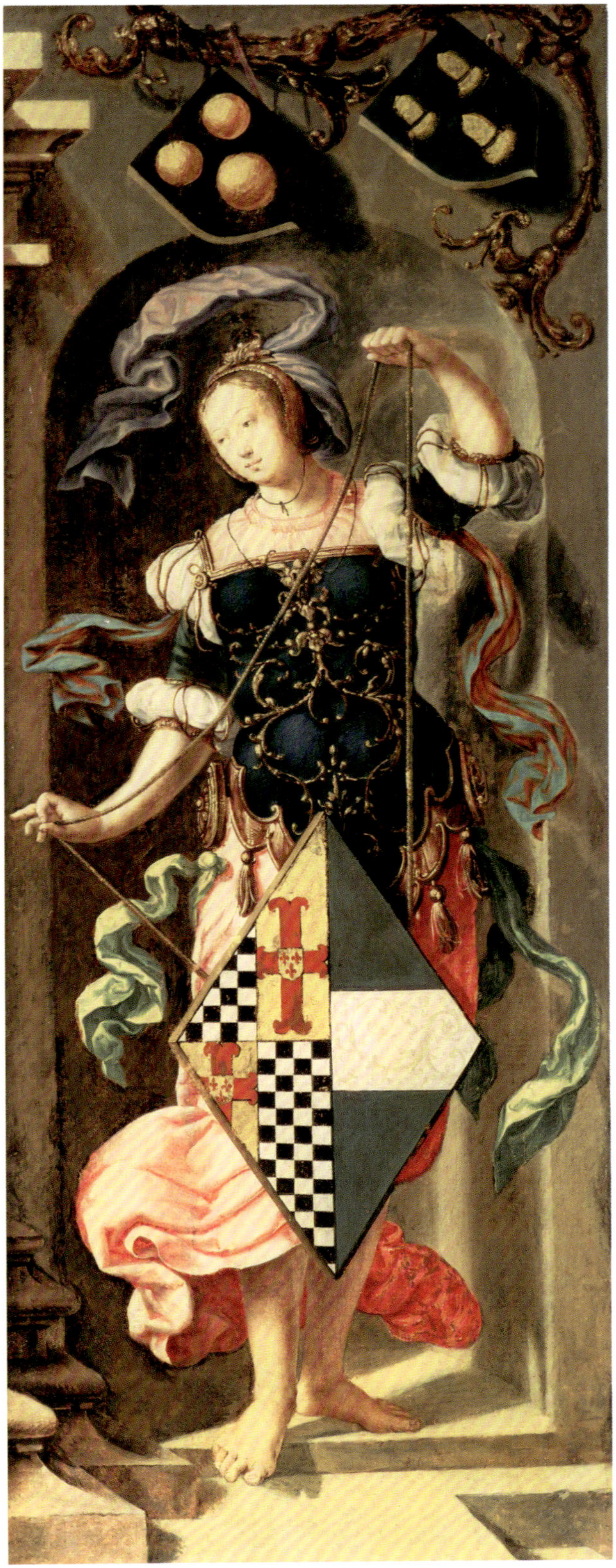

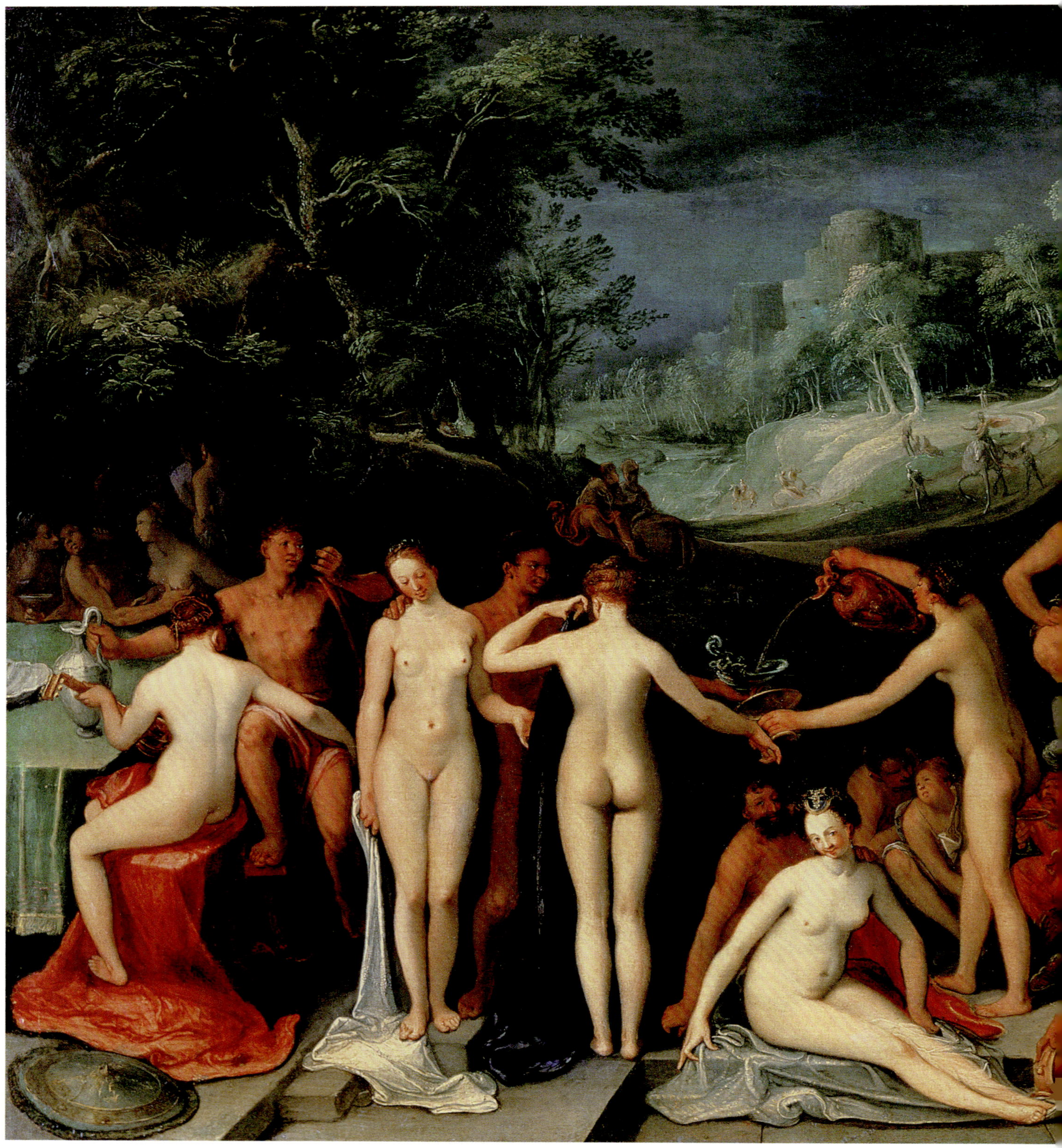

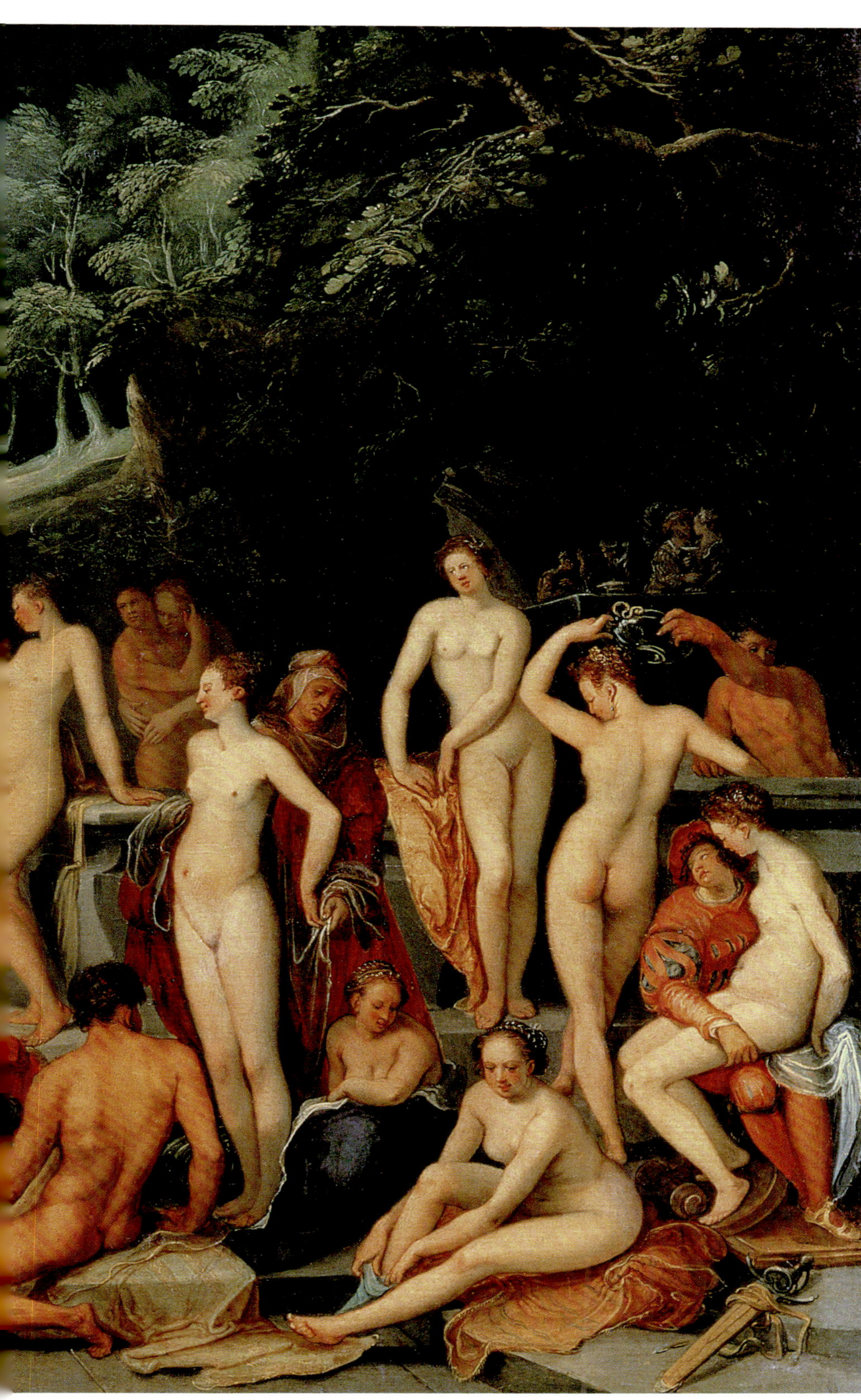

Karel van Mander (1548–1606)

The Love Garden

Le Jardin d'amour

Der Liebesgarten

El jardín del amor

O Jardim do Amor

De liefdestuin

1602, Oil on canvas/Huile sur toile, 45 × 70 cm

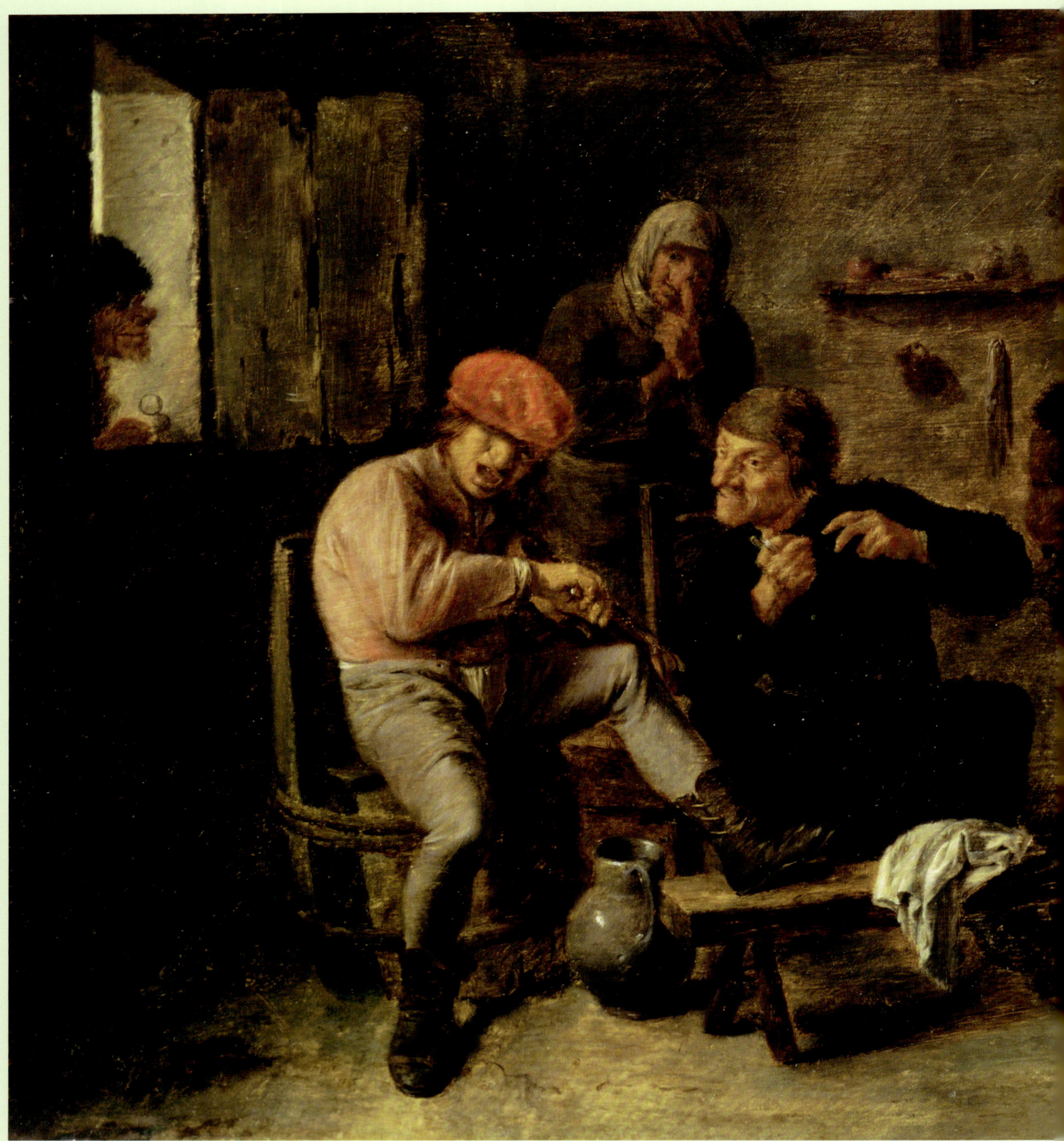

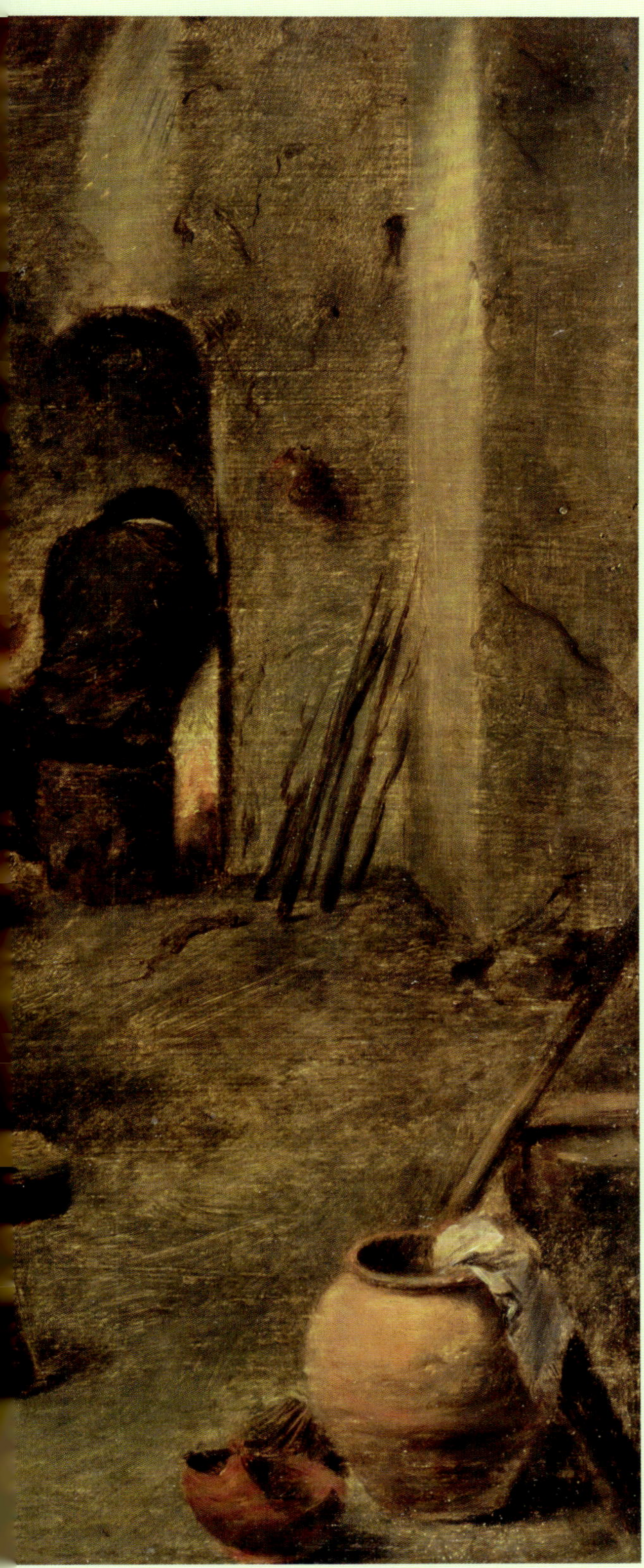

FLEMISH PAINTING OF THE 17TH AND 18TH CENTURIES
LA PEINTURE FLAMANDE DES XVIIE ET XVIIIE SIÈCLES
FLÄMISCHE MALEREI DES 17. UND 18. JAHRHUNDERTS
PINTURA FLAMENCA DE LOS SIGLOS XVII Y XVIII
PINTURA FLAMENGA DO SÉCULO XVII E VXIII
VLAAMSE SCHILDERKUNST VAN DE 17E EN 18E EEUW

Adriaen Brouwer (1605/6–38)

Tavern Scene (The Village Fiddler)

Paysant écoutant un « violoneux »

Wirtshausszene (Der Dorfgeiger)

Escena de taberna (el violinista de pueblo)

Cena numa Taberna (O Violinista da Aldeia)

In de taveerne (De dorpsviolist)

1634–38, Oil on wood/Huile sur bois, 25 × 33,5 cm

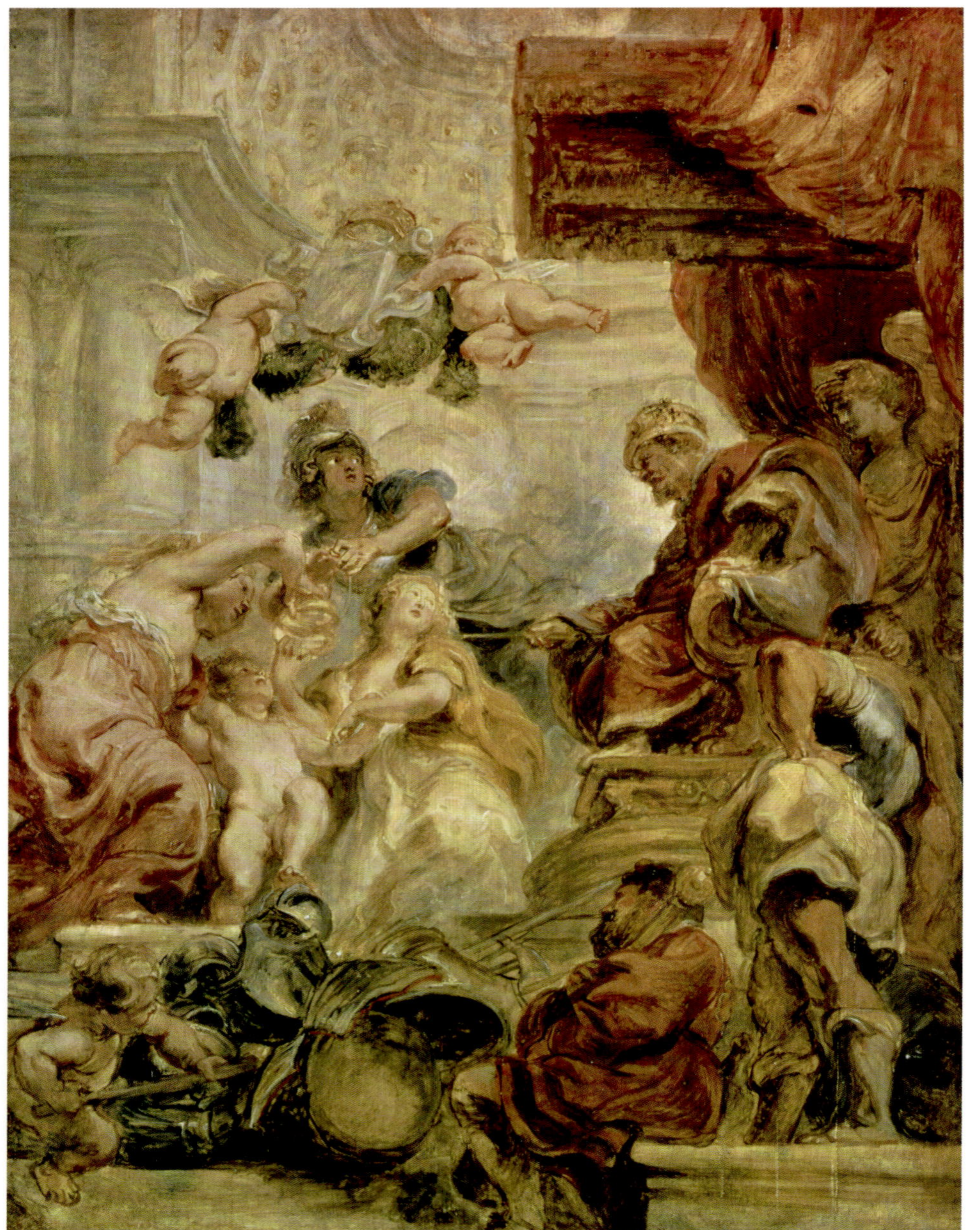

Flemish Painting
of the 17th and 18th Centuries

Flemish painting of the 17th and 18th centuries is housed in five rooms of the New Hermitage. Works include 22 paintings and countless drawings by Rubens, 24 pieces by his pupil Anthonis van Dyck, and large-scale works by Frans Snyders and other contemporaries.

La peinture flamande
des XVIIᵉ et XVIIIᵉ siècles

La peinture flamande des XVIIᵉ et XVIIIᵉ siècles est installée dans cinq salles du Nouvel Ermitage. La collection impressionnante offre vingt-deux tableaux de Rubens, à côté de ses nombreux dessins, vingt-quatre œuvres de son élève Antoine van Dyck et des tableaux de grand format de Frans Snyders et d'autres contemporains.

Flämische Malerei
des 17. und 18. Jahrhunderts

In fünf Räumen der Neuen Eremitage ist die flämische Malerei des 17. und 18. Jahrhunderts untergebracht. Die eindrucksvolle Kollektion präsentiert 22 Gemälde von Rubens, nebst Zeichnungen, 24 Werke seines Schülers Anthonis van Dyck sowie großformatige Werke von Frans Snyders und weiteren Zeitgenossen.

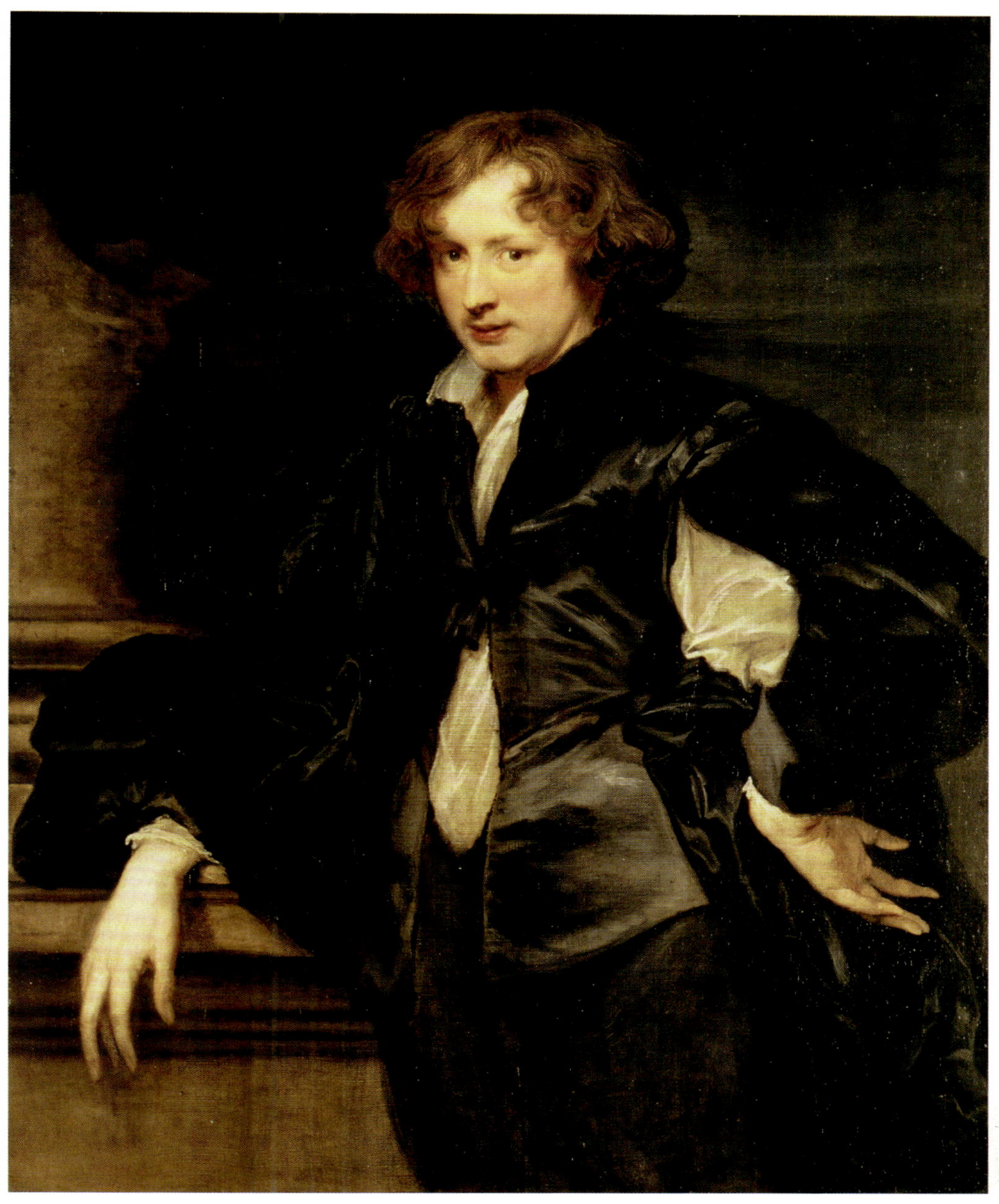

Anthonis van Dyck (1599–1641)

Self-Portrait
Autoportrait
Selbstbildnis
Autorretrato
Autorretrato
Zelfportret

c. 1622/23, Oil on canvas/Huile
sur toile, 116,5 × 93,5 cm

Pintura flamenca
de los siglos XVII y XVIII

La pintura flamenca de los siglos XVII y XVIII
está alojada en cinco salas del Nuevo Hermitage.
La impresionante colección presenta 22 pinturas de
Rubens, además de dibujos, 24 obras de su alumno
Anthonis Van Dyck así como obras de gran formato de
Frans Snyders y otros coetáneos.

Pintura flamenga
do século XVII e VXIII

A pintura flamenga dos séculos XVII e XVIII está
acomodada em cinco salas do Novo Hermitage.
A impressionante coleção apresenta 22 pinturas de
Rubens, além de desenhos, 24 obras do seu aluno
Anthonis van Dyck, bem como obras de grande formato
de Frans Snyders e de outros contemporâneos.

Vlaamse schilderkunst
van de 17e en 18e eeuw

In vijf zalen van de Nieuwe Hermitage is de Vlaamse
schilderkunst van de zeventiende en achttiende eeuw
ondergebracht. Tot de imposante collectie behoren 22
schilderijen van Rubens, 24 doeken van zijn leerling
Anthonis van Dyck, werken op groot formaat van Frans
Snyders en andere tijdgenoten, en tekeningen.

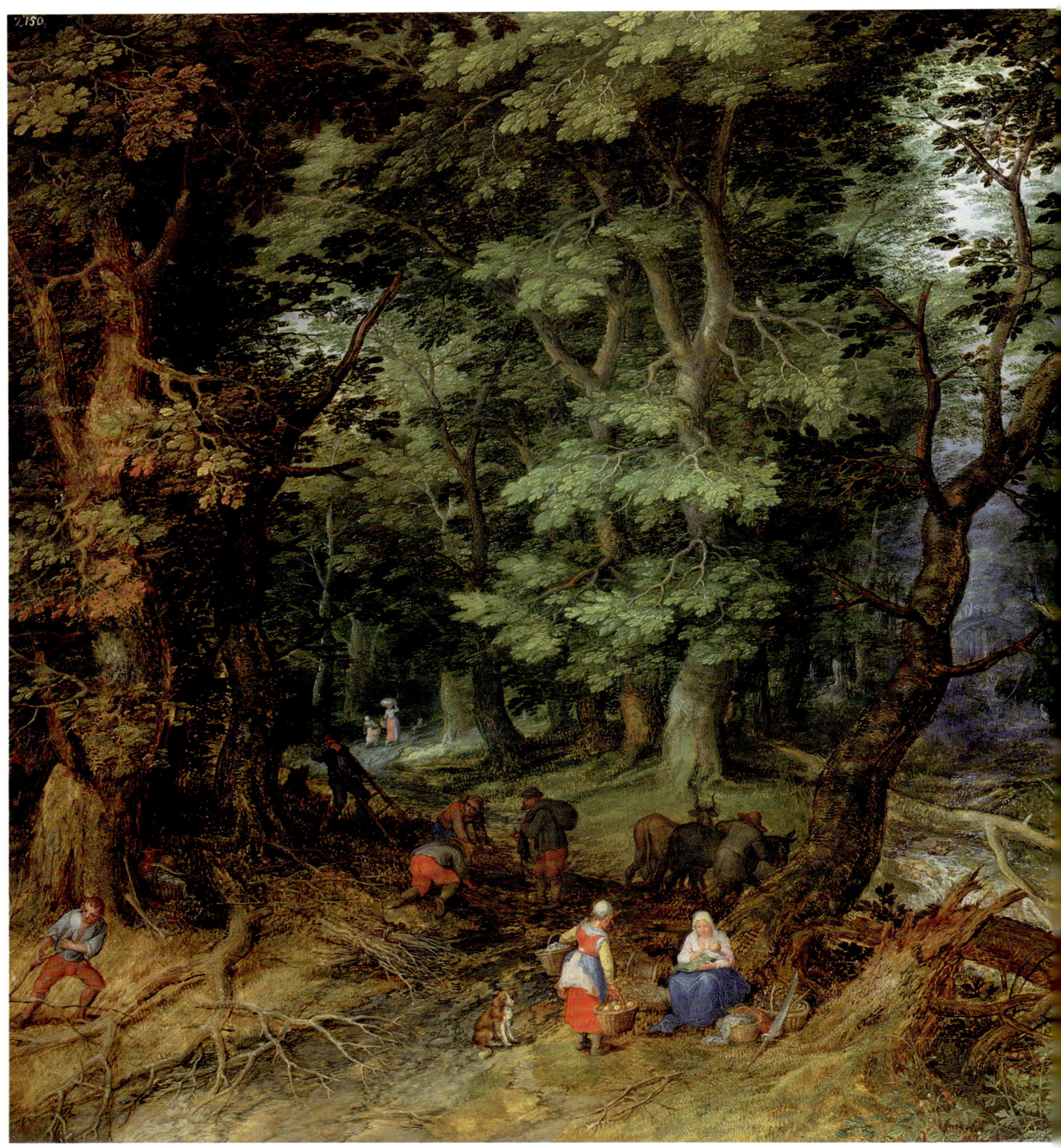

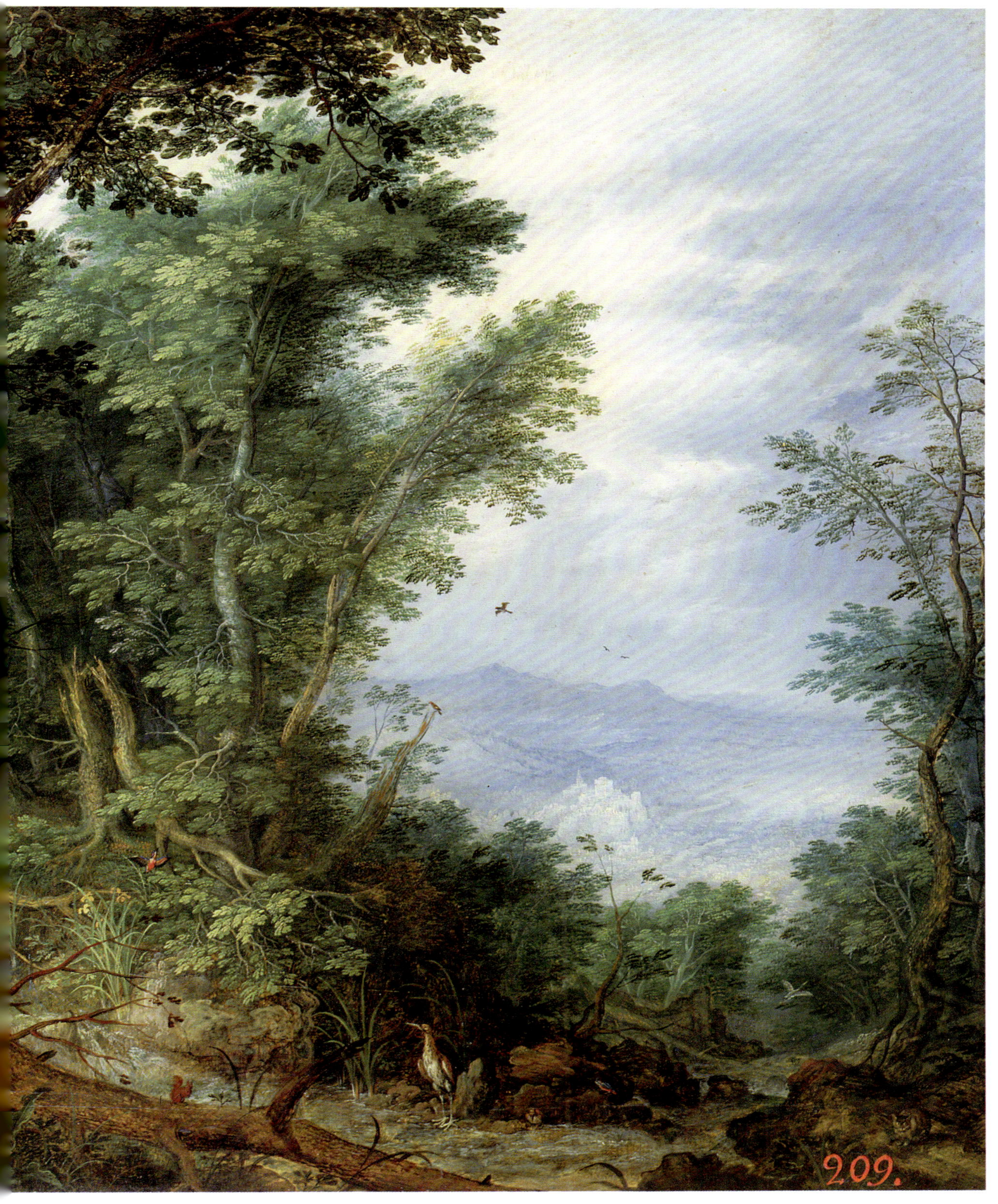

Jan Brueghel de Oude/the Elder/l'Ancien (1568–1625)

Forest Landscape *or* Rest on the Flight into Egypt

Lisière d'une forêt *ou* La Fuite en Égypte

Waldlandschaft *oder* Ruhe auf der Flucht nach Ägypten

Paisaje de bosque *o* Descanso durante la huida a Egipto

Paisagem Florestal *ou* Descanso na Fuga para o Egito

Boslandschap *of* Rust tijdens de vlucht naar Egypte

1607, Oil on wood/Huile sur bois, 51,5 × 91,5 cm

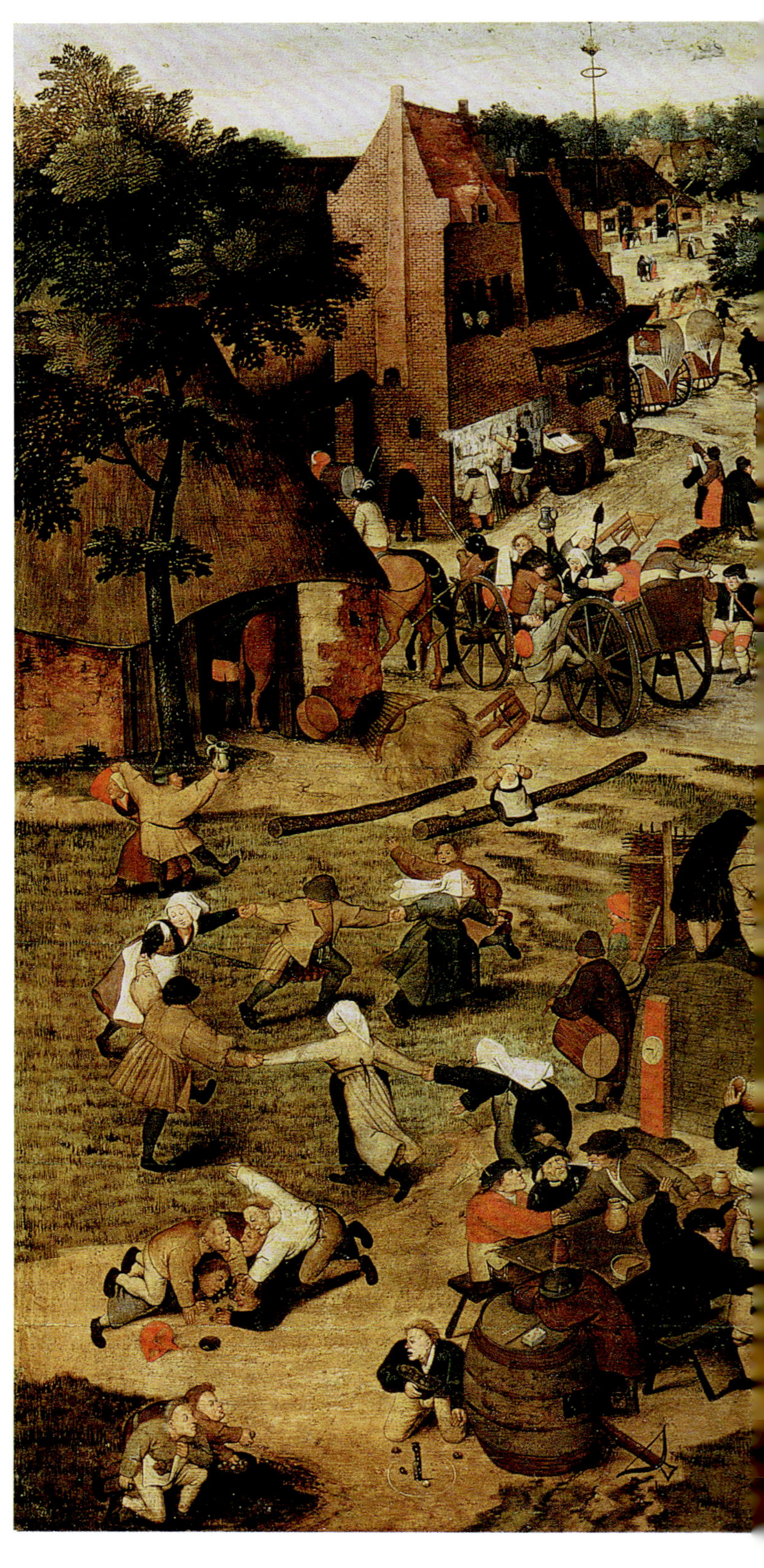

Pieter Brueghel de Jonge/the Younger/le Jeune (c. 1564–1638)

Fairground with Theatrical Performance

Foire avec représentation théâtrale

Kirmes mit Theateraufführung

Feria con representación teatral

Feira com Apresentação Teatral

Kermis mit toneelvoorstelling

c. 1600–35, Oil on wood/Huile sur bois, 111 × 164,5 cm

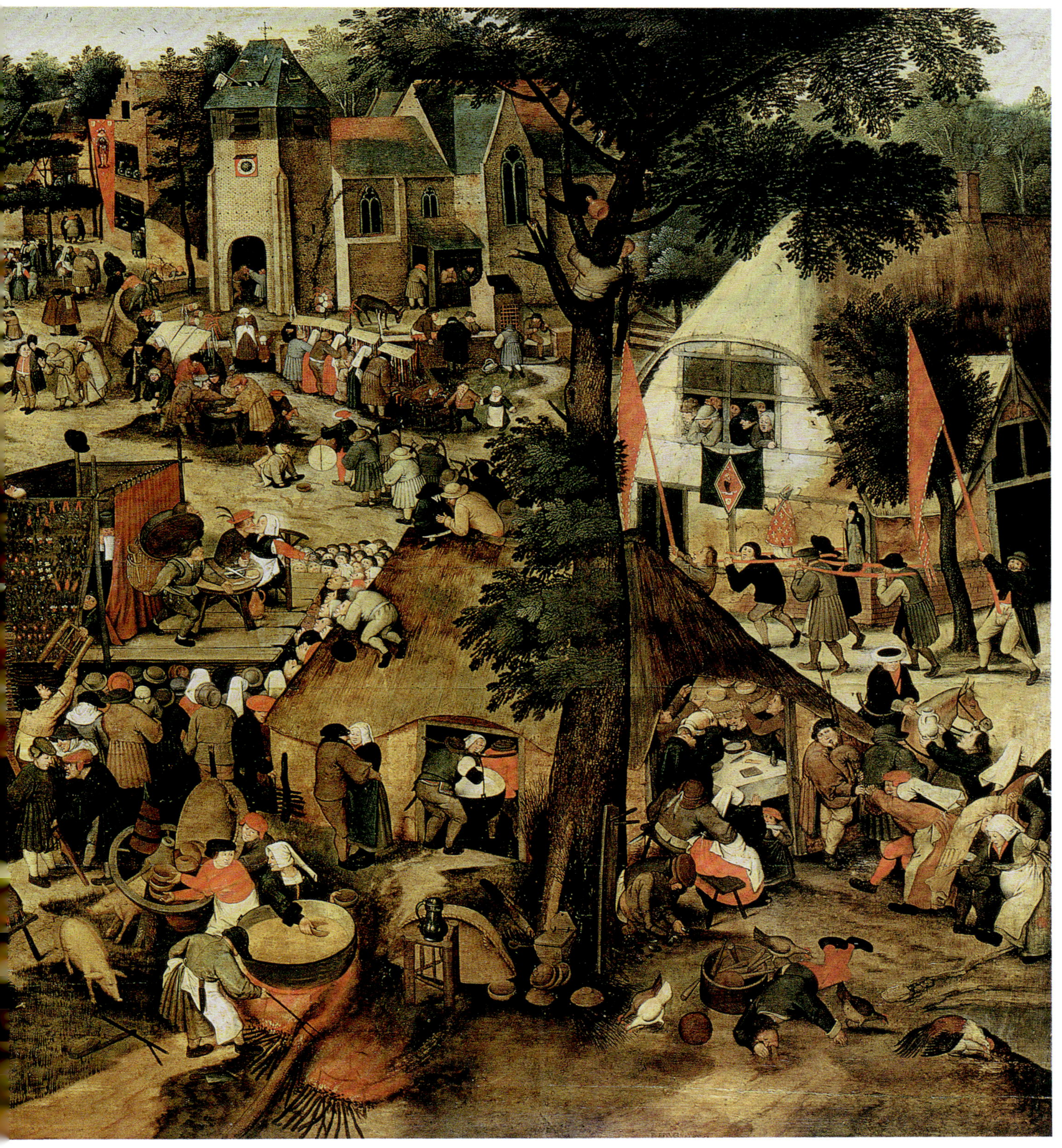

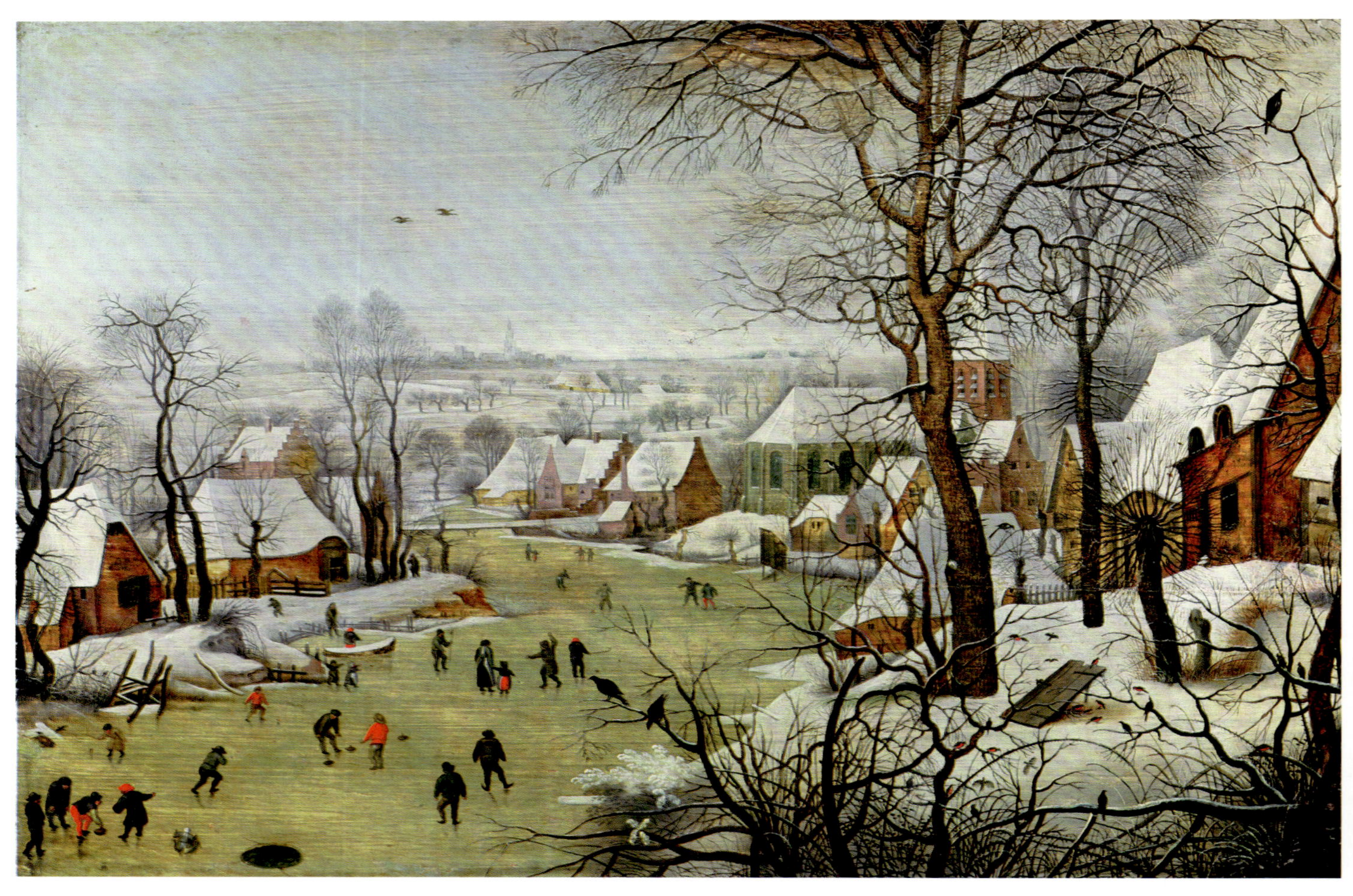

Peter Brueghel de Jonge/the Younger/le Jeune (c. 1564–1638)

Winter Landscape with Birdtrap

Paysage d'hiver avec patineurs

Winterlandschaft mit Vogelfalle

Paisaje invernal con trampa para pájaros

Paisagem de Inverno com Armadilha para Pássaros

Winterlandschap met schaatsers en vogelval

1615–20, Oil on wood/Huile sur bois, 38,5 × 57,8 cm

Jacob Jordaens (1593–1678)

Madonna and Child in Garland

La Vierge à l'Enfant

Muttergottes mit Kind
im Blumenkranz

Virgen con niño en
corona de flores

Virgem e Menino em
Coroa de Flores

Madonna met Kind in
een bloemenkrans

c. 1618, Oil on canvas/Huile
sur toile, 104,5 × 73,5 cm

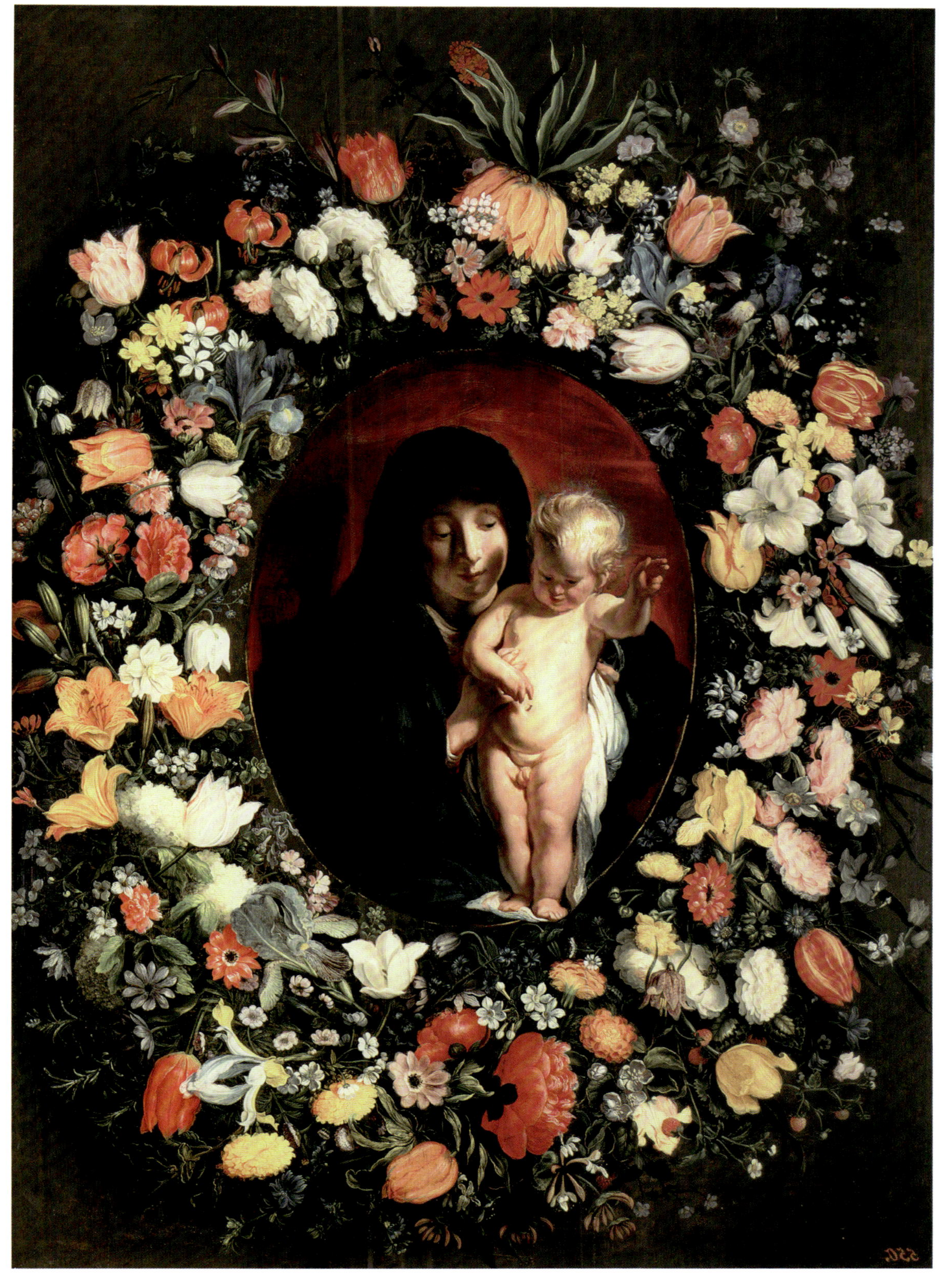

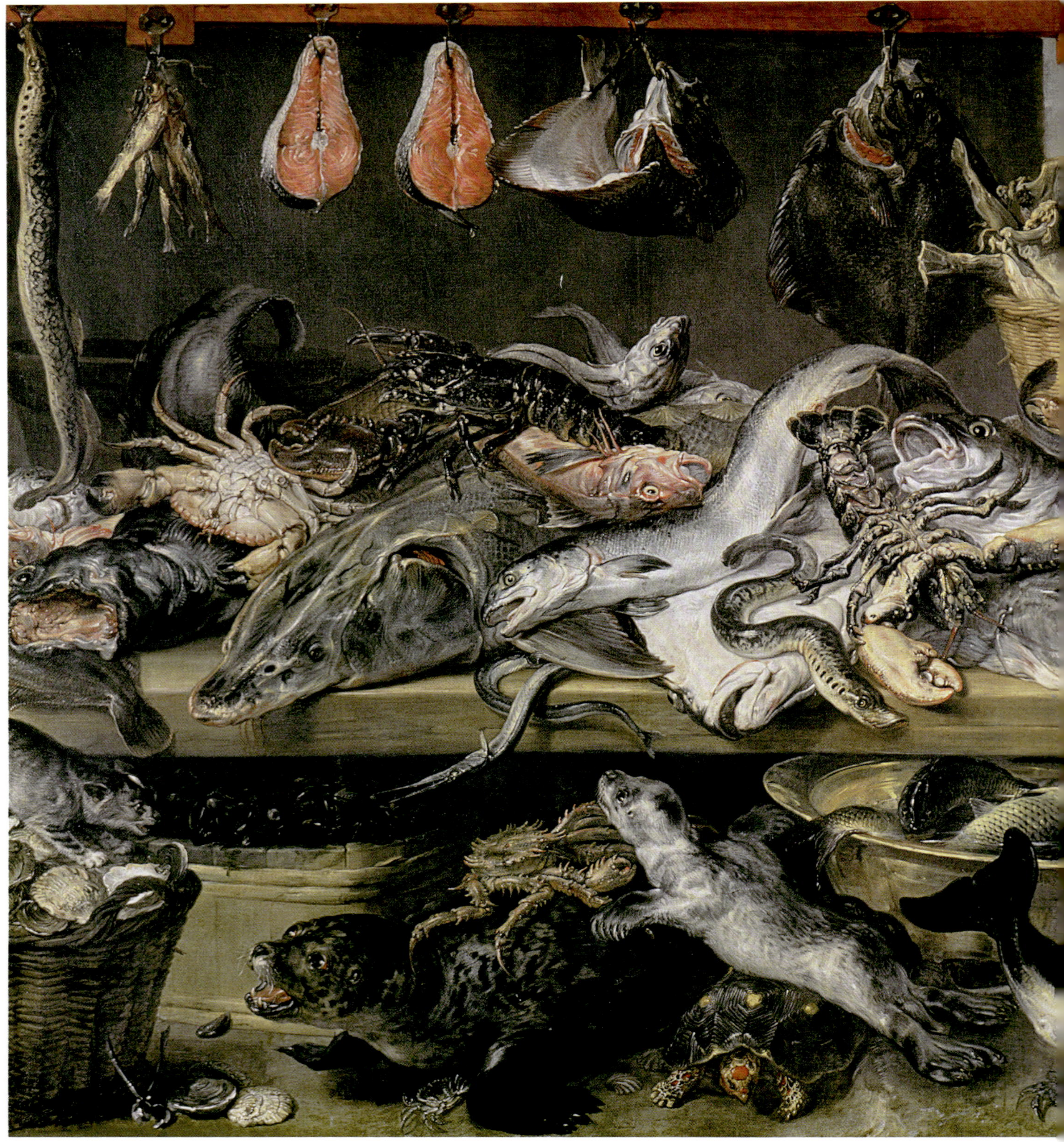

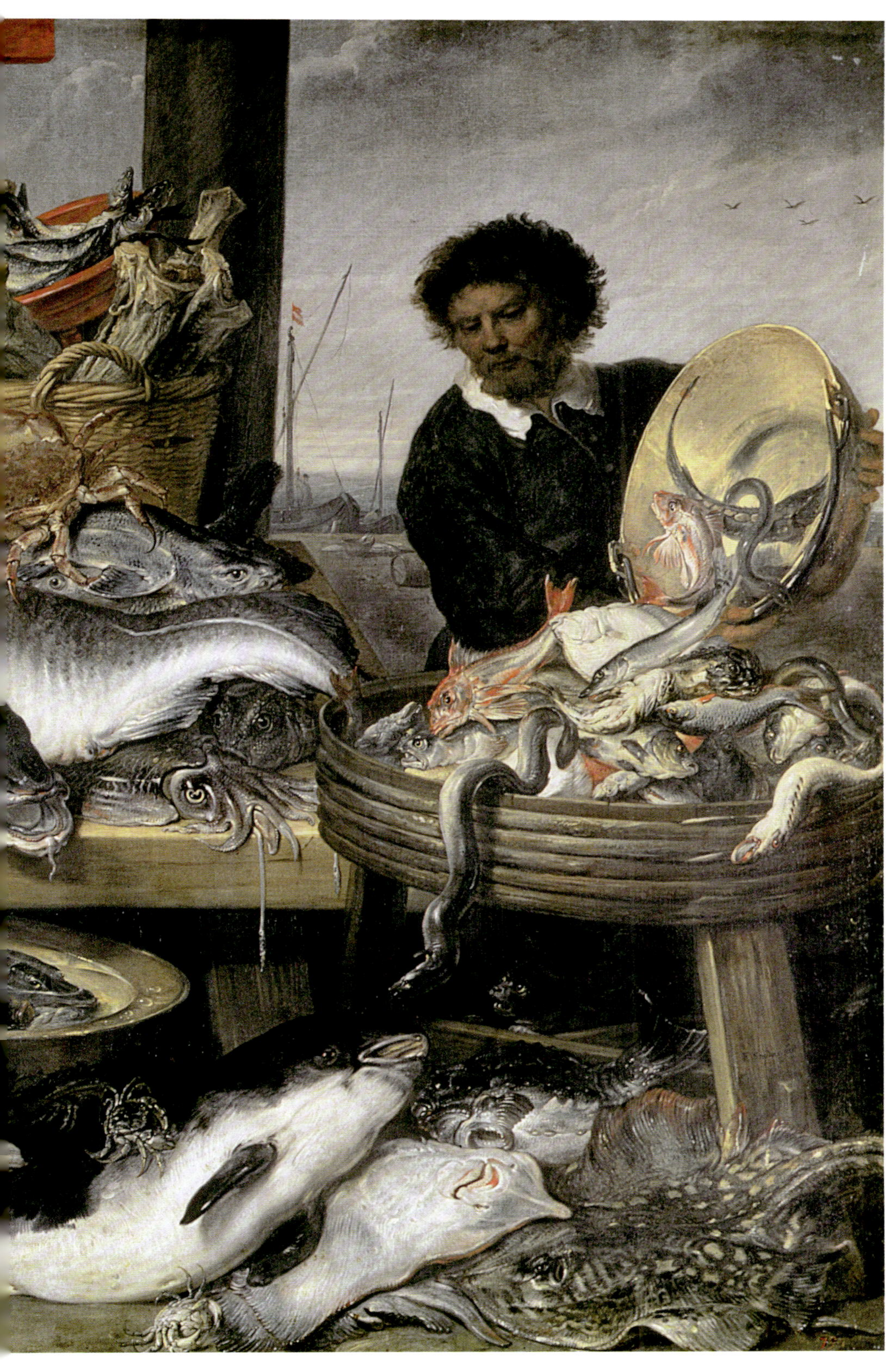

Frans Snyders (1579–1657)

The Fish Market

Marchand de poisson à son étal

Der Fischmarkt

El mercado de pescado

O Mercado de Peixe

De vismarkt

1620, Oil on canvas/Huile sur toile, 210,5 × 340 cm

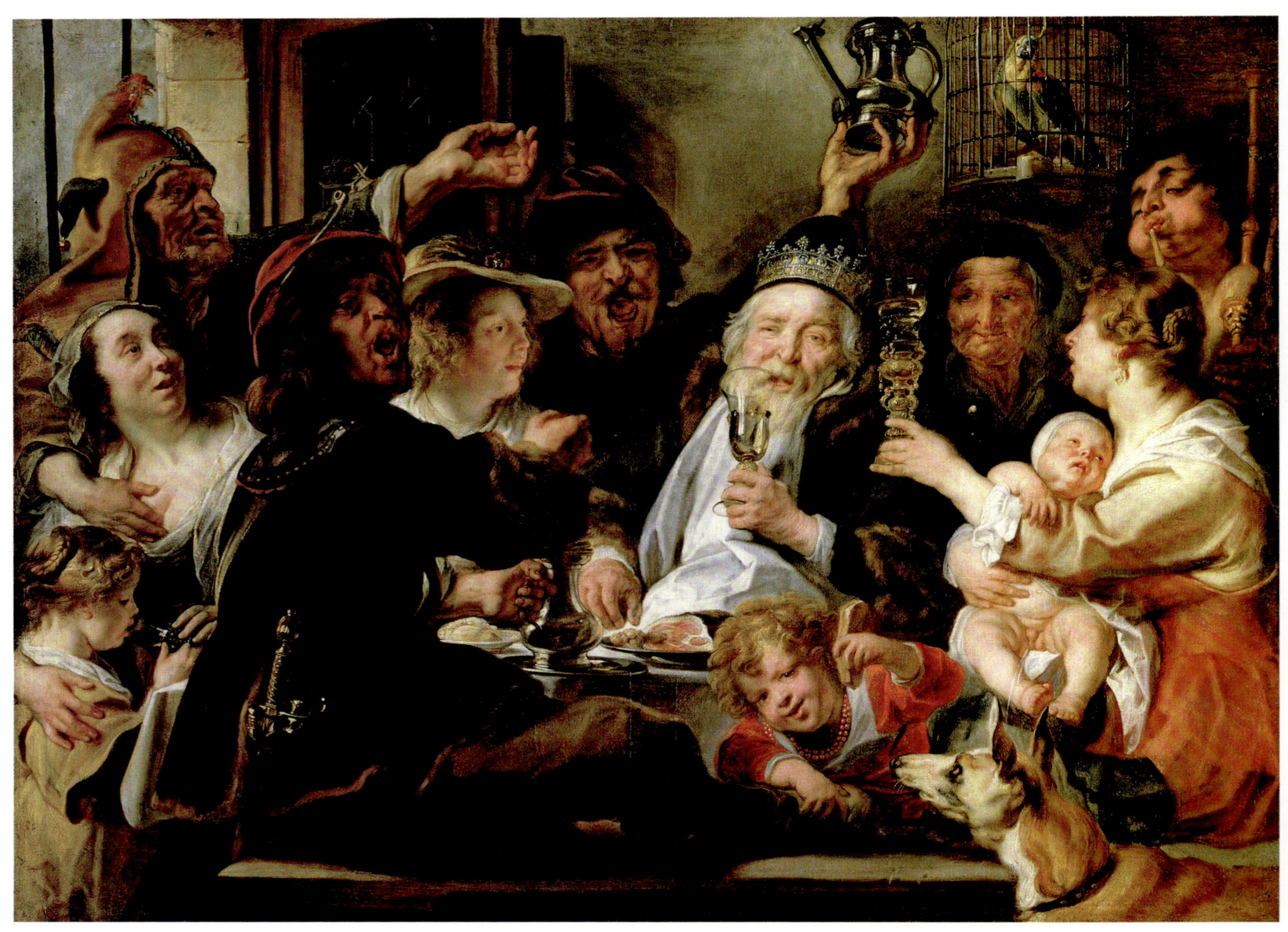

Jacob Jordaens (1593–1678)

The Bean King (The King Drinks)

Le Roi boit

Der Bohnenkönig (Der König trinkt)

El rey de las habas (El rey bebiendo)

O Rei do Feijão (O Rei Bebe)

De Bonenkoning (De koning drinkt)

c. 1638, Oil on canvas/Huile sur toile, 160 × 213 cm

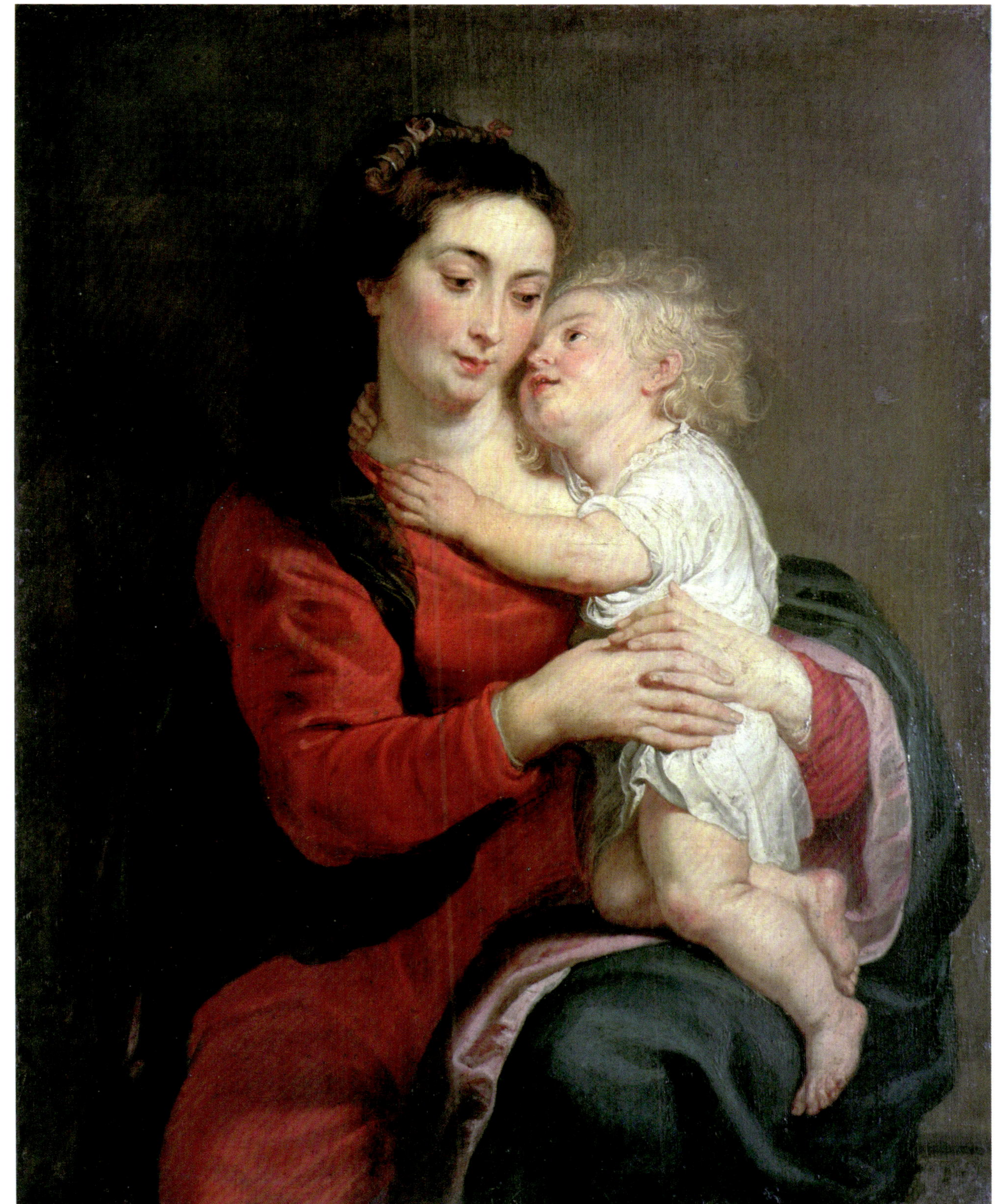

*Peter Paul
Rubens
(1577–1640)*

Madonna
with Child

Madonne à
l'Enfant

Muttergottes
mit Kind

Virgen con niño

Virgem e o
Menino

Madonna
met Kind

n. d., Oil on
canvas/Huile sur
toile, 108 × 84 cm

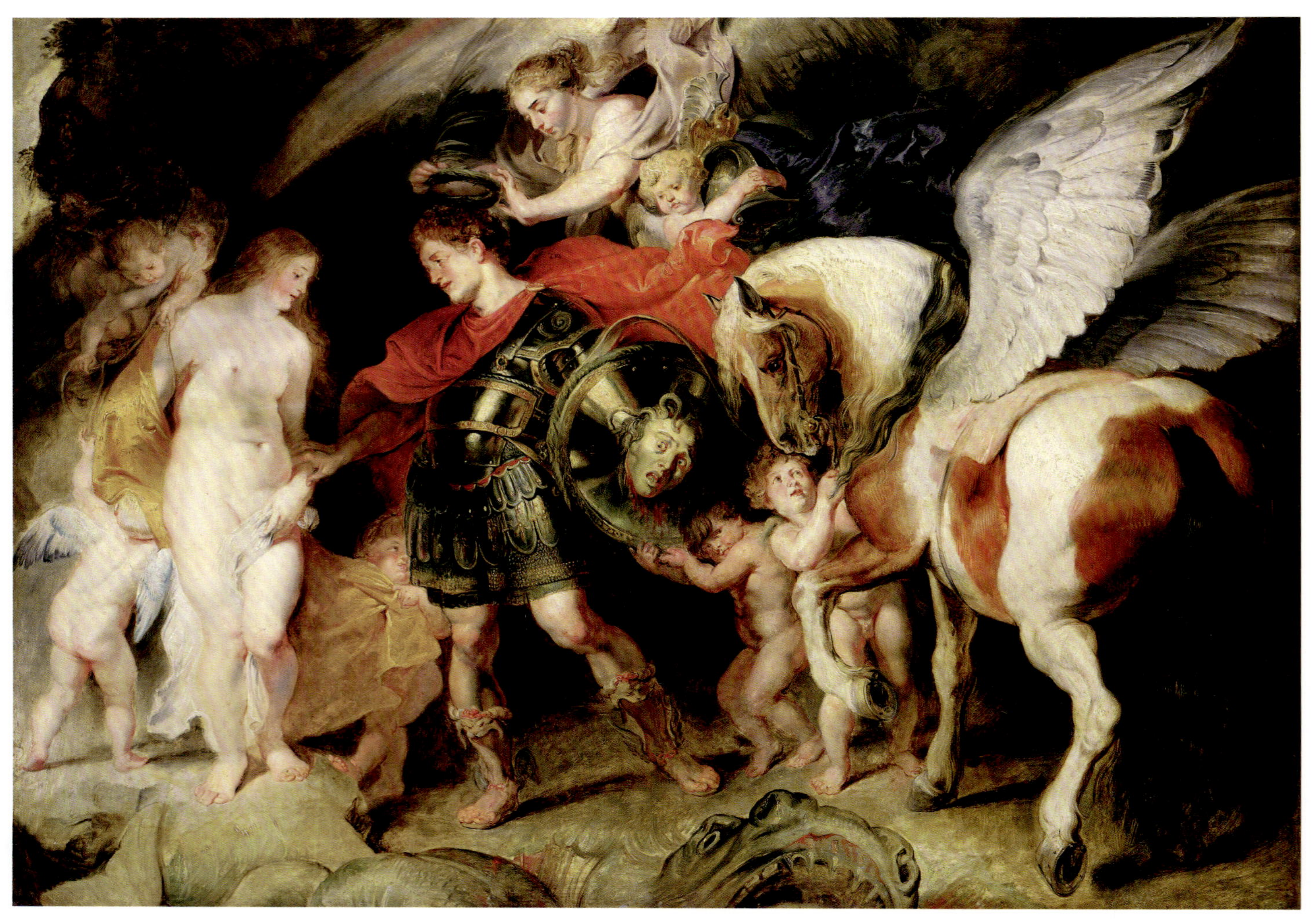

Peter Paul Rubens (1577–1640)

Perseus Freeing Andromeda

Persée et Andromède

Perseus befreit Andromeda

Perseo libera a Andrómeda

Perseu Liberta Andrómeda

Perseus bevrijdt Andromeda

c. 1622, Oil on canvas/Huile sur toile, 99,5 × 139 cm

Peter Paul Rubens (1577–1640)

The Union of Fire and Water

L'Union de la Terre et de l'Eau

Die Vereinigung von Feuer und Wasser

La unión de fuego y agua

A União de Fogo e Água

De vereniging van vuur en water

c. 1618, Oil on canvas/Huile sur toile, 222,5 × 180,5 cm

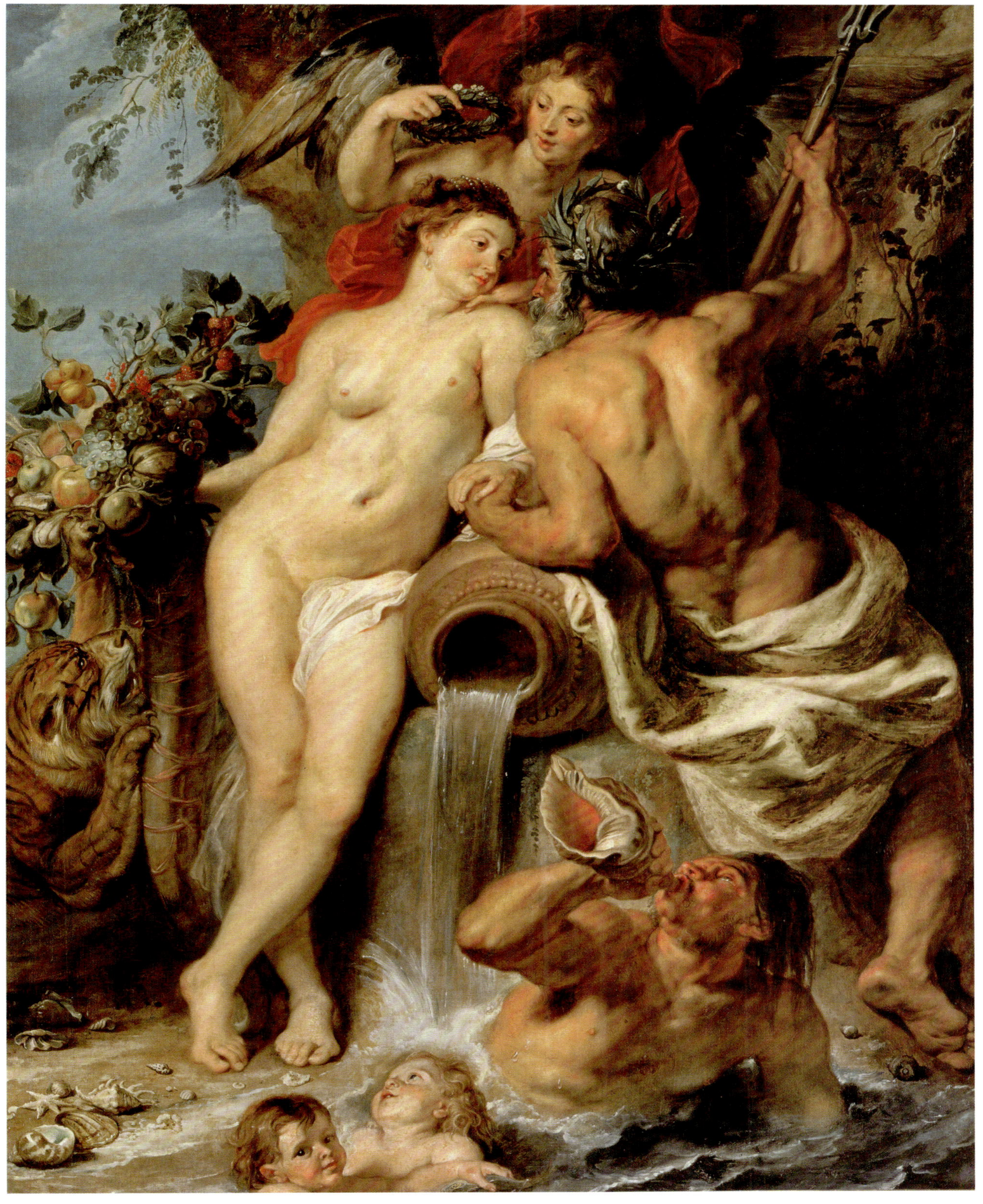

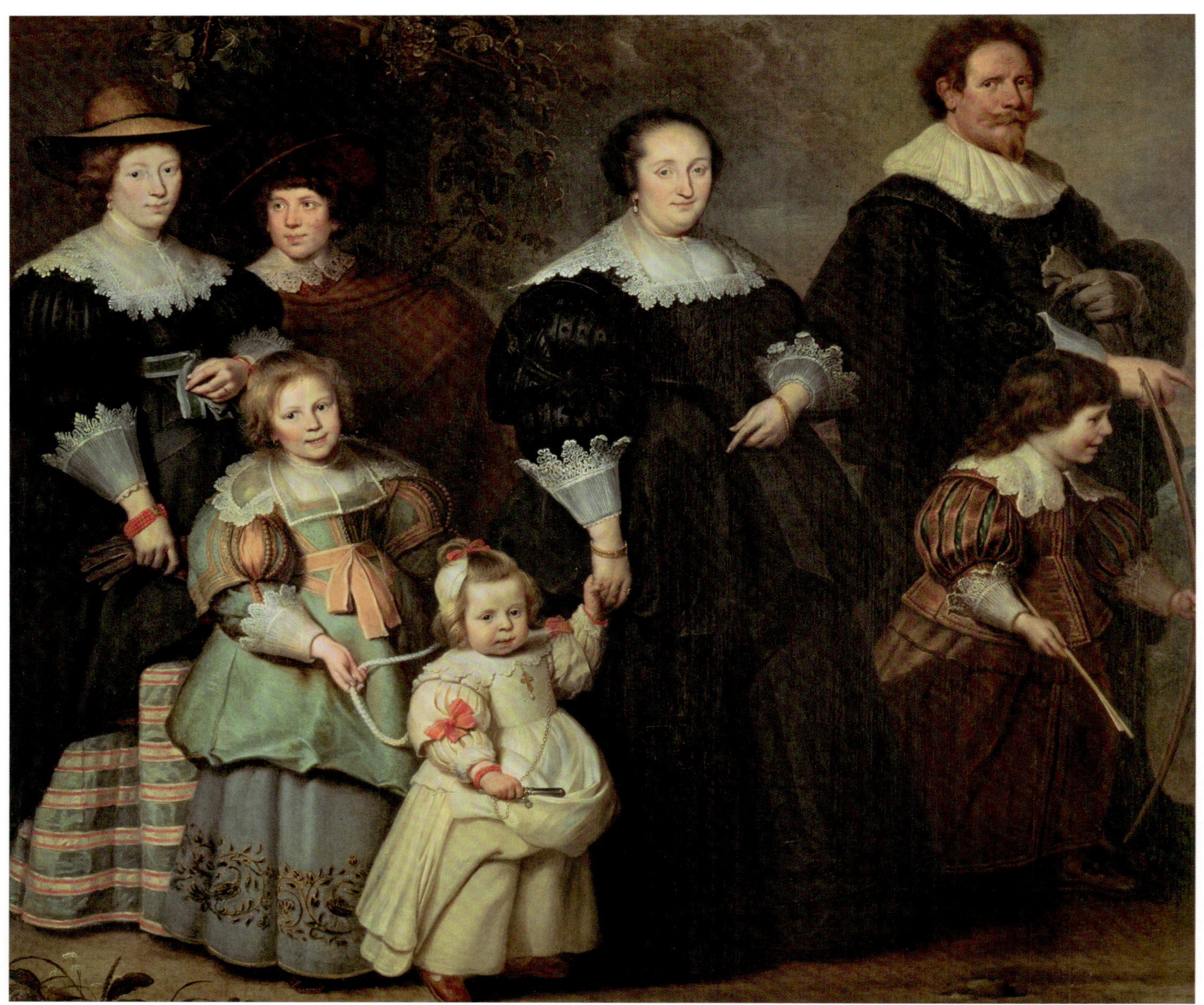

Cornelis de Vos (1584–1651)

Family Portrait

Portrait de famille

Familienporträt

Retrato de familia

Retrato de Família

Familieportret

1634, Oil on canvas/Huile sur toile, 185,5 × 221 cm

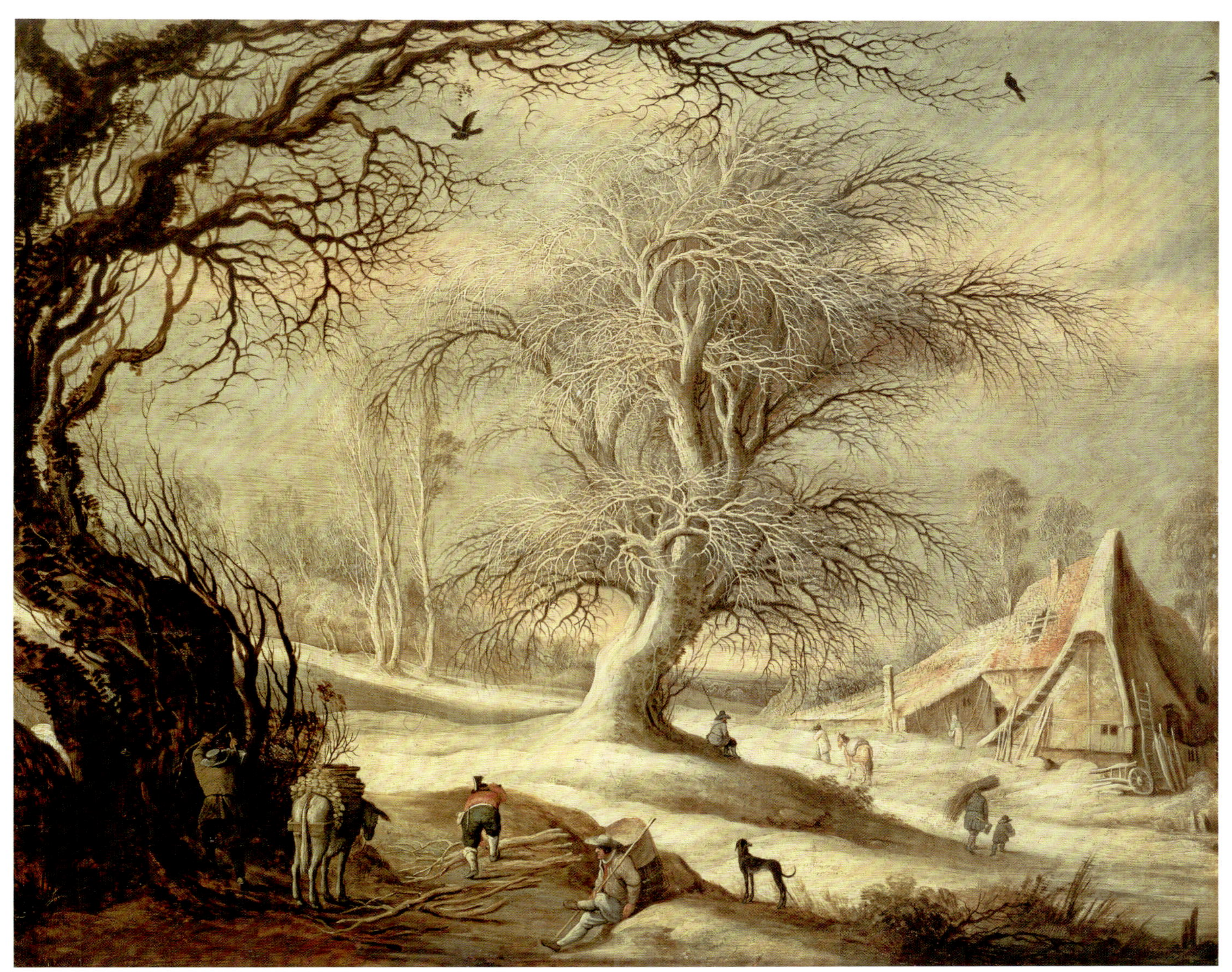

Gijsbrecht Lijttens (1586–c. 1656)

Winter Landscape

Paysage d'hiver avec bûcherons

Winterlandschaft

Paisaje invernal

Paisagem de Inverno

Winterlandschap

n.d., Oil on wood/Huile sur bois, 71,5 × 89 cm

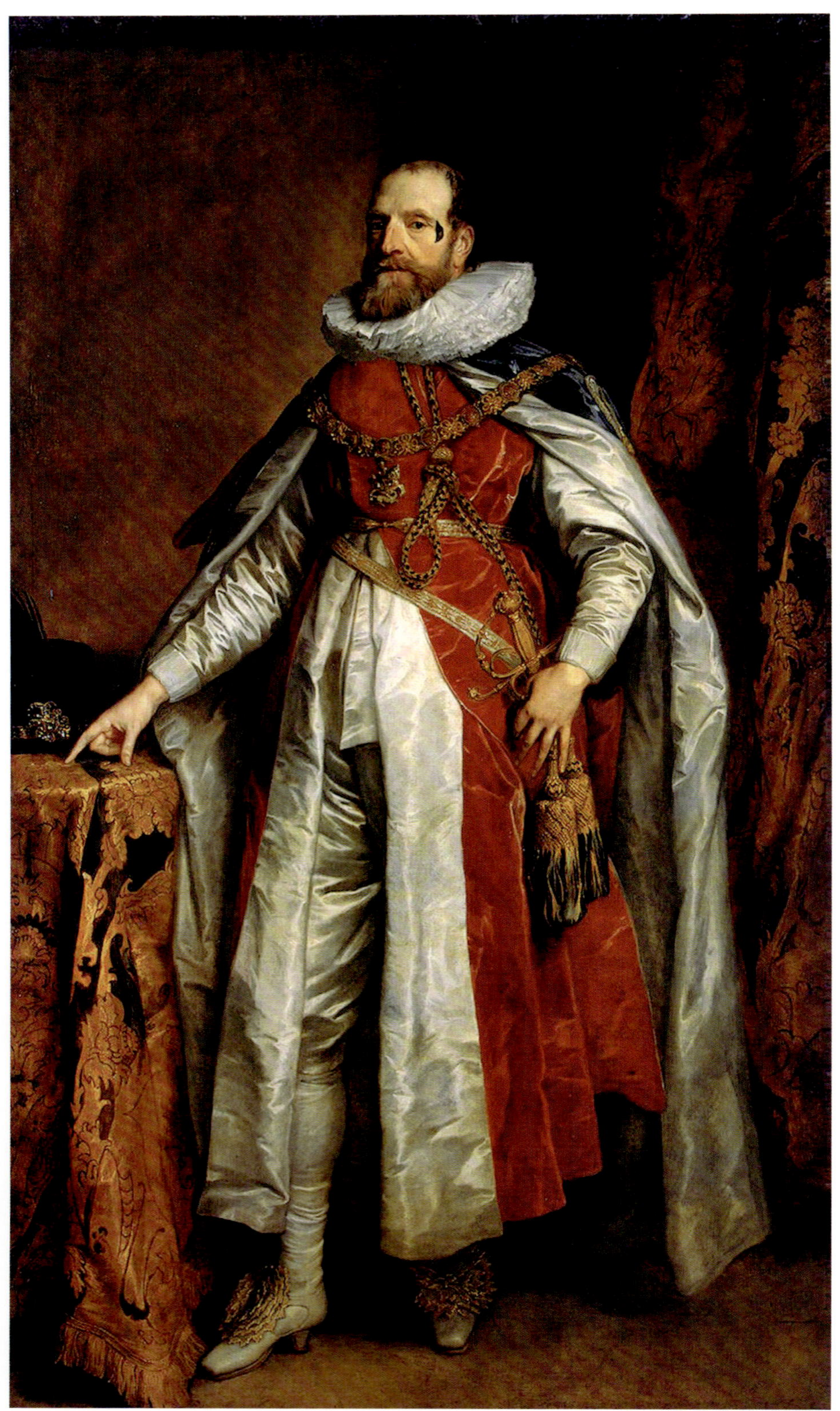

Anthonis van Dyck (1599–1641)

Henry Danvers, 1st Earl of Danby

Henry Danvers, comte Danby

Henry Danvers, 1st Earl of Danby

Henry Danvers, Primer Earl de Danby

Henry Danvers, 1st Earl of Danby

Henry Danvers, 1st Earl of Danby

c. 1630, Oil on canvas/Huile sur toile, 223 × 130,6 cm

Anthonis van Dyck (1599–1641)

Family Portrait

Portrait de famille

Familienporträt

Retrato de familia

Retrato de Família

Familieportret

1621, Oil on canvas/Huile sur toile, 113,5 × 93,5 cm

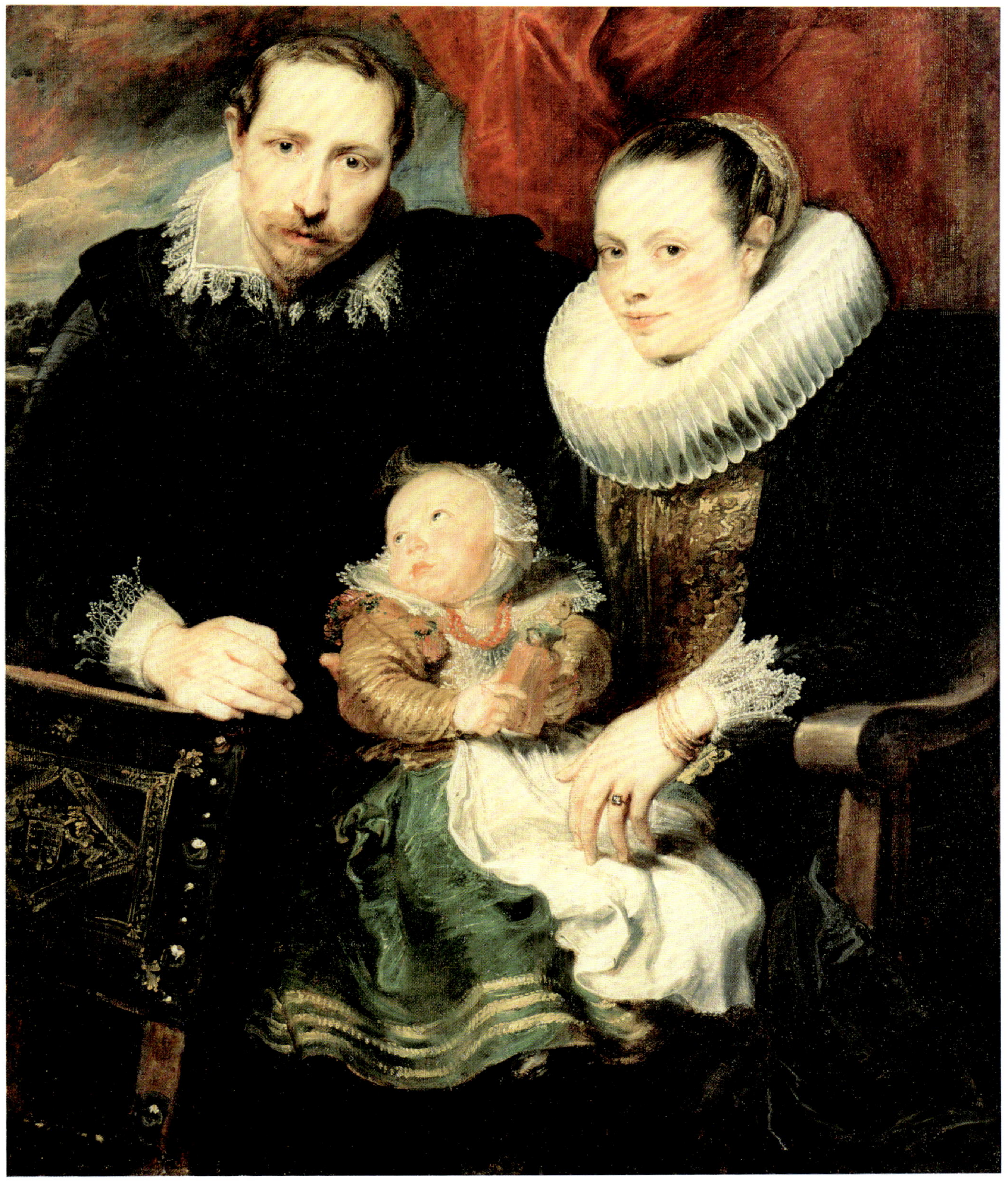

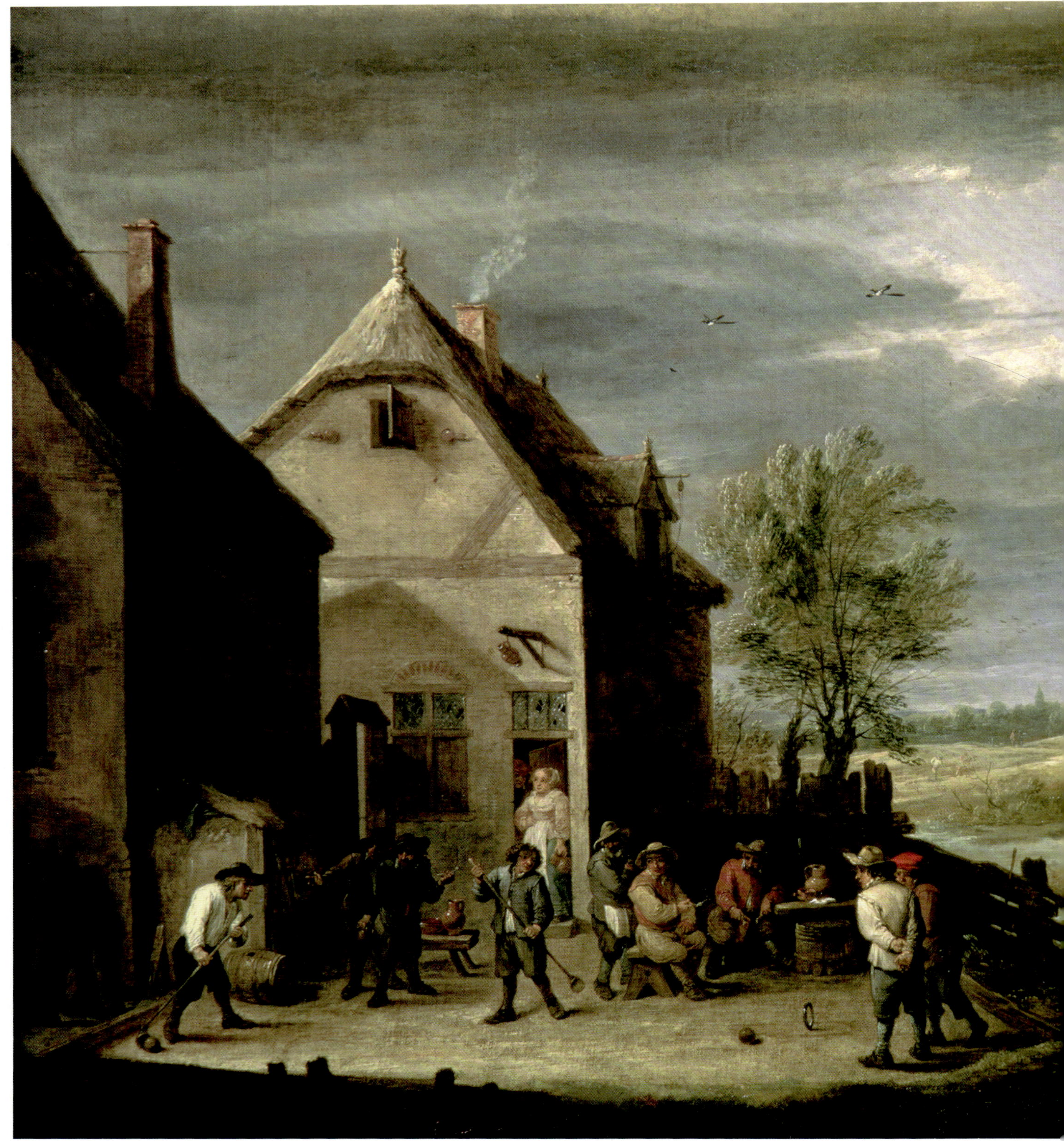

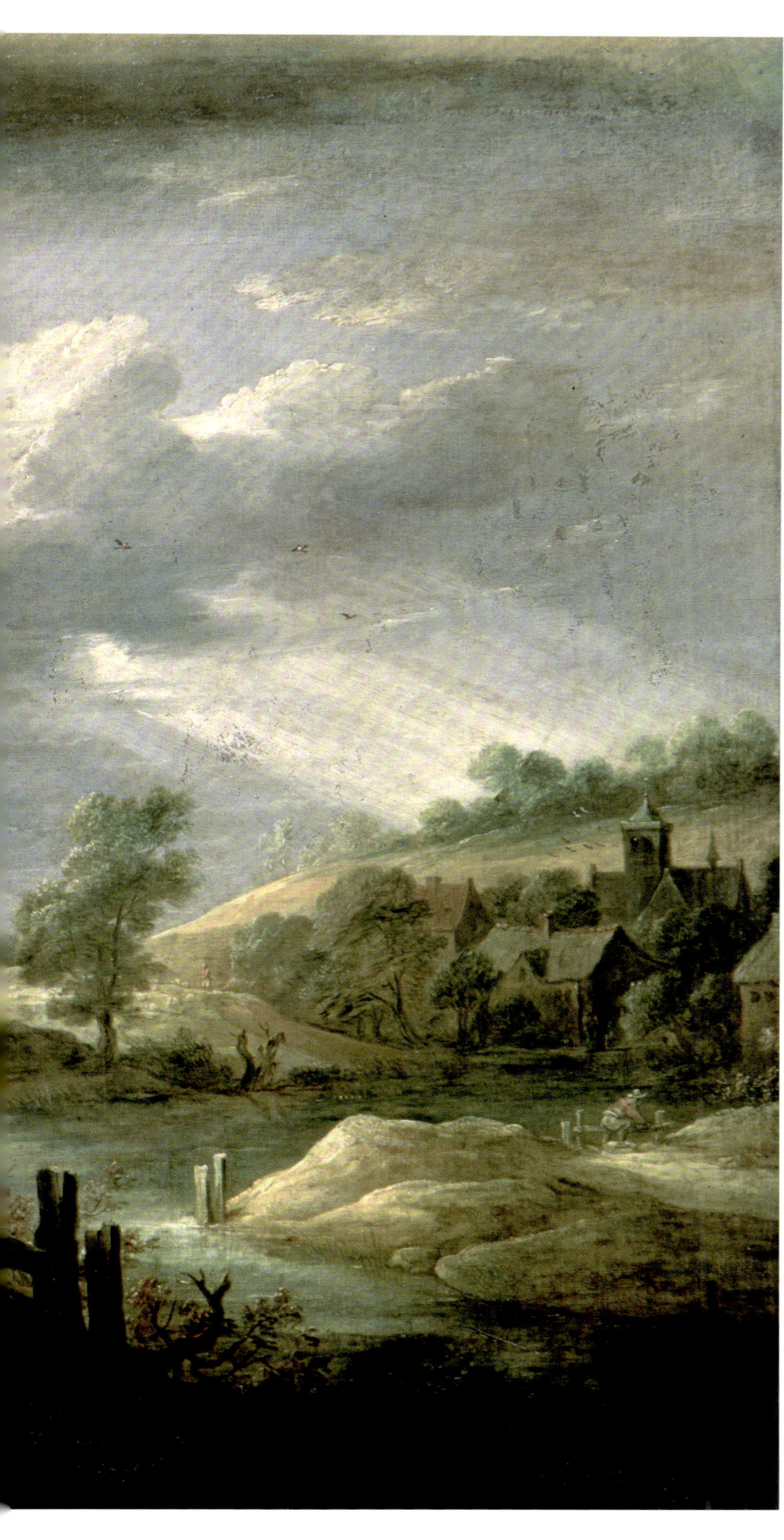

David Teniers de Jonge/the Younger/le Jeune (1610−90)

Peasants Playing Bowls

Paysans jouant aux boules

Bauern beim Boulespiel

Campesinos jugano a la petanca

Camponeses a Jogar Petanca

Boeren spelen jeu de boules

c. 1640, Oil on canvas/Huile sur toile, 61,5 × 89,5 cm

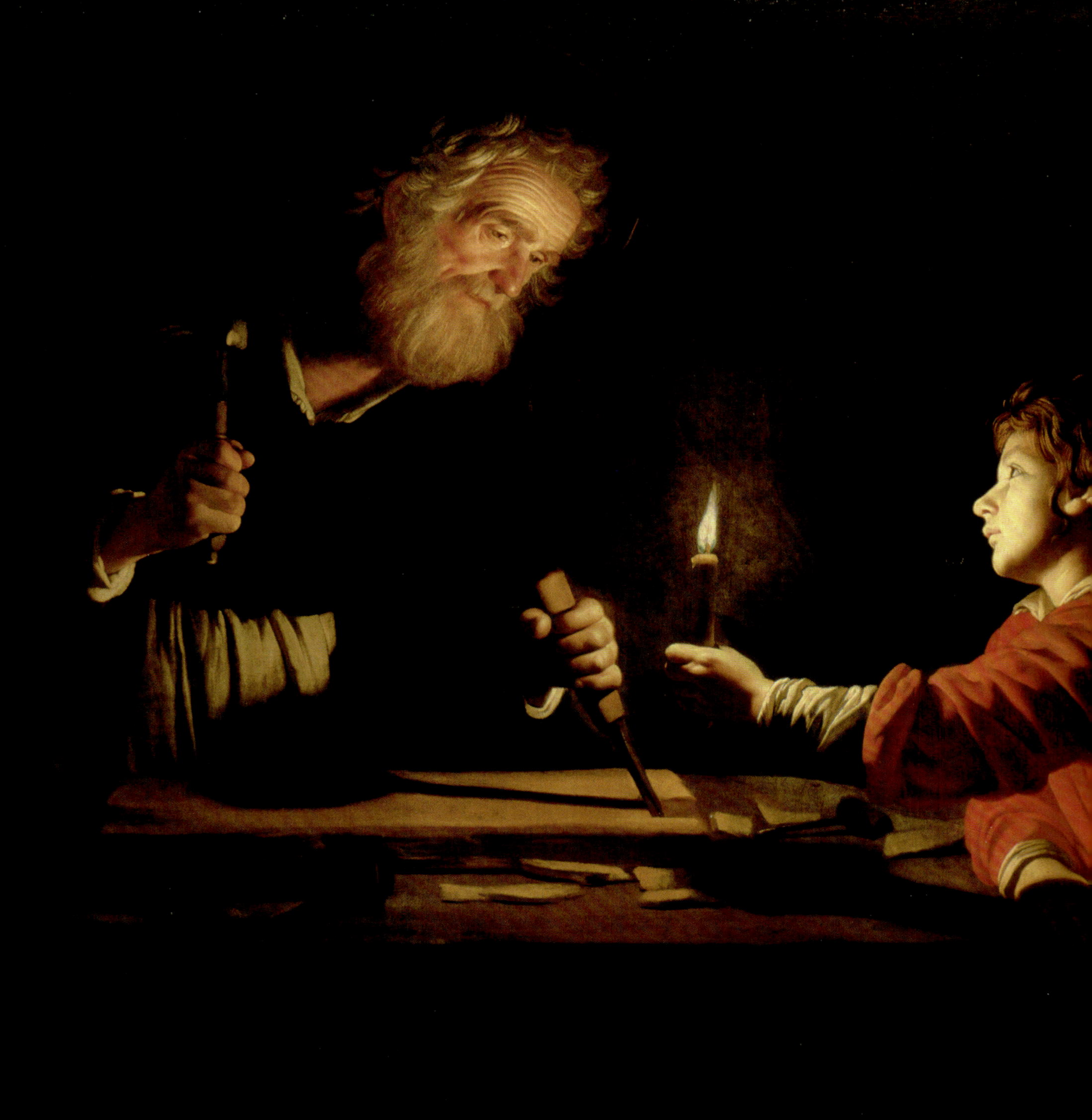

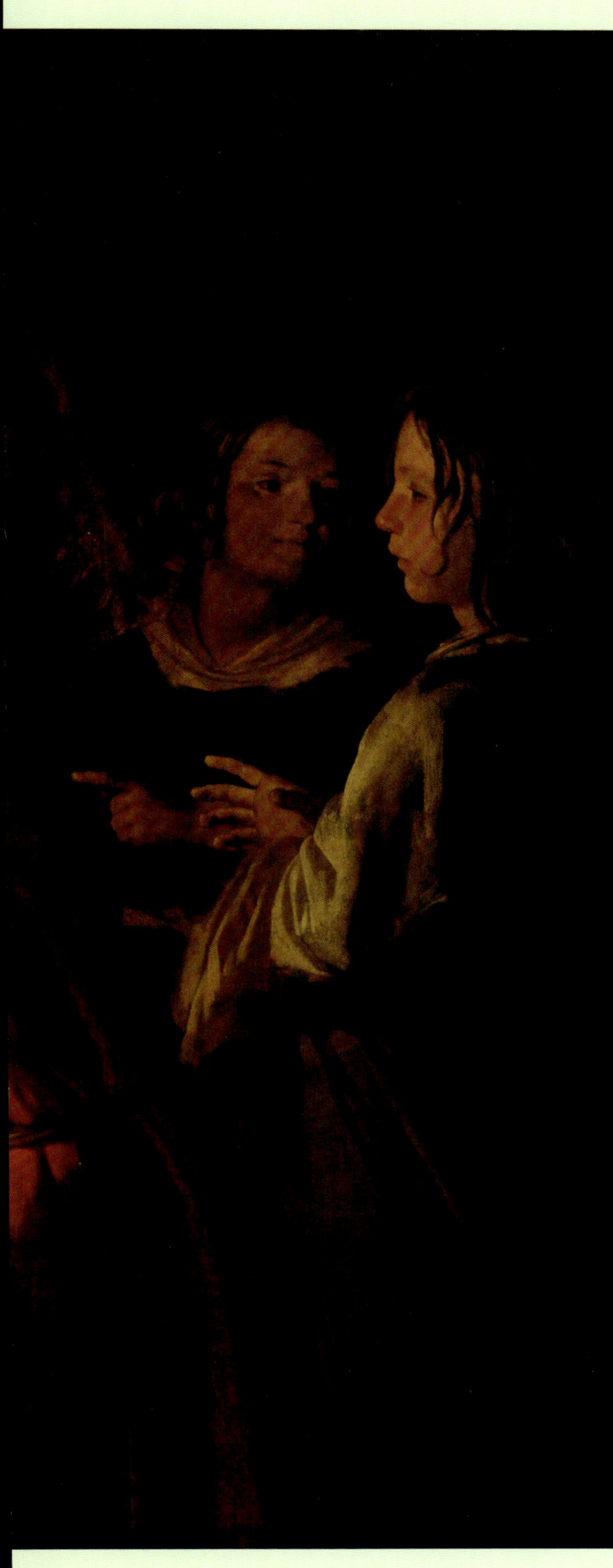

DUTCH PAINTING OF THE 17TH–19TH CENTURY
LA PEINTURE HOLLANDAISE DU XVIIᴱ–XIXᴱ SIÈCLES
NIEDERLÄNDISCHE MALEREI DES 17.–19. JAHRHUNDERTS
PINTURA HOLANDESA DEL SIGLOS XVII – XIX
PINTURA HOLANDESA DO SÉCULOS XVII – XIX
HOLLANDSE MEESTERS VAN DE 17E TOT EN MET 19E EEUW

Gerrit van Honthorst (1590–1656)

The Childhood of Christ

Le Christ dans l'atelier de Joseph

Die Kindheit Christi

La infancia de Cristo

A Infância de Cristo

De jeugd van Christus

c. 1620, Oil on canvas/Huile sur toile, 137 × 185 cm

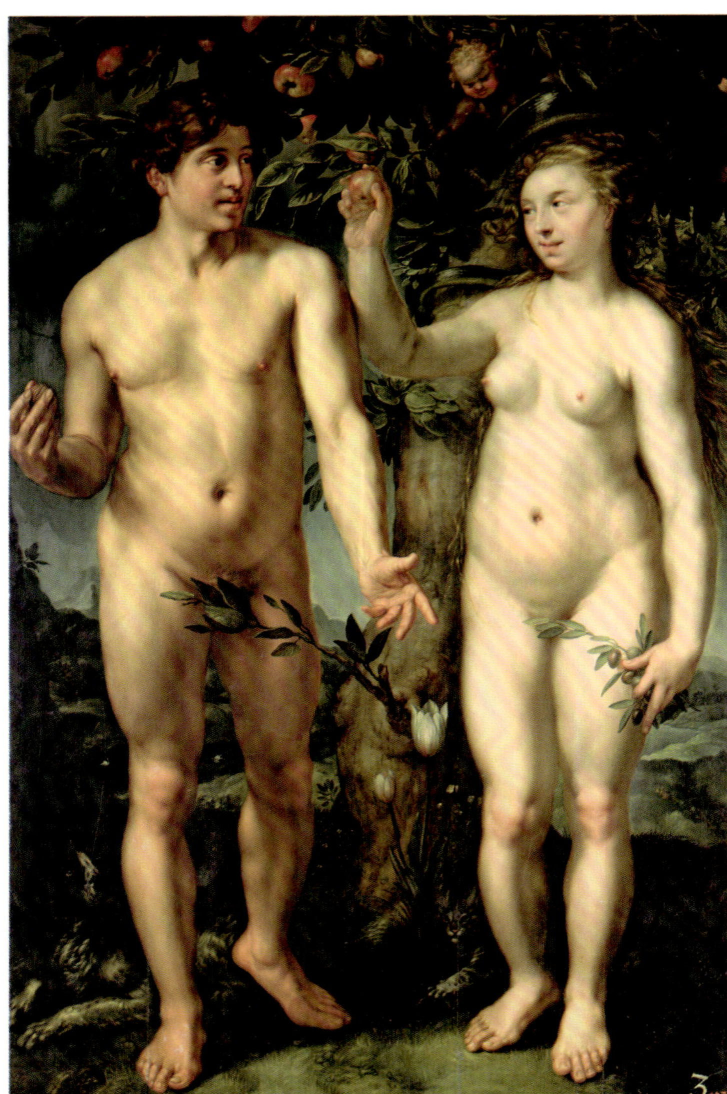

Hendrick Goltzius (1558–1617)

Adam and Eve
Adam et Ève
Adam und Eva
Adán y Eva
Adão e Eva
Adam en Eva

1608, Oil on wood/Huile sur bois, 203,5 × 134 cm

Vincent van Gogh (1853–90)

The Lilac Bush
Le Buisson de lilas
Der Fliederbusch
El arbusto de lilas
O Arbusto de Lilases
Seringenstruik

1889, Oil on canvas/Huile sur toile, 73 × 92 cm

Dutch Painting of the 17th–19th Century

The collection of seventeenth-century Dutch painting is massive, with more than 1,000 pieces. One room is exclusively dedicated to Rembrandt and his pupils. The collection holds more than 20 Rembrandt works, making it the largest collection of the artist's work outside the Netherlands. The landscapes of Jan van Goyen and Jacob van Ruisdael, genre scenes by Pieter de Hoochs and Jan Steens, and still lifes by Willem Claesz Hedas and Willem Kalfs further round out the collection.

Another room with works by Vincent van Gogh is dedicated to 19th century Dutch painters.

La peinture hollandaise du XVIIᵉ– XIXᵉ siècles

La collection de peinture hollandaise du XVIIᵉ siècle compte plus de mille œuvres. Une salle entière est consacrée à Rembrandt et à ses élèves – car la collection abrite plus de vingt tableaux de Rembrandt : c'est la plus grande en dehors des Pays-Bas. Des paysages de Jan van Goyen et Jacob van Ruisdael complètent cet impressionnant ensemble, à côté de scènes de genre de Pieter de Hooch et de Jan Steen, et de natures mortes signées Willem Claesz Heda et Willem Kalf.

Une autre salle, comportant des œuvres de Vincent van Gogh, est consacrée aux peintres hollandais du XIXᵉ siècle.

Niederländische Malerei des 17.–19. Jahrhundert

Über 1000 Stücke zählt die Sammlung niederländischer Malerei des 17. Jahrhunderts. Ein Saal ist allein Rembrandt und seinen Schülern gewidmet, denn die Sammlung beherbergt mehr als 20 Rembrandt-Werke, die größte Rembrandt-Sammlung außerhalb der Niederlande. Landschaften von Jan van Goyen oder Jacob van Ruisdael komplettieren neben Genreszenen Pieter de Hoochs oder Jan Steens sowie Stillleben Willem Claesz Hedas oder Willem Kalfs die eindrucksvolle Sammlung.

Ein weiterer Saal mit van Gogh-Werken widmet sich der niederländischen Malerei des 19. Jahrhunderts.

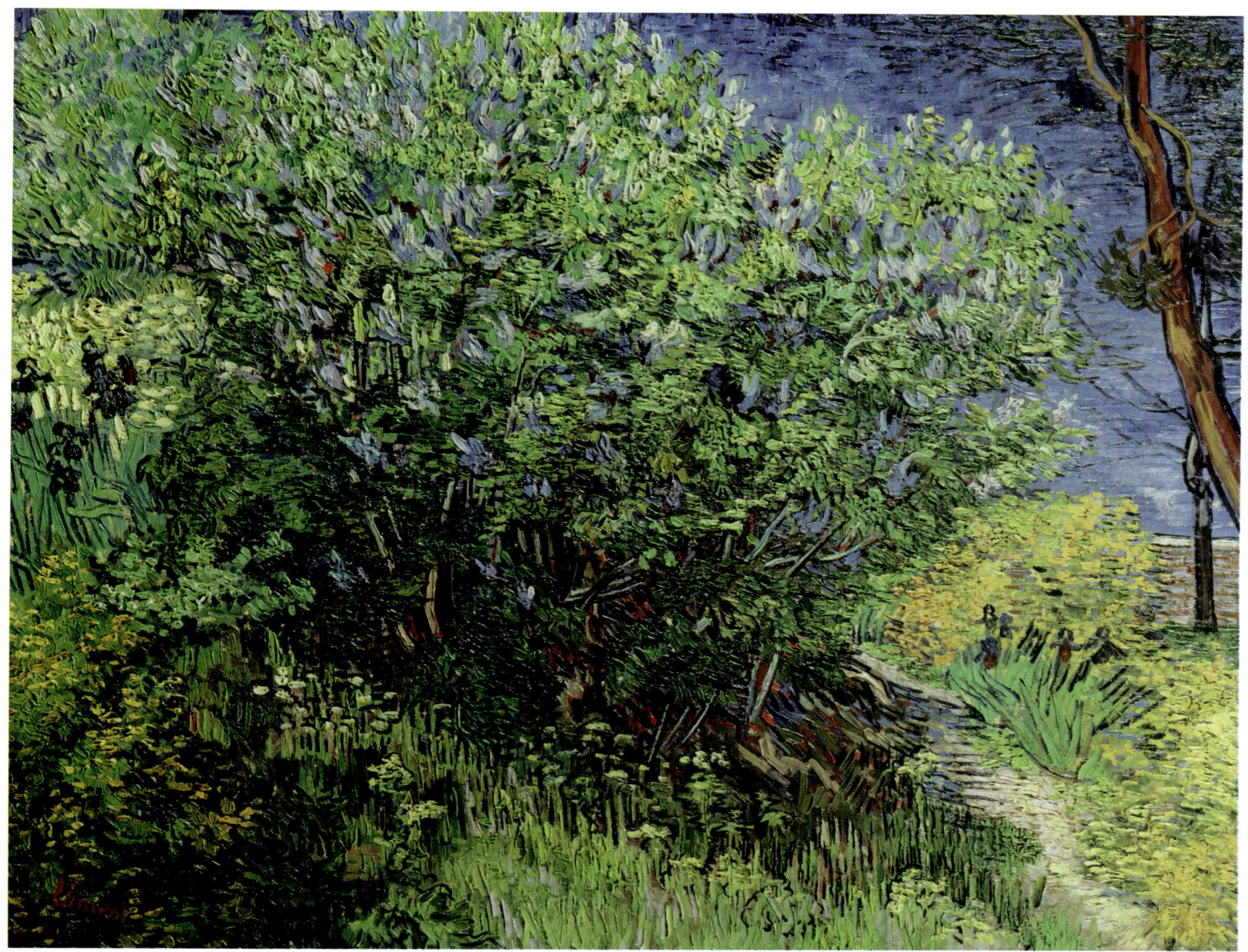

Pintura holandesa
del siglos XVII–XIX

Más de 1.000 piezas conforman la colección de pintura holandesa del siglo XVII. Una de las salas está dedicada exclusivamente a Rembrandt y a sus alumnos, así que la colección incluye más de 20 obras de Rembrandt, la mayor colección sobre Rembrandt fuera de Holanda. Paisajes de Jan van Goyen y Jacob van Ruisdael completan la impresionante colección, además de escenas de género de Pieter de Hooch y Jan Steens así como naturalezas muertas de Willem Claesz Heda y Willem Kalfs.

Otra sala con pinturas de Van Gogh se dedica a la pintura holandesa del siglo XIX.

Pintura holandesa
do séculos XVII–XIX

A coleção de pintura holandesa do século XVII conta com mais de 1000 objetos. Um único salão é dedicado apenas a Rembrandt e aos seus alunos, pois a coleção abrange mais de 20 obras de Rembrandt, sendo esta a maior coleção deste artista situada fora dos Países Baixos. As paisagens de Jan van Goyen ou de Jacob van Ruisdael, além das cenas de género de Pieter de Hooch ou de Jan Steen, bem como as naturezas-mortas de Willem Claesz Hedas ou de Willem Kalfs completam a impressionante coleção.

Uma outra sala com obras de van Gogh também é dedicada à pintura holandesa do século XIX.

Hollandse meesters van de
17e tot en met 19e eeuw

De collectie Hollandse meesters van de zeventiende eeuw telt ruim duizend werken. Eén zaal allen al is gewijd aan Rembrandt en zijn leerlingen, want tot de verzameling behoren ruim twintig doeken van Rembrandt – de omvangrijkste collectie buiten Nederland. Landschappen van Jan van Goyen en Jacob van Ruisdael, genrestukken van Pieter de Hooch en Jan Steen, en stillevens van Willem Claesz Heda en Willem Kalf completeren deze imposante verzameling.

Eén zaal is gewijd aan de Nederlandse schilderkunst van de negentiende eeuw, met doeken van Vincent van Gogh.

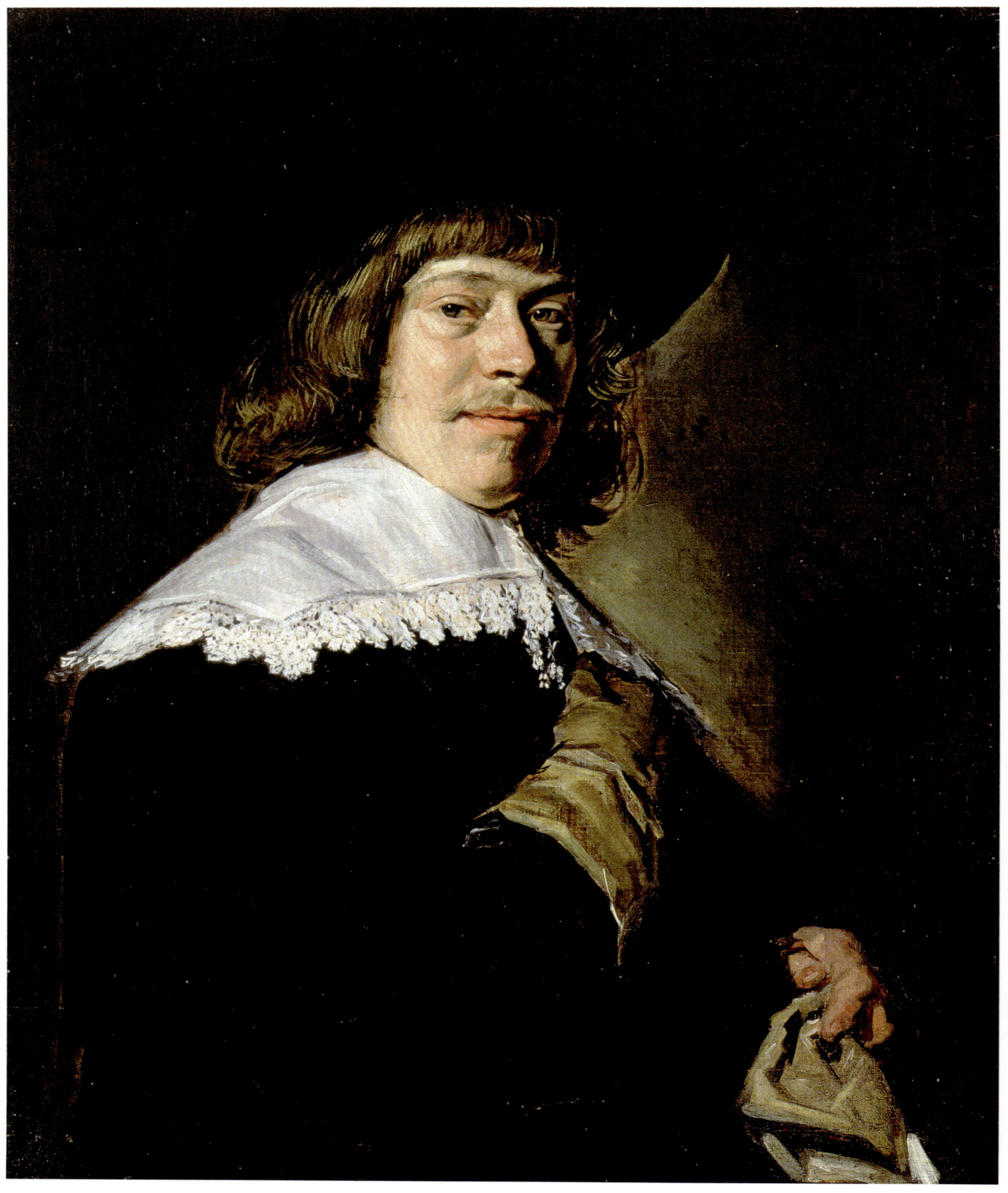

Frans Hals
(1580–1666)

Portrait of a
Young Man
with Glove

Jeune
Homme
au gant

Bildnis
eines jungen
Mannes mit
Handschuh

Retrato de
un joven
con guante

Retrato de
um Jovem
Homem
com Luva

Portret van
een jongeman
met
handschoen

c. 1650, Oil
on canvas/
Huile sur toile,
80 × 66,5 cm

Frans Hals
(1580–1666)

Portrait of
a Man

Portrait
d'homme

Bildnis eines
Mannes

Retrato de
un hombre

Retrato de
um Homem

Portret van
een man

c. 1661, Oil
on canvas/
Huile sur toile,
84,5 × 67 cm

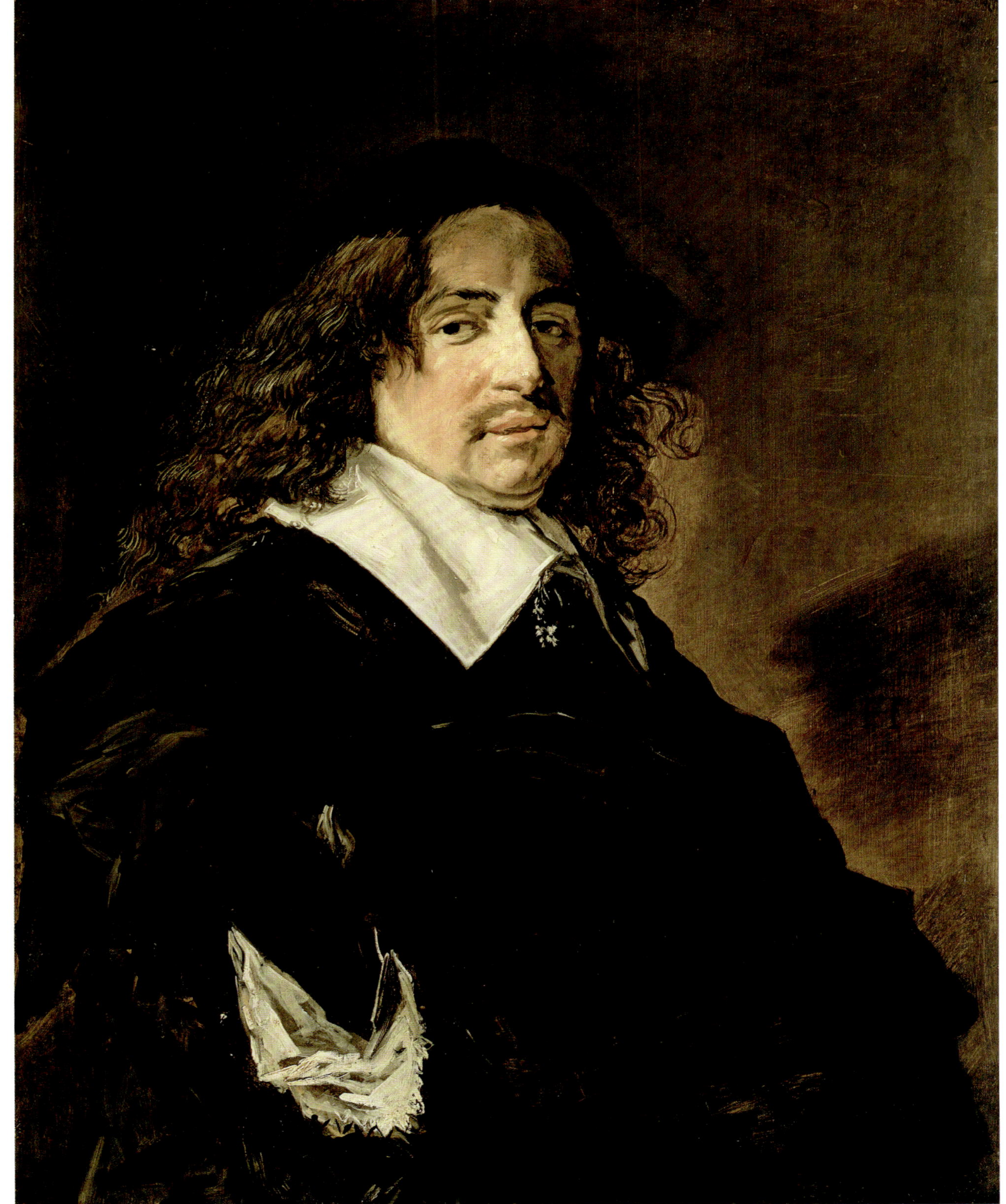

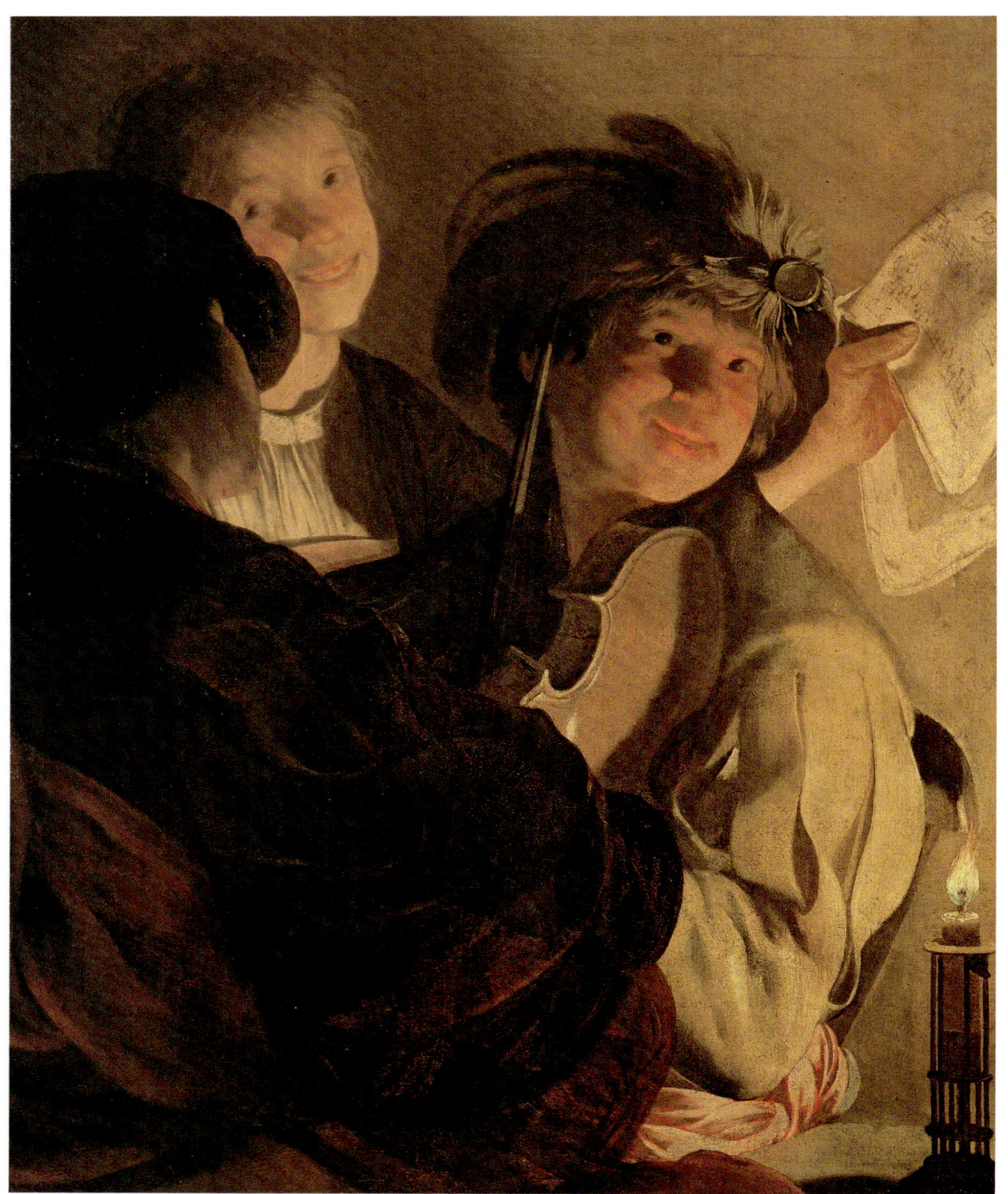

Hendrick Jansz. Terbrugghen (1588–1629)

Concert	Konzert	Concerto
Concert	Concierto	Concert

1626, Oil on canvas/Huile sur toile, 102 × 83 cm

Gerrit van Honthorst (1590–1656)

A Musician
Un musicien
Ein Musiker
Un músico
Um Músico
Een muzikant

1624, Oil on canvas/Huile sur toile, 84 × 66,5 cm

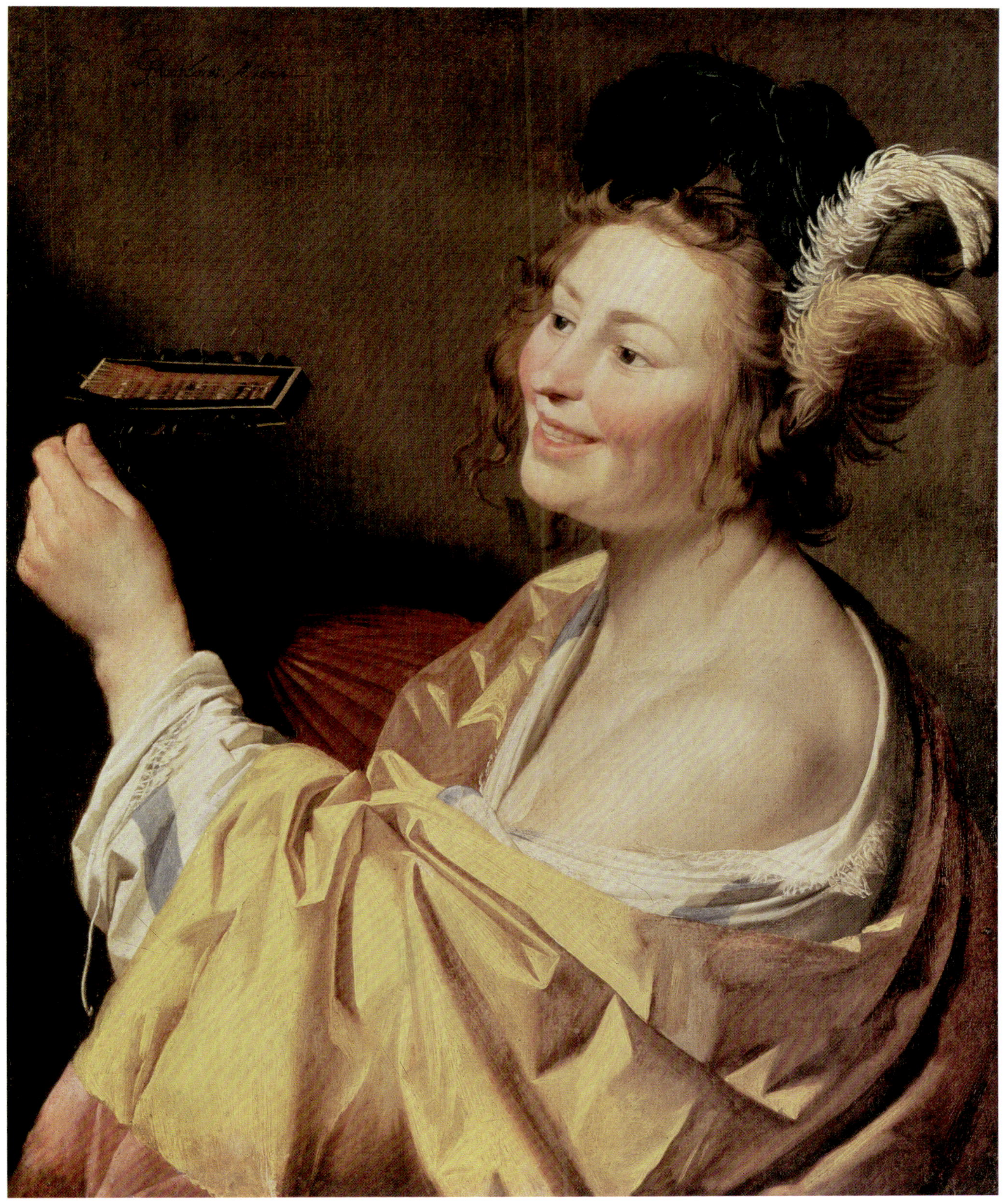

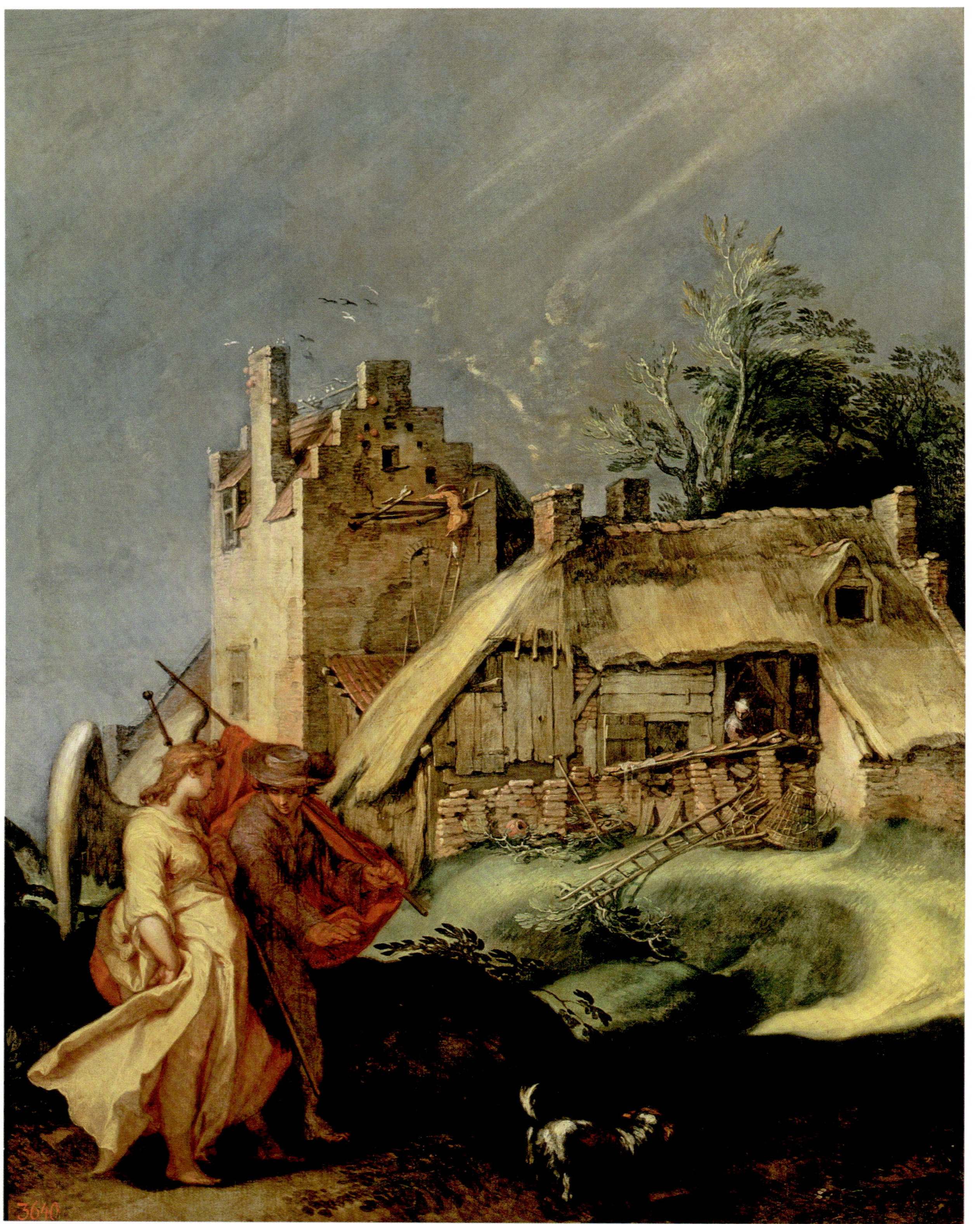

Abraham
Bloemaert
(1566-1651)

Landscape with
Tobias and
the Angel

Paysage avec
Tobie et l'Ange

Landschaft mit
Tobias und
dem Engel

Paisaje con Tobías
y el ángel

Paisagem com
Tobias e o Anjo

Landschap met
Tobias en de engel

c. 1600, Oil on
canvas/Huile sur
toile, 139 × 107,5 cm

Jacob Gerritsz.
Cuyp (1594–1651)

The Vintner

Le Vigneron

Der Weinbauer

El vinicultor

O Viticultor

De wijnbouwer

1628, Oil on canvas/
Huile sur toile,
112 × 107 cm

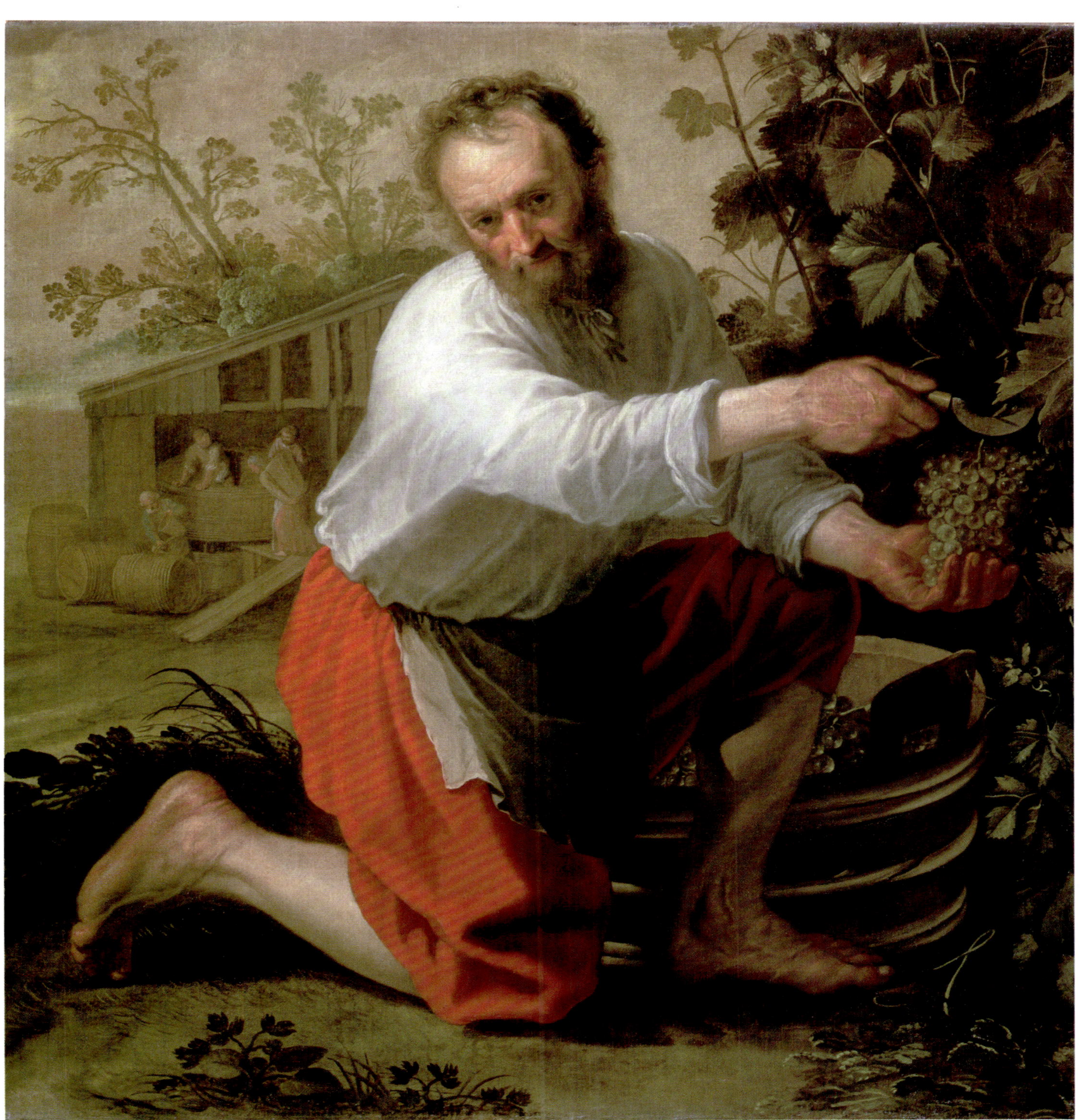

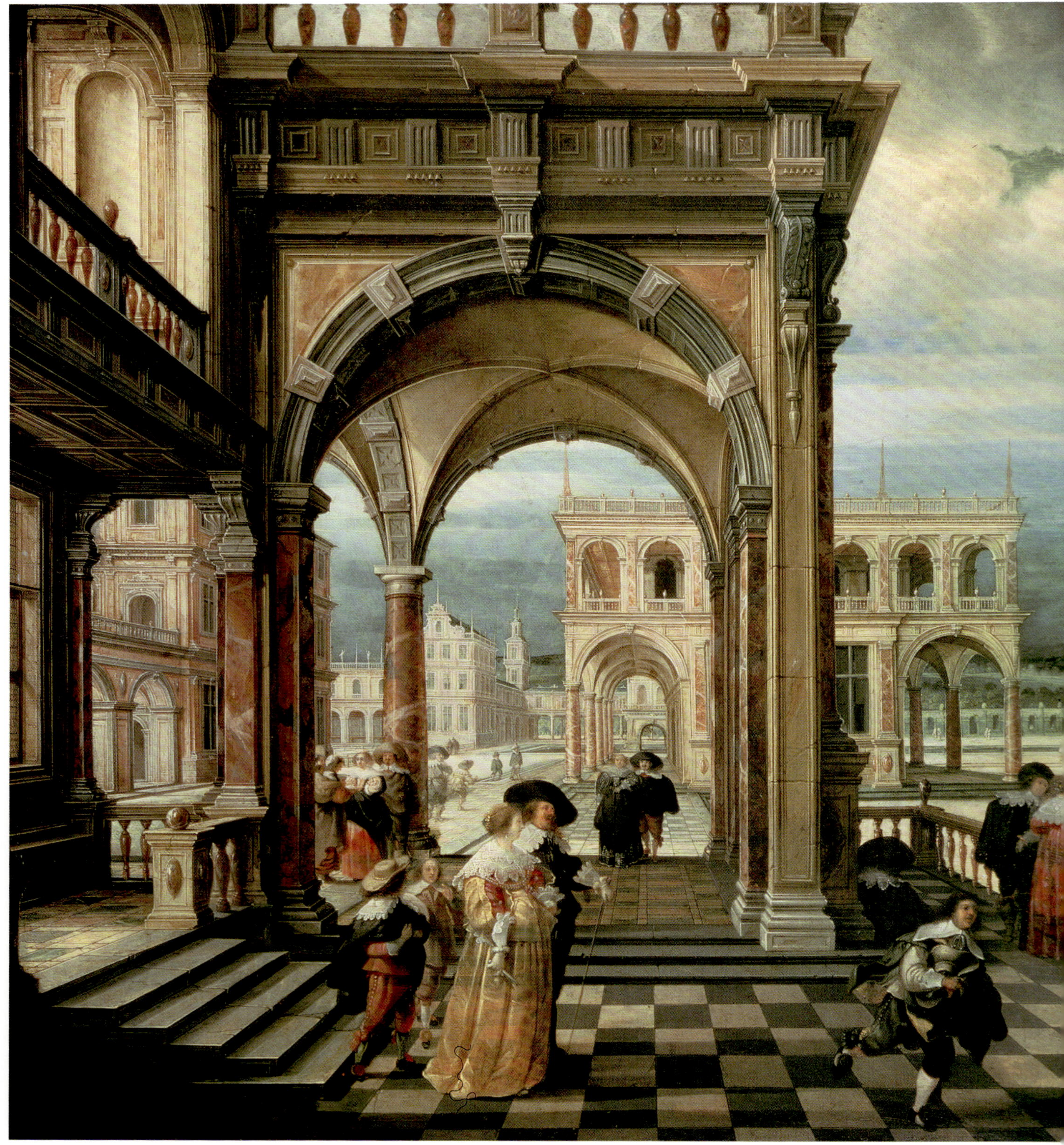

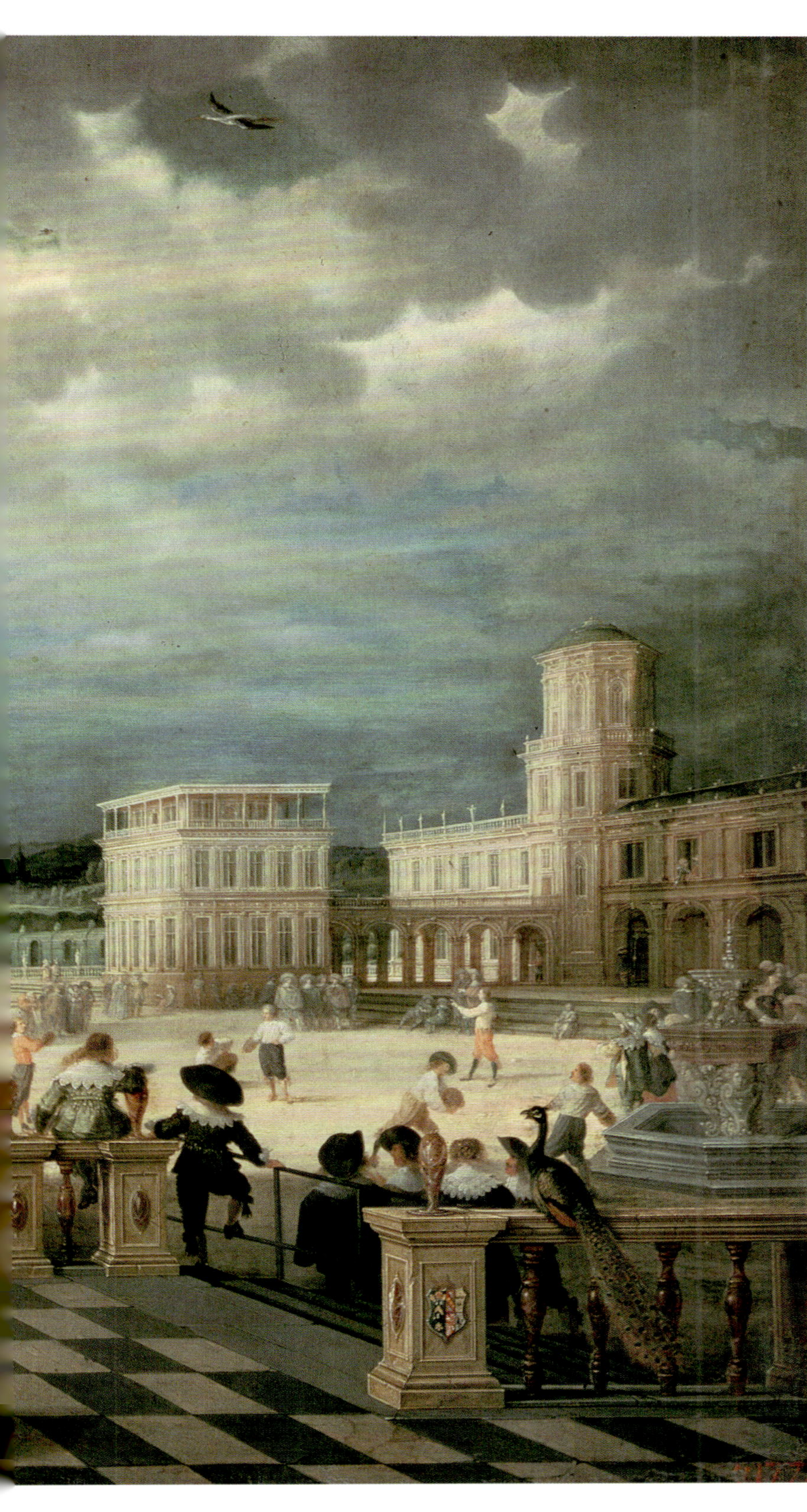

Hendrick van Steenwyck de Jonge (c. 1580–b./a. 1649)
Italian Palace
Palais italien
Italienischer Palast
Palacio italiano
Palácio Italiano
Italiaans paleis
1623, Oil on copper/Huile sur cuivre, 54,5 × 80 cm

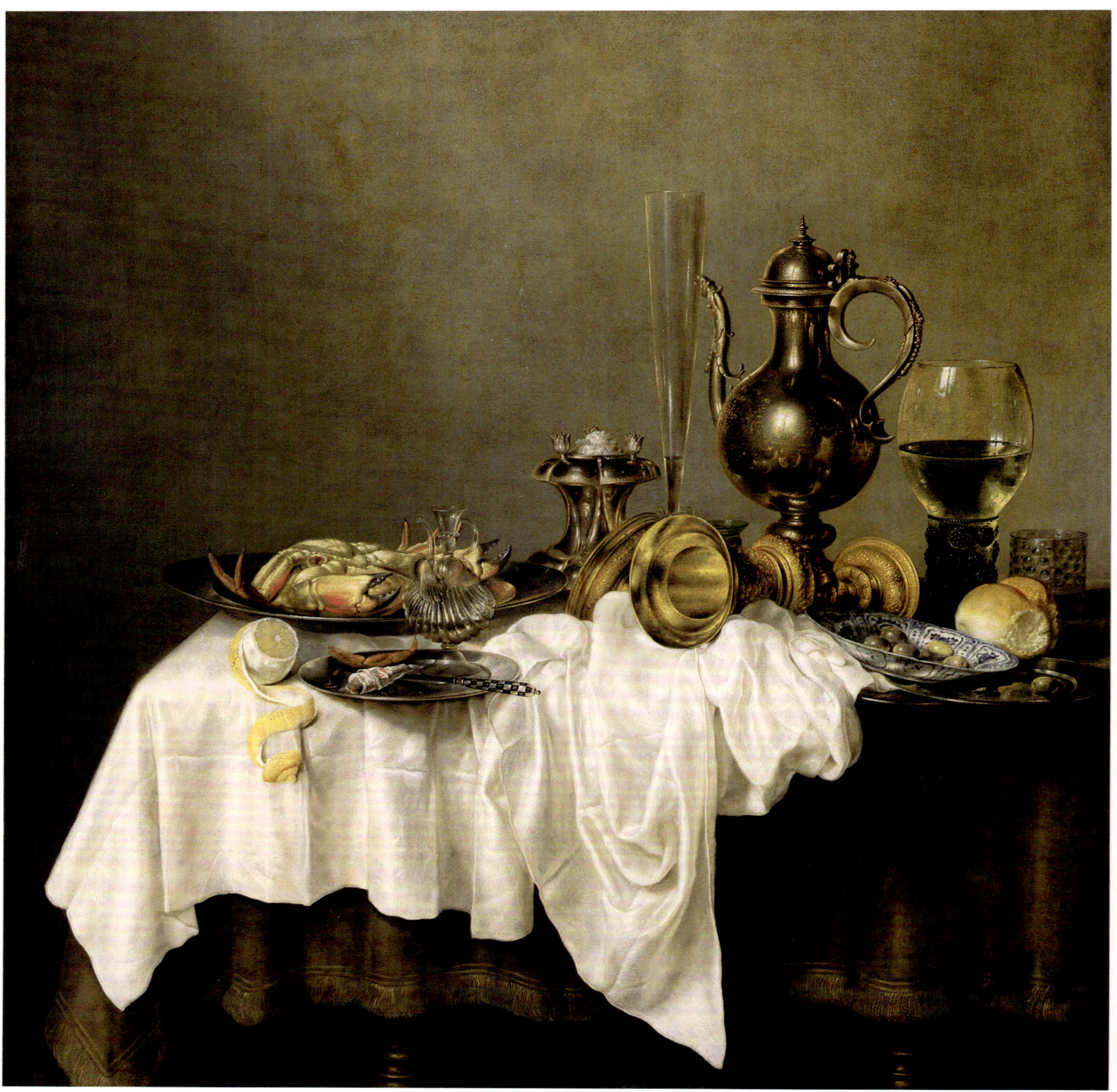

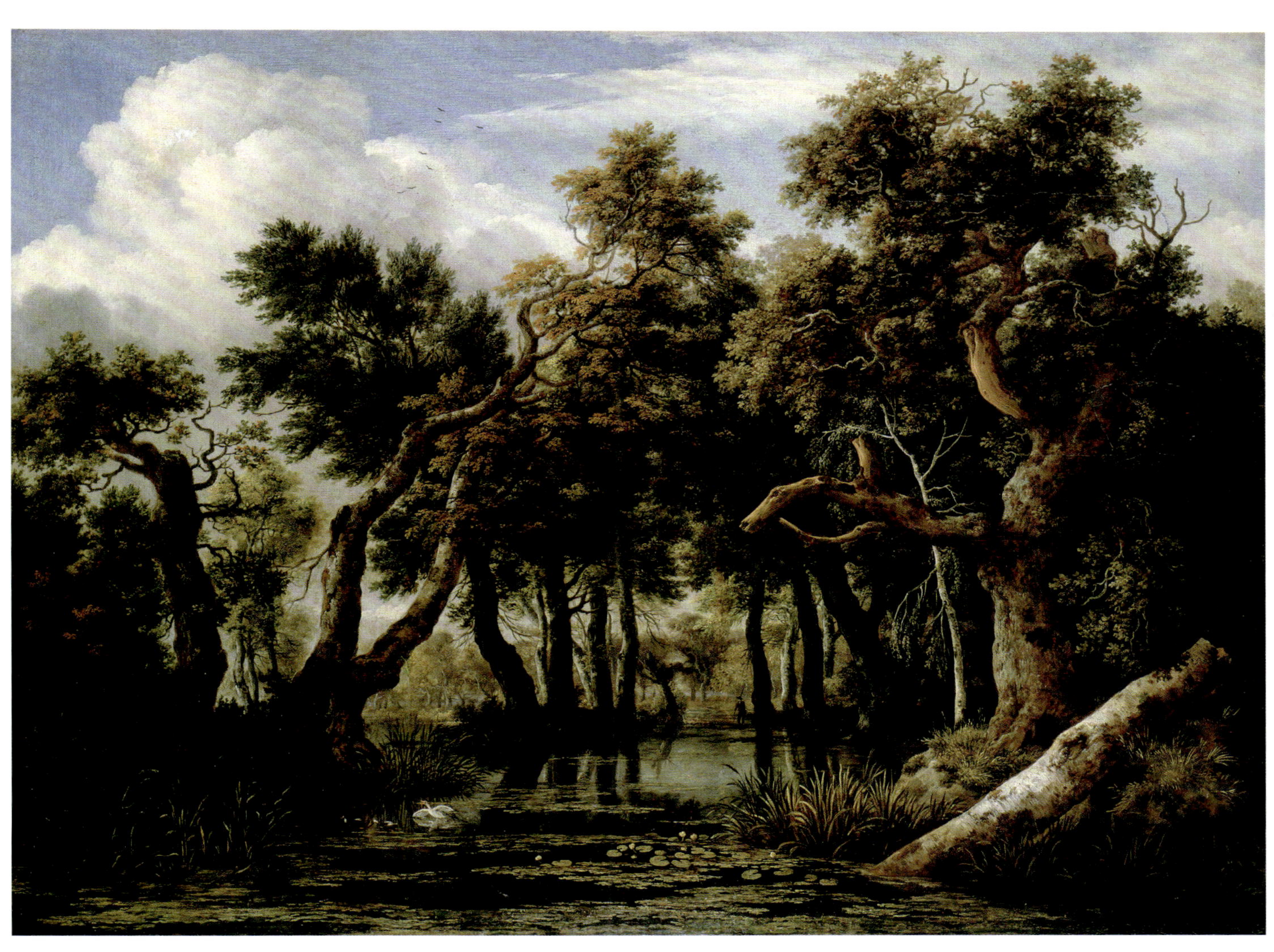

Willem Claesz. Heda (1594–1680)

Still Life with Crab

Nature morte au crabe

Stillleben mit Krebs

Bodegón con cangrejo

Natureza-Morta com Caranguejo

Stilleven met een krab

1648, Oil on canvas/Huile sur toile, 118 × 118 cm

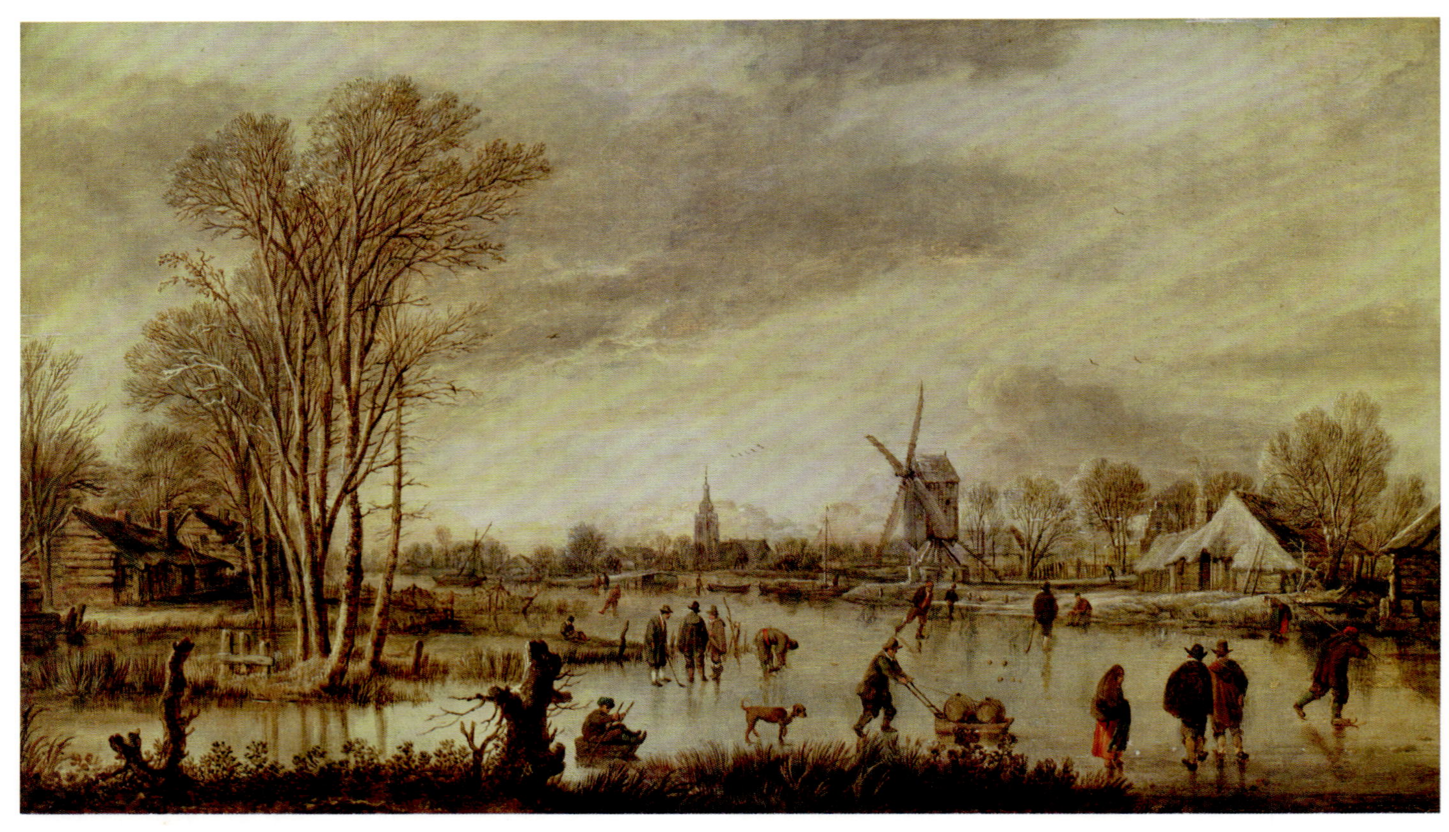

Aert van der Neer (1603–77)

River in Winter

Rivière en hiver

Fluss im Winter

Río en invierno

Rio no Inverno

Rivier in de winter

c.1645, Oil on wood/Huile sur bois, 35,5 × 62 cm

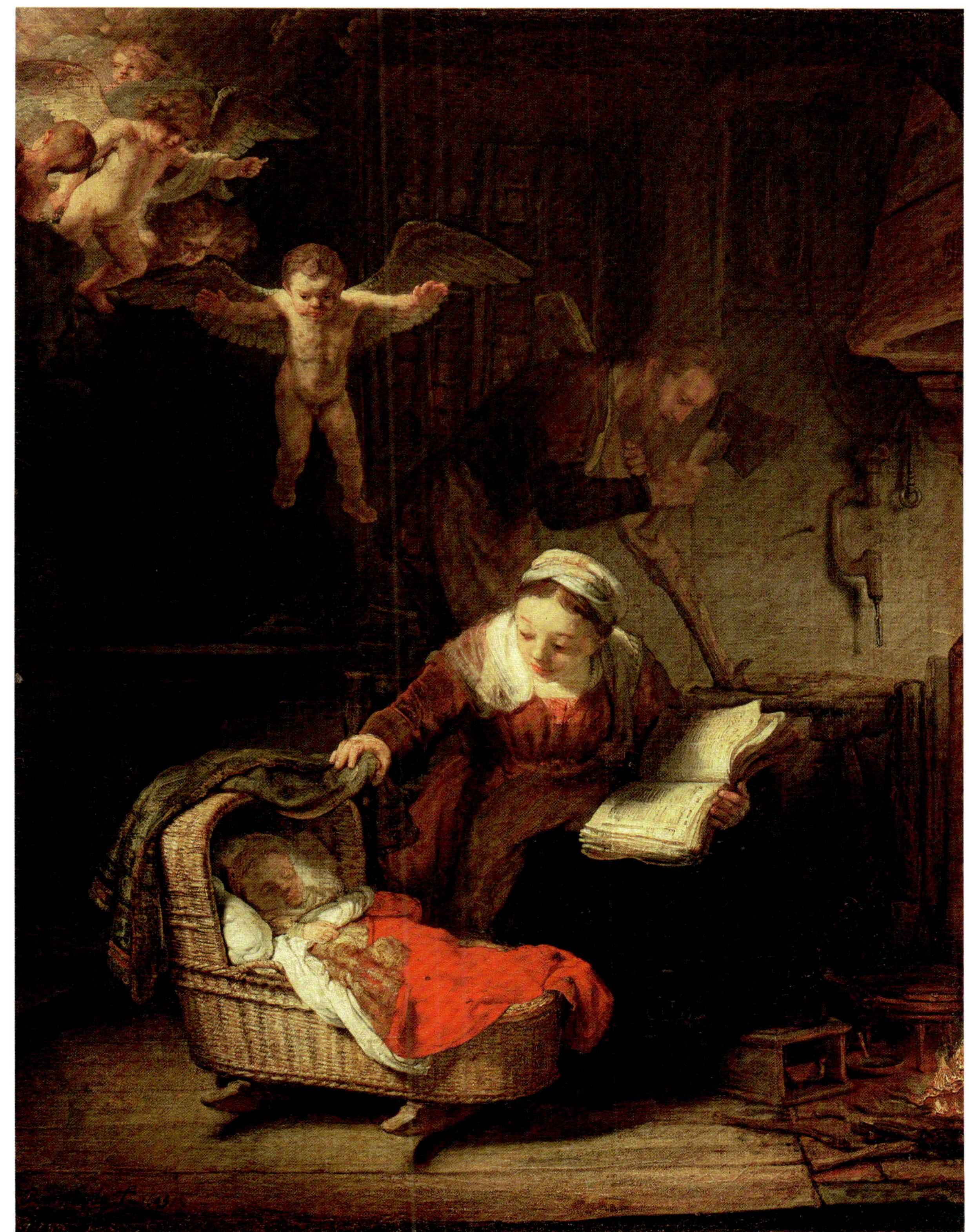

*Rembrandt Harmensz.
van Rijn (1606–69)*

The Holy Family
La Sainte Famille
Die Heilige Familie
La Sagrada Familia
A Sagrada Família
De Heilige Familie

1645, Oil on canvas/
Huile sur toile,
117 × 91 cm

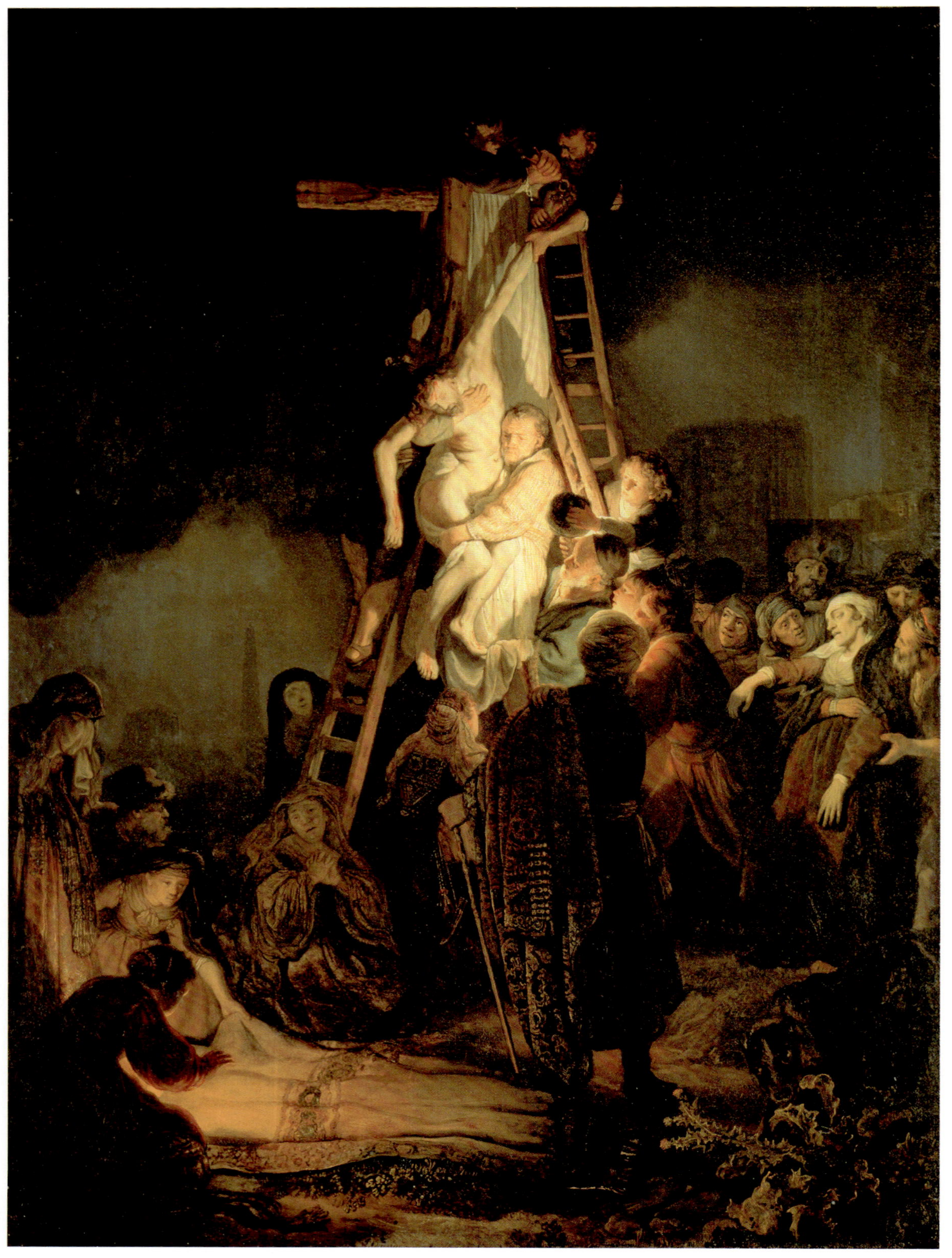

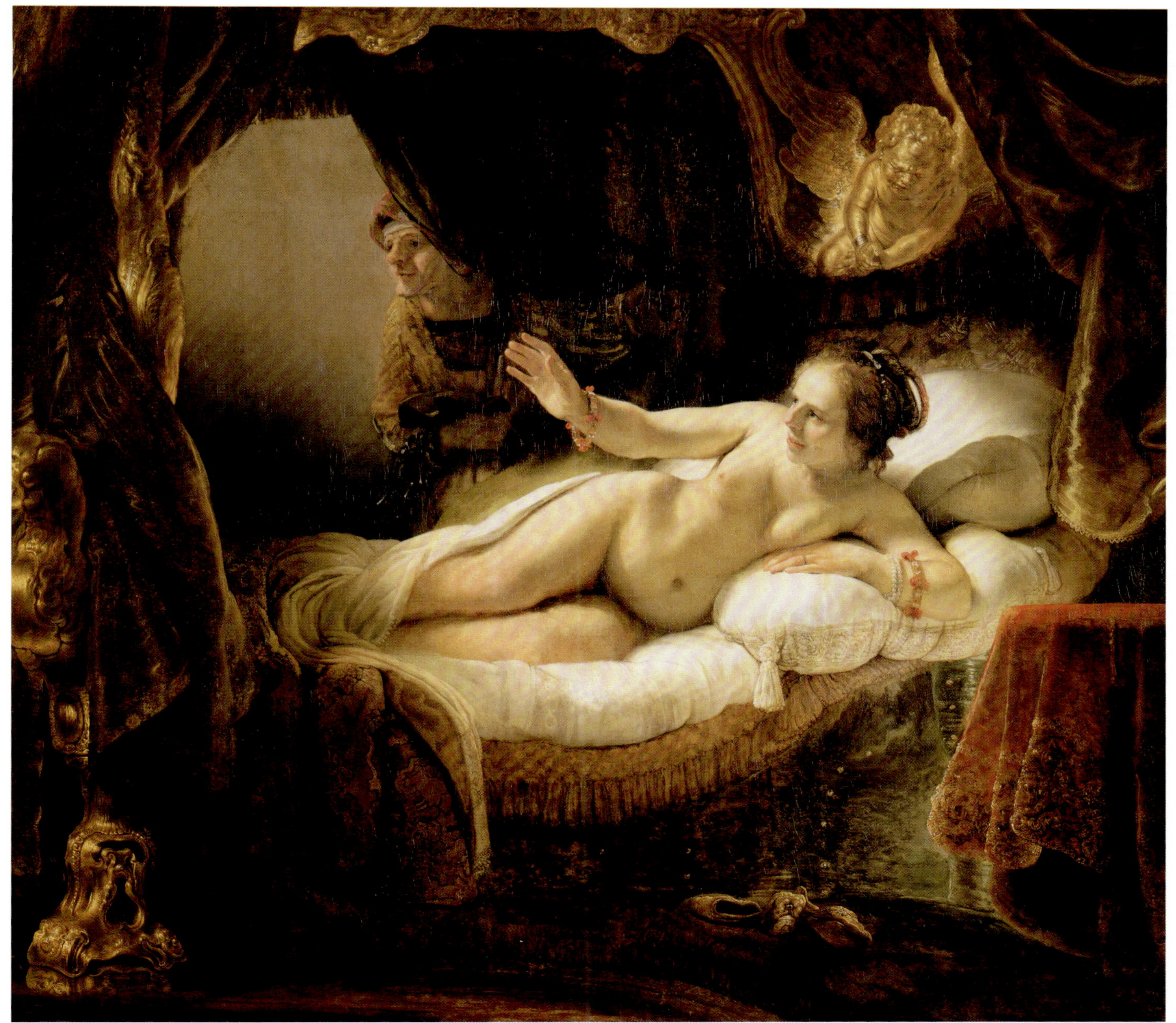

Rembrandt Harmensz. van Rijn (1606–69)

Danae

Danaé

Danae

Danae

Dánae

Danae

1636, Oil on canvas/Huile sur toile, 185 × 202,5 cm

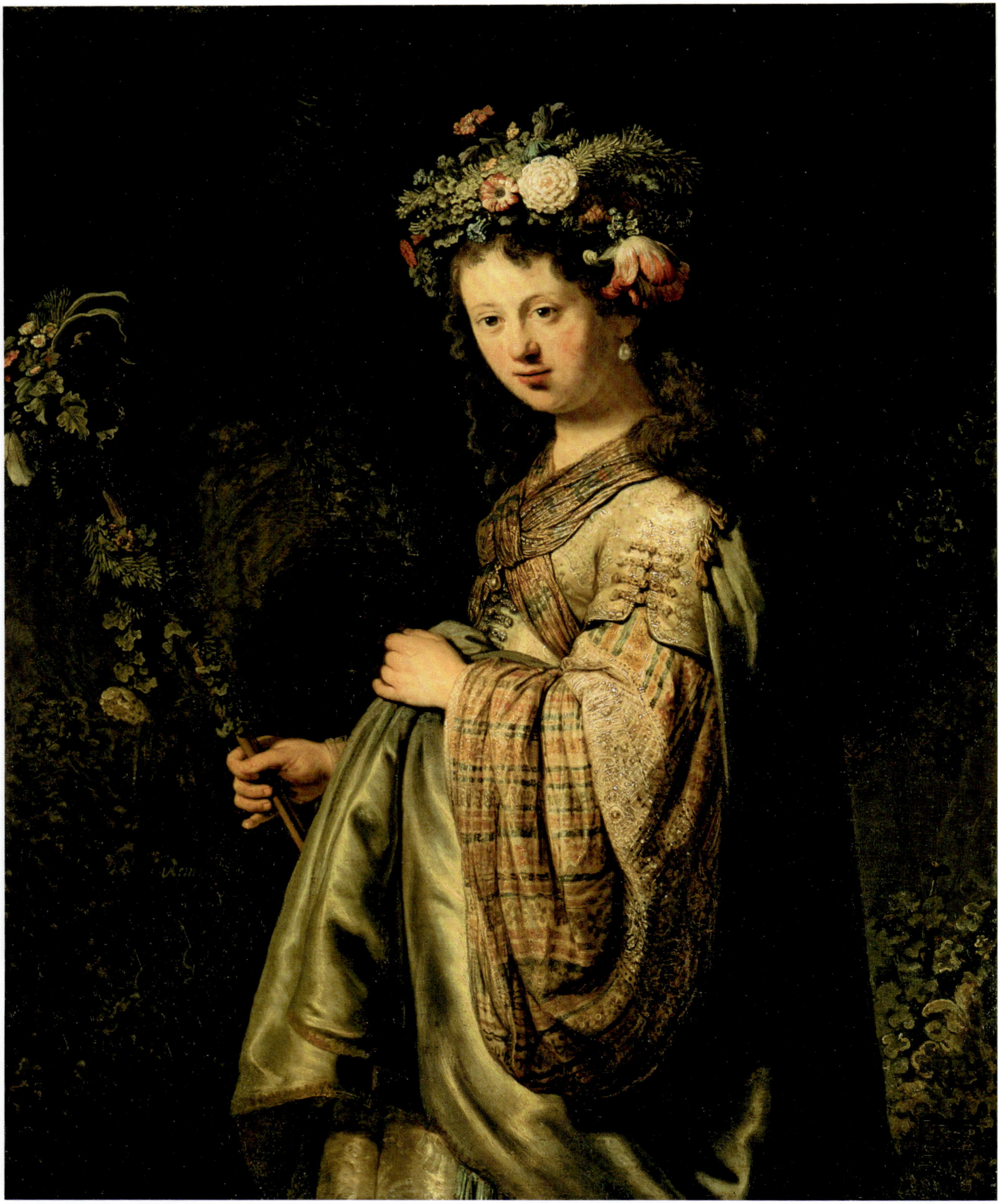

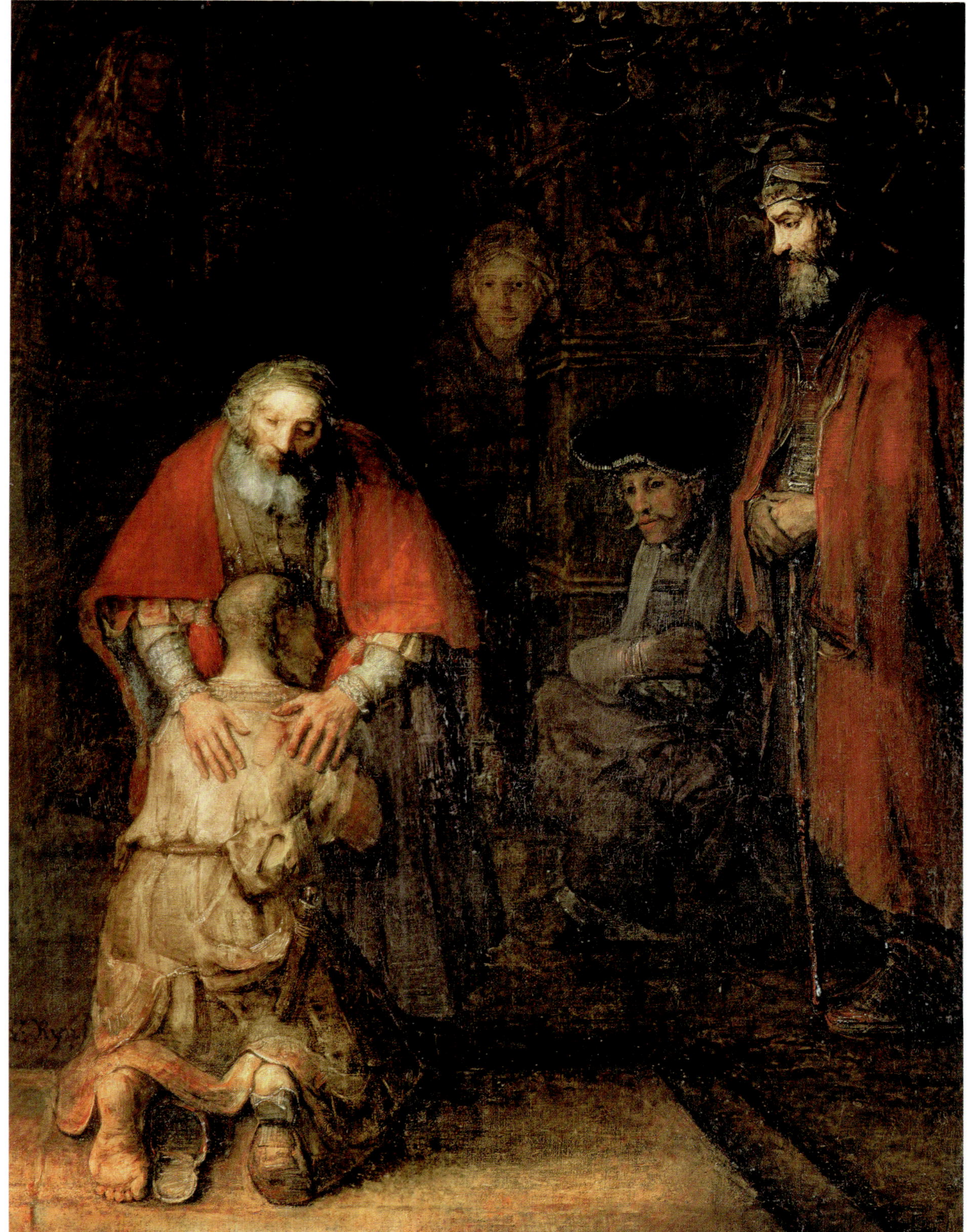

Rembrandt Harmensz.
van Rijn (1606–69)

Saskia as Flora

Flore

Saskia als Flora

Saskia como Flora

Saskia como Flora

Saskia als Flora

1634, Oil on canvas/
Huile sur toile,
125 × 101 cm

Rembrandt Harmensz.
van Rijn (1606–69)

The Return of the
Prodigal Son

Le Retour du
fils prodigue

Die Rückkehr des
verlorenen Sohnes

El retorno del
hijo pródigo

O Regresso do
Filho Pródigo

De terugkeer van
de verloren zoon

c. 1668/69, Oil on
canvas/Huile sur
toile, 262 × 205 cm

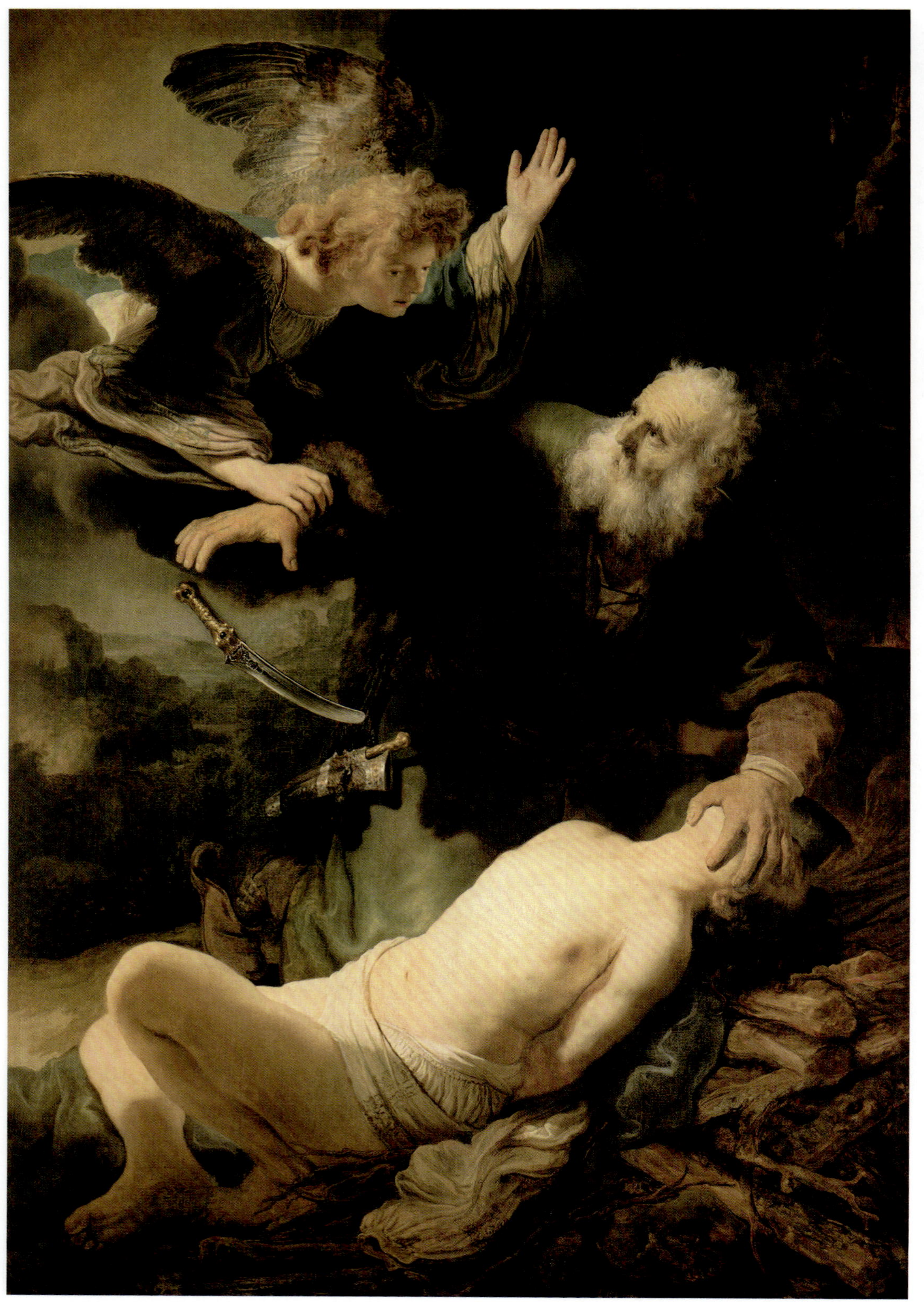

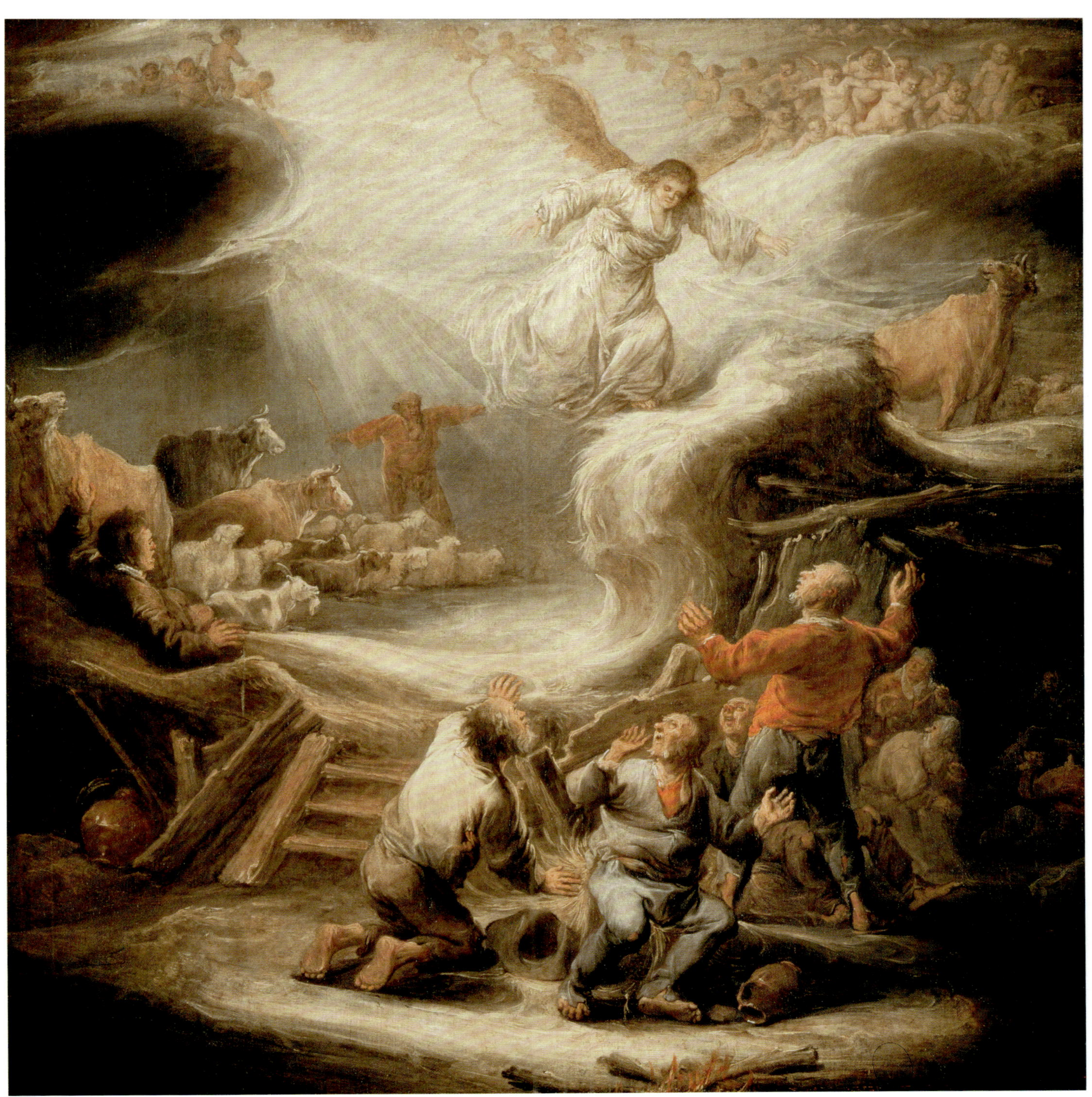

*Gerard
ter Borch
(1617–81)*

The Glass of
Lemonade

Le Verre de
citronnade

Das Glas
Limonade

El vaso de
limonada

O Copo de
Limonada

**Het glas
limonade**

1660, Oil
on canvas,
transferred
from panel/
Huile sur toile,
transposée d'un
bois, 67 × 54 cm

*Willem Kalf
(1619–93)*

Still Life with
Akelei Goblet

La Desserte

Stillleben mit
Akeleipokal

El postre
(bodegón)

Natureza-
Morta com
Pocal

Stilleven met
beker met
akeleien

1653/54, Oil
on canvas/
Huile sur toile,
105 × 87,5 cm

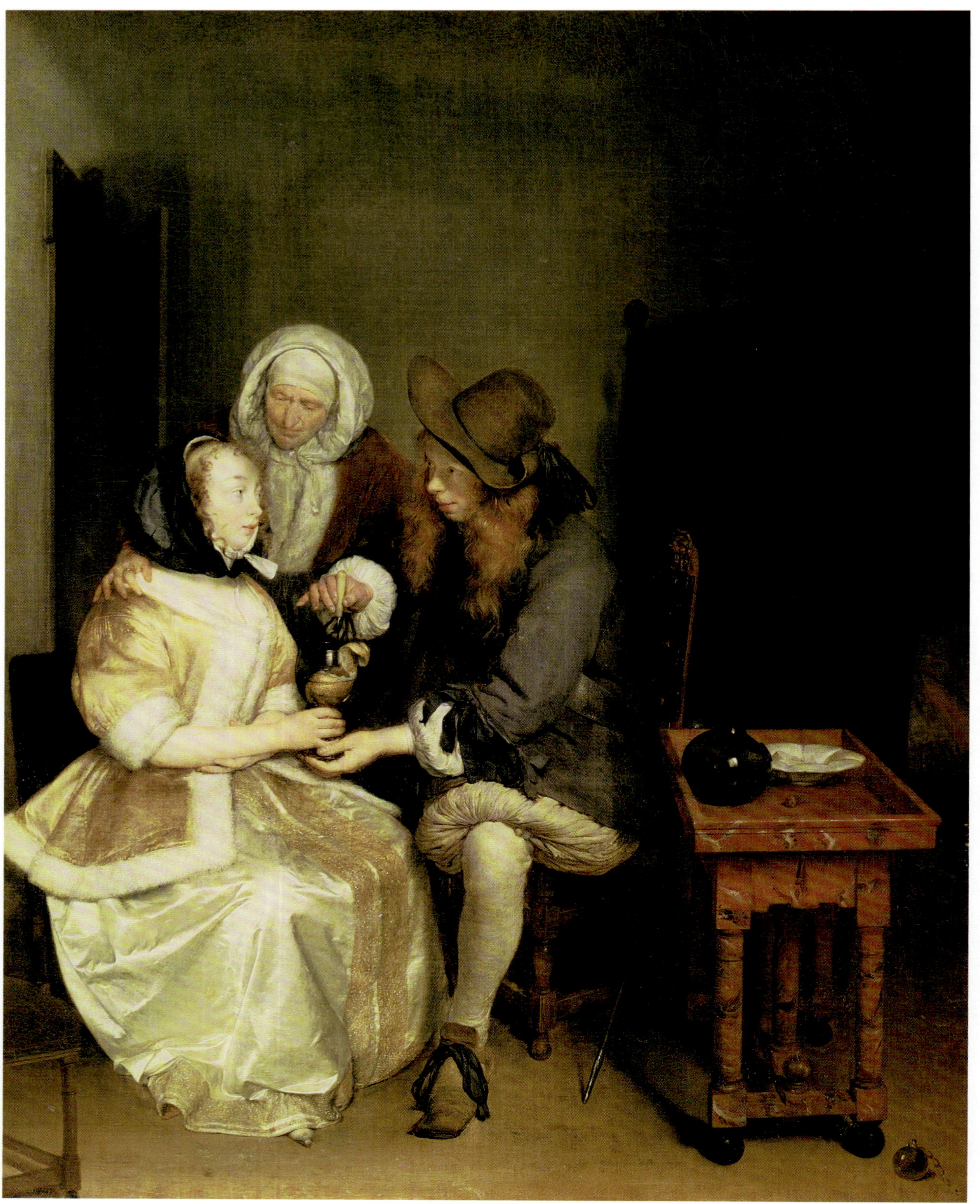

214

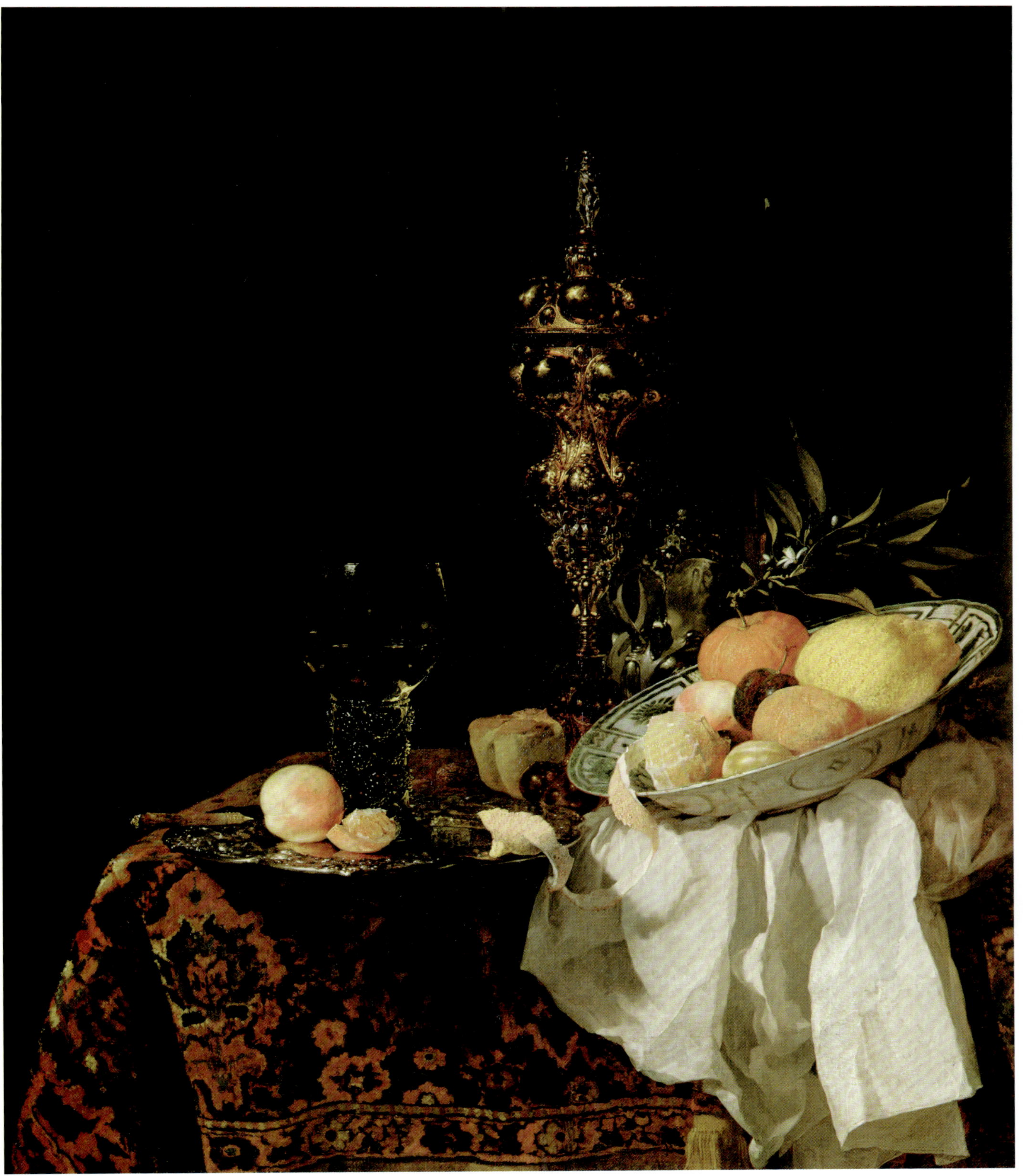

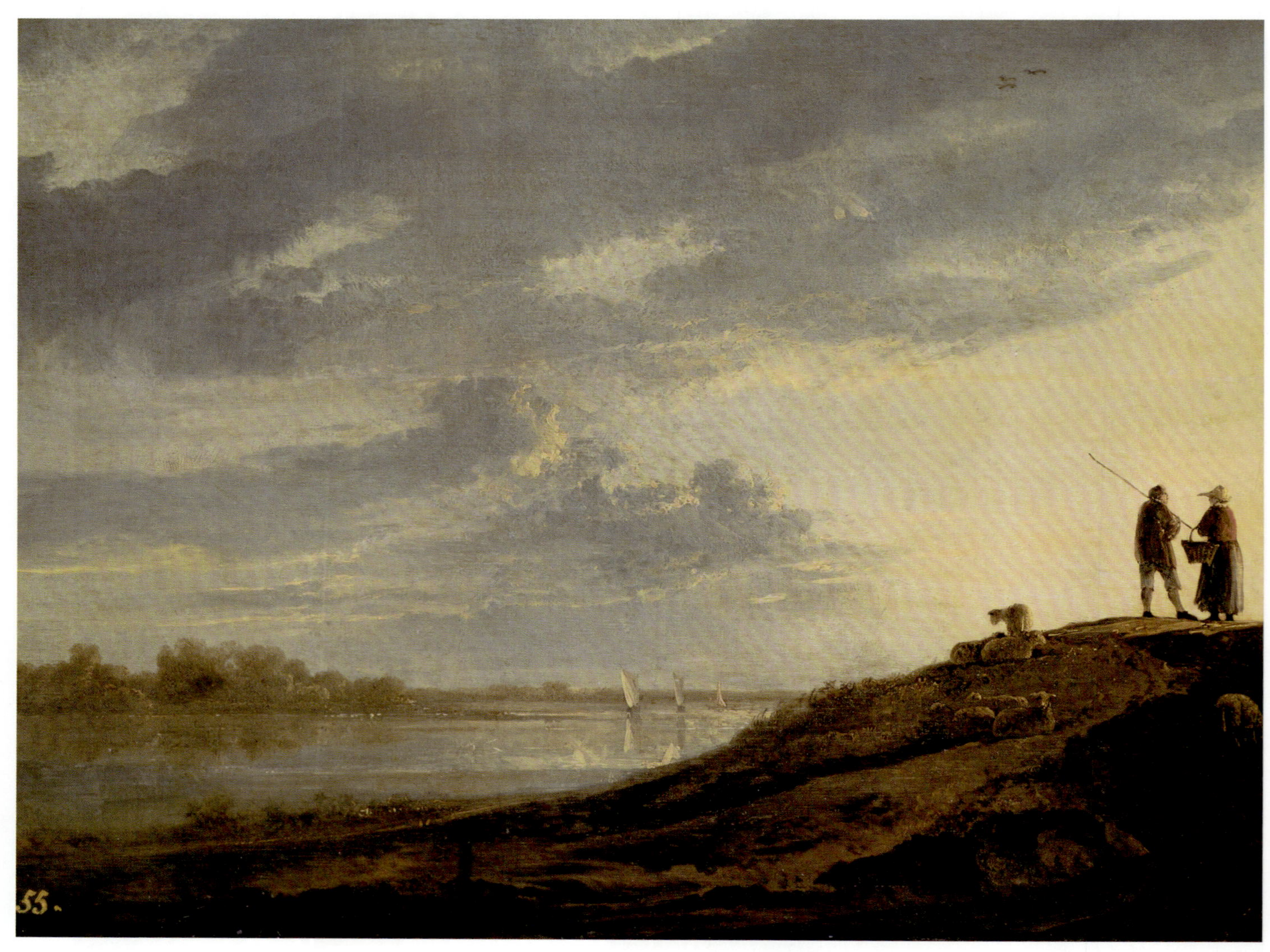

Aelbert Cuyp (1620–91)

Sunset over a River

Rivière au soleil couchant

Sonnenuntergang über einem Fluss

Puesta de sol sobre un río

Pôr-do-Sol sobre um Rio

Zonsondergang boven de rivier

c. 1650–59, Oil on canvas/Huile sur toile, 38,5 × 53 cm

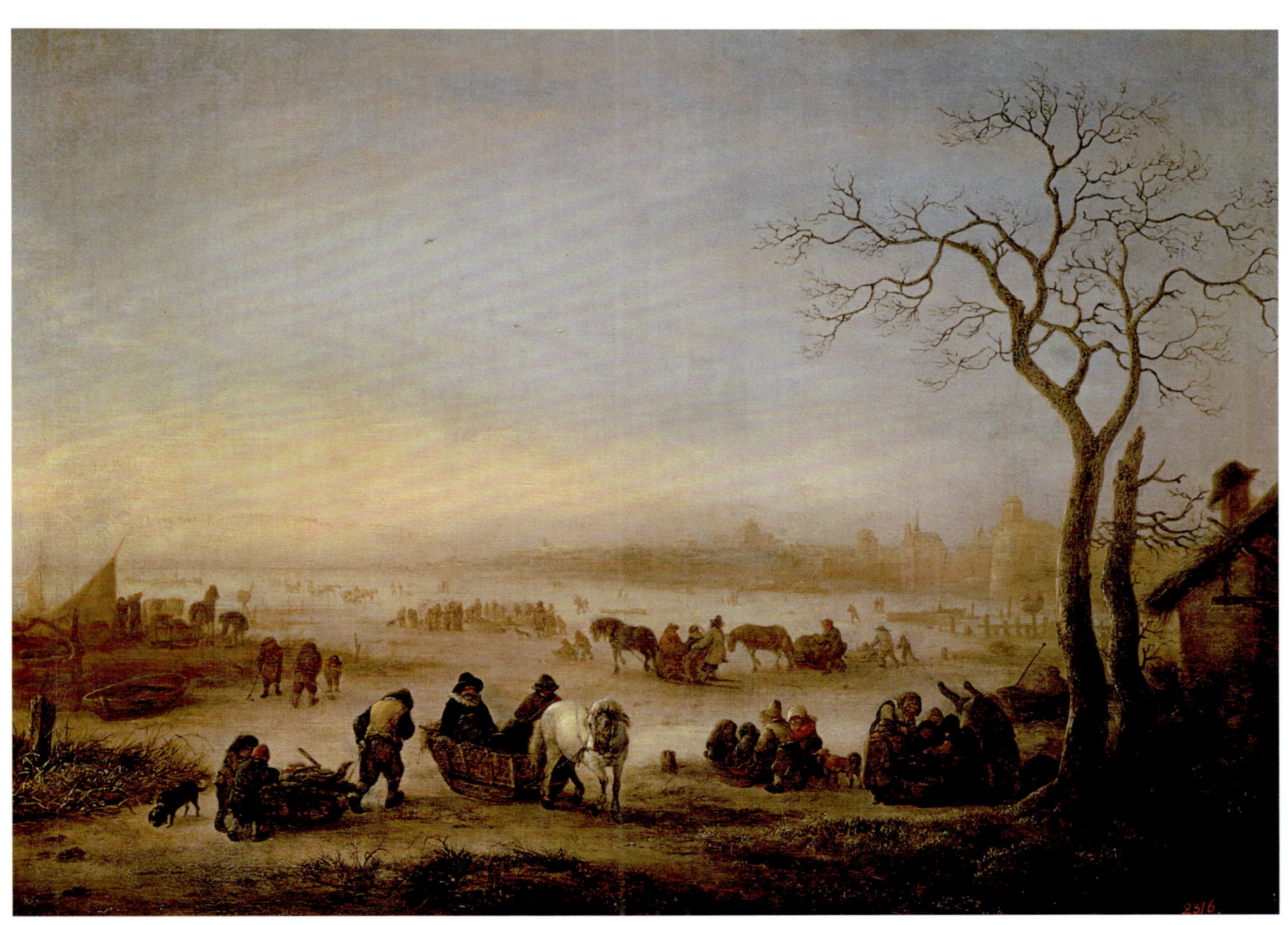

Isaac van Ostade (1621–49)

The Frozen Lake

Lac gelé

Der zugefrorene See

El lago congelado

O Lago Gelado

Het bevroren meer

1648, Oil on canvas/Huile sur toile, 59 × 80,5 cm

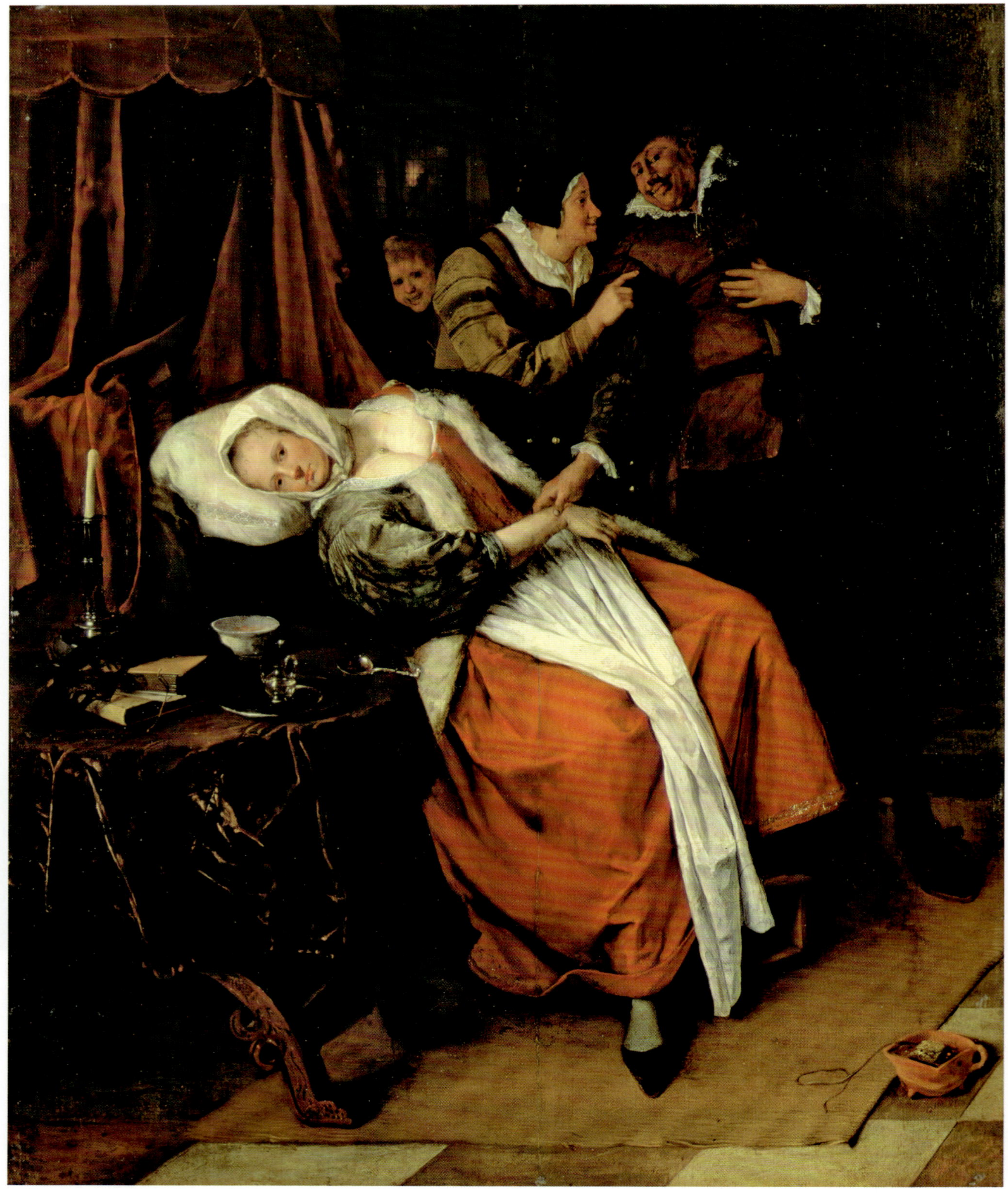

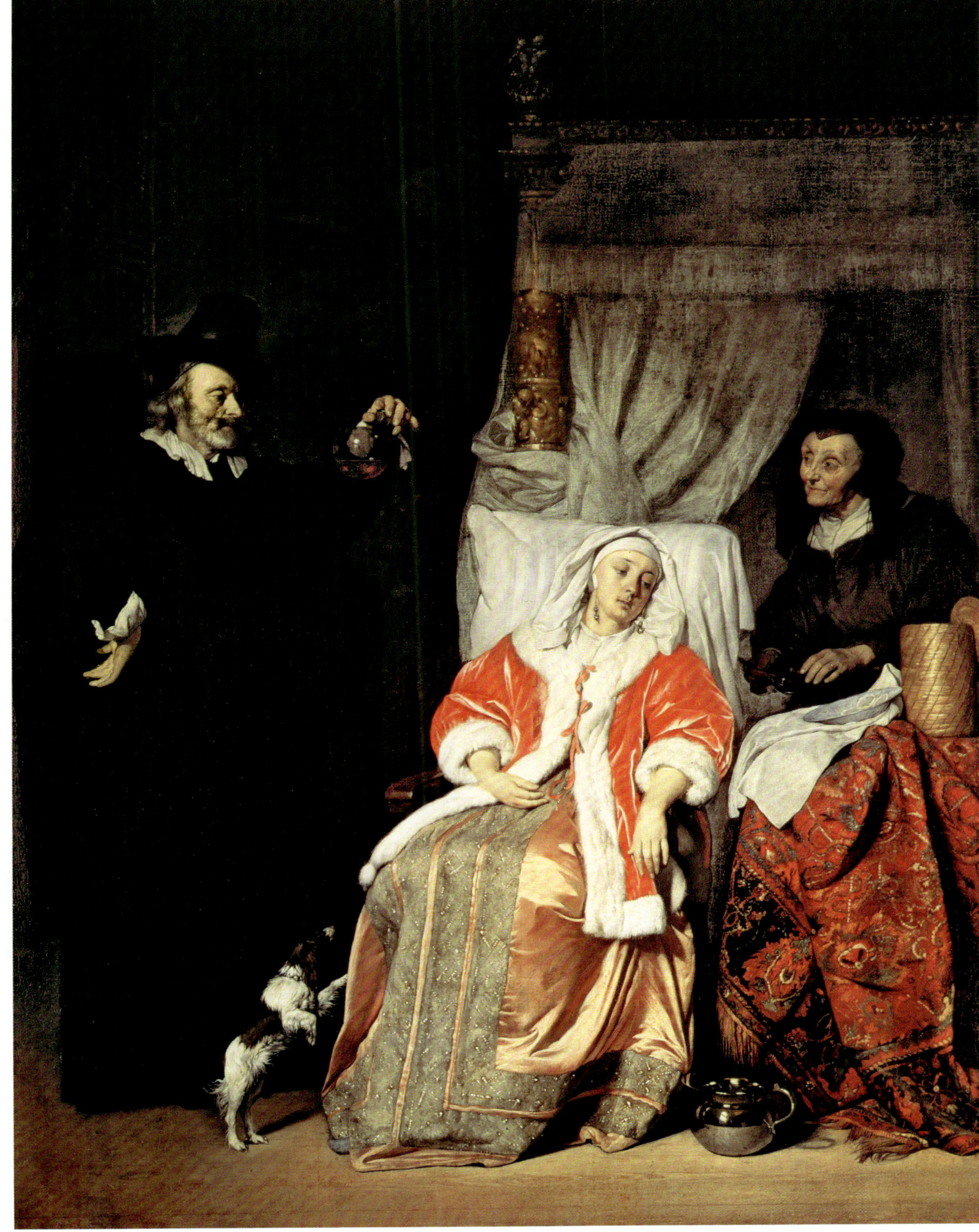

Jan Steen
(c. 1625–79)

The Patient and
the Doctor

La Malade et
le médecin

Die Patientin
und der Arzt

La paciente y
el médico

A Paciente e
o Médico

De patiënte
en de arts

c. 1660–69, Oil on
canvas/Huile sur
toile, 62,5 × 51 cm

Gabriel Metsu
(1629–67)

The Patient and
the Doctor

La Malade et
le médecin

Die Patientin
und der Arzt

La paciente y
el médico

A Paciente e
o Médico

De patiënte
en de arts

c. 1660–69, Oil on
canvas/Huile sur
toile, 61,5 × 47,5 cm

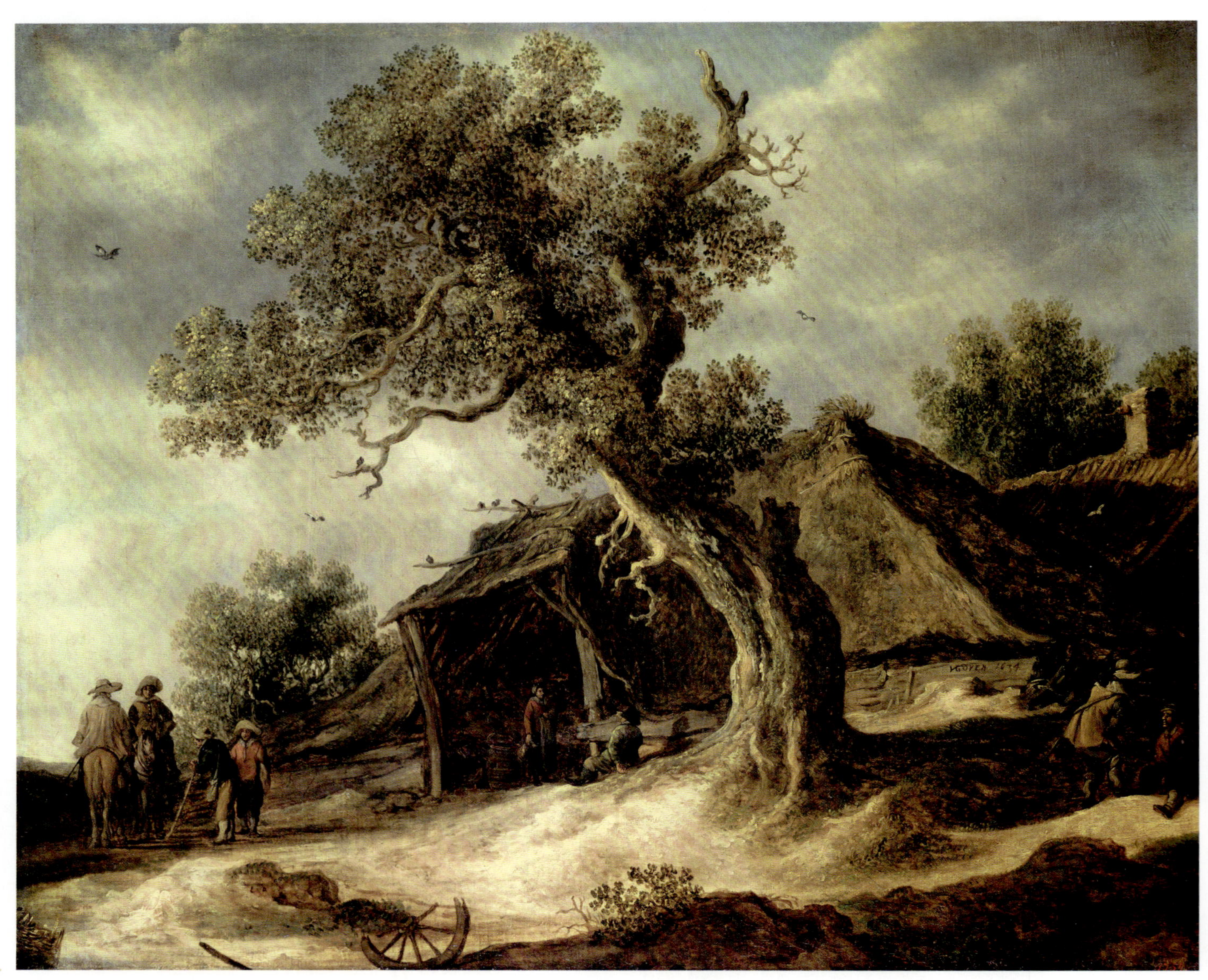

Jacob van Ruisdael (c. 1628–82)

Landscape with Oaks

Paysage avec un chêne

Landschaft mit Eiche

Paisaje con roble

Paisagem com Carvalho

Landschap met een eikenboom

c. 1652, Oil on canvas/Huile sur toile, 87 × 105 cm

Samuel van Hoogstraten (1627–78)

Boy Looking Out a Window

Jeune garçon regardant à travers la fenêtre

Junge, der aus dem Fenster schaut

Joven mirando por la ventana

Rapaz Olhando pela Janela

Jongen die uit het raam kijkt

c. 1647, Oil on canvas/Huile sur toile, 42 × 36 cm

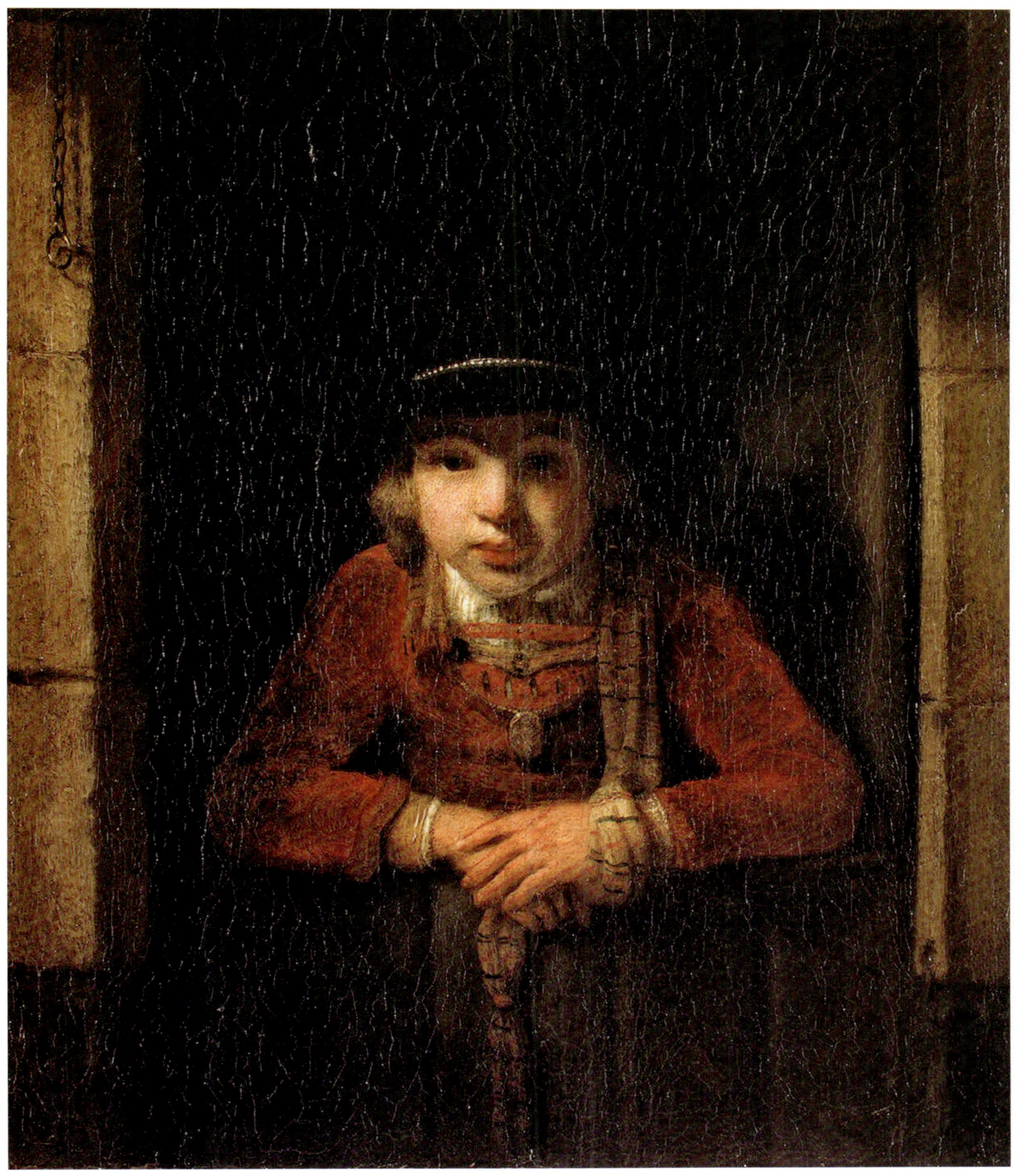

Gabriel Metsu
(1629–67)

Breakfast

Le Petit Déjeuner

Das Frühstück

El desayuno

O Pequeno-Almoço

Het ontbijt

c. 1660, Oil on
canvas/Huile sur
toile, 56 × 42 cm

Pieter de Hooch
(1629–84)

Soldier and
Servant Woman

Intérieur avec un
homme offrant
à une femme un
verre de vin

Soldat und Dienerin

Soldado y sierva

Soldado e Criada

Soldaat en
dienstmeisje

c. 1653, Oil on
canvas/Huile sur
toile, 53 × 42 cm

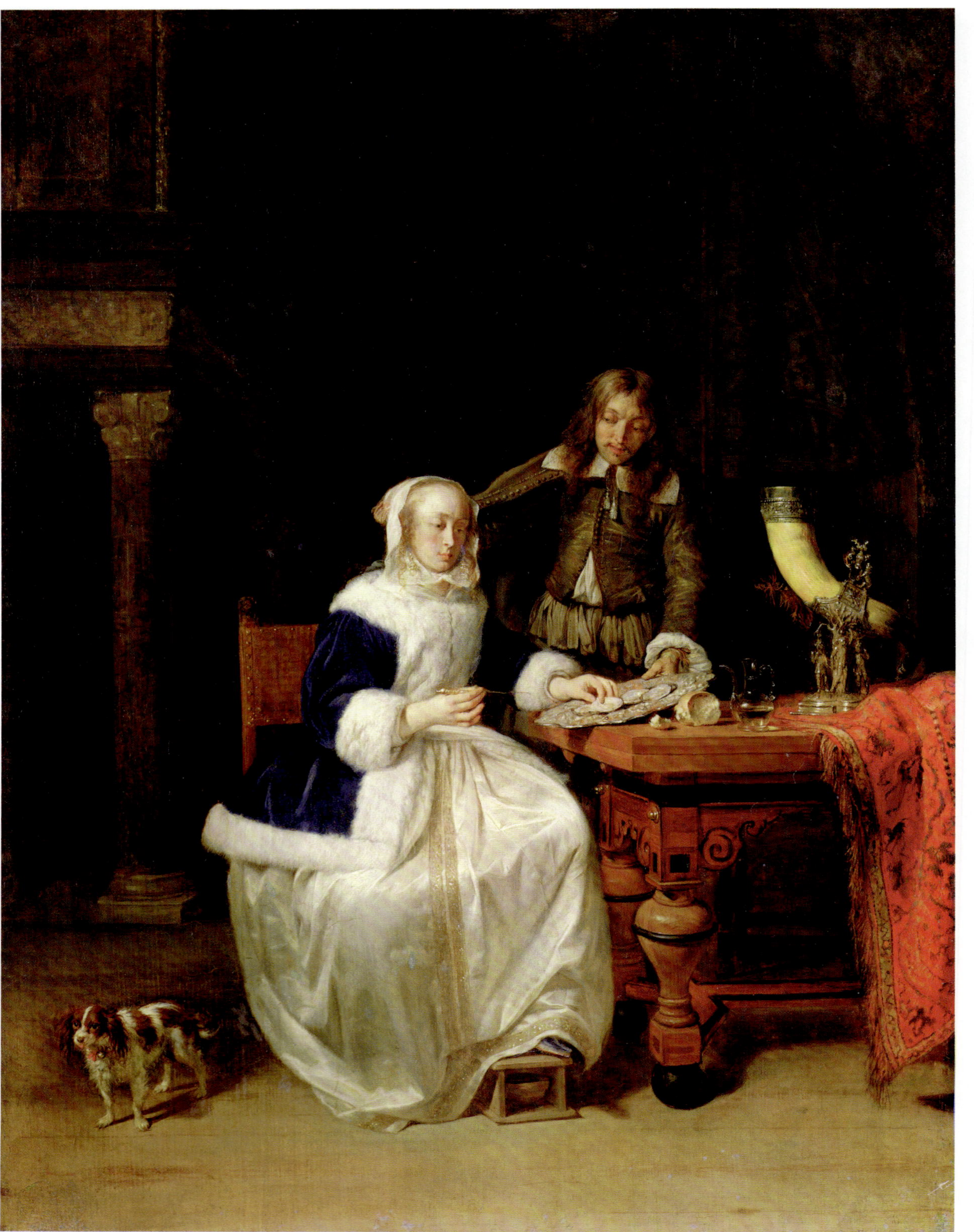

222

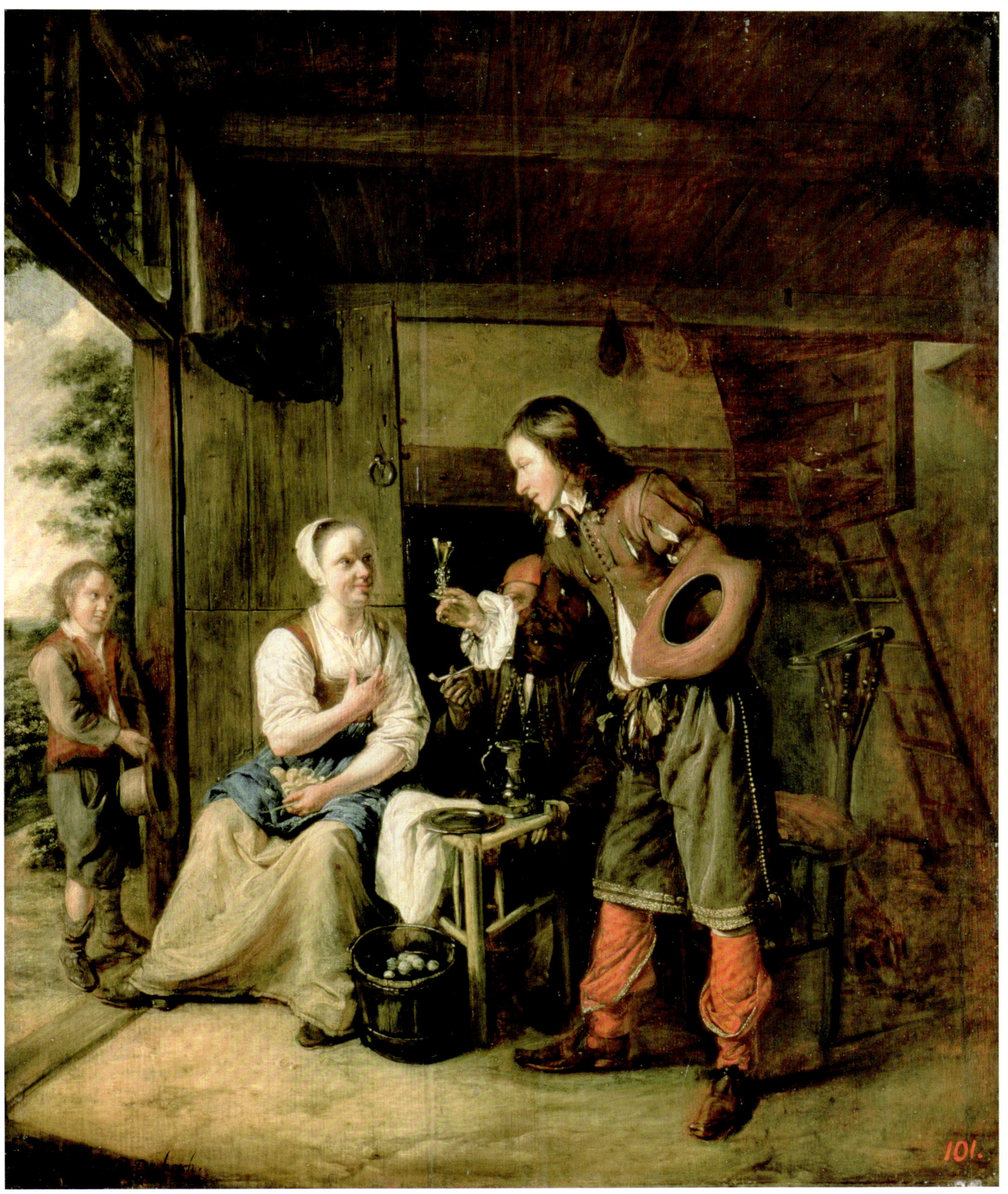

101.

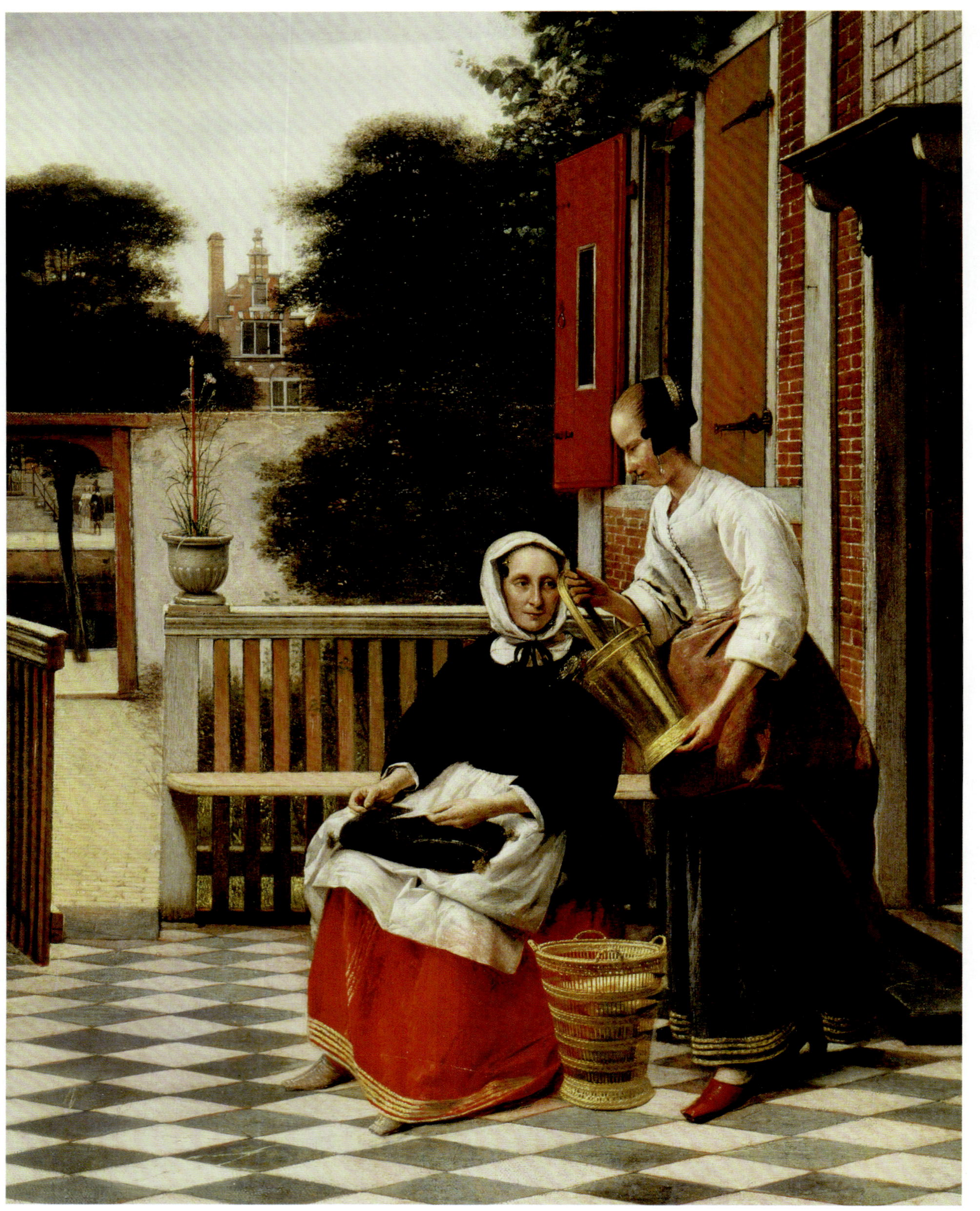

Pieter de Hooch
(1629–84)

A Lady with
her Maid

Une dame et
sa servante

Eine Dame mit
ihrer Magd

Una dama con
su criada

Uma Senhora
e a sua Criada

Een mevrouw
en haar meid

c. 1660, Oil on
canvas/Huile sur
toile, 53 × 42 cm

Frans van Mieris
(1635–81)

The Morning
Toilette of a
Young Lady

Matinée d'une
jeune dame

Die
Morgentoilette
einer jungen
Dame

El aseo matinal
de una joven

A Toilette
Matinal de uma
Jovem Dama

Het
ochtendtoilet
van een jonge
vrouw

1659/60, Oil
on cardboard/
Huile sur carton,
51,5 × 39,5 cm

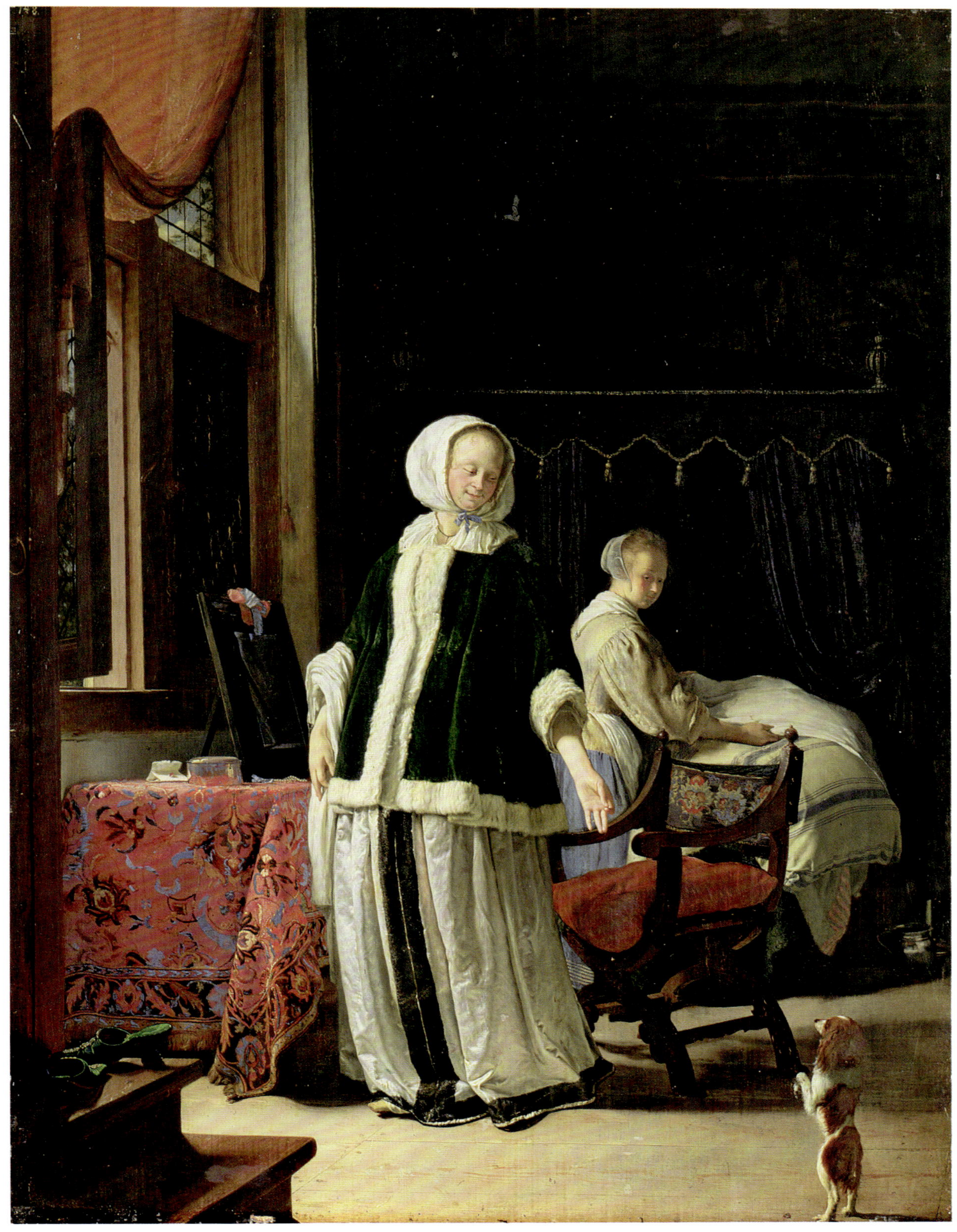

Jacob Hendrik Maris (1837–99)
Landscape with Windmills
Paysage aux moulins
Landschaft mit Windmühlen
Paisaje con molinos
Paisagem com Moinhos
Landschap met windmolens
1890–95, Oil on canvas/Huile sur toile, 46 × 73 cm

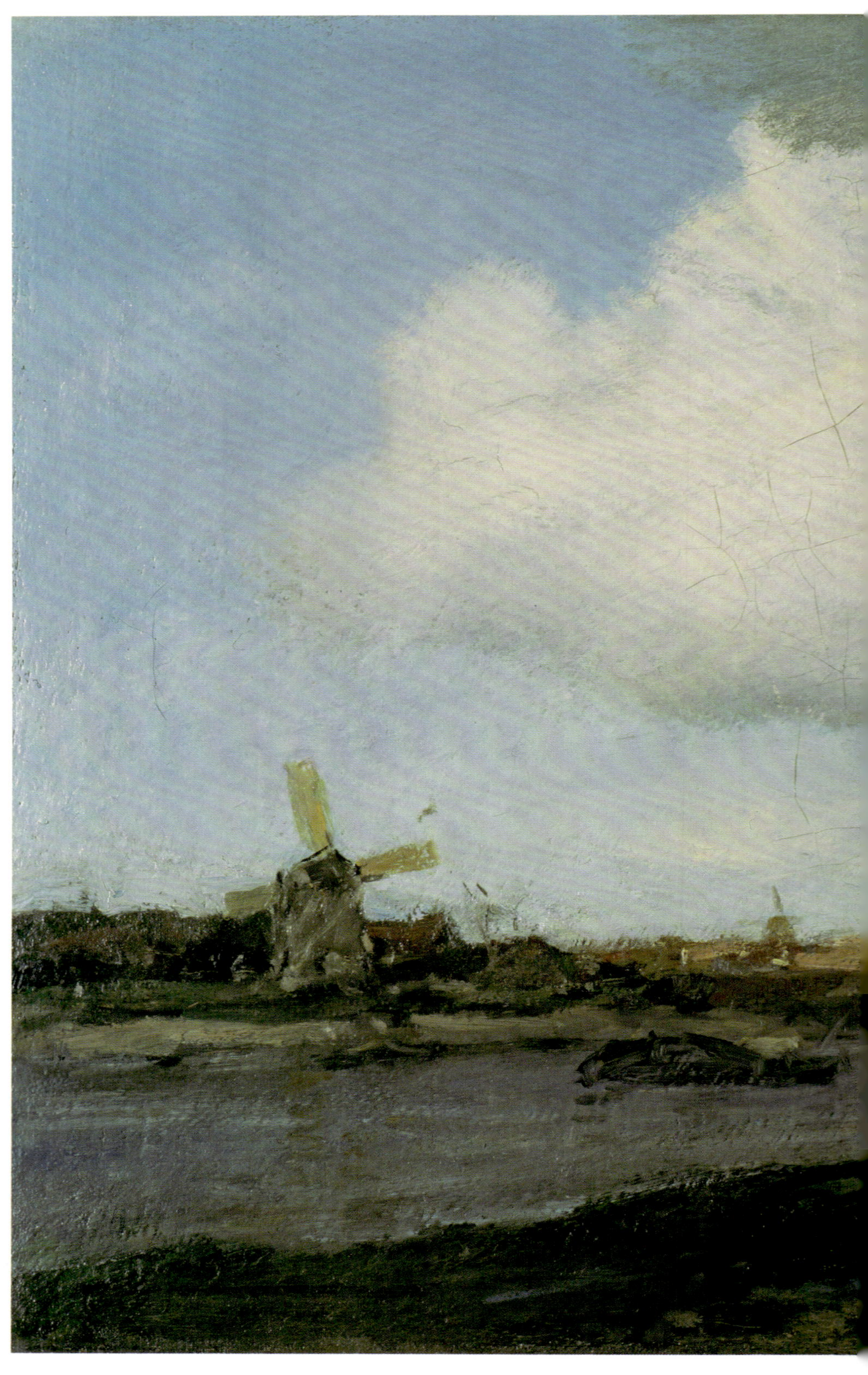

226

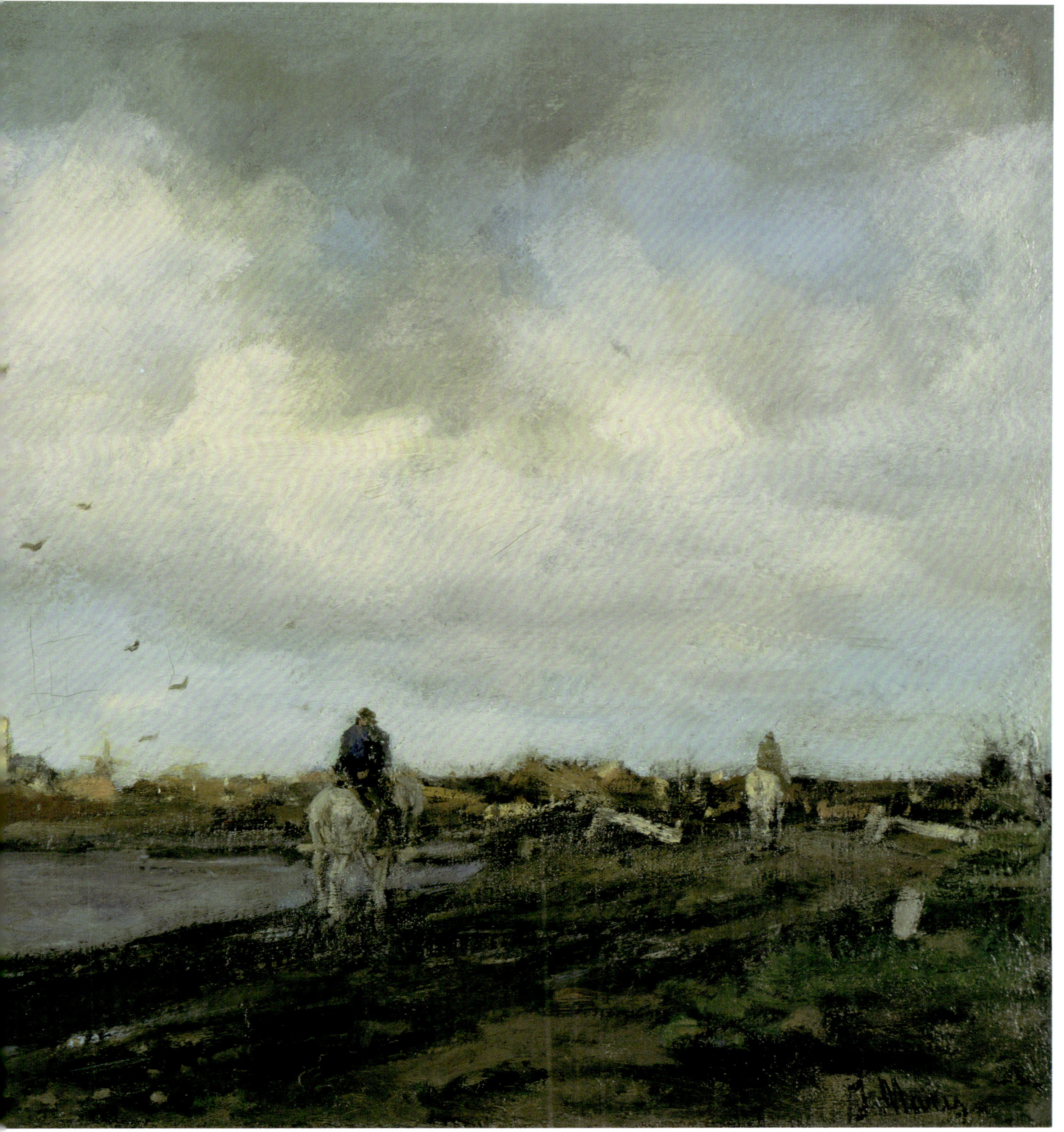

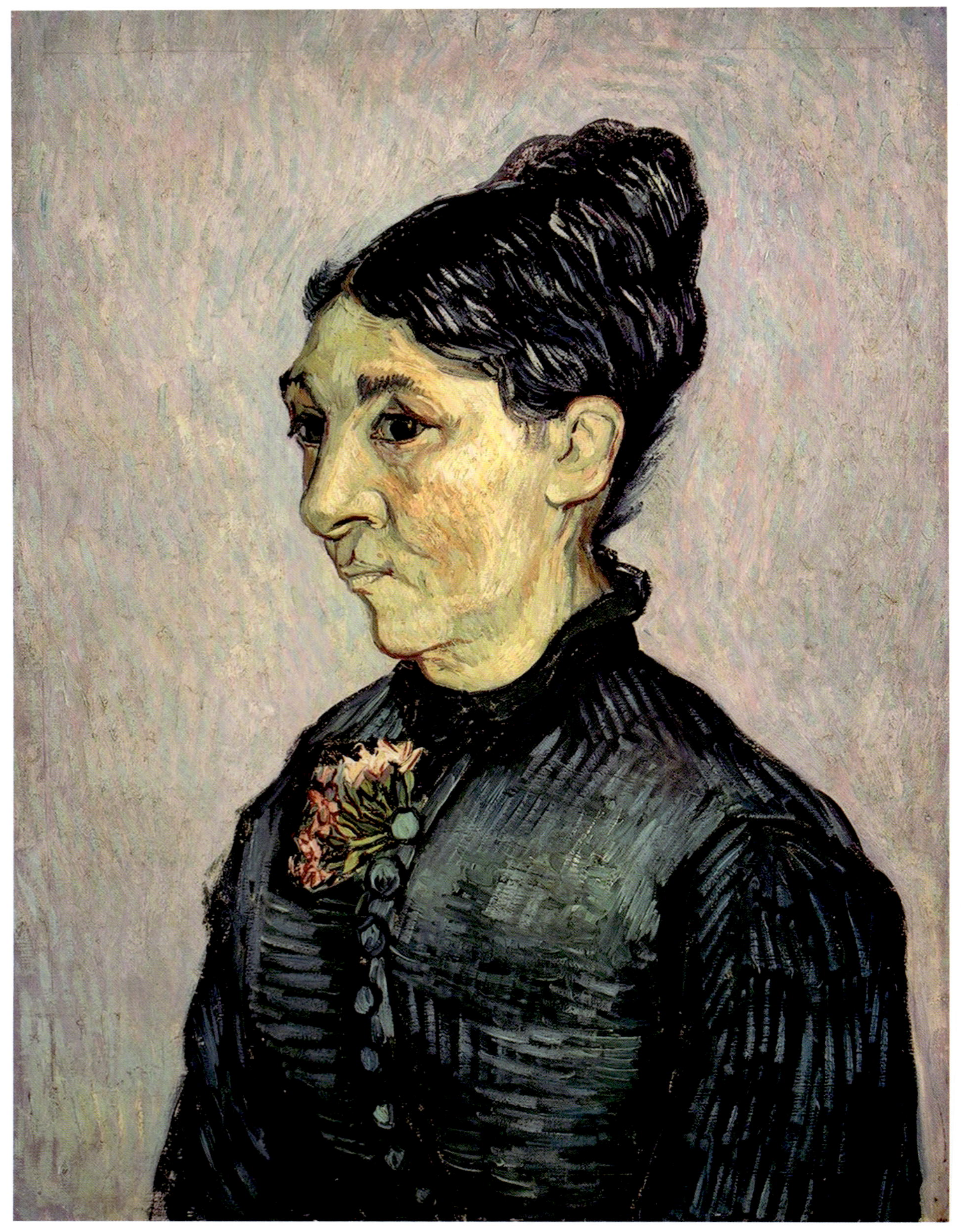

Vincent van Gogh
(1853–90)

Madame Jeanne Trabuc

1889, Oil on canvas/Huile
sur toile, 63,7 × 48 cm

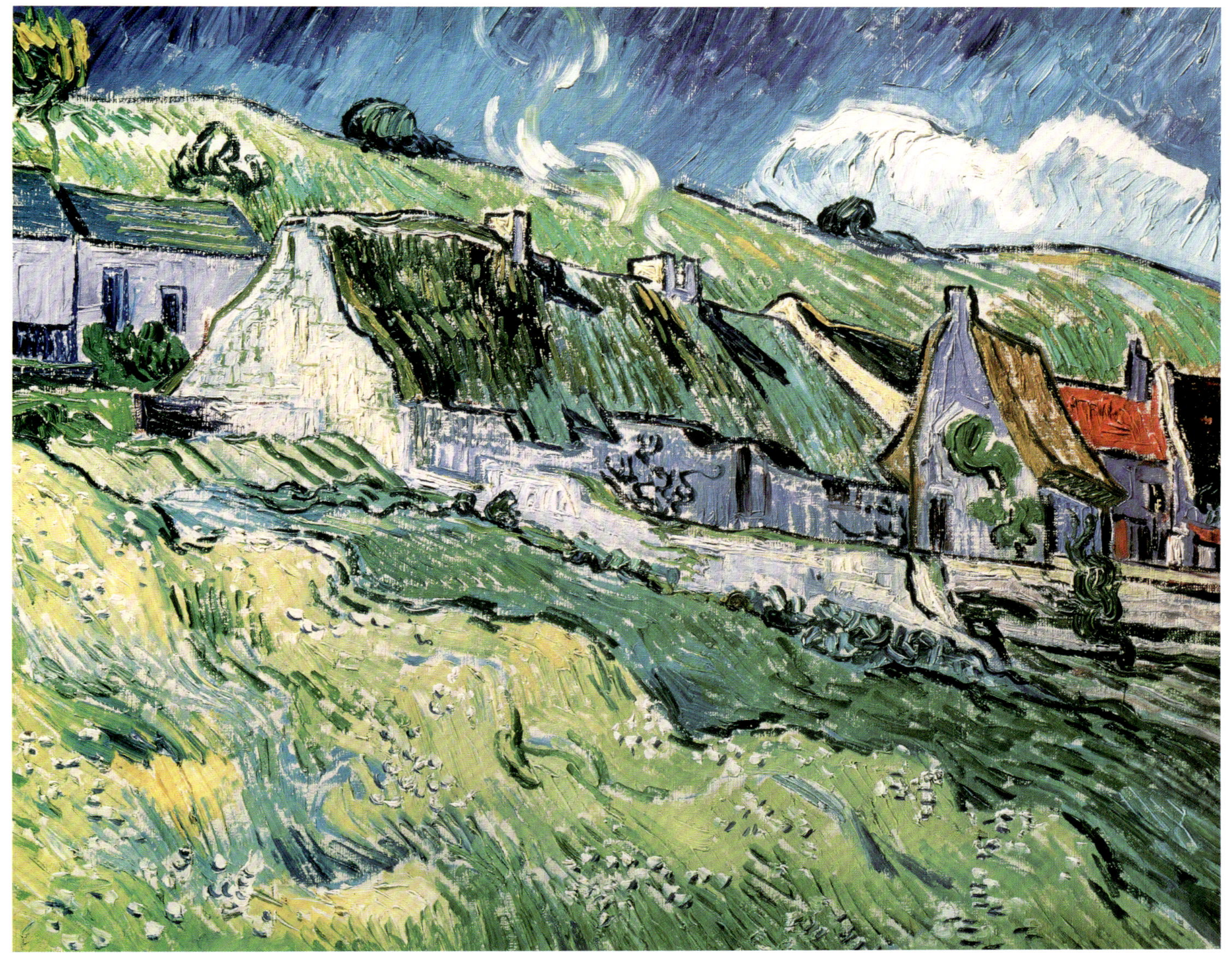

Vincent van Gogh (1853–90)

Houses in Auvers-sur-Oise

Les Chaumières

Häuser in Auvers-sur-Oise

Casas en Auvers-sur-Oise

Casas em Auvers-sur-Oise

Huizen in Auvers-sur-Oise

1890, Oil on canvas/Huile sur toile, 59 × 72 cm

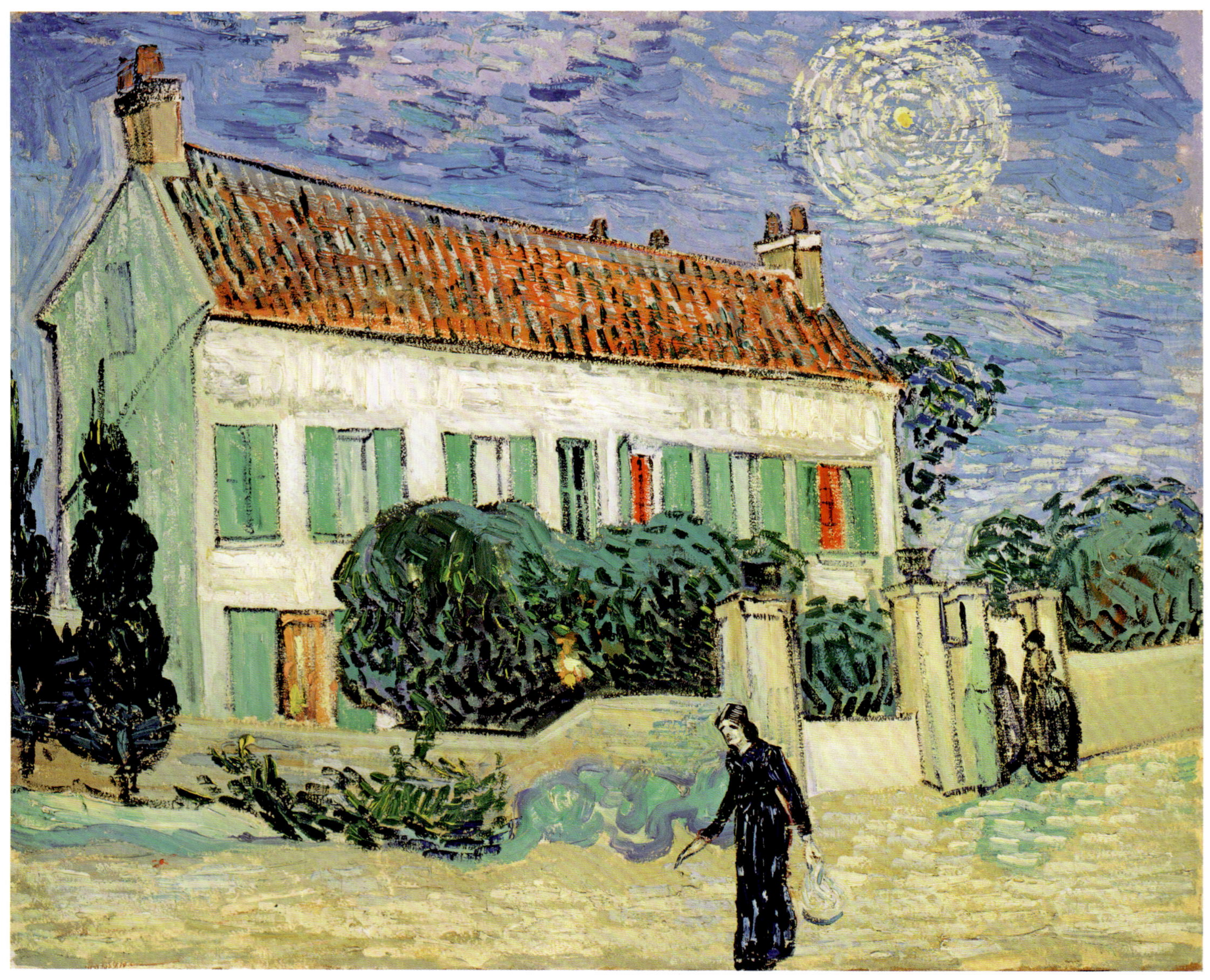

The White House at Night
La Maison blanche, la nuit
Das weiße Haus bei Nacht
La casa blanca por la noche
A Casa Branca à Noite
Het witte huis bij nacht

1890, Oil on canvas/Huile sur toile, 59 × 72,5 cm

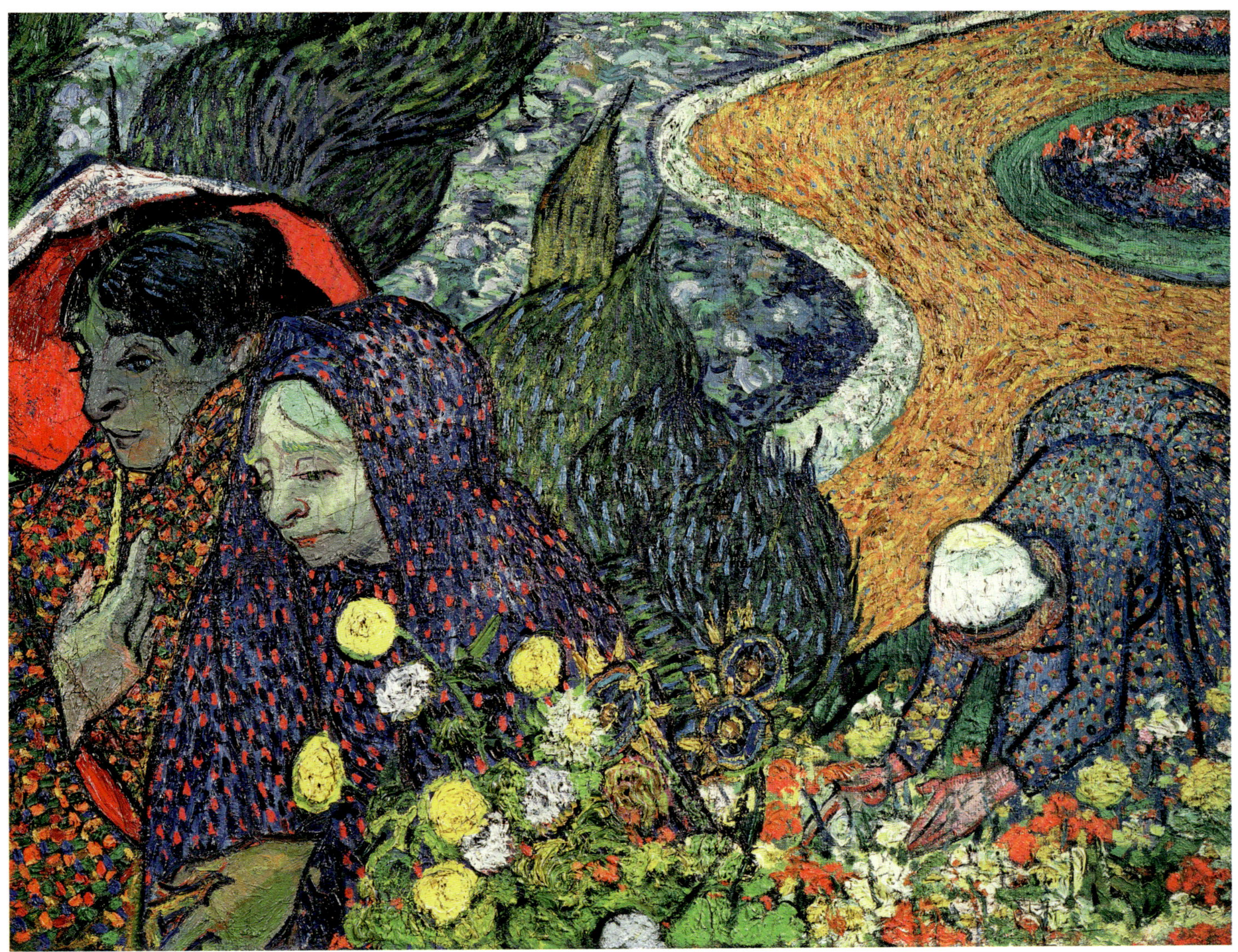

Vincent van Gogh (1853–90)

The Ladies of Arles (Memories of the Garden at Etten)

Promenade à Arles (Souvenir du jardin à Etten)

Die Damen von Arles (Erinnerung an den Garten in Etten)

Las mujeres de Arles (recuerdo de los jardines de Etten)

As Damas de Arles (Memória do Jardim em Etten)

De vrouwen van Arles (Herinnering aan de tuin in Etten)

1888, Oil on canvas/Huile sur toile, 73 × 92 cm

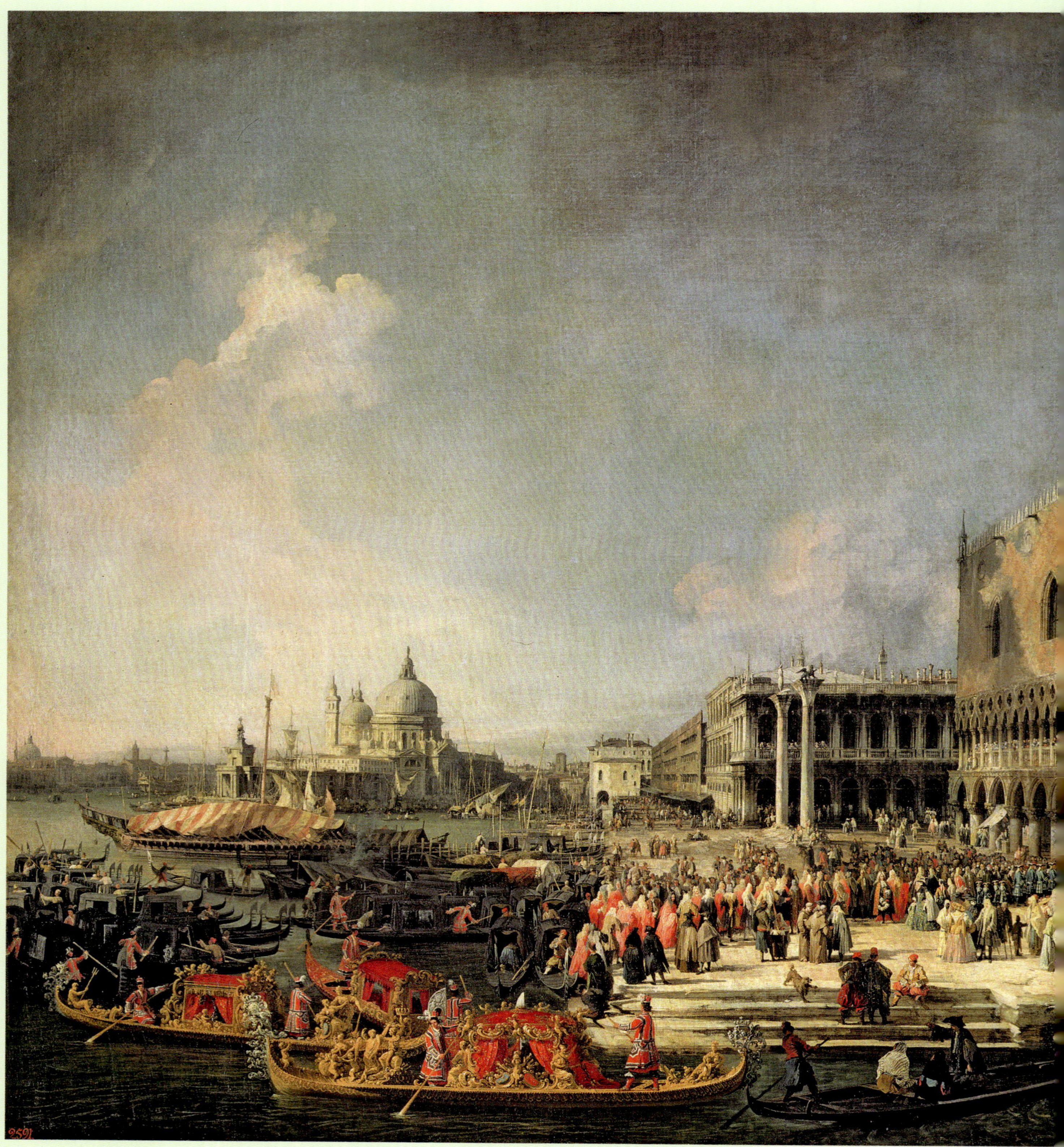

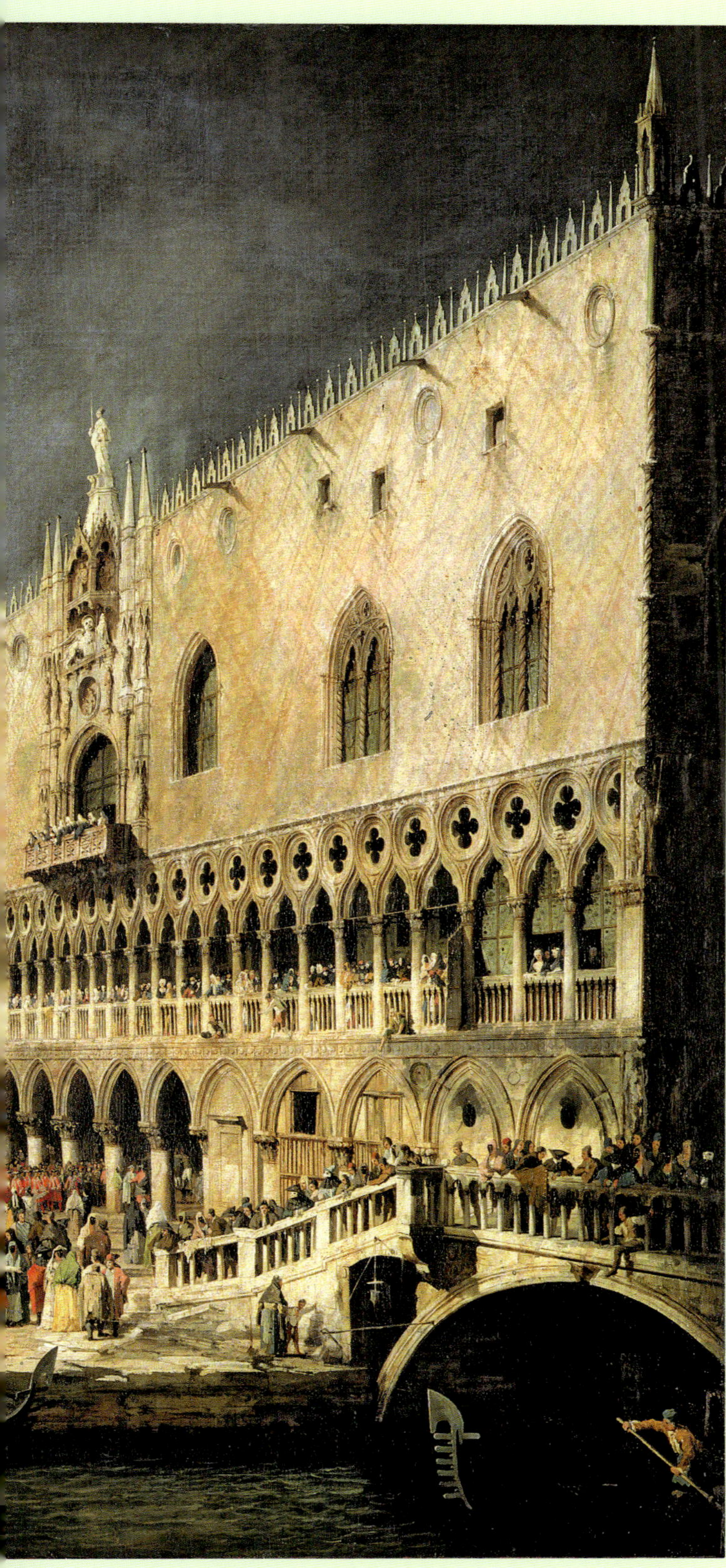

Giovanni Antoni Canal (Canaletto) (1697–1768)
Reception of the French Ambassador in Venice
Réception de l'ambassadeur de France à Venise
Der Empfang des französischen Botschafters in Venedig
La recepción del embajador francés en Venecia
A Receção do Embaixador Francês em Veneza
De ontvangst van de Franse ambassadeur in Venetië
1726/27, Oil on canvas/Huile sur toile, 181 × 259,5 cm

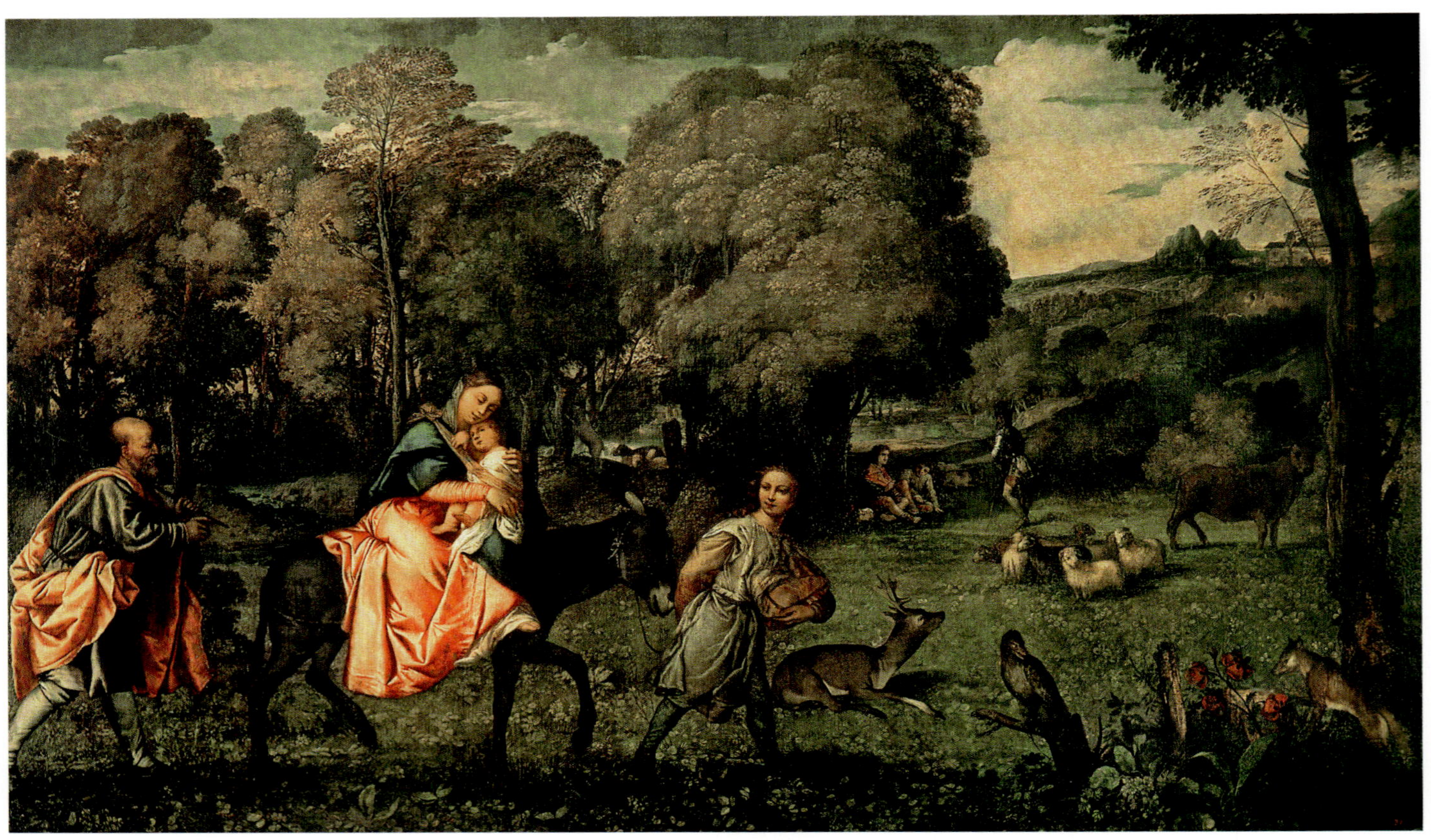

Italian Painting

The collection of Italian painting is led by a work by Leonardo da Vinci, the *Madonna with the Flower* (c. 1478) although the latter is now ascribed by many art historians to his da Vinci's pupils. Originals by Raphael such as the *Holy Family* (c. 1506) are also at the Hermitage. Other highlights include works by Titian, Giorgione, Veronese, Caravaggio, Annibale Carracci, Luca Giordano, Salvator Rosa, Tiepolo, and Francesco Guardi.

La peinture italienne

La collection de peinture italienne comporte la *Madone Benois* (v. 1478) de Léonard de Vinci – que beaucoup d'historiens d'art attribuent plutôt aujourd'hui au cercle de Léonard. Des originaux de Raphaël ont également trouvé le chemin de l'Ermitage, comme la *Sainte Famille* (v. 1506). On peut également admirer d'autres chefs-d'œuvre signés Titien, Giorgione, Véronèse, Caravage, Annibal Carrache, Luca Giordano, Salvator Rosa, Tiepolo et Francesco Guardi.

Italienische Malerei

Die Sammlung der italienischen Malerei wird von einem Werk Leonardo da Vincis angeführt, der *Madonna mit der Blume* (um 1478), die heute viele Kunstwissenschaftler aber dem Leonardo-Umkreis zuschreiben. Auch Originale von Raffael, wie die *Heilige Familie* (um 1506), haben ihren Weg in die Eremitage gefunden. Weitere Höhepunkte sind Werke von Tizian, Giorgione, Veronese, Caravaggio, Annibale Carracci, Luca Giordano, Salvator Rosa, Tiepolo und Francesco Guardi.

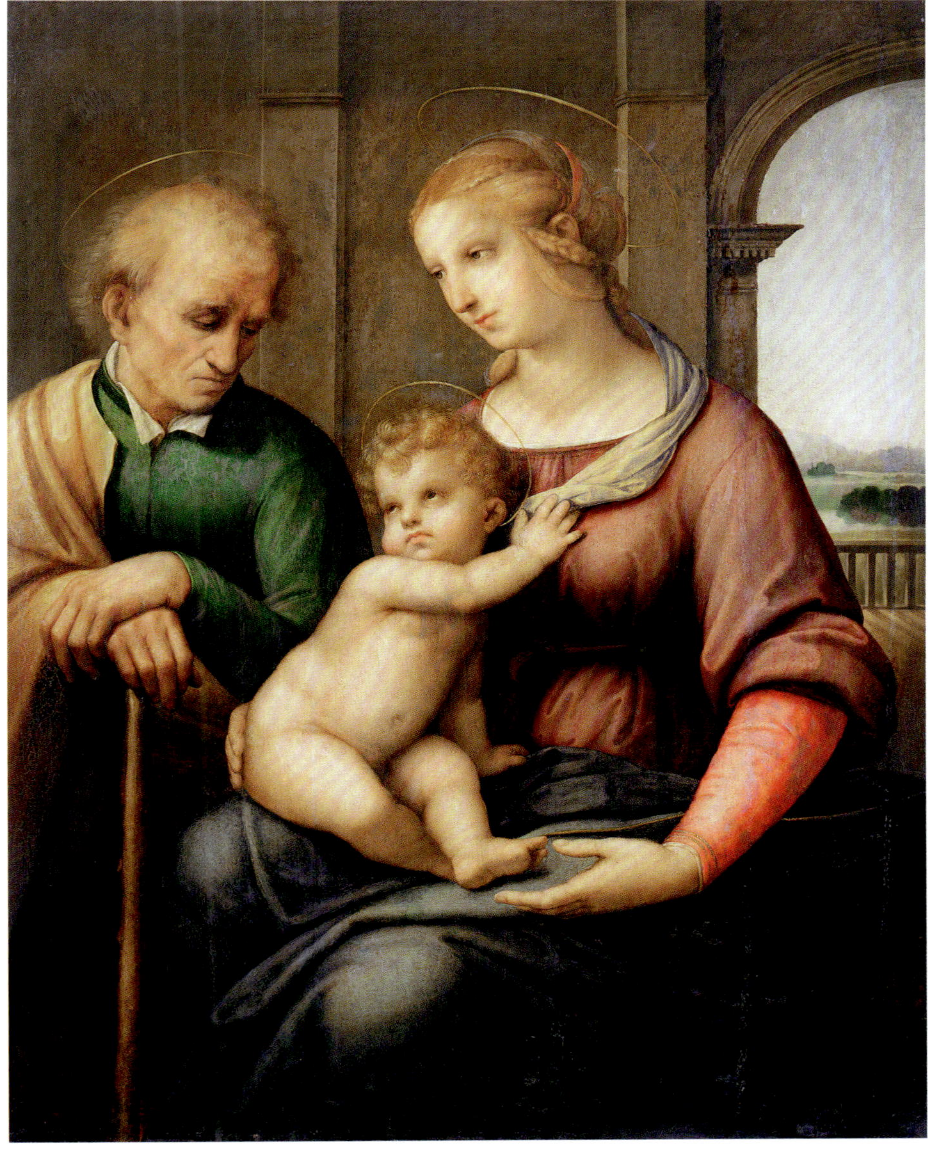

Pintura italiana

La colección de pintura italiana está liderada por
una obra de Leonardo da Vinci, la *Virgen de la flor*
(alrededor 1478), que son atribuidas hoy en día por
muchos investigadores a pintores de su entorno.
También llegaron hasta el Hermitage algunos originales
de Rafael, como la *Sagrada Familia* (alrededor 1506).
Otras obras importantes incluyen trabajos de Tiziano,
Giorgione, Veronese, Caravaggio, Annibale Carracci,
Luca Giordano, Salvator Rosa, Tiepolo y Francesco
Guardi.

Pintura italiana

A coleção de pintura italiana é liderada por uma obra de
Leonardo da Vinci, a *Madona Benois* (aproximadamente
1478) que, no entanto, é atualmente atribuída por
muitos investigadores de arte ao âmbito circundante
de Leonardo. Também obras originais de Rafael,
como *A Sagrada Família* (aproximadamente 1506)
encontraram o seu caminho até ao Hermitage. Outros
pontos altos são as obras de Ticiano , Giorgione,
Veronese, Caravaggio, Annibale Carracci, Luca
Giordano, Salvator Rosa, Tiepolo e Francesco Guardi.

Italiaanse schilderkunst

De collectie Italiaanse schilderkunst wordt aangevoerd
door een werk van Leonardo da Vinci, de *Madonna met
een bloem* (c. 1478), die veel kunstwetenschappers nu
aan de kring rond Leonardo toeschrijven. Ook originele
werken van Rafaël, waaronder de *Heilige Familie* (c.
1506), hebben hun weg naar de Hermitage gevonden.
Andere topstukken zijn werken van Titiaan, Giorgione,
Veronese, Caravaggio, Annibale Carracci, Luca
Giordano, Salvator Rosa, Tiepolo en Francesco Guardi.

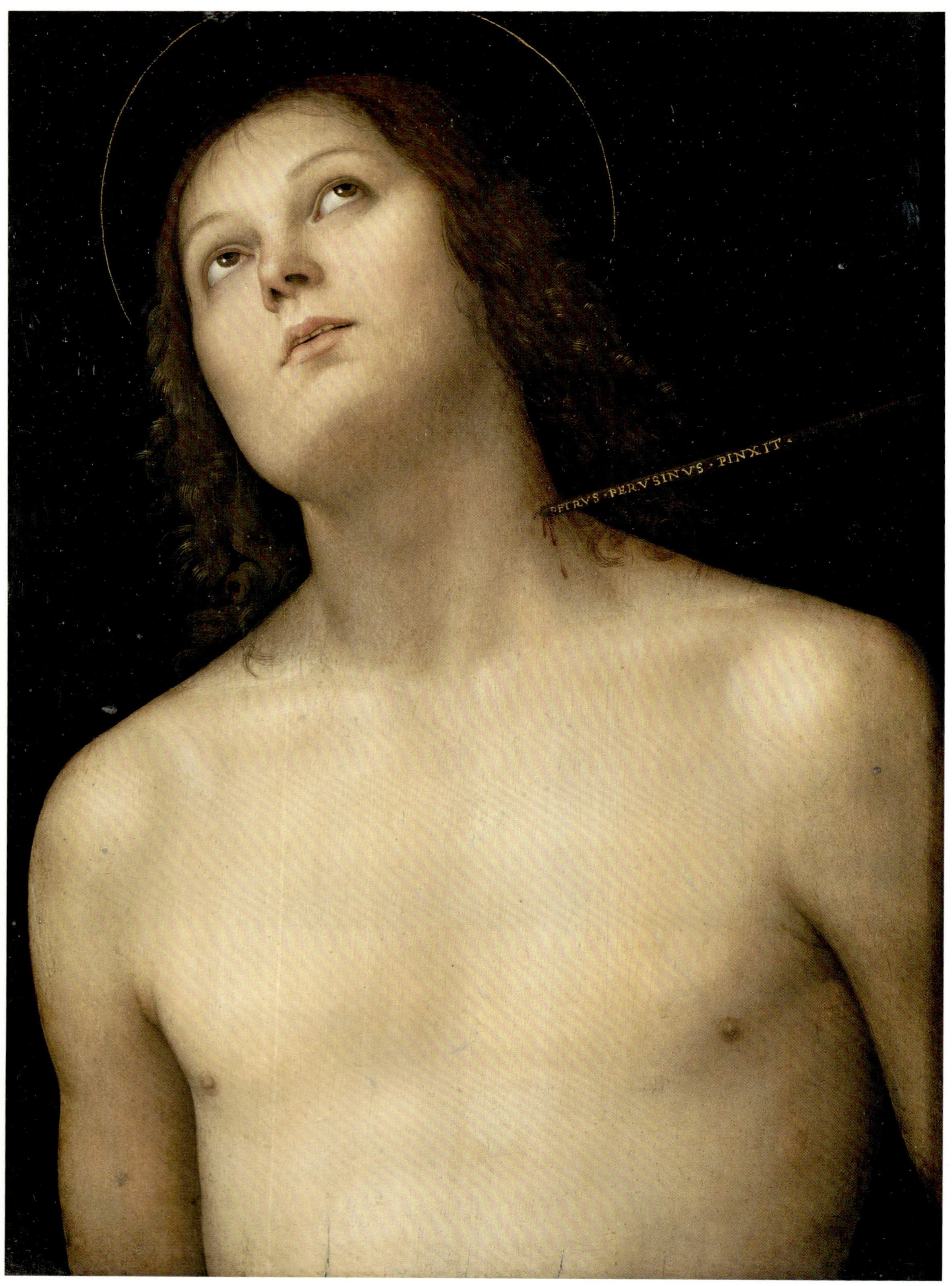

Pietro Perugino
(c. 1445–1523)

Saint Sebastian

Saint Sébastien

Der heilige Sebastian

San Sebastión

São Sebastião

De heilige Sebastiaan

c. 1493/94, Tempera and oil on wood/Tempera et huile sur bois, 53,8 × 39,5 cm

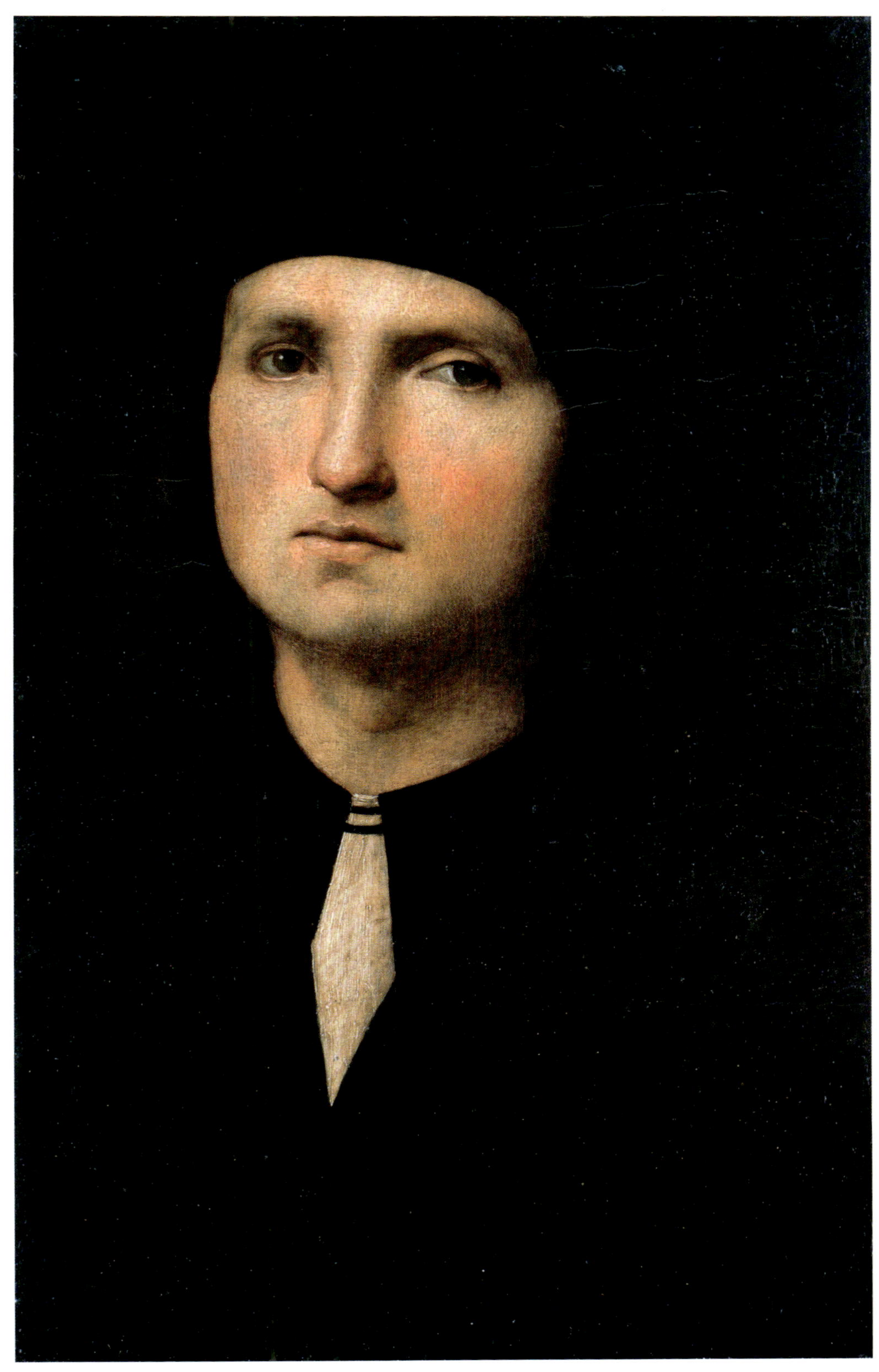

Pietro Perugino (c. 1445–1523)
Portrait of a Young Man
Portrait d'un jeune homme
Bildnis eines jungen Mannes
Retrato de un hombre joven
Retrato de um Jovem Homem
Portret van een jongeman

c. 1500, Oil on canvas, transferred from panel/Huile
sur toile, transposée d'un bois, 40,5 × 25,5 cm

This wonderful image of the Madonna image by Leonardo da Vinci was first acquired by the Hermitage in 1914 from the Benois Collection in Petrograd (the most expensive art purchase ever recorded at the time) and hung suspended together with the *Madonna Litta* in the Hermitage's Leonardo room. Leonardo portrays the relationship between mother and child with a particular intimacy. Using the blurred contours of the *sfumato* technique that he had invented, the master has created flowing and extremely atmospheric transitions between the components of the image.

Cette magnifique Vierge à l'Enfant du jeune Vinci a été acquise en 1914 auprès de la collection Benois, à Pétrograd (ce fut, à l'époque, le tableau le plus cher du monde), et accrochée alors avec la *Madone Litta* dans la salle Vinci. Leonardo a merveilleusement réussi à exprimer la tendre intimité d'une mère avec son enfant. Grâce à la technique du *sfumato* développée par lui, qui estompe les contours, le maître a créé des passages fluides et extrêmement aérés entre les divers éléments du tableau.

Dieses wunderbare Madonnen-Bild von Leonardo da Vinci wurde erst 1914 aus der Sammlung Benois in Petrograd erworben (es war damals das teuerste je verkaufte Gemälde) und zusammen mit der *Madonna Litta* im Leonardo-Saal aufgehängt. Als von besonderer Innigkeit schildert Leonardo die Beziehung zwischen Mutter und Kind. Mit der von ihm entwickelten Maltechnik des *Sfumato,* in der die Konturen verschwimmen, schuf der Meister fließende und äußerst atmosphärische Übergänge zwischen den Bestandteilen des Bildes.

Esta fantástica Virgen de Leonardo da Vinci se compró en 1914 de la colección Benois en Petrogrado (fue en su momento la venta de un cuadro más cara de la historia) y se expone, junto a la *Madonna Litta,* en la sala Leonardo. Leonardo presenta la relación madre-hijo con una intimidad especial. Con su propia técnica del *sfumato,* en la que los contornos se desdibujan, el maestro creó transiciones atmosféricas y muy fluidas entre los diversos elementos de la imagen.

Esta maravilhosa pintura da Virgem de Leonardo da Vinci foi apenas adquirida em 1914 da coleção de Benois em Petrogrado (naquela altura foi a obra mais dispendiosa alguma vez adquirida) e pendurada juntamente com a obra *Madona Litta* no salão dedicado a Leonardo. Leonardo retrata a relação entre mãe e filho com uma intimidade especial. Através da técnica de pintura do *sfumato* por ele desenvolvida, na qual os contornos se esbatem, o mestre criou passagens fluidas e extremamente evocativas entre as partes constituintes da pintura.

Dit beeldschone Madonna-schilderij van Leonardo da Vinci werd pas in 1914 uit de Benois-collectie in Petrograd (nu Sint-Petersburg) aangekocht (het was destijds het duurste schilderij ooit verkocht) en samen met de *Madonna Litta* in de Leonardo-zaal opgehangen. Leonardo schildert de relatie tussen moeder en kind als een bijzonder innige. Met de door hem ontwikkelde *sfumato*-schildertechniek die contouren laat vervagen, realiseerde de meester vloeiende en bijzonder sfeervolle overgangen tussen de samenstellende delen van het schilderij.

Leonardo da Vinci (1452–1519)
Madonna with Flower (Madonna Benois)
La Madone Benois
Madonna mit der Blume (Madonna Benois)
Virgen con flor (Madonna Benois)
Madona Benois (Virgem Benois)
Madonna met een bloem (Madonna Benois)
1478–80, Oil on canvas, transferred from panel/
Huile sur toile, transposée d'un bois, 49,5 × 33 cm

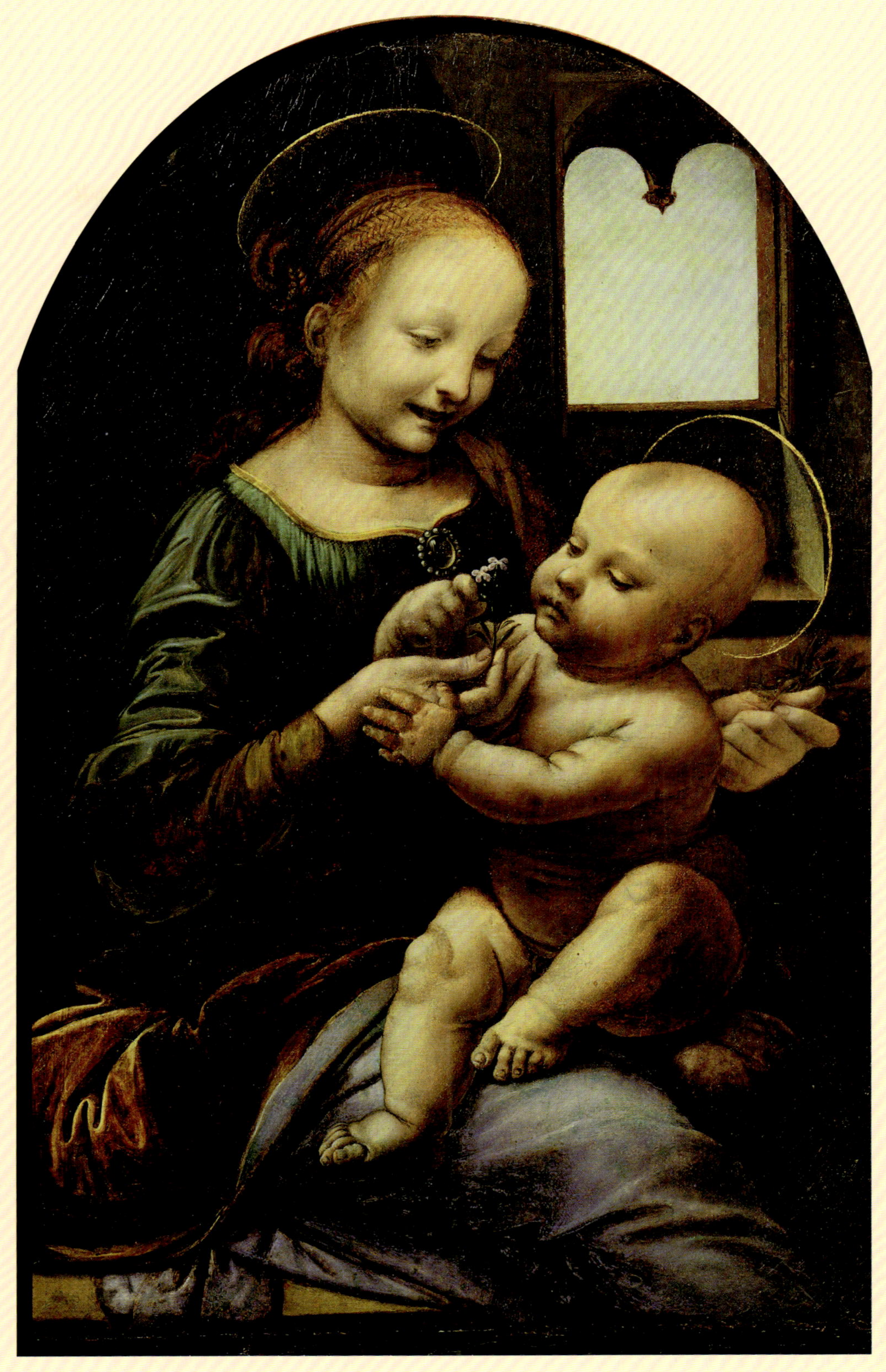

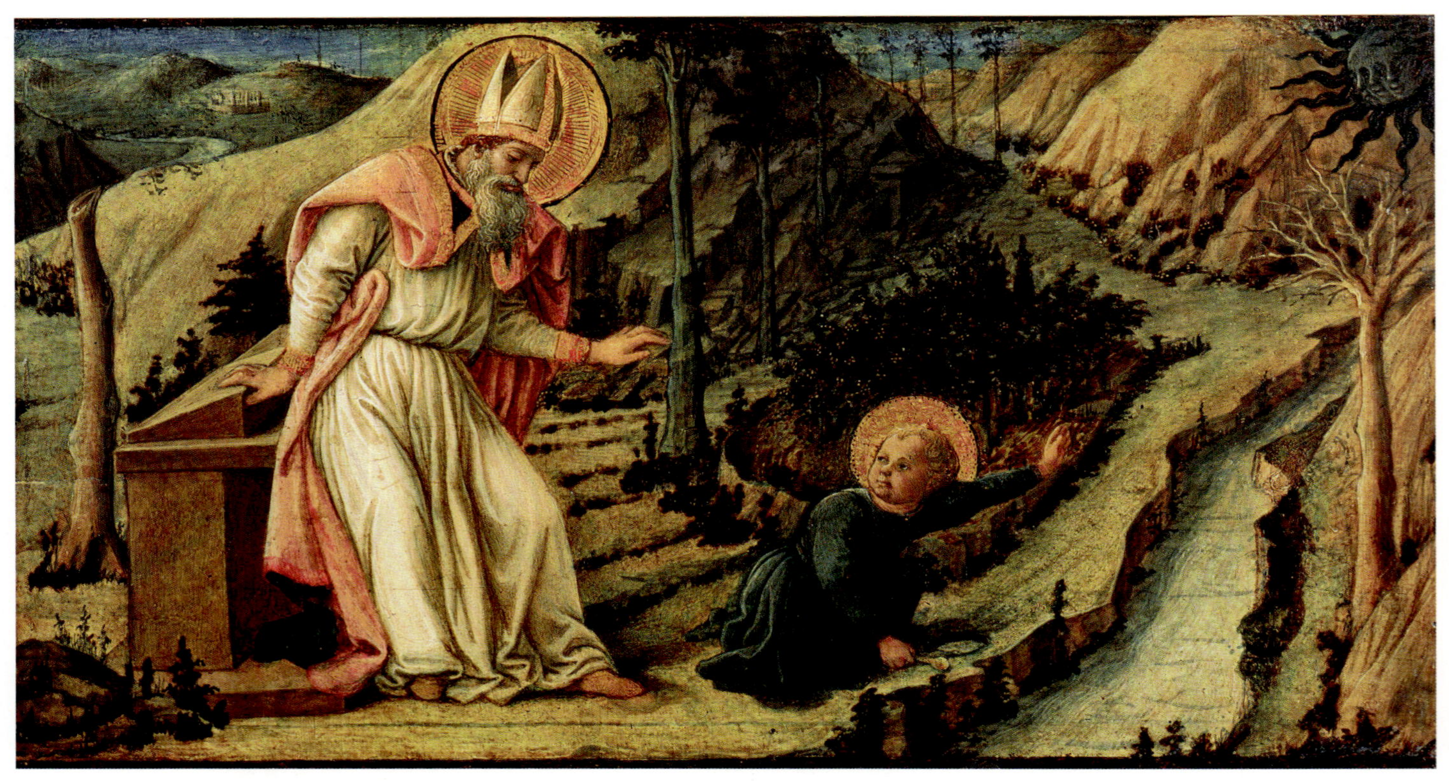

Filippino Lippi (c. 1457–1504)

The Vision of St. Augustine

La Vision de saint Augustin

Die Vision des heiligen Augustinus

La visión de San Agustín

A Visão de São Agostinho

Het visioen van de heilige Augustinus

c. 1480, Tempera and oil on wood/Tempera et huile sur bois, 28 × 51,5 cm

Sebastiano del Piombo (S. Luciani) (c. 1485–1547)

Cardinal Reginald Pole

Cardinal Reginald Pole

Kardinal Reginald Pole

Cardenal Reginald Pole

Cardinal Reginald Pole

Kardinaal Reginald Pole

1540, Oil on canvas/Huile sur toile, 112 × 94,5 cm

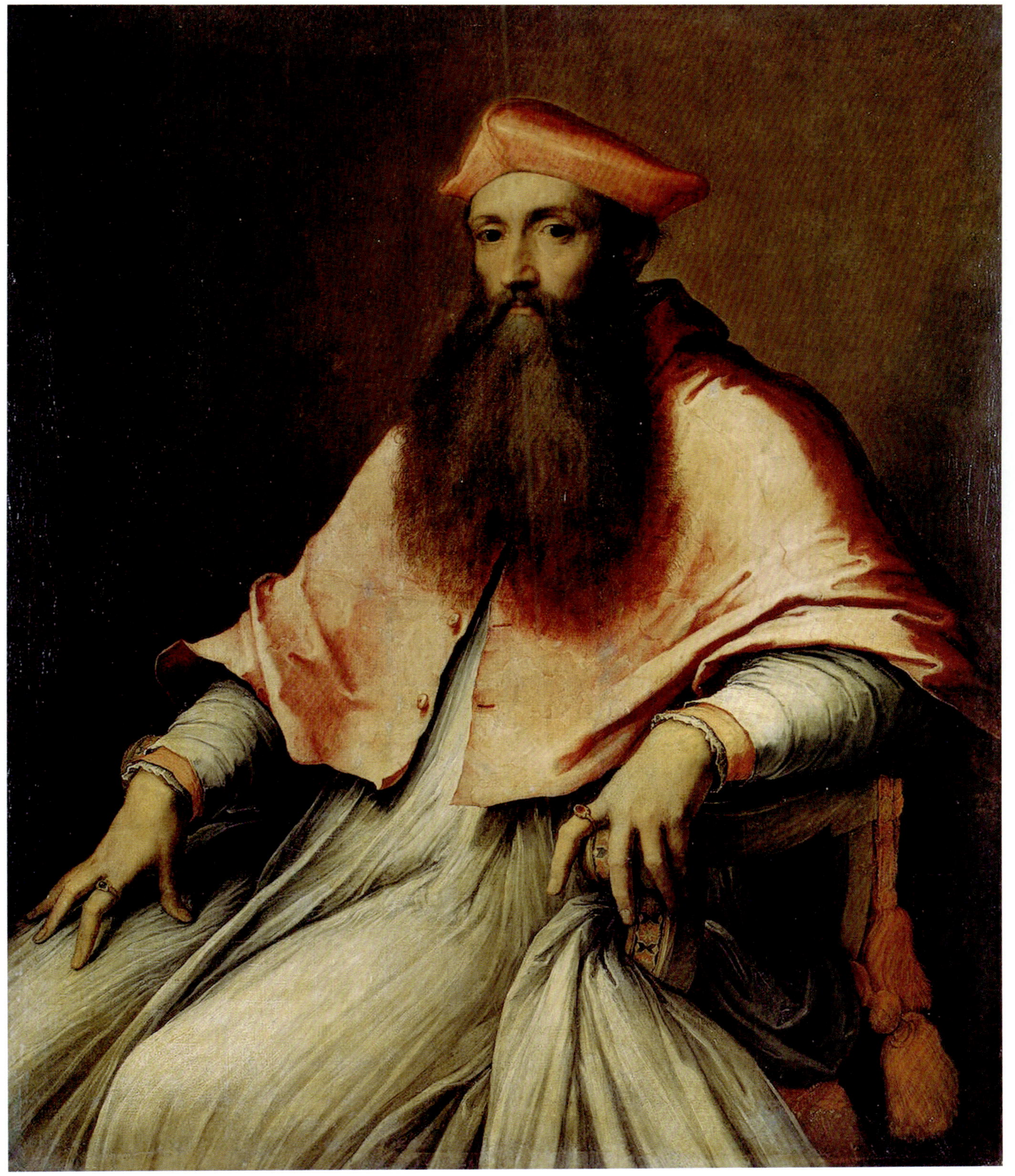

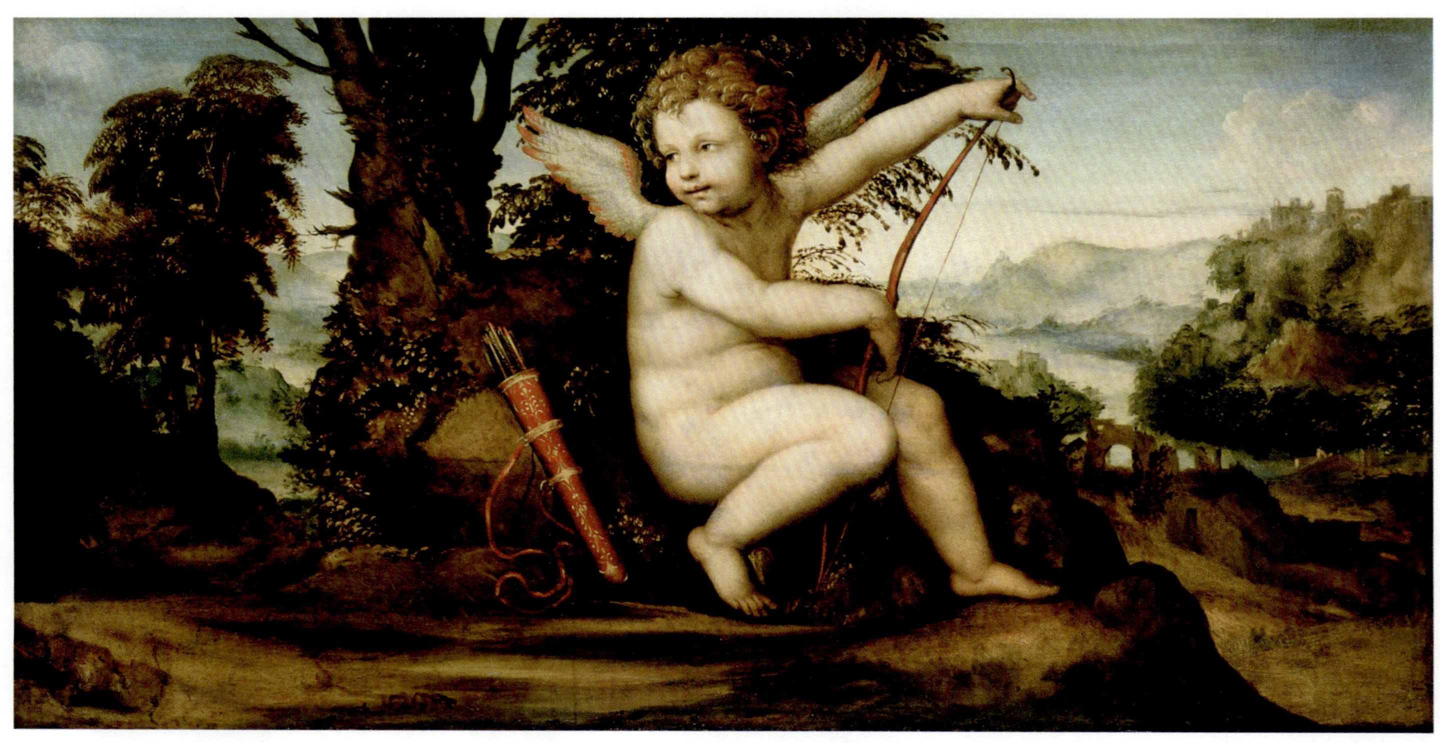

Sodoma (Giovanni Antonio Bazzi) (1477–1549)

Cupid in a Landscape

Amour dans un paysage

Amor in einer Landschaft

Amor en un paisaje

Amor numa Paisagem

Amor in een landschap

1510, Oil on canvas, transferred from panel/Huile sur toile, transposée d'un bois, 68 × 129 cm

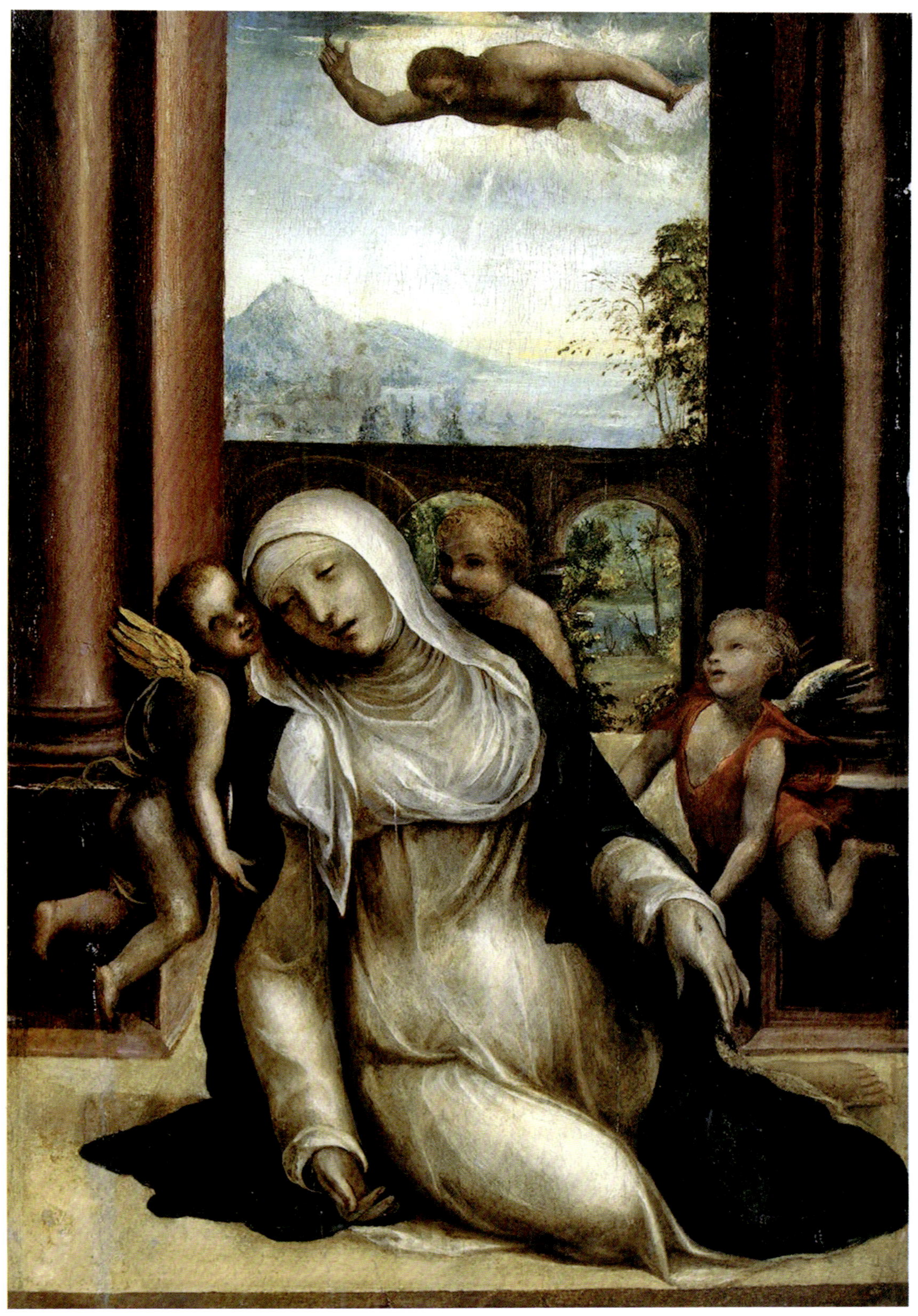

Sodoma (Giovanni Antonio Bazzi)
(1477–1549)

Stigmata and Fainting of
St. Catherine of Siena

L'Évanouissement de sainte
Catherine dû aux stigmates

Stigmatisierung und Ohnmacht
der heiligen Katharina von Siena

Estigmatización y desmayo de
Santa Catalina de Siena

Estigmatização e Desmaio de
Santa Catarina de Siena

Stigmatisering en bezwijming van
de heilige Catharina van Siena

16th century/XVIe siècle, Oil on canvas/
Huile sur toile, 46 × 30 cm

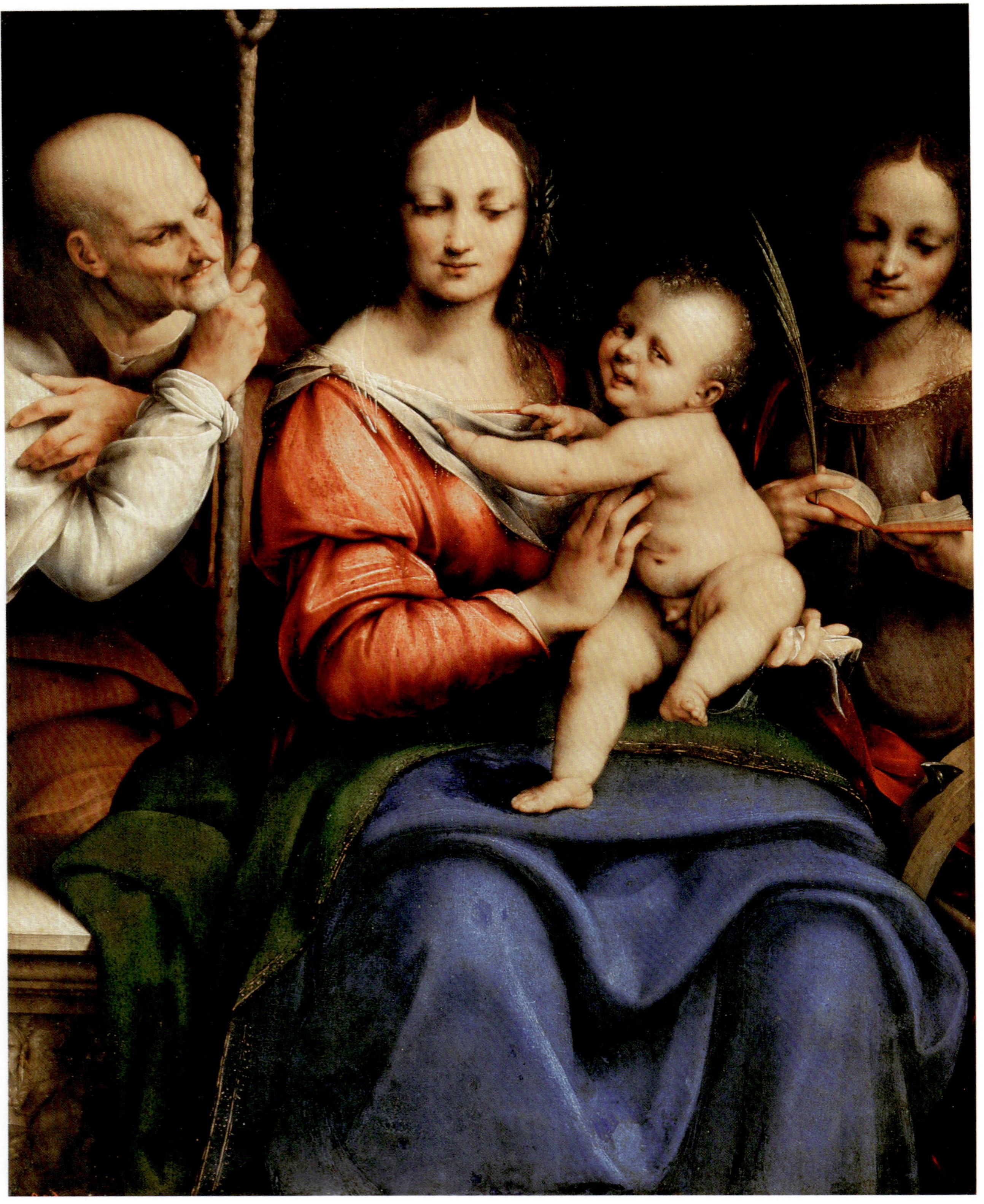

Cesare da Sesto (1477–1523)

The Holy Family with St. Catherine

La Sainte Famille avec sainte Catherine

Die Heilige Familie mit der heiligen Katharina

La Sagrada Familia con Santa Catalina

A Sagrada Família com Santa Catarina

De Heilige Familie met de heilige Catharina

1515–20, Oil on canvas, transferred from panel/ Huile sur toile, transposée d'un bois, 89 × 71 cm

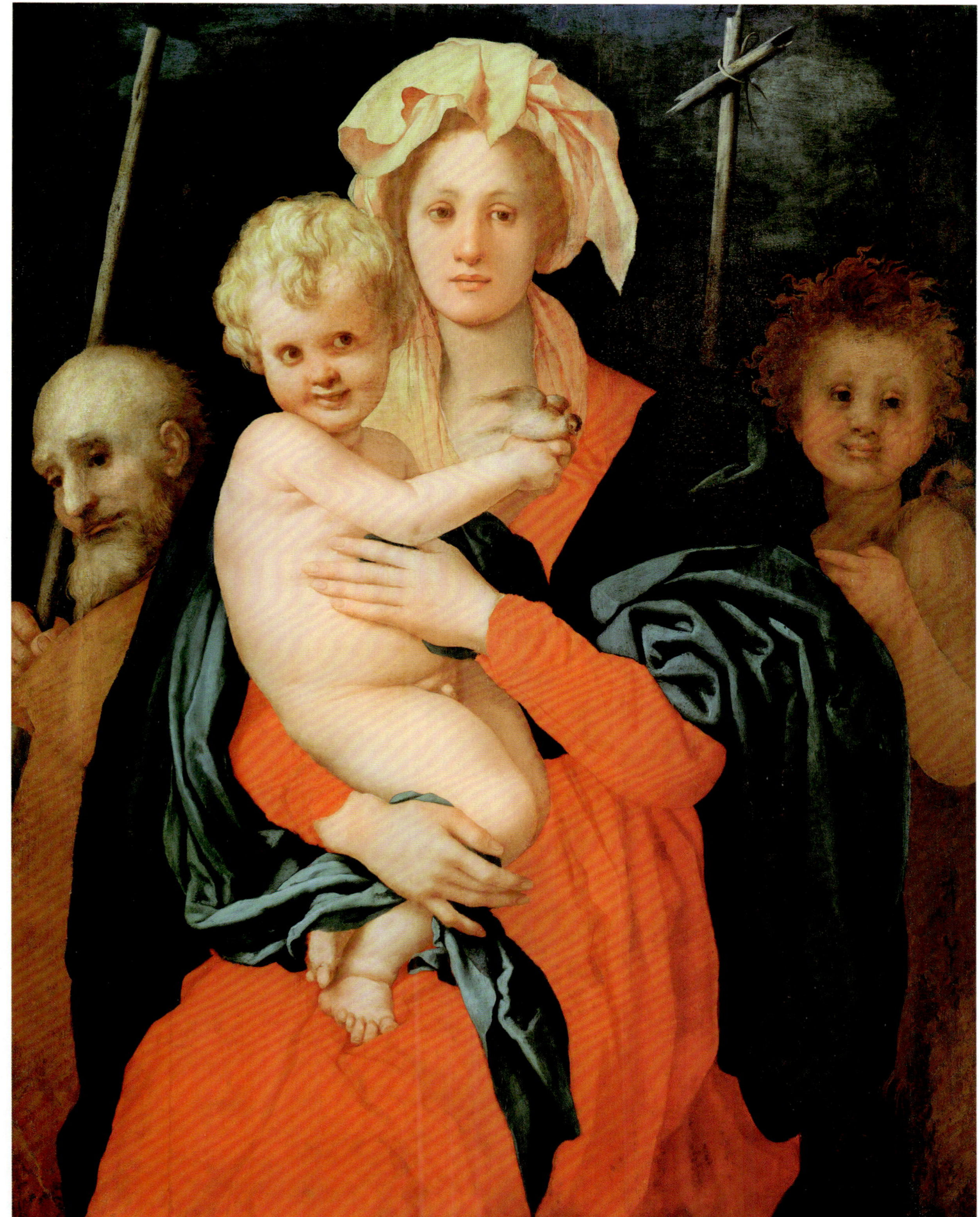

Jacopo Pontormo
(1494–1557)

Madonna and
Child with St.
Joseph and John
the Baptist

La Vierge et
l'Enfant avec saint
Joseph et saint
Jean Baptiste

Madonna und Kind
mit dem heiligen
Josef und Johannes
dem Täufer

Virgen con niño
junto a San José y
San Juan Bautista

Virgem e o Menino
com São José e
João Batista

Madonna en Kind
met de heilige
Jozef en Johannes
de Doper

c. 1520, Oil on
canvas, transferred
from panel/Huile sur
toile, transposée d'un
bois, 120 × 98,5 cm

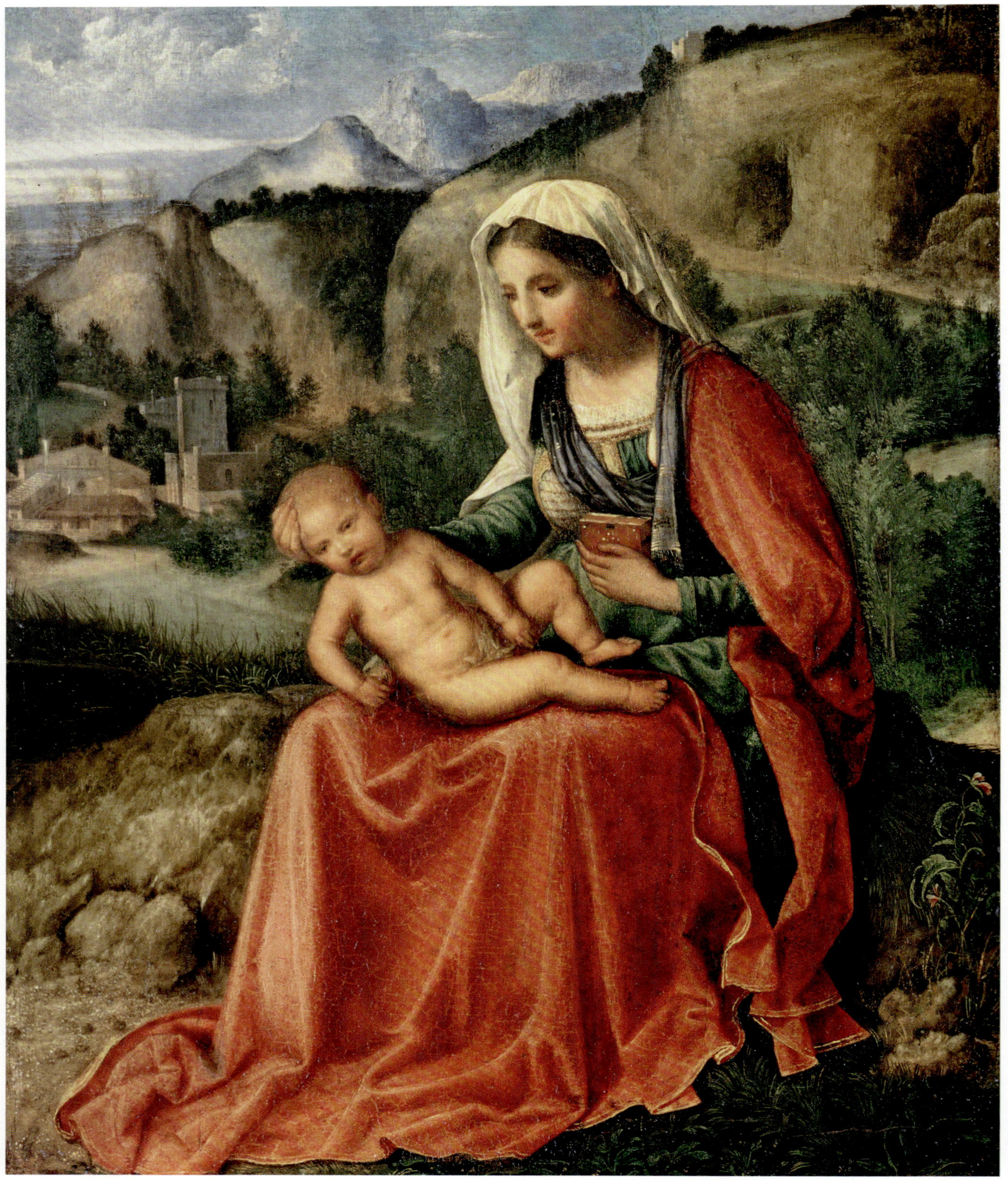

*Giorgione
(Giorgio da
Castelfranco)
(c. 1478–1510)*

Madonna
and Child in
a Landscape

La Vierge et
l'Enfant dans
un paysage

Madonna und
Kind in einer
Landschaft

Virgen con
niño en un
paisaje

Virgem e o
Menino numa
Paisagem

Madonna en
Kind in een
landschap

c. 1503, Oil
on canvas/
Huile sur toile,
44 × 36,5 cm

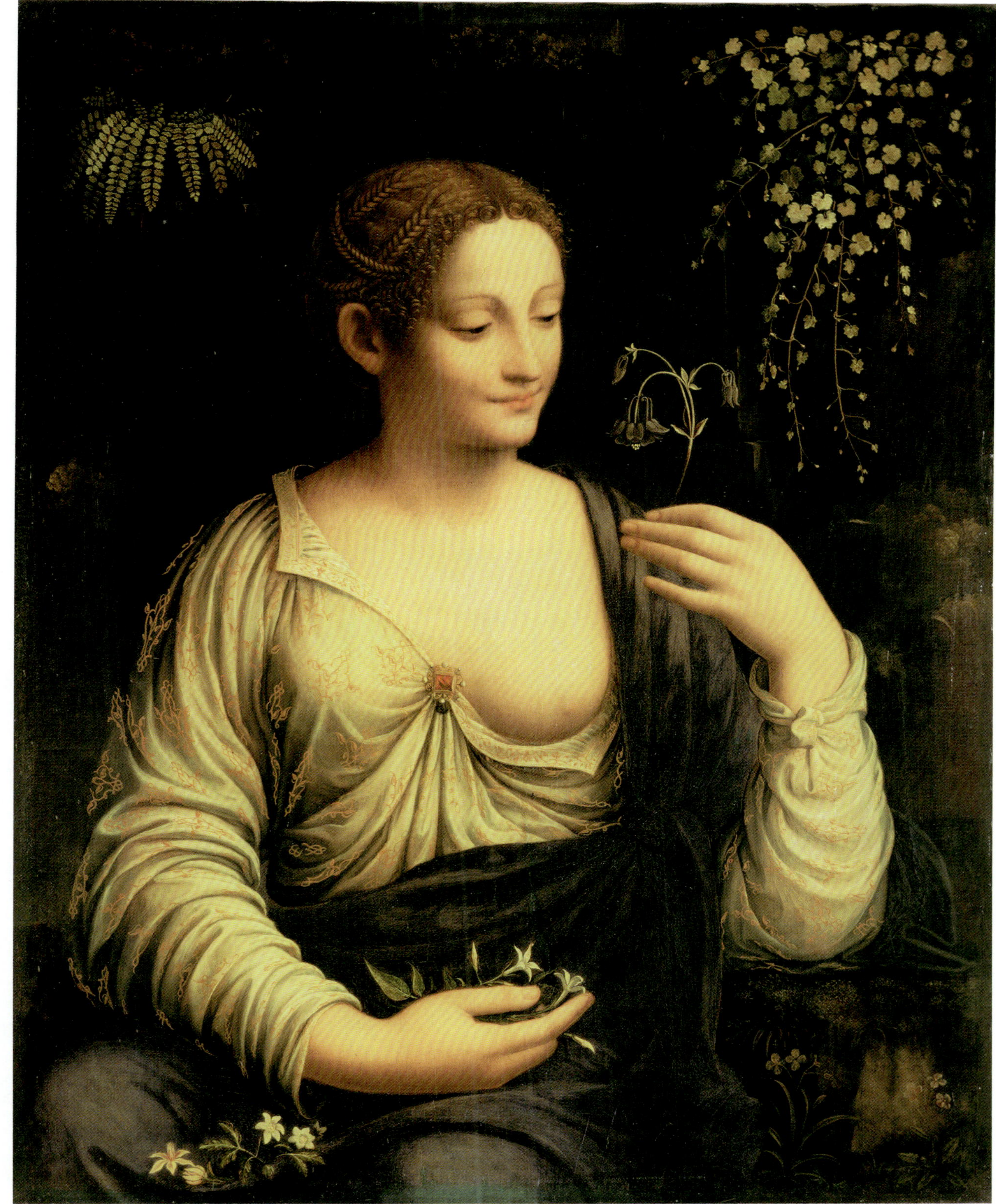

*Francesco
Melzi
(1493–1570)*

Flora

c. 1520, Oil
on canvas,
transferred
from panel/
Huile sur toile,
transposée
d'un bois,
76 × 63 cm

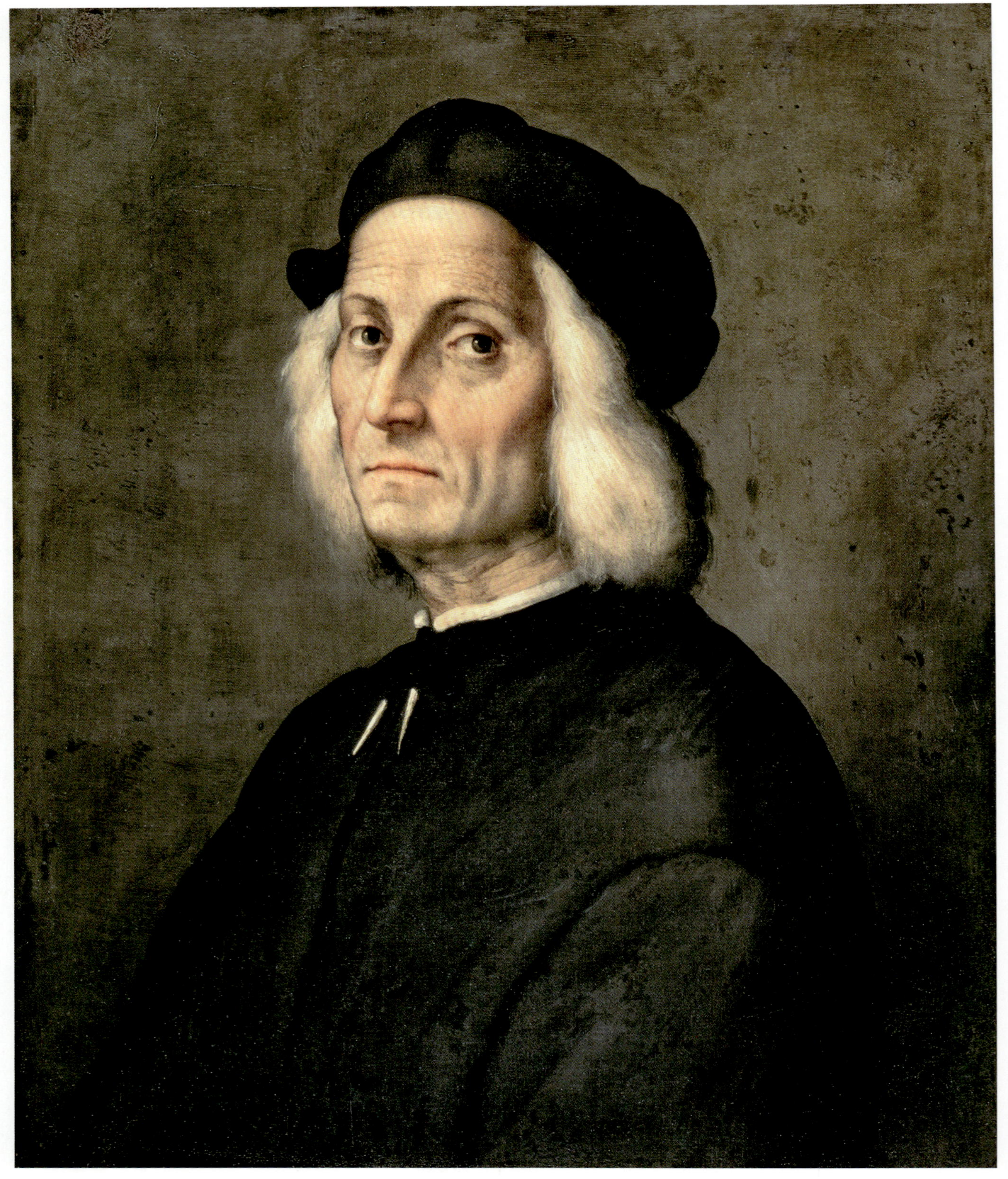

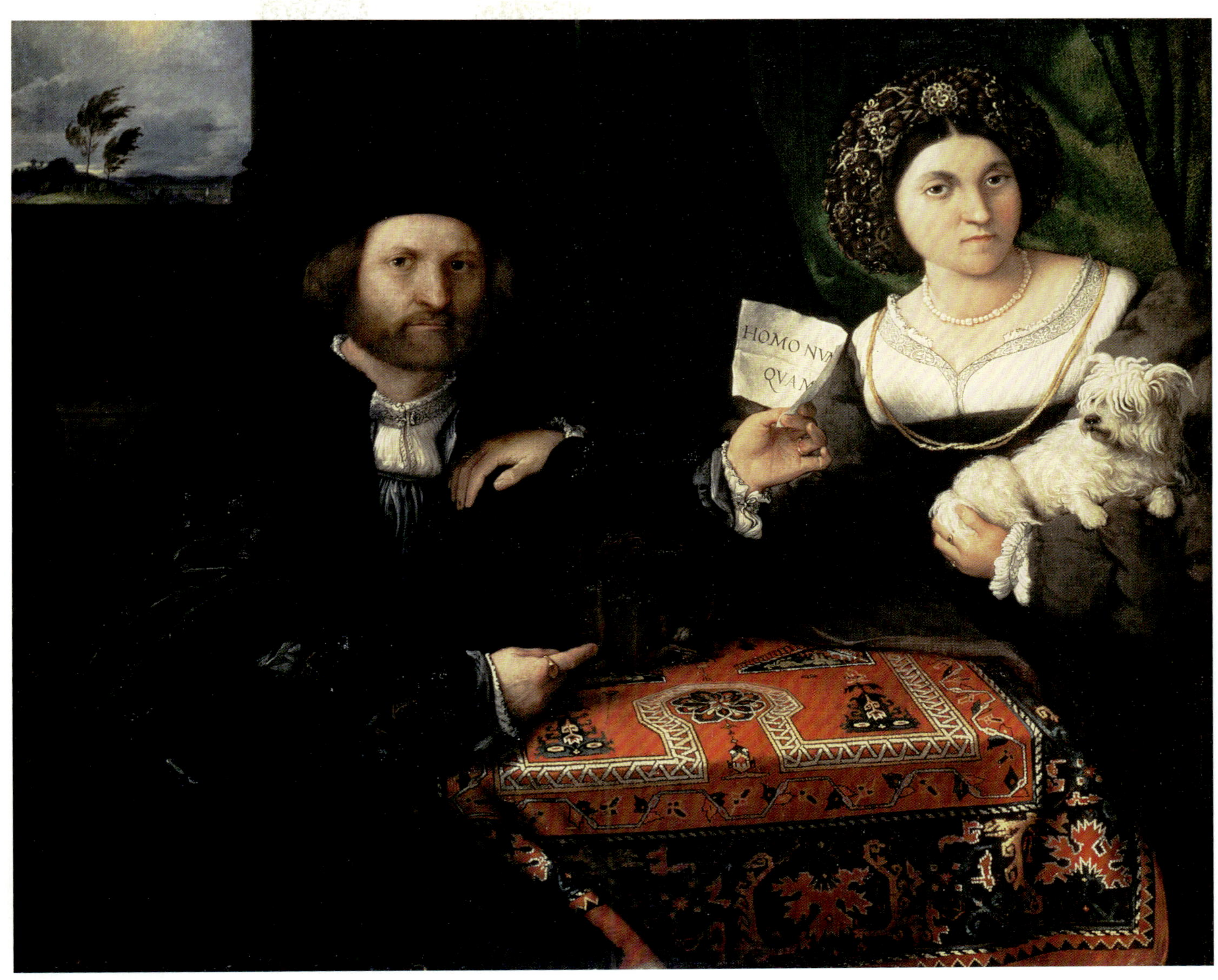

Ridolfo Ghirlandaio (1483–1561)

Portrait of an Old Man

Portait d'un vieillard

Bildnis eines alten Mannes

Retrato de un hombre joven

Retrato de um Velho Homem

Portret van een oude man

c. 1520, Oil on canvas, transferred from panel/
Huile sur toile, transposée d'un bois, 61 × 50,5 cm

Lorenzo Lotto (c. 1480–1556)

Married Couple

Portrait d'un couple

Ehepaar

Matrimonio

Casal

Echtpaar

c. 1523/24, Oil on canvas/Huile sur toile, 96 × 116 cm

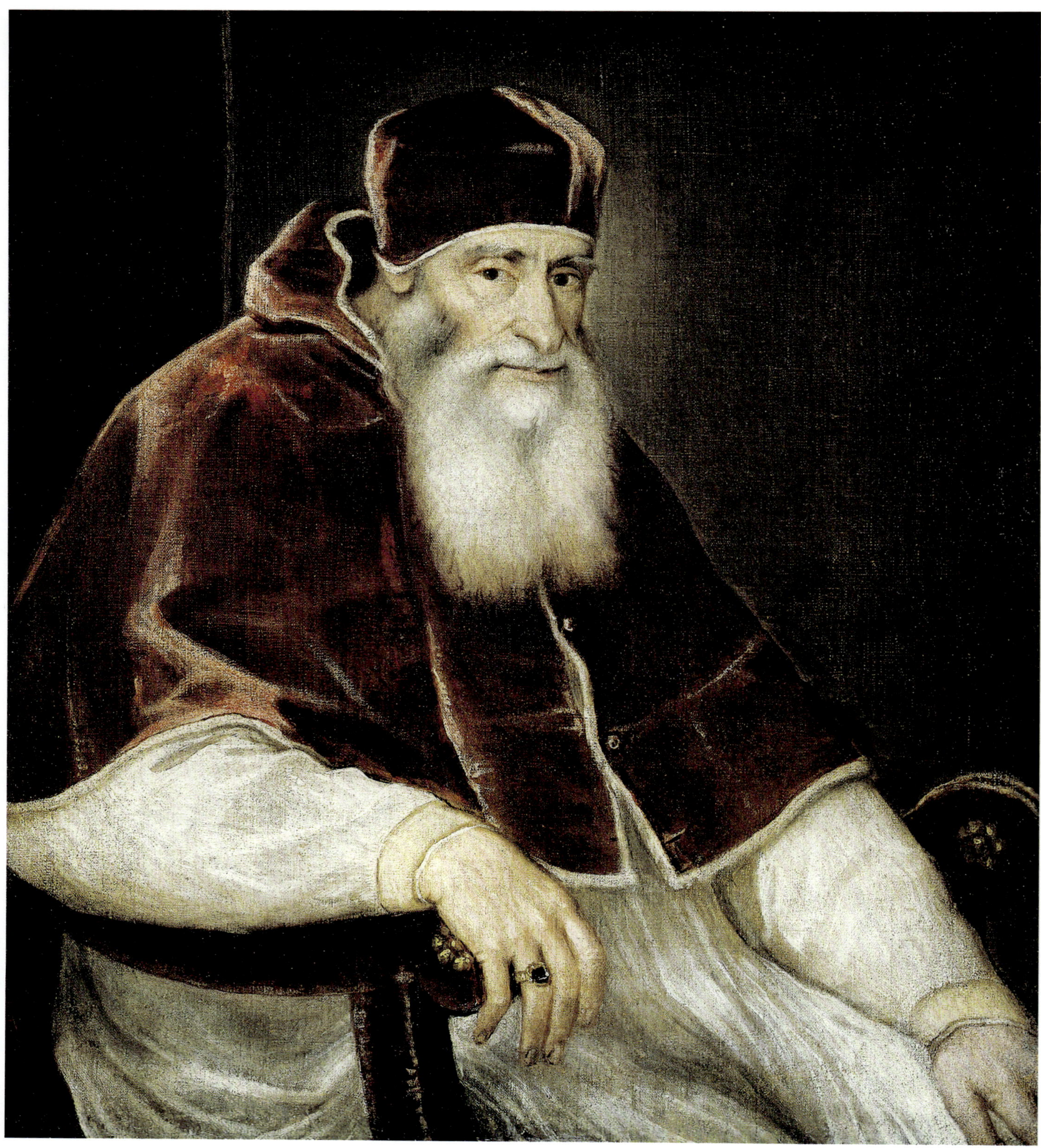

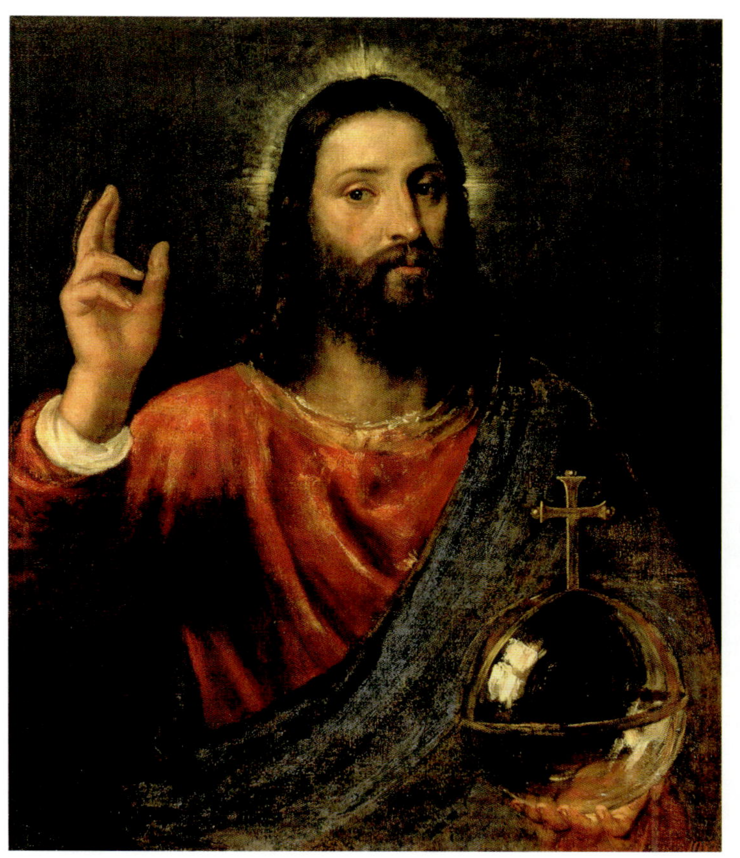

Tizian (Tiziano Vecellio) (c. 1488–1576)

Christ the Redeemer

Le Christ bénissant

Christus der Erlöser

Cristo redentor

Cristo o Salvador

Christus de Verlosser

c. 1570, Oil on canvas/Huile sur toile, 96 × 80 cm

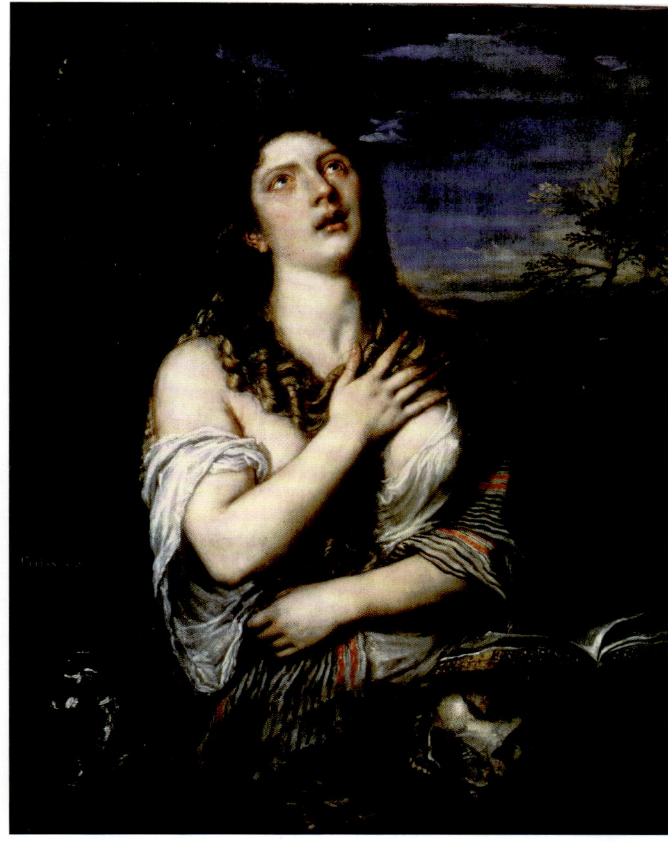

Tizian (Tiziano Vecellio) (c. 1488–1576)

Mary Magdalene

Marie Madeleine repentante

Maria Magdalena

María Magdalena

Maria Madalena

Maria Magdalena

1560, Oil on canvas/Huile sur toile, 119 × 97 cm

Tizian (Tiziano Vecellio) (c. 1488–1576)

Pope Paul III

Le Pape Paul III

Papst Paul III.

Papa Pablo III

Papa Paulo III

Paus Paulus III

1545/46, Oil on canvas/Huile sur toile, 98 × 79 cm

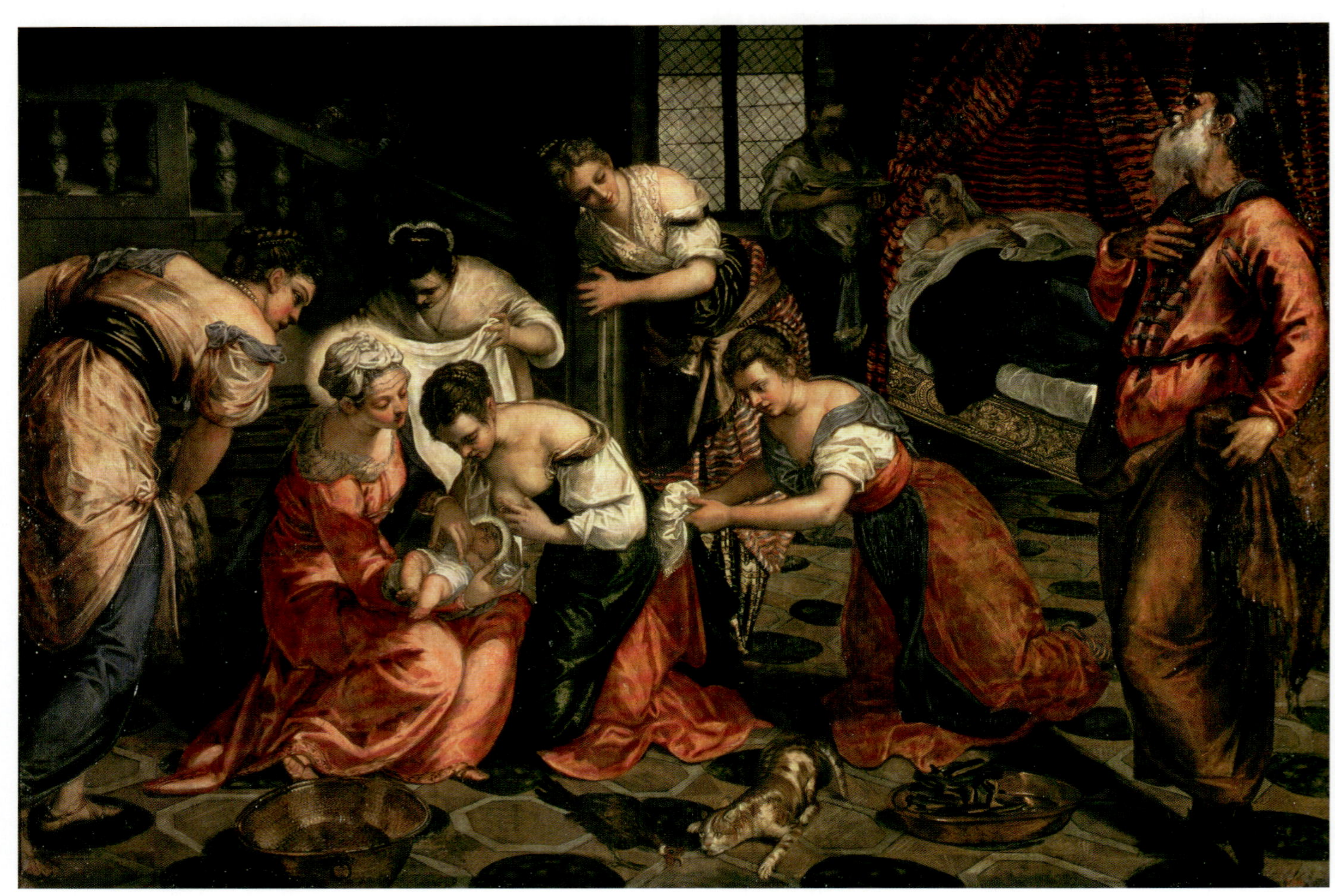

The Birth of John the Baptist

La Nativité de saint Jean-Baptiste

Die Geburt Johannes des Täufers

El nacimiento de San Juan Bautista

O Nascimento de João Batista

De geboorte van Johannes de Doper

1550, Oil on canvas/Huile sur toile, 181 × 266 cm

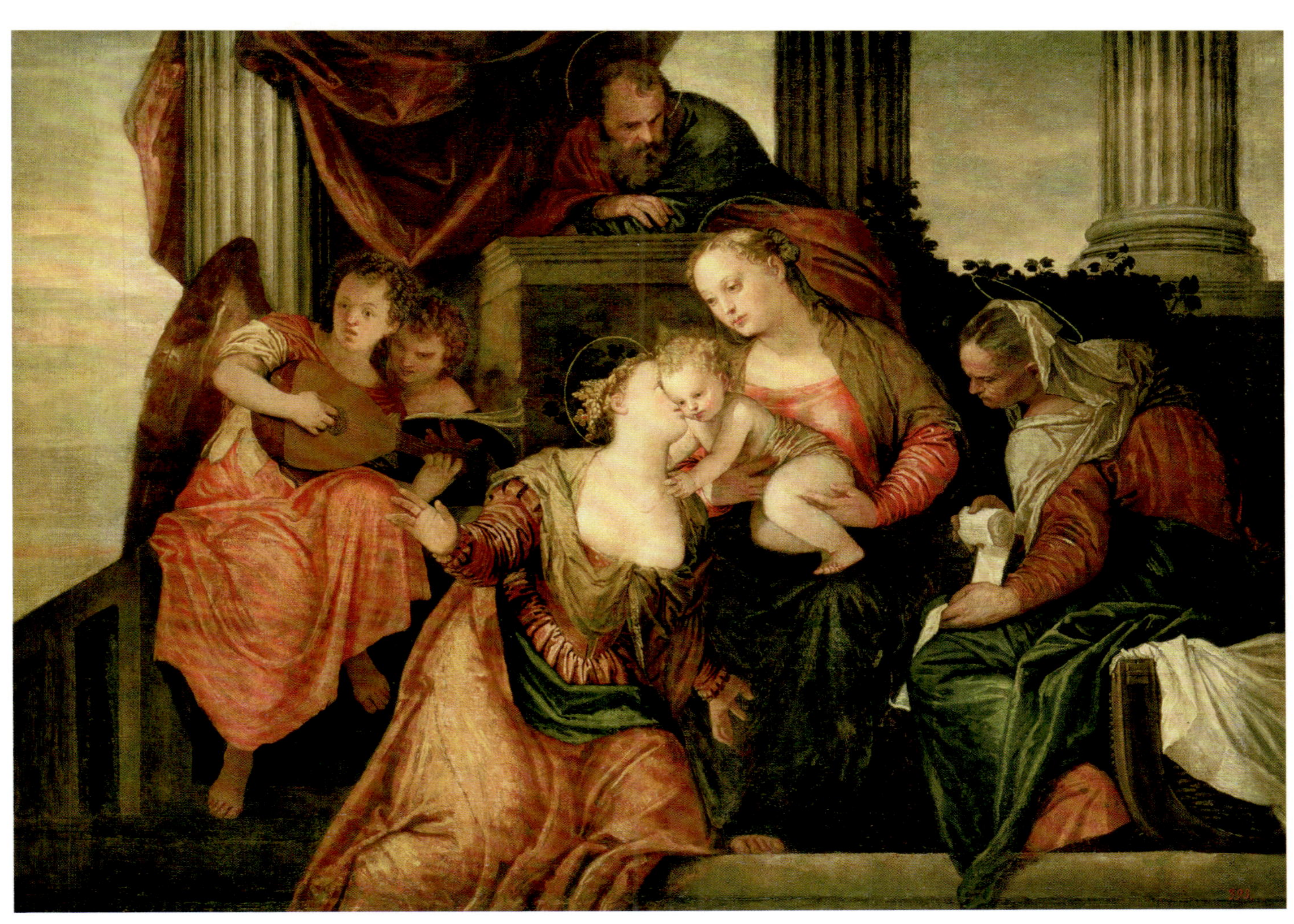

Paolo Veronese (Paolo Caliari) (1528–88)
The Mystical Marriage of St. Catherine
Le Mariage mystique de sainte Catherine
Die mystische Vermählung der heiligen Katharina
La boda mística de Santa Catalina de Siena
O Místico Casamento de Santa Catarina
Het mystieke huwelijk van de heilige Catharina
1547/48, Oil on canvas/Huile sur toile, 145,5 × 205 cm

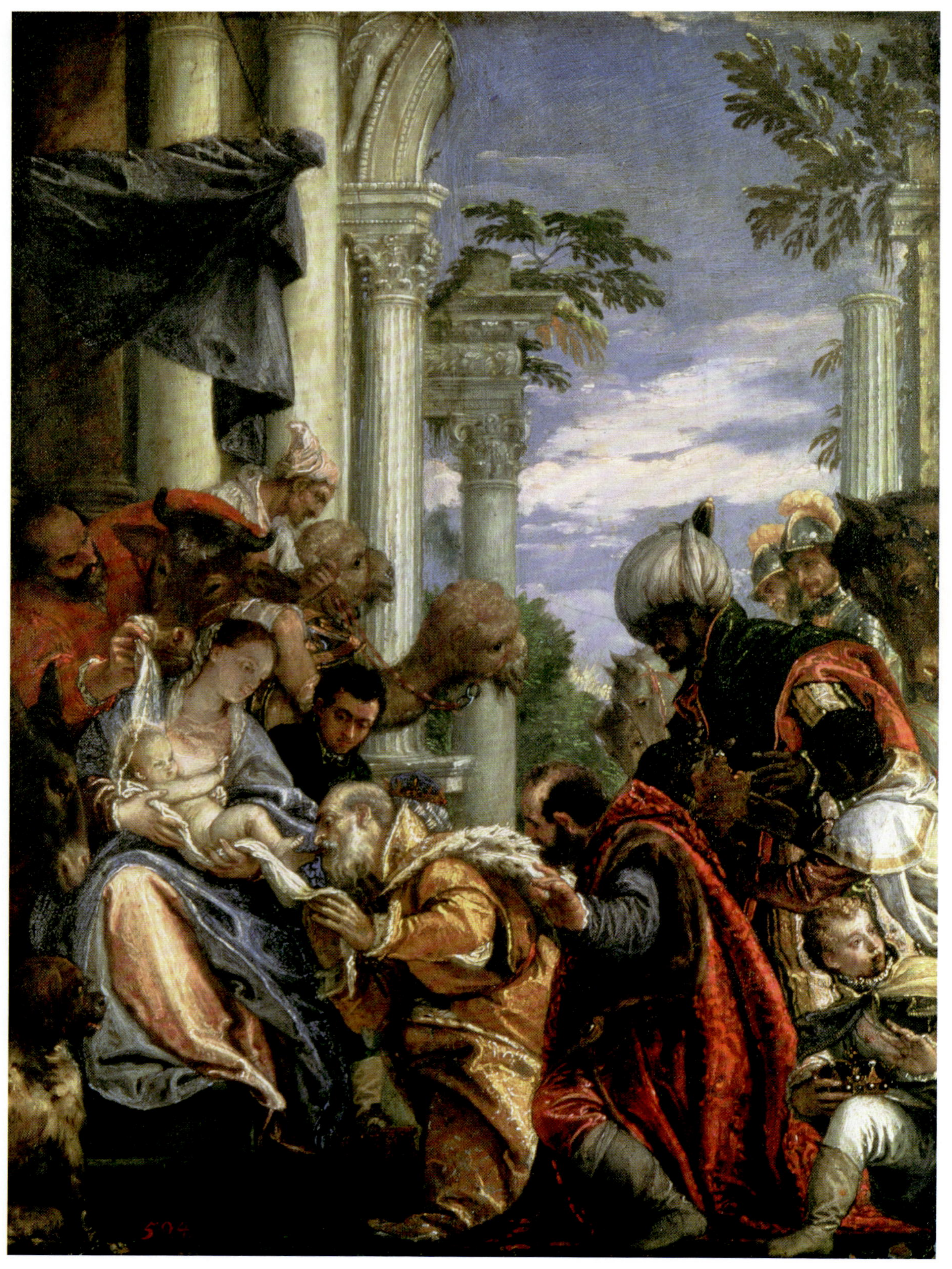

*Paolo Veronese (Paolo
Caliari) 1528–88*

The Adoration of the Magi

L'Adoration des Mages

Die Anbetung der Könige

La adoración de los
Reyes Magos

A Adoração dos Reis

De aanbidding door
de koningen

c. 1570–79, Oil on copper/
Huile sur cuivre, 45 × 34,5 cm

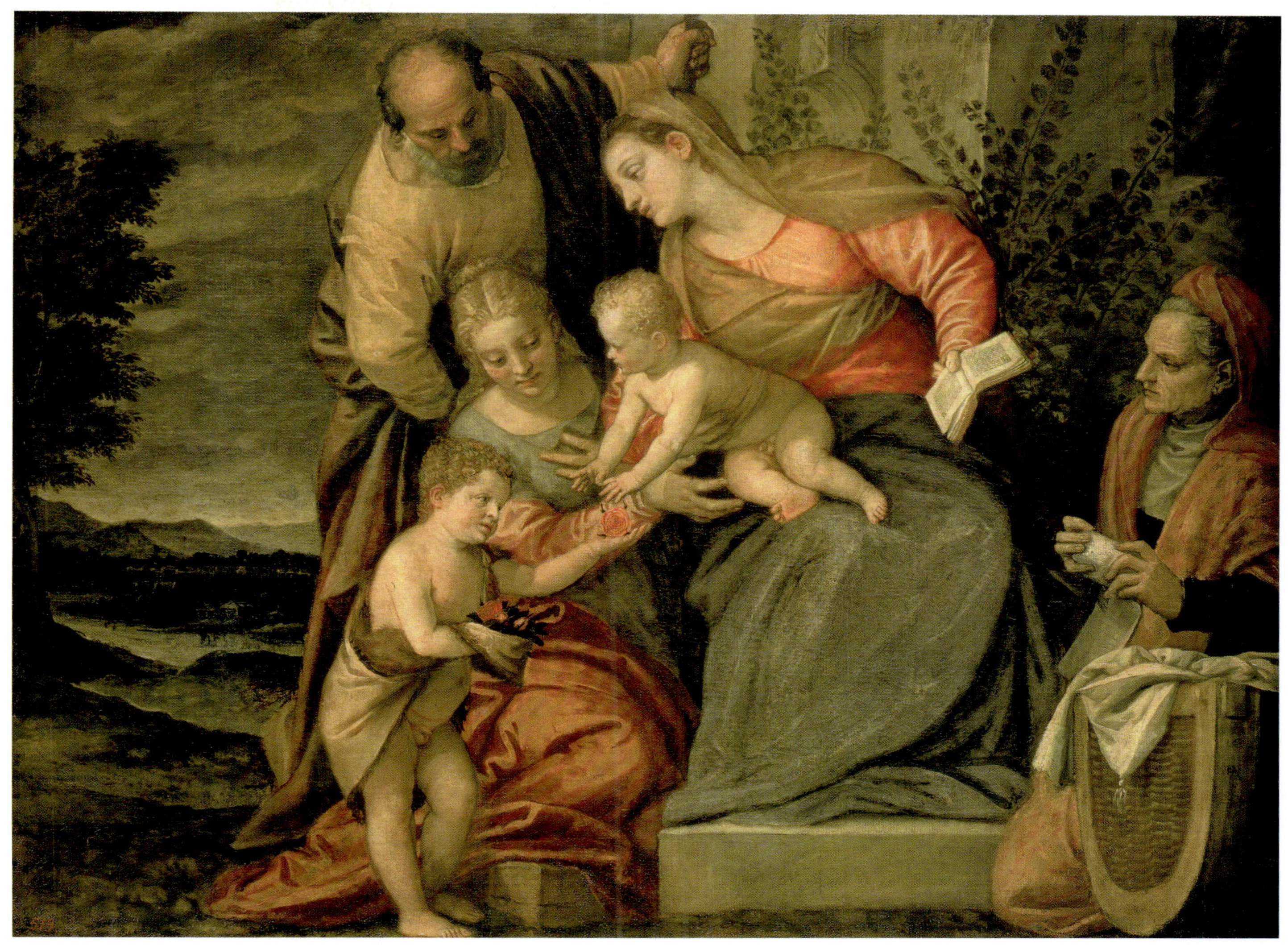

The Holy Family with St. Elizabeth and John the Baptist

La Sainte Famille avec sainte Catherine, sainte Anne et saint Jean

Die Heilige Familie mit der heiligen Elisabeth und Johannes dem Täufer

La Sagrada Familia con Santa Isabel y San Juan Bautista

A Sagrada Família com Santa Elisabete e João Batista

De Heilige Familie met de heilige Elisabeth en Johannes de Doper

1580–82, Oil on canvas/Huile sur toile, 120 × 159 cm

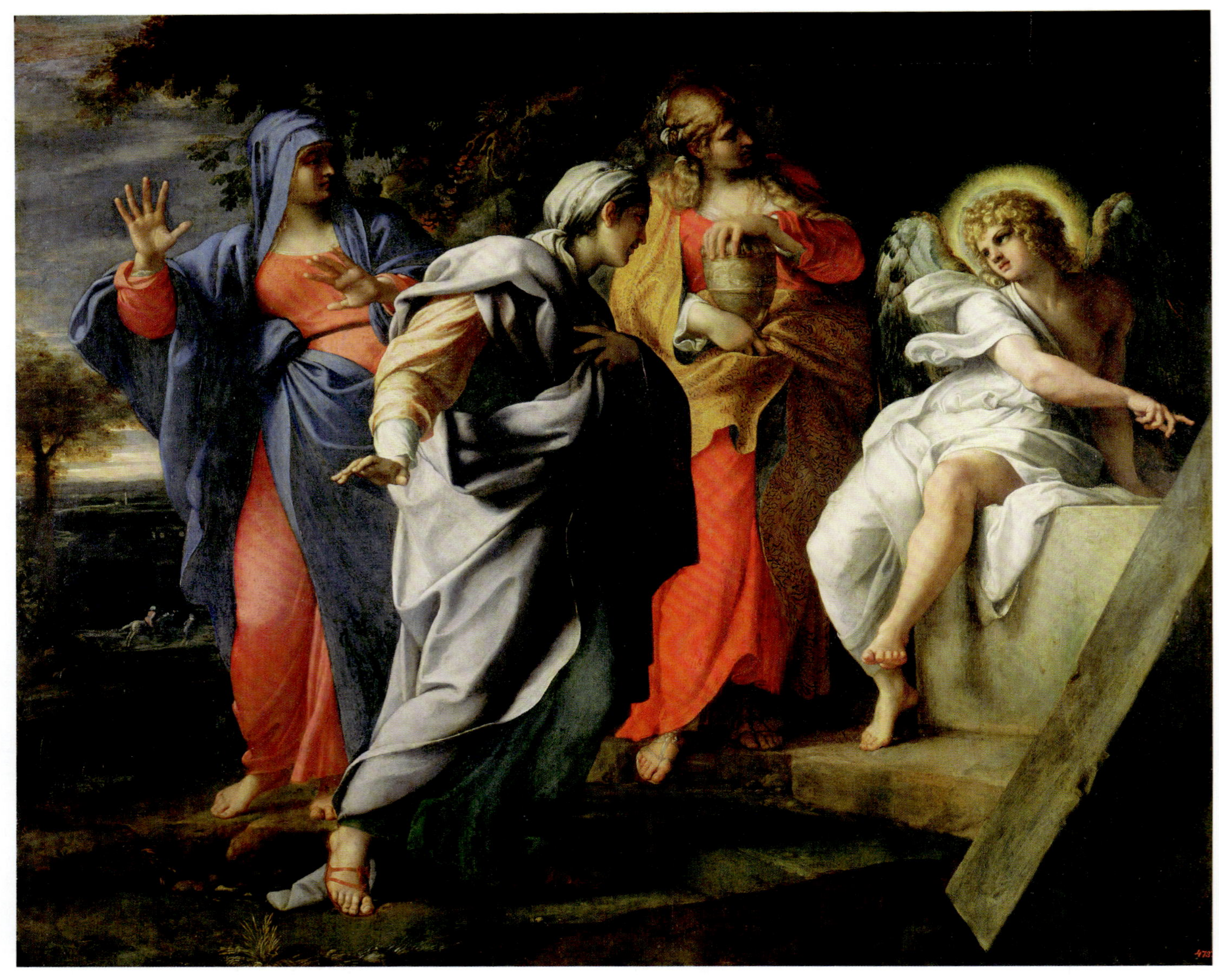

Annibale Carracci (1560–1609)

The Three Women at the Tomb of Christ

Les Saintes Femmes au tombeau du Christ

Die drei Frauen am Grab Christi

Las tres mujeres en la tumba de Cristo

As Três Mulheres no Túmulo de Cristo

De drie vrouwen aan het graf van Christus

c. 1590, Oil on canvas/Huile sur toile, 121 × 145,5 cm

Nicolas Régnier (1591–1667)

St. John the Baptist

Saint Jean-Baptiste

Johannes der Täufer

San Juan Bautista

João Batista

Johannes de Doper

1615–20, Oil on canvas/Huile sur toile, 179 × 142 cm

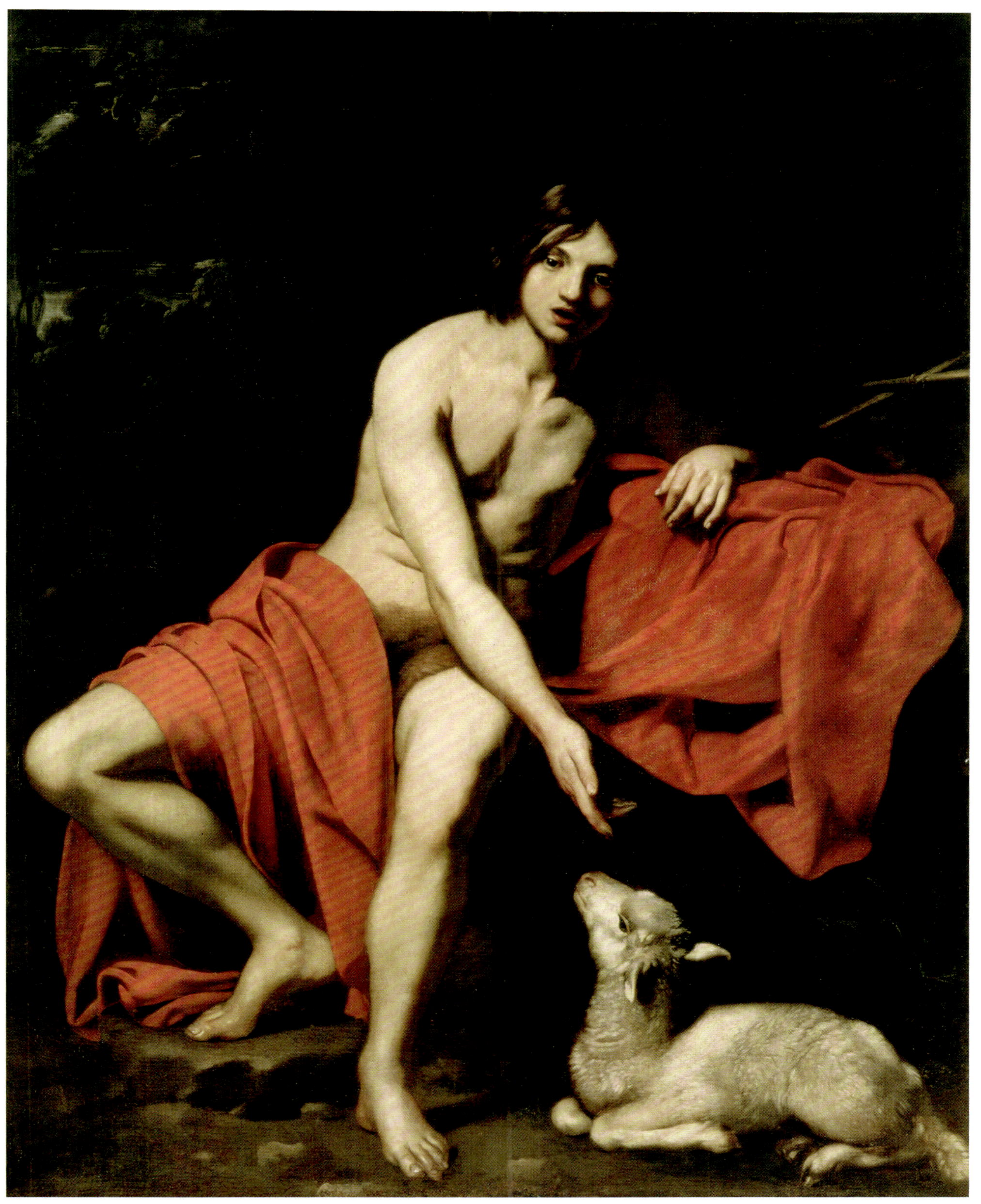

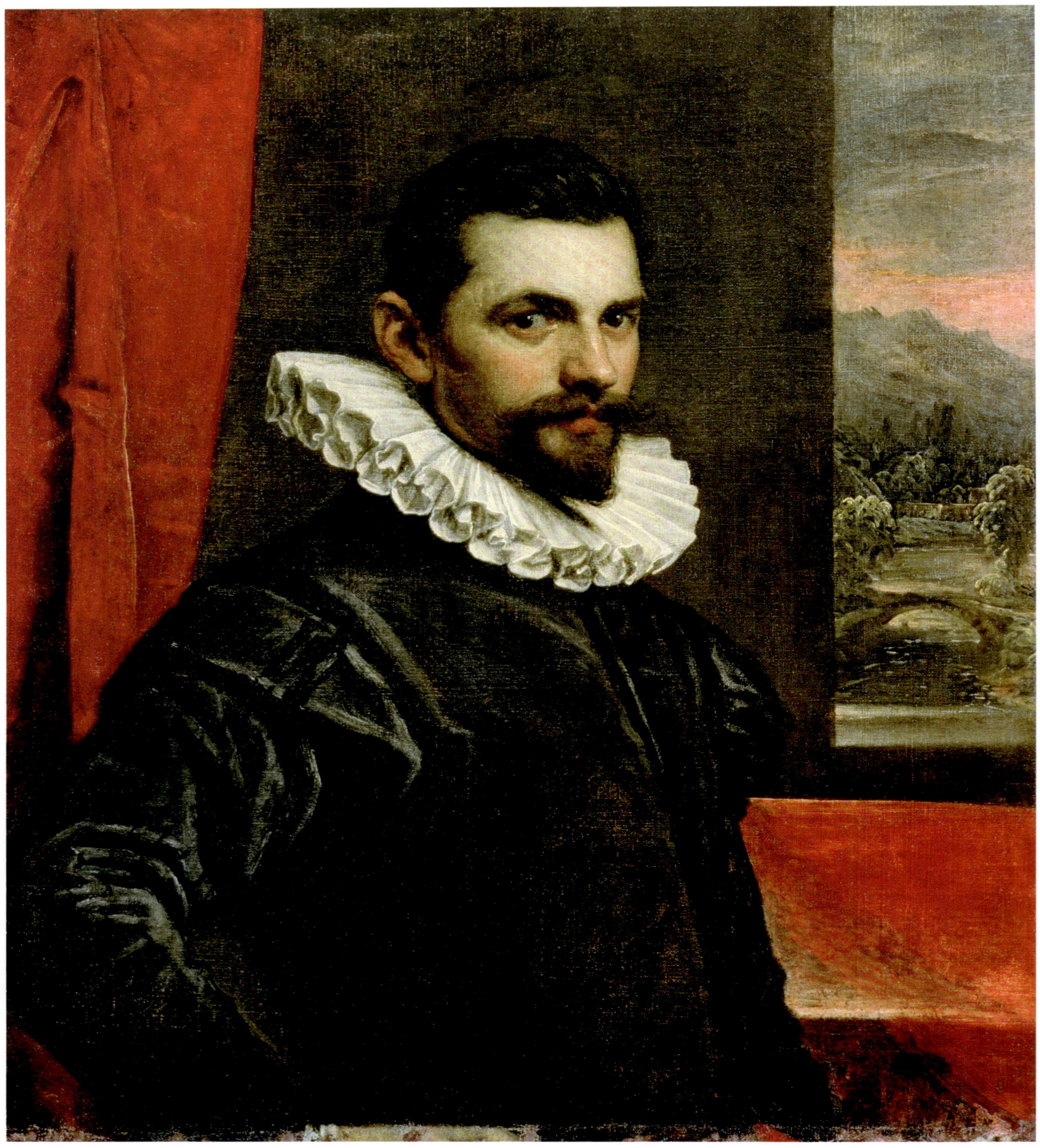

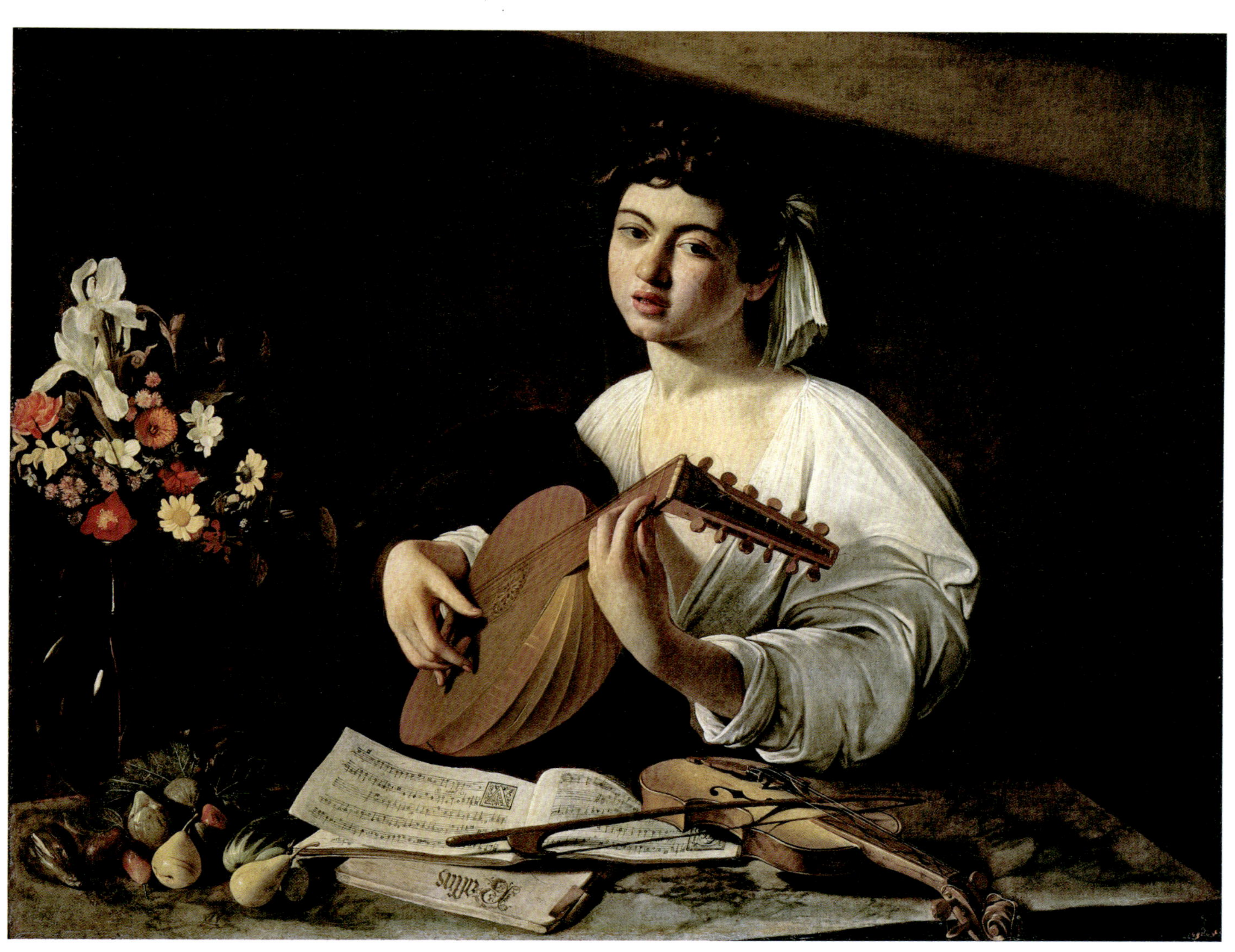

Domenico Tintoretto (Domenico Robusti) (1560–1635)

Francesco Bassano (?)

1586–89, Oil on canvas/Huile sur toile, 79 × 71 cm

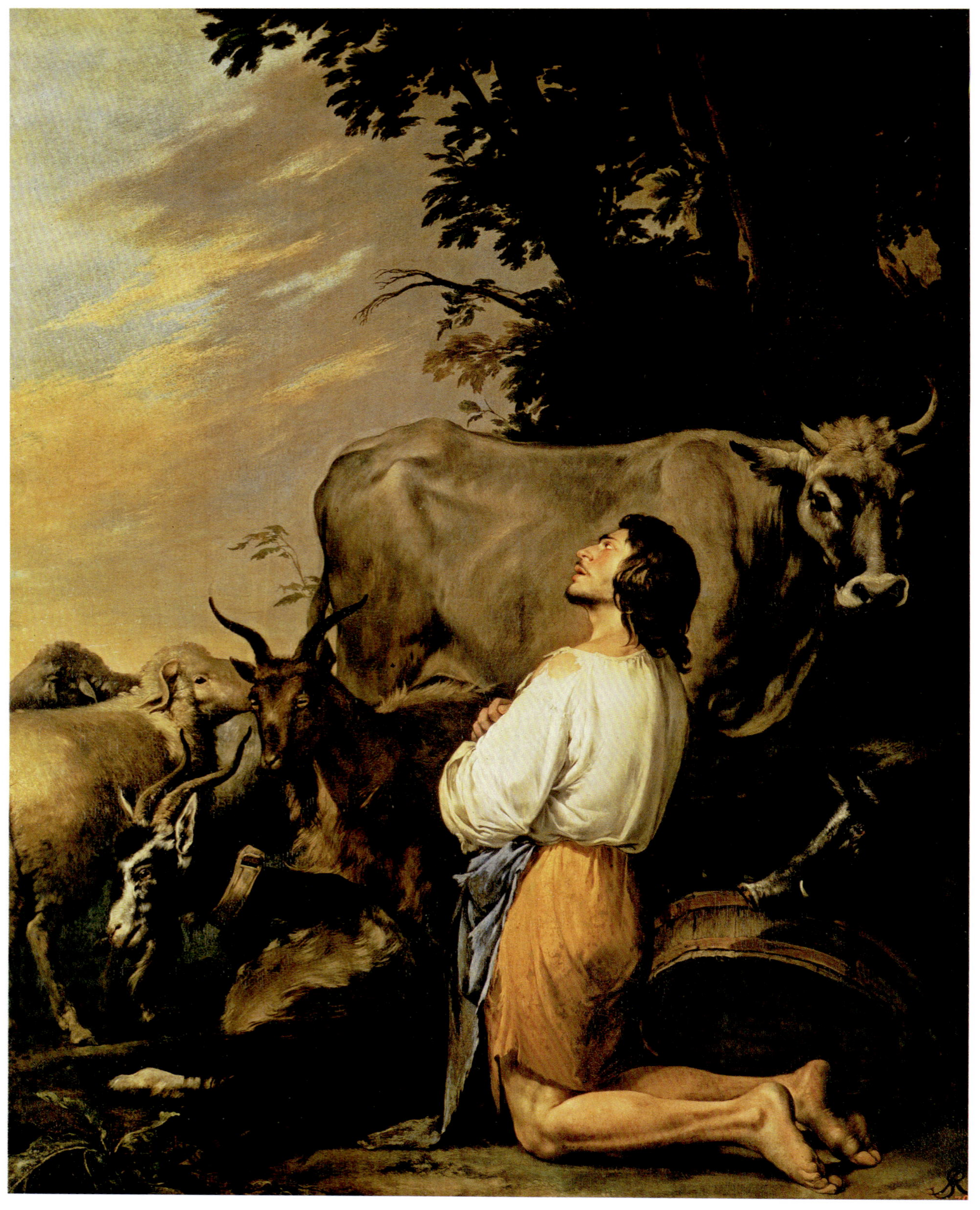

*Salvator Rosa
(1615–73)*

The Prodigal
Son

Le Fils
prodigue

Der verlorene
Sohn

El hijo pródigo

O Filho
Pródigo

De verloren
zoon

c. 1650–55,
Oil on canvas/
Huile sur toile,
253,5 × 201 cm

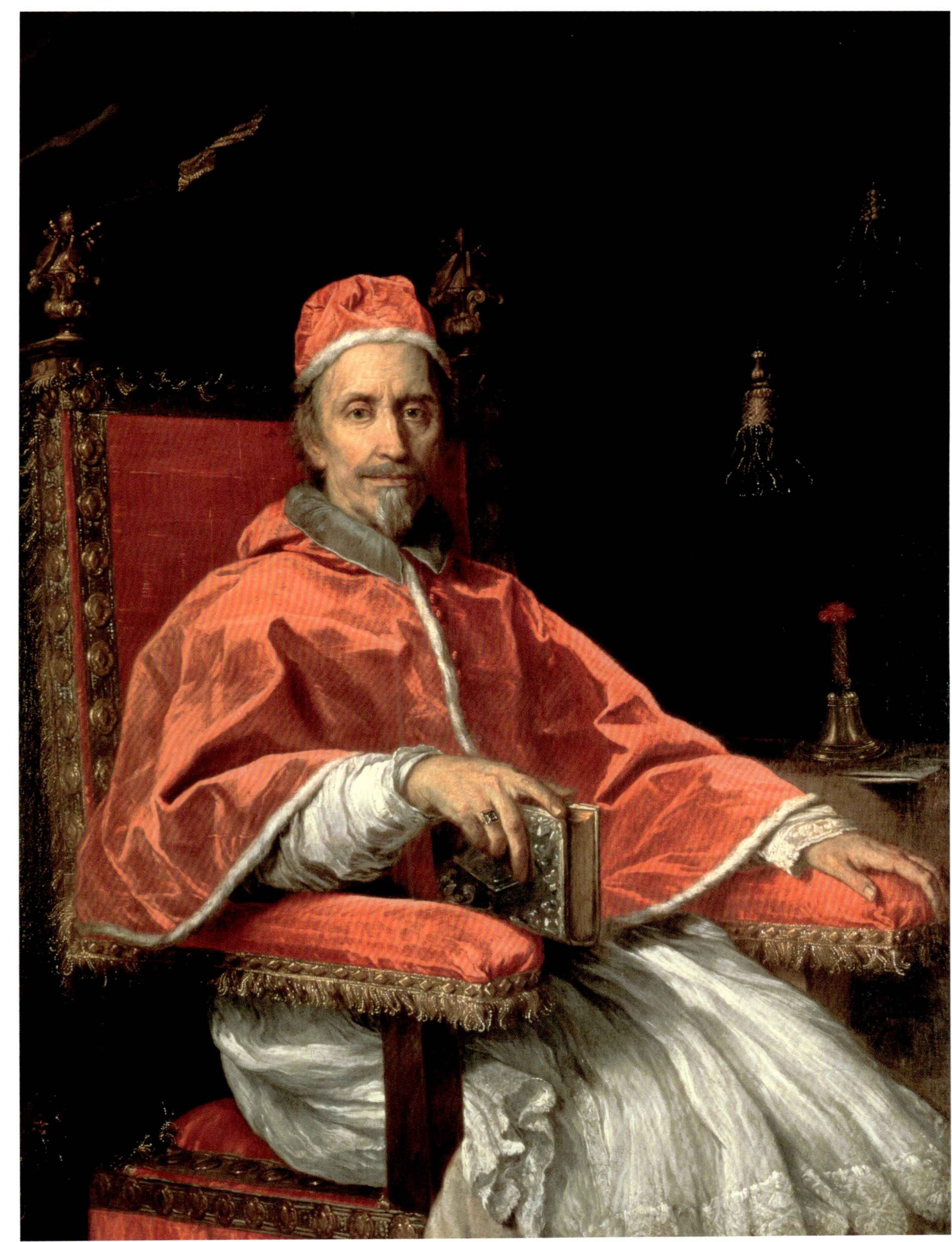

Carlo Maratta
(1625–1713)

Pope Clement IX

Le Pape Clément IX

Papst Clemens IX.

El papa Clemente IX

Papa Clemente IX

Paus Clemens IX

c. 1669, Oil on canvas/Huile
sur toile, 153 × 118,5 cm

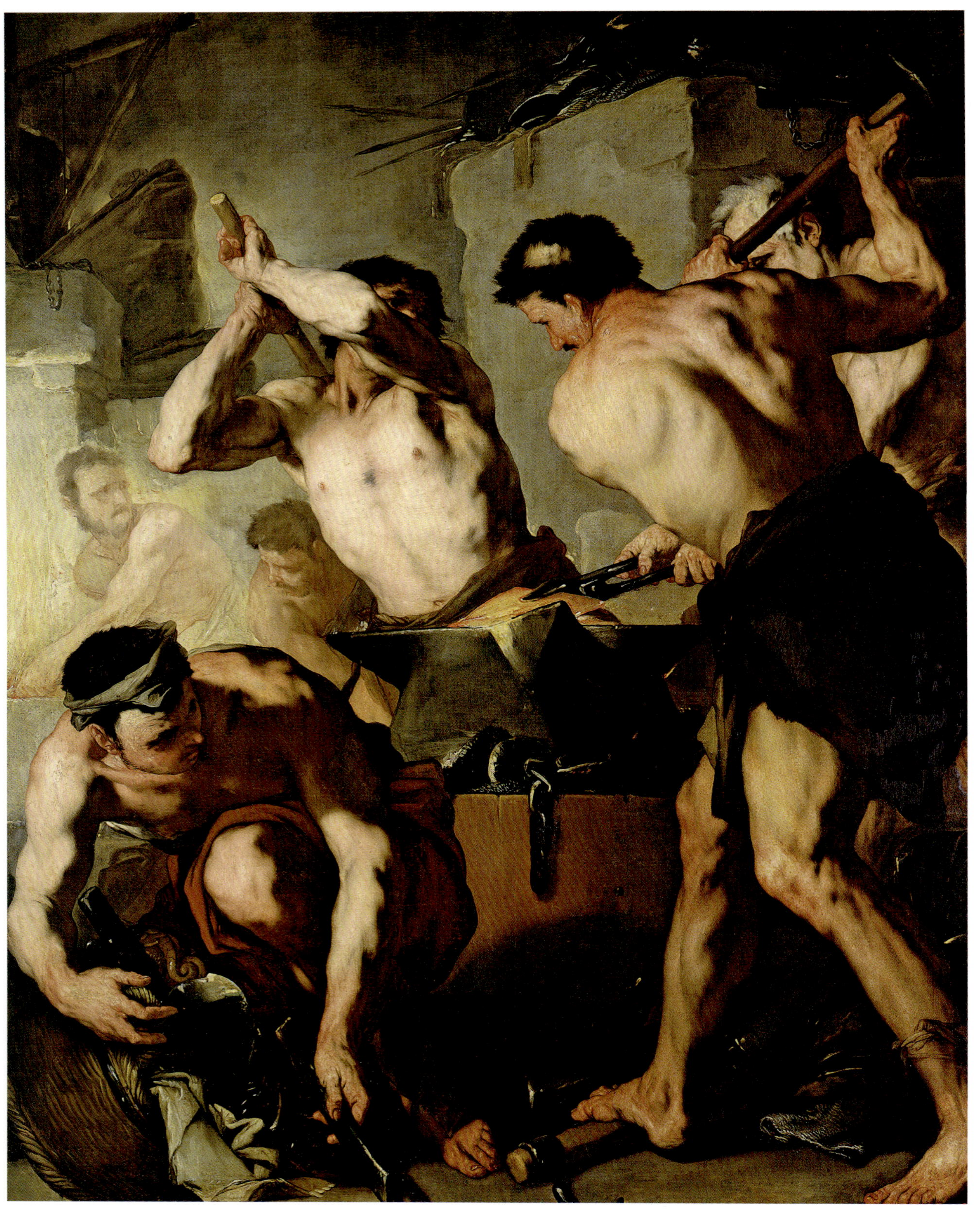

Luca Giordano
(1634–1705)

The Forge
of Vulcan

La Forge de
Vulcain

Die Schmiede
des Vulkan

La fragua de
Vulcano

Os Ferreiros
do Vulcão

De smidse van
Vulcanus

c. 1660, Oil
on canvas/
Huile sur toile,
192,5 × 151,5 cm

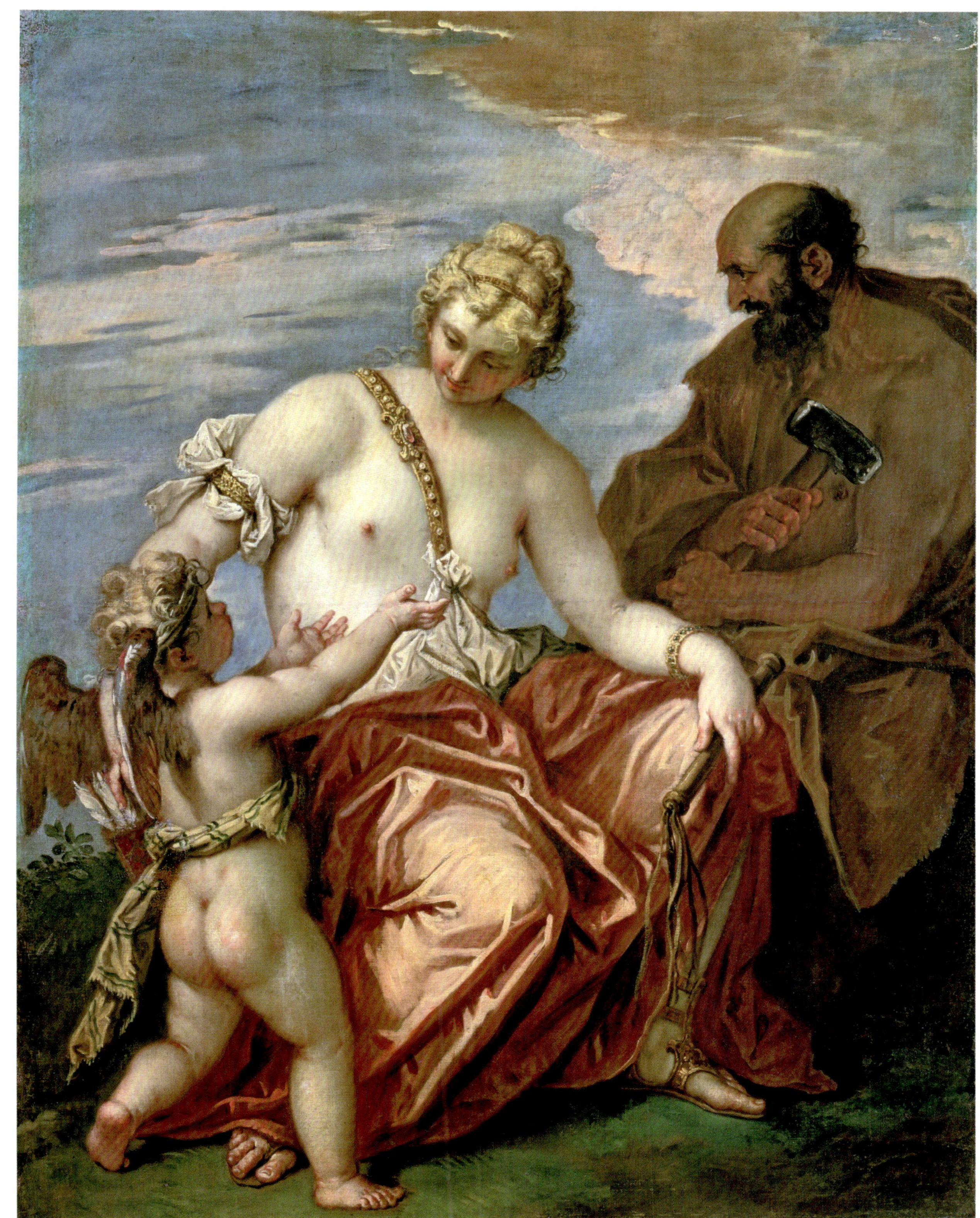

Sebastiano Ricci
(1659–1734)

Venus, Vulcan,
and Cupid

Vénus, Cupidon
et Vulcain

Venus, Vulkan
und Amor

Venus, Vulcano
y Amor

Vénus, Vulcão
e Amor

Venus, Vulcanus
en Amor

c. 1695, Oil
on canvas/
Huile sur toile,
154,5 × 126,5 cm

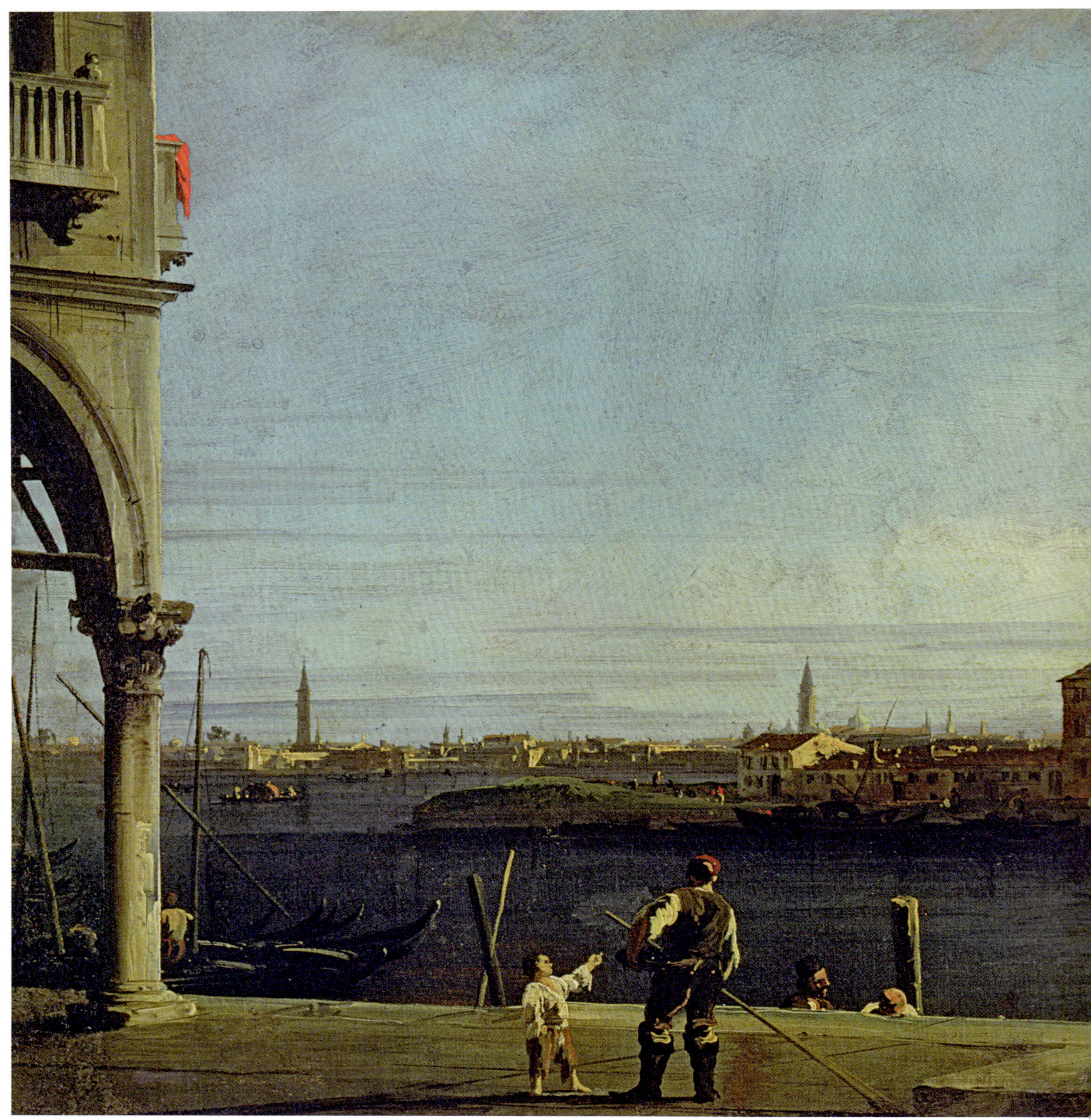

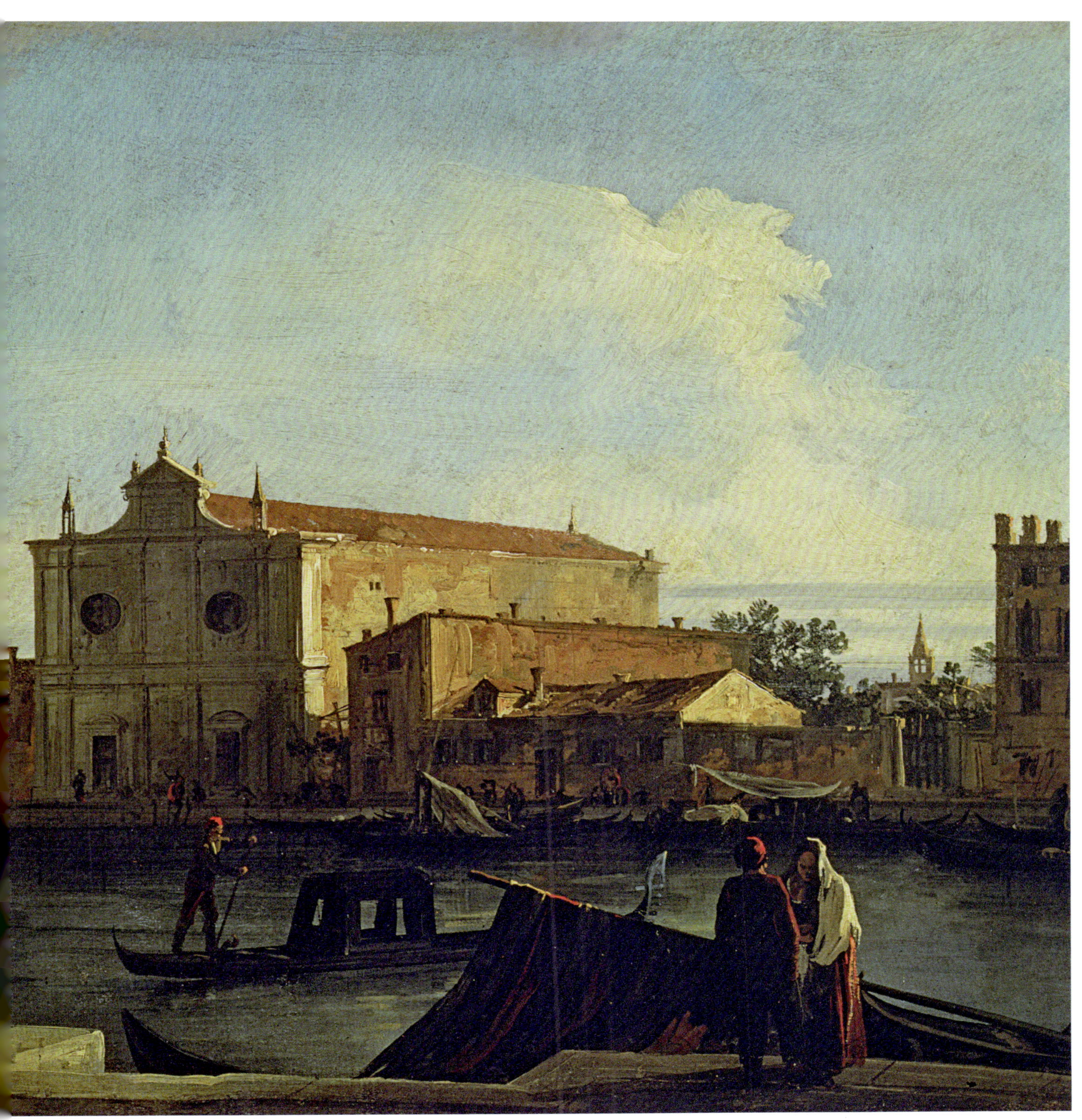

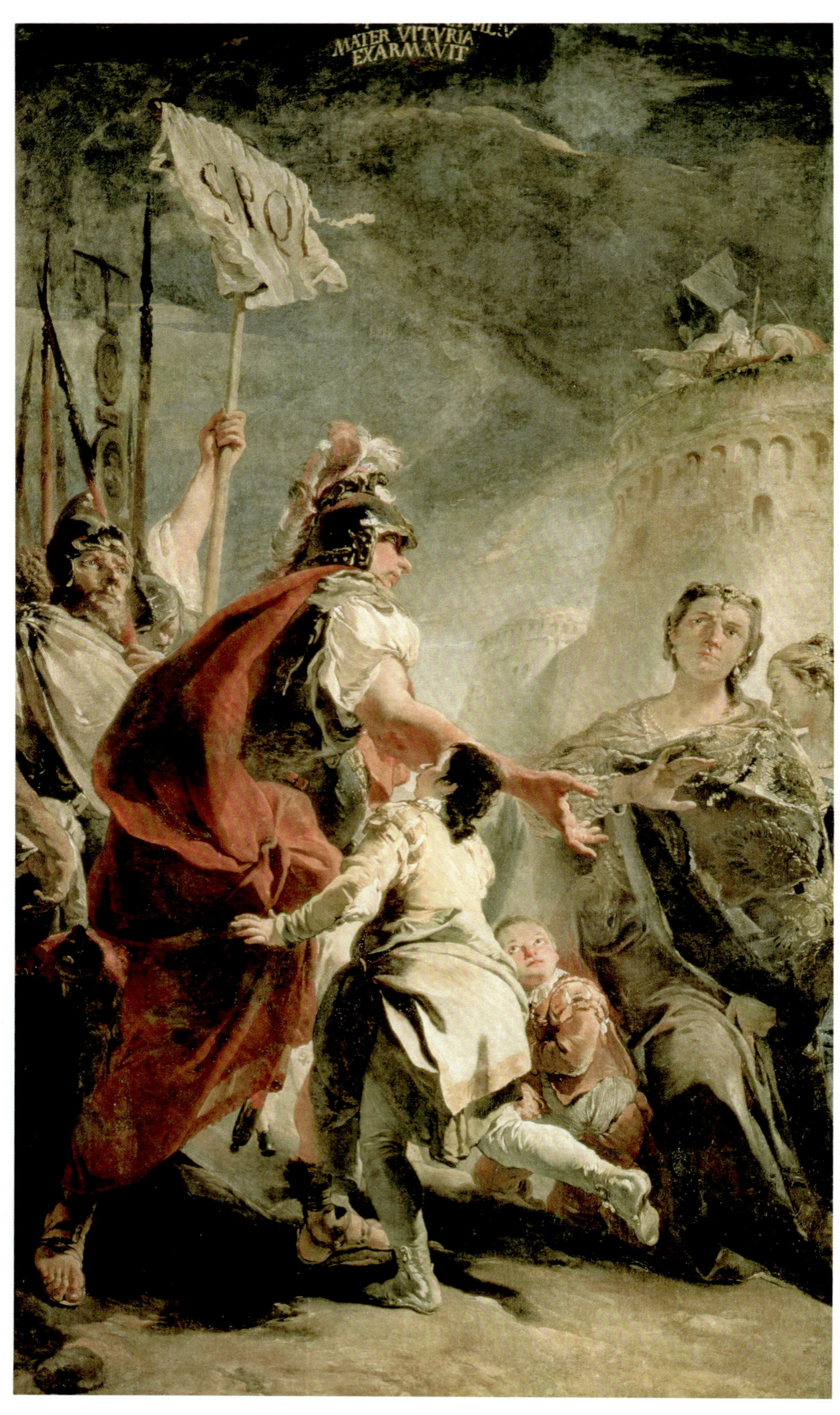

Giovanni Battista Tiepolo (1696–1770)
Coriolanus near Rome
Coriolan devant les murs de Rome
Coriolanus in der Umgebung von Rom
Coriolano en los alrededores de Roma
Coriolano nas Imediações de Roma
Coriolanus in de omgeving van Rome
c. 1730, Oil on canvas/Huile sur toile, 387 × 224 cm

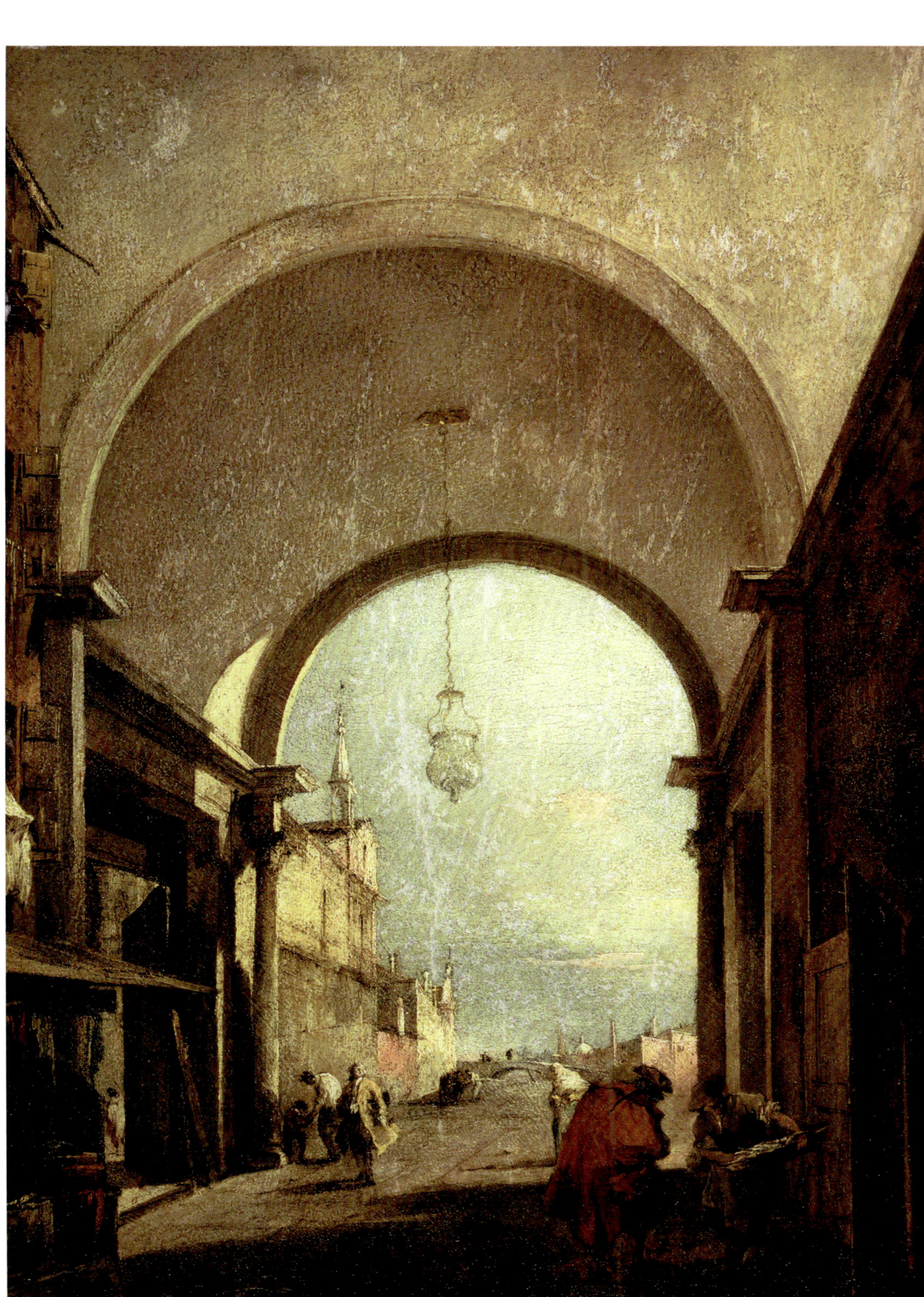

pp. 264/265

Giovanni Antoni Canal (Canaletto)
(1697–1768)

The Church of S.Giovanni
dei Battuti in Murano

Vue de l'église San Giovanni dei
Battuti sur l'île de Murano

Die Kirche S.Giovanni dei
Battuti in Murano

La iglesia S.Giovanni dei
Battuti en Murano

A Igreja S. Giovanni dei
Battuti em Murano

De S.Giovanni dei Battuti in Murano

1725–28, Oil on canvas/Huile
sur toile, 66 × 127,5 cm

Francesco Guardi (1712–93)

Cityscape

Vue urbaine

Stadtansicht

Vista de ciudad

Vista da Cidade

Stadsgezicht

c. 1775–80, Oil on wood/Huile
sur bois, 52 × 38,5 cm

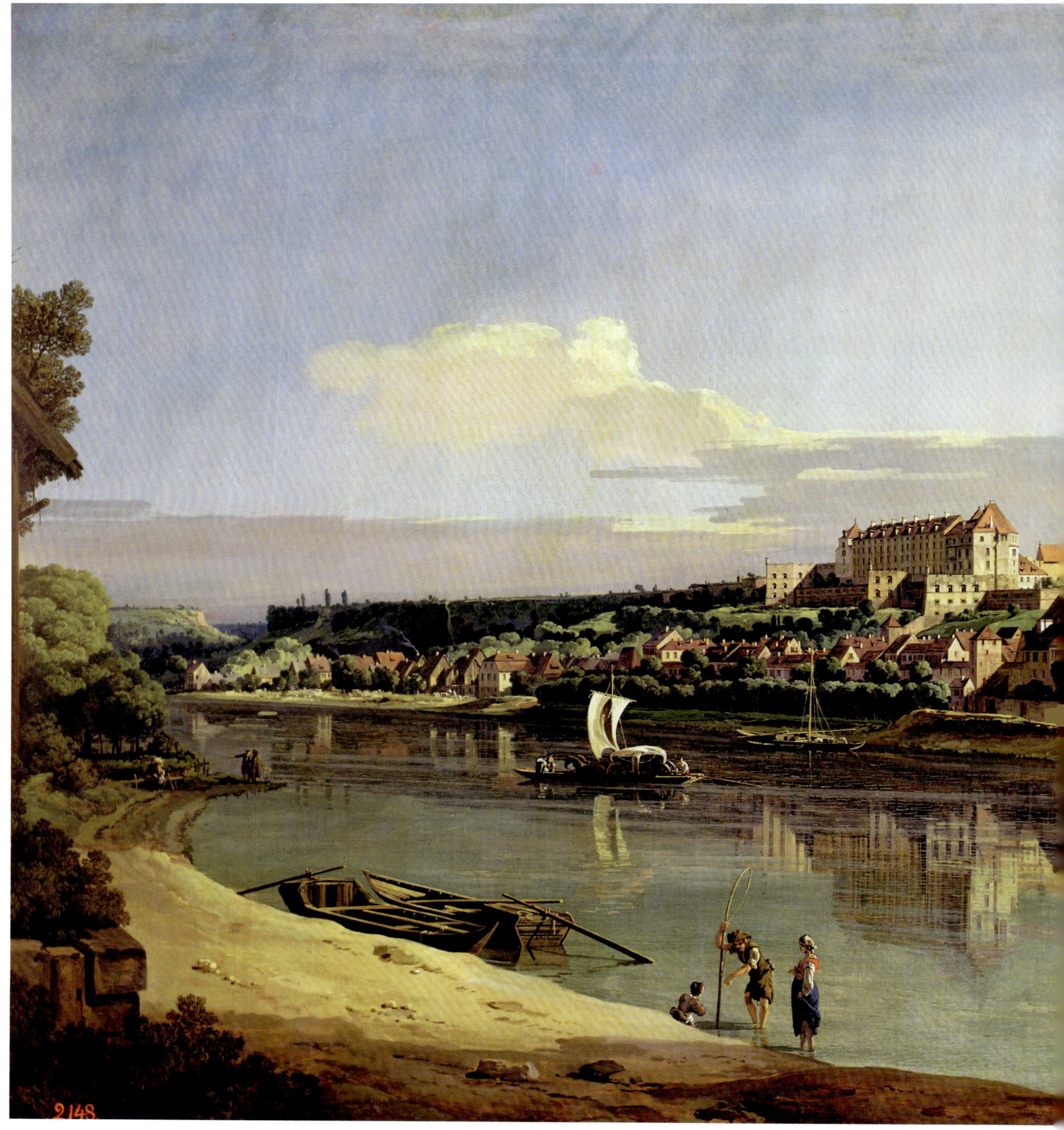

2148

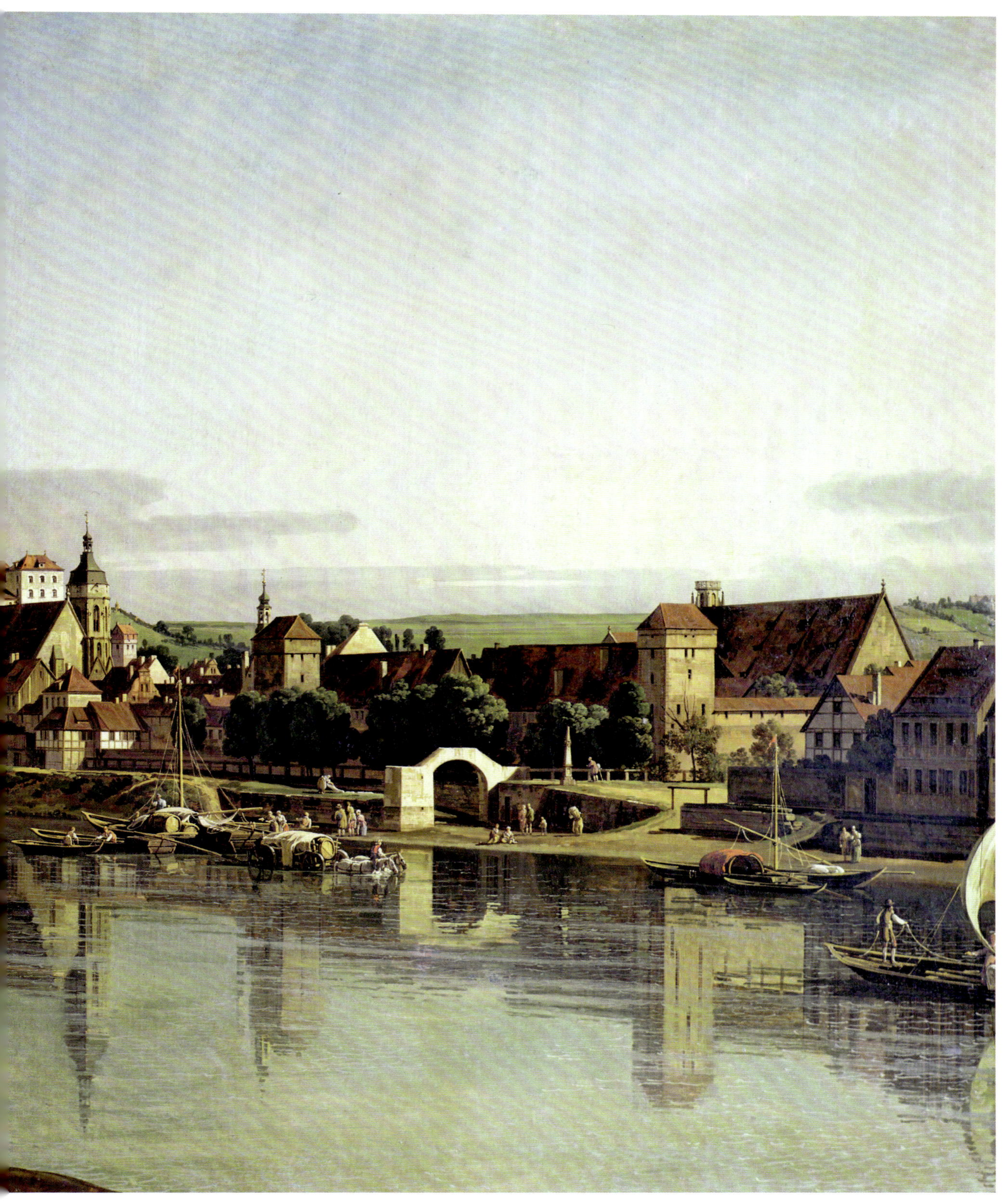

*Bernardo
Bellotto
(Canaletto)
(1720–80)*

Pirna from
the Right
Bank of
the Elbe

Pirna vue
depuis la
rive droite
de l'Elbe

Pirna vom
rechten
Elbufer aus

Pirna desde la
orilla derecha
del Elba

Pirna a partir
da Margem
Direita
do Elba

Uitzicht op
Pirna vanaf de
rechteroever
van de Elbe

c. 1753, Oil
on canvas/
Huile sur toile,
133 × 237,5 cm

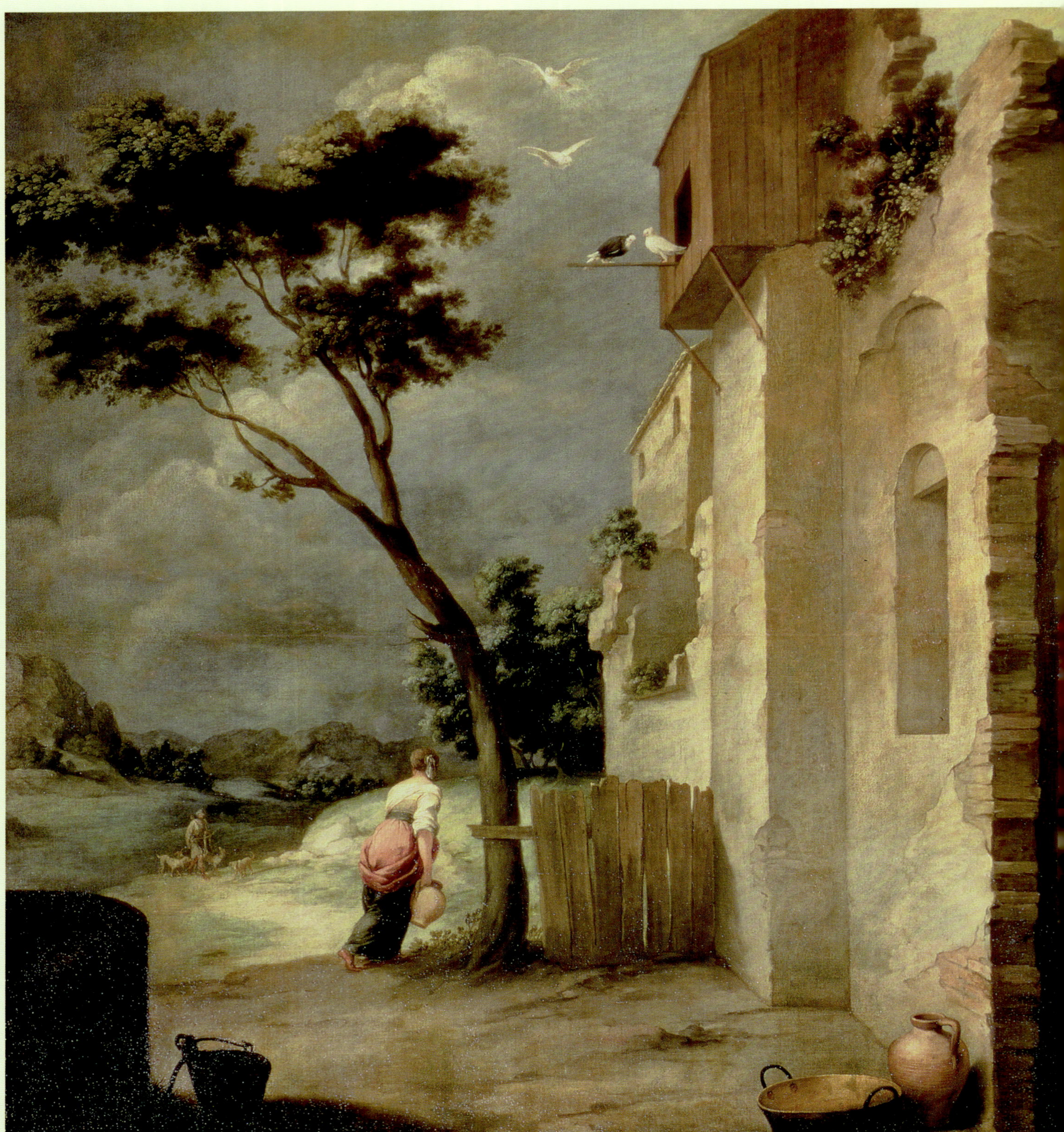

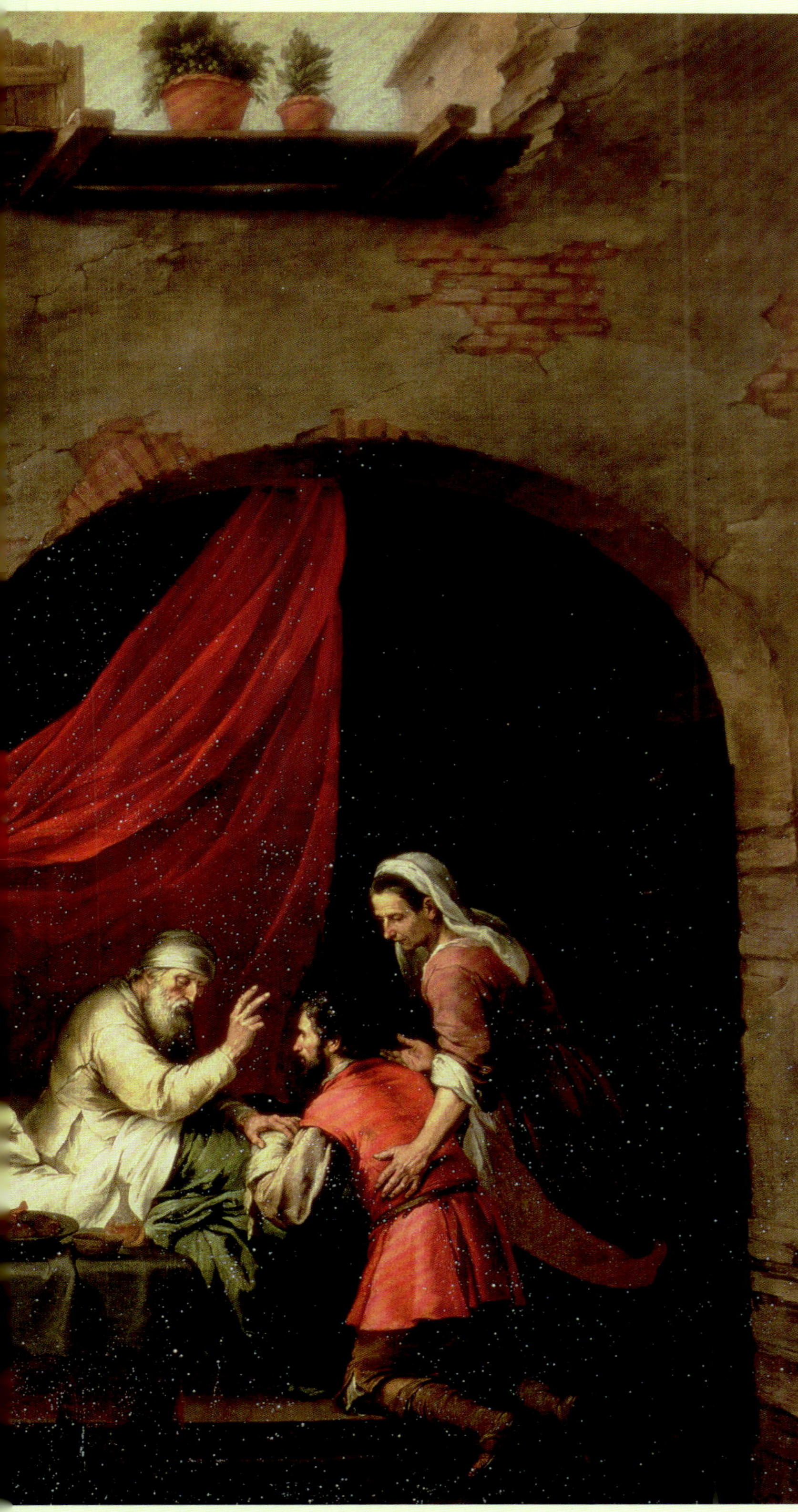

Bartolomé Esteban Murillo (1618–82)
Isaac blessing Jacob
Isaac bénissant Jacob
Isaak segnet Jakob
Isaac bendice a Jacob
Isaac Abençoa Jacó
Izaäk zegent Jacob
c. 1660, Oil on canvas/Huile sur toile, 245 × 357,5 cm

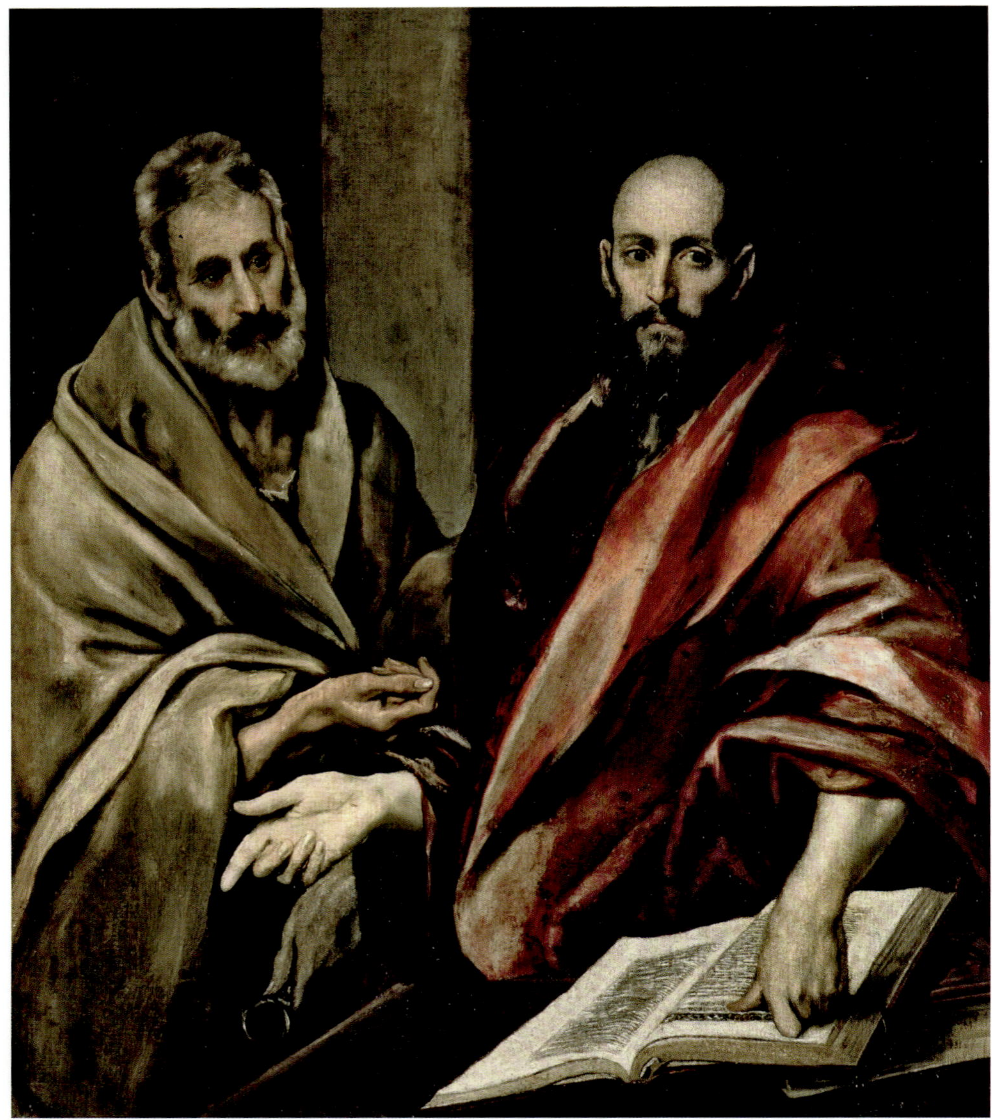

Spanish Painting

The 150 paintings in the Spanish collection is displayed in two rooms of the New Hermitage. The 16th century is represented by two works by El Greco, including the double portrait of *Saints Peter and Paul*. With 13 works, Bartolomé Esteban Murillo receives special attention. The collection is further enriched by other outstanding 17th-century artists, including pieces by Francisco de Zurbarán, Diego Velázquez, and Jusepe de Ribera. Goya's portrait of *Antonia Zárate* represents the 19th century.

La peinture espagnole

Les quelque 150 peintures que compte la collection espagnole se trouvent dans deux salles du Nouvel Ermitage. Le XVIᵉ siècle y est représenté par deux œuvres du Greco, dont *Les Apôtres saint Pierre et saint Paul*. L'œuvre de Bartolomé Esteban Murillo attire particulièrement l'attention, avec 13 tableaux. Des œuvres d'autres artistes exceptionnels du XVIIᵉ siècle enrichissent la collection, tels Francisco de Zurbarán, Diego Velázquez et Jusepe de Ribera. Le XIXᵉ siècle est représenté entre autres par Francisco de Goya et son Portrait de *Doña Antonia Zárate*.

Spanische Malerei

Die rund 150 Gemälde umfassende Sammlung spanischer Malerei befindet sich in zwei Sälen der Neuen Eremitage. Das 16. Jahrhundert wird durch zwei Werke El Grecos, darunter das Doppelporträt der *Heiligen Peter und Paul* vertreten. Mit 13 Gemälden erfährt das Werk Bartolomé Esteban Murillos besondere Aufmerksamkeit. Zudem bereichern Werke weiterer herausragender Künstler des 17. Jahrhunderts die Sammlung, darunter Francisco de Zurbarán, Diego Velázquez und Jusepe de Ribera. Aus dem 19. Jahrhundert ist Francisco de Goya mit dem Porträt *Antonia Zárate* vertreten.

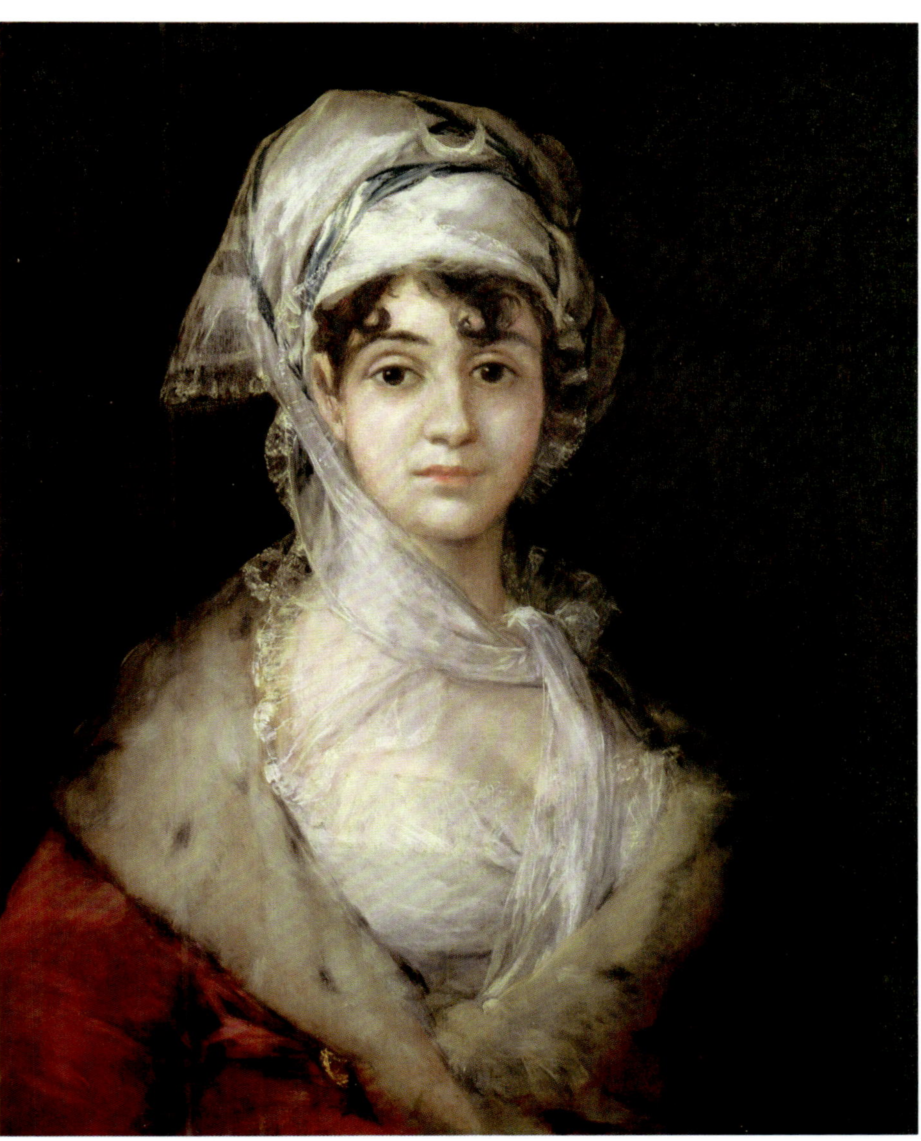

Pintura española

Las aproximadamente 150 pinturas de la colección de pintura española están alojadas en dos salas del Nuevo Hermitage. El siglo XVI está representado por dos obras de El Greco, entre ellos el doble retrato de *San Pedro y San Pablo*. El trabajo de Bartolomé Esteban Murillo recibe una atención especial con trece pinturas. Además, enriquecen la colección las obras de otros artistas destacados del siglo XVII, entre ellos Francisco de Zurbarán, Diego Velázquez y José de Ribera. El siglo XIX está representado con el retrato de *Antonia Zárate* de Francisco de Goya.

Pintura espanhola

A coleção de pintura espanhola, que abrange cerca de 150 obras, encontra-se em duas salas do Novo Hermitage. O século XVI está representado por duas obras de El Greco, entre as quais o retrato duplo de *São Pedro e São Paulo*. Com 13 pinturas, a obra de Bartolomé Esteban Murillo é alvo de uma especial atenção. Além disso, obras de outros excelentes artistas do século XVII, entre eles, Francisco de Zurbarán, Diego Velázquez e Jusepe de Ribera enriquecem a coleção. Do século XIX encontra-se representado Francisco de Goya com o retrato de *Antonia Zárate*.

Spaanse schilderkunst

De rond 150 werken tellende collectie Spaanse schilderkunst is in twee zalen in de Nieuwe Hermitage ondergebracht. De zestiende eeuw is vertegenwoordigd met twee doeken van El Greco, waaronder het dubbelportret *De heiligen Petrus en Paulus*. Met dertien doeken neemt Bartolomé Esteban Murillo een bijzondere plaats in. De collectie wordt verder verrijkt met werk van andere grote schilders uit de zeventiende eeuw, onder wie De Zurbarán, Velázquez en De Ribera. De negentiende eeuw is vertegenwoordigd met Francisco de Goya, met diens portret van *Antonia Zárate*.

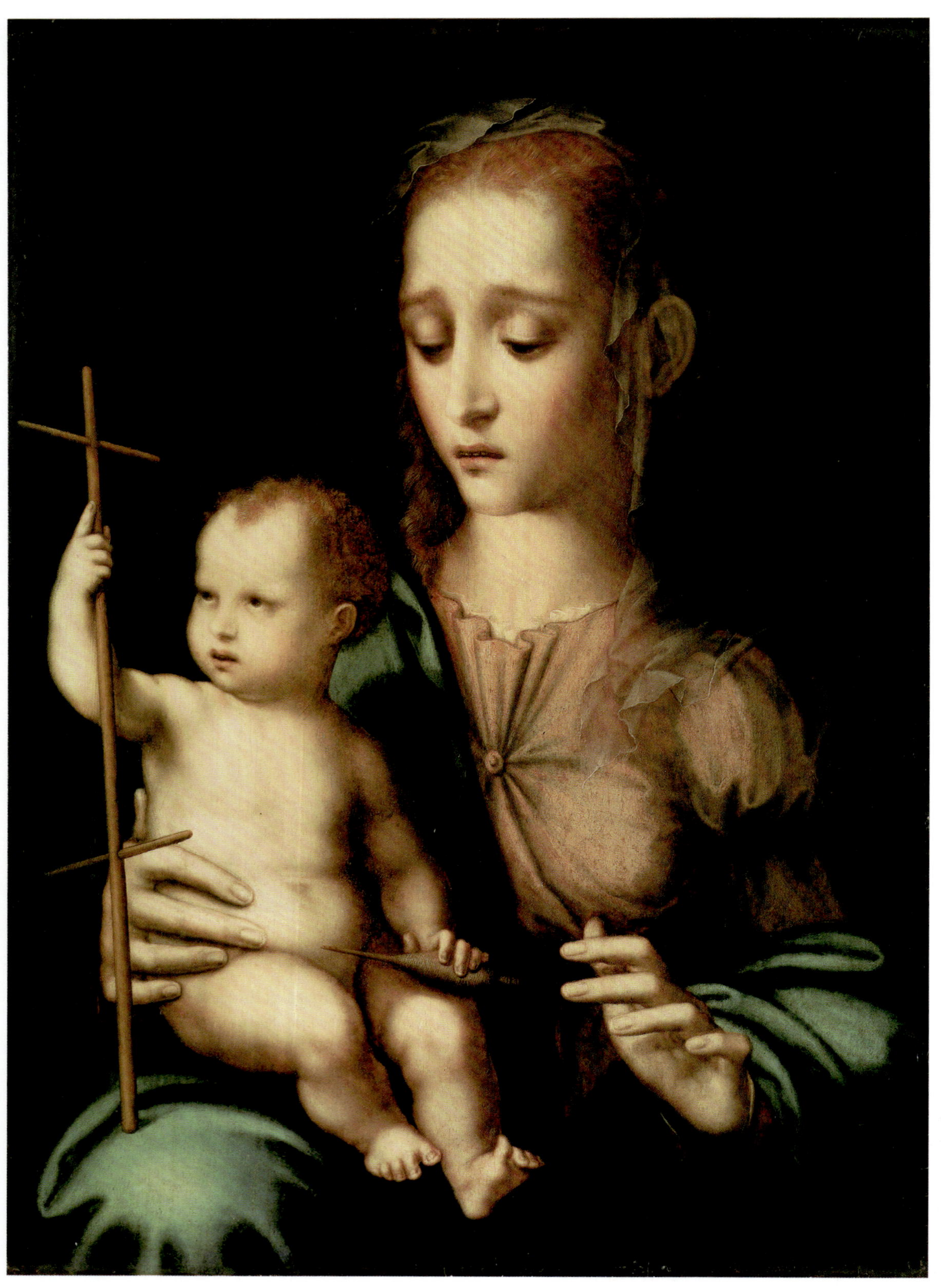

Luis de Morales (c. 1509–86)

Madonna and Child
with a Spindle

La Vierge et l'Enfant
à la bobine de fil

Madonna und Kind
mit einer Spindel

La Virgen del huso

A Virgem e o Menino com Fuso

Madonna en Kind
met een spintol

c. 1570–79, Oil on canvas,
transferred from panel/
Huile sur toile, transposée
d'un bois, 71,5 × 52 cm

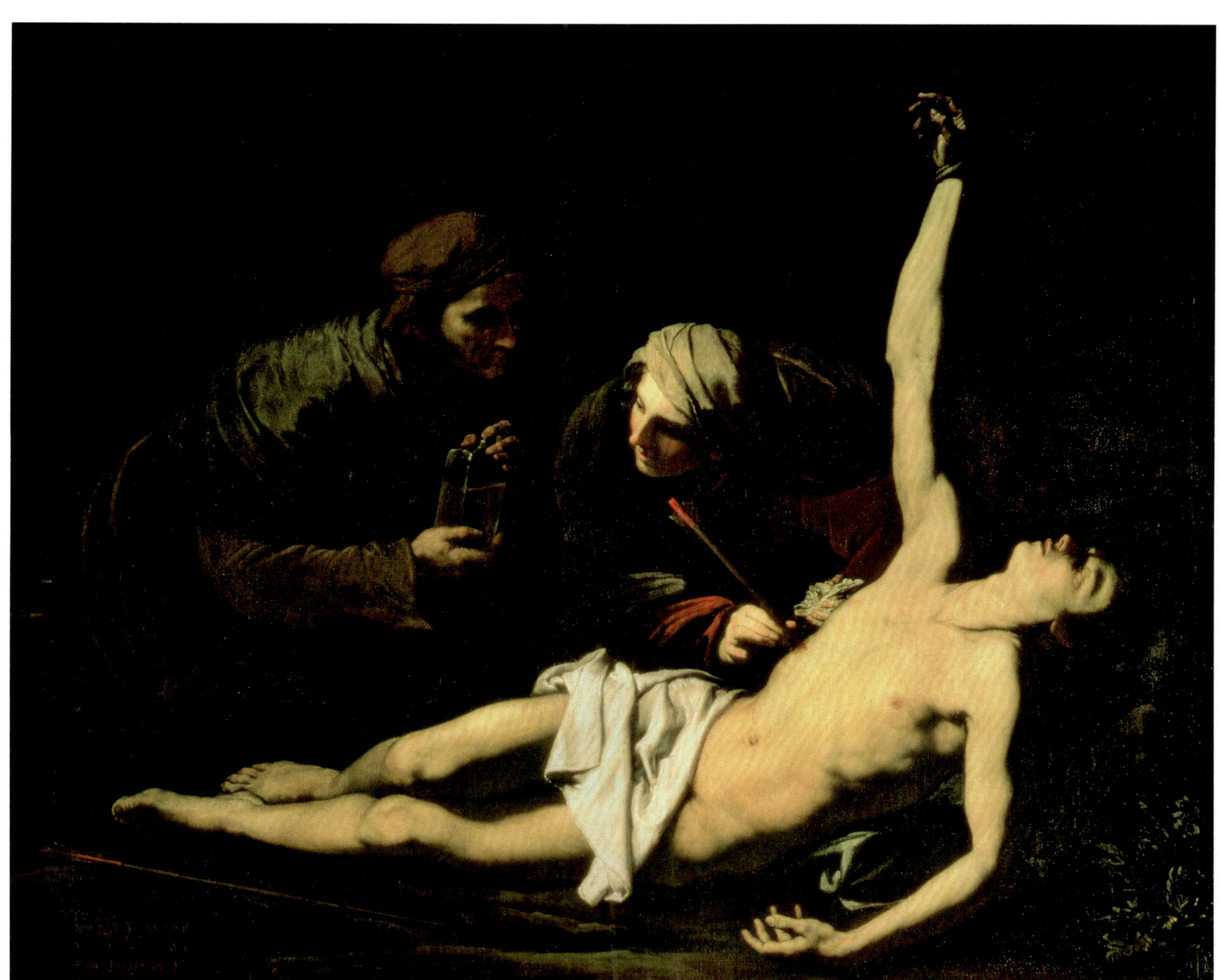

Jusepe de Ribera (Lo Spagnoletto) (c. 1590–1652)

St. Sebastian Nursed Back to Health by St. Irene

Saint Sébastien, sainte Irène et sainte Lucine

Der heilige Sebastian wird von der heiligen Irene gesund gepflegt

San Sebastián curado por Santa Irene

São Sebastião é Curado por Santa Irene

De heilige Sebastiaan wordt door de heilige Irene verpleegd

1628, Oil on canvas/Huile sur toile, 156 × 188 cm

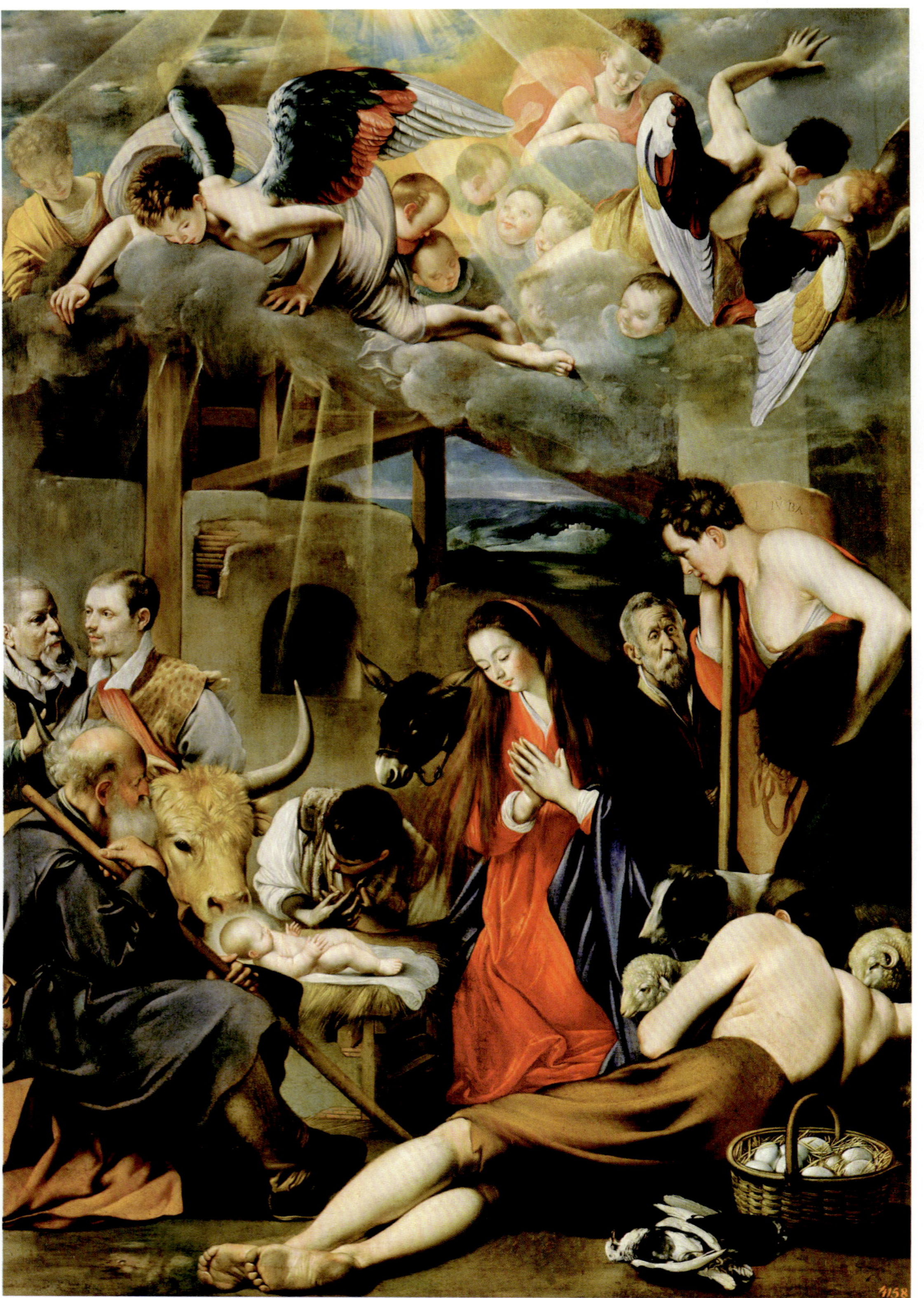

Fray Juan Bautista Maíno (1581–1649)
The Adoration of the Shepherds
Adoration des bergers
Die Anbetung der Hirten
La adoración de los pastores
A Adoração dos Pastores
De aanbidding door de herders
c. 1613, Oil on canvas/Huile
sur toile, 143,5 × 100,5 cm

Jusepe de Ribera (Lo Spagnoletto)
(c. 1590–1652)
St. Onuphrius
Saint Onuphre
Der heilige Onuphrius
San Onofre
São Onofre
De heilige Onuphrius
1637, Oil on canvas/Huile
sur toile, 130 × 104 cm

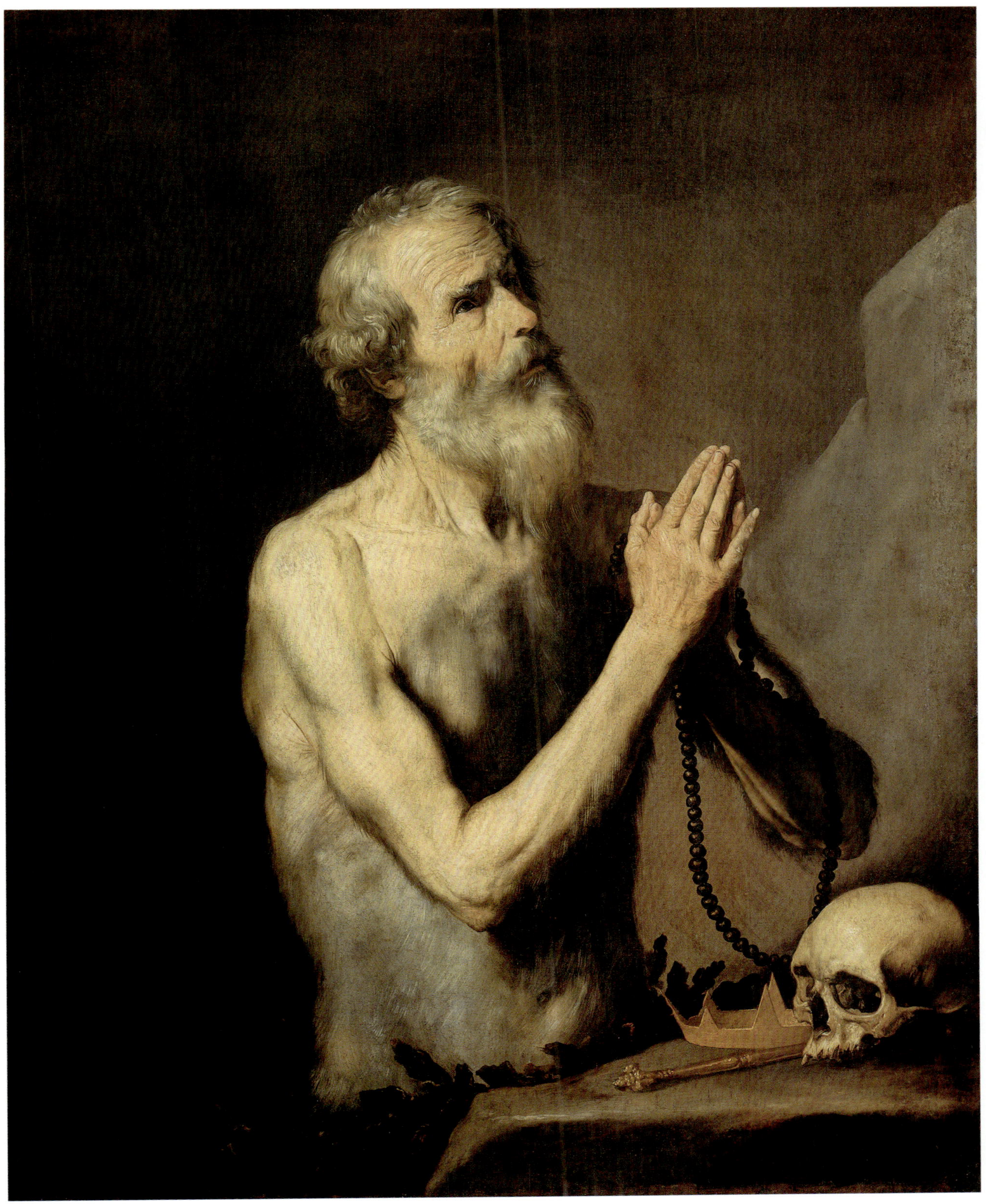

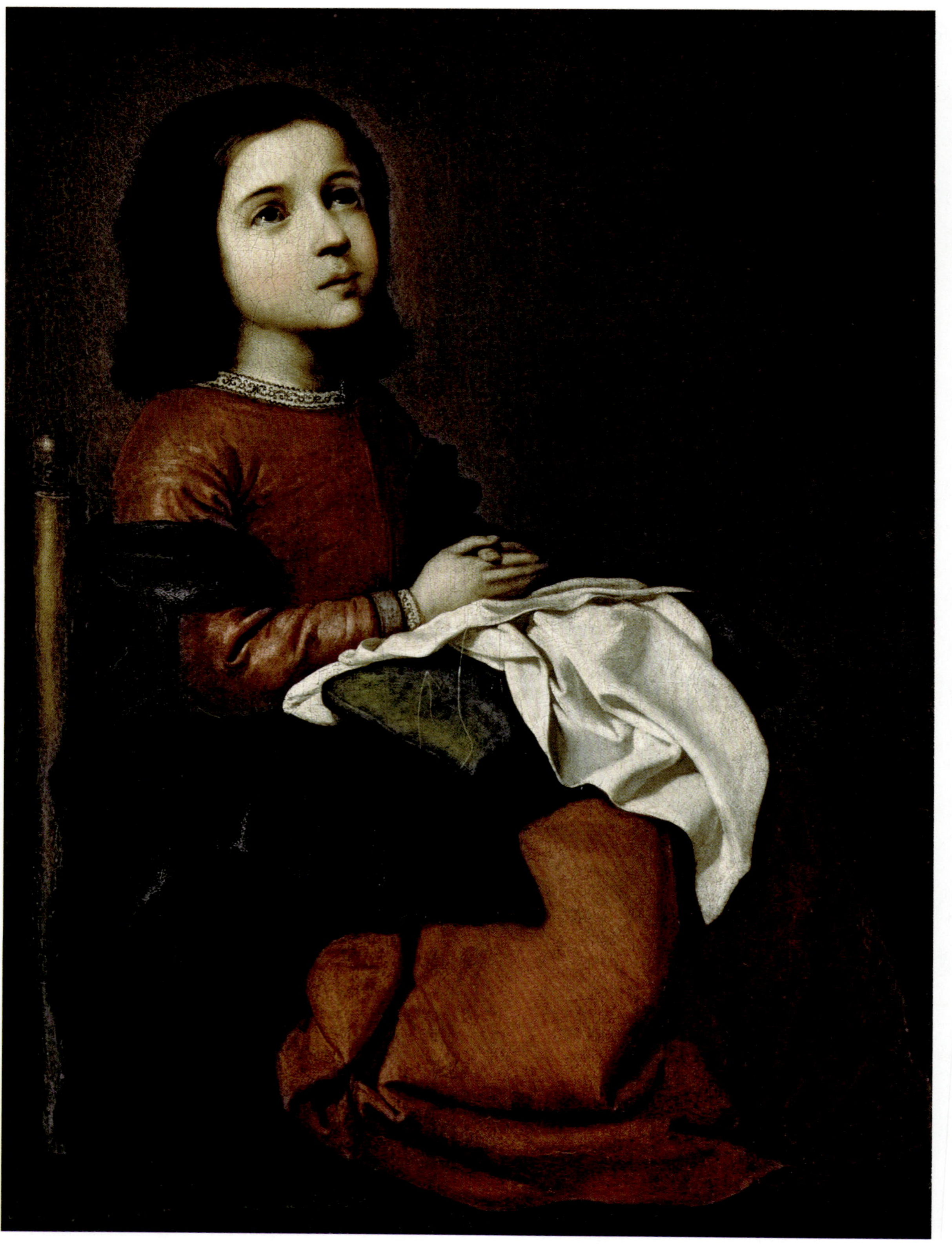

Francisco de Zurbarán
(1598–1664)

The Childhood of
the Virgin Mary

L'Enfance de la Vierge

Die Kindheit der
Jungfrau Maria

La infancia de la Virgen

A Infância da
Virgem Maria

De jeugd van de
Maagd Maria

c. 1658–60, Oil on
canvas/Huile sur toile,
73,5 × 53,5 cm

Diego Velázquez
(1599–1660)

Luncheon

Trois Hommes à table

Das Mittagessen

La comida

O Almoço

De lunch

c. 1617, Oil on canvas/Huile
sur toile, 108,5 × 102 cm

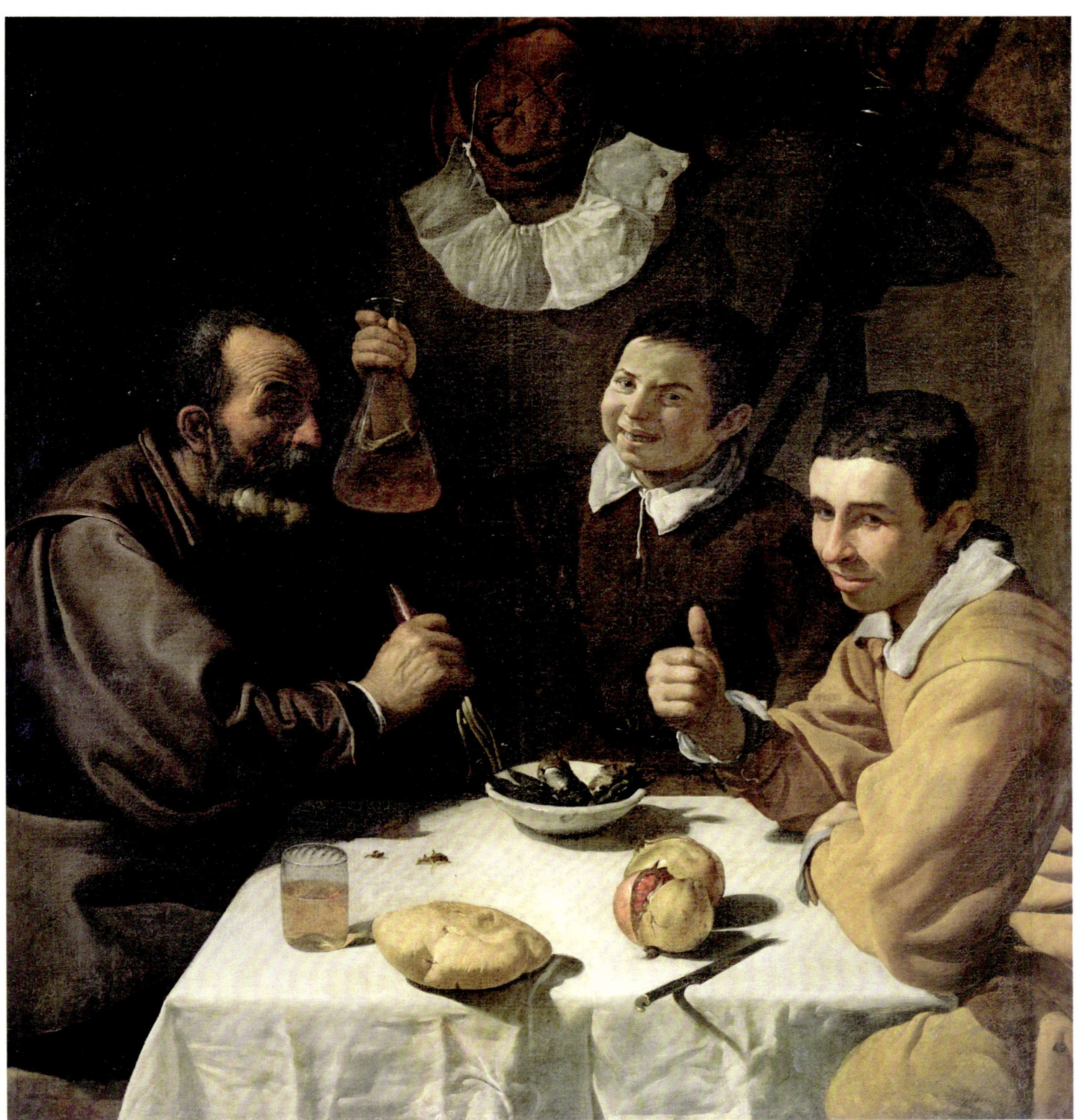

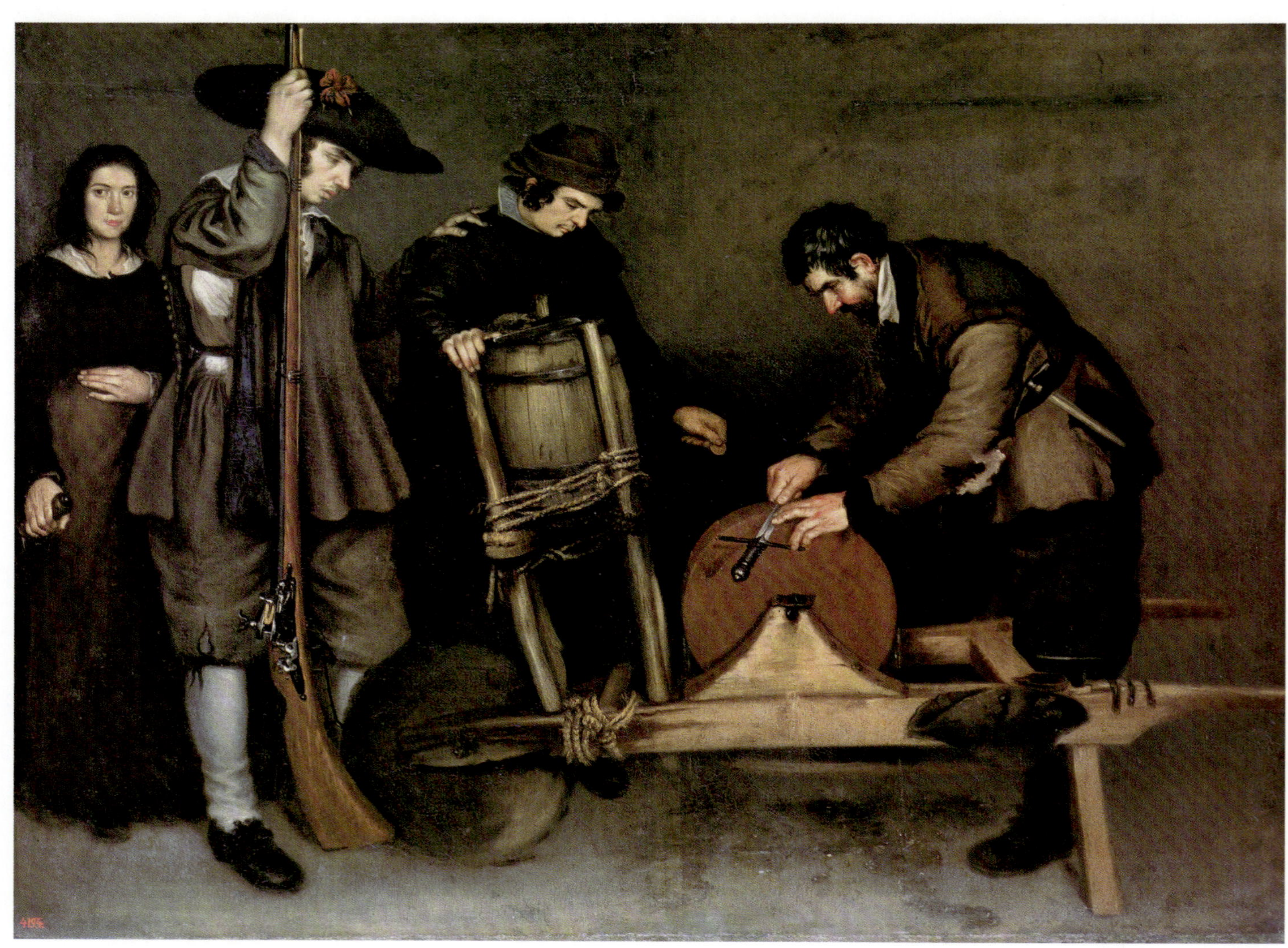

Antonio Puga (1602–48)

The Knife Grinder

Le Rémouleur

Der Messerschleifer

El afilador

Amolador de Facas

De messenslijper

1635–40, Oil on canvas/Huile sur toile, 120 × 160 cm

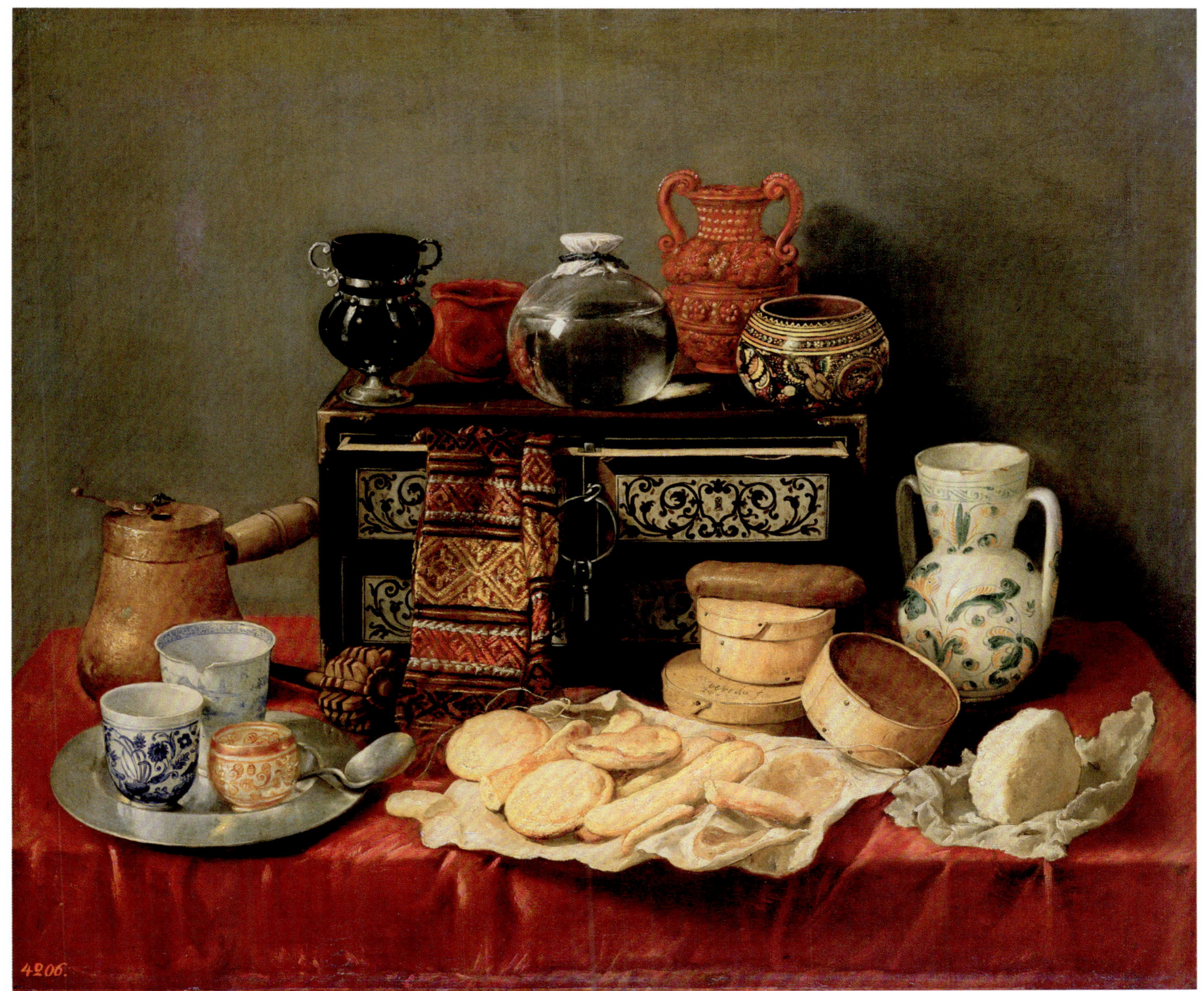

Antonio Pereda y Salgado (1611–78)

Still Life with Ebony Box

Nature morte

Stillleben mit Ebenholzkasten

Bodegón con cajón de ébano

Natureza-Morta com Armário de Ébano

Stilleven met ebbenhouten kistje

1652, Oil on canvas/Huile sur toile, 80 × 94 cm

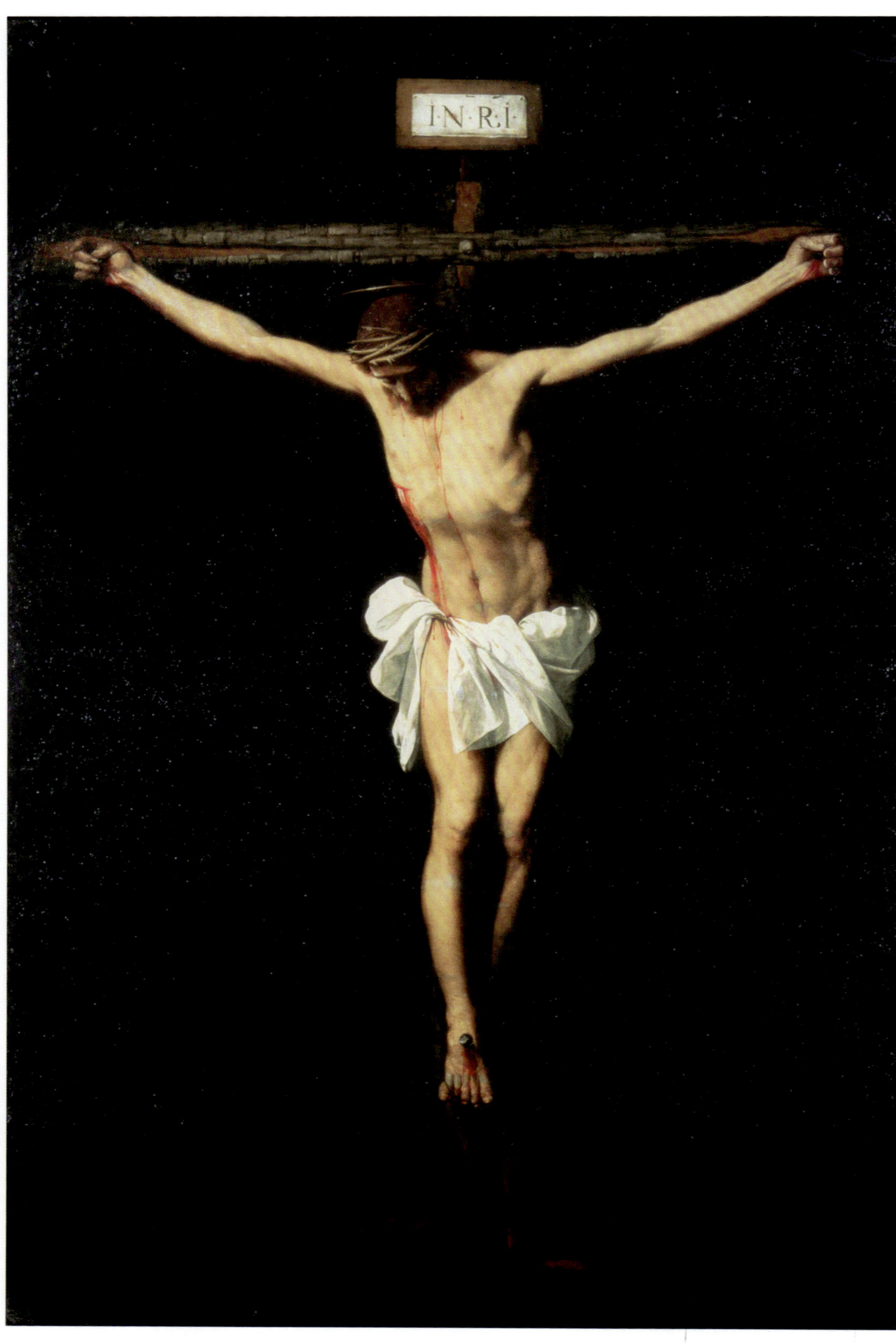

Alonso Cano (attr.) (1601–67)

The Crucified

Crucifixion

Der Gekreuzigte

Cristo crucificado

O Crucificado

De gekruisigde

c. 1636–38, Oil on canvas/Huile
sur toile, 265 × 173 cm

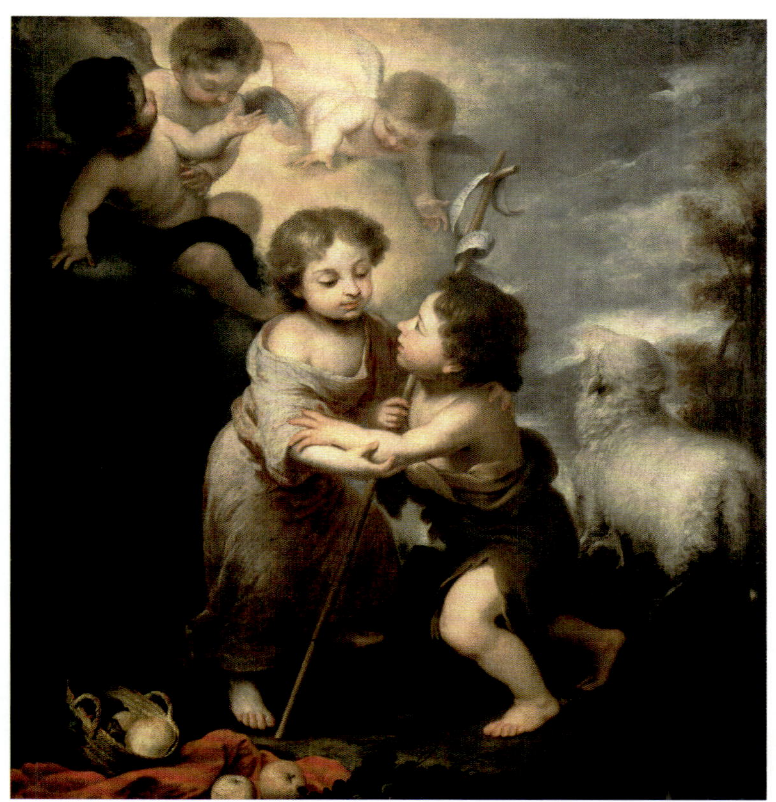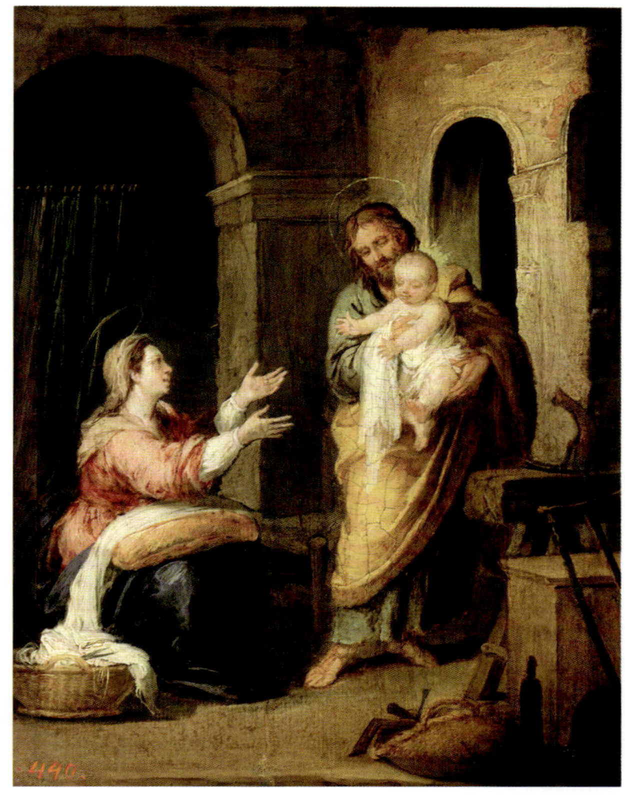

Bartolomé Esteban Murillo (1618–82)

The Christ Child and Saint John the Baptist

L'Enfant Jésus et le petit saint Jean

Das Christuskind und Johannes der Täufer

El niño Jesús y San Juan Bautista

Cristo e João Batista

Het Christuskind en Johannes de Doper

c. 1650, Oil on canvas/Huile sur toile, 124 × 115 cm

Bartolomé Esteban Murillo (1618–82)

The Holy Family

La Sainte famille

Die Heilige Familie

La Sagrada Familia

A Sagrada Família

De Heilige Familie

c. 1665, Oil on panel/Huile sur panneau, 24 × 18 cm

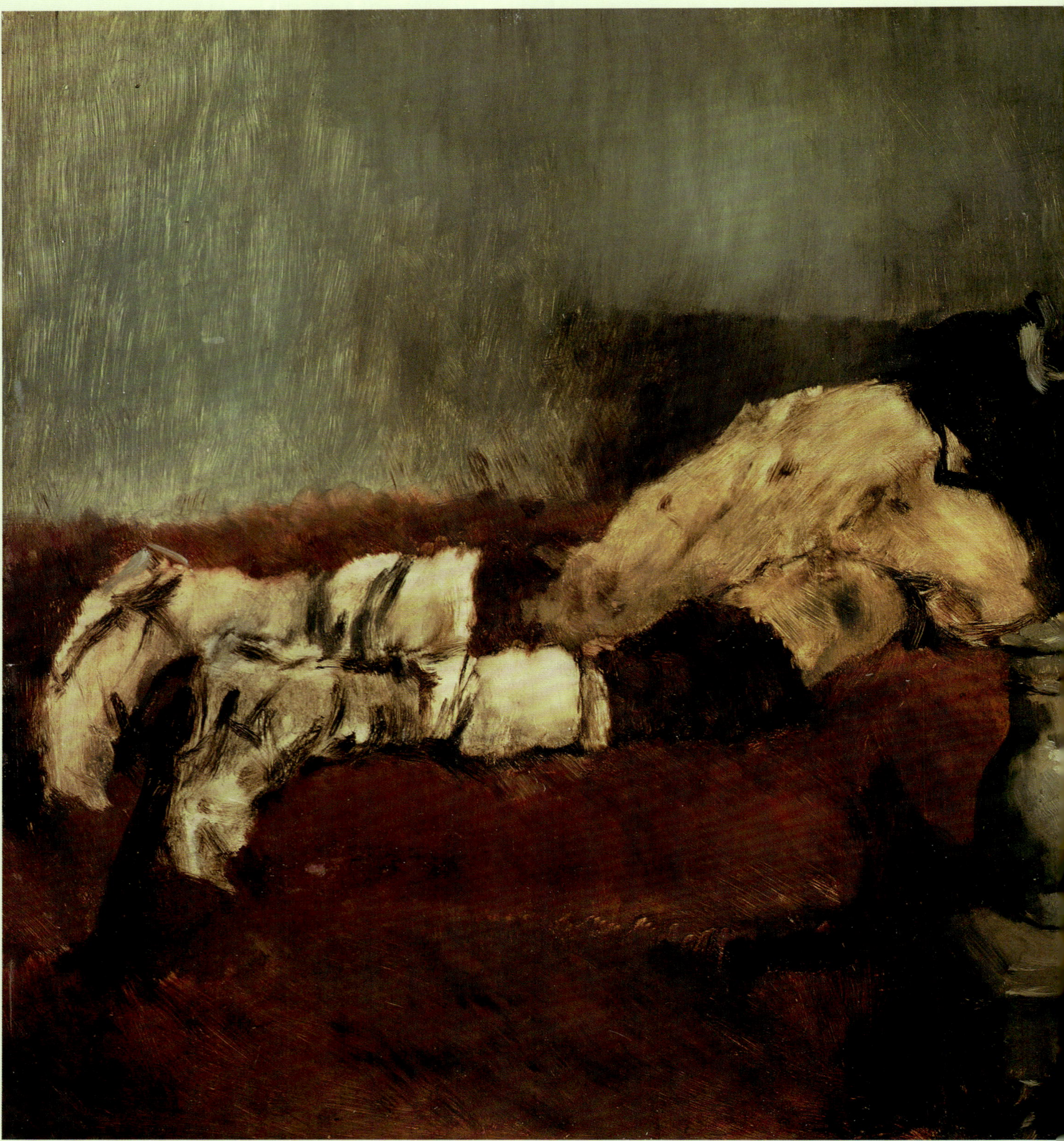

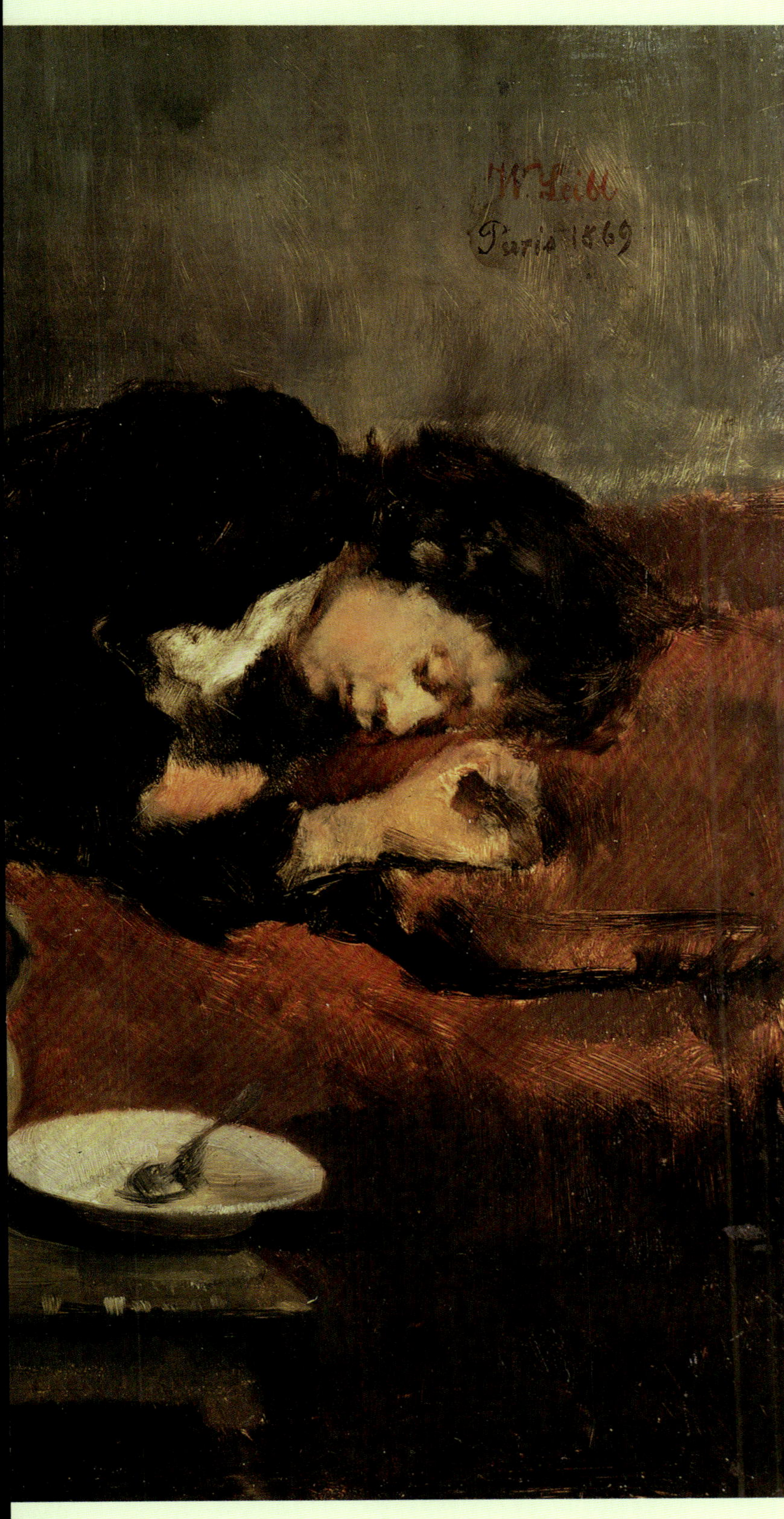

GERMAN PAINTING
LA PEINTURE ALLEMANDE
DEUTSCHE MALEREI
PINTURA ALEMANA
PINTURA ALEMÃ
DUITSE SCHILDERKUNST

Wilhelm Leibl (1844–1900)
Sleeping Farmboy
Jeune Savoyard dormant
Schlafender Bauernjunge
Joven campesino dormido
Jovem Camponês Dormindo
Slapende boerenjongen
1869, Oil on wood/Huile sur toile, 44 × 64 cm

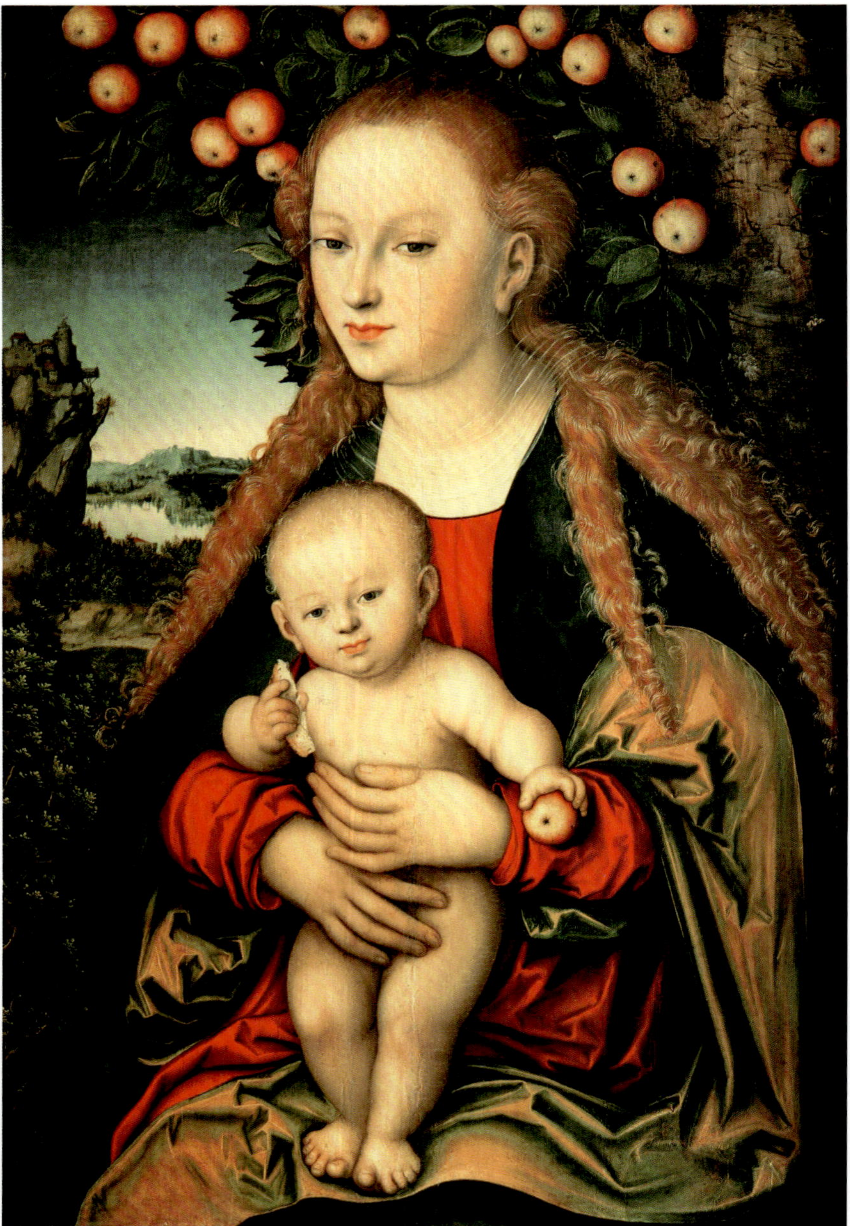

German Painting

Five works by Lucas Cranach the Older , including *Venus and Cupid,* as well as *Madonna and Child Under the Apple Tree,* are the stars of the German collection. A particular focus is on German painting of the 18th century. This is the second largest collection of this period outside Germany. Artists represented include Johann Friedrich Tischbein and Caspar David Friedrich.

La peinture allemande

Cinq tableaux de Lucas Cranach l'Ancien – dont *Vénus et Amour* et *La Vierge et l'Enfant sous le pommier* – forment la fierté de la collection de peinture allemande. La peinture des XVIIIe et XIXe siècles y est fortement représentée : il s'agit de la deuxième plus grande collection hors d'Allemagne. On y trouve aussi des tableaux de Johann Friedrich Tischbein et Caspar David Friedrich.

Deutsche Malerei

Fünf Werke von Lucas Cranach d. Ä., darunter *Venus und Amor* sowie *Madonna mit Kind unter dem Apfelbaum,* sind der Stolz der Sammlung deutscher Malerei. Einen Schwerpunkt bildet die Malerei des 18. Jahrhunderts; es handelt sich um die zweitgrößte Sammlung außerhalb Deutschlands. Hierunter befinden sich auch Werke von Johann Friedrich Tischbein und Caspar David Friedrich.

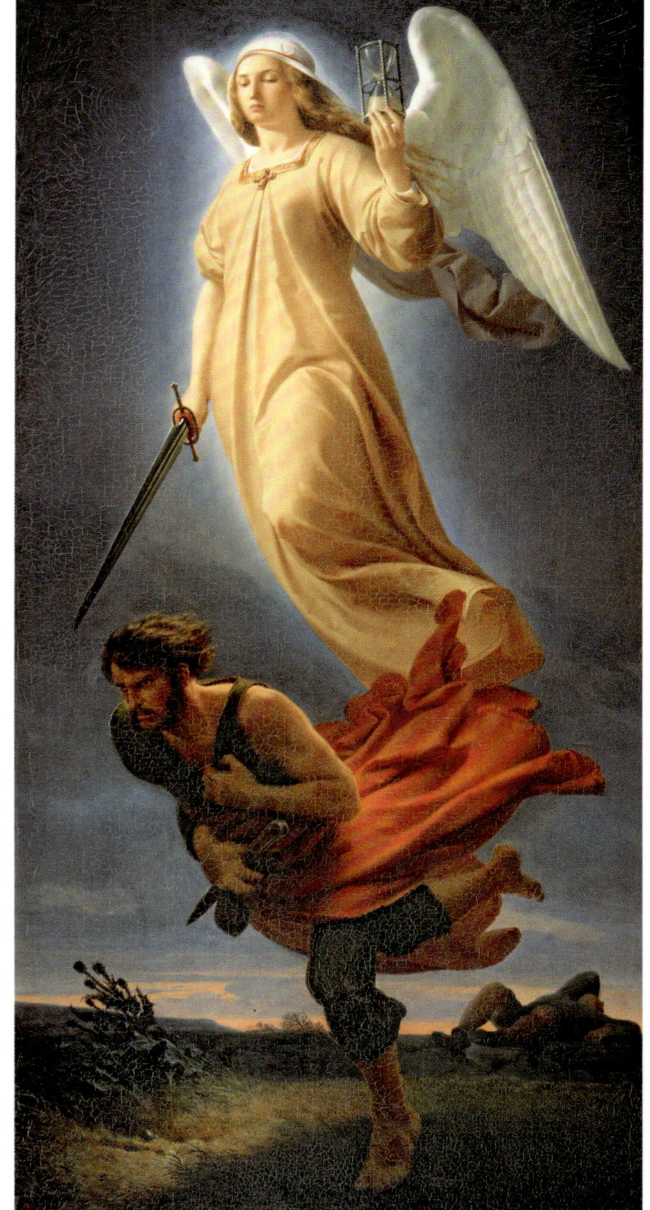

Pintura alemana

Cinco obras de Lucas Cranach el Viejo, incluyendo *Venus y Cupido* y *La Virgen y el Niño bajo un manzano,* son el orgullo de la colección de pintura alemana. Un punto clave fundamental de la pintura del siglo XVIII; se trata de la segunda mayor colección fuera de Alemania. Entre otras se encuentran obras de Johann Friedrich Tischbein y Caspar David Friedrich.

Pintura alemã

Cinco obras de Lucas Cranach, o Velho, entre as quais *Vénus e Amor,* bem como *A Virgem e o Menino sob uma Macieira,* são o orgulho da coleção de pintura alemã. Um ponto forte é formado pela pintura do século XVIII. Trata-se da segunda maior coleção que se situa fora da Alemanha. Entre as obras, encontram-se também pinturas de Johann Friedrich Tischbein e de Caspar David Friedrich.

Duitse schilderkunst

De trots van de collectie Duitse schilderkunst zijn de werken van Lucas Cranach de Oudere, waaronder *Venus en Cupido* en *Madonna met Kind onder de appelboom.* Een zwaartepunt vormt de schilderkunst van de achttiende eeuw – de op één na omvangrijkste collectie buiten Duitsland, met werken van Johann Friedrich Tischbein en Caspar David Friedrich.

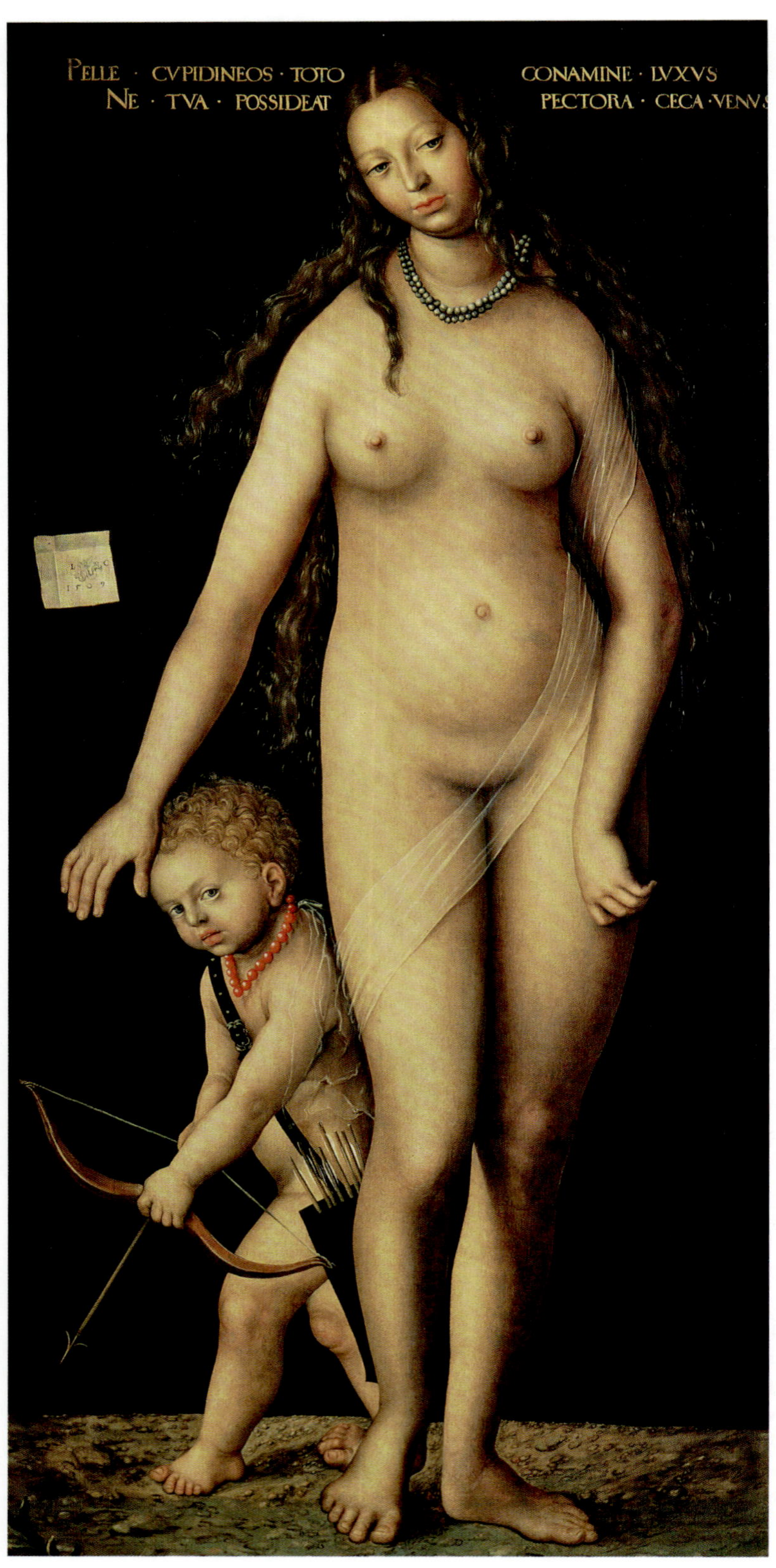

Lucas Cranach der Ältere/the Elder/l'ancien

Venus and Cupid

Vénus et Amour

Venus und Amor

Venus y Cupido

Vénus e Amor

Venus en Amor

1509, Oil on canvas/Huile sur toile, 213 × 102 cm

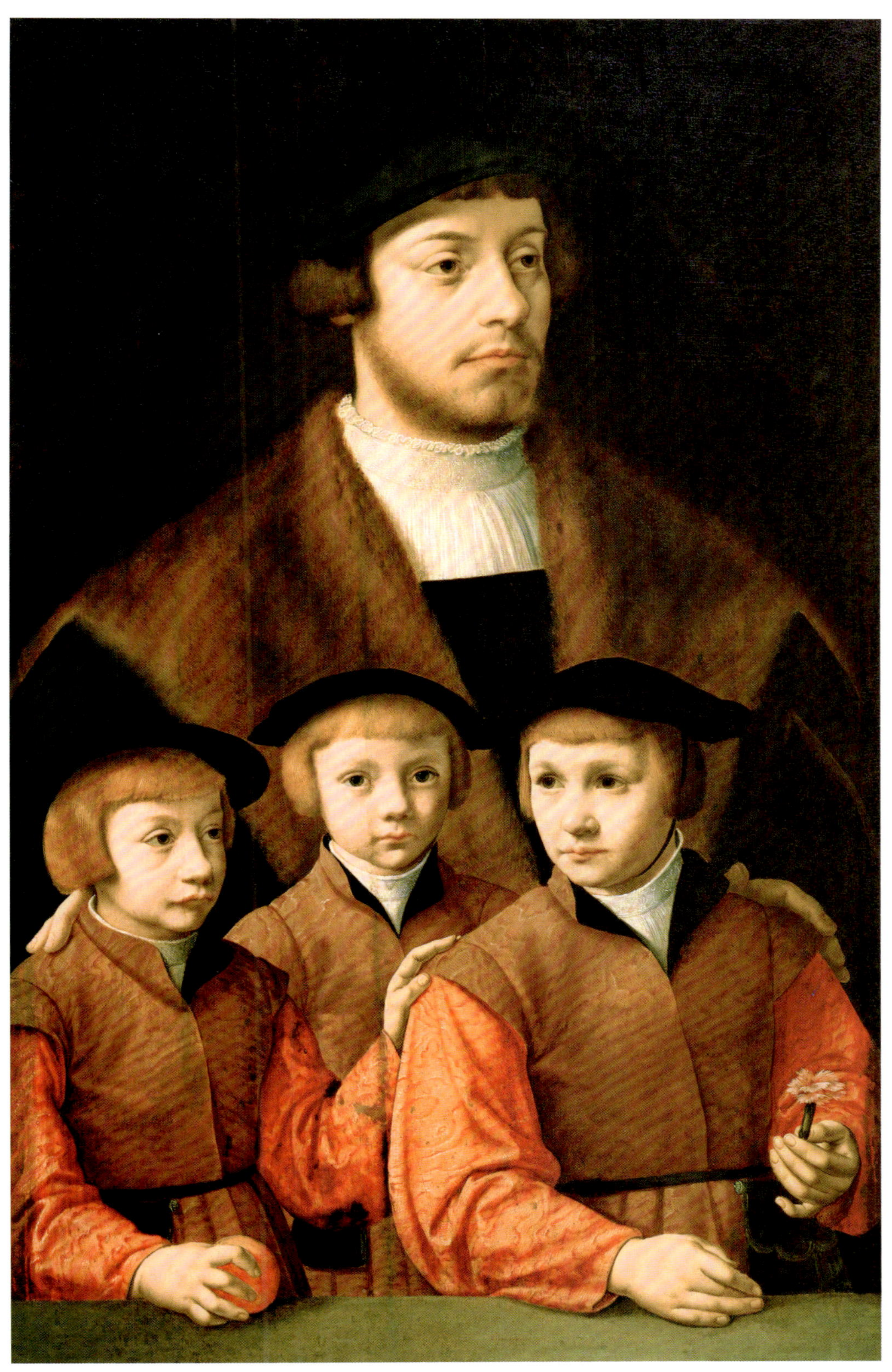

*Bartholomäus Bruyn der Ältere/the Elder/l'Ancien
(1493–1555)*
A Man with his Three Sons
Portrait d'un homme et ses trois fils
Ein Mann mit seinen drei Söhnen
Hombre con sus tres hijos
Um Homem com os Seus Três Filhos
Een man met zijn drie zonen
c. 1530–49, Oil on canvas/Huile sur toile, 75,5 × 46 cm

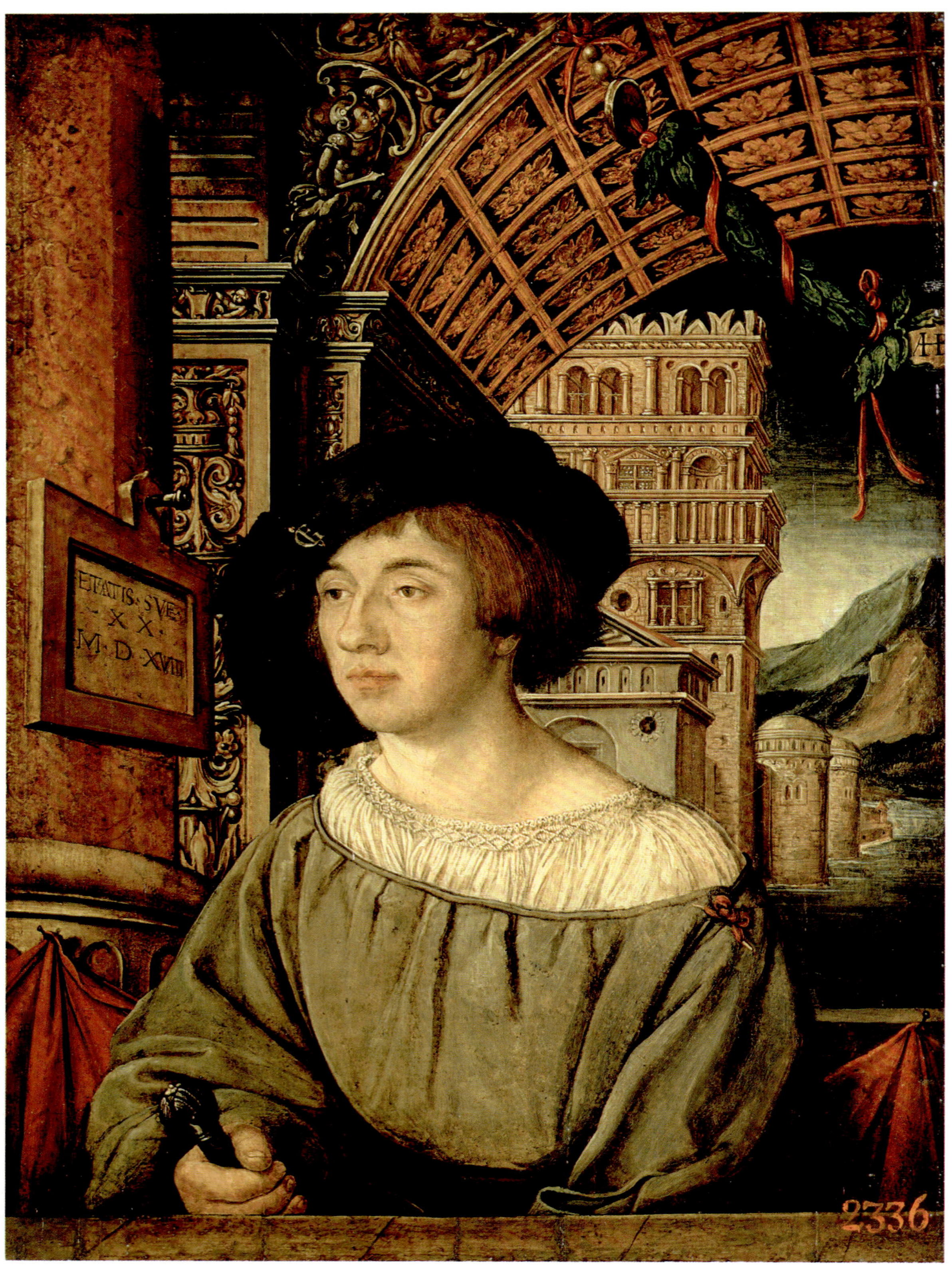

Ambrosius Holbein
(c. 1495–c. 1519)

Portrait of a Young Man

Portrait d'un jeune homme

Porträt eines
jungen Mannes

Retrato de un joven

Retrato de um
Jovem Homem

Portret van een jonge man

1518, Oil on wood/Huile
sur bois, 44 × 32,5 cm

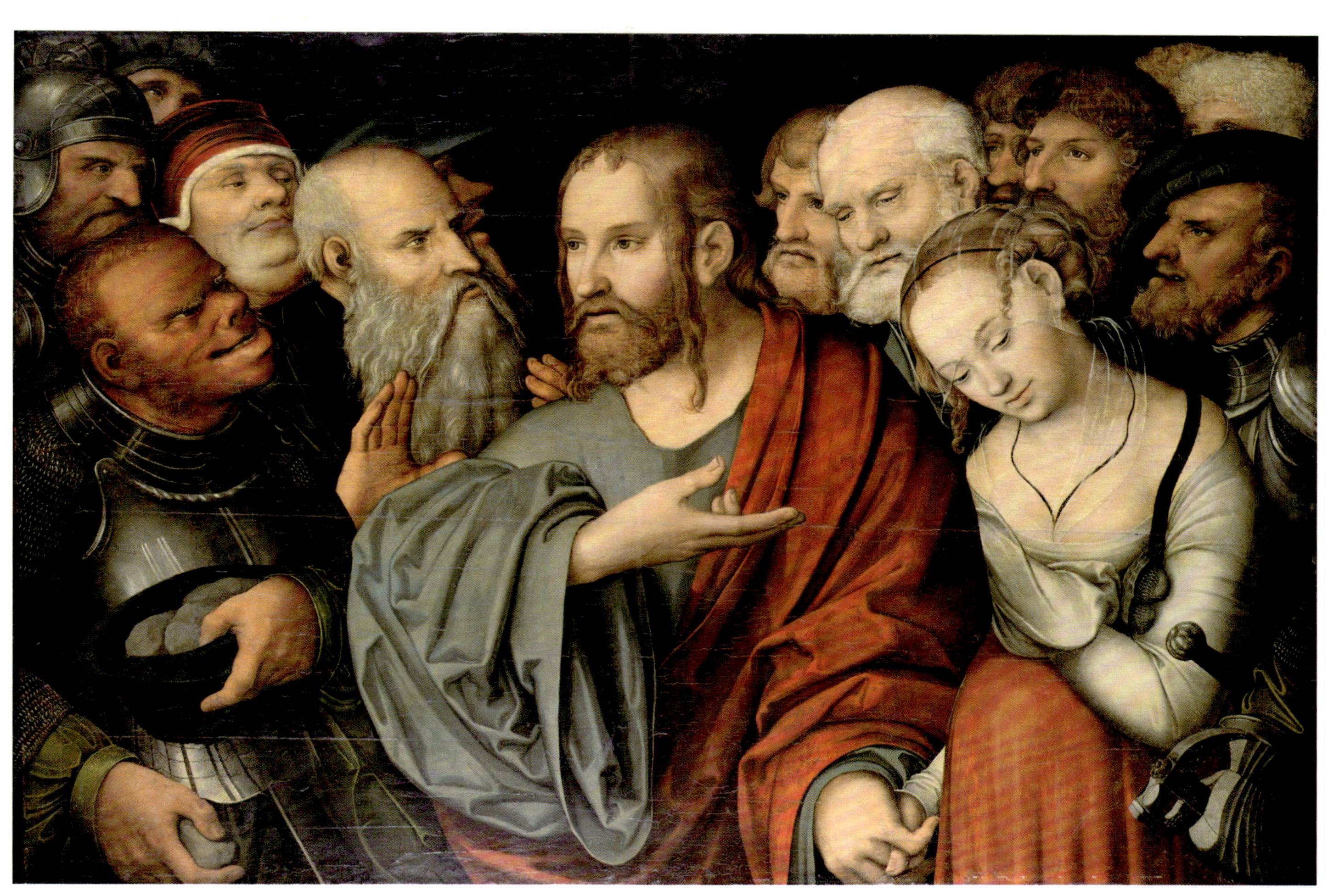

Lucas Cranach der Jüngere/the Younger/le Jeune (1515–86)

Christ and the Adulterous Woman

Le Christ et la femme adultère

Christus und die Ehebrecherin

Cristo y la adúltera

Cristo e a Adúltera

Christus en de overspelige vrouw

c. 1532, Oil on wood/Huile sur bois, 84 × 123 cm

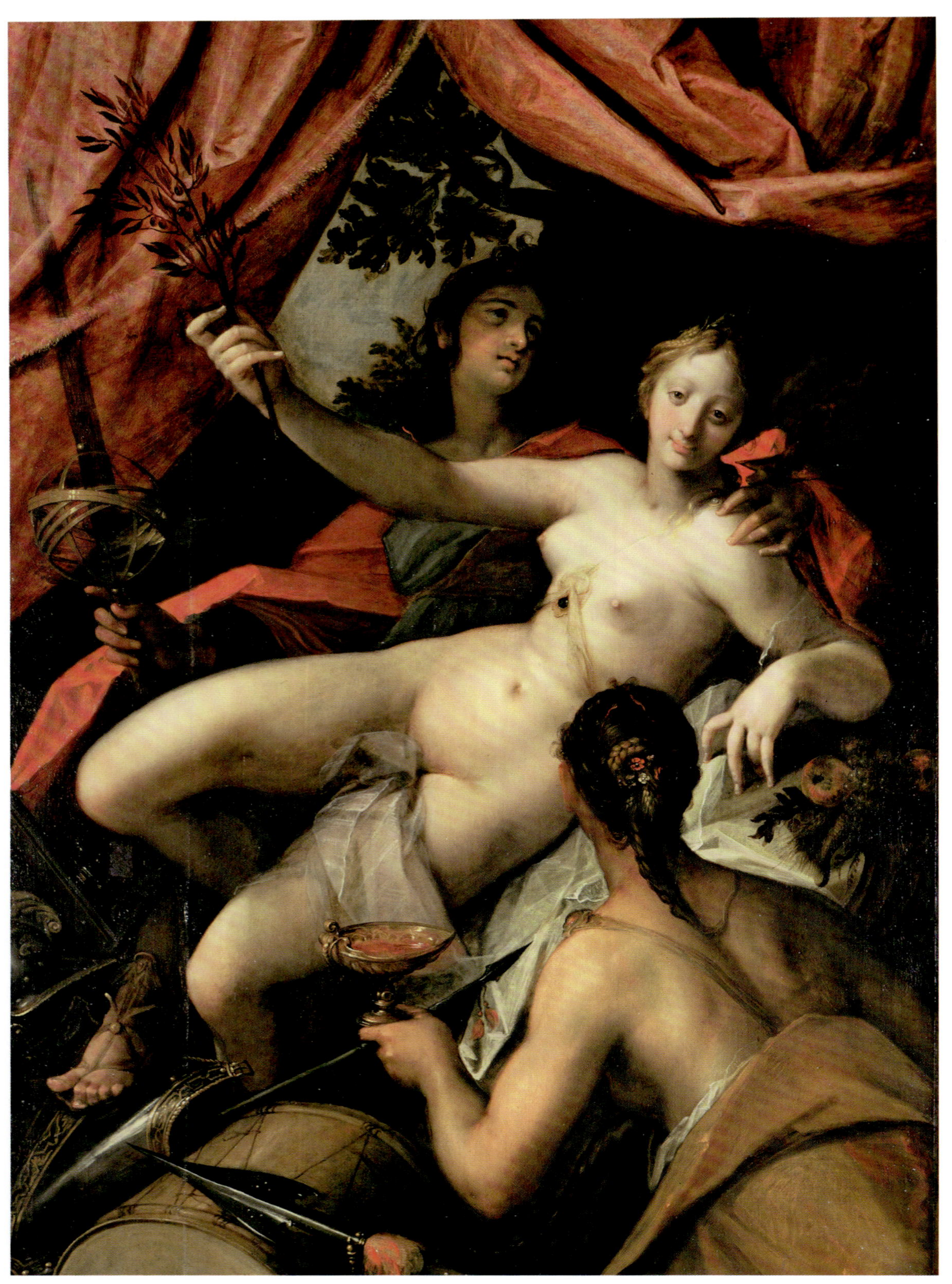

Hans von Aachen (1552–1616)

Allegory of Peace, Art,
and Prosperity

Allégorie de la Paix, de
l'Art et de l'Abondance

Allegorie der Friedens, der
Kunst und des Wohlstands

Alegoría de la Paz, el
Arte y el Bienestar

Alegoria da Paz, da Arte
e da Abundância

Allegorie van de Vrede, de
Kunst en de Welvaart

1602, Oil on wood/Huile
sur bois, 197 × 142 cm

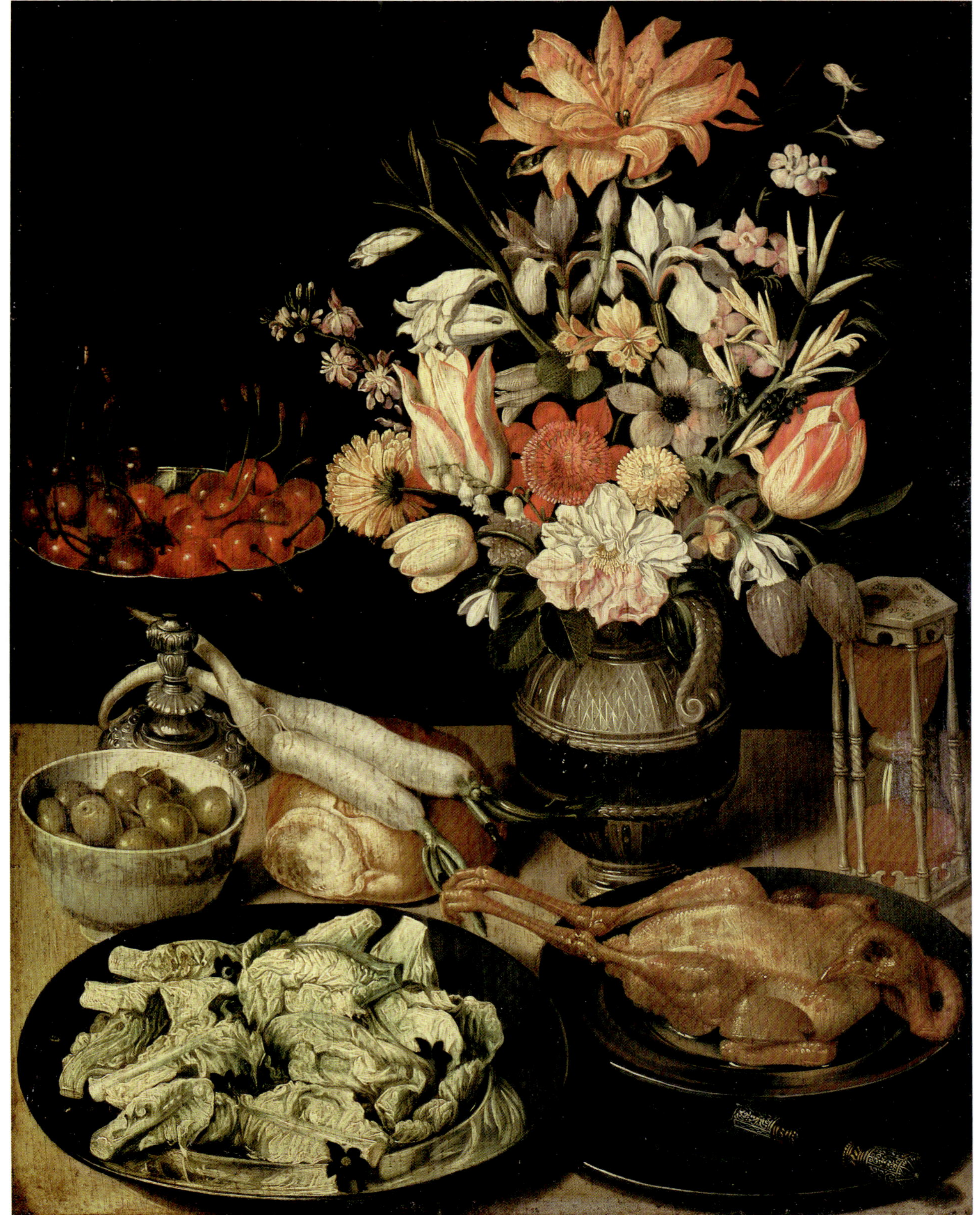

Georg Flegel
(1566–1638)

Still Life with
Flowers

Nature morte avec
fleurs et collation

Stillleben mit
Blumen

Bodegón con flores

Natureza-Morta
com Flores

Stilleven met
bloemen

1630–35, Oil on
wood/Huile sur
bois, 52,5 × 41 cm

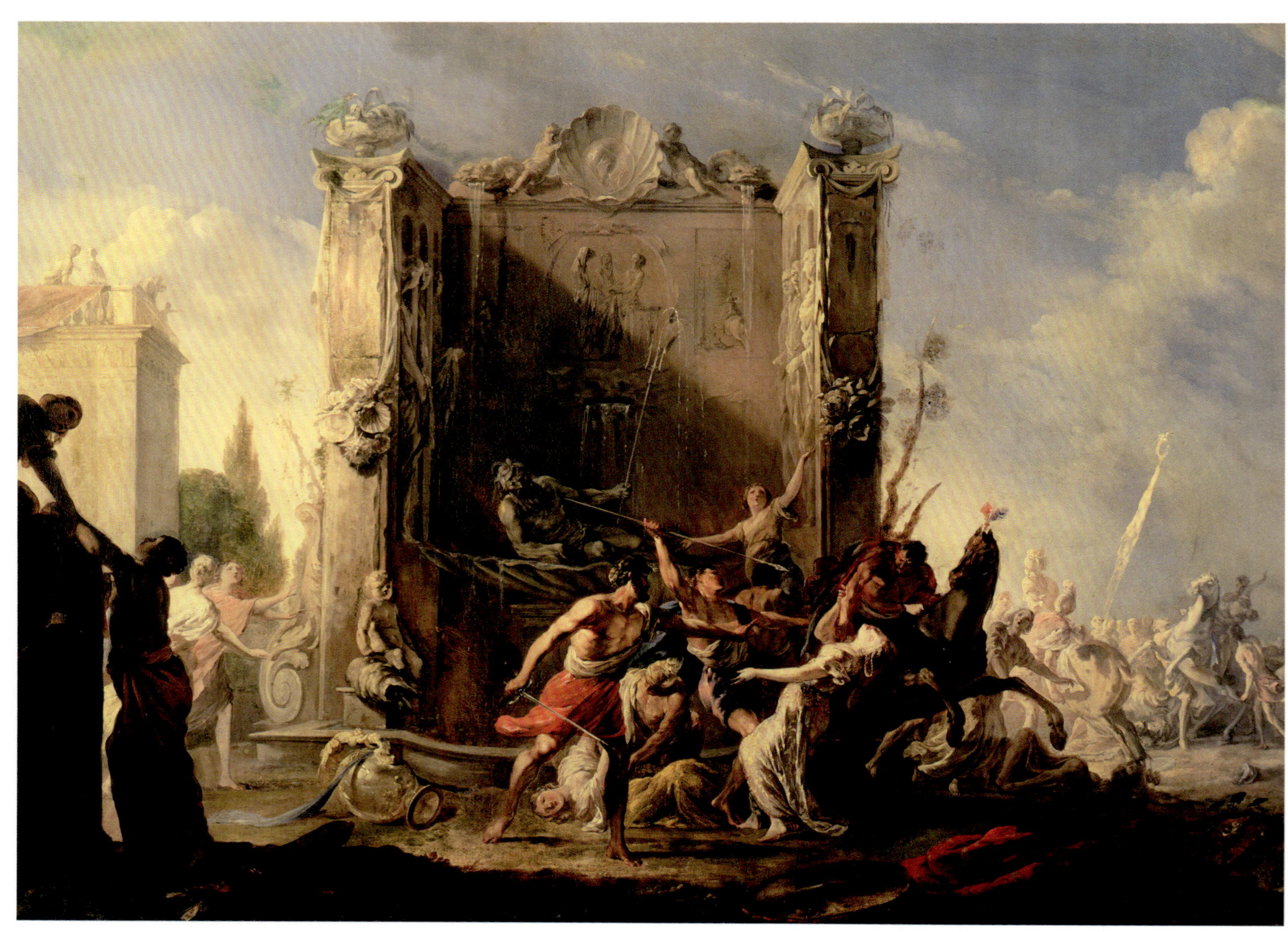

Johann Heinrich Schönfeld (1609–c. 1684)

The Rape of the Sabines

L'Enlèvement des Sabines

Der Raub der Sabinerinnen

El rapto de las Sabinas

O Rapto das Sabinas

De roof van de Sabijnse maagden

1631–50, Oil on canvas/Huile sur toile, 98,5 × 134 cm

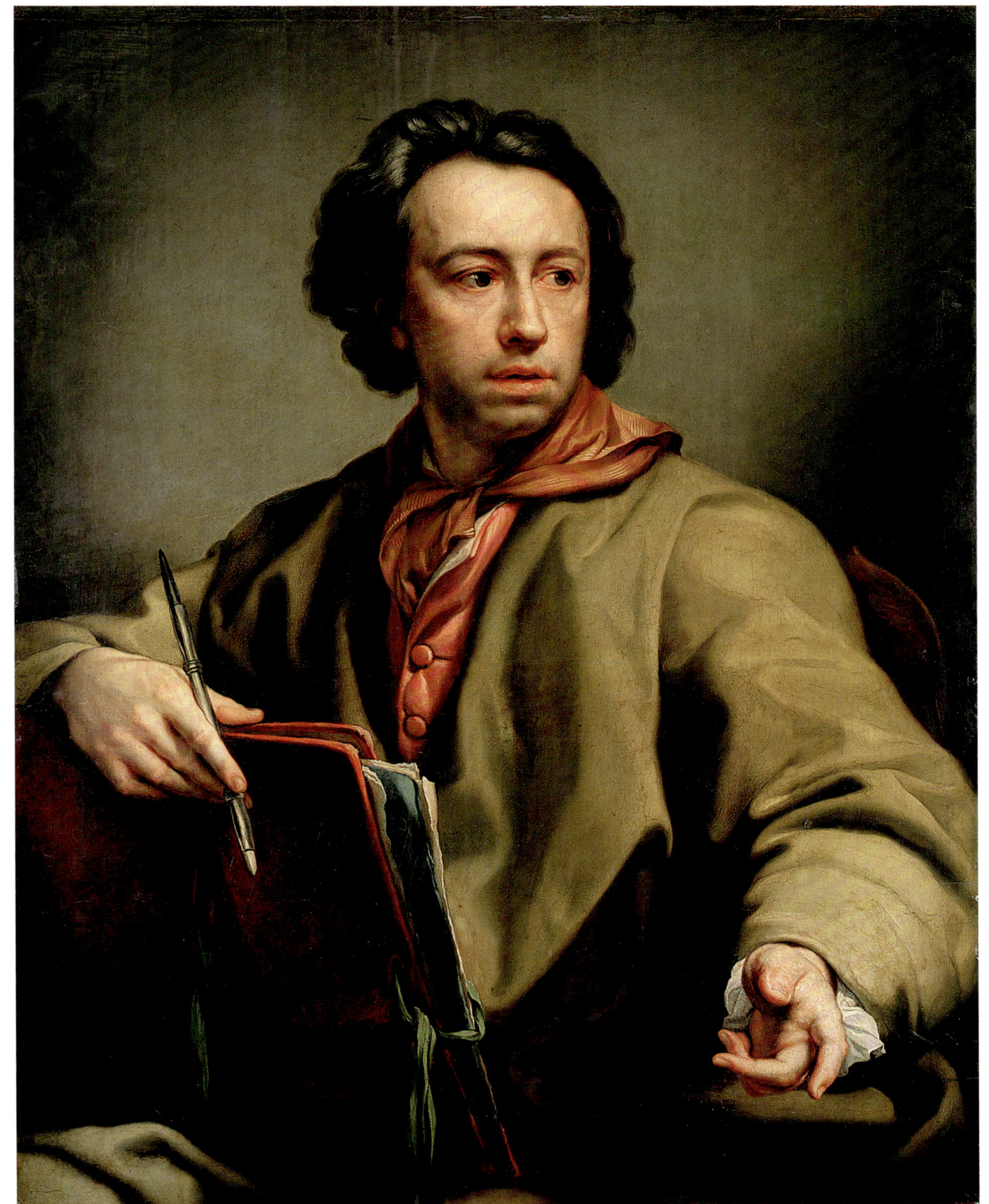

Anton Raphael
Mengs (1728–79)

Self-Portrait

Autoportrait

Selbstporträt

Autorretrato

Autorretrato

Zelfportret

c. 1775, Oil on
wood/Huile sur
bois, 102 × 77 cm

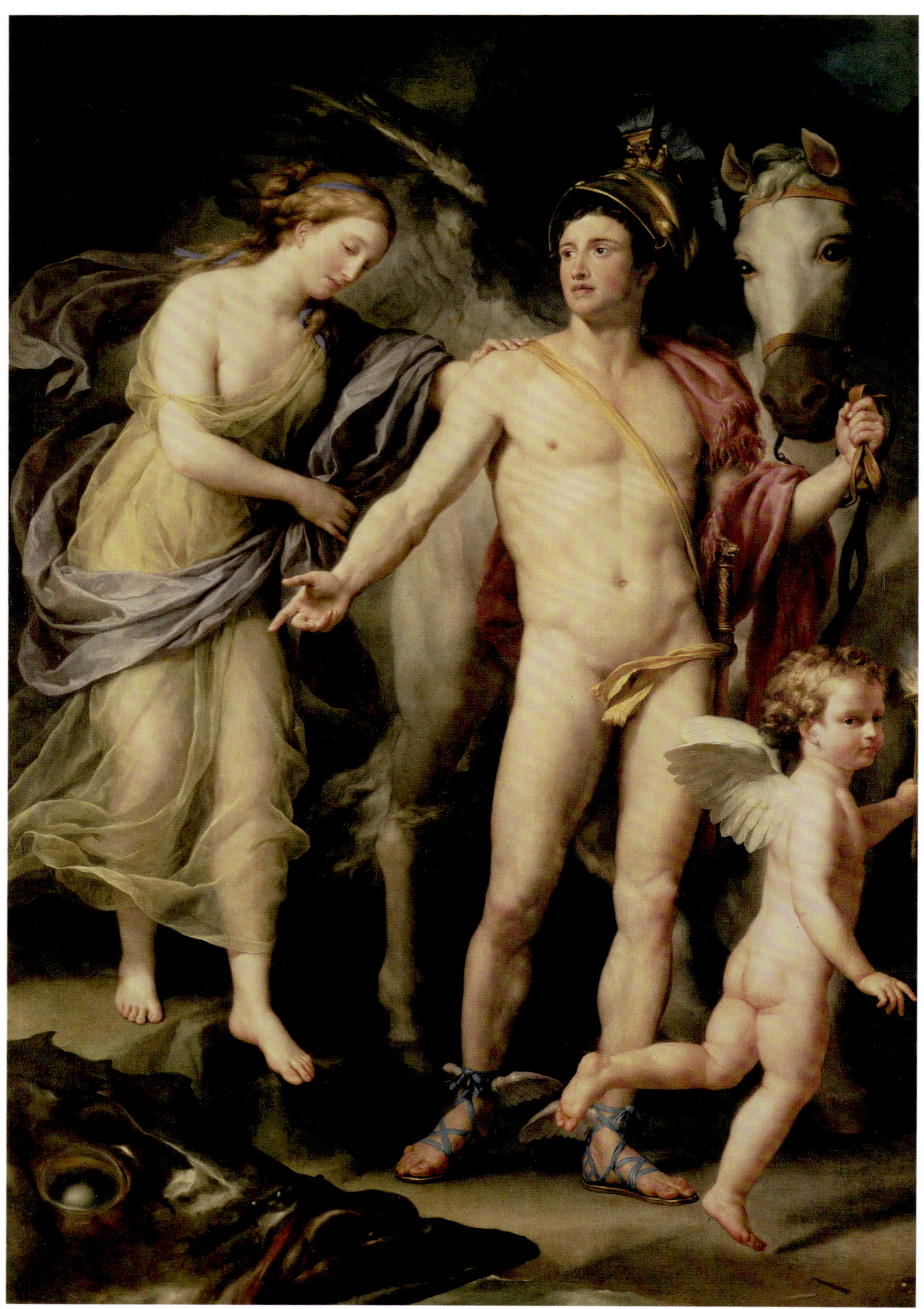

Anton Raphael Mengs (1728–79)
Perseus and Andromeda
Persée et Andromède
Perseus und Andromeda
Perseo y Andrómeda
Perseu e Andrómeda
Perseus en Andromeda

1778, Oil on canvas/Huile sur toile, 227 × 153,5 cm

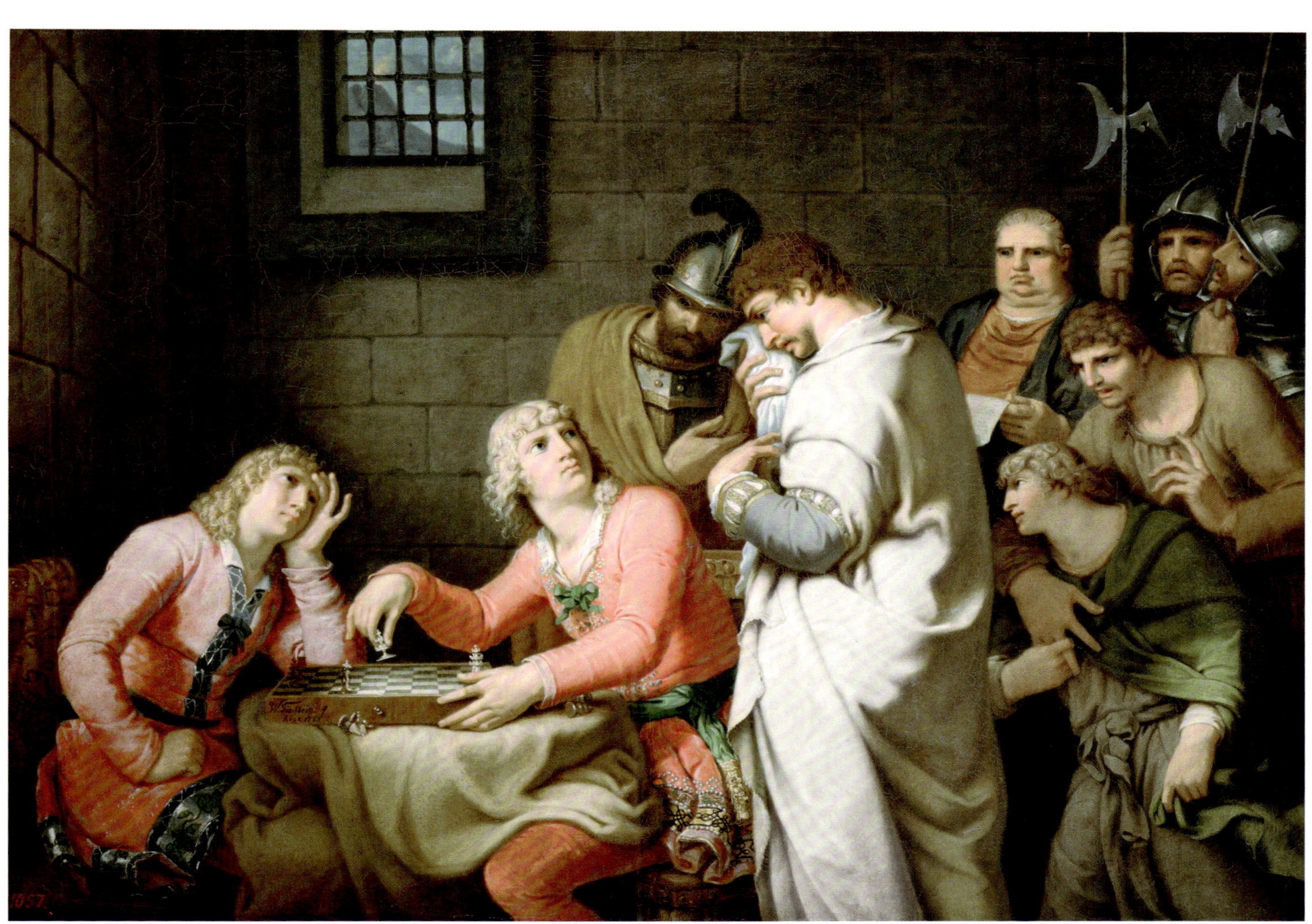

Johann Heinrich Wilhelm Tischbein (1751–1829)

Conradin of Swabia and Friedrich of Baden Awaiting their Verdict

Conradin de Souabe et Frédéric d'Autriche jouant aux échecs en attendant la sentence de mort

Konradin von Schwaben und Friedrich von Baden erwarten ihr Urteil

Conradino de Suabia y Federico I de Baden-Baden aguardan su sentencia

Conradin da Suábia e Frederick de Baden Esperam a Sentença

Konradin von Schwaben en Friedrich von Baden wachten op hun veroordeling

1785, Oil on canvas/Huile sur toile, 65,5 × 91,5 cm

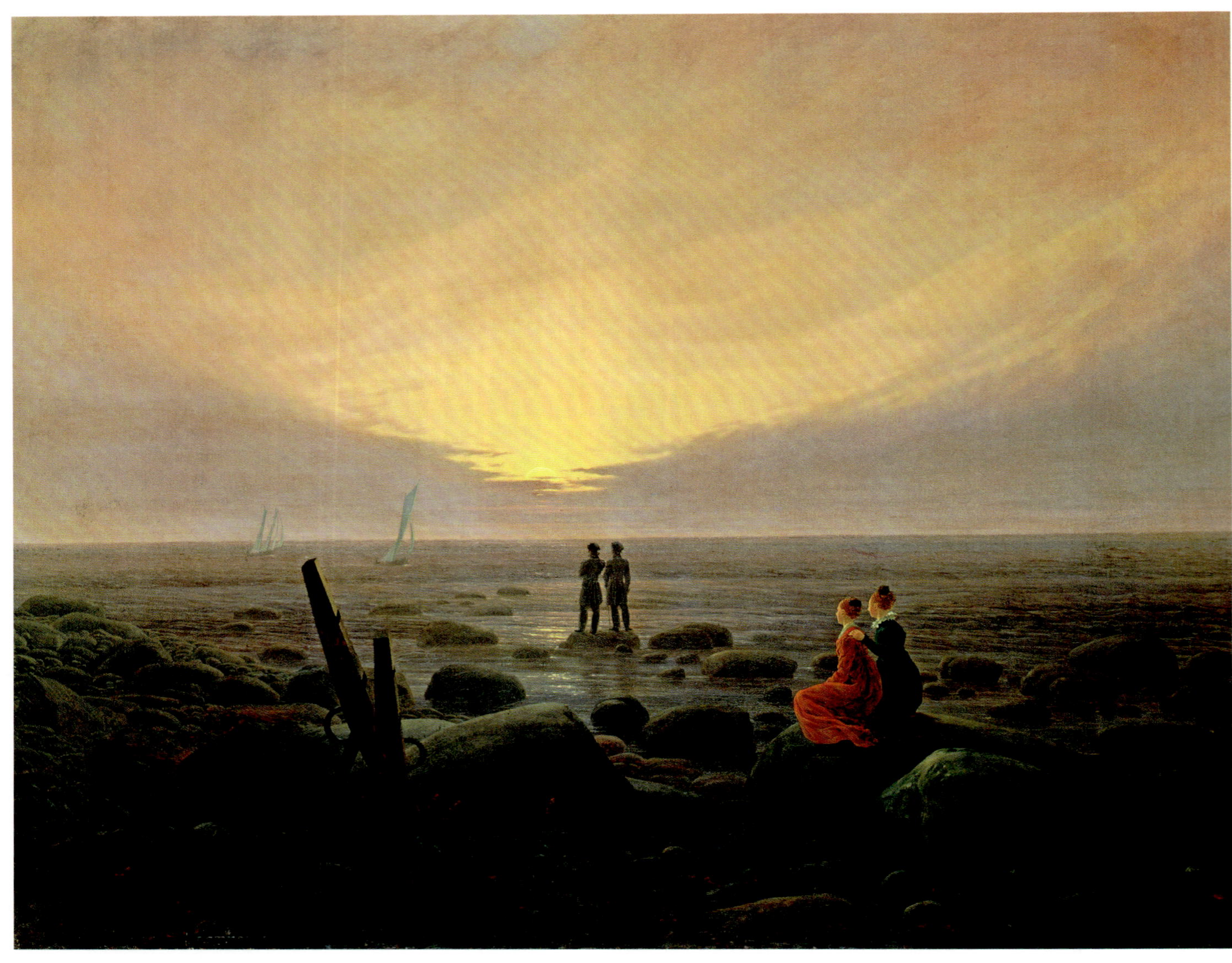

Caspar David Friedrich (1774–1840)

Moonrise by the Sea

Lever de lune sur la mer

Mondaufgang am Meer

Salida de la luna en el mar

Lua Nascente no Mar

Maanopgang boven zee

1821, Oil on canvas/Huile sur toile, 135 × 170 cm

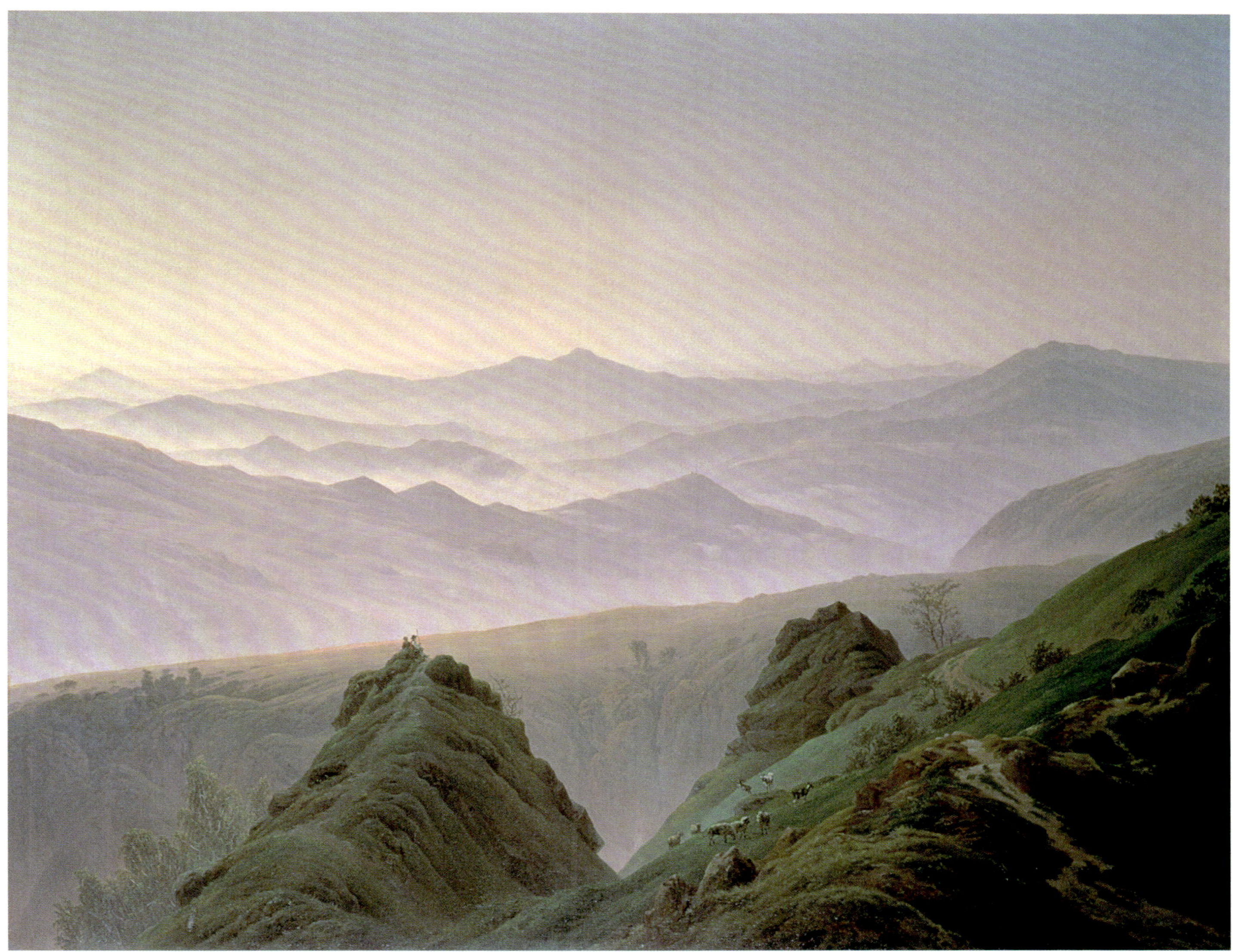

Caspar David Friedrich (1774–1840)

The Morning in the Mountains

Matin dans les montagnes

Der Morgen im Gebirge

Mañana en las montañas

A Manhã na Montanha

Ochtend in het gebergte

c. 1832, Oil on canvas/Huile sur toile, 135 × 170 cm

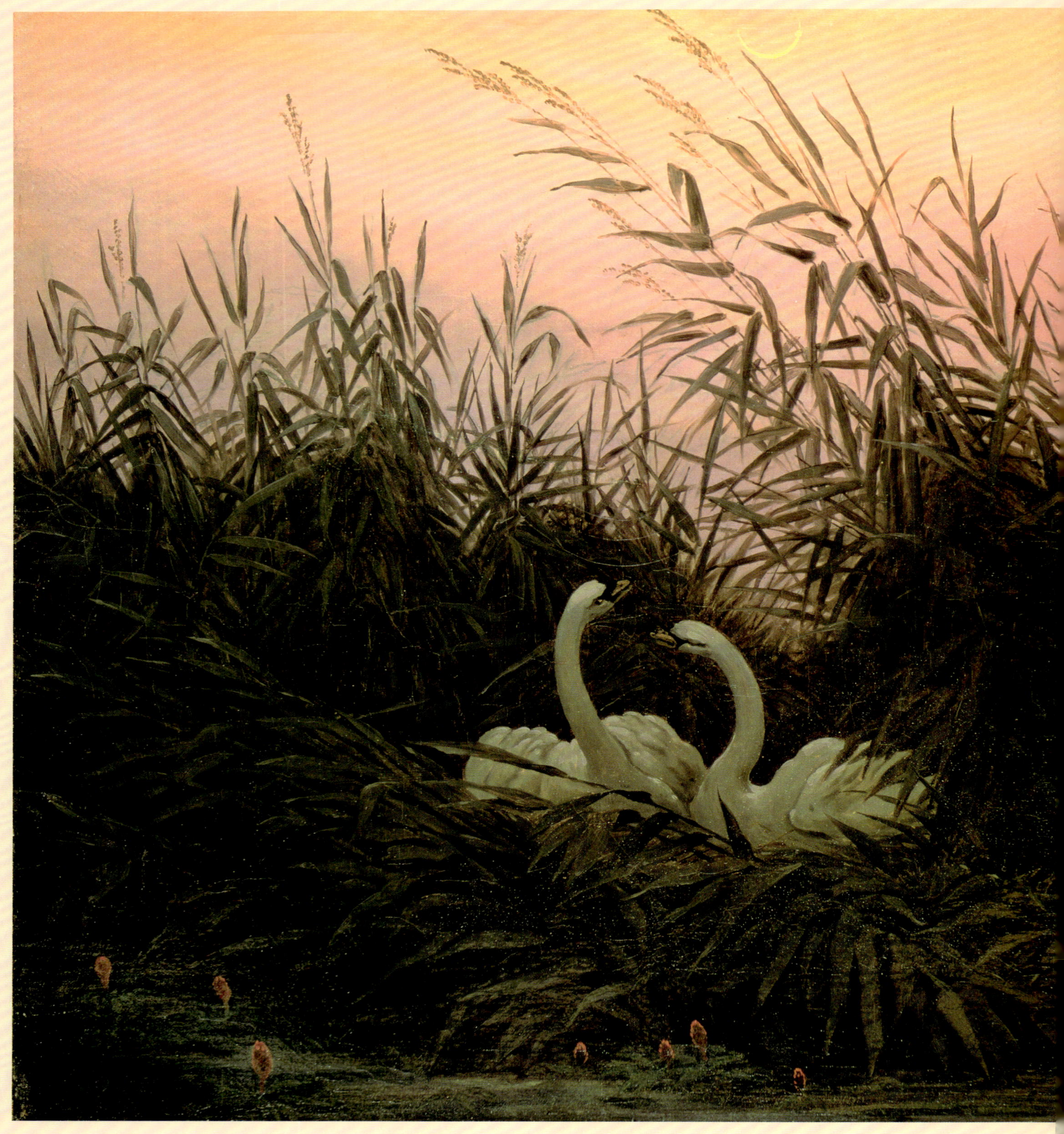

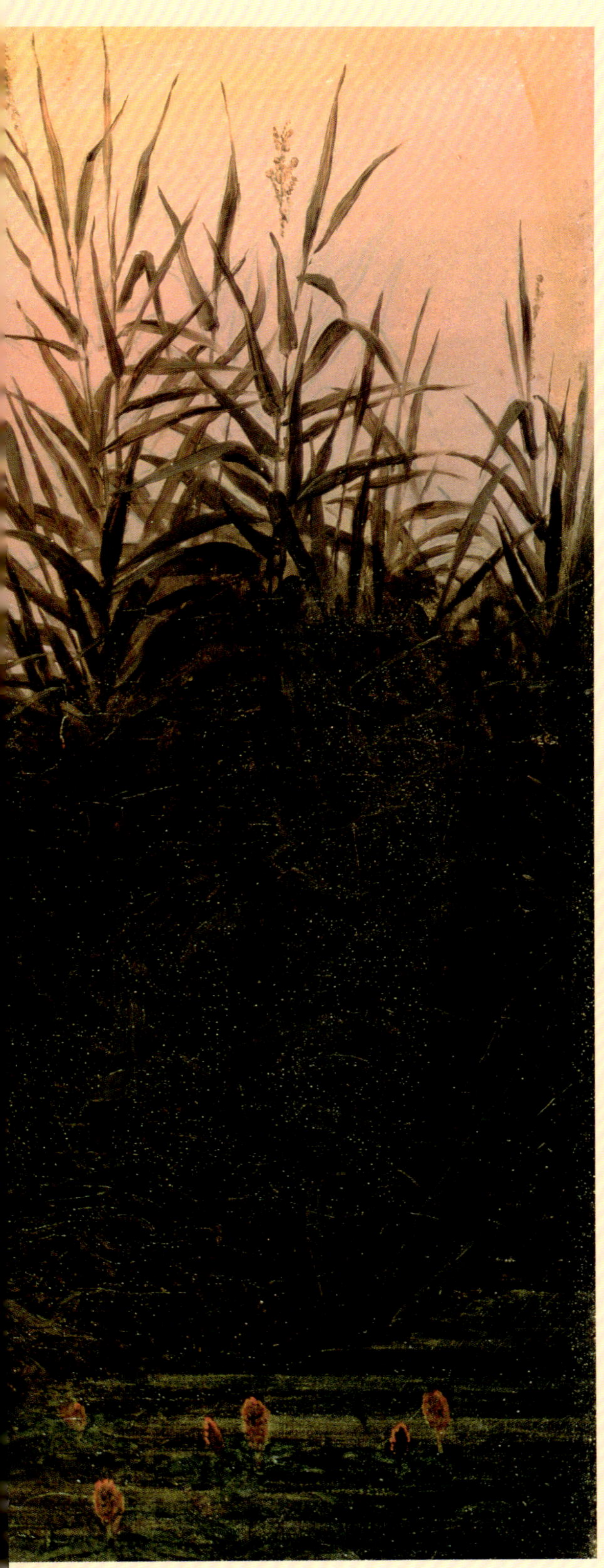

Caspar David Friedrich (1774–1840)

Swans in the Reeds at the First Dawn
Cygnes dans les roseaux à la première aube
Schwäne im Schilf beim ersten Morgenrot
Cisnes entre los juncos al amanecer
Cisnes entre Juncos na Alvorada
Zwanen tussen het riet
c. 1820–32, Oil on canvas/Huile sur toile, 33 × 44 cm

Caspar David Friedrich painted the motif of swans in the reeds several times. As with other works by the German painter, one can understand the image as a symbolic allegory of the afterlife. The swans symbolize this because of their reputation of singing most beautifully when dying, with the joyful expectation of death as the transition to eternal life. The evening star, which is also the morning star, can be seen at the top of the image, representing the connection between death and resurrection.

Caspar David Friedrich a maintes fois représenté le motif des cygnes dans les roseaux. Comme dans les autres tableaux du peintre romantique allemand, on peut comprendre cette œuvre comme une allégorie symbolique du passage dans l'au-delà. Les cygnes – dont les chants sont les plus beaux juste avant leur mort – symbolisent dans cette perspective l'attente sereine du trépas comme passage à la vie éternelle. Reconnaissable tout en haut du tableau, l'étoile du Soir est dans le même temps celle du Matin – ce qui exprime métaphoriquement l'union intime de la Mort et de la Résurrection.

Caspar David Friedrich hat das Motiv der Schwäne im Schilf mehrfach dargestellt. Wie bei anderen Bildern des deutschen Malers kann man das Bild als eine symbolische Allegorie des Jenseits verstehen. Die Schwäne versinnbildlichen wegen ihrer Eigenschaft, im Sterben am schönsten zu singen, die freudige Erwartung des Todes als Übergang zum ewigen Leben. So bezeichnet auch der – ganz oben im Bild zu erkennende – Abendstern, der zugleich der Morgenstern ist, die Verbindung von Tod und Auferstehung.

Caspar David Friedrich pintó en varias ocasiones el tema de los cisnes entre juncos. Como en otras imágenes del pintor alemán, podemos entender el cuadro como una alegoría simbólica del más allá. Los cisnes representan, dado el hecho de que su canto más bello ocurre al morir, la espera ferviente de la muerte como transición hacia la vida eterna. La estrella de la tarde, reconocible en la parte superior, es a la vez estrella de la mañana y marca la unión de la muerte y la resurrección.

Caspar David Friedrich representou várias vezes o motivo dos cisnes entre os juncos. Tal como noutras pinturas do pintor alemão, a obra pode ser entendida como uma alegoria simbólica do além. Dada a característica canção do cisne no momento da sua morte, os mesmos simbolizam a esperança alegre da morte como passagem para a vida eterna. Deste modo, a estrela da noite visível na parte superior da pintura, que é simultaneamente a estrela da manhã, corresponde à ligação entre a morte e a ressurreição.

Caspar David Friedrich heeft vaker zwanen tussen het riet geschilderd. Net als bij andere schilderijen van de Duitse schilder kan het werk als een symbolische voorstelling van de andere wereld worden opgevat. Omdat van zwanen wordt gezegd dat ze zingend hun dood tegemoet gaat, symboliseren ze de blijde verwachting van de dood als overgang naar het eeuwige leven. Zo betekent ook de – langs de bovenrand van het schilderij te ontwaren – avondster, die ook morgenster is, de verbinding tussen dood en opstanding.

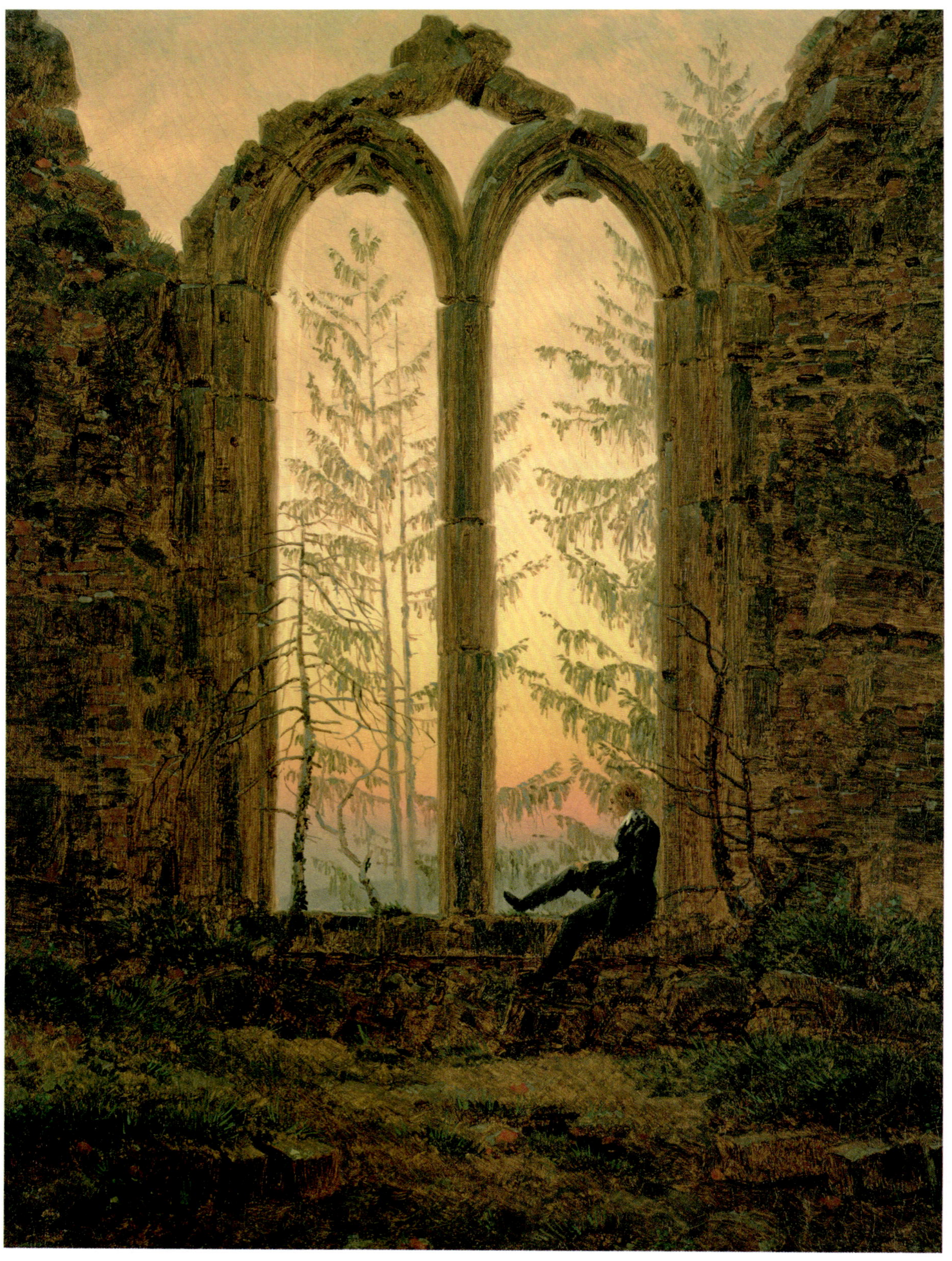

Caspar David Friedrich
(1774–1840)

Ruins of Oybin Monastery
(The Dreamer)

Le Rêveur

Klosterruine Oybin
(Der Träumer)

Claustro en ruinas en
Oybin (el soñador)

Ruina do Convento
Oybin (O Sonhador)

Kloosterruïne Oybin
(De Dromer)

c. 1835, Oil on canvas/
Huile sur toile, 27 × 21 cm

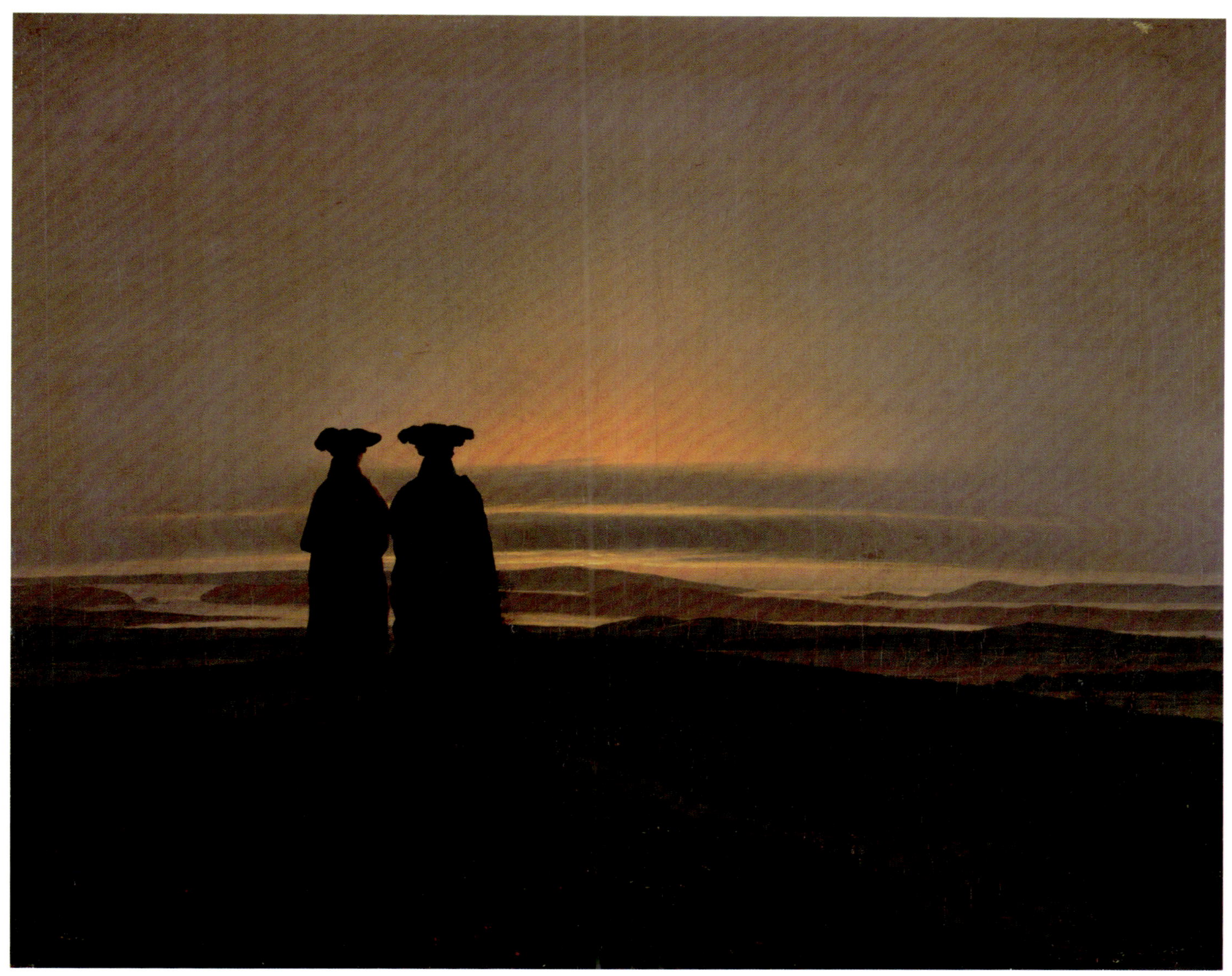

Caspar David Friedrich (1774–1840)

Evening Landscape with Two Men

Paysage du soir avec deux hommes

Abendlandschaft mit zwei Männern

Paisaje nocturno con dos hombres

Paisagem Noturna com Dois Homens

Avondlandschap met twee mannen

c. 1830–35, Oil on canvas/Huile sur toile, 25 × 31 cm

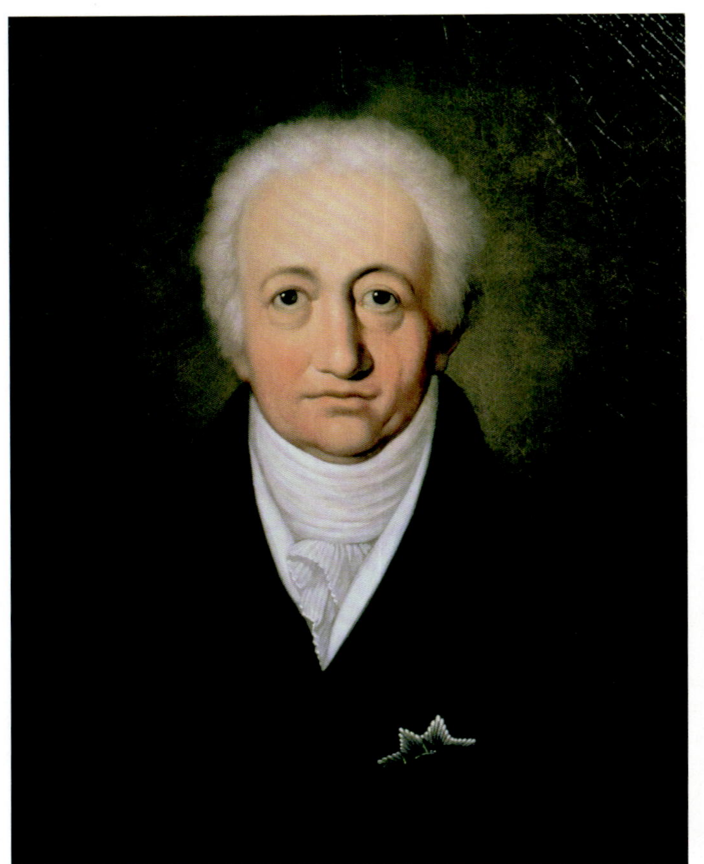

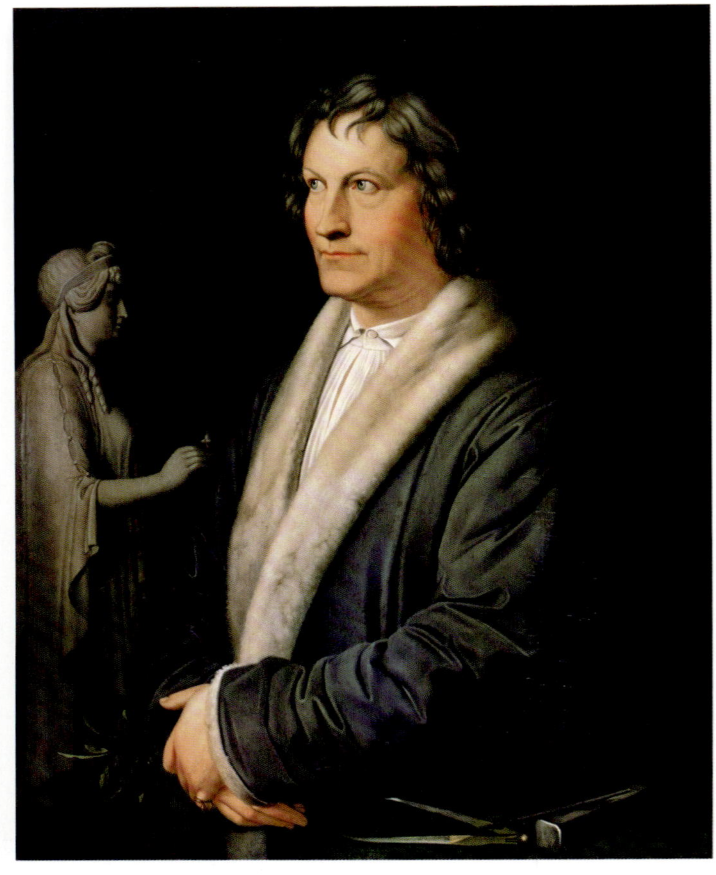

Johann Wolfgang von Goethe

1818, Oil on canvas/Huile sur toile, 73 × 57 cm

The Sculptor Berthel Thorvaldsen

Portrait du sculpteur Bertel Thorvaldsen

Der Bildhauer Berthel Thorvaldsen

El escultor Berthel Thorvaldsen

O Escultor Berthel Thorvaldsen

Beeldhouwer Berthel Thorvaldsen

c. 1820, Oil on canvas/Huile sur toile, 47 × 37 cm

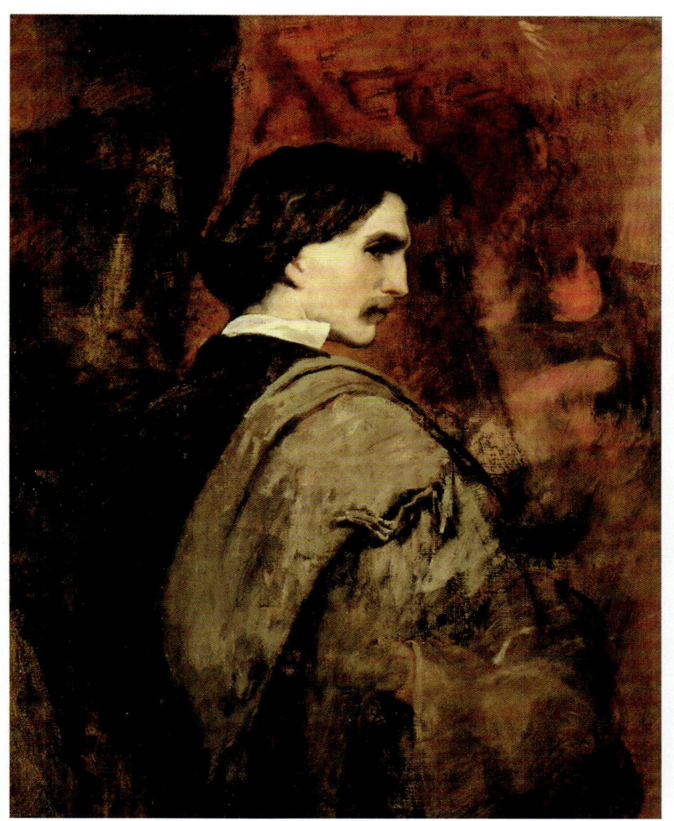

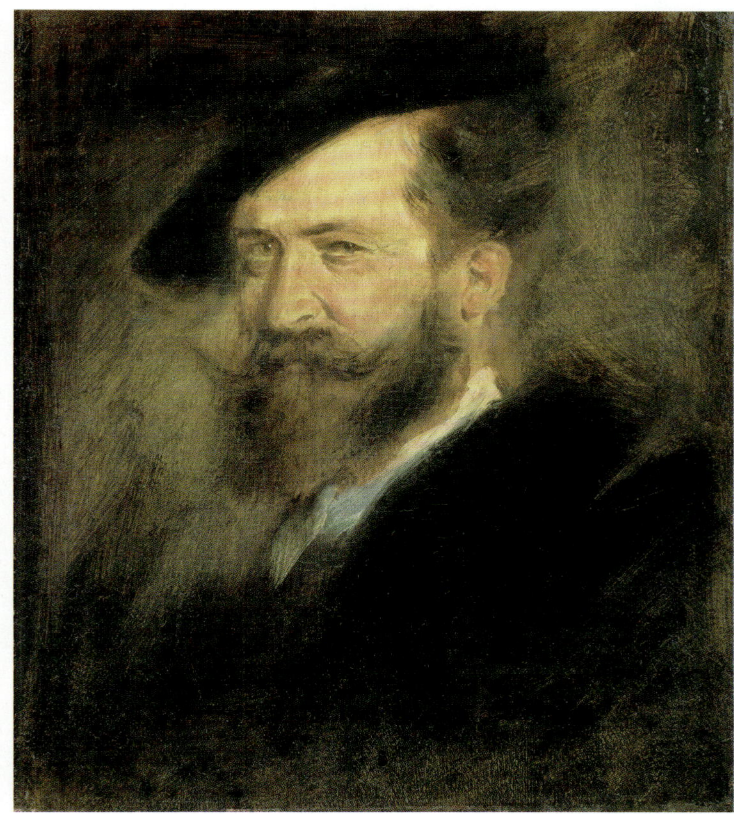

Anselm Feuerbach (1829–80)

Self-Portrait

Autoportrait

Selbstbildnis

Autorretrato

Autorretrato

Zelfportret

c. 1854–58, Oil on canvas/Huile sur toile, 92 × 73 cm

Franz Lenbach (1836–1904)

The Artist Wilhelm Busch

L'artiste Wilhelm Busch

Der Künstler Wilhelm Busch

El artista Wilhelm Busch

O Artista Wilhelm Busch

Kunstenaar Wilhelm Busch

c. 1878, Oil on canvas/Huile sur carton, 54 × 47,5 cm

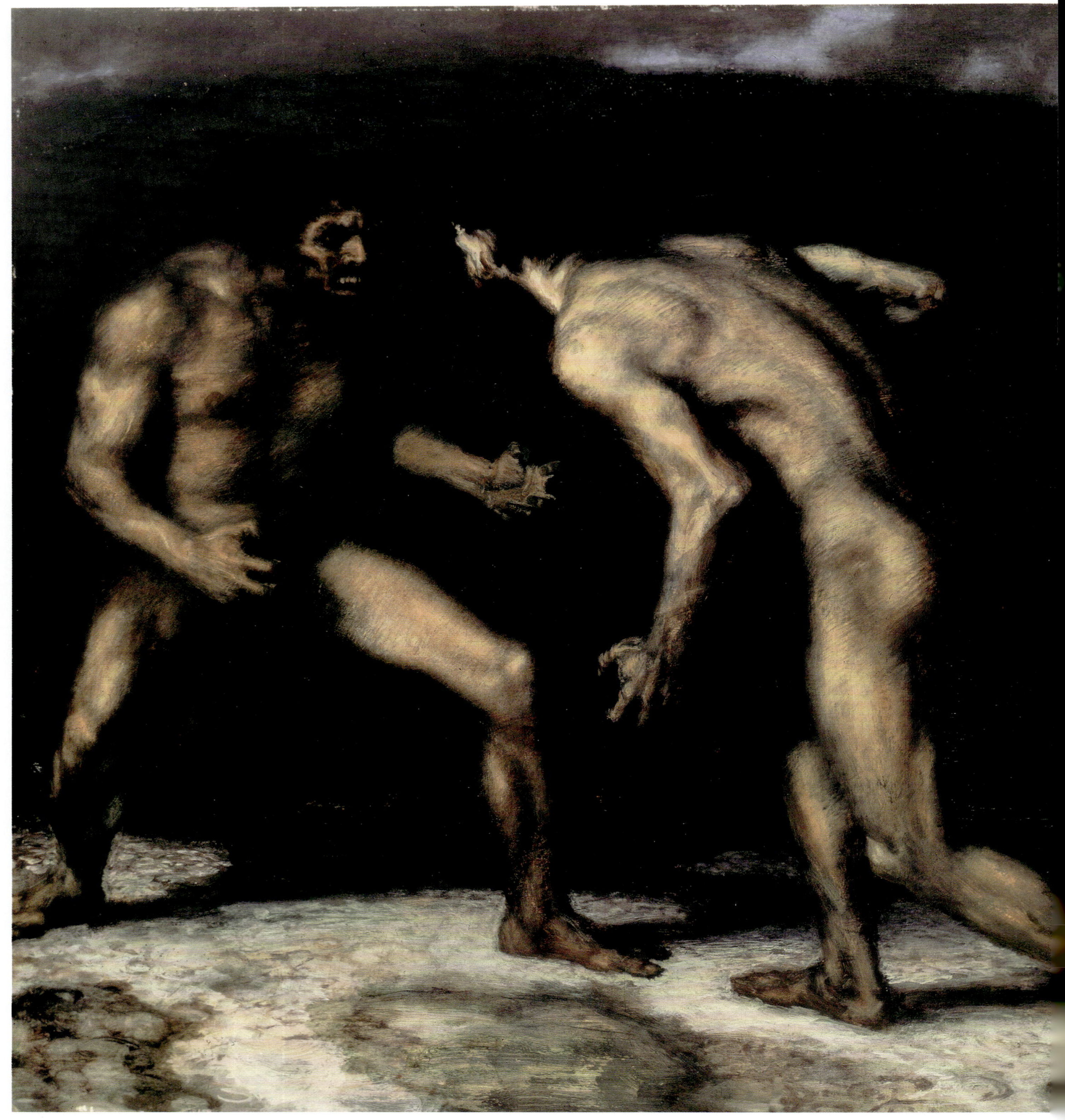

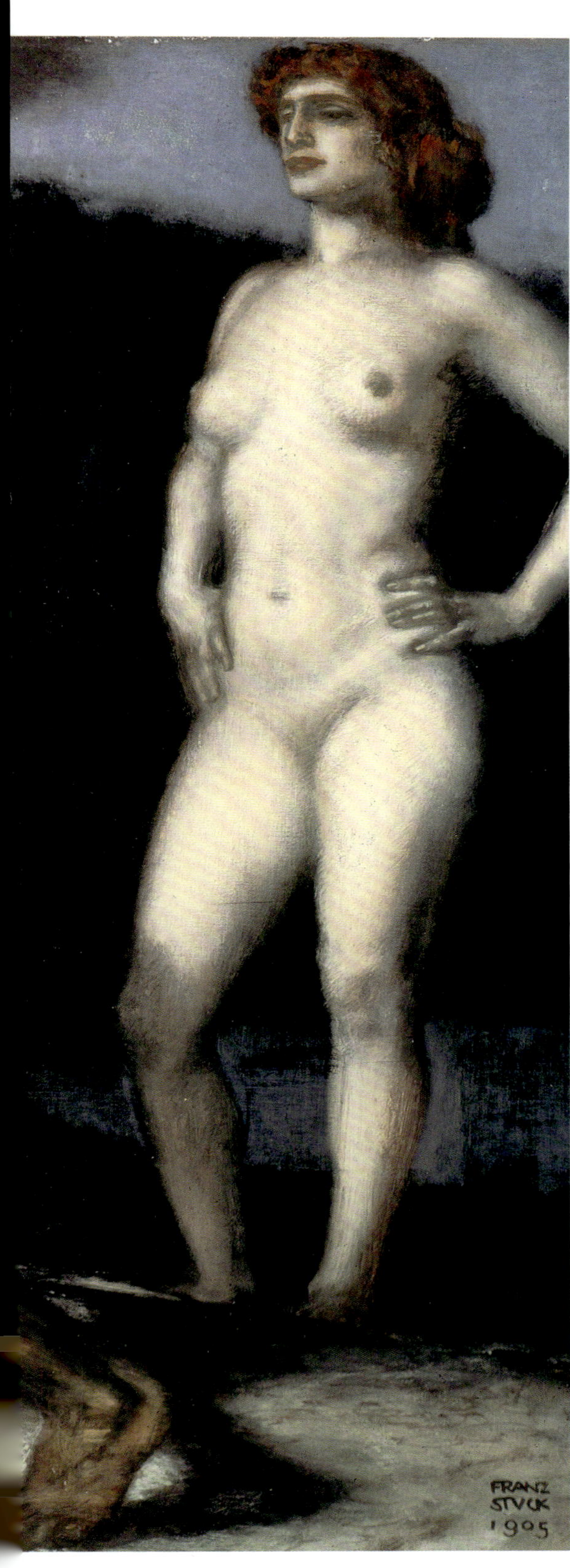

Franz von Stuck (1863–1928)

Fighting for a Woman

Combat pour une femme

Der Kampf ums Weib

La lucha por la mujer

A Luta por uma Mulher

De strijd om een vrouw

1905, Oil on wood/Huile sur bois, 90 × 117 cm

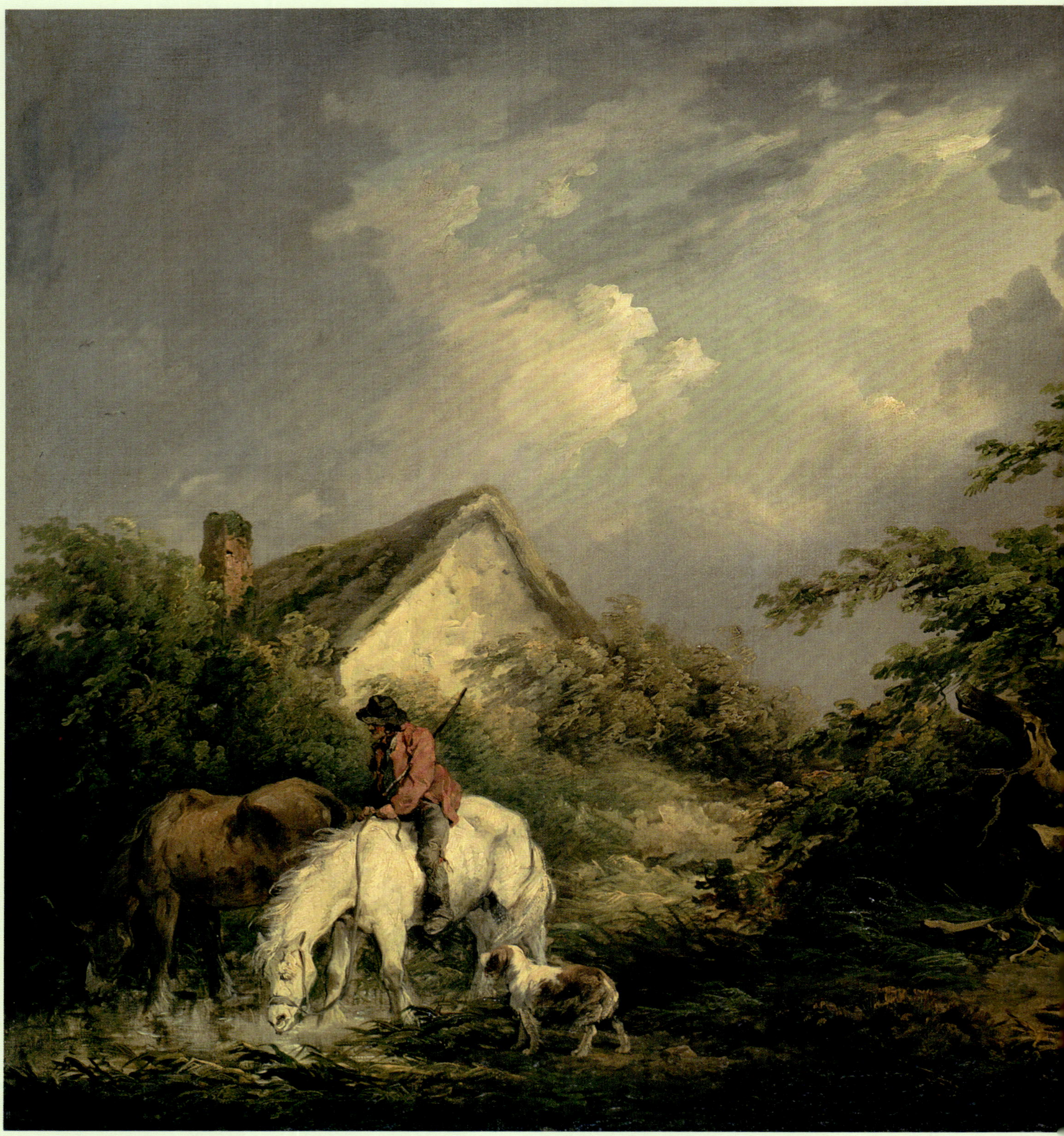

BRITISH PAINTING
LA PEINTURE ANGLAISE
BRITISCHE MALEREI
PINTURA BRITÁNICA
PINTURA INGLESA
BRITSE SCHILDERKUNST

George Morland (1763–1804)
The Approaching Storm
Avant l'orage
Der aufziehende Sturm
La tormenta se acerca
Aproximação da Tempestade
De naderende storm
1791, Oil on canvas/Huile sur toile, 85 × 117 cm

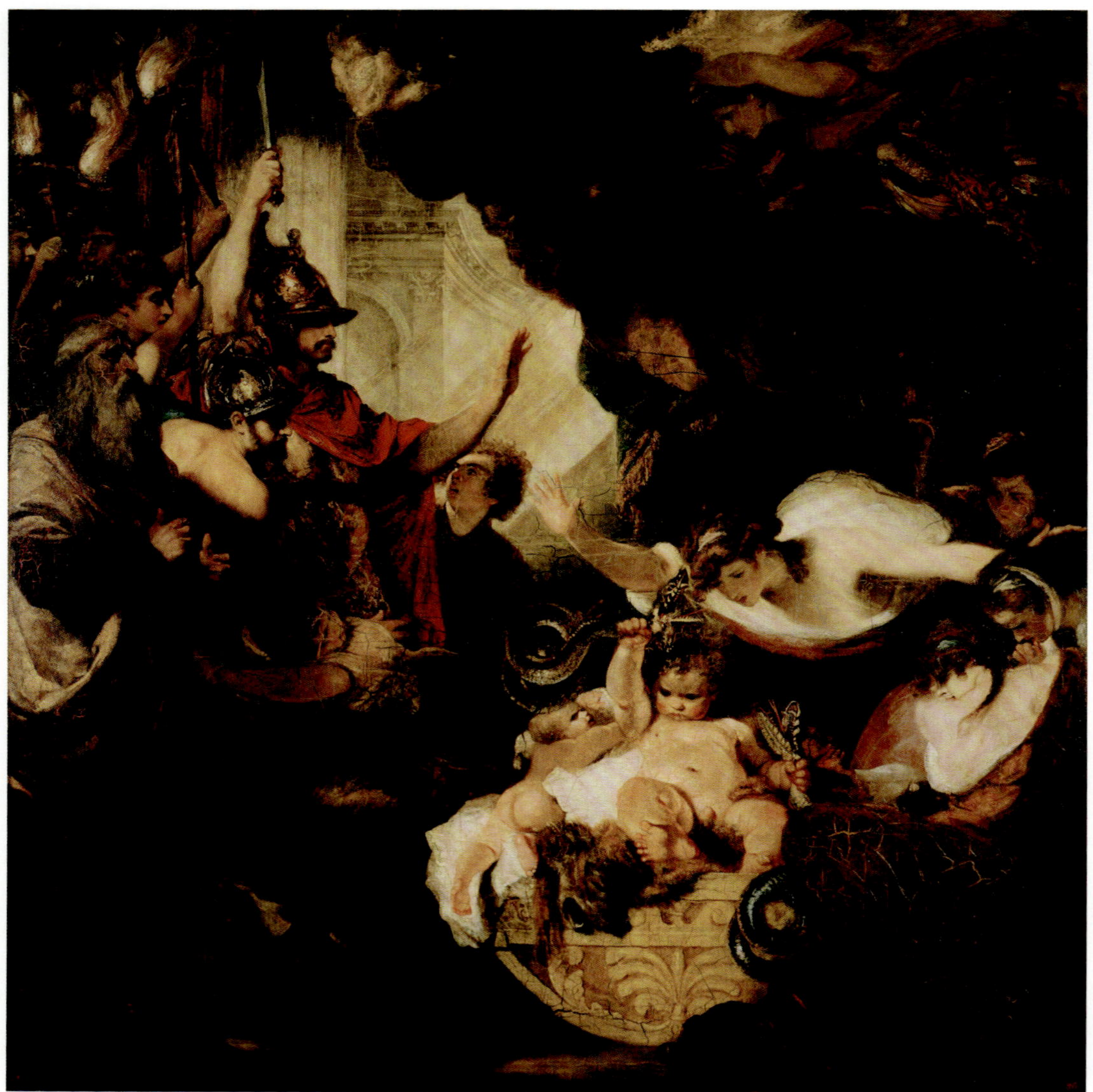

British Painting

With more than 450 works, the Hermitage features
an extensive collection of British artists from the
16th to 19th centuries. The 18th century, when British
painting really began to flourish, is particularly
strongly represented. There are some unusual works in
the collection, including history paintings by Joshua
Reynolds as well as examples of British portraiture,
such as the *Woman in Blue,* the only work by Thomas
Gainsborough in the Hermitage. The 19th century is
also represented with portraits by Thomas Lawrence
and his contemporaries, some of which are markedly
romantic.

La peinture anglaise

Avec plus de 450 tableaux, l'Ermitage possède une
vaste collection d'artistes anglais du XVIe au XIXe siècle.
Le XVIIIe siècle y est particulièrement représenté : c'est
l'apogée de la peinture anglaise. S'y trouvent aussi des
œuvres peu communes telles que des tableaux d'histoire
de Joshua Reynolds, mais aussi des exemples de l'art
du portrait comme la *Dame en bleu,* seule œuvre de
Thomas Gainsborough à l'Ermitage. Le XIXe siècle est
représenté par des portraits de Thomas Lawrence et de
contemporains, en partie influencés par le romantisme
allemand.

Britische Malerei

Mit über 450 Werken besitzt die Eremitage eine
umfangreiche Sammlung britischer Künstler des
16.–19. Jahrhunderts. Besonders stark vertreten ist
das 18. Jahrhundert, die Blütezeit der britischen
Malerei. Darunter befinden sich auch ungewöhnliche
Werke, wie beispielsweise Historienstücke von
Joshua Reynolds, aber auch Beispiele der britischen
Porträtmalerei, wie die *Frau in Blau,* das einzige Werk
von Thomas Gainsborough in der Eremitage. Auch
das 19. Jahrhundert wird durch Porträts von Thomas
Lawrence und Zeitgenossen, teils deutlich romantisch
beeinflusst, abgebildet.

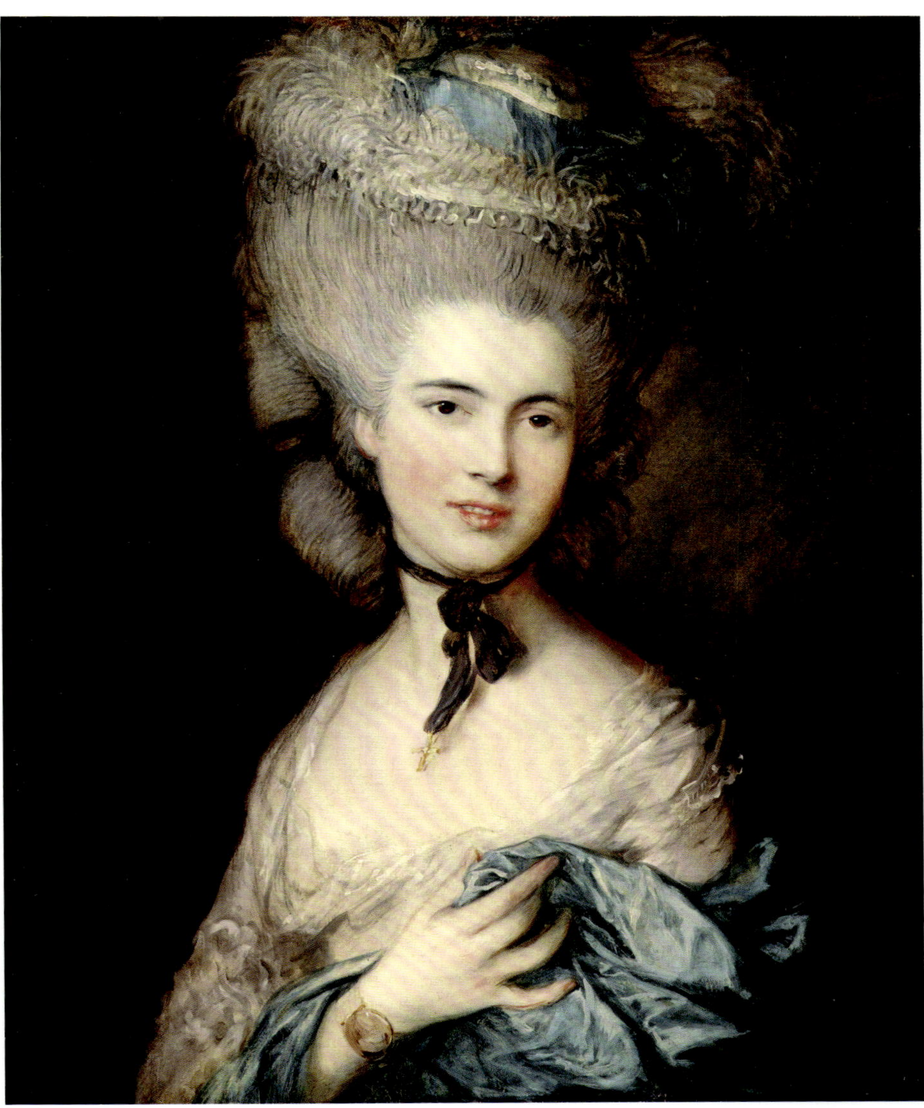

Pintura británica

Con más de 450 obras, el Hermitage cuenta con una amplia colección de artistas británicos de los siglos XVI al XIX. Particularmente bien representado se encuentra el siglo XVIII, la edad de oro de la pintura británica. Entre otras se encuentran también obras inusuales, como piezas históricas de Joshua Reynolds, así como ejemplos de retratos británicos, como *La mujer de azul,* la única obra de Thomas Gainsborough en el Hermitage. El siglo XIX también está representado por retratos de Thomas Lawrence y otros artistas contemporáneos, notablemente influenciados por retratos románticos.

Pintura inglesa

Com mais de 450 obras, o Hermitage possui uma abrangente coleção de artistas britânicos do século XVI ao século XIX. O século XVIII está especialmente bem representado, tratando-se da época do florescimento da pintura britânica. Entre as pinturas encontram-se também obras invulgares, como, por exemplo, peças históricas de Joshua Reynolds, mas também exemplos da pintura britânica de retratos, como a *Senhora de Azul,* a única obra de Thomas Gainsborough no Hermitage. Também o século XIX se encontra reproduzido através de retratos de Thomas Lawrence e dos seus contemporâneos, em parte de influência claramente romântica.

Britse schilderkunst

Met ruim 450 stukken bezit de Hermitage een grote collectie werken van Britse kunstenaars van de zestiende tot en met de negentiende eeuw, met de nadruk op de achttiende eeuw, de bloeitijd van de Britse schilderkunst. Deze collectie omvat ook ongewone doeken, zoals historiestukken van Joshua Reynolds, en voorbeelden van Britse portretkunst, zoals *Portret van een dame in het blauw,* het enige doek van Thomas Gainsborough in de Hermitage. De negentiende eeuw is vertegenwoordigd met portretten van Thomas Lawrence en zijn tijdgenoten, die door de Romantiek zijn beïnvloed.

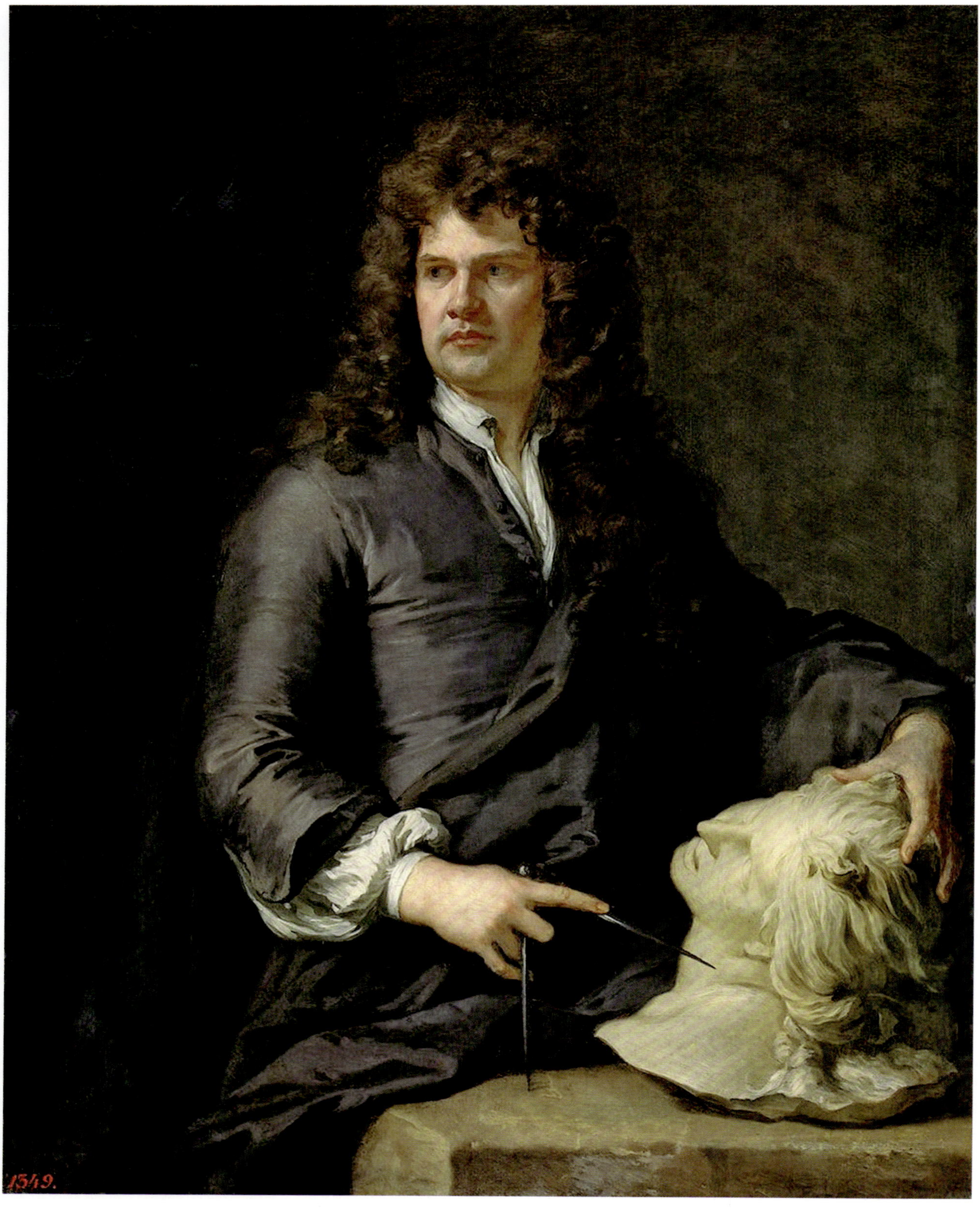

Sir Godfrey Kneller (1646–1723)

Grinling Gibbons

c. 1690, Oil on canvas/ Huile sur toile, 125,5 × 101 cm

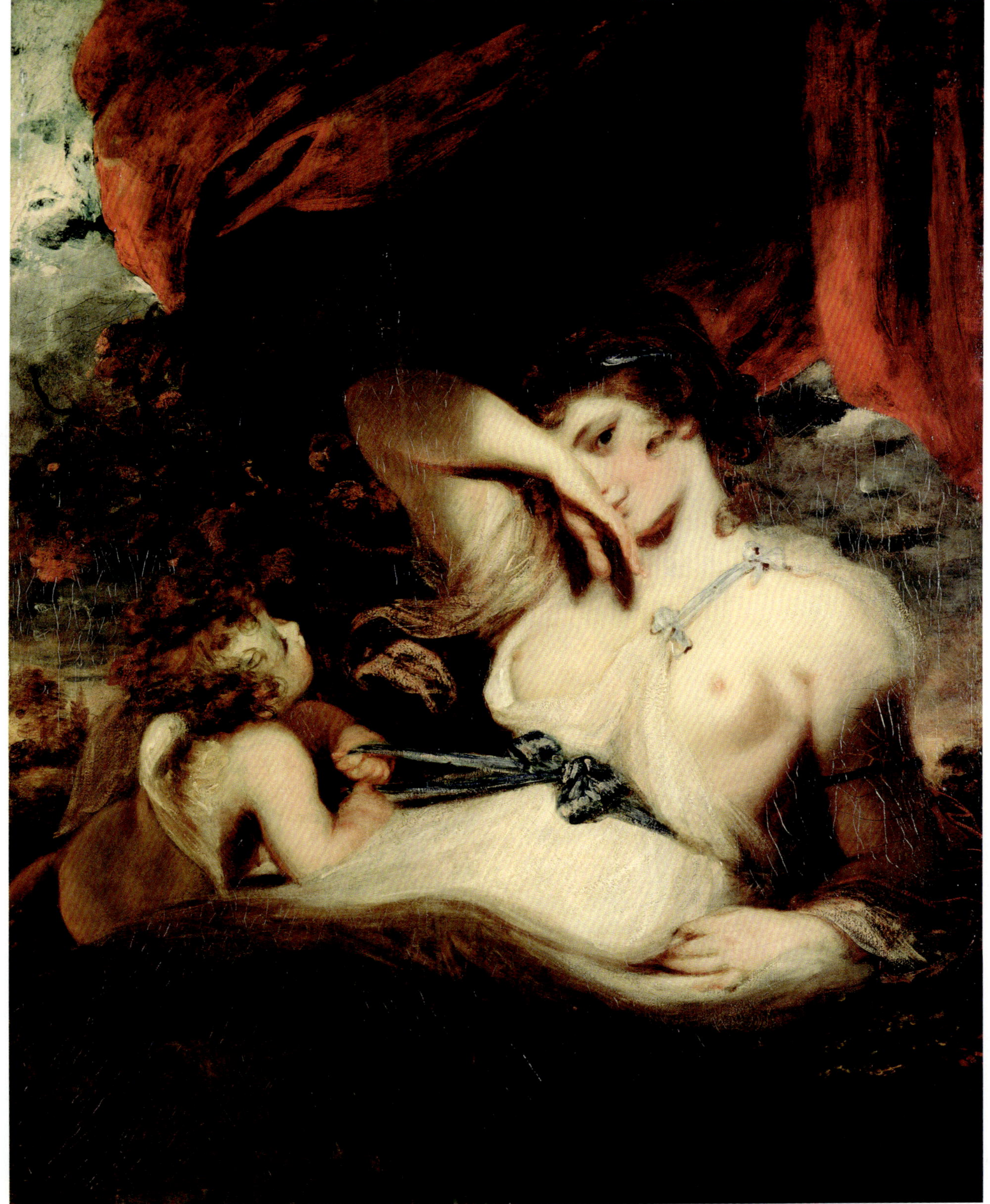

*Joshua
Reynolds
(1723–92)*

Cupid
Unfastening
the Belt of
Venus

L'Amour
dénouant
la ceinture
de Vénus

Amor löst
den Gürtel
der Venus

Amor abre
el cinturón
de Venus

Amor Solta o
Cinto de Vénus

Amor trekt de
ceintuur van
Venus los

1788, Oil
on canvas/
Huile sur toile,
127,5 × 101 cm

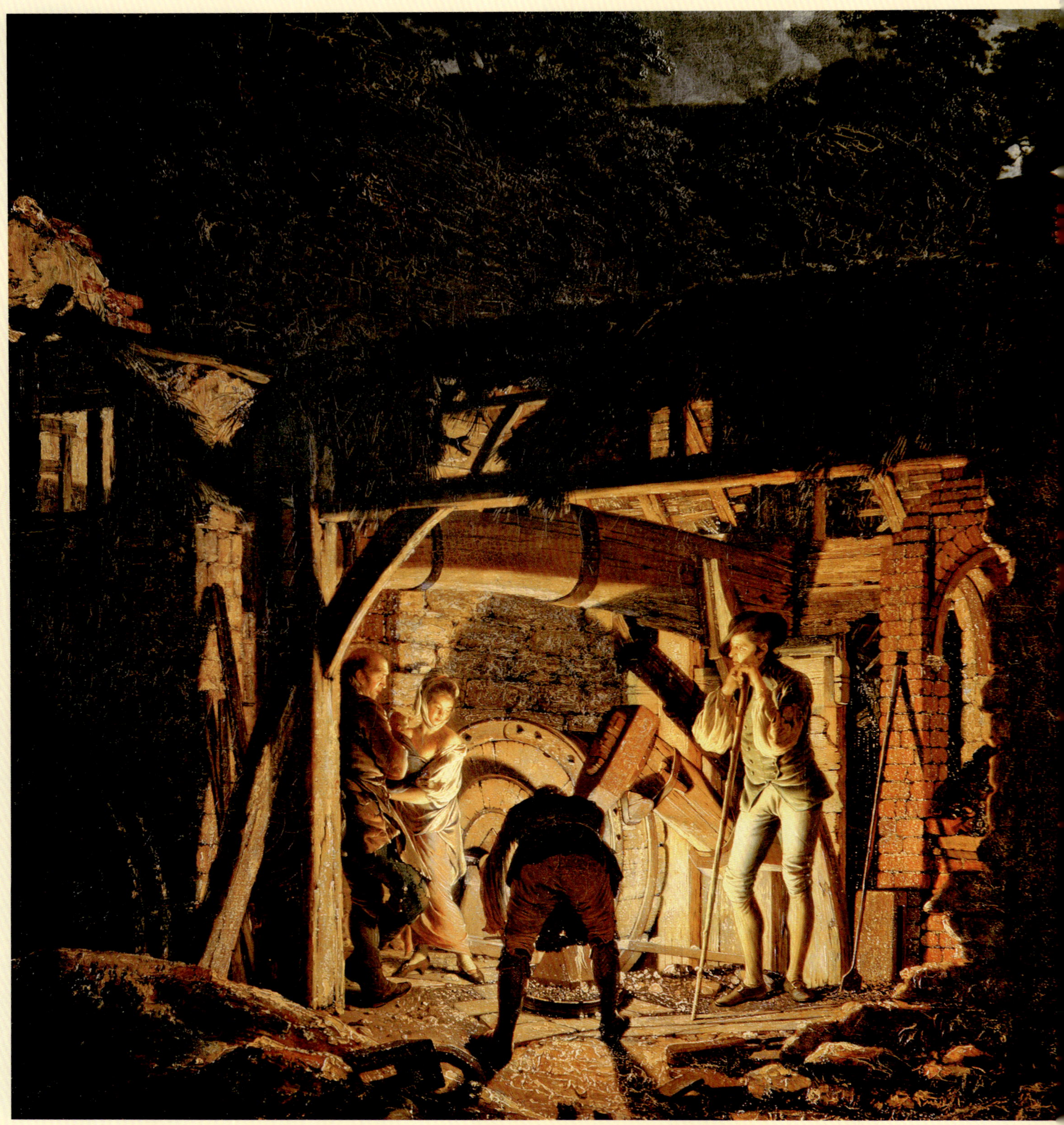

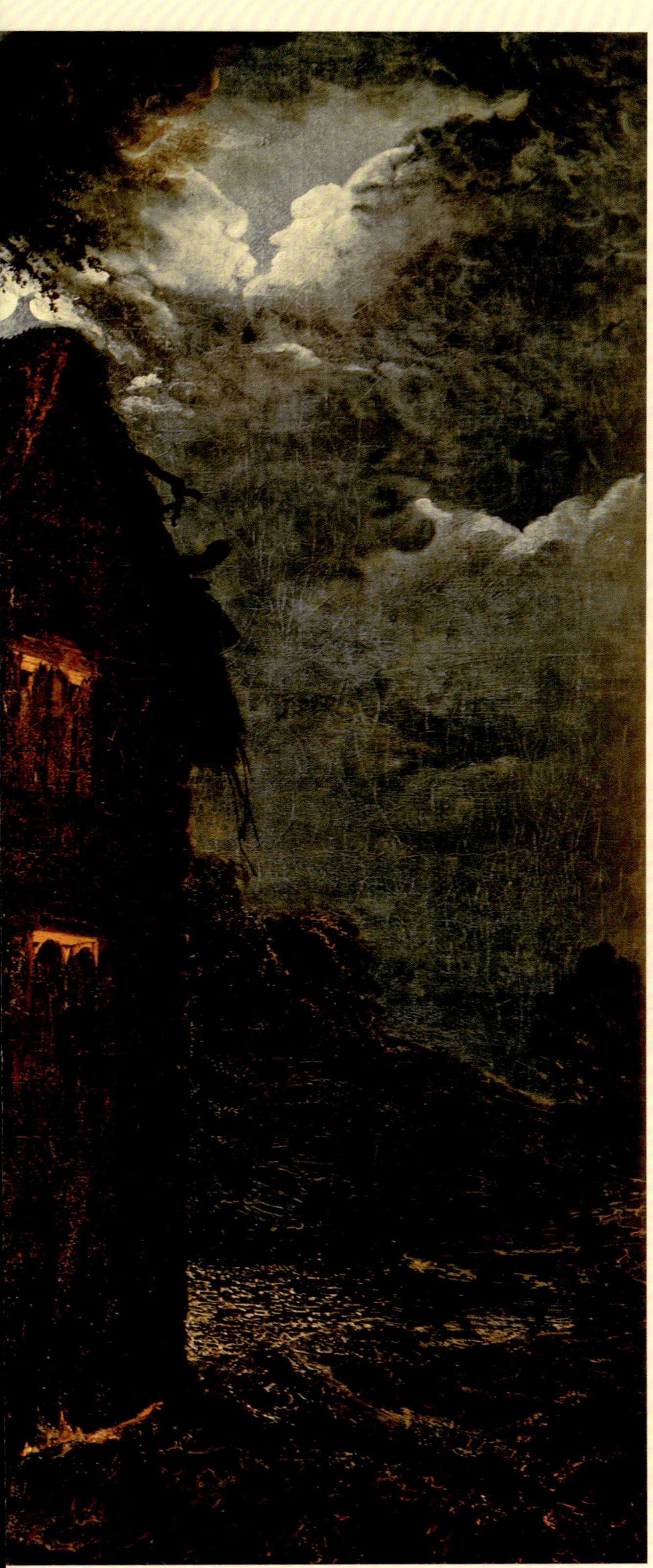

Joseph Wright of Derby (1734–97)
The Ironforge
Une forge vue de l'extérieur
Die Eisenschmiede
La fragua
Os Ferreiros
De smederij
1773, Oil on canvas/Huile sur toile, 105 × 140 cm

Joseph Wright of Derby was a master of nocturnes and the presentation of artificial sources of light, in this respect a descendant of Caravaggio. In this image, the fire in the forge cuts through the darkness of the night. The moon has retreated behind large clouds and lends them a threatening heft with its radiance, The haunting scene can be understood as a prelude to the industrial revolution that would propel Europe into a new era soon after this work was completed.

Joseph Wright of Derby fut un maître des scènes nocturnes et de la représentation des éclairages artificiels. Il était en ce sens et pour ainsi dire un héritier de Caravage et du luminisme. Dans ce tableau, c'est le feu de la forge qui éclaire la nuit ténébreuse. La lune est masquée par de lourds nuages auxquels ses rayons donnent leur volume menaçant. Cette scène d'allure fantomatique doit être comprise aussi comme une sorte de prémonition symbolique de la révolution industrielle qui va – peu de temps après ce tableau (1773) – propulser toute l'Europe dans une ère nouvelle.

Joseph Wright of Derby war ein Meister der Nachtstücke und der Darstellung künstlicher Lichtquellen – in dieser Hinsicht sozusagen ein Nachfahre von Caravaggio. In diesem Bild erhellt das Feuer der Schmiede die dunkle Nacht. Der Mond hat sich hinter großen Wolken zurückgezogen und gibt ihnen durch seine Strahlen ihr bedrohlich wirkendes Volumen. Die gespenstisch anmutende Szene ist auch als ein Vorspiel zur industriellen Revolution zu verstehen, die bald nach Entstehen des Bildes ganz Europa in eine neue Zeit katapultieren sollte.

Joseph Wright of Derby era un maestro de las obras nocturnas y de la representación de fuentes luminosas artificiales, constituyendo en este aspecto un descendiente de Caravaggio. El fuego de la fragua ilumina en este cuadro la oscura noche. La luna se ha retirado detrás de grandes nubes y les otorga, con sus rayos, un volumen que se antoja amenazador. La en principio fantasmal escena ha de entenderse también como preludio de la Revolución Industrial, que poco después de la creación de esta pintura catapultaría a Europa a una nueva era.

Joseph Wright of Derby era um mestre das obras noturnas e da representação de fontes de luz artísticas, podendo-se dizer deste ponto de vista que se trata de um sucessor de Caravaggio. Nesta obra, o fogo ilumina a noite escura aos ferreiros. A lua esconde-se atrás de grandes nuvens e através dos seus raios atribui-lhes um volume de efeito ameaçador. A cena de aparência fantasmagórica deverá também ser entendida como prelúdio relativamente à Revolução Industrial, que logo após a criação desta obra viria a catapultar toda a Europa numa nova era.

Joseph Wright of Derby was een meester in nachtstukken en het weergeven van verschillende soorten kunstlicht; in dit opzicht was hij een nazaat van Caravaggio. Op dit schilderij zorgt het vuur van de smid voor licht in de donkere nacht. De maan is achter grote wolken verdwenen en door zijn stralen lijken die wolken nóg groter dan ze in werkelijkheid zijn. Het tafereel ademt een spookachtige sfeer en kan worden gezien als een opmaat tot de industriële revolutie, die ertoe leidde dat kort nadat Wright of Derby dit schilderij voltooide in heel Europa een nieuwe tijd aanbrak.

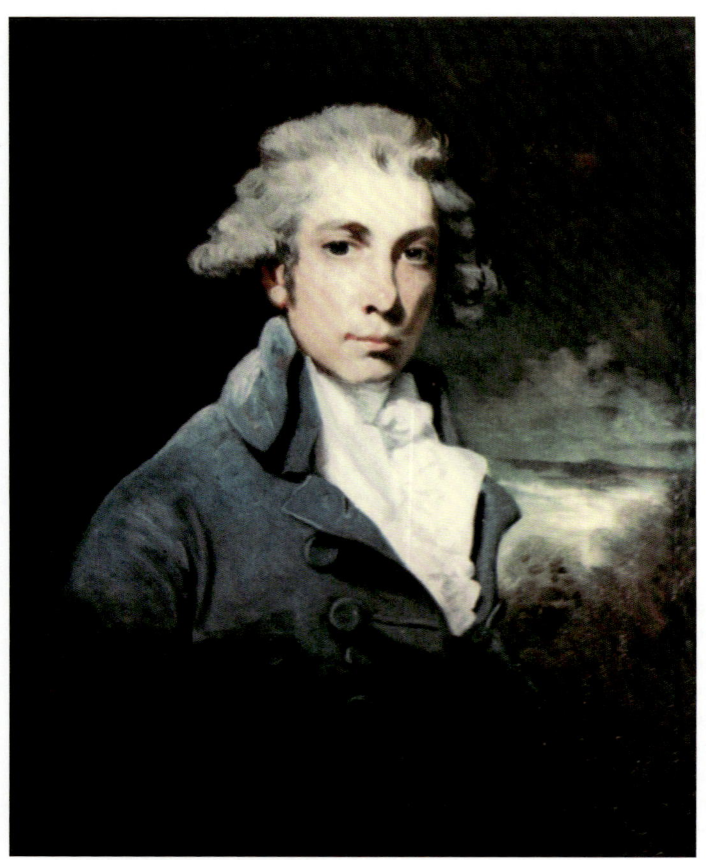

John Hoppner (1758–1810)
Richard Brinsley Sheridan
1780–90, Oil on canvas/Huile sur toile, 77 × 64,5 cm

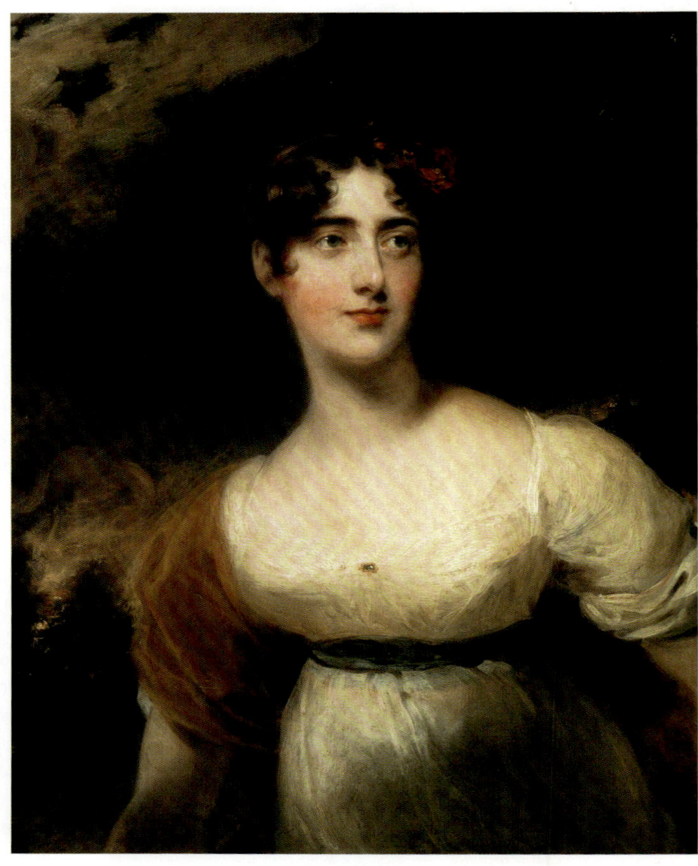

Thomas Lawrence (1769–1830)
Lady Emily Harriet Wellesley-Pole (Lady Raglan)
c. 1815, Oil on wood/Huile sur panneau, 76 × 63 cm

Sir Thomas Lawrence (1769–1830)
Prince Mikhail Semyonovich Vorontsov
Le Comte S. R. Vorontsov
Fürst Michail Semjonowitsch Woronzow
Mijaíl Semiónovich Vorontsov
Príncipe Mijaíl Semiónovich Vorontsov
Vorst Michail Semjonovitsj Vorontsov
1821, Oil on canvas/Huile sur toile, 143 × 113 cm

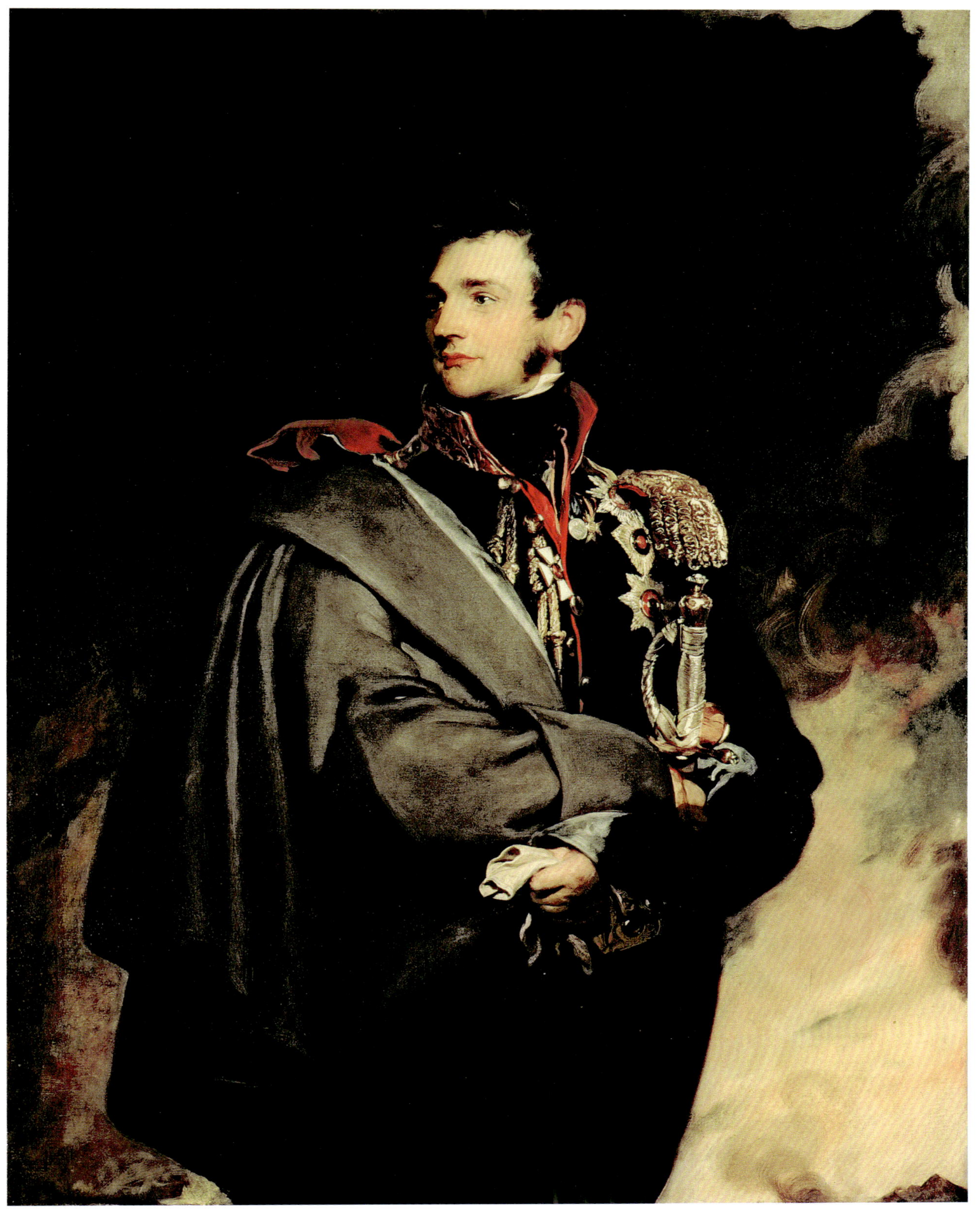

Marianna Butenschön, *Ein Zaubertempel für die Musen. Die Ermitage in St. Petersburg,* Köln 2008

Natalya Gritsay, *Seventeenth- and eighteenth-century Flemish painting: State Hermitage Museum Catalogue,* New Haven 2008

Oleg Yakovlevich Neverov & Dmitry Pavlovich Alexinsky, *The Hermitage,* New York 2010

Nikolai N. Nikulin (Ed.), *Netherlandish painting: fifteenth and sixteenth centuries,* Firenze 1989

Geraldine Norman, *The Hermitage,* London 1997

B. B. Piotrovsky (Ed.), *The Hermitage catalogue of Western European painting. Gosudarstvennyj Ermitaz,* Leningrad/St. Petersburg 1983

Mikhail Piotrovsky, *The Hermitage: the history of the buildings and collections,* St. Petersburg 2000

Witali Suslow (Hrsg.), *Die Ermitage: Westeuropäische und russische Kunst,* Leipzig 1988